The Lotus® Guide to Learning 1-2-3® Release 2.2

THE LOTUS® GUIDE TO

LEARNING 1-2-3®
RELEASE 2.2

Lotus
Books®

ADDISON-WESLEY PUBLISHING COMPANY, INC.

Reading, Massachusetts Menlo Park, California New York
Don Mills, Ontario Wokingham, England Amsterdam Bonn
Sydney Singapore Tokyo Madrid San Juan

This book is part of the Lotus Learning Series.

Library of Congress Cataloging-in-Publication Data
The Lotus guide to learning 1-2-3 Release 2.2.
p. cm. — (Lotus learning series)
ISBN 0-201-52320-5
1. Lotus 1-2-3 (Computer program) 2. Business—Data processing.
3. Electronic spreadsheets. 4. IBM Personal Computer—Programming.
I. Lotus Development Corporation. II. Series.
HF5548.4.L67L655 1989 005.36'9—dc20 89-17783

Editor: Anna Typrowicz
Cover Designer: Celia Miller
Cover Illustrator: David Bishop

ISBN 0-201-52320-5
ABCDEFGHIJ-AL-89
First printing, September 1989

Contents

About This Book xi
What is 1-2-3? xi
How to Use This Book xiii
Conventions Used in This Guide xiv

PART I WORKSHEETS, GRAPHICS, AND DATABASES 1

Chapter 1 Getting Started 2
Preliminary Steps 3
The Computer Keyboard 6
Starting 1-2-3 7
Leaving 1-2-3 16

Chapter 2 Basic Skills 18
The 1-2-3 Screen 20
1-2-3 Menus 22
Moving Around the Worksheet 25
Other 1-2-3 Keys 28
Ranges 29
Using the Undo Feature 35
Files 37
The 1-2-3 Help Facility 45
The File Commands 46

Chapter 3 Creating a Worksheet 47
Building a Worksheet 51
Entering Data in the Worksheet 53
Editing Data 59
Changing the Appearance of the Worksheet 62
Saving the File 68

Formulas 69
Formatting Values in Cells 86
The Help Facility 91
Naming a Range 91
Linking Files 99
Transposing Ranges 109
Splitting the Screen 111
Erasing Ranges 114
Text Editing 115
What-If Calculations 117
Creating and Saving Worksheets 119
Printing the Worksheet 119
The Main Menu Command Structure 123
The Worksheet Commands 124
The Range Commands 125
The Print Commands 125

Chapter 4 **Creating Graphs 126**
Graph Types 128
Graph Settings Sheets 133
Graphing With /Graph Group 135
Creating a Bar Graph 142
Creating a Pie Chart 156
What-If Graphics 164
Printing a Graph 168
The Graph Commands 177
The PrintGraph Menu Tree 178

Chapter 5 **Creating a Database 179**
Setting Up a Database 183
Refining the Appearance of the Database 191
Saving the File 197
Sorting Database Records 197
Querying the Database 207
Finding Data Records 213
Extracting Records 217
Replacing Information in the Database 223
Saving the File 227
The Data Commands 228

Chapter 6 **Formatting and Printing with Allways 229**
Starting Allways 231
The Allways Screen 235
The Allways Menu 236
Allways Function Keys 237
Getting Help 237
Returning to 1-2-3 238
Formatting with Allways 242
Including Graphs 257
Printing with Allways 266
Allways Menu Command Structure 270
The Allways Main Menu Commands 270
The Worksheet Commands 270
The Format Commands 271
The Graph Commands 271
The Layout Commands 272
The Print Commands 272
The Display Commands 273

Chapter 7 **Tips 274**
Worksheet 275
Functions and Formulas 293
Database 298
Printing 301
Graphics 309
Allways 315

PART II **1-2-3 MACROS 321**

Chapter 8 **Getting Started with Macros 323**
Basic Information About Macros 324
Keystroke Macros 326
The Advanced Macro Commands 326
Entering Macros 327
Protecting Data 329
Using Macros 330
Simple Macros 330
1-2-3 Special Keys 339
A Summary of Macro Basics 343
Macro Troubleshooting Checklist 346

Chapter 9 **1–2–3's Learn Feature 347**
Cell-Formatting Macro 351
File Table Macro 356
Correcting Mistakes 363
Saving the Macros 365
Adding to a Learn Range 365

Chapter 10 **Building Advanced Macros 367**
Advanced Macro Command Structure 368
Using Advanced Macro Commands 373
Correcting a Macro with STEP Mode 381
Summary of Advanced Macros 385
Troubleshooting Checklist 386
The Advanced Macro Commands 387

Chapter 11 **A Collection of Utility Macros 403**
Entering the Macros 405
Range Naming Macros 406
File Saving Macro 408
Date and Time Macros 410
Single and Double Line Macros 416
Pointer-Movement Macros 420
Looping Macro 423
Form Letter Macro 428
Print Macros 435
Creating a Range Name Table 438

Chapter 12 **Creating a Macro Library 441**
The Macro Library Manager 442
Starting the Macro Library Manager 443
The Macro Library Manager Menu 447
Saving Macros in a Library 448
Using Macros in a Library 451
Removing a Library From Memory 453
Using a Library for Storing Data 453
Editing a Library 459
Working with the Macro Library Manager 464

Chapter 13 **Application Macros 467**
The Graph Application 470
The Database Application 493
The Form Letter Application 517

Chapter 14 **A Macro Menu 537**
How the Macro Menu Works 539
Creating the Sales Expenses Worksheet 540
Creating the Macro Menu 554
Creating the Macro Menu Routines 560
Testing the Macro Menu 577
Refining the Macro Menu 583
Invoking the Macro Menu Automatically 594

Appendix A **Working with 1–2–3 Add-In Programs 596**
Attaching an Add-In 597
Invoking an Add-In 599
Detaching Add-Ins 599
Attaching and Invoking Add-Ins Automatically 600

Appendix B **Using 1–2–3 Over a Network 603**
Sharing Data Files 603
Printing on a Network 606

Appendix C **Quick Reference 607**
1–2–3 Keys 607
Allways Keys 611
File Names 612
Label Prefixes 613
Operators and Precedence Numbers 614
1–2–3 @Functions 615
Macro Key Names 620
Advanced Macro Command Summary 621
Menu Trees 625
Allways Menu Trees 625
Macro Library Manager Menu Tree 631
PrintGraph Menu Tree 632

Index **633**

About This Book

WHAT IS 1–2–3?

1-2-3, the leading spreadsheet for IBM personal computers and compatibles, is a fully-integrated package that provides the tools you need to increase your productivity and improve your decision making.

1–2–3 lets you create:

- **Worksheets** to calculate numbers, test assumptions, and analyze results
- **Graphs**, drawn from numeric data in the worksheet, to illustrate and emphasize trends
- **Databases** to organize and manage information such as personnel data.

1–2–3 also lets you create **macros** to automate tasks you perform frequently or to build applications for yourself or for others. The simplest 1–2–3 macros are stored sequences of keystrokes that perform particular tasks, such as saving your work. More sophisticated macros use the 1–2–3 **advanced macro commands**, which are a powerful built-in programming language. Using advanced macro commands, you can design your own menus, branch to routines, and create for loops.

1–2–3 Release 2.2 Additions

1–2–3 Release 2.2 has introduced some important enhancements both to increase the power of 1–2–3 and to make it easier to use:

- **File linking** allows you to refer to data in other files in the worksheet you're currently working on. This gives you a way of consolidating information from several worksheets (perhaps a series of monthly budgets) in a summary worksheet.

- In earlier releases of 1–2–3, the program would recalculate all of the cells and formulas in the worksheet when you made a change in the worksheet. Now 1–2–3 uses a technique called **minimal recalculation** to recalculate only formulas or cells that are affected by a change to the worksheet. Calculation in worksheets therefore takes place very quickly.
- An **undo feature** lets you reverse the changes you made to the worksheet, allowing you to change your mind or correct mistakes quickly.
- **Setting sheets** show you related settings on a single screen. When creating a graph or printing, for example, you can see all the applicable settings at a glance so you know exactly what they are as you change them.
- The **Graph Group command** lets you create a graph in one step based on a group of contiguous data ranges. This saves you from specifying data ranges for the graph individually.
- The **Allways** add-in allows you to create and print **presentation-quality worksheets** right from 1–2–3. Using Allways, you can mix spreadsheet data with graphics, and include different fonts, boldface, underlining, boxes, and shading to enhance the appearance of your worksheets.
- To help you create keystroke macros, 1–2–3 Release 2.2 includes a **learn feature** that records your keystrokes automatically as a macro. This gives you a quick way to create macros and minimize typing or syntax errors in the macros.
- You create macros directly in the worksheet. In earlier releases of 1–2–3, the use of a macro was restricted to the worksheet that contained it, unless you re-entered or copied the macro in another worksheet. To allow you to use your macros with more than one worksheet, 1–2–3 Release 2.2 provides the **Macro Library Manager** add-in. With this add-in, you can save macros in a macro library for use in any worksheet. Macros in a library are no longer tied to a specific worksheet.
- 1–2–3 Release 2.2 is "**network-ready**," meaning you can share 1–2–3 data and program files with other 1–2–3 users in your work group over a local area network, even if the other users are using 1–2–3

Release 2.01 or Release 3. You can reserve files and protect them with passwords. You can also print your worksheets on shared printers.

With 1–2–3, you never have to switch disks; you can go from worksheet to database to graphics and back. A single keystroke can start the Allways add-in so you can format and print professional-looking worksheets, and a single keystroke returns you to the basic 1–2–3 environment. The same is true for the Macro Library Manager add-in.

You can use the 1–2–3 worksheet and database functions independently with excellent results. Used in conjunction with graphics, however, they comprise a powerful productivity tool. You can, for example, enter information into a database, move to a worksheet and calculate the latest numeric information for the database, and then graph that information in any one of a number of different graphic formats. You can print your work at any time. And if you're doing a special report or presentation, you can use Allways to format and print your worksheet.

Once you're familiar with the basic features of 1–2–3, you can try your hand at creating macros to make it quicker and easier to perform tasks that you frequently perform.

HOW TO USE THIS BOOK

This book is a hands-on guide for the new 1-2-3 user. It is designed to introduce 1-2-3 and its functionality. You'll learn through a series of hands-on exercises that will involve creating a worksheet and entering and manipulating data, drawing a bar graph and a pie chart from the worksheet data you created, producing a formatted presentation-quality printout of the worksheet and graph you created, generating and manipulating a database, and automating your work with macros.

This book is written for 1-2-3 Release 2.2. Users of earlier releases of 1–2–3 may still find the book useful, but should be aware that Release 2.2 contains many new features not found in earlier releases. The (2.2) symbol has been used to indicate these new features.

The *Guide* is not a substitute for the 1-2-3 manuals, but it will familiarize you with 1-2-3 so you can be up and working productively while exploring the manuals at your own pace.

You cannot expect to master 1-2-3 all at once, but you can work while you are learning. You'll be surprised at how quickly you'll be able to use 1-2-3 to accomplish some sophisticated tasks.

This book contains two parts. Part I covers the basics of working with worksheets, graphs, and databases. It also includes a chapter on formatting and printing with Allways to produce presentation-quality worksheets and graphs. Part II teaches you the fundamentals of 1-2-3 macros so you can automate your work and create quite sophisticated applications.

The following reading path is suggested:

- Begin by going through Chapters 1 to 3. This will give you a good foundation in 1–2–3 and worksheet skills.
- Depending on your interests, then turn either to Chapter 4 (graphs) or Chapter 5 (databases).
- Before turning to Chapter 6 (Allways), complete Chapters 3 and 4; you'll need the worksheet and graphs from those chapters so you can format them with Allways.
- Chapter 7 contains various tips about using 1–2–3; refer to this chapter at any time.
- Once you've mastered some of the fundamentals of 1–2–3 (worksheet, graphs, and databases), go on to Part II where you can learn how to use macros to automate 1–2–3 tasks.

Clear explanations with keystroke directions and liberal screen illustrations and diagrams direct you throughout the *Guide*. The important point is to go at your own pace and enjoy yourself while you're learning. That's what this book is designed for.

CONVENTIONS USED IN THIS GUIDE

This section describes the typographical conventions used in *The Lotus Guide to Learning 1–2–3.*

References to Keys

In the exercises, special keys (such as Enter) are represented by keycaps that show the word or symbol as it appears on the keyboard. For example, [→] is the keycap for the right arrow key. The function keys (F1, F2, and so on) are represented by keycaps marked with the 1-2-3 function name, for example, [HELP] or [NAME]. To help you identify the function key, the keycap is followed by the function key identification (F1, F2, and so on) in parentheses, for example, [HELP] (F1). The function-key template will also help you to familiarize yourself with the location of functions. Some function keys perform more than one function, and require you first to press and hold down the Alt key and then to press a function key, for example, [UNDO] (Alt-F4).

In the text of the *Guide*, all the keys are referred to by name, followed by the function key identification in parentheses, for example, Help (F1). Enter in the text is the Enter key; in a keystroke direction Enter appears as a keycap with a bent left arrow: [↵].

The Keystroke Terminology

The *Guide* teaches by leading you through keystroking sequences. Each sequence is preceded by one or more paragraphs that explain what you are about to do and what will happen on the screen.

To avoid confusion, read this text first. Wait until you reach the actual keystroke directions to begin typing.

The following terminology is used in the *Guide*'s keystroking directions.

Press: This means to strike or press a key. It is used primarily with arrow keys, special keys, function keys, and the Enter key.

Press: [↵]

Type: Type also means to strike or press a key. It is used primarily with the standard typewriter keys.

Type: **60000**

Any data you must enter appears in this type: **Quarter 1**.

Move to: This directs you to reposition the cell pointer in a certain place on the screen. (The cell pointer marks your position on the 1-2-3 screen.)

Move to: cell D3 (in a worksheet)

Select: This directs you to select a specific command from a menu.

A **menu** is a list of commands that appears in a line across the top of the screen.

Select: Worksheet

Many commands in a menu bring up a submenu from which you choose another command. Selecting the first command replaces the menu with the submenu. In the *Guide,* all the commands in such a sequence are listed on different lines in the keystroking direction. The commands for erasing a worksheet involve such a sequence. The keystroke directions look like this:

Select: Worksheet
Erase
Yes

Sample Keystrokes

The following keystrokes are representative:

Move to: cell A3
Type: Salary
Press: ↵
Move to: cell A5
Type: 22700
Press: ↵

These directions say: move the cell pointer to A3 in the worksheet, type Salary, press Enter to enter it in A3, move the cell pointer to cell A5, type the number 22700, and press Enter to enter the number in cell A5.

Suppose you want to see a list of worksheet files in the current directory. The following keystrokes direct you to display the list.

Press: [/]
Select: File
List
Worksheet

These directions say: press / (the slash key) to call up the menu, and select the commands **File**, **List**, and **Worksheet**. 1-2-3 will then list any worksheet files it finds in the current directory.

Other Conventions

Commands and new terms in the *Guide* appear in **boldface**.

References to indicators on the screen appear in UPPERCASE, for example, READY or UNDO.

Within text, file names, range names, @functions, and advanced macro commands appear in UPPERCASE, for example, INCOME.WK1 or {PANELOFF}. Within keystroke instructions, they appear in lowercase because that's the way you're most likely to type them. (You can type them in either upper or lowercase).

Part I: Worksheets, Graphics, and Databases

1

Getting Started

Before you begin using this *Guide* you must take some steps to prepare.

This chapter explains:

- The installation procedure
- The computer keyboard
- Starting 1–2–3
- Setting up your directory and/or drive correctly for the exercises in this book
- Leaving 1–2–3.

PRELIMINARY STEPS

Checklist

1. Check the *Setting Up 1–2–3* manual to make sure you have the hardware you need to run 1–2–3.
2. Gather all the materials necessary for the exercises:
   - The 1–2–3 **disks**

Figure 1.1
1–2–3 Disks

- The **function-key template** that comes with the 1–2–3 package. The template fits over the computer's function keys and indicates special uses of those keys in 1–2–3.
- A **data disk** if you're working on a two-diskette computer. You need a blank, formatted disk on which to save the sample files you'll create during the exercises.

  New disks must be formatted before they can be used. Formatting checks the condition of the disk and prepares it to store information. Formatting is done with the Disk Operating System (DOS), the program that contains basic commands that operate the computer. The procedure is described in the *Setting Up 1–2–3* manual.

3. Make sure you complete the necessary initial procedures.

   For a two-diskette computer, the initial procedures include:

(2.2) - Initializing 1–2–3—recording your name and your company's name on the original System Disk (5.25″ systems) or System, Help, and PrintGraph Disk (3.5″ systems). This procedure is very important; it identifies you as the licensed owner of your copy of 1–2–3, and 1–2–3 won't work without it. You need to complete this procedure only once.
- Making a copy of each of the 1–2–3 disks. These copies are called **backups**.
- Running the 1–2–3 Install program to tailor 1–2–3 to your particular computer system.

All of these procedures are discussed in detail in the *Setting Up 1-2-3* manual.

For a hard-disk computer, the initial procedures include:

2.2 ▪ Initializing 1-2-3—recording your name and your company's name on the original System Disk (5.25″ systems) or System, Help, and PrintGraph Disk (3.5″ systems). This procedure is very important; it identifies you as the licensed owner of your copy of 1-2-3, and 1-2-3 won't work without it. You need to complete this procedure only once.

- Making a directory that contains just the 1-2-3 program files.
- Copying the 1-2-3 disks into the directory you created.
- Running the 1-2-3 Install program to tailor 1-2-3 to your particular computer system.
- Running the Allways Setup program to tailor Allways to your particular computer system.

All of these procedures are discussed in detail in the *Setting Up 1-2-3* manual.

The 1-2-3 Install Program

Installing 1-2-3 is a simple process during which you select **drivers** for each piece of equipment in your computer system. Selecting drivers involves going through lists of the different kinds of equipment (such as printers and monitors) that can be used to run 1-2-3. On each list you indicate which particular piece of equipment you have. When you have selected all the necessary drivers, 1-2-3 collects them in a special file called a **driver set**.

You don't need to install 1-2-3 to start using the program, but installing allows you to view and print graphs and to print worksheet files.

The finished driver set must have a name. 1-2-3 automatically names the driver set 123.SET unless you specify otherwise. Using another name is only necessary if you want to create more than one driver set. For example, you may want to be able to run 1-2-3 on a hard-disk computer at the office and a two-diskette computer at home. Most first-time users need only one driver set; in this case, the name 1-2-3 gives the driver set is adequate. (Additional driver sets can be created at any time in the future; a driver set can also be changed, or edited, at any time.)

The Allways Setup Program

The Allways add-in lets you format and print presentation-quality worksheets. Allways has its own setup (installation) procedure. The 1-2-3 driver set you create with the 1-2-3 Install program does not work with Allways. Allways has its own drivers, and you must select the appropriate drivers for your system before you can use Allways.

> NOTE: To use the Allways add-in, you must have a hard-disk and at least 512K of conventional memory.

Before using the Allways Setup program, install 1-2-3. The Allways Setup program needs to know the name of the directory that contains the 1-2-3 program files. When you run the Setup program, it copies Allways to your hard disk and lets you select the equipment you are planning to use with Allways. For details of this procedure, see the *Setting Up 1-2-3* manual.

THE COMPUTER KEYBOARD

The computer keyboard has five sections:

1. Typewriter Section

   The typewriter section works just like a standard typewriter keyboard. Letter and number keys are in their usual places. Holding the Shift key down and typing a letter key at the same time produces a capital letter. (The Shift key often has an upward arrow rather than the word Shift on the keycap.)

2. Pointer-Movement Keys

   To the right of the typewriter section are four keys, each of which has an arrow on the keycap. These keys are used to move the **cell pointer**. (The cell pointer is a highlighted block that marks your position on the screen.)

The set of keys combined with, or next to, the arrow keys move the cell pointer in large jumps.

The pointer-movement keys are described in detail in Chapter 2.

3. Special Keys

   On either side of the typewriter section, there are a number of keys unique to the computer, such as the Ctrl (Control) key. The names of these keys also vary from one computer to another.

   Also included in this section are some standard typewriter keys, such as Tab, Shift, and Backspace.

4. The Enter Key

   The Enter key often has a left-facing bent arrow on the keycap. It is also called the Return key or Carriage Return key on some computers.

   The Enter key is actually part of the special keys section, but it is treated separately here because it has particular importance. The Enter key is similar to the key on an electric typewriter that makes the move from the end of one line to the beginning of the next. It does that in 1–2–3, but it also does much more.

   In many instances, you press Enter after selecting a command or typing data to register (or enter) your action with 1–2–3. Enter is probably the most frequently used key on the computer keyboard.

5. Function Keys

   Most computers have a set of keys called function keys. They vary in number from 10 to 12 depending on the computer, and are usually labeled F1, F2, and so on. These keys are assigned specific functions by the software being used. In 1–2–3, they do such things as recalculate the worksheet or display Help screens.

STARTING 1–2–3

Once you have completed the preliminary steps outlined earlier in this chapter, you are ready to work with 1–2–3. The procedure for starting up the program differs for a two-diskette computer and a hard-disk computer. Read the section that pertains to your computer system.

Two-Diskette Computer

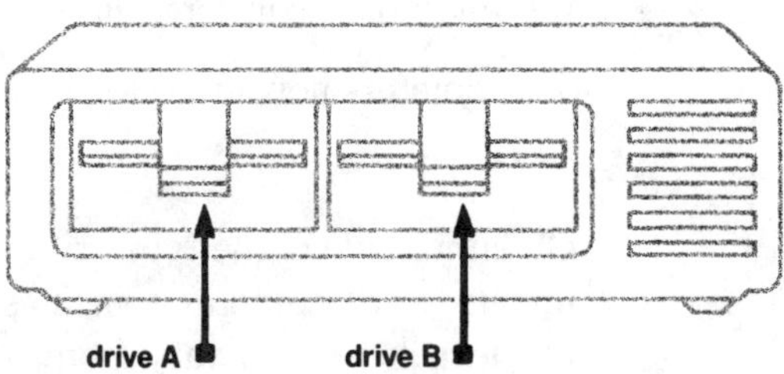

Figure 1.2 Two-diskette computer

Whenever you start 1–2–3, you must first load DOS into the computer's memory. Place your DOS disk in drive A, close the door, and turn on the computer.

If DOS asks you to do so, type the date and time. (Many computers have internal clocks that set the date and time for you. In that case, you won't be asked for the date and time.)

The DOS **prompt** will then appear. The prompt can differ from computer to computer, but will usually be something like A> or A:>. At this point you can start 1–2–3. If you have any questions about loading DOS, consult your DOS manual.

You can start 1–2–3 in one of two ways: directly from DOS or from the Lotus Access system. Starting from DOS has the advantage of giving you more of your computer's memory to work with, and saves the step of going through the Access system, so this is the method the *Guide* recommends.

The steps that follow assume that the computer is on and the DOS prompt is on the screen.

1. Insert the 1–2–3 System Disk (5.25″ system) or System, Help, and PrintGraph Disk (3.5″ system) in drive A and close the door.

2. Insert the data disk into drive B and close the door.

3. With the DOS prompt on the screen:

   Type: 123
   Press: ↵

   If you created more than one driver set or if you named the driver set anything other than 1–2–3:

Type: 123 driver name
Press: ↵

Be sure to type the specific name of the driver set you created, for example, **PORTABLE**.

1-2-3 displays a logo screen, which contains the information you entered when you initialized 1-2-3, and then displays the worksheet.

> NOTE: To start 1-2-3 from the Access system you would type **lotus** instead of **123**. The Access menu appears on the screen. From here you can choose one of the following: the 1-2-3 Program, the PrintGraph Program (to print a graph), the Translate Utility (to read files from certain other programs), the Install program (to indicate the type of printer and other additional equipment you have), or Exit back to DOS. The pointer is highlighting 1-2-3, so just press Enter to confirm the selection. You will first see the logo screen and then the 1-2-3 worksheet.

Customizing 1-2-3 for this Guide

During the course of working through this book, you will be creating a number of files. In some cases, the files you create in one chapter will be used in other chapters, so you will want to save the files.

When you first use 1-2-3, it is set up to save the files you create on a data disk in the same drive that was used to start 1-2-3, in this case, drive A. You will probably want to change this. Users with two-diskette systems usually save files on a disk in drive B. This allows you to use the Help facility on either the Help Disk (5.25″ system) or System, Help, and PrintGraph Disk (3.5″ system). One of these must be inserted in drive A.

(2.2) Default Settings Sheet

To change the drive where 1-2-3 will save files, you will work on a special screen called a **setting sheet**. 1-2-3 Release 2.2 introduced setting sheets to help you see a group of 1-2-3 settings at a glance. As you change a setting, the setting sheet reflects the change you made so you can easily keep track of your settings. The setting sheet that you will see shortly shows the **default settings** for 1-2-3. These settings affect every 1-2-3 session and include printer settings, clock display formats, and the current drive and/or directory setting.

You will now display the default settings sheet so you can instruct 1-2-3 to save your files on a disk in drive B.

If you started 1–2–3 according to the earlier directions, you now have a blank worksheet on the screen.

Press: / (slash key)

A menu (a list of choices or commands) appears at the top of the screen above the worksheet. You are going to select Worksheet from this menu, and then Global, Default, and Directory from the menus that follow.

To select an item from a menu, either highlight the item by moving the pointer with the Right key and pressing Enter or type the first letter of the item, such as **d** for Default.

Select: Worksheet
Global
Default

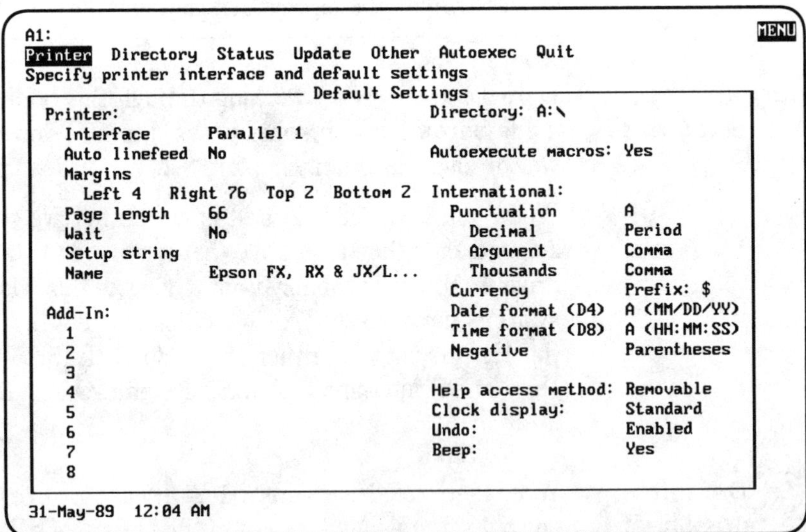

```
A1:                                                                MENU
Printer  Directory  Status  Update  Other  Autoexec  Quit
Specify printer interface and default settings
                           Default Settings
  Printer:                                     Directory: A:\
    Interface      Parallel 1
    Auto linefeed  No                          Autoexecute macros: Yes
    Margins
      Left 4   Right 76  Top 2  Bottom 2       International:
    Page length    66                            Punctuation        A
    Wait           No                              Decimal          Period
    Setup string                                   Argument         Comma
    Name           Epson FX, RX & JX/L...          Thousands        Comma
                                                 Currency           Prefix: $
  Add-In:                                        Date format (D4)   A (MM/DD/YY)
    1                                            Time format (D8)   A (HH:MM:SS)
    2                                            Negative           Parentheses
    3
    4                                          Help access method: Removable
    5                                          Clock display:      Standard
    6                                          Undo:               Enabled
    7                                          Beep:               Yes
    8

31-May-89  12:04 AM
```

Figure 1.3 Default settings sheet

The default settings sheet shows all of the default settings for 1–2–3. Notice the directory setting in the upper right corner reads A:\. To change a setting, you select items from the menu above the setting sheet and the choices you make are reflected on the setting sheet.

Select: Directory

Instead of the menu, you see a line that reads **Enter default directory: A:**. You want to change the A:\ to B:\.

Press: ESC to erase the A:\
Type: b:\
Press: ↵

Notice that on the setting sheet it now says **B:\ next to Directory.** You are going to make the change permanent by selecting Update from the menu. Unless you select Update, the change you make applies only to the current 1-2-3 session.

Select: Update
Select: Quit

The worksheet is back on the screen. You can now remove the System Disk (5.25" systems) and replace it with the Help Disk. On 3.5" systems, leave the System, Help, and PrintGraph Disk in drive A.

Go on to "Leaving 1-2-3" later in this chapter.

Hard-Disk Computer

Figure 1.4 Hard-disk system

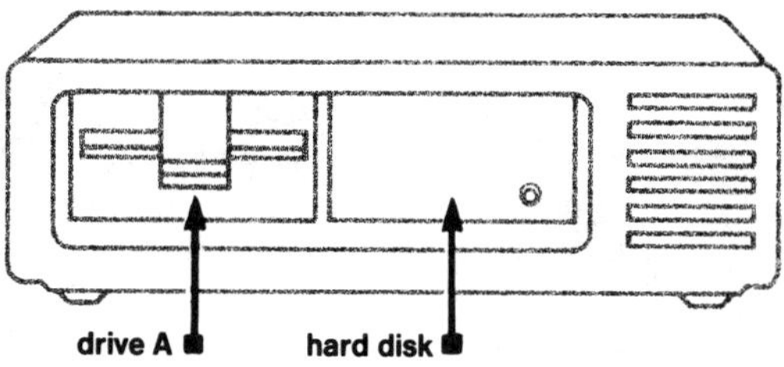

Whenever you start 1-2-3, you must first load DOS into the computer's memory. Most people with a hard-disk computer use the hard disk (and not the diskette drive) as the main source on the computer. In this case, DOS is copied directly onto the hard disk so that it's loaded into the computer's memory automatically when the computer is turned on.

A hard disk has a main directory (called the **root directory**) that lists all the programs and files that are stored on the hard disk. Most people also create subdirectories into which specific programs and files are copied. You name a subdirectory when you create it. For example, it's a good idea to create a subdirectory to hold all the 1-2-3 disks and name that subdirectory 123. If the hard disk contains subdirectories, all the subdirectory names are listed in the root directory. DOS is often copied into the root directory.

If you have any questions about copying DOS onto the hard disk or creating subdirectories, consult your DOS manual. The *Setting Up 1-2-3* manual gives instructions for creating a subdirectory for 1-2-3.

To load DOS on a hard-disk system, turn on the computer. If asked to do so, type the date and time. (Many computers have internal clocks that set the date and time for you. In that case, you won't be asked for the date and time.) You should then see the DOS prompt on the screen. This prompt will vary from computer to computer, but will generally be something like C> or D>.

Creating a Directory for Your Worksheet Files

During the course of working through this book, you will be creating a number of files. In some cases, the files you create in one chapter will be used in other chapters, so you will want to save the files.

When you first use 1-2-3, it is set up to save the files you create in the same directory that was used to start 1-2-3, for example, C:\123. You will probably want to change this so that your data files are kept in a separate directory from the one containing the 1-2-3 program files.

For the exercises in this *Guide*, you should create a separate subdirectory to hold the files you'll create. The following directions tell you how to create a new subdirectory named TEMP. Once you start 1-2-3, you'll instruct it to save the files in this directory.

Starting in the DOS root directory (the DOS prompt will be C> or D>):

Type: md temp
Press: [↵]

This creates a new subdirectory named TEMP. For more information about creating subdirectories, refer to your DOS manual.

You're now ready to start 1-2-3.

Starting 1-2-3 from a Hard-Disk Computer

You can start 1-2-3 in one of two ways: directly from DOS or from the Lotus Access system. Starting from DOS has the advantage of giving you more of your computer's memory to work with, and saves the step of going through the Access system, so this is the method the *Guide* recommends.

The steps that follow assume that the computer is on, DOS is installed on the hard disk, all the 1-2-3 disks have been copied onto the hard disk, and the DOS prompt is on the screen.

1. Be sure the DOS prompt is displayed on the screen AND that you are in the directory into which you copied the 1-2-3 disks.

   If 1-2-3 is in a subdirectory, then:

   Type: CD\subdirectory name

   > NOTE: Be sure to type the name of the specific subdirectory you created, for example, 123.

   Press: ↵

2. With the DOS prompt on the screen:

   Type: 123
   Press: ↵

   If you created more than one driver set or if you named the driver set anything other than 1-2-3:

   Type: 123 driver name
   Press: ↵

   Be sure to type the specific name of the driver set you created, for example, PORTABLE.

   1-2-3 displays a logo screen, which contains the information you entered when you initialized 1-2-3, and then displays the worksheet.

> NOTE: To start 1-2-3 from the Access system you would type lotus instead of 123. The Access menu appears on the screen. From there you can choose one of the following: the 1-2-3 Program, the PrintGraph Program (to print a graph), the Translate Utility (to read files from certain other programs), the Install program (to indicate the type of printer and other additional equipment you have), or Exit back to DOS. The pointer is highlighting 1-2-3, so just press Enter to confirm the selection. You will first see the logo screen and then the 1-2-3 worksheet.

Customizing 1–2–3 for this Guide

You have already created a new subdirectory named TEMP for the files you'll create while going through the exercises in this *Guide*. You must now instruct 1–2–3 to save files in this directory instead of the one from which you started 1–2–3 (for example, C:\123).

(2.2) Default Setting Sheet

To change the directory where 1–2–3 will save files, you will work on a special screen called a **setting sheet**. 1–2–3 Release 2.2 introduced setting sheets to help you see a group of 1–2–3 settings at a glance. As you change a setting, the setting sheet reflects the change you made so you can easily keep track of your settings. The setting sheet that you will see shortly shows the **default settings** for 1–2–3. These settings affect every 1–2–3 session and include printer settings, clock display formats, and the current drive and/or directory setting.

You will now display the default settings sheet so you can instruct 1–2–3 to save your files in your newly created directory C:\TEMP.

If you started 1–2–3 according to the earlier directions, you now have a blank worksheet on the screen.

Press: [/] (slash key)

A menu (a list of choices or commands) appears at the top of the screen above the worksheet. You are going to select Worksheet from this menu, and then Global, Default, and Directory from the menus that follow.

To select an item from a menu, highlight the item either by moving the pointer with the Right key and pressing Enter, or type the first letter of the item, such as **d** for Default.

Select: Worksheet
Global
Default

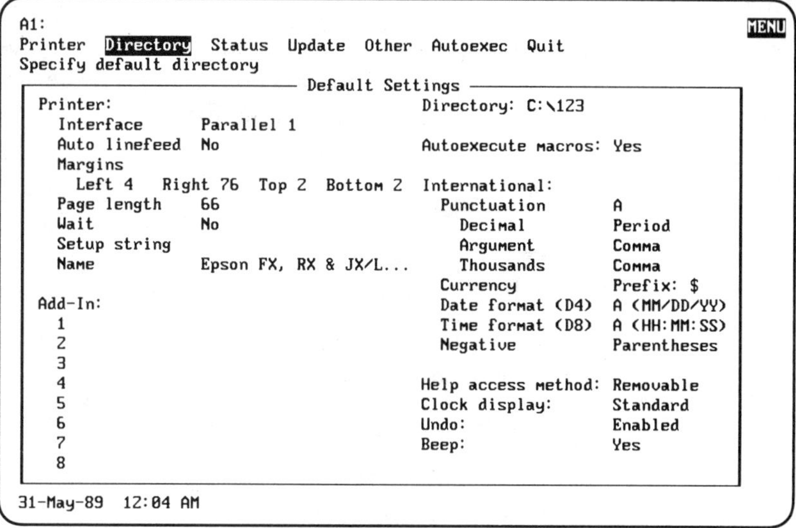

Figure 1.5 Default setting sheet

The default settings sheet shows all of the default settings for 1-2-3. Notice the directory setting in the upper right corner lists the name of the directory from which you started 1-2-3, for example, C:\123. To change a setting, you select items from the menu above the setting sheet and the choices you make are reflected on the setting sheet.

Select: Directory

Instead of the menu, you see a line that reads **Enter default directory:** followed by the name of the subdirectory that contains the 1-2-3 files. You want to change this directory to C:\TEMP:

Press: ESC to erase the current directory setting
Type: c:\temp
Press: ↵

Notice that on the setting sheet it now says **C:\TEMP** next to Directory. You are going to make the change permanent by selecting Update from the menu. Unless you select Update, the change you make applies only to the current 1-2-3 session.

Select: Update
Select: Quit

The worksheet is back on the screen.

LEAVING 1–2–3

At any point while going through this book you can stop working and leave 1–2–3. Before you do so, however, be sure you save your work in a worksheet file (with the **File Save** command) as described in the next chapter.

To leave 1–2–3:

Press: / (slash)
Select: Quit

1–2–3 now asks you to confirm. To leave 1–2–3, select Yes; to change your mind and stay, select No.

Select: Yes

2.2 If you haven't saved your work, 1–2–3 will warn you and ask you whether to save the worksheet or not.

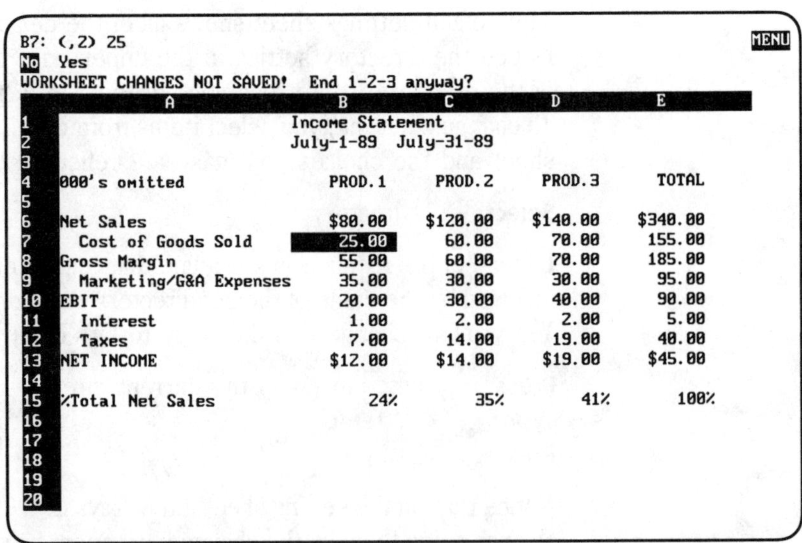

Figure 1.6 The leaving without saving warning

If you don't care about the changes you've made, select Yes to leave 1–2–3; otherwise, select No to save them.

When you're ready to start using 1-2-3 again, just follow the procedures outlined earlier. On a hard-disk computer, start in the directory that contains the 1-2-3 files (or make sure this directory is on your DOS path; for details, refer to your DOS manual). On a two-diskette system, insert the System Disk (5.25" systems) or System, Help, and PrintGraph Disk (3.5" systems) in drive A. Then type **123** at the DOS prompt.

2

Basic Skills

This chapter introduces the basics of 1–2–3:

- The 1–2–3 screen
- 1–2–3 menus and how to select from them
- Movement around the worksheet
- 1–2–3 function and special keys
- Ranges
- (2.2) The undo feature
- Files
- The Help facility

As in all the chapters in the book, you learn by actually keystroking through some simple tasks.

Before You Start

You should begin this and every other chapter by starting 1–2–3. Each chapter begins with the following reminder.

For a two-diskette computer

- 1–2–3 should be set up to save files on a disk in drive B.
- The data disk should be in drive B.
- Once you've started 1–2–3, the Help Disk (5.25″ systems) or System, Help, and PrintGraph Disk (3.5″ systems) should be in drive A.

For a hard-disk computer

- 1–2–3 should be set up to save files in a subdirectory called TEMP.
- All the 1–2–3 disks should be copied in their own subdirectory on the hard disk.

The first step is to review some terminology. Start up 1–2–3 if you haven't already done so. Instructions are in Chapter 1.

THE 1–2–3 SCREEN

When you start 1–2–3, the screen displays a blank worksheet. The worksheet is where you enter and calculate data.

Figure 2.1
1–2–3 worksheet

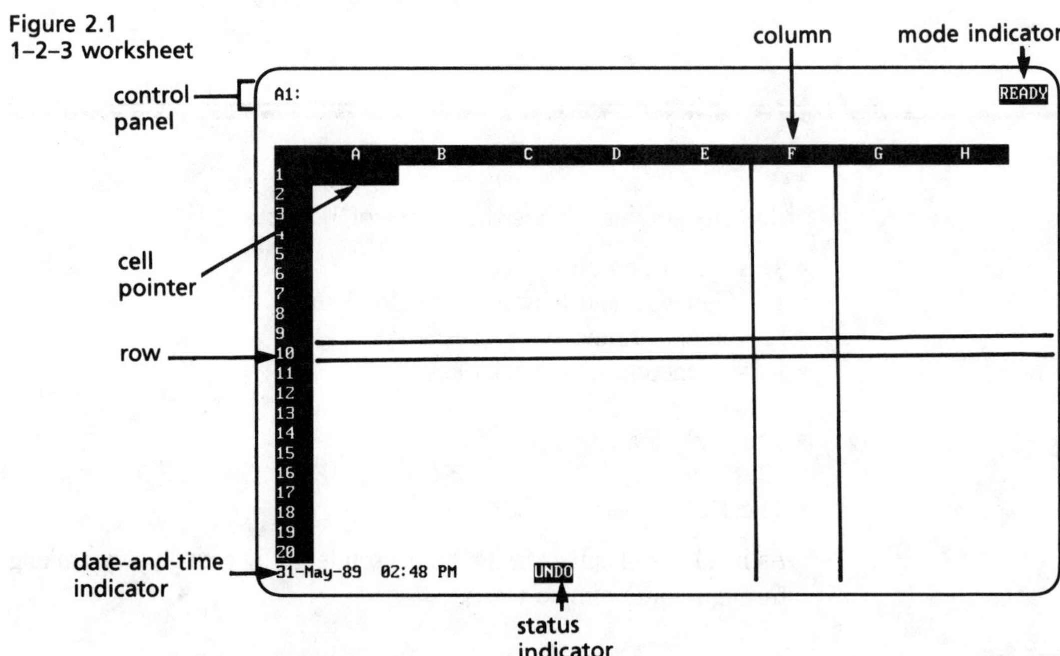

Look at the screen. The worksheet is bordered by a row of letters across the top and by a column of numbers down the left side. The horizontal rows and vertical columns form a pattern of boxes called cells. All data is entered into cells. The highlighted rectangle on the screen is called the cell pointer; it marks the current cell in the worksheet.

The 1–2–3 worksheet is very large: it has 256 columns (labeled A to IV) and 8,192 rows (numbered 1 to 8192). Obviously, you can't see an entire worksheet of this size on the screen at one time. The screen provides a window that displays a small portion of the worksheet.

The cell address of the current cell is always displayed in the first line of the control panel, which is at the upper-left corner of the screen above the worksheet. The current cell is A1. As you can see, a cell address consists of a column letter followed by row number. Whenever you create a new worksheet, the cell pointer is positioned at the intersection of column A and row 1, which is cell A1.

Parts of the Worksheet

Columns	256 columns labeled A through IV.
Rows	8,192 rows labeled 1 through 8192.
Cells	Rectangular boxes formed by the intersection of a column and a row. A cell is identified by its cell address, made up of the column letter plus the row number—for example, the cell in the upper-left corner of the worksheet has the cell address A1.
Cell pointer	The highlighted area that marks the current cell.
Control panel	The area across the top of the screen at the left side, consisting of three lines.
First line	The line that indicates the current cell's address and contents.
Second line	The line that displays menu items and prompts. Also, an entry is displayed here as you type it into a cell or edit it.
Third line	The line that displays submenus and descriptions of menu items highlighted in the second line. Prompts are also displayed here.
Mode indicator	The indicator that shows the current mode of operation. The mode indicator changes as you work to show, for example, that you are entering a value or a label, editing an entry, or making an error. Because the worksheet is now ready to receive data, the mode indicator reads READY.
Status indicator	The box that shows the status of the worksheet. Status indicators include UNDO, which shows that you can undo 1-2-3 operations, and CAPS, which indicates that the Caps Lock key is on.

Date-and-time indicator (2.2)

The 1–2–3 clock normally displays the current date and time. You can turn off its display or adjust it to an international format. With 1–2–3 Release 2.2, you can also display the name of the worksheet file you're working on instead of the date and time. (You change the date-and-time indicator with **/Worksheet Global Default Other Clock.**)

1–2–3 MENUS

1–2–3 is a menu-driven program. When you press / (slash), the main menu appears in the second line of the control panel above the worksheet. The menu offers a variety of commands to accomplish different tasks. 1–2–3 leads you through a command sequence by displaying clear explanations of each command in the third line of the control panel, directly below the menu.

Press: /

Figure 2.2 1–2–3 main menu

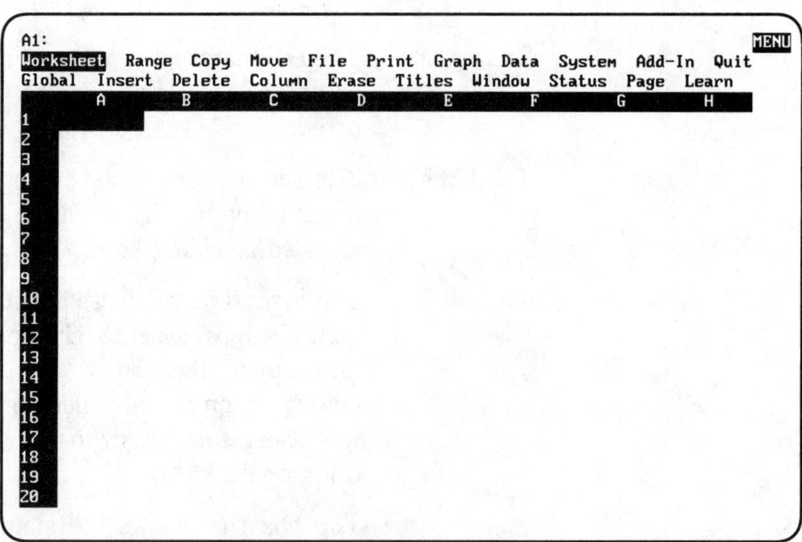

The main 1–2–3 menu is displayed in the second line of the control panel. Notice that the mode indicator reads MENU after you press /.

The main menu contains commands that control various aspects of the 1-2-3 program. Four of these commands are used to manipulate worksheet data: **Worksheet**, **Range**, **Copy**, and **Move**. Both **Worksheet** and **Range** have submenus with their own sets of commands. **Graph** and **Data**, which let you create graphs and work with databases respectively, also have their own submenus. **Print** controls all the specifications
2.2 involved in printing a document. **Add-In** is a new 1-2-3 Release 2.2 command that lets you run add-in programs (such as Allways, which is described in Chapter 6) with 1-2-3 to extend its power. The remaining commands manage 1-2-3 system functions: **File** has commands to manipulate files, **System** lets you use DOS commands during a 1-2-3 session, and **Quit** exits the program.

When the pointer is highlighting a command in the second line of the control panel, a description of that command appears on the third line below. Move the pointer along the list of commands and look at the different descriptions.

Notice that the pointer works with a circular movement. Pressing the Right arrow key when the last command on the right is highlighted brings the pointer back to the first command on the left, in this case, **Worksheet**. Try it:

Press: [→] 11 times

Selecting from a Menu

You can make a selection from a menu in either of two ways:

- Move the pointer to a command with the arrow keys and then press Enter.
- Type the first letter of the command you want to use. If you type the first letter of the command, you do not need to move the pointer nor do you need to press Enter.

As you become proficient with 1-2-3, you'll find that typing the first letter of the command is quicker than highlighting the command. Make a selection now by typing the first letter of **Worksheet**:

Type: w

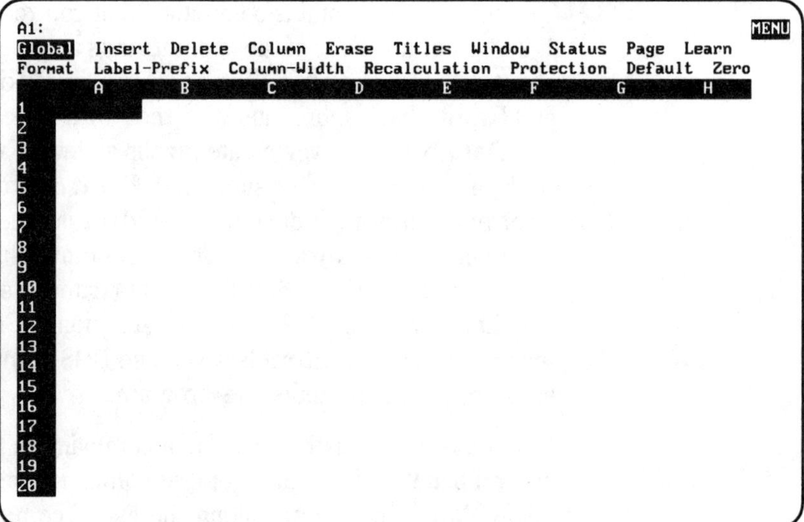

Figure 2.3
/Worksheet menu

The Worksheet submenu, previously displayed in the third line of the control panel, appears in the second line.

> NOTE: The keystroke directions in this book simply tell you to select a command. You can use either of the above methods to make the selection. If, however, you choose to highlight a command, don't forget to press Enter. All Enter keystrokes that appear in the directions are for other purposes and should not be confused with selecting a command.

It's not uncommon to call up a menu by mistake or to decide not to complete a command once you are already in the command sequence. The Esc key takes you backwards through a menu sequence, replacing the current menu with the one previous to it. Try it:

Press: ESC twice

The first time you press Esc, the main menu replaces the Worksheet submenu; the second time, the main menu disappears, leaving the line blank.

The uniformity of the 1-2-3 command structure and the clarity of its commands make the program simple to use. You'll be surprised at how quickly you'll find yourself issuing commands by typing letters without even looking up at the menu.

MOVING AROUND THE WORKSHEET

Working in the worksheet involves moving from one cell to another and entering data. 1-2-3 offers a number of ways of moving around the worksheet quickly and efficiently.

First, you can move the cell pointer one cell at a time with the arrow keys. Experiment with the arrow keys now. Watch the screen to see their effects.

Press: Each of the arrow keys a few times

You'll notice that 1-2-3 beeps each time the cell pointer hits the edge of the worksheet.

Second, you can use Goto (F5), which allows you to make larger jumps. After pressing Goto (F5), type a cell address and press Enter. (You can type cell addresses in either uppercase or lowercase letters.)

Press: GOTO (F5)
Type: **Z75**
Press: ↵ note the position of the cell pointer

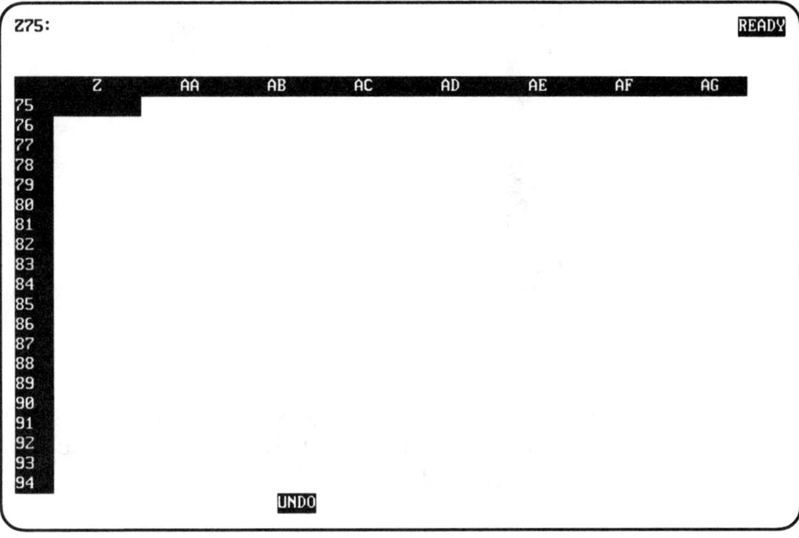

Figure 2.4
Cell Z75

Press: HOME

Several keys, known as the **pointer-movement keys**, let you move the pointer around the worksheet by cell, window, and blocks of data. You're going to enter some data in the worksheet and experiment with the pointer-movement keys. The pointer should be in cell A1. If it is not, press Home.

Data that you type is entered into the cell occupied by the cell pointer. The data, however, does not appear in the cell as you are typing. Instead, as you type, the entry appears in the second line of the control panel. When you're done, you insert the completed entry into the cell by pressing Enter. The cell pointer remains on the cell.

Type: 3000
Press: ↵

Figure 2.5
Entering a number

You can also enter data and move the pointer to an adjacent cell with any one of the arrow keys. Unlike Enter, the arrow keys enter the data into the cell and move the pointer to the next cell. Try it:

Press: →
Type: 4000 →
5000 →
6000 ↵

Figure 2.6
Numbers entered across a row

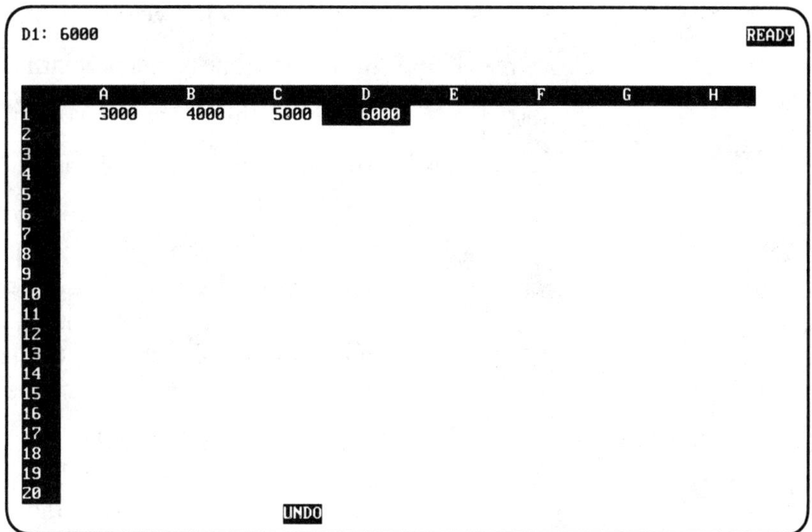

The PgUp and PgDn keys move the cell pointer one window height.

Press: PGDN
PGUP

The Big Left (Ctrl-Left) and Big Right (Ctrl-Right) keys move the screen right and left one window width. (In the keystroke instructions in this book, keys linked with a hyphen must be pressed simultaneously; for example, hold down Ctrl, press Right, then release both keys.)

Press: BIG RIGHT (Ctrl-Right)
BIG LEFT (Ctrl-Left)

Pointer-Movement Keys

The following table lists all the keys and key combinations that you can use to move around the worksheet. Keys linked with a hyphen must be pressed simultaneously.

→ ← ↑ ↓	Move the pointer one cell in each direction.
PGUP	Moves up one window height.
PGDN	Moves down one window height.

BIG RIGHT	Moves right one window width. (Ctrl-Right)
BIG LEFT	Moves left one window width. (Ctrl-Left)
HOME	Moves to the upper-left corner of the worksheet.
END HOME	Moves to the last cell into which you've entered information.
END → END ← END ↑ END ↓	If the pointer is on a blank cell, it moves in the arrow's direction to the first filled cell or to the edge of the worksheet. If the pointer is on a filled cell, it moves in the arrow's direction to the last filled cell before a blank cell or to the edge of the worksheet. When you press End, the word END appears as the status indicator; the word disappears when you press an arrow key to complete the command.
GOTO	Moves to the cell address you specify.

OTHER 1–2–3 KEYS

In addition to the pointer-movement keys, 1–2–3 includes function keys to perform special operations and some other keys that have special uses which may be helpful while creating a worksheet.

Function Keys

Depending on your computer, the function keys are usually located either to the left of the typewriter section or directly above it. The keys are usually labeled F1, F2, and so on.

1–2–3 has assigned special functions to 10 function keys. Each of the 10 function keys (except for F6) performs two different functions: one when you press the function key alone and the other when you hold down Alt and then press the function key.

Earlier in this chapter, you used the Goto (F5) key to move to a specific cell in the worksheet. As you work your way through the exercises in this *Guide*, you'll be introduced to many other 1–2–3 function keys. For a complete list of the keys, see Appendix C, the "Quick Reference" section of this *Guide*.

Special Keys

You may find the following additional keys useful as you work with 1-2-3:

NUM LOCK — Num Lock allows you to use the numeric keypad to type numbers; it disables the arrow keys. Press Num Lock once to turn Num Lock on, and again to turn it off. Notice that NUM appears in the status line when you're using the numeric keypad for numbers.

CAPS LOCK — Caps Lock capitalizes lowercase letters and makes capital letters lowercase. It affects only letters you're typing, and it does not replace the Shift key. Press Caps Lock once to turn Caps Lock on, and again to turn it off. Notice that CAPS appears in the status line when Caps Lock is on.

SCROLL LOCK — When Scroll Lock is on, the arrow keys move the window one column or row at a time. When Scroll Lock is off, the arrow keys move the cell pointer. Press Scroll Lock once to turn Scroll Lock on, and again to turn it off. SCROLL appears in the status line when Scroll Lock is on.

Other special keys will be discussed in the exercises.

RANGES

Many 1-2-3 commands involve working with ranges. A **range** is a cell or group of adjacent cells in the worksheet. A range can be one cell, a single row or column of cells, or a block of cells composed of many rows and columns. It must, however, be a rectangular block. The four numbers you entered earlier, for example, occupy the range of cells from A1 to D1. 1-2-3 prompts use the addresses of two opposite corners of the range to identify it. For example, the notation A1..D1 identifies the range of numbers you entered.

Figure 2.7 Ranges

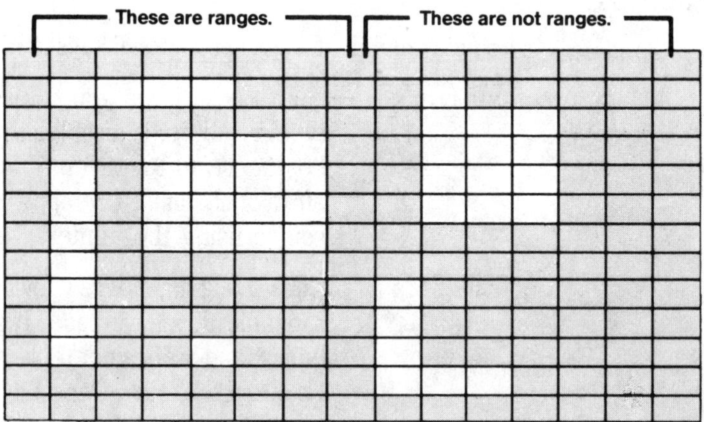

Ranges are one of the significant features of an electronic worksheet. They can be used to copy or move sections of the worksheet; to format an entire area quickly; and to erase, print, and name a group of cells.

You are going to copy data in the A1..D1 range to another section of the worksheet. Copying is a two-step process in which you first indicate the range to be copied FROM and then indicate the place you want it copied TO. Prompts in the second line of the control panel guide you through the process.

Press: HOME

/

Select: Copy

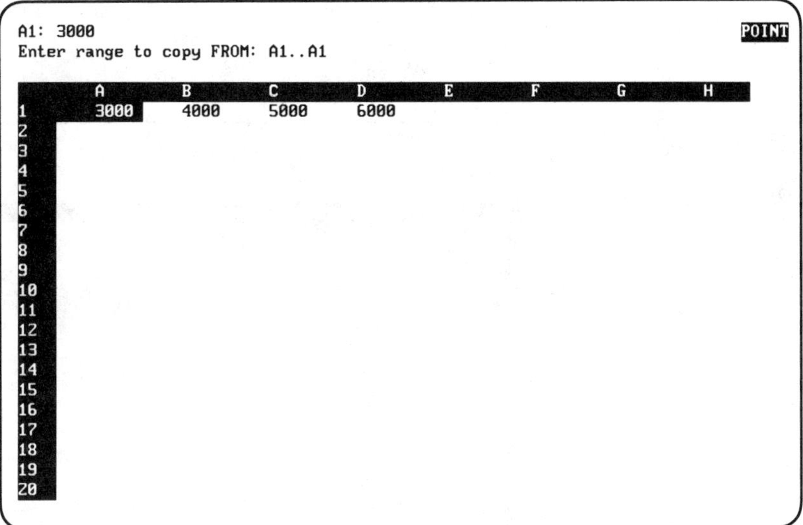

Figure 2.8 /Copy FROM prompt

Notice that the mode indicator reads POINT and the second line of the control panel displays a prompt asking you to indicate the range of cells to copy. The notation A1..A1 appears beside the prompt; it shows the current position of the cell pointer (which is also a one-cell range). The second cell address in the notation will change when you highlight the range to be copied.

You can indicate a range in two ways: (1) type the cell addresses that comprise the range, or (2) expand the highlight so that all the cells in the range are highlighted. To expand the highlight, you must first anchor the range. You can tell if the range is anchored by looking at the notation beside the prompt. A cell address (A1) means the range is not anchored, whereas a range notation (A1..A1) shows it is anchored. The range is automatically anchored for several 1-2-3 commands, including **/Copy**.

> NOTE: If the range is anchored in the wrong place, press Esc to release the anchor, reposition the cell pointer, and press . (period) to reanchor the range. You can also press Backspace to release the anchor, in which case the cell pointer returns to the cell it was highlighting before 1-2-3 entered POINT mode.

You will expand the highlight to complete the **Copy** command.

Press: → three times

Figure 2.9 /Copy FROM range highlighted

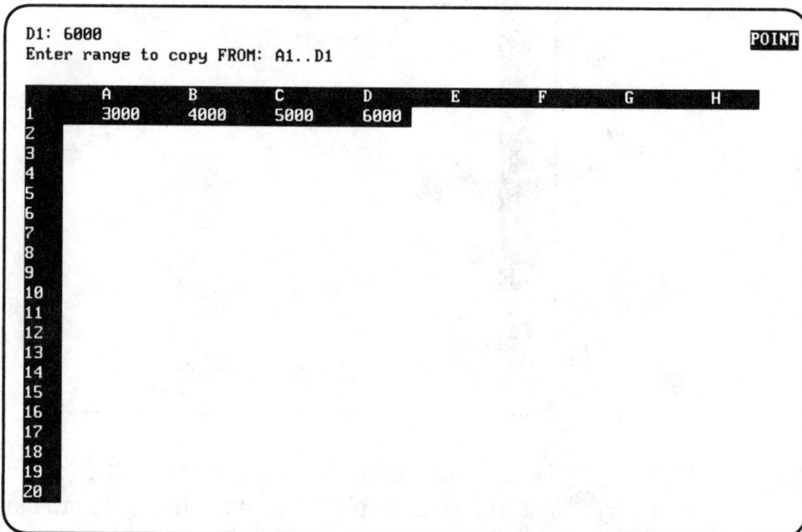

Press: ↵

Figure 2.10 /Copy TO prompt

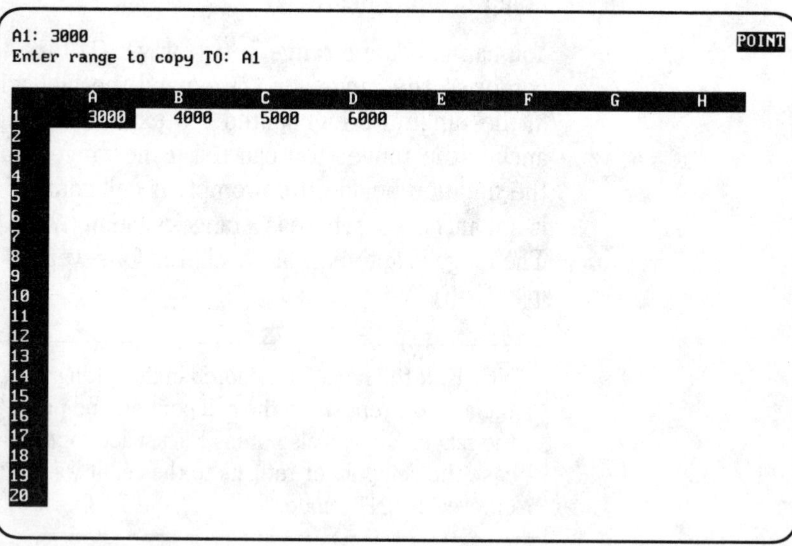

Pressing Enter confirms the specified range. The second line of the control panel then displays a second prompt asking you to indicate where you want the range copied to. Notice that the notation beside the second prompt is a cell address (A1). This means that the range is not anchored. You must now move the cell pointer to the place in the worksheet where you want to copy the range. You do not have to specify a full range equal in size to that occupied by the data to be copied; you only need to indicate the first cell of the range that will contain the data.

Before copying a range, make sure there is no data in the area where you want to copy the data. /**Copy** will write over any data that is already there.

Move to: cell A5

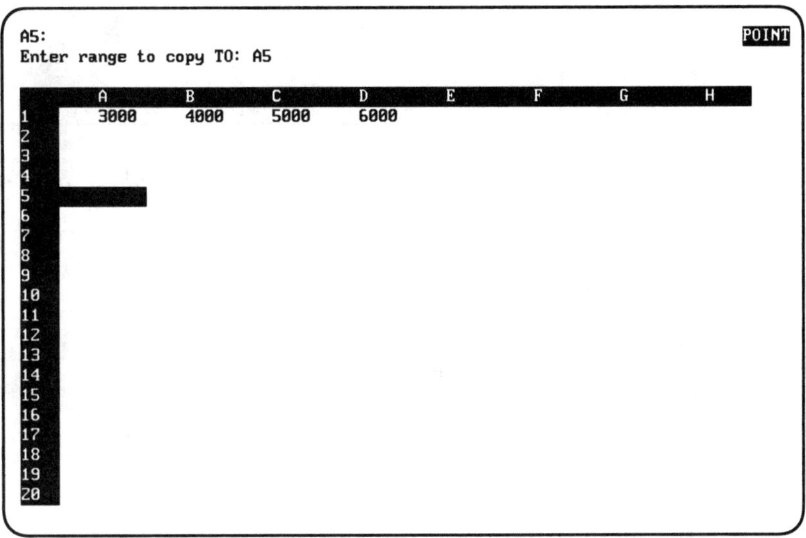

Figure 2.11
/Copy TO range highlighted

Press: [↵]

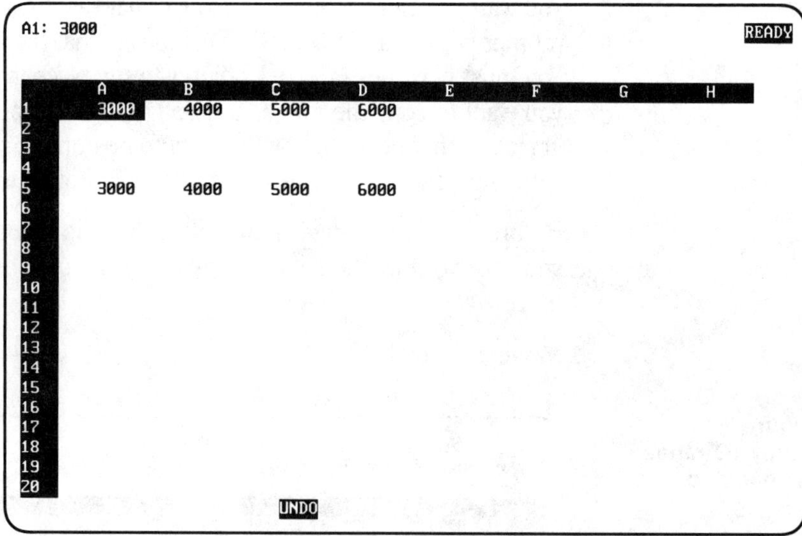

Figure 2.12
Copied data

Pressing Enter completes the second step. It also activates **/Copy**.

Now you will erase all the data from the worksheet. Unlike copying, erasing is a one-step process: you indicate the range to be erased and then press Enter. A prompt in the control panel guides you. This time you'll type the range rather than point to it. (You only need to type one period between the two cell addresses.)

Press: [/]
Select: Range
Erase

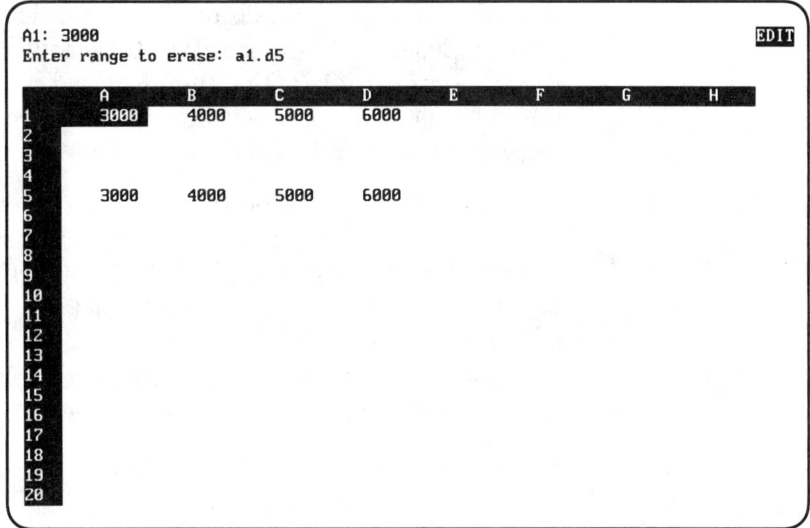

Figure 2.13 /Range Erase prompt

Type: a1.d5
Press: ↵

NOTE: To erase the worksheet, you can also press / and select **Worksheet**, **Erase**, and **Yes**.

(2.2) USING THE UNDO FEATURE

1–2–3 Release 2.2 includes an important feature—undo—that serves as a safeguard against time-consuming mistakes. The undo feature allows you to press Undo (Alt-F4) almost any time 1–2–3 is in READY mode to cancel the most recent operation that changed worksheet data and/or settings.

For example, suppose you accidentally replace a complicated formula in a cell with a number. If the undo feature is on, you can press Undo (Alt-F4) right after entering the number. 1–2–3 will erase the number and restore the formula to the cell. Sometimes you may use a command whose effect you don't like or didn't expect. For example, you may accidentally copy a large range of data in such a way that it writes over part of your worksheet. By pressing Undo (Alt-F4), the copied data will be removed and the original data restored.

You know the undo feature is on if the status line at the bottom of the screen includes the UNDO indicator. (The feature is on by default when you first start using 1–2–3.) If the UNDO indicator is not on the status line and you want to use the undo feature, select **/Worksheet Global Default Other Undo Enable.**

1–2–3 essentially lets you undo any step you took since it was last in READY mode. A step may be as simple as making an entry in a cell or as complex as using a series of commands to create a graph. Some 1–2–3 commands, however, cannot be undone. You can't for example, undo a command such as **/File Erase** which deletes a file or undo commands that activate the printer. For a complete list of exceptions, see Chapter 1 of the 1–2–3 *Reference Manual.*

To use the undo feature, press Undo (Alt-F4)—hold down Alt, press F4, and then release both keys.

As you work through the exercises in this book, remember to use the Undo (Alt-F4) key should you make mistakes. You will generally be able to undo them. The illustrations include the UNDO indicator to remind you of the existence of the undo feature.

You will now undo the result of the **Range Erase** command you just used.

Press: UNDO (Alt-F4)

Figure 2.14 Erased range restored

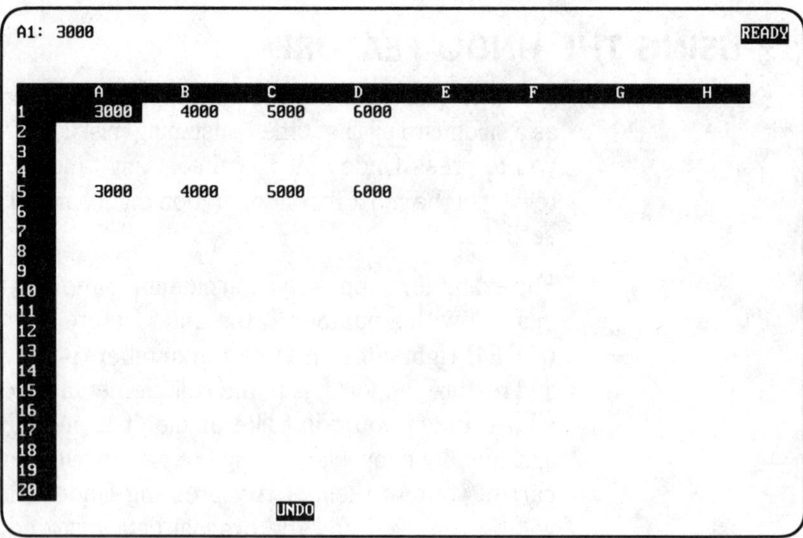

The worksheet now appears the way it was before you used /**Range Erase**.

Next enter a label and then press Undo (Alt-F4) to remove the entry:

Move to: cell A8
Type: Net Sales
Press: ↵

Net Sales is now in cell A8.

Press: UNDO (Alt-F4)

1–2–3 erases the entry and restores the worksheet to the way it looked before you entered the label.

The other benefit of the undo feature is that you can change your mind about what you undid. For example, if you want to restore the 'Net Sales' entry, you can press Undo (Alt-F4) again. Try this now:

Press: UNDO (Alt-F4)

The entry reappears.

If you start using the undo feature and it doesn't work quite the way you expected, refer to Chapter 1 of the 1–2–3 *Reference Manual* for a complete explanation of the feature.

FILES

All the work you do with 1–2–3 is done in the worksheet area on the screen. You then permanently save the contents of each worksheet in a file on a disk. That file contains your work, and it's available at any time for you to use and change as necessary. Electronic files are similar to traditional file folders; a disk containing electronic files is analogous to a filing cabinet containing folders.

Figure 2.15 Files

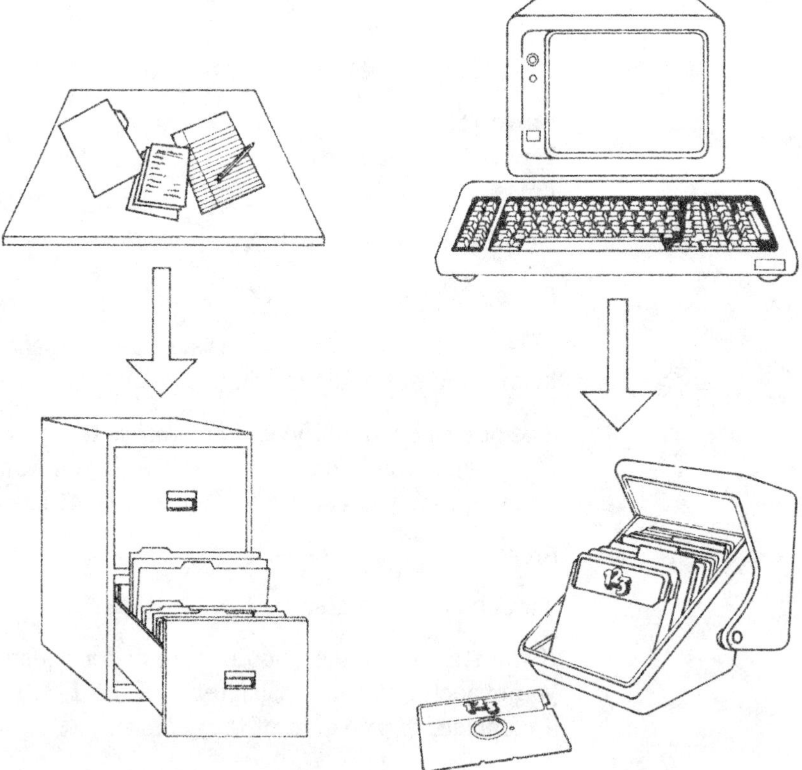

While working with 1-2-3, all the work you do is stored in the temporary memory of the computer (called random access memory, or RAM). None of the changes are permanent until you save the worksheet in a file on disk. Thus it is a good idea to save your work periodically—don't wait until you have completed all the desired changes to the worksheet, unless you have very few changes to make. Saving a worksheet in 1-2-3 takes only a few seconds and leaves the worksheet on the screen, so saving periodically will take little time. Develop the habit of saving your work every 10 to 15 minutes.

As you have seen, whenever you start up 1-2-3, it displays a blank worksheet. 1-2-3 always assumes that you want to start a new worksheet. In many cases, of course, you will actually want to work on an existing worksheet saved in a file. The following section explains how to name and save files, and then how to retrieve them.

Saving Files

You will start with a blank worksheet on your screen. You will enter a number in that worksheet and then save the worksheet in a file.

Press: [/]
Select: Worksheet
Erase
Yes
Type: 1000
Press: [↵]

To save a worksheet in a file, you must first specify a file name of up to eight characters. All 1-2-3 worksheet files have a .WK1 extension at the end of the file name. 1-2-3 adds this extension automatically; you don't have to type it.

Press: [/]
Select: File
Save

The prompts you see in the control panel above the worksheet when saving a file are slightly different for a two-diskette computer and a hard-disk computer.

- On a two-diskette computer, you'll see the following in the control panel:

  Enter save file name: B:\

  The B: indicates that the file will be saved on the disk in drive B. The name of the file will appear to the right of the B:\ as you type it. Pressing Enter enters the name. You're going to name the file ONE:

  Type: one [↵]

- On a hard-disk computer, you will see the following in the control panel:

  Enter save file name: C:\TEMP\

  This example assumes that you changed the default directory to TEMP, as described in Chapter 1. The C:\TEMP*.WK1 indicates that the file will be saved in a subdirectory called TEMP on the hard disk. As you type the name of the file, it will appear to the right of the second backslash (\). Pressing Enter then enters the name. You're going to name the file ONE:

Type: one [↵]

After you type the name, the mode indicator changes to WAIT while the worksheet is saved in the file (this won't take long because the worksheet is a small one).

Notice that the worksheet still remains on the screen after you save it.

Retrieving Files

Retrieving an existing file is a simple, straightforward process using the **File Retrieve** command. In this example, you will erase the current worksheet (the file named ONE) from the screen, and then recover it by retrieving the file. You will start by erasing the worksheet:

Press: [/]
Select: Worksheet
Erase
Yes

Now you're going to issue the command that will retrieve the file named ONE from the disk and make it the current worksheet:

Press: [/]
Select: File
Retrieve

1-2-3 responds with a prompt in the second line of the control panel asking you to identify the file to retrieve.

- On a two-diskette computer:

  Name of file to retrieve: B:*.wk?

- On a hard-disk computer:

  Name of file to retrieve: C:\TEMP*.wk?

The files stored on the disk are listed in the third line of the control panel. At this point, the only file listed is ONE.WK1 because it is the only file on the disk.

To select the file to be retrieved, simply highlight the name and press Enter. ONE.WK1 is already highlighted, so you are just going to press Enter:

Press: ↵

The mode indicator flashes WAIT, the red light on the disk drive flashes, and the file named ONE.WK1 appears on the screen. (You can tell it is the same file because the 1000 you entered is now back on the screen.)

(2.2) Retrieving a File When You Start 1–2–3

1–2–3 Release 2.2 has a feature that allows you to retrieve a file when you start 1–2–3 from DOS. This means that, instead of starting off with a blank worksheet, you start off with the worksheet you specified when you started 1–2–3.

To retrieve a worksheet when you start 1–2–3, you type **123** as usual at the DOS prompt, and follow it with a space, a hyphen, the letter **w**, and the name of your worksheet file. For example, you would type **123 -wfeb** to retrieve a file named FEB.WK1.

If the worksheet file is in a different directory or drive, you can precede the file name with a path. For example, you would type **123 -wc: \temp\income** if you wanted to retrieve a file named INCOME.WK1 from a directory named TEMP on the C drive.

Saving an Amended File

Whenever you finish working on any file, new or old, be sure to save the latest version of it before you retrieve another file. The worksheet currently in memory (on the screen) is always erased from memory when you retrieve another file.

When you select **/File Save** for a file that has been saved once already, 1–2–3 still displays the save prompt in the second line of the control panel, but it now lists the current name of the file as well. A small blinking cursor is positioned right after the name. You have two options at this point: you can change the file name or you can save the amended file under the old name.

To change the name of the file, type a new name (without the .WK1 extension) and press Enter. This results in two files: the old file with the old name and a new file with any changes you have made and a new name.

Usually, however, you will not want to change the name of the file—you will simply want to save the changes to the existing file. In this case, you simply press Enter when the old file name appears. 1–2–3 then gives you three choices:

Cancel Replace Backup

Cancel aborts the **/File Save** operation; the new file is not saved at all (you can repeat the procedure to save it). The file currently saved under that name is left intact.

Replace saves the amended worksheet on the screen by writing over the old version of the file.

(2.2) Backup is a feature new to 1–2–3 Release 2.2. It allows you to have two versions of the worksheet: the most recent one and the previous (**backup**) one. Having a backup can be useful should something go wrong with the worksheet you're working on. You can then retrieve the backup file, which means that you at least have a recent version of your work to go with.

Choosing Backup keeps the previous version of the file under the same name, but with a .BAK extension instead of .WK1. The amended worksheet then becomes the new .WK1 file. Suppose you make some changes to a worksheet named INCOME. If you select the backup option when saving the worksheet, INCOME.BAK will be the version of the worksheet that you began with (prior to the changes you made); INCOME.WK1 will include all the changes you made.

You are now going to replace the existing file ONE with a changed worksheet. First you're going to add some data to distinguish the new file.

Press: [↓]
Type: 5000 [↵]

Now save the revised file. You will accept the name offered (ONE) and then instruct 1–2–3 to replace the existing file with the revised one:

Press: [/]
Select: File
Save
Press: [↵]
Select: Replace

Some Final Notes on Retrieving Files

This section describes the process for retrieving files when there is more than one file on the disk. It gives you more practice in the fundamental skills of saving and retrieving files.

The first step is to create a new worksheet and save it under the file named TWO. You will begin by erasing the worksheet currently on the screen:

Press: [/]
Select: Worksheet
Erase
Yes

A blank worksheet appears on the screen. You will enter some data and save the file. When you select the commands to save this file, you'll notice that the name of the first file you created appears in the third line of the control panel. Again, you'll simply type in the new file name.

Type: 2000 [↵]
Press: [/]
Select: File
Save
Type: two [↵]

You now have two separate files, named ONE and TWO. At this point, erase the current worksheet and take the time to create and save four more small files on the same disk. Type a number in each worksheet to distinguish one file from the next (try 3000, 4000, 5000, and 6000) and name them THREE, FOUR, FIVE, and SIX respectively. It's important here that you create a total of six files.

After you create the six files, you will select **/File Retrieve** so you can see the list of files on the screen.

Press: [/]
Select: File
Retrieve

You should see the following in the control panel (this is for a hard-disk computer; for a two-diskette computer you would see B:*.wk?):

```
Name of file to retrieve: C:\TEMP\*.wk?
FIVE.WK1     FOUR.WK1     ONE.WK1     SIX.WK1     THREE.WK1
```

Notice two things: first, 1–2–3 lists the files in alphabetical order (rather than in the order in which you saved them); second, 1–2–3 lists only five names on the screen at one time even though there are six files on the disk.

You will frequently have more than six files on a disk or in a subdirectory on the hard disk. To see all the file names, you can press Name (F3):

Press: NAME (F3)

The list of files appears on the screen in the area where the worksheet normally appears.

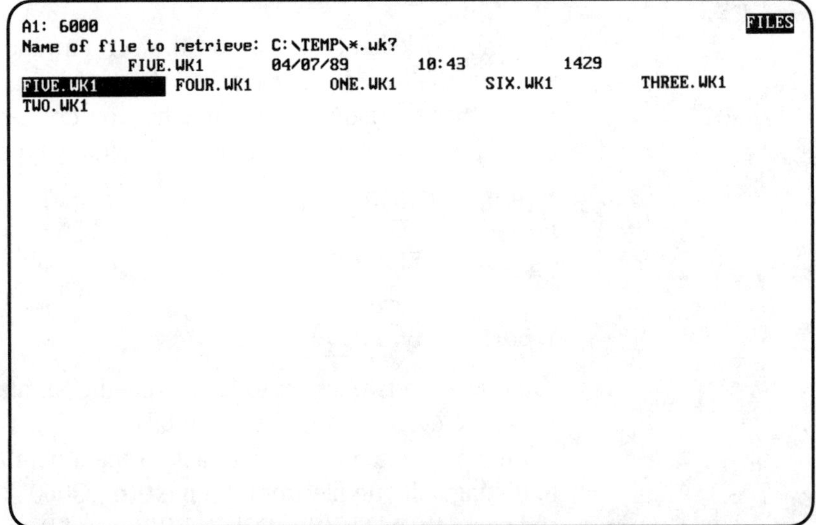

Figure 2.16 File list produced with NAME (F3)

To select one of the listed files in order to retrieve it, use the arrow keys to move the pointer among the file names. To make a selection, press Enter when the pointer is highlighting the file you want to retrieve.

You can also type the name of the file you want to retrieve. You cannot, however, just type the first letter of the file (as you can when selecting a command); you must type the full name of the file.

Once you've selected the file, the list of files is replaced by the file you've retrieved.

THE 1–2–3 HELP FACILITY

1–2–3's Help facility provides detailed information about how the program works and how to use it. Pressing Help (F1) while you are working with a worksheet brings up a Help screen that deals with the specific task that you are doing at the moment. If you want additional help, you can highlight a topic mentioned on the Help screen and press Enter, and you will see another screen on that topic.

To use the Help facility on a two-diskette system, you must keep the Help Disk (5.25" systems) or System, Help, and PrintGraph Disk (3.5" systems) in drive A. Continue to keep your data disk in drive B.

To use the Help facility on a hard-disk system, you must have the Help files in the same directory on the hard disk as the one that contains the 1–2–3 program files.

THE FILE COMMANDS

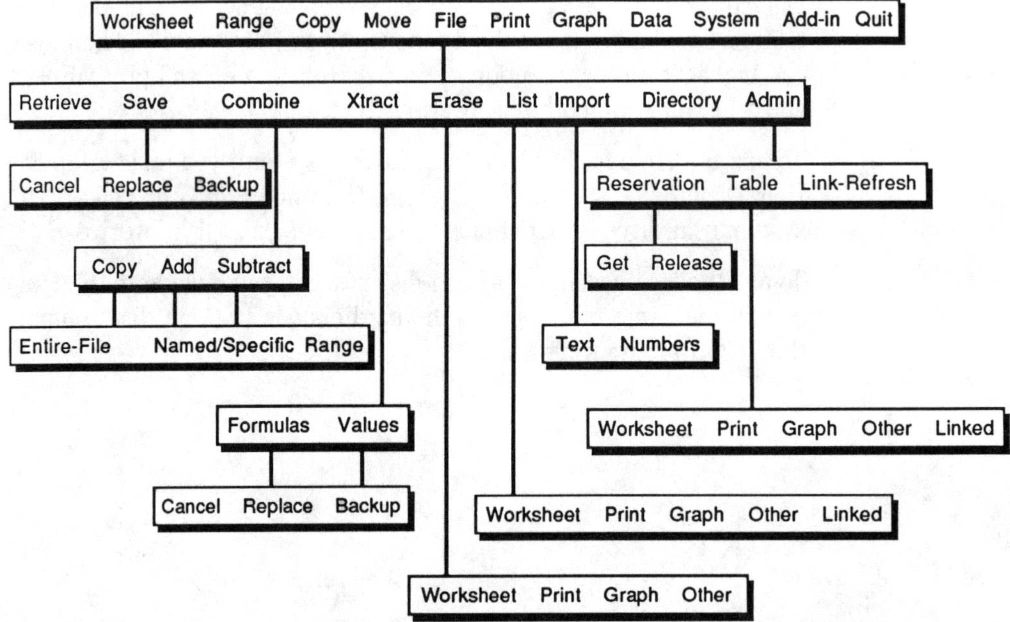

3

Creating a Worksheet

This chapter teaches the basic skills involved in creating a worksheet. It covers the following topics:

- Entering labels (text)
- Entering values (numbers)
- Making changes to the data
- Changing the appearance of the worksheet
- Entering and copying formulas
- Formatting values in cells
- Using named ranges
- (2.2) Linking files
- Transposing ranges
- Splitting the screen
- Text editing
- Performing what-if calculations
- Printing the worksheet

A Traditional Spreadsheet

A spreadsheet is a structure for numeric or financial calculations. It is an integral tool for all business operations. A traditional spreadsheet is a ledger whose columns and rows intersect to form a pattern of boxes, each of which holds a value. Many values in a spreadsheet depend on other values entered elsewhere in the spreadsheet. Thus, changing one value requires that you change all the other values related to it.

For example, a ledger containing the operating expenses of a company is a spreadsheet. One column contains the salary figures of all employees; the total of that column represents the total compensation paid by the company. That total is then entered in another column detailing monthly expenditures. If the salary of an employee or, as is frequently the case, the number of employees changes, you must go back and recalculate the entire column. You must also recalculate any figure that uses the total compensation.

Figure 3.1
Traditional spreadsheet

PAYROLL

	NAME	1 REGULAR PAY	2 FEDERAL TAX	3 STATE TAX	4 FICA	5 DEDUCTIONS	6 NET PAY	
1	Haunton, Lee	500 00	62 24	21 24	35 25	11 00	370 27	1
2	Jones, Doris	650 00	97 50	32 50	45 76	6 50	467 74	2
3	Levitt, David	650 00	80 93	27 63	45 76	11 00	484 68	3
4	Pinto, Maria	375 00	56 25	18 75	26 40	3 00	270 60	4
5	Seaver, Helen	575 00	71 58	24 43	40 48	11 00	427 51	5
6	Tan, Chiaw	500 00	62 24	21 24	35 25	11 00	370 27	6
7	Tobias, Albert	825 00	123 75	41 25	58 08	3 00	598 92	7
8	Wagner, Suzi	915 00	156 06	55 08	64 63	11 00	628 23	8
9	Williams, Carol	425 00	52 91	18 06	29 92	6 50	317 61	9
10	Yang, Shin-Chan	500 00	75 00	25 00	35 20	3 00	361 80	10
11								11
12	Total	5915 00	838 46	285 18	416 73	77 00	4297 63	12

The fundamental structure for storing and organizing data in 1–2–3 is the worksheet. A **worksheet** is a grid made up of rows and columns. Each intersection of a row and column forms a cell in which you can store data. The worksheet therefore retains the basic format of the paper spreadsheet, but it makes the maintenance of your financial data much easier and allows sophisticated operations that would be quite demanding if you did them manually.

Related numbers entered in different cells in the worksheet can be dynamically linked together—when you change one value, all other values related to it change automatically. In the case of the payroll ledger, for example, you would just have to enter a corrected salary figure in its proper cell, and all the related numbers would adjust accordingly.

Before You Start

For a two-diskette computer

- 1–2–3 should be set up to save files on a disk in drive B.
- The data disk should be in drive B.
- The Help Disk (5.25″ systems) or System, Help, and PrintGraph Disk (3.5″ systems) should be in drive A.

For a hard-disk computer

- 1-2-3 should be set up to save files in a subdirectory named TEMP.
- All the 1-2-3 disks should be copied in their own subdirectory on the hard disk.

The 1-2-3 Worksheet

As you move through the examples in this chapter, you will learn the basics of the 1-2-3 worksheet. The keystrokes and commands for setting up and maintaining a worksheet are one of the first steps.

When you start the program, 1-2-3 automatically displays a blank worksheet. If, however, you begin this chapter after having read another one, or if you've experimented with 1-2-3, the screen may already contain data. Begin by clearing the screen and creating a new worksheet.

Press: /
Select: Worksheet
Erase
Yes

Figure 3.2
Blank worksheet

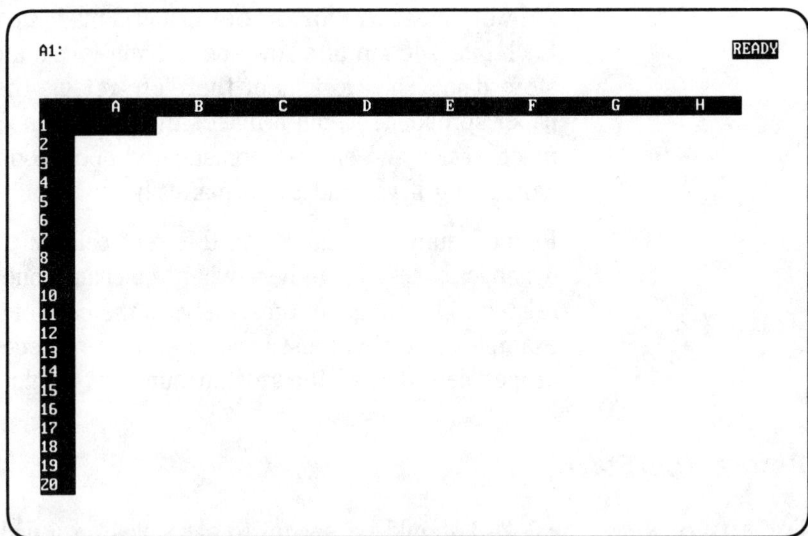

A blank worksheet is displayed on the screen. READY appears in the upper right corner, indicating 1-2-3 is ready for you to enter data or select commands.

BUILDING A WORKSHEET

In Chapter 2, you saw how to enter data in a worksheet, learned about ranges, used two worksheet commands (/**Copy** and /**Range Erase**), and undid changes to the worksheet. In this section you'll learn more about moving around a worksheet and using various 1-2-3 commands by building an income statement. The sample income statement is a simplified version of one that a company might use to analyze product sales and expenses.

First, look at the various parts of the completed income statement.

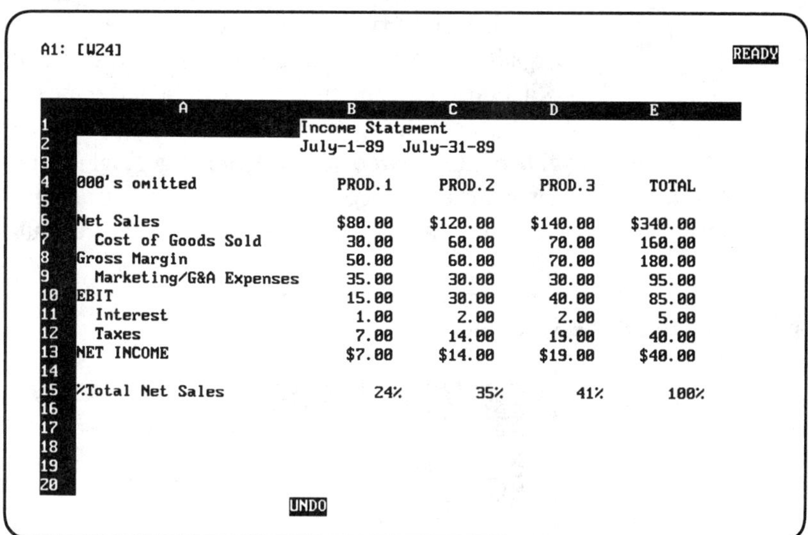

A1: [W24] READY

	A	B	C	D	E
1		Income Statement			
2		July-1-89	July-31-89		
3					
4	000's omitted	PROD.1	PROD.2	PROD.3	TOTAL
5					
6	Net Sales	$80.00	$120.00	$140.00	$340.00
7	Cost of Goods Sold	30.00	60.00	70.00	160.00
8	Gross Margin	50.00	60.00	70.00	180.00
9	Marketing/G&A Expenses	35.00	30.00	30.00	95.00
10	EBIT	15.00	30.00	40.00	85.00
11	Interest	1.00	2.00	2.00	5.00
12	Taxes	7.00	14.00	19.00	40.00
13	NET INCOME	$7.00	$14.00	$19.00	$40.00
14					
15	%Total Net Sales	24%	35%	41%	100%
16					
17					
18					
19					
20					

UNDO

Figure 3.3 Completed income statement

The Income Statement

Net Sales	Net revenue for sales of products 1, 2, and 3.
Cost of Goods Sold	The amount it costs to manufacture each product.
Gross Margin	Net Sales minus Cost of Goods Sold.
Marketing/G&A	Marketing, General and Administrative. For example, advertising, rent, salaries, and utilities.
EBIT	Earnings Before Interest and Taxes—that is, Gross Margin minus Marketing/G&A expenses.

Interest	Interest on loans, and so on.
Taxes	Federal, state, and local taxes.
Net Income	Earnings Before Interest and Taxes minus Interest and Taxes—the actual profit that this company makes on its products.
% Total Net Sales	The percentage of Net Sales that each product's sales represent—for example, Product 1's $80,000 is 24 percent of the total sales.

Notice that the data is interrelated. Many of the values result from adding or subtracting two or more other values. For example, Gross Margin equals Net Sales minus Cost of Goods sold ($50,000 = $80,000 – $30,000). The interrelation of data is the most essential characteristic of the worksheet; the worksheet's ability to recalculate automatically those interrelated values when any single value is changed is its most singular advantage. The illustration shows those values that must be entered manually and those that 1-2-3 calculates automatically.

Figure 3.4
Different kinds of values

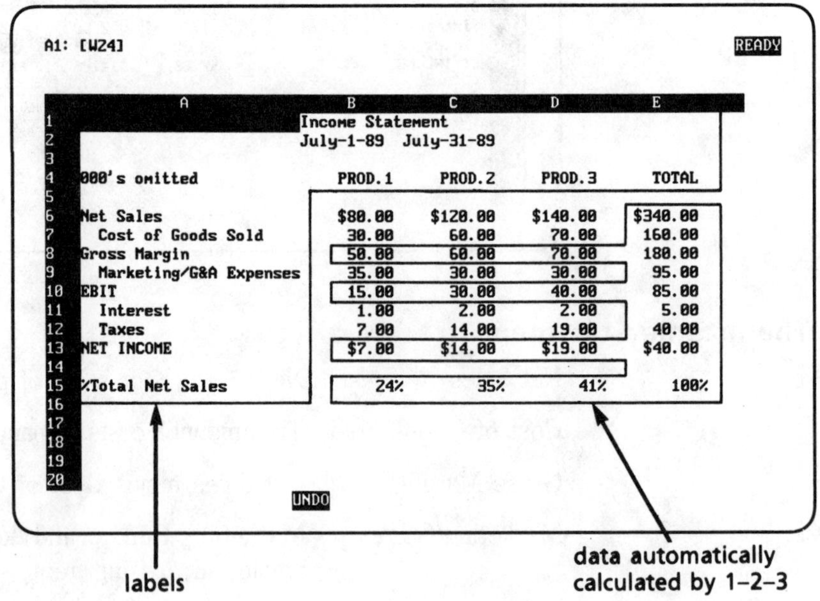

A1: [W24] READY

	A	B	C	D	E
1		Income Statement			
2		July-1-89	July-31-89		
3					
4	000's omitted	PROD.1	PROD.2	PROD.3	TOTAL
5					
6	Net Sales	$80.00	$120.00	$140.00	$340.00
7	Cost of Goods Sold	30.00	60.00	70.00	160.00
8	Gross Margin	50.00	60.00	70.00	180.00
9	Marketing/G&A Expenses	35.00	30.00	30.00	95.00
10	EBIT	15.00	30.00	40.00	85.00
11	Interest	1.00	2.00	2.00	5.00
12	Taxes	7.00	14.00	19.00	40.00
13	NET INCOME	$7.00	$14.00	$19.00	$40.00
14					
15	%Total Net Sales	24%	35%	41%	100%
16					
17					
18					
19					
20					

UNDO

Think of a worksheet as a whole comprised of two parts: a basic structure and the numbers you enter into that structure. The basic structure is designed for a specific purpose, such as an income statement, an expense report, or a general ledger. It includes labels that describe the kind of information available, formatting specifications that control the worksheet's physical appearance (column width, the display of numbers, and so forth), and formulas that tell the computer how to calculate the values entered in certain cells.

The numeric data from which 1-2-3 automatically calculates any formulas is entered into this structure.

ENTERING DATA IN THE WORKSHEET

There are two kinds of worksheet entries: labels and values. In most cases, **labels** are letters or words; they can be titles, captions that describe what is in a column or row, or special characters. **Values** can be numbers or they can be formulas that calculate numbers.

1-2-3 distinguishes between a label entry and a value entry by the first character. Because labels are usually words and values are usually numbers, 1-2-3 assumes that an entry beginning with a letter is a label and one beginning with a number is a value. For example, Net Sales and Total are labels; 100 and 80 are values.

Certain entries, however, such as those that begin with symbols, are ambiguous. The following rules apply:

- 1-2-3 will interpret the entry as a value if the first character is one of the following:

  0 1 2 3 4 5 6 7 8 9 + – (. @ # $

- 1-2-3 will interpret the entry as a label if the first character is not one of the characters listed above.

> NOTE: In some cases, a label may begin with a number (for example, 4th Quarter); a formula in a value can begin with a letter (for example, A3+A4). See "Special Entries" later in this chapter for information about these exceptions.

Entering Labels

Begin the Income Statement by entering the first label (the worksheet should be blank). As you enter the label, you'll notice that the mode indicator reads LABEL.

Move to: cell A5
Type: Net Sales [↵]

Figure 3.5 First label entered

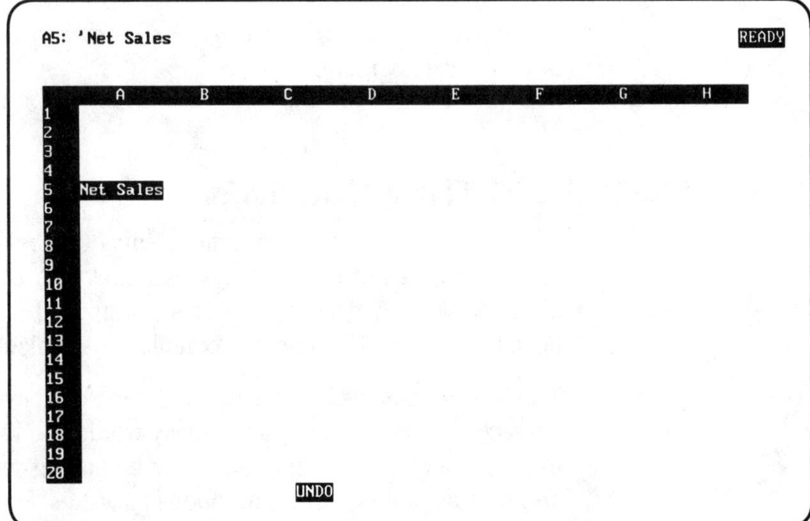

Now look at the first line of the control panel:

A5: 'Net Sales

1–2–3 recognizes that the entry is a label and automatically puts an apostrophe (') before it. This symbol, one of a number of **label prefixes**, indicates that this entry is a label, aligned at the left side of the cell.

> NOTE: If you make a mistake while typing the entry, use the Backspace or Del keys to remove the error, and then retype the entry. If you notice the mistake after pressing Enter, correct it by moving the cell pointer to the cell, typing the correct entry, and pressing Enter. (You'll learn more about editing entries below.)

Enter the remaining labels in Column A. Remember, you can press Down instead of Enter to enter the label in the cell and move the cell pointer to the next cell. Follow the keystrokes for the next three labels.

Move to: cell A6
Press: SPACE two times
Type: Cost of Goods Sold ↓
Gross Margin ↓
Press: SPACE two times
Type: Marketing /G&A Expenses
Press: ↓

Copy the rest of the labels from Figure 3.6 into Column A. Remember to leave two blank spaces (press the space bar twice) at the beginning of labels that are indented.

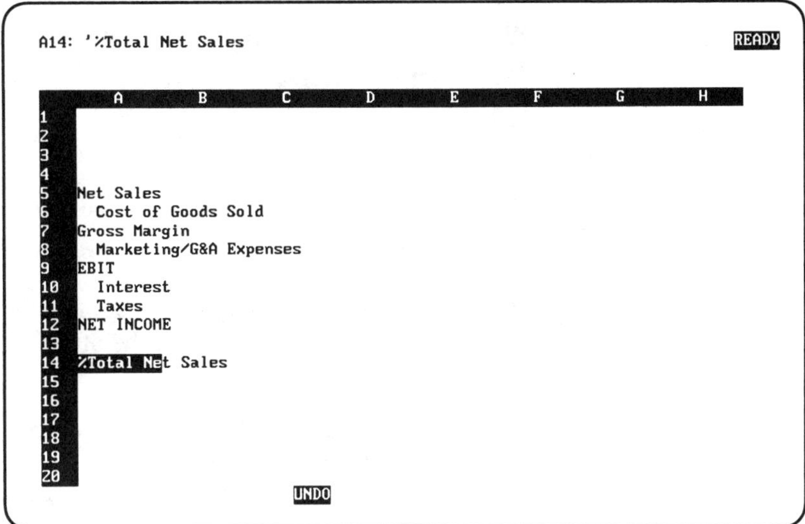

Figure 3.6 Labels in column A

Widening a Column

Some of the labels run over into columns B and C. Column widths can be adjusted to fit any data you need to enter. You will now widen column A before entering the rest of the labels.

Move to: any cell in column A
Press: [/]
Select: Worksheet
Column
Set-Width
Type: 24 [↵]

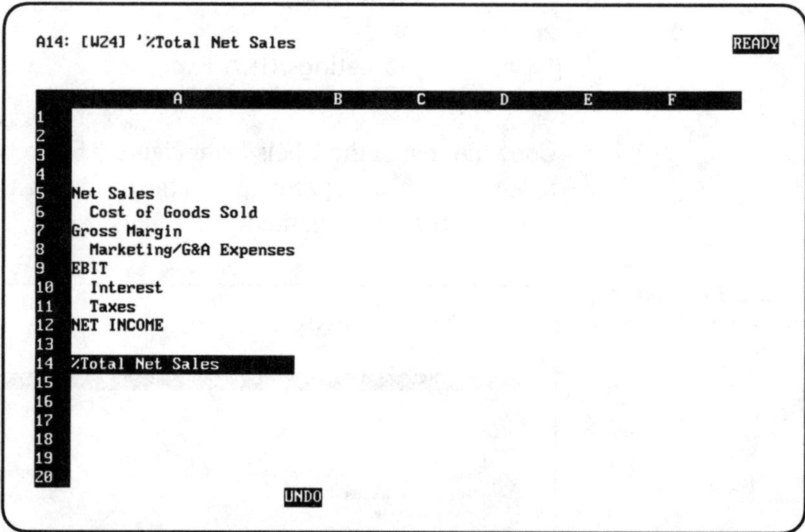

Figure 3.7
Column A widened

Column A went from 9 to 24 spaces wide, and the cell pointer expanded to fill the wider column. Notice that the other columns did not change; they remained 9 spaces wide.

The width of column A is now set at a number other than the initial setting. 1-2-3 indicates the exact width with a message in the first line of the control panel. Notice that [W24] follows the cell address in that line.

Now you will enter the column labels in row 4.

Move to: cell B4
Type: PROD.1 [→]
PROD.2 [→]
PROD.3 [→]
TOTAL [↵]

Next enter the title and date. (The dates will run together. You'll fix them later.)

Move to: cell B1
Type: Income Statement [↓]
July-2-89 [→]
Aug-1-89 [↵]

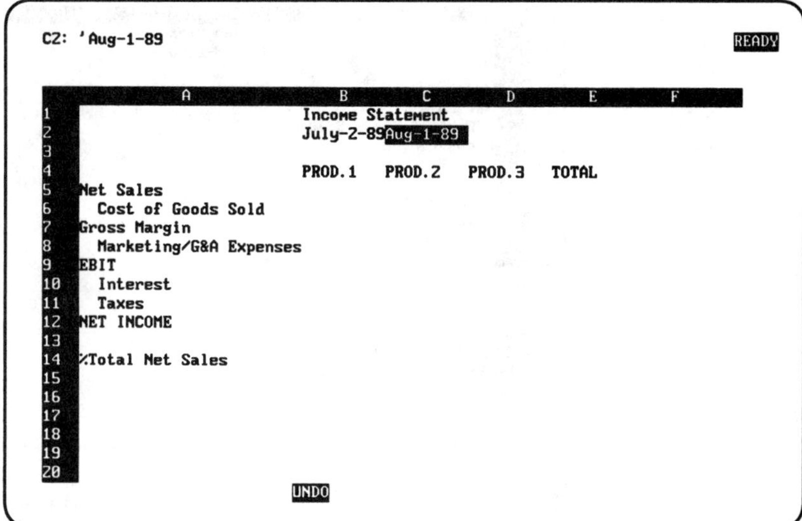

Figure 3.8 More labels entered

Notice that the title contains more characters than the cell can display, so the label overflows into cell C1. This type of entry is called a **long label**. 1-2-3 stores the long label only in cell B1, leaving cell C1 blank. You can see this by moving the cell pointer back to B1 and C1 and looking at the first line of the control panel.

Entering Values

You have entered the labels, and the basic structure of the worksheet is complete. The next step is to enter the values. Enter Net Sales values for Products 1, 2, and 3. You'll notice that the mode indicator will read VALUE as soon as you start to type a value.

Move to: cell B5
Type: 80 [→]
120 [→]
140 [↵]

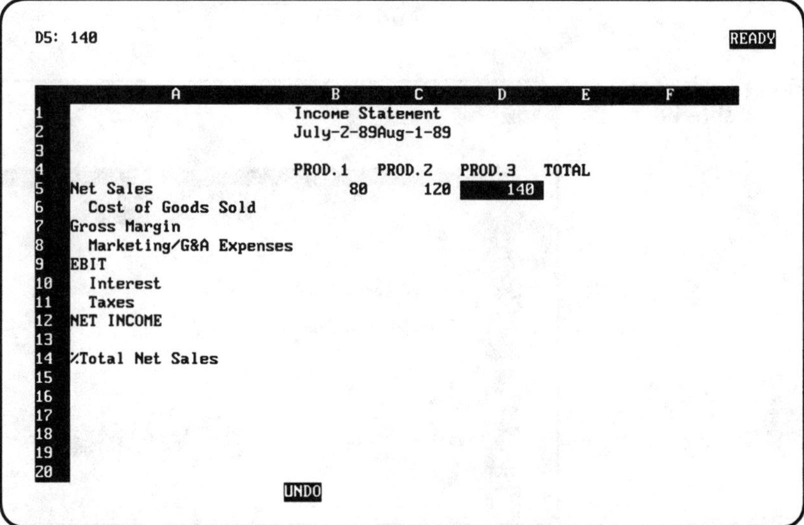

Figure 3.9
First three values entered

The worksheet now contains both labels and values. The initial settings of 1-2-3 cause labels to appear on the left side of the cell and values on the right side.

Enter the Cost of Goods Sold values for Products 1, 2, and 3:

Move to: cell B6
Type: 30 [→]
60 [→]
70 [↵]

Finally, enter the following data. (The blank rows will be filled in later.)

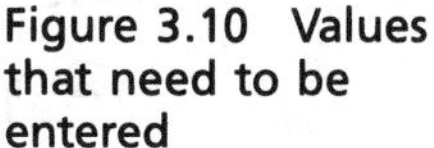

Figure 3.10 Values that need to be entered

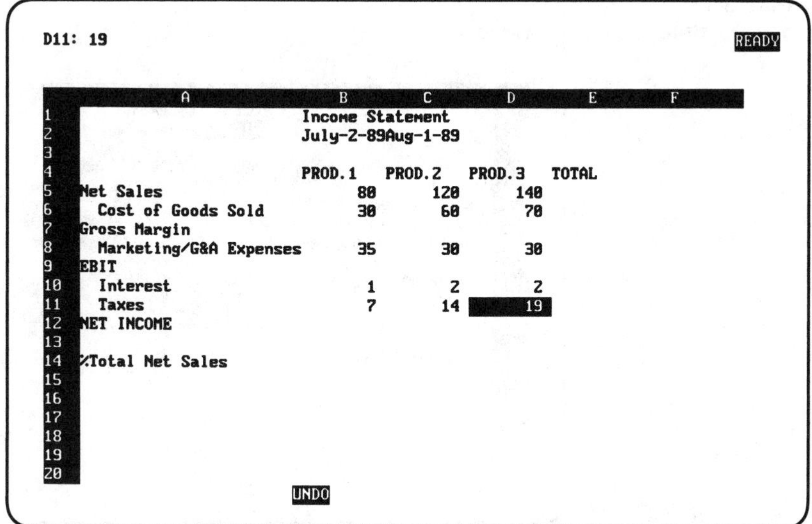

When you're finished, your screen should look exactly like the one pictured in Figure 3.10.

EDITING DATA

You can edit or change entries in the worksheet in two ways. First, you can move the cell pointer to the cell that contains the entry you want to change, type a new entry, and press Enter or an arrow key. This method is the best choice for replacing an entire entry.

Second, you can use the Edit (F2) key, which is the best way to make a minor change in a long entry. Edit (F2) lets you edit the entry in the second line in the control panel. In this example, you are going to use Edit (F2) to change the dates. The mode indicator will read EDIT.

Move to: cell B2
Press: EDIT (F2)
← four times
DEL
Type: 1 ↵

Figure 3.11
Changed date

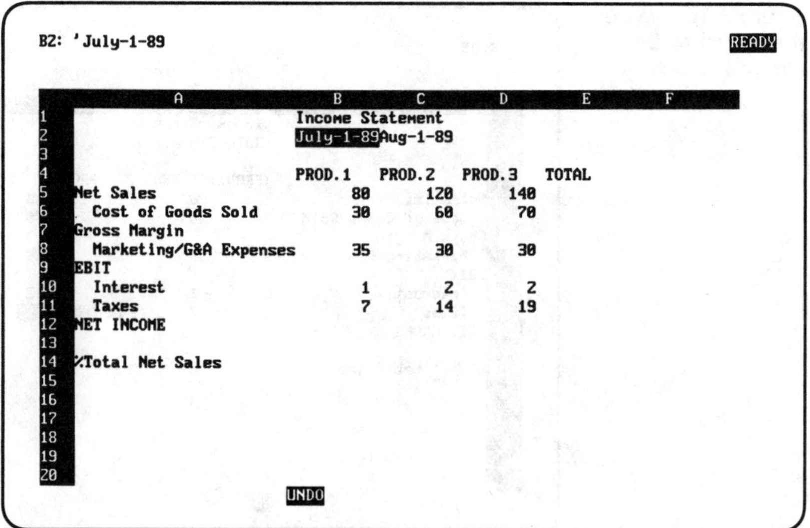

The corrected label is entered. You are now going to change the other date to July 31st the same way.

Move to: cell C2

Press: EDIT (F2)

HOME

→

DEL four times

Type: July-3 ↵

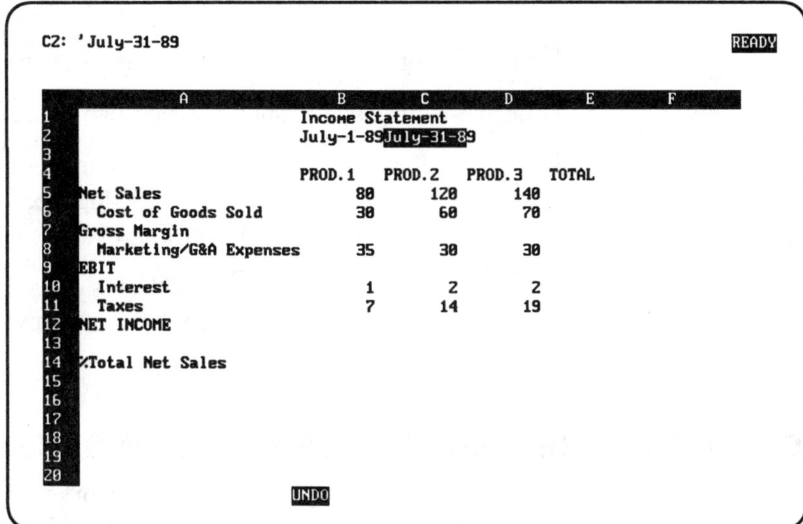

Figure 3.12 Second date edited

Editing Keys

Use the following keys when editing entries:

EDIT (F2) — Lets you start editing; the mode indicator reads EDIT. Pressing Enter turns editing off and returns the mode indicator to READY.

↵ — Replaces the original entry with the edited one.

ESC — Lets you stop editing and leaves the original entry intact.

BACKSPACE — Erases the character to the left and moves left.

DEL — Erases the character the cursor is on.

HOME — Moves to the first character of the entry. (If your entry is a label, the first character will be a label prefix.)

END — Moves to the last character of the entry.

← →	Moves one character at a time.
CTRL → or TAB	Moves five characters to the right.
CTRL ← or SHIFT TAB	Moves five characters to the left.
INS	Switches between inserting text by moving existing text over (INS mode) and writing over text (OVR mode).
↑ ↓	Completes editing and moves cell pointer up/down one row.

CHANGING THE APPEARANCE OF THE WORKSHEET

1-2-3 offers flexibility in adapting the worksheet for both appearance and functionality. The worksheet is readily adjustable, as you saw above when you widened a column. Other structural changes are equally simple.

Inserting a Row

A blank row is easily inserted into the worksheet. You will now insert one between the rows with the Product and Net Sales labels. Begin by placing the pointer in the row below where you want the new row to appear.

Move to: any cell in row 5
Press: /
Select: Worksheet
Insert
Row
Press: ↵

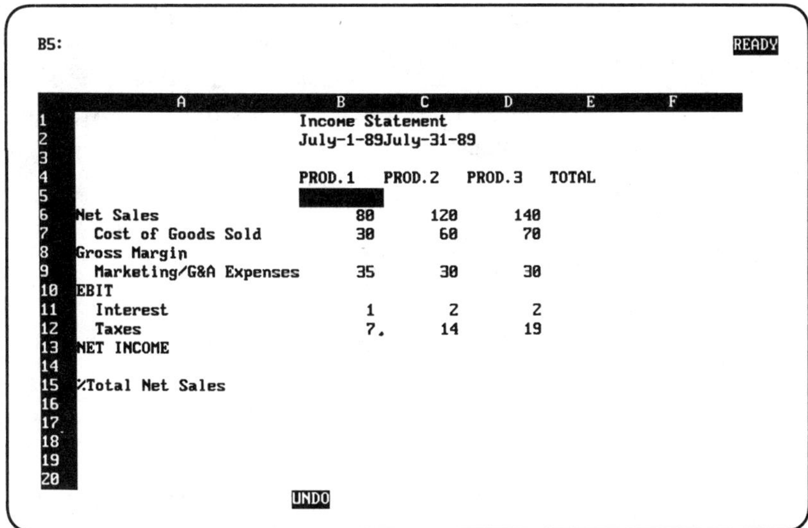

Figure 3.13 Blank row inserted

Notice that each cell in the worksheet below the new row now has a new address. Net Sales, for example, was in A5 and is now in A6. This simple example shows how an electronic worksheet makes automatic adjustments; 1-2-3 can do even more. For instance, if the worksheet contains a formula and you insert or delete a row or column within that range, all the cell references in the formulas change to reflect the new row/column relationships.

Right-Aligning Labels

Labels positioned in various ways can improve the appearance of the worksheet. A choice of three label prefixes determines the placement of the label within a cell. The apostrophe is 1-2-3's initial setting. 1-2-3 automatically places an apostrophe before a label and aligns the label on the left side of the cell. When you change the position of the label within the cell with **/Range Label**, the prefix changes. A double quotation mark (‘‘) indicates that the label is aligned on the right side of the cell. A caret (^) shows the label is centered in the cell.

You can change label prefixes manually, one at a time. Or you can change the alignment of all the labels in a range with a single command. (You can even change the initial setting from the apostrophe to one of the other label prefixes.)

You are going to place the column labels on the right of their cells so they line up with the numbers below (numbers automatically appear at the right side of cells). You will use the **Range Label** command. The label prefix will change from an apostrophe (') to a double quotation mark (").

Move to: cell B4
Press: /
Select: Range
Label
Right
Press: END
→
↵

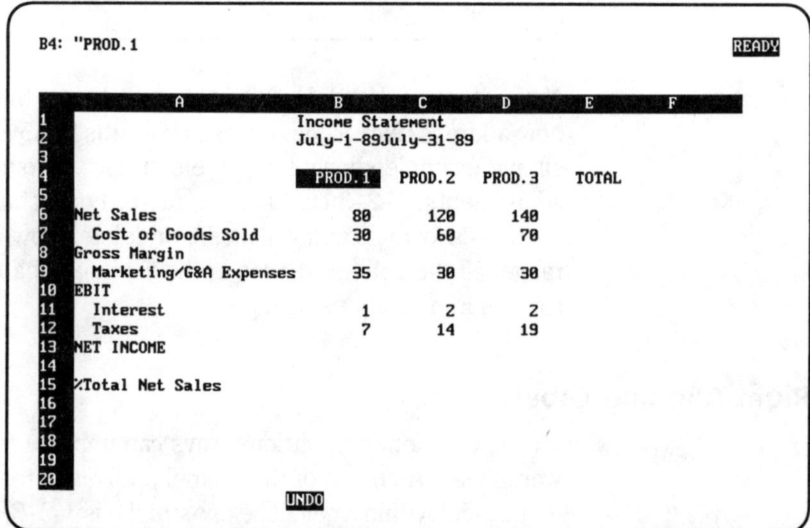

Figure 3.14 Right-aligned labels

The **Range Label** command instantly right-aligned all the labels in row 4. Now move the cell pointer through a few of them and look in the first line of the control panel. The new prefix " appears before each label.

Changing Column Widths

1–2–3 initially sets all columns to be nine characters wide. Column width is one of the **global settings**, which control the entire worksheet.

You can either change the width of columns manually (as you did with column A earlier) or you can change the global setting so that all columns (*except* any column that you've set manually) change to the new width.

(2.2) When you change one of the global settings, 1-2-3 displays a setting sheet showing all its global settings. A **setting sheet** is a special screen that is new to 1-2-3 Release 2.2. It helps you keep track of the changes you're making by showing you the current settings for all the options. You change the settings by selecting the appropriate commands from the menu that appears above the setting sheet.

You are going to change the column widths on the Income Statement from 9 to 11 to make the worksheet easier to read. The worksheet will automatically be displayed as you do this so that you can see the effect of the adjustment.

Move to: any cell in column B
Press: /
Select: Worksheet
Global

1-2-3 now displays the global settings sheet on the screen. Notice that column width is currently set to 9.

Figure 3.15
Global settings

```
B4: "PROD.1                                                          MENU
Format  Label-Prefix  Column-Width  Recalculation  Protection  Default  Zero
Fixed  Sci  Currency  ,  General  +/-  Percent  Date  Text  Hidden
                         Global Settings
   Conventional memory:  173682 of 362096 Bytes (47%)
   Expanded memory:      (None)

   Math coprocessor:     (None)

   Recalculation:
     Method              Automatic
     Order               Natural
     Iterations          1

   Circular reference:   (None)

   Cell display:
     Format              (G)
     Label prefix        ' (left align)
     Column width        9
     Zero suppression    No

   Global protection:    Disabled
```

Select: Column-Width
Press: [→] two times

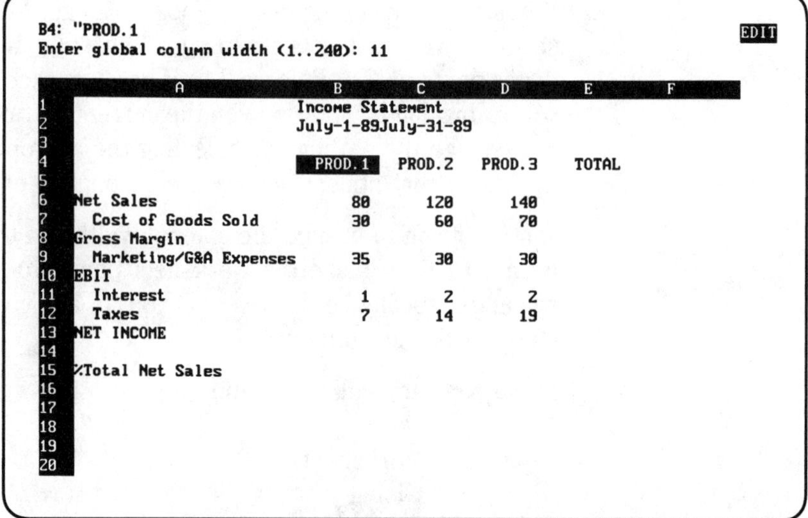

Figure 3.16 Prompt for column width

Notice that the prompt in the second line of the control panel changes as you widen the columns by pressing Right. You can type in the new column width instead of pressing arrows, but using the arrow key lets you see the effect of the change immediately. For example, notice that the date labels in row 2 are now separated. Stop when **Enter global column width (1..240):** reads **11**.

Press: [↵]

> NOTE: The width of column A did not change because earlier you set the width of this column manually with the **Worksheet Column Set-Width** command. That command sets individual columns and takes precedence over global settings that control the entire worksheet.

If you decide at a later point that you want to change the global column width, simply select **/Worksheet Global Column-Width** again.

Special Entries

1-2-3 automatically identifies each entry you type as a label or value by looking at the first character. Sometimes, however, the first character is misleading. For example, you may want to enter a label that begins with a number, such as 1st Product.

To use this kind of label, you would manually type a label prefix (usually ') before the first character: **'1st Product**. This tells the program that the entry is a label. The prefix does not appear in the cell, but you will see it in the first line of the control panel when the cell pointer is in the cell.

All of the values entered in the Income Statement represent numbers in the thousands, but the last three zeros have been left out. You indicate this abbreviation by entering **000's omitted**—a label that begins with a number—at the top of the Income Statement. First try entering it without the prefix:

Move to: cell A4
Type: 000's omitted ↵

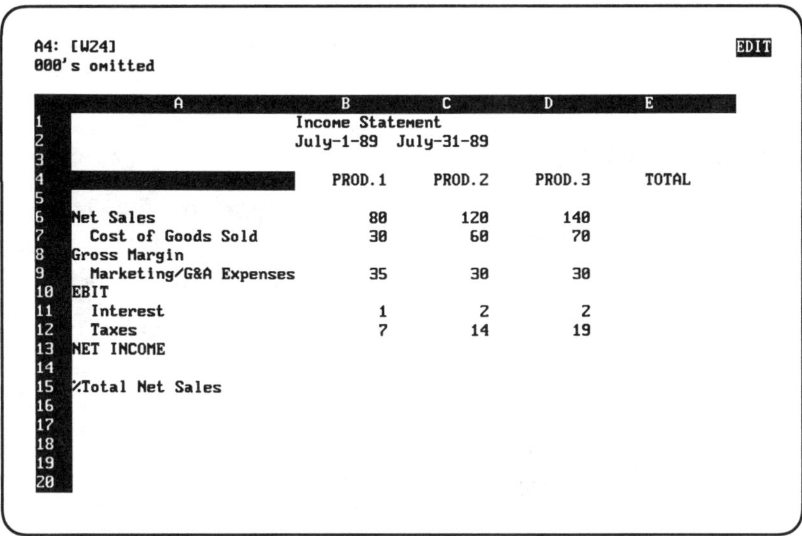

Figure 3.17
Entering 000's omitted

The computer beeps and the mode indicator reads EDIT. The initial 0 tells 1-2-3 the entry is a value, but the program will not accept a value that contains alphabetical characters.

Try it again with a label prefix. Keep your eye on the mode indicator; once you have typed the apostrophe, the indicator will read LABEL.

Press: ESC twice
Type: '000's omitted ↵

Figure 3.18 000's omitted entered correctly

```
A4: [W24] '000's omitted                                              READY

          A                  B          C          D          E
1                         Income Statement
2                         July-1-89  July-31-89
3
4   000's omitted              PROD.1     PROD.2     PROD.3     TOTAL
5
6   Net Sales                      80        120        140
7     Cost of Goods Sold           30         60         70
8   Gross Margin
9     Marketing/G&A Expenses       35         30         30
10  EBIT
11    Interest                      1          2          2
12    Taxes                         7         14         19
13  NET INCOME
14
15  %Total Net Sales
16
17
18
19
20
                        UNDO
```

SAVING THE FILE

You've created the basic structure of the worksheet and entered some data. Before proceeding, save what you've done. Develop the habit of saving your work every 15 minutes or so.

When saving a file that has been previously named and saved, 1-2-3 provides the file name; you only need to press Enter. New files, however, need to be given a file name. Name this file INCOME.

Press: /
Select: File
Save

Any files you've already created will be listed in the third line of the control panel. In the second line, you'll see the prompt **Enter save file name: C:\TEMP*.wk1**. (This is for a hard-disk computer; if you have a two-diskette computer, the prompt will read B:*.WK1). Simply type in the file name.

Type: income

Figure 3.19 Prompt for saving file

```
A4: [W24] '000's omitted                                              EDIT
Enter name of file to save: C:\TEMP\INCOME.wk1

        A                    B          C          D          E
1                        Income Statement
2                        July-1-89  July-31-89
3
4  000's omitted             PROD.1     PROD.2     PROD.3     TOTAL
5
6  Net Sales                    80        120        140
7    Cost of Goods Sold         30         60         70
8  Gross Margin
9    Marketing/G&A Expenses     35         30         30
10 EBIT
11   Interest                    1          2          2
12   Taxes                       7         14         19
13 NET INCOME
14
15 %Total Net Sales
16
17
18
19
20
```

Press: ↵

The disk drive light goes on while the file is being saved.

FORMULAS

Formulas are another important element of the worksheet. They perform both simple and sophisticated mathematical operations. Formulas allow 1–2–3 to recalculate all related values to reflect whatever changes you make.

Formulas contain references to particular cells (indicated by their cell addresses) and specify the mathematical operations to be performed on the values within those cells. 1–2–3 looks at the values in each of the cells listed in the formula when it performs a calculation.

This section explains how to enter formulas and provides an introduction to the powerful built-in formulas of 1–2–3, called @functions (“at” functions).

Entering a Formula

You enter a formula in the worksheet just as you would any other entry—by typing it in a cell. A formula is a value, but it often contains cell references, so many times it begins with the plus sign (+) to indicate that a formula follows (for example, +A1+B7, +C3/5.2).

The basic way to create a formula is to enter a cell address or a value, then a mathematical operator, then another address or value, and so on. This is similar to the way a formula is entered on a calculator.

The most frequently used mathematical operators are:

+ add
– subtract
* multiply
/ divide

You can enter a formula in three ways: (1) by pointing to cells to be included (as you'll do in this example), (2) by typing the formula, or (3) by selecting named ranges from a list (named ranges are discussed later in this chapter). (The Edit (F2) and Goto (F5) keys do not function while you are pointing to a cell in a formula.)

A formula being entered appears in the second line of the control panel. When you press Enter or an arrow key, the result of the formula appears in the cell in the worksheet.

You are going to enter a formula for the Total Net Sales for Products 1, 2, and 3. It will add the values in cells B6, C6, and D6. Begin by moving the cell pointer to the cell that will contain the formula.

Move to: cell E6
Type: +
Move to: cell B6 (the mode indicator reads POINT)
Type: + (the cell pointer moves back to cell E6)
Move to: cell C6
Type: +
Move to: cell D6
Press: ↵

Figure 3.20
Formula entered

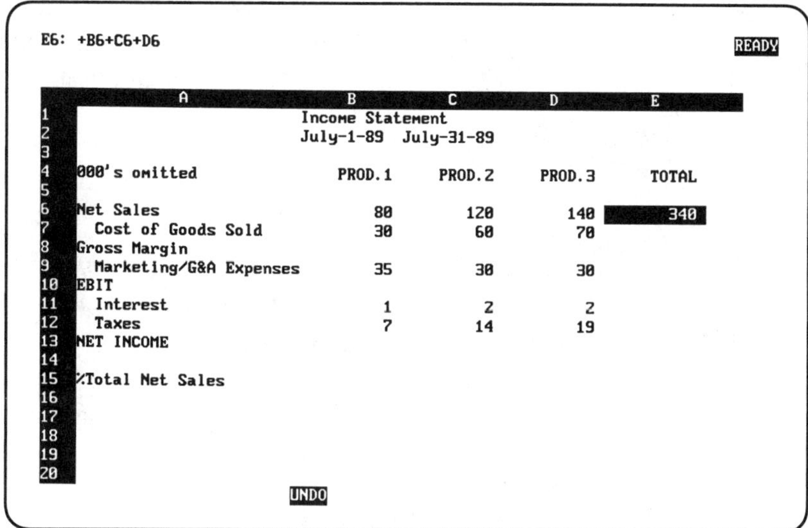

The value 340 appears in cell E6, and the formula +B6+C6+D6 appears in the first line of the control panel.

> NOTE: To look at any formula stored in the worksheet, move the cell pointer to the cell containing the formula. Although a value may be displayed in the cell, the formula itself appears in the control panel. You can edit a formula as you would any other entry—type over it or use the Edit (F2) key.

@Functions

In addition to standard arithmetical calculations, 1-2-3 can perform many special-purpose calculations. Each of these begins with the @ ("at") character; thus, they are called **@functions** ("at" functions). The various @functions make it easy to build sophisticated calculations in the worksheet.

An @function is made up of three parts:

1. The @ symbol, which must appear as the first character.
2. The name of the function, typed in either uppercase or lowercase letters.

3. One or more arguments enclosed in parentheses (the **argument** specifies the data the function works on and can be anything from a single value to a range of cells, depending on the particular function).

For example:

@SUM(A1..A10) The argument, A1..A10, is the range of cells that will be added by the @SUM function.

@SQRT (16) The argument, 16, is what the @SQRT function will find the square root of.

You just calculated Total Net Sales by pointing to each cell and building the formula cell by cell. Now you are going to enter a similar formula with the function @SUM. The function will add the Cost of Goods Sold for Products 1, 2, and 3 to calculate the Total in cell E7.

Move to: cell E7
Type: **@sum(b7.d7)** (the period in the formula tells 1-2-3 that this is a range)
Press: ↵

Figure 3.21
@SUM entered

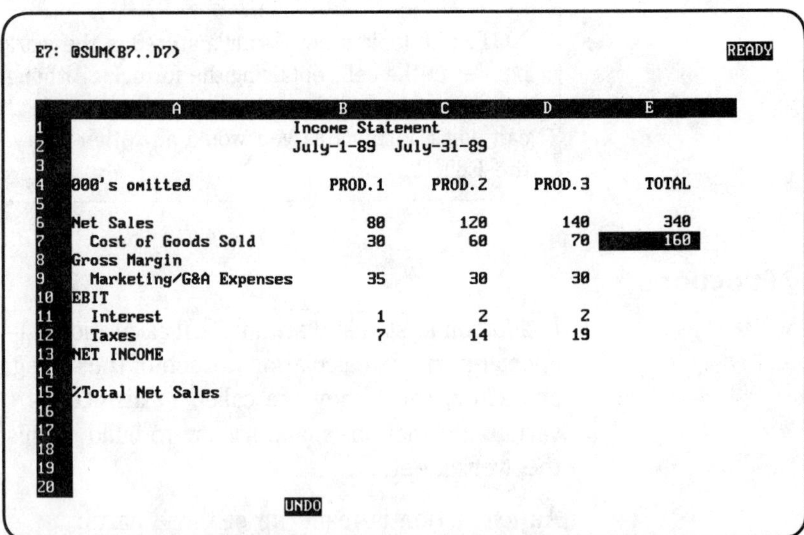

E7: @SUM(B7..D7) READY

	A	B	C	D	E
1		Income Statement			
2		July-1-89	July-31-89		
3					
4	000's omitted	PROD.1	PROD.2	PROD.3	TOTAL
5					
6	Net Sales	80	120	140	340
7	Cost of Goods Sold	30	60	70	160
8	Gross Margin				
9	Marketing/G&A Expenses	35	30	30	
10	EBIT				
11	Interest	1	2	2	
12	Taxes	7	14	19	
13	NET INCOME				
14					
15	%Total Net Sales				
16					
17					
18					
19					
20					

UNDO

The number 160 appears in cell E7, and the formula appears in the first line of the control panel.

The @functions have a number of advantages that provide great flexibility:

- You can use a range in a formula. For example, instead of individually typing 10 numbers you want to add, use the function @SUM and a range: @SUM(A1..A10).
- They perform advanced calculations of many kinds:

Mathematical:	@COS	the cosine of a number
	@EXP	e raised to a number
	@SQRT	the square root of a number
Statistical:	@AVG.......	the average of a list
	@STD	the standard deviation of a list
	@VAR.......	the variance of a list
Financial:	@FV	the future value of a series of payments at a certain interest rate
	@PMT	a loan payment, based on the specified principal and interest

> NOTE: These are only a few of the advanced calculations 1-2-3 can perform using @functions.

- You can use logical arithmetic, that is, make an entry depend on certain conditions. For example, the logical function @IF(A1 >5,300,0) means that if the value in A1 is greater than 5, the formula will resolve to 300; if the value is not greater than 5, the formula will resolve to 0.
- Other kinds of @functions help you do such things as look up a value in a table, convert a number into a string (string functions), or change a date into a serial number (date and time functions).

> NOTE: These functions are described in detail in the 1-2-3 *Reference Manual*.

Copying a Formula

/Copy is one of the most frequently used worksheet commands. You've seen how it can copy the contents of a cell or a range of cells to another place in the worksheet.

/Copy works differently when copying cells containing formulas. Rather than copying the value displayed in the cell, it copies the formula displayed in the control panel. Copying formulas instead of typing them individually in every place they are needed saves time and keystrokes.

> NOTE: The **Range Value** command copies cell values (the results of formulaic calculations) rather than formulas.

Remember, copying is a two-step process: (1) point to what you want to copy FROM, and (2) point to where you want to copy TO.

On the Income Statement, you are going to use the same formula to calculate Total Gross Margin (adding the three cells to the left of the Total column) that you used to obtain Total Cost of Goods Sold. Instead of typing the formula over again, you will copy it from cell E7 to E8.

Move to: cell E7
Press: /
Select: Copy

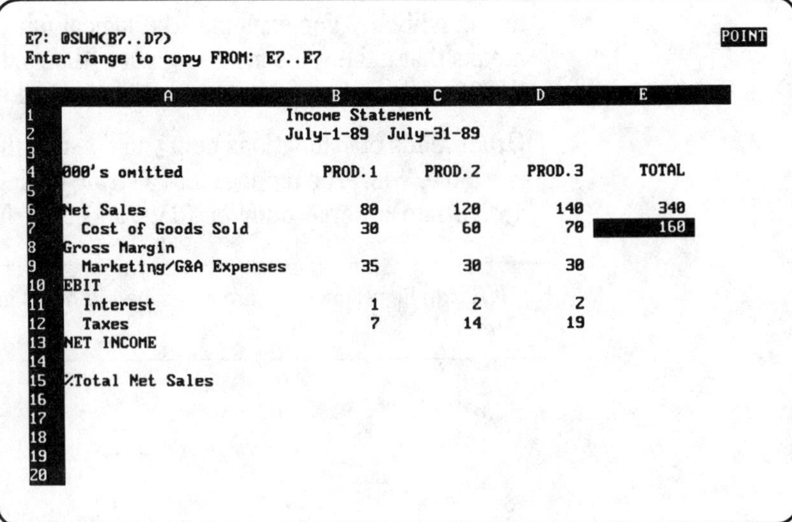

E7: @SUM(B7..D7)
Enter range to copy FROM: E7..E7 POINT

	A	B	C	D	E
1		Income Statement			
2		July-1-89	July-31-89		
3					
4	000's omitted	PROD.1	PROD.2	PROD.3	TOTAL
5					
6	Net Sales	80	120	140	340
7	Cost of Goods Sold	30	60	70	160
8	Gross Margin				
9	Marketing/G&A Expenses	35	30	30	
10	EBIT				
11	Interest	1	2	2	
12	Taxes	7	14	19	
13	NET INCOME				
14					
15	%Total Net Sales				
16					
17					
18					
19					
20					

Figure 3.22 /Copy FROM prompt

The prompt in the control panel reads: **Range to copy FROM: E7..E7.** Because you're copying the one-cell range marked by the cell pointer, you don't need to point to a range.

Press: ↵

The new prompt in the second line of the control panel reads **Range to copy TO: E7.**

Press: ↓
↵

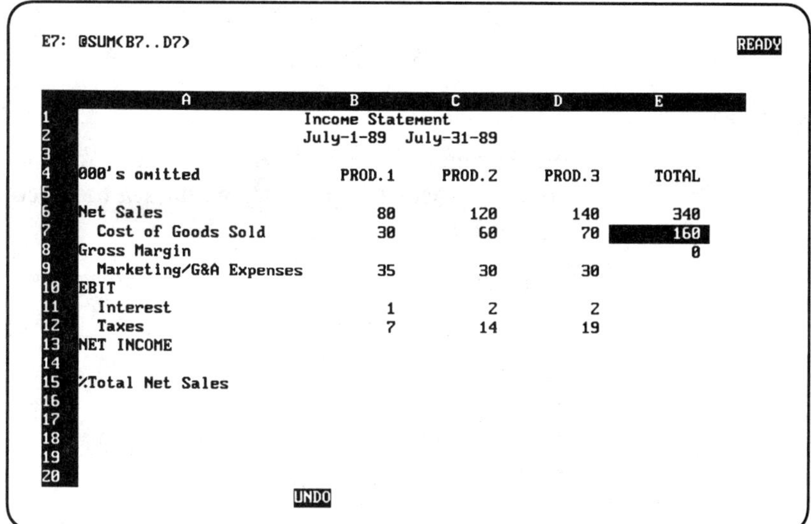

Figure 3.23
Copied formula

Move to cell E8 and look at the first line of the control panel; 1-2-3 has copied the formula. (You'll see in a moment why the two formulas look different.) The number 0 appears in cell E8 because you haven't yet entered values in cells B8, C8, or D8. When you do fill in the values, 1-2-3 will display a value other than 0 in E8.

Relative Cell Addresses

Look at the original formula in cell E7. Now look at the copy you made in cell E8. They are different because 1-2-3 automatically adjusted the cell references in the formula to reflect the different position of the copied formula. Such adjustable cell addresses are called **relative cell addresses.**

1-2-3 reads the original formula, @SUM(B7..D7), as "Add the contents of the three cells immediately to the left and place the answer here." When you copied the formula to E8, its meaning, "Add the contents of the three cells immediately to the left...," stayed the same relative to its new location. Those cells are now B8, C8, and D8; thus, the copied formula reads @SUM(B8..D8).

1-2-3 considers all cell addresses in formulas to be relative cell addresses unless you specify otherwise. This means that a copied formula performs the same operation no matter where it is placed. (The alternative to a relative cell address is called an **absolute cell address**; it is discussed later in this chapter.)

Copying a Formula to a Range

You just copied a formula to a single cell. You can also copy one formula to many places by specifying a range in the second step of the copying process.

You will now copy the formula in E8 down the entire Total column on the Income Statement.

Move to: cell E8
Press: /
Select: Copy
Press: ↵

Figure 3.24
/Copy TO prompt

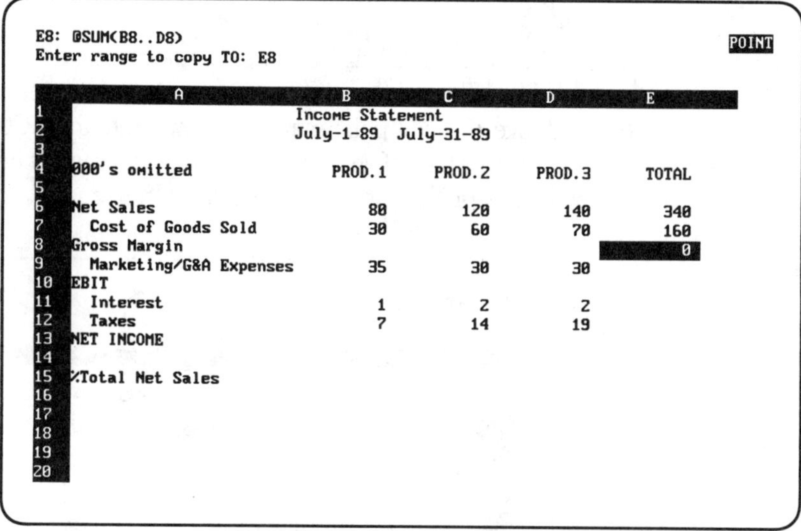

After accepting E8..E8 as the range to copy FROM, the prompt **Enter range to copy TO: E8** appears.

Move to: cell E9
Press: [.] (period) to anchor the range
Move to: cell E13

Figure 3.25
Highlighted range for copy

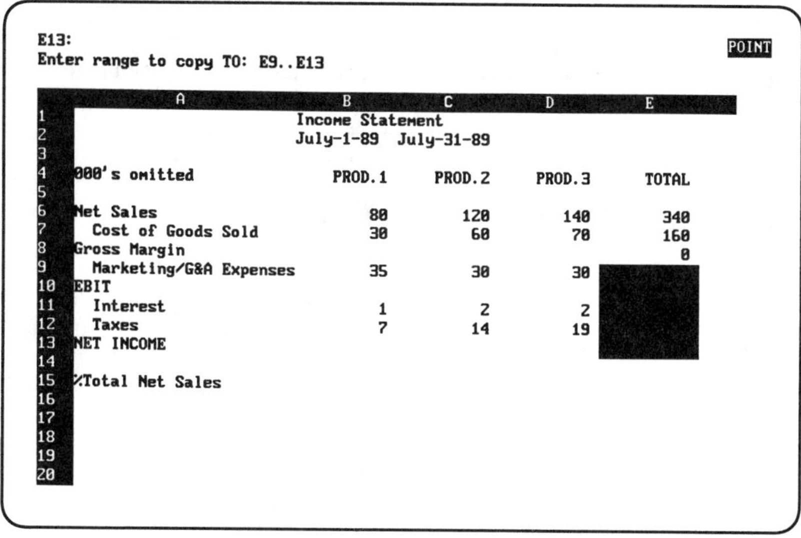

Press: ↵

When the formula has been copied, zeros will appear in some cells of the Total Column because you have not yet entered all the values. Move the cell pointer up and down the Total Column while looking at the first line of the control panel, and you'll see that the formula has been copied with relative cell addresses.

Figure 3.26
Copied formula

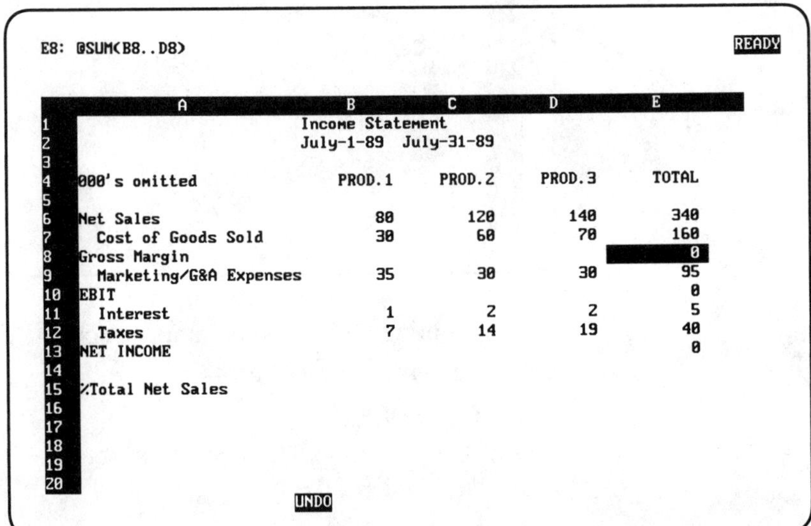

E8: @SUM(B8..D8)   READY

	A	B	C	D	E
1		Income Statement			
2		July-1-89	July-31-89		
3					
4	000's omitted	PROD.1	PROD.2	PROD.3	TOTAL
5					
6	Net Sales	80	120	140	340
7	Cost of Goods Sold	30	60	70	160
8	Gross Margin				0
9	Marketing/G&A Expenses	35	30	30	95
10	EBIT				0
11	Interest	1	2	2	5
12	Taxes	7	14	19	40
13	NET INCOME				0
14					
15	%Total Net Sales				
16					
17					
18					
19					
20					

UNDO

2.2 NOTE: If you accidentally copy a formula to the wrong cell(s), use the undo feature (press Undo (Alt-F4)) to cancel what you did.

Completing the Income Statement

Enter the remaining data for the Income Statement according to the following directions. Notice what happens to the Total Column as you add new information in each row.

Enter a formula for Gross Margin for Product 1: Net Sales minus Cost of Goods Sold.

Move to: cell B8
Type: +b6−b7 ↵

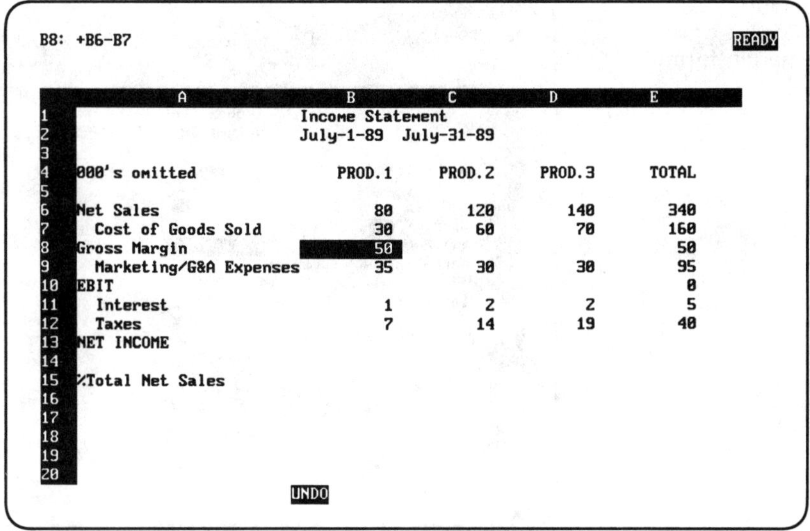

B8: +B6-B7 READY

	A	B	C	D	E
1		Income Statement			
2		July-1-89	July-31-89		
3					
4	000's omitted	PROD.1	PROD.2	PROD.3	TOTAL
5					
6	Net Sales	80	120	140	340
7	Cost of Goods Sold	30	60	70	160
8	Gross Margin	50			50
9	Marketing/G&A Expenses	35	30	30	95
10	EBIT				0
11	Interest	1	2	2	5
12	Taxes	7	14	19	40
13	NET INCOME				
14					
15	%Total Net Sales				
16					
17					
18					
19					
20					

UNDO

Figure 3.27
Formula for gross margin

Copy the Gross Margin formula for Products 2 and 3.

Press: [/]
Select: Copy
Press: [↵] for the FROM range
Move to: cell C8 for the TO range
Press: [.] to anchor the range
Move to: cell D8 to highlight the range
Press: [↵]

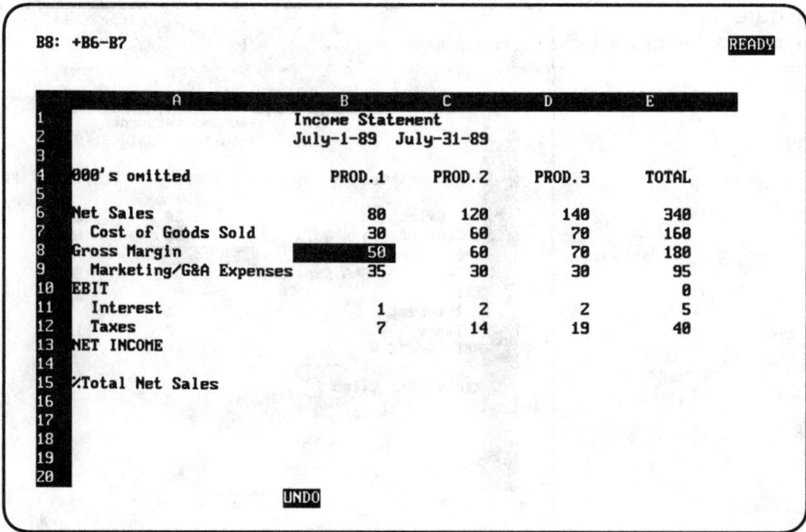

B8: +B6-B7 READY

	A	B	C	D	E
1		Income Statement			
2		July-1-89	July-31-89		
3					
4	000's omitted	PROD.1	PROD.2	PROD.3	TOTAL
5					
6	Net Sales	80	120	140	340
7	Cost of Goods Sold	30	60	70	160
8	Gross Margin	50	60	70	180
9	Marketing/G&A Expenses	35	30	30	95
10	EBIT				0
11	Interest	1	2	2	5
12	Taxes	7	14	19	40
13	NET INCOME				
14					
15	%Total Net Sales				
16					
17					
18					
19					
20					

UNDO

Figure 3.28 Copied gross margin formula

You are going to enter a formula to compute EBIT: Gross Margin minus Marketing/G&A Expenses. The formula is basically the same as the one for Gross Margin: subtract the cell one row above from the cell two rows above. Enter this formula in range B12..D12 by copying it from row 8 (Gross Margin).

Move to: cell B8
Press: [/]
Select: Copy
Press: [↵] for the FROM range
Move to: cell B10 for the TO range
Press: [.] to anchor the range
Move to: cell D10 to highlight the range
Press: [↵]

Figure 3.29 EBIT formula copied

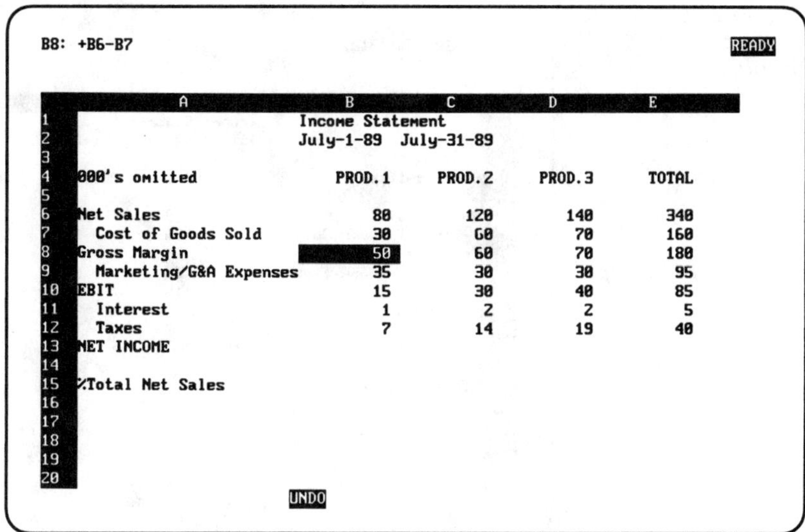

Enter the formula to compute Net Income for Product 1: EBIT minus Interest plus Taxes.

Move to: cell B13
Type: +b10−(b11+b12) [↵]

Notice how parentheses are used to group the different parts of the formula. Any calculations inside parentheses take place first.

Copy the formula to cells C13 and D13.

Press: [/]
Select: Copy
Press: [↵]
Move to: cell C13
Press: [.]
Move to: cell D13
Press: [↵]

Figure 3.30
Copied net income formula

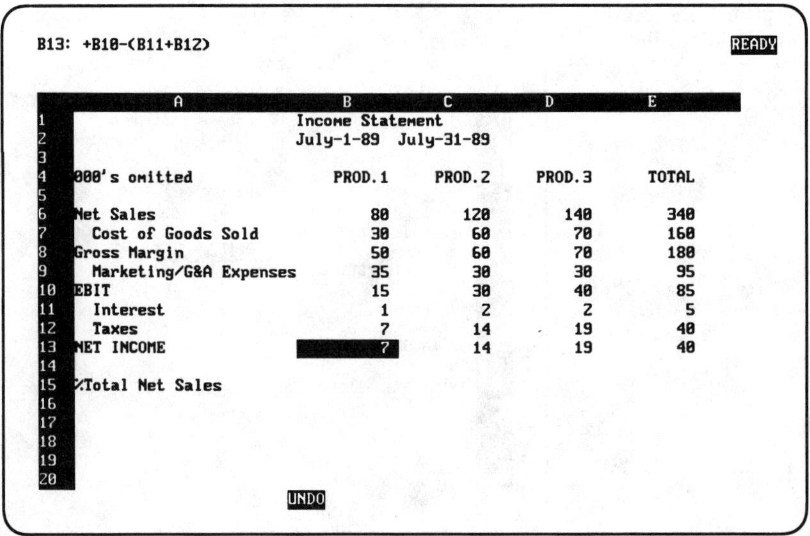

B13: +B10-(B11+B12) READY

	A	B	C	D	E
1		Income Statement			
2		July-1-89	July-31-89		
3					
4	000's omitted	PROD.1	PROD.2	PROD.3	TOTAL
5					
6	Net Sales	80	120	140	340
7	Cost of Goods Sold	30	60	70	160
8	Gross Margin	50	60	70	180
9	Marketing/G&A Expenses	35	30	30	95
10	EBIT	15	30	40	85
11	Interest	1	2	2	5
12	Taxes	7	14	19	40
13	NET INCOME	7	14	19	40
14					
15	%Total Net Sales				
16					
17					
18					
19					
20					

UNDO

Save the worksheet file again. You named it the first time you saved it, so now you only need to accept the file name when it is displayed. 1-2-3 indicates that a file with that name already exists and asks if you want to replace it, that is, replace the saved file with the altered worksheet containing data you've added or changed.

Press: [/]
Select: File
Save
Press: [↵]
Select: Replace

Absolute Cell Addresses

All the formulas entered and copied to this point have relative cell addresses. The addresses changed when you copied a formula from one location on the worksheet to another.

Sometimes, however, you do not want to copy a formula using relative cell addresss. For example, you have yet to enter formulas to calculate the % Total Net Sales. These figures will show each product's proportion of the month's total net sales.

To obtain the percentage of the total net sales for Product 1, you divide that product's net sales in cell B6 ($80,000) by the total net sales in cell E6 ($340,000). The percentage for Product 2 would be obtained by dividing its net sales in cell C6 ($120,000) by the total net sales in cell E6. The same pattern would be followed for Product 3. You would put the following formulas in cells B15, C15, and D15 to calculate each product's percentage of the total net sales:

For Product 1 .... +B6/E6
For Product 2 .... +C6/E6
For Product 3 .... +D6/E6

Notice that the first cell address in each formula is different but that the second is the same for each formula. If you were to enter the first formula in cell B15 and then copy it to cells C15 and D15 (as you did earlier), the result would look like this:

Figure 3.31 Incorrect use of relative addresses

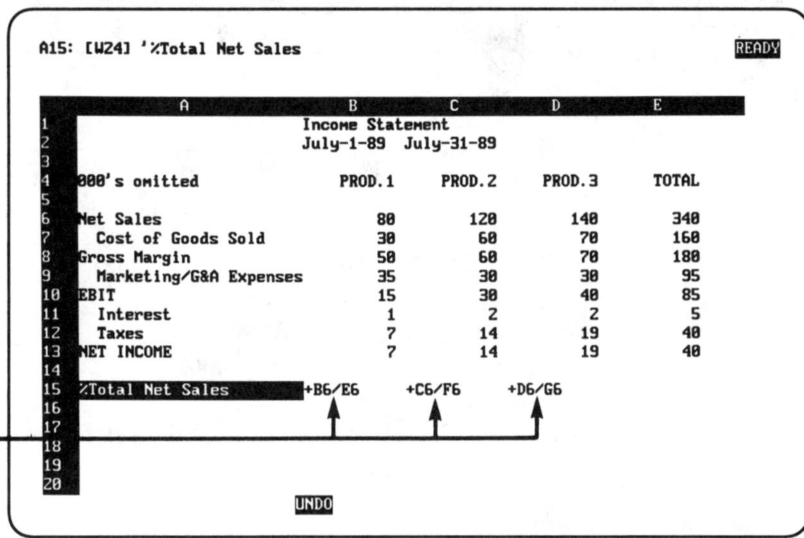

A15: [W24] '%Total Net Sales READY

	A	B	C	D	E
1		Income Statement			
2		July-1-89	July-31-89		
3					
4	000's omitted	PROD.1	PROD.2	PROD.3	TOTAL
5					
6	Net Sales	80	120	140	340
7	Cost of Goods Sold	30	60	70	160
8	Gross Margin	50	60	70	180
9	Marketing/G&A Expenses	35	30	30	95
10	EBIT	15	30	40	85
11	Interest	1	2	2	5
12	Taxes	7	14	19	40
13	NET INCOME	7	14	19	40
14					
15	%Total Net Sales	+B6/E6	+C6/F6	+D6/G6	
16					
17					
18					
19					
20					

UNDO

Each formula divides the value located nine cells above it by the value three cells to the right of the first value.

The diagram above shows that the second cell addresses in the formulas for Products 2 and 3 are not what you want. They refer to cells that are three cells to the right of the first cell, and in this case, these are blank. Because cell addresses in formulas are interpreted to be relative, copying the formula changes the cell addresses relative to the location of the original formula.

To type a formula with an absolute cell address, you use the Abs (F4) key to indicate that a cell address remains the same (absolute) whenever the formula is copied. Abs (F4) places a $ (dollar sign) before both the column letter and the row number in the cell address.

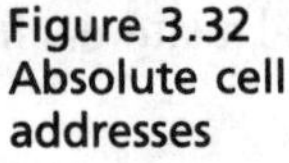

Figure 3.32
Absolute cell addresses

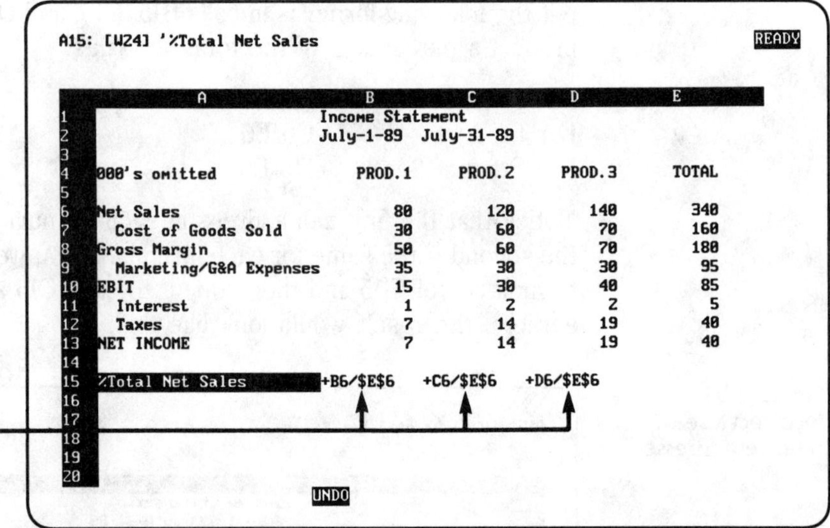

Each formula divides the value located nine cells above it by the value in cell E6.

Enter the necessary formula with the absolute cell address in cell B15:

Move to: cell B15
Type: + (signaling a value)
Move to: cell B6
Type: / (indicating division)
Move to: cell E6
Press: ABS (F4) making E6 an absolute cell address
↵

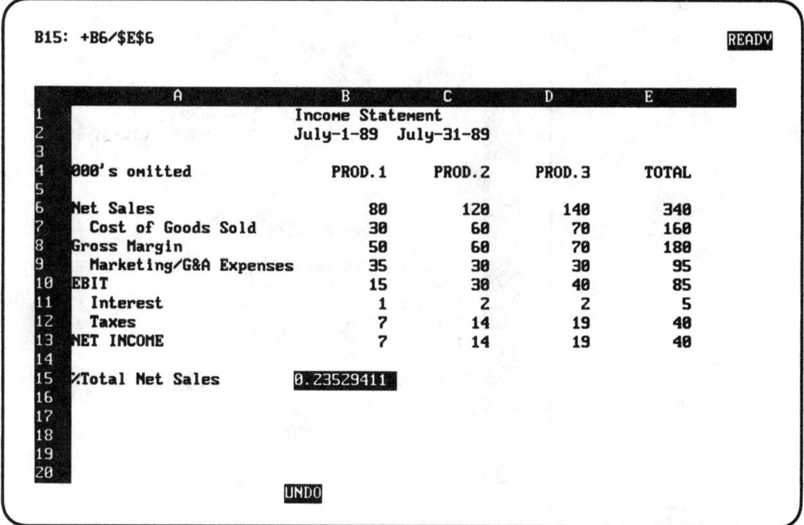

Figure 3.33 Result of formula using absolute address

The answer, 0.23529411, appears in cell B15. Notice that Abs (F4) inserted a $ before E and before 6 in the first line of the control panel. This means that the cell address E6 in this formula will remain E6 no matter where the formula is moved. (The cell address B6 will change—it is still a relative cell address.)

Copy this formula across the rest of the % Total Net Sales row:

Move to: cell B15
Press: [/]
Select: Copy
Press: [↵] for the FROM range
Move to: cell C15
Press: [.]
Move to: cell E15 to expand the highlight
Press: [↵]

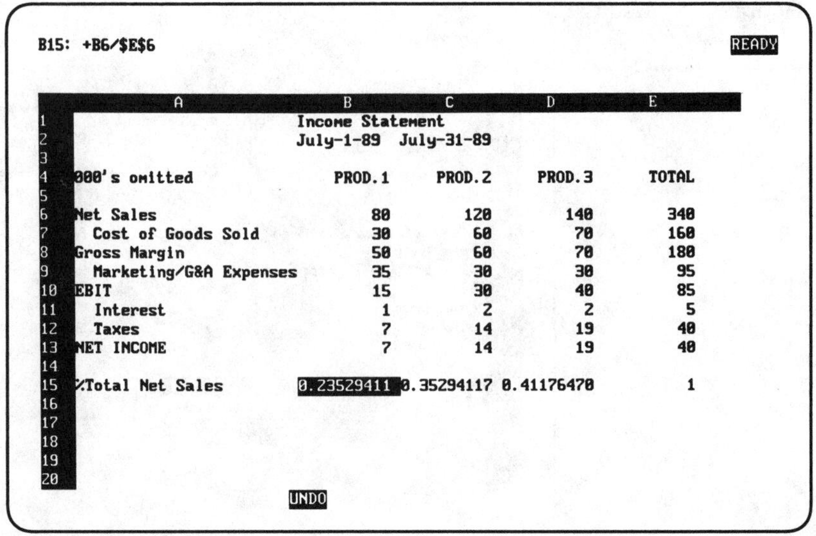
B15: +B6/$E$6 READY

	A	B	C	D	E
1		Income Statement			
2		July-1-89	July-31-89		
3					
4	000's omitted	PROD.1	PROD.2	PROD.3	TOTAL
5					
6	Net Sales	80	120	140	340
7	Cost of Goods Sold	30	60	70	160
8	Gross Margin	50	60	70	180
9	Marketing/G&A Expenses	35	30	30	95
10	EBIT	15	30	40	85
11	Interest	1	2	2	5
12	Taxes	7	14	19	40
13	NET INCOME	7	14	19	40
14					
15	%Total Net Sales	0.23529411	0.35294117	0.41176470	1
16					
17					
18					
19					
20					

UNDO

Figure 3.34
Copied formula

The formula with the absolute cell address (referring to cell E6) has been copied. Use the arrow keys to look at the formula in each cell. Notice that the first cell address in each formula (B6, C6, D6) has changed—without a $ symbol it remains a relative cell address—but that the second, absolute cell address ($E$6) has stayed the same.

FORMATTING VALUES IN CELLS

All the values entered in the Income Statement are displayed in the cells as unformatted numbers. Values within cells can be formatted; you can add dollar signs, insert commas, or round off decimal places. As you would expect, you can format one cell or a range of cells. The following list shows the options available with the **Range Format** command.

Fixed	Rounds to a fixed number of decimal places: 1125.62.
Sci	Displays in exponential notation: 1.13E+03.
Currency	Shows as dollars and cents: $1,125.62.
, (Comma)	Adds commas to long numbers: 1,125.62; places negative values in parentheses.

General	Has no fixed number of decimal places: 1125.621 (the initial setting format).
+/–	Displays in pictograph form.
Percent	Multiplies by 100 and adds a % sign: .42 = 42%.
Date	Formats into one of several date formats: for example, DD-MMM-YY (02-Sep-89).
Text	Displays formulas in cells, not the values.
Hidden	Hides cell entries.
Reset	Returns to the global default format (General, if not changed).

NOTE: Formatting a value only changes the way it is displayed. The value itself is not changed.

You are going to format the cells in the bottom row of the Income Statement to display their contents as percentages with no decimal places.

Move to: cell B15
Press: [/]
Select: Range
Format
Percent
Type: 0 [↵] (for 0 decimal places)
Move to: cell E15 to highlight the range
Press: [↵]

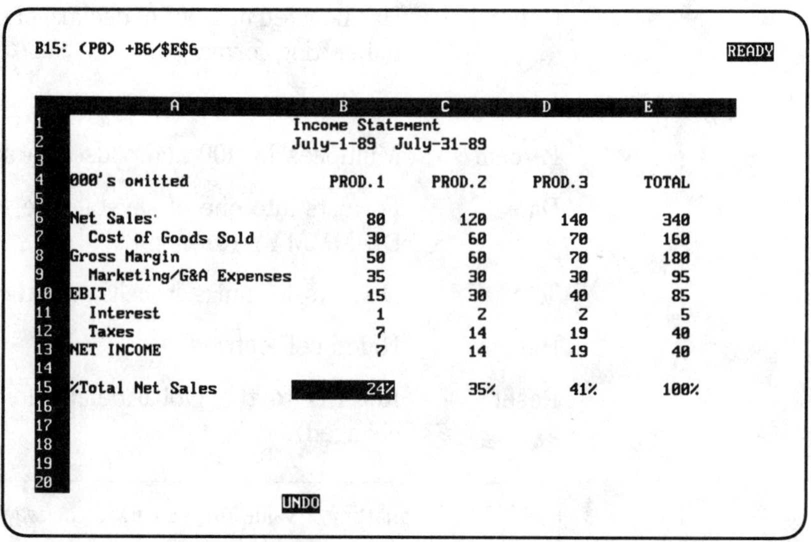
B15: (P0) +B6/$E$6 READY

	A	B	C	D	E
1		Income Statement			
2		July-1-89 July-31-89			
3					
4	000's omitted	PROD.1	PROD.2	PROD.3	TOTAL
5					
6	Net Sales	80	120	140	340
7	Cost of Goods Sold	30	60	70	160
8	Gross Margin	50	60	70	180
9	Marketing/G&A Expenses	35	30	30	95
10	EBIT	15	30	40	85
11	Interest	1	2	2	5
12	Taxes	7	14	19	40
13	NET INCOME	7	14	19	40
14					
15	%Total Net Sales	24%	35%	41%	100%
16					
17					
18					
19					
20					

UNDO

Figure 3.35
% Total net sales formatted as percentages

Look at the first line of the control panel as you move through the cells in the bottom row of the Income Statement. Notice that (P0) now appears before the contents of the cell shown in the control panel. This means the format is "Percent, 0 decimal places."

Now format all the rows except for Net Sales and Net Income in the , (comma) format with two decimal places:

Move to: cell B7
Press: [/]
Select: Range
Format
[,]
Press: [↵] for 2 decimal places
Move to: cell E7
Press: [↓] five times to highlight the range B7..E12

Figure 3.36 Range highlighted for comma format

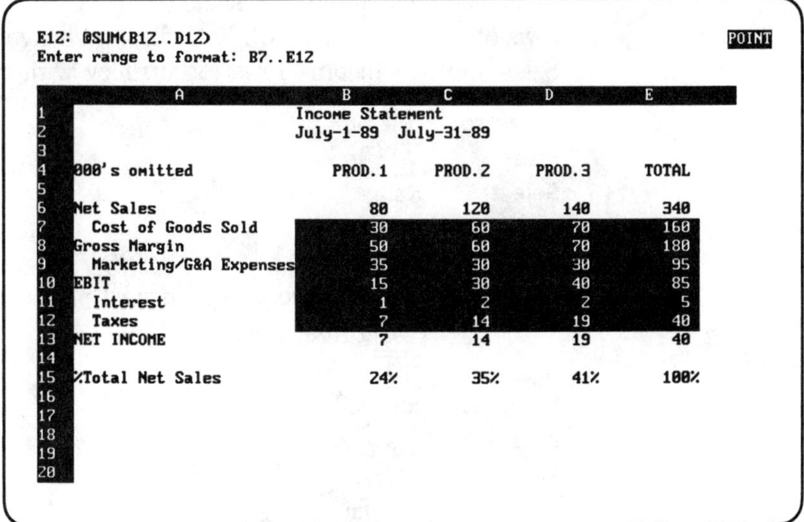

Press: ↵

Figure 3.37 Comma format in worksheet

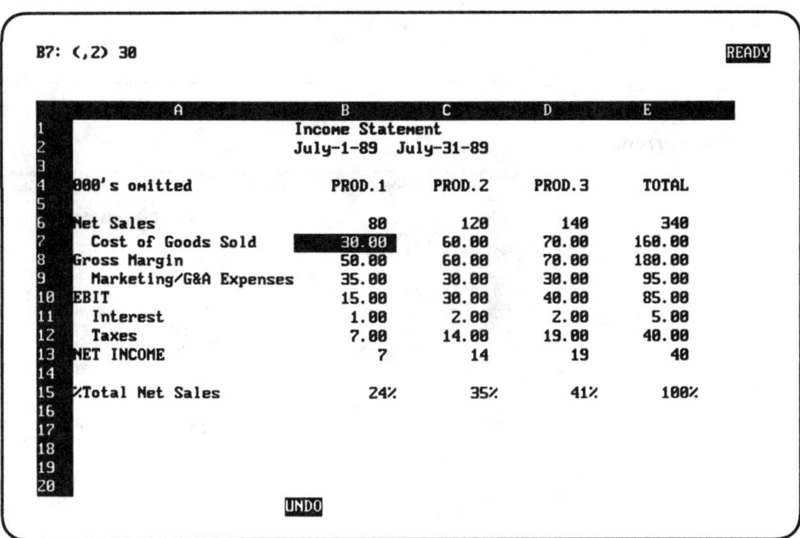

The values in rows 7 to 12 now appear in the comma (,) format with two decimal places.

In an income statement, it's customary to format the top and bottom rows of figures as currency. You will now change the format of the Net Sales and Net Income rows to currency with two decimal places:

Move to: cell B6
Press: /
Select: Range
Format
Currency
Press: ↵ to accept two decimal places
→ three times
↵
Move to: cell B13
Press: /
Select: Range
Format
Currency
Press: ↵ to accept two decimal places
→ three times
↵

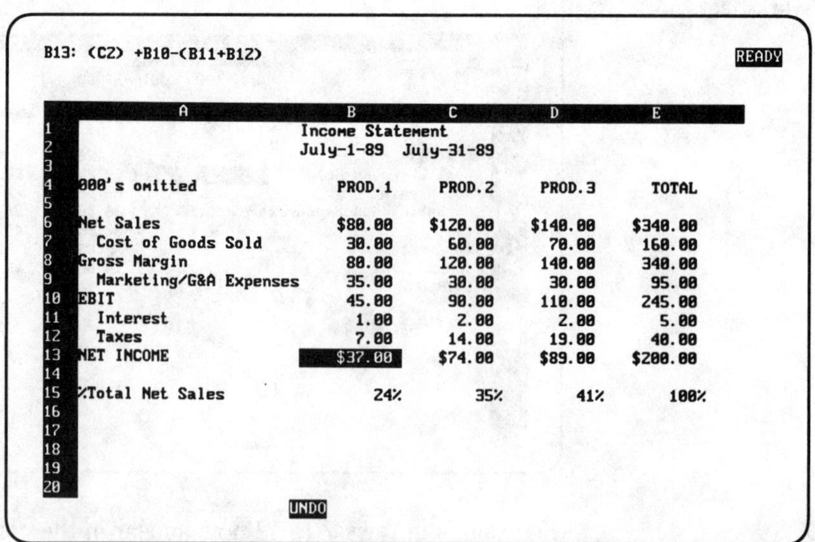
B13: (C2) +B10-(B11+B12) READY

	A	B	C	D	E
1		Income Statement			
2		July-1-89	July-31-89		
3					
4	000's omitted	PROD.1	PROD.2	PROD.3	TOTAL
5					
6	Net Sales	$80.00	$120.00	$140.00	$340.00
7	Cost of Goods Sold	30.00	60.00	70.00	160.00
8	Gross Margin	80.00	120.00	140.00	340.00
9	Marketing/G&A Expenses	35.00	30.00	30.00	95.00
10	EBIT	45.00	90.00	110.00	245.00
11	Interest	1.00	2.00	2.00	5.00
12	Taxes	7.00	14.00	19.00	40.00
13	NET INCOME	$37.00	$74.00	$89.00	$200.00
14					
15	%Total Net Sales	24%	35%	41%	100%
16					
17					
18					
19					
20					

UNDO

Figure 3.38 Net sales and net income as currency

(2.2) If you have a hard-disk computer and are interested in producing high-quality printouts that include other kinds of formatting such as bold, underlining, shades, and different typefaces, you can use the Allways program that is part of the 1–2–3 Release 2.2 package. Chapter 6 takes you through exercises that format and print this Income Statement worksheet with Allways.

THE HELP FACILITY

You can call up a Help screen at any point (even in the middle of a command sequence). Each Help message is tailored to what is currently on the screen. Pressing Esc will return you to the worksheet.

NOTE: Remember, to use Help on a two-diskette computer, the Help Disk (5.25″ systems) or System, Help, and PrintGraph Disk (3.5″ systems) must be in drive A; on a hard-disk computer, the Help files must be copied into the same subdirectory as the 1–2–3 System Disk.

NAMING A RANGE

You've seen how frequently ranges are used in a worksheet. Instead of typing or highlighting a range, you can specify a **range name** for that range of cells. Naming a range of cells makes a worksheet much easier to use. For example, it is easier to use a name like Total to refer to the cells in a range than it is to remember that cells E6 through E15 comprise the range.

After creating a range name, you can use the name with any command that calls for a range, from copying and moving to formatting and graphing. When prompted to specify a range, simply type the name. Range names are created with the **Range Name Create** command. They are automatically saved with the worksheet so they remain available for future work sessions (unless you choose to delete them).

Creating a Range Name

First you'll give the name NET_SALES to the cells in the Net Sales row (B6..D6). The two-step process is similar to that you've used with other worksheet commands. At the first prompt **Enter name:** you will type the name of the range. (Range names can be up to 15 characters long, and should not contain any spaces.)

Move to: cell B6
Press: [/]
Select: Range
Name
Create
Type: **net_sales** [↵]

When you see **Enter range: B6..B6** in the control panel, highlight the range to be named NET_SALES.

Press: [→] twice to move to cell D6

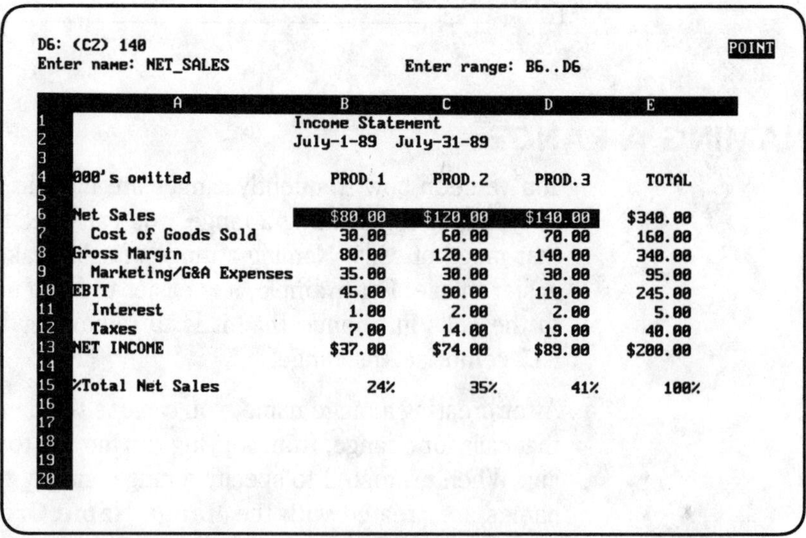

D6: (C2) 140 POINT
Enter name: NET_SALES Enter range: B6..D6

	A	B	C	D	E
1		Income Statement			
2		July-1-89	July-31-89		
3					
4	000's omitted	PROD.1	PROD.2	PROD.3	TOTAL
5					
6	Net Sales	$80.00	$120.00	$140.00	$340.00
7	Cost of Goods Sold	30.00	60.00	70.00	160.00
8	Gross Margin	80.00	120.00	140.00	340.00
9	Marketing/G&A Expenses	35.00	30.00	30.00	95.00
10	EBIT	45.00	90.00	110.00	245.00
11	Interest	1.00	2.00	2.00	5.00
12	Taxes	7.00	14.00	19.00	40.00
13	NET INCOME	$37.00	$74.00	$89.00	$200.00
14					
15	%Total Net Sales	24%	35%	41%	100%
16					
17					
18					
19					
20					

Figure 3.39
NET_SALES range highlighted

Press: [↵]

Name a second range that includes the cells in the Gross Margin row.

Move to: cell B8
Press: [/]
Select: Range
Name
Create

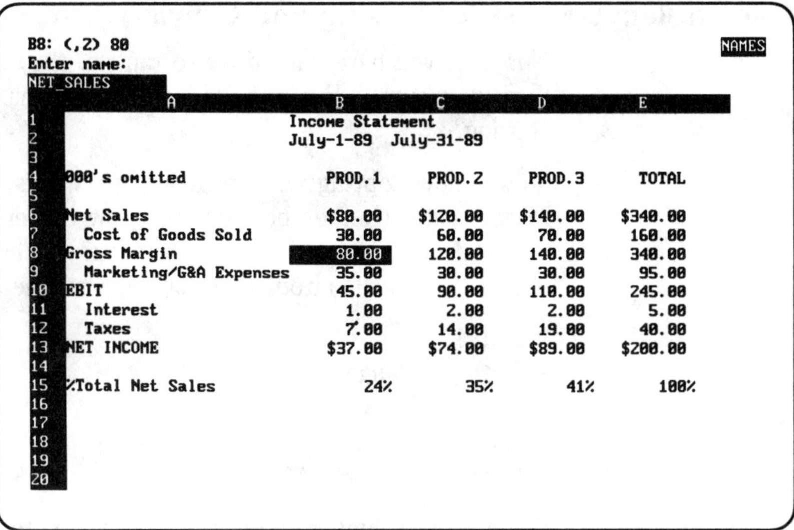

Figure 3.40 Prompt for range name

Look at the third line of the control panel. Below the prompt **Enter name:** you'll see NET_SALES. Each range name you create will now be listed when you select **/Range Name Create**. When there are more names that fit the width of the control panel, use the arrow keys to see the complete list or press Name (F3) for a full-screen list. The names will disappear when you type in a range name.

Type: gross_margin [↵]
Press: [→] twice
[↵]

Name a third range that includes the cells in the Net Income row:

Move to: cell B13
Press: [/]
Select: Range
Name
Create

Two range names are now listed in the control panel.

Type: net_income [↵]
Press: [→] twice
[↵]

Using a Range Name for Erasing and Copying

Now that you have named these ranges, they can be used wherever they are required. For example, using a range name can save time when copying.

To see how copying with range names works, first erase the Gross Margin data. (Remember that this row contains formulas that were copied from the Net Sales row.) You will select the range name (GROSS_MARGIN) from a list that appears when you press Name (F3).

Press: [/]
Select: Range
Erase
Press: [NAME] (F3)
Select: GROSS_MARGIN

Some of the values in the worksheet change to reflect the loss of data (rows 10 and 13 show negative values). Now you'll replace the original formulas in the Gross Margin row by copying them from the EBIT row. Instead of indicating the TO range by highlighting it in the worksheet, you will use its range name. At the /**Copy** command prompts, you will highlight the EBIT range and then select the range name for the Gross Margin range after you press Name (F3).

Move to: cell B10
Press: [/]
Select: Copy
Press: [→] twice
[↵]
[NAME] (F3)
Select: GROSS_MARGIN

The formulas are copied from the EBIT row to the Gross Margin range and recalculated with the related values. The worksheet should look just as it did before you erased the range.

Using a Range Name in Formulas

(2.2) Range names can also be used in a formula. 1-2-3 Release 2.2 offers a convenient shortcut to typing range names in formulas with the Name (F3) key. When you type a formula and get to the point where you need to specify a range, you can press Name (F3) and 1-2-3 will display all the named ranges in the worksheet. Just highlight the one you want and press Enter. For example, if you wanted to use the @SUM function on a range named SALES, you would type **@sum(**, press Name (F3), select SALES from the list 1-2-3 displays, type **)**, and press Enter. Using Name (F3) also saves you from trying to remember and type the range names in the worksheet.

Earlier you entered this formula for the Total Gross Margin: @SUM (B8..D8). The range of cells in B8..D8 is the same range you named GROSS_MARGIN. Thus the formula can also be written @SUM (GROSS_MARGIN).

Move to: cell E8

Figure 3.41 Range name in formula

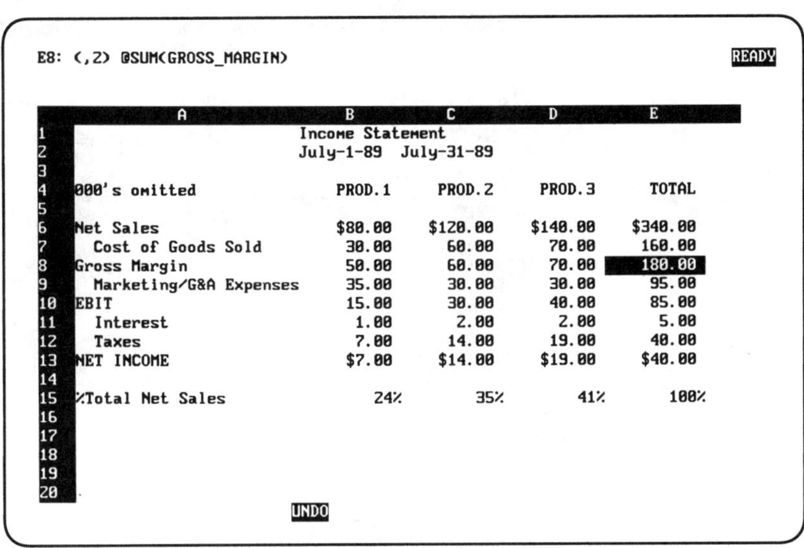

E8: (,2) @SUM(GROSS_MARGIN) READY

	A	B	C	D	E
1		Income Statement			
2		July-1-89	July-31-89		
3					
4	000's omitted	PROD.1	PROD.2	PROD.3	TOTAL
5					
6	Net Sales	$80.00	$120.00	$140.00	$340.00
7	Cost of Goods Sold	30.00	60.00	70.00	160.00
8	Gross Margin	50.00	60.00	70.00	180.00
9	Marketing/G&A Expenses	35.00	30.00	30.00	95.00
10	EBIT	15.00	30.00	40.00	85.00
11	Interest	1.00	2.00	2.00	5.00
12	Taxes	7.00	14.00	19.00	40.00
13	NET INCOME	$7.00	$14.00	$19.00	$40.00
14					
15	%Total Net Sales	24%	35%	41%	100%
16					
17					
18					
19					
20					

UNDO

Look at the first line of the control panel. When you named the range earlier, 1-2-3 automatically changed the formula display by replacing the cell addresses B8..D8 with the range name GROSS_MARGIN. If you move to cell E13, you will see that 1-2-3 also substituted the range name NET_INCOME for the cell addresses B13..D13. If you decide to delete the range names, 1-2-3 will redisplay the cell addresses in the formulas.

Creating a Range Name Table

You've already named three ranges in the Income Statement: Net Sales, Gross Margin, and Net Income. In a large worksheet, you might name several ranges to help copy formulas or identify sections of the worksheet to which you refer regularly.

One way of locating a range that you have saved is by using the Goto (F5) and Name (F3) keys.

Press: GOTO (F5)
NAME (F3)

Figure 3.42
GOTO prompt

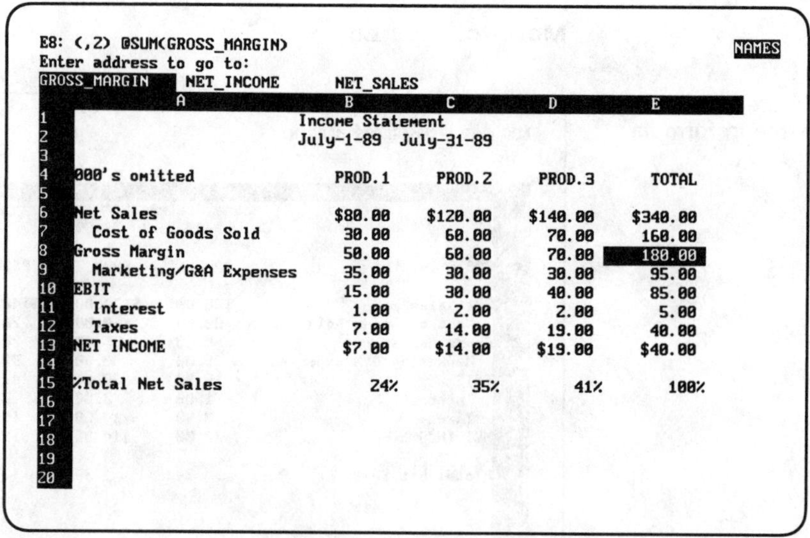

E8: (,2) @SUM(GROSS_MARGIN) NAMES
Enter address to go to:
GROSS_MARGIN NET_INCOME NET_SALES

	A	B	C	D	E
1		Income Statement			
2		July-1-89	July-31-89		
3					
4	000's omitted	PROD.1	PROD.2	PROD.3	TOTAL
5					
6	Net Sales	$80.00	$120.00	$140.00	$340.00
7	Cost of Goods Sold	30.00	60.00	70.00	160.00
8	Gross Margin	50.00	60.00	70.00	180.00
9	Marketing/G&A Expenses	35.00	30.00	30.00	95.00
10	EBIT	15.00	30.00	40.00	85.00
11	Interest	1.00	2.00	2.00	5.00
12	Taxes	7.00	14.00	19.00	40.00
13	NET INCOME	$7.00	$14.00	$19.00	$40.00
14					
15	%Total Net Sales	24%	35%	41%	100%
16					
17					
18					
19					
20					

Select: NET_INCOME

The cell pointer moves to the first cell in the named range, in this case, cell B13.

If you press Name (F3) twice after you press Goto (F5), 1-2-3 displays a full-screen list of the range names in the worksheet and lists the range address of the highlighted range name.

Press: GOTO (F5)
NAME (F3) twice

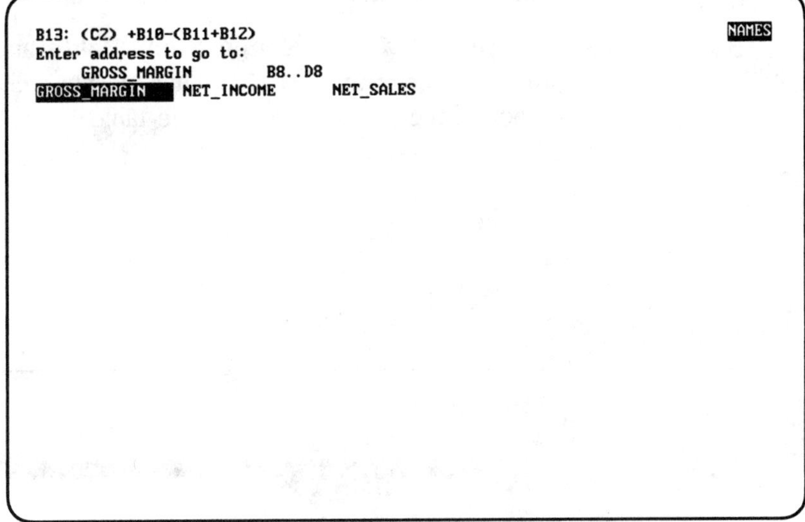

Figure 3.43 Full-screen list of range names

Press: ↵

An even better way of keeping track of range names—especially when there are many of them—is to create a range name table. Then you can see the names and locations of all the range names in a worksheet at one time.

A range name table is created in the worksheet. It takes two columns: one for range names and one for the cell addresses. When deciding where to locate the table, be sure to go far enough beyond the worksheet data you've already entered so that you have sufficient room to continue the worksheet. You should also widen the first column of the table so that it is large enough to display the range names.

You're going to create a range name table of the three ranges you've named for the Income Statement. Move to a blank area of the worksheet and widen the first column.

Press: BIG RIGHT (Ctrl-Right)
Move to: cell G1
Press: /

Select: Worksheet
Column
Set-Width
Type: 16 [↵]

Next you will select **/Range Name Table** and press Enter at the prompt **Enter range: G1..G1**. This accepts cell G1 as the upper-left corner of the range to contain the table.

Press: [/]
Select: Range
Name
Table
Press: [↵]

Figure 3.44
Range name table

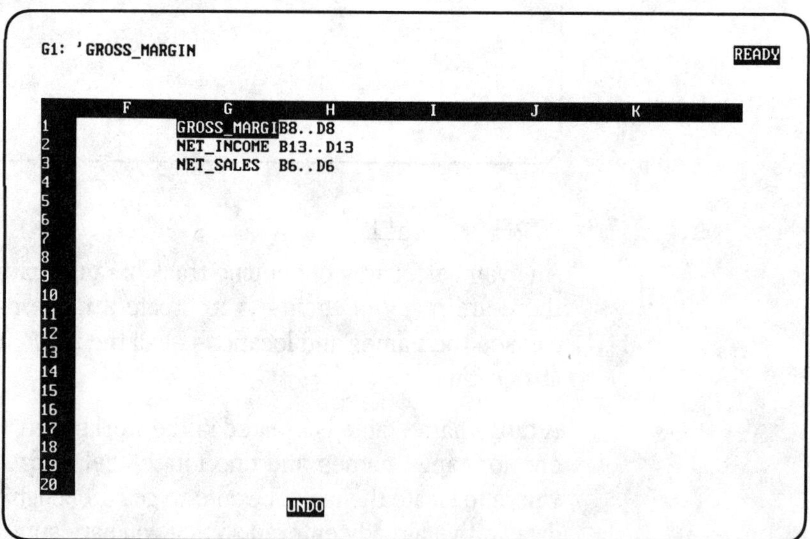

A table of all the named ranges for this worksheet appears in columns G and H. Notice that the table is in alphabetical order and contains the upper-left and lower-right cell address for each range.

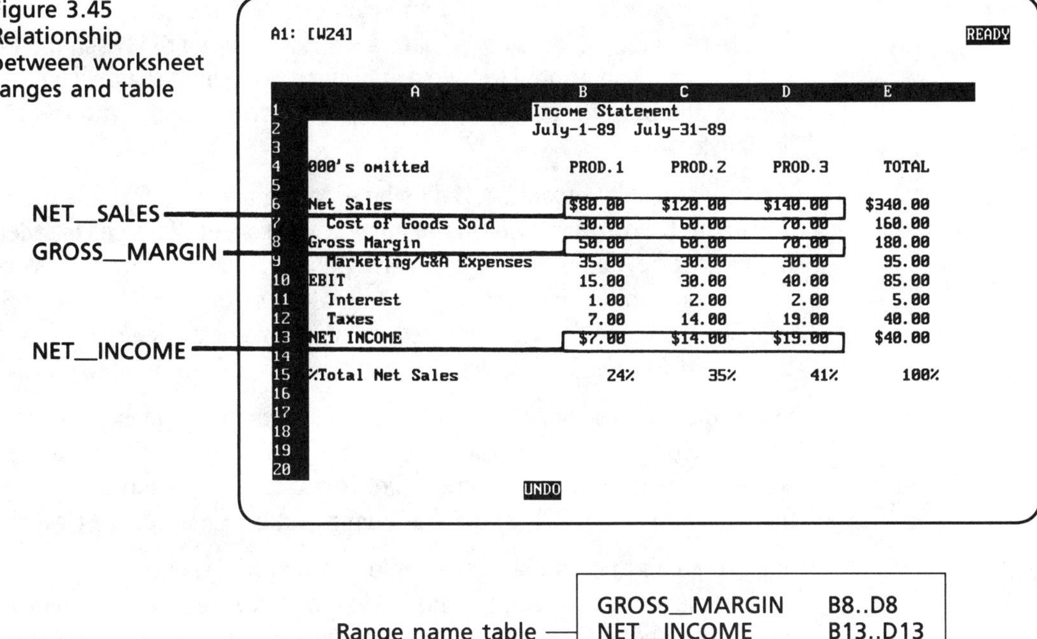

Figure 3.45 Relationship between worksheet ranges and table

Range name table

GROSS__MARGIN	B8..D8
NET__INCOME	B13..D13
NET__SALES	B6..D6

Press: HOME to return to the upper-left corner of the worksheet

> NOTE: Once you have created the table, you can see it at any time. If you give the table itself a range name (such as RN__TABLE), you can see it by pressing Goto (F5) and typing the name.

(2.2) LINKING FILES

File linking is an important 1-2-3 Release 2.2 feature that allows you to use values from cells in other worksheet files in the current worksheet (the worksheet that is currently in memory and on the screen). File linking saves you the trouble of manually changing the current worksheet to account for a change made to another file. The feature is especially useful if you want to consolidate data from a number of files to a summary worksheet.

In this chapter, you've created an income statement for the month of July. In real life, you're likely to have a similar statement for each month of the year. If you wanted to have a summary worksheet that highlighted certain numbers for each product, you could do so easily with the file linking feature.

You create a link between two files by entering a special formula called a **linking formula** in a cell in the current worksheet. This cell is called the **target cell** because it will receive data. The linking formula refers to a cell in another file; this cell is called the **source cell** because it supplies the data. For the same reason, the current worksheet is called the **target file** and the file with the source cell is called the **source file**.

Once you enter the linking formula, 1-2-3 copies the value in the source cell to the target cell. The value of the target cell is automatically updated whenever you retrieve the target file. If you change data in the source file, the target file will reflect the changes next time you retrieve it.

You are going to create a very simple summary worksheet that tracks net income for your three products during the third quarter (July, August, and September). This summary worksheet (which will be the target file) will have a linking formula for the net income figure for each of your three products. To save you from remembering cell addresses in the INCOME file, you will start by assigning range names to the three net income cells.

Figure 3.46
Income statement

A1: [W24] READY

	A	B	C	D	E
1		Income Statement			
2		July-1-89	July-31-89		
3					
4	000's omitted	PROD.1	PROD.2	PROD.3	TOTAL
5					
6	Net Sales	$80.00	$120.00	$140.00	$340.00
7	Cost of Goods Sold	30.00	60.00	70.00	160.00
8	Gross Margin	50.00	60.00	70.00	180.00
9	Marketing/G&A Expenses	35.00	30.00	30.00	95.00
10	EBIT	15.00	30.00	40.00	85.00
11	Interest	1.00	2.00	2.00	5.00
12	Taxes	7.00	14.00	19.00	40.00
13	NET INCOME	$7.00	$14.00	$19.00	$40.00
14					
15	%Total Net Sales	24%	35%	41%	100%
16					
17					
18					
19					
20					

UNDO

If it's not on the screen, retrieve the INCOME worksheet:

Press: [/]
Select: File
Retrieve
INCOME.WK1

You will name the three net income cells PROD1, PROD2, and PROD3:

Move to: cell B13
Press: [/]
Select: Range
Name
Create
Type: prod1 [↵]
Press: [↵] to accept B13 as the cell to name
Move to: cell C13
Press: [/]
Select: Range
Name
Create
Type: prod2 [↵]
Press: [↵] to accept C13 as the cell to name

Now assign the name PROD3 to D13.

You're now ready to create the summary worksheet. Save the Income Statement (so the new range names are saved) and then erase the worksheet:

Press: [/]
Select: File
Save
Press: [↵]
Select: Replace
Press: [/]
Select: Worksheet
Erase
Yes

Creating the Summary Worksheet

The summary worksheet will contain a framework of labels plus some linking formulas. Start by entering the labels.

Move to: cell C2
Type: '3rd Quarter Net Income (don't forget the apostrophe)
Press: [↵]
Move to: cell B4
Type: PROD.1 [→]
PROD.2 [→]
PROD.3 [↵]
Move to: cell A6
Type: July [↓]
August [↓]
September [↵]

Right-align the labels in row 4 so they line up with the numbers that will appear below them.

Move to: cell B4
Press: [/]
Select: Range
Label
Right
Press: [→] twice
[↵] to accept B4..D4 as the range

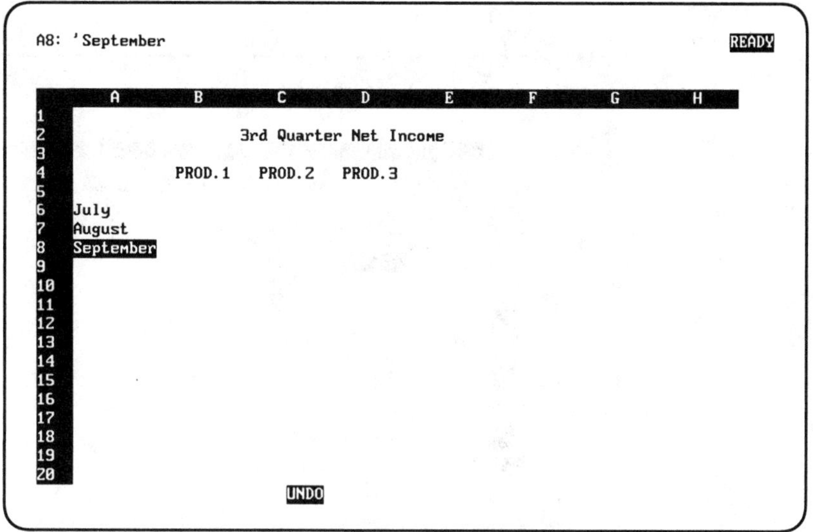

Figure 3.47
Labels in summary worksheet

Your worksheet should look just like Figure 3.47.

Entering the Linking Formulas

Now the structure of the worksheet is in place, you can enter the linking formulas for the month of July. A linking formula has the following structure:

+ <<file name>>cell reference

It begins with a + (plus sign) and is followed by the name of the source file in double angle brackets and the address or range name of the source cell. The name of your source file is INCOME.WK1 and the cell reference is one of three range names you just created (PROD1, PROD2, or PROD3).

Start by creating a linking formula for product 1.

Move to: cell B6
Type: + <<income>>prod1
Press: ↵

Figure 3.48
Linked cell

linking formula in target file

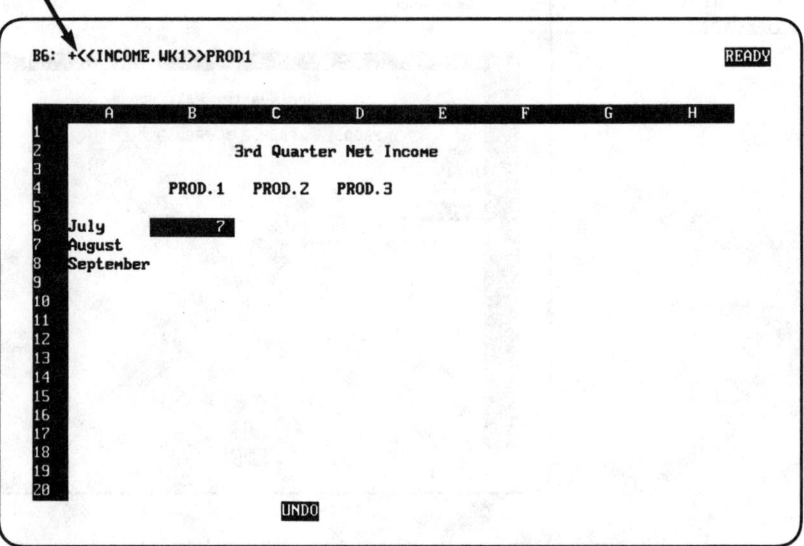

Cell B6 now shows the result of the linking formula: 7. This is the content of the cell named PROD1 in the INCOME worksheet file. Notice the control panel shows the actual formula.

Create linking formulas for products 2 and 3.

Move to: cell C6
Type: **+ << income >> prod2** ↵
Move to: cell D6
Type: **+ << income >> prod3** ↵

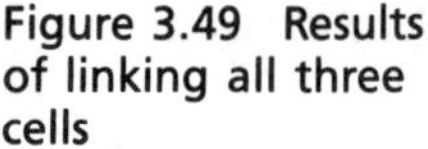

Figure 3.49 Results of linking all three cells

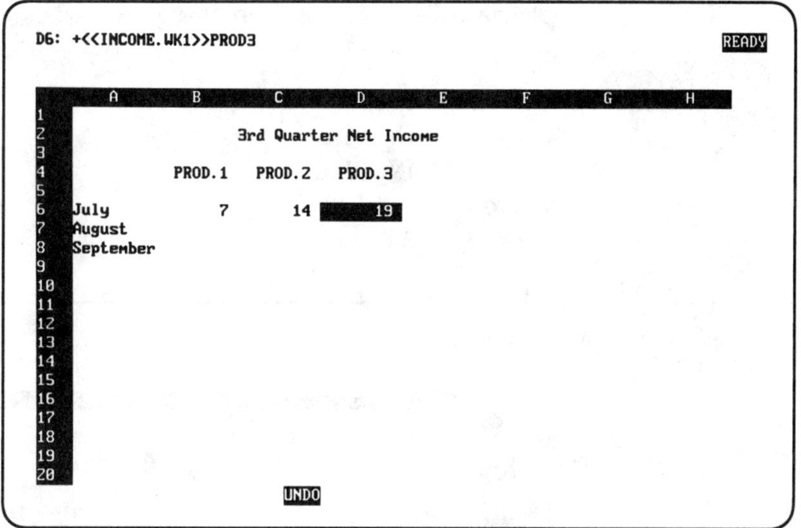

In this case, all three linking formulas referred to the same file, but to different cells in it. You could, however, have links to many different worksheet files in the same target file. For example, if you had separate files for the August and September income statements, you would simply use the names of those files instead of INCOME.WK1 in your formulas.

> NOTE: If the source file is in another drive and/or directory, include the path to the file within the double angle brackets, for example, <<C:\SALES\FEB>>.

Updating Linked Data

One of the benefits of creating links between files is that you can make a change in the target file that will automatically be reflected in the source file the next time you retrieve it. You can see how this works by changing a number in the INCOME.WK1 file.

First save the summary worksheet. Call it NETINC.

Press: [/]
Select: File
Save
Type: netinc [↵]

Retrieve INCOME.WK1 and change the taxes for product 1 to 3.

Press: /
Select: File
Retrieve
INCOME
Move to: cell B12
Type: 3 ↵

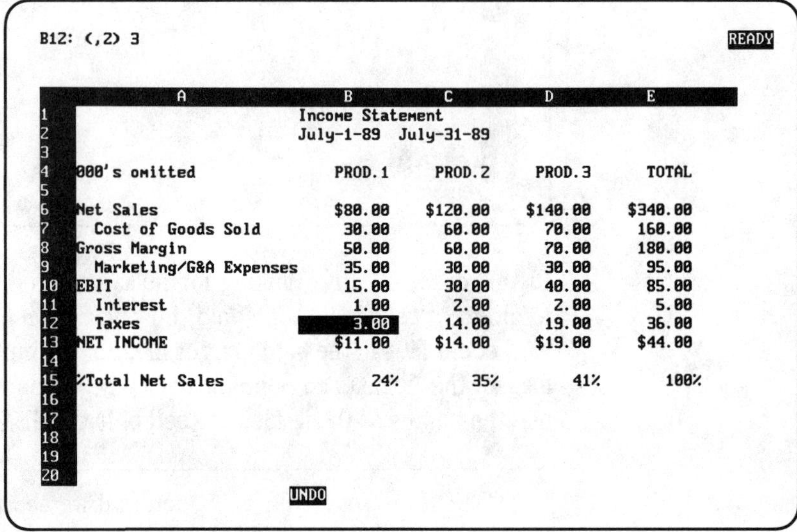
B12: (,2) 3 READY

	A	B	C	D	E
1		Income Statement			
2		July-1-89	July-31-89		
3					
4	000's omitted	PROD.1	PROD.2	PROD.3	TOTAL
5					
6	Net Sales	$80.00	$120.00	$140.00	$340.00
7	Cost of Goods Sold	30.00	60.00	70.00	160.00
8	Gross Margin	50.00	60.00	70.00	180.00
9	Marketing/G&A Expenses	35.00	30.00	30.00	95.00
10	EBIT	15.00	30.00	40.00	85.00
11	Interest	1.00	2.00	2.00	5.00
12	Taxes	3.00	14.00	19.00	36.00
13	NET INCOME	$11.00	$14.00	$19.00	$44.00
14					
15	%Total Net Sales	24%	35%	41%	100%
16					
17					
18					
19					
20					

UNDO

Figure 3.50 Changed taxes for product 1

Notice that the net income for product 1 is now 11.

Save the worksheet and retrieve NETINC to see the change to the linked cell.

Press: /
Select: File
Save
Press: ↵
Select: Replace
Press: /
Select: File
Retrieve
NETINC

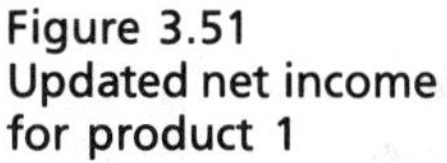

Figure 3.51
Updated net income for product 1

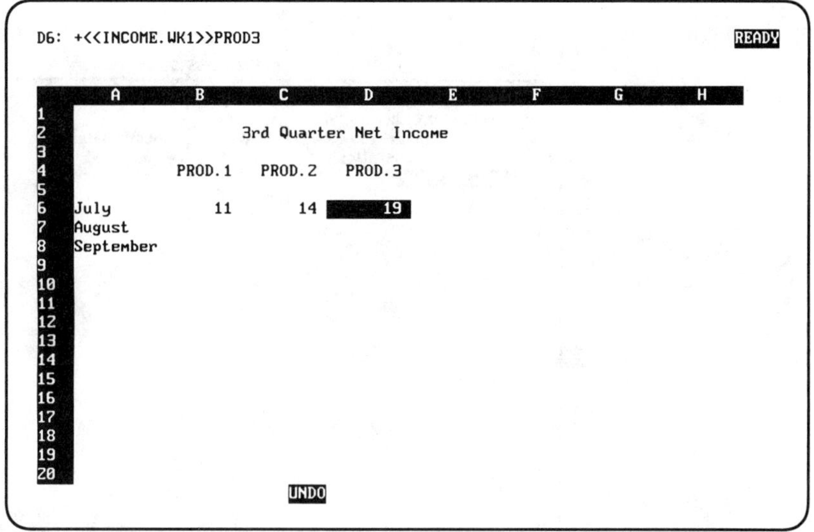

1-2-3 automatically updated the net income for product 1 when you retrieved the worksheet.

You can use the cell that contains a link (the target cell) in any 1-2-3 formula. For example, once you had data for August and September in your summary net income worksheet, you could calculate the average net income for each product with the @AVG function.

Listing Linked Files

If the target worksheet contains links to several other files, you may want to see a list of those files. You can do so with the **File List Linked** command. You have links to only one file, but try this command now to see how it works.

Press: /
Select: File
List
Linked

Figure 3.52 File list of linked files

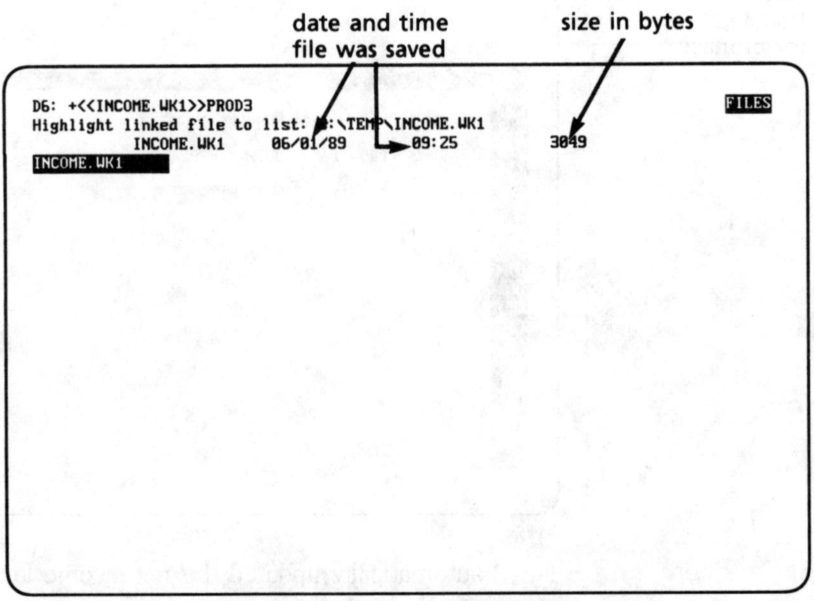

One file, INCOME.WK1, is listed and highlighted. If you had several files listed, you could highlight the name of any one of them to see additional information about it: its drive and directory, the date and time it was last saved, and its size (in bytes).

Press: [↵] to return to READY mode

Before continuing to the next chapter, retrieve INCOME again and change the taxes in cell B12 back to 7 (you don't need to save NETINC first).

Press: [/]
Select: File
Retrieve
INCOME
Move to: cell B12
Type: 7 [↵]

Now save the income statement.

Press: [/]
Select: File
Save

Press: ↵
Select: Replace

TRANSPOSING RANGES

/Range Trans changes (transposes) a column to a row or a row to a column. (If the range you're transposing contains any formulas, 1-2-3 replaces them with their values in the copy.) This command is extremely helpful when building a detailed worksheet involving labels or values that you have already typed. For example, you could create a small worksheet below the Income Statement to show total costs for each product over a three-month period. In this expenses worksheet, the labels PROD.1, PROD.2, and PROD.3 need to run down the side of the worksheet rather than across the top.

Create the expenses sheet below the Income Statement. First, add a title to it and enter monthly labels.

Move to: cell A19
Type: Monthly Expenses →
June →
July →
August ↵

Figure 3.53
Monthly expenses labels

D19: 'August READY

	A	B	C	D	E
1		Income Statement			
2		July-1-89	July-31-89		
3					
4	000's omitted	PROD.1	PROD.2	PROD.3	TOTAL
5					
6	Net Sales	$80.00	$120.00	$140.00	$340.00
7	Cost of Goods Sold	30.00	60.00	70.00	160.00
8	Gross Margin	50.00	60.00	70.00	180.00
9	Marketing/G&A Expenses	35.00	30.00	30.00	95.00
10	EBIT	15.00	30.00	40.00	85.00
11	Interest	1.00	2.00	2.00	5.00
12	Taxes	7.00	14.00	19.00	40.00
13	NET INCOME	$7.00	$14.00	$19.00	$40.00
14					
15	%Total Net Sales	24%	35%	41%	100%
16					
17					
18					
19	Monthly Expenses	June	July	August	
20					

UNDO

Next you will copy the product labels from the Income Statement to the Monthly Expenses section. Following the procedure you've used before, you will first indicate the range you want to copy and then the range you want to copy to. Follow the prompts.

Move to: cell B4—the beginning of the range to be transposed
Press: [/]
Select: Range
Trans
Press: [→] twice
[↵]
Move to: cell A20
Press: [↵]
Move to: cell A22

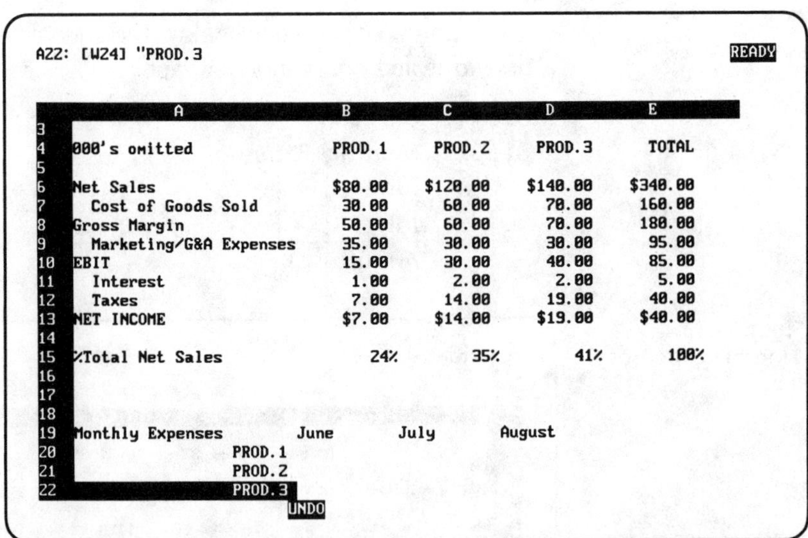

A22: [W24] "PROD.3 READY

	A	B	C	D	E
3					
4	000's omitted	PROD.1	PROD.2	PROD.3	TOTAL
5					
6	Net Sales	$80.00	$120.00	$140.00	$340.00
7	Cost of Goods Sold	30.00	60.00	70.00	160.00
8	Gross Margin	50.00	60.00	70.00	180.00
9	Marketing/G&A Expenses	35.00	30.00	30.00	95.00
10	EBIT	15.00	30.00	40.00	85.00
11	Interest	1.00	2.00	2.00	5.00
12	Taxes	7.00	14.00	19.00	40.00
13	NET INCOME	$7.00	$14.00	$19.00	$40.00
14					
15	%Total Net Sales	24%	35%	41%	100%
16					
17					
18					
19	Monthly Expenses	June	July	August	
20	PROD.1				
21	PROD.2				
22	PROD.3				

UNDO

Figure 3.54
Transposed labels

When you move the cell pointer down to rows 21 and 22, you can see that the labels are transposed from column labels to row labels. Notice that the label prefix (the double quotation) has been copied with the labels as well, causing them to be right-aligned in column A.

SPLITTING THE SCREEN

If a worksheet is longer than twenty rows or wider than eight columns, it is too large to fit on some screens. You can move around the worksheet to view it quickly and easily using the pointer-movement keys, but 1-2-3 also has a feature that allows you to see two separate sections of the worksheet at the same time.

Using **/Worksheet Window**, you can create a second window on the screen that contains a range of cells from any area of the worksheet. This feature allows you to keep track of more than one area at once; you can see the effects of changes in one range on cells in another.

In the Monthly Expenses worksheet you just created, the range of transposed labels starts in row 22. This means the area is out of view when you're looking at the entire Income Statement. Here you will create another window on the screen that will allow you to view both the majority of the Income Statement and the Monthly Expenses at the same time.

Press: [HOME] to place row 1 at the top of the screen
Move to: cell A14
Press: [/]
Select: Worksheet
Window

The Window menu offers the choice of either a horizontal or a vertical window (as well as synchronized or unsynchronized windows, options that are covered below). The highlight is on Horizontal, and the third line of the control panel reads Split the screen horizontally at the current row.

Select: Horizontal

Figure 3.55
Split screen

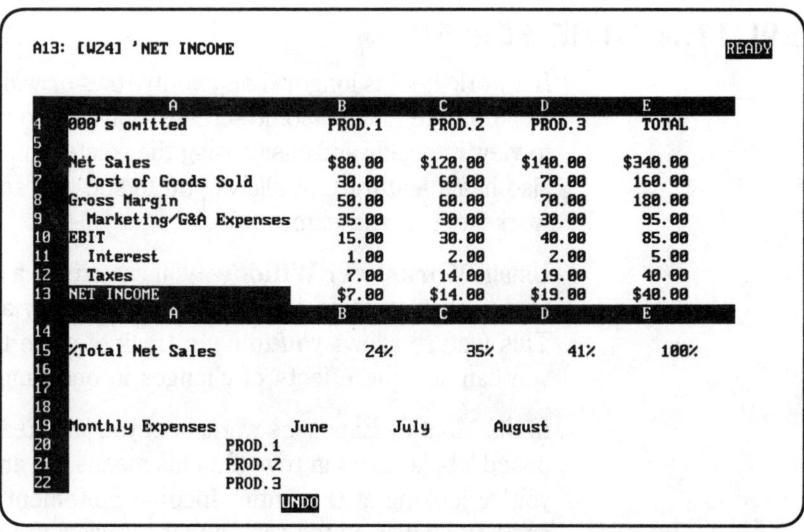

A new row of column letters appears between rows 13 and 14, separating the two windows. Notice that the bottom row is now row 19.

The cell pointer is currently in the top window. You can move the cell pointer between the two windows with the Window (F6) key. Move the cell pointer to the bottom window and scroll down:

Press: WINDOW (F6)
Move to: cell A22 using ↓

Figure 3.56 Moving down a window

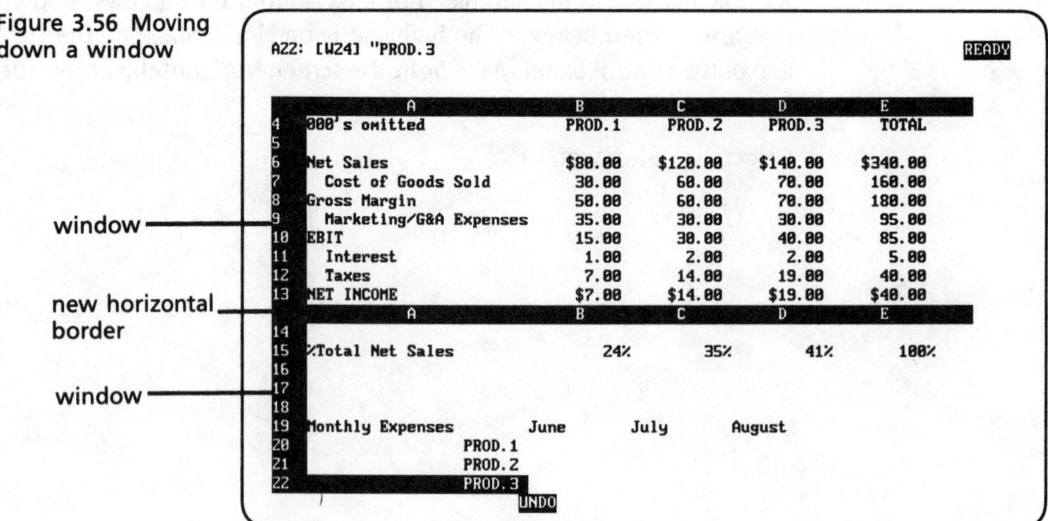

The range containing the Monthly Expenses labels is now visible on the screen.

Experiment with Window (F6) and the arrow keys to see how you can move between and around the two windows. Notice that when the screen moves right or left, both windows scroll together.

You can also make the two windows scroll separately. Use **/Worksheet Window Sync** and **/Worksheet Window Unsync** to control this feature.

Move to: any cell in column A
Press: [/]
Select: Worksheet
Window
Unsync

No difference is immediately visible, but now when you scroll one window to the left or right, the other window remains stationary.

Press: [→] until the cell pointer is in column G

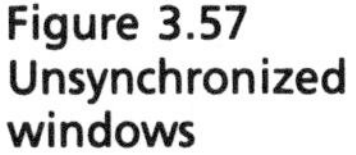
Figure 3.57 Unsynchronized windows

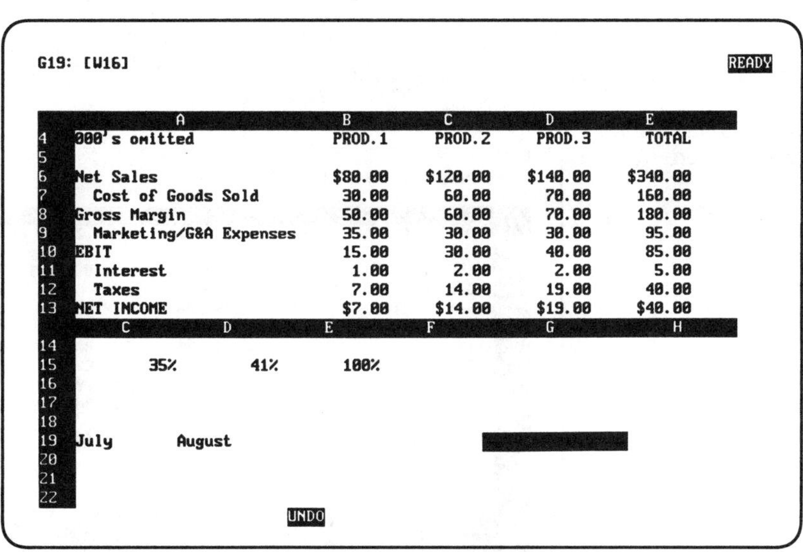

When you are through moving around the two windows, clear them from the screen:

Press: [/]
Select: Worksheet
Window
Clear

ERASING RANGES

/Range Erase is used to remove parts of the worksheet that you no longer need. The command erases the cell contents of the specified range, but it leaves the cell formats intact.

In this example, the range of monthly expenses is no longer necessary. Use **/Range Erase** to replace the labels with blanks.

Move to: cell A19
Press: [/]
Select: Range
Erase

The second line of the control panel reads Enter range to erase: A19..A19. Highlight the range.

Press: [↓] three times
[→] three times

Figure 3.58 Range to be erased

```
D22:                                                          POINT
Enter range to erase: A19..D22

               A                  B         C         D         E
4  000's omitted               PROD.1    PROD.2    PROD.3     TOTAL
5
6  Net Sales                   $80.00   $120.00   $140.00   $340.00
7    Cost of Goods Sold         30.00     60.00     70.00    160.00
8  Gross Margin                 50.00     60.00     70.00    180.00
9    Marketing/G&A Expenses     35.00     30.00     30.00     95.00
10 EBIT                         15.00     30.00     40.00     85.00
11   Interest                    1.00      2.00      2.00      5.00
12   Taxes                       7.00     14.00     19.00     40.00
13 NET INCOME                   $7.00    $14.00    $19.00    $40.00
14
15 %Total Net Sales               24%       35%       41%      100%
16
17
18
19 Monthly Expenses         June      July      August
20                     PROD.1
21                     PROD.2
22                     PROD.3
23
```

Press: [↵]

TEXT EDITING

The 1-2-3 worksheet has features that let you do a small amount of text editing in the worksheet. You can enter a few lines of text to document portions of the worksheet or include a memo.

As you have seen, 1-2-3 allows a label to be longer than the cell in which it is entered. The label overflows into adjacent cells, provided they are blank. **/Range Justify** acts on the label, breaking the lines so they fit into a range of any width you specify.

You'll write a short memo at the bottom of the Income Statement. When you enter the sentence into cell A21, do not press Enter until you reach the end of the sentence. Then use **/Range Justify** to fit the sentence into a block across columns A and B.

Move to: cell A19
Type: Memo to All Departments [↵]
Press: [↓] twice
Type: All products are currently showing a profit, but we should keep an eye on product 1. [↵]

Figure 3.59
Long label

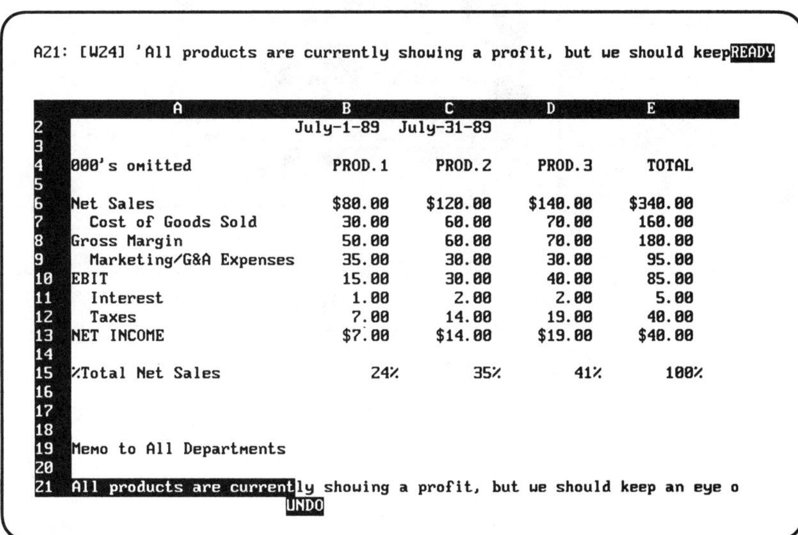

A21: [W24] 'All products are currently showing a profit, but we should keep READY

	A	B	C	D	E
2		July-1-89	July-31-89		
3					
4	000's omitted	PROD.1	PROD.2	PROD.3	TOTAL
5					
6	Net Sales	$80.00	$120.00	$140.00	$340.00
7	Cost of Goods Sold	30.00	60.00	70.00	160.00
8	Gross Margin	50.00	60.00	70.00	180.00
9	Marketing/G&A Expenses	35.00	30.00	30.00	95.00
10	EBIT	15.00	30.00	40.00	85.00
11	Interest	1.00	2.00	2.00	5.00
12	Taxes	7.00	14.00	19.00	40.00
13	NET INCOME	$7.00	$14.00	$19.00	$40.00
14					
15	%Total Net Sales	24%	35%	41%	100%
16					
17					
18					
19	Memo to All Departments				
20					
21	All products are currently showing a profit, but we should keep an eye o				

UNDO

The sentence extends across the screen, and the last characters are not visible.

Press: /
Select: Range
Justify

The second line of the control panel will read **Enter justify range: A21..A21**. You want the text to extend across columns A and B.

Press: → to expand the highlight to cell B21
↵
↓ twice

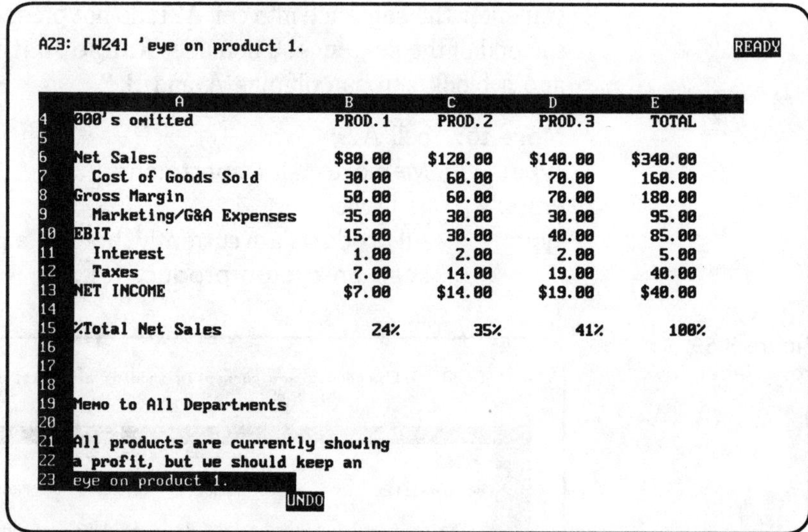

A23: [W24] 'eye on product 1. READY

	A	B	C	D	E
4	000's omitted	PROD.1	PROD.2	PROD.3	TOTAL
5					
6	Net Sales	$80.00	$120.00	$140.00	$340.00
7	Cost of Goods Sold	30.00	60.00	70.00	160.00
8	Gross Margin	50.00	60.00	70.00	180.00
9	Marketing/G&A Expenses	35.00	30.00	30.00	95.00
10	EBIT	15.00	30.00	40.00	85.00
11	Interest	1.00	2.00	2.00	5.00
12	Taxes	7.00	14.00	19.00	40.00
13	NET INCOME	$7.00	$14.00	$19.00	$40.00
14					
15	%Total Net Sales	24%	35%	41%	100%
16					
17					
18					
19	Memo to All Departments				
20					
21	All products are currently showing				
22	a profit, but we should keep an				
23	eye on product 1.				

UNDO

Figure 3.60
Justified text

The text is broken into three lines that spread across columns A and B. If you move the cursor down column A, you will see that there are now three labels, located in cells A21, A22, and A23. To edit the text, you would move to one of those cells and press Edit (F2).

WHAT-IF CALCULATIONS

Changing Sample Values

If the electronic worksheet's automatic recalculation is the key to greater efficiency, its use in what-if scenarios is the key to better decision making. The two examples that follow illustrate the what-if potential of 1–2–3.

1. What if Net Sales for Product 1 increased by 12%? What effect would this have on Net Income?

Move to: cell B6

Type: **100*112%** [↵] (to increase the amount by 12%)

Figure 3.61
Changed values

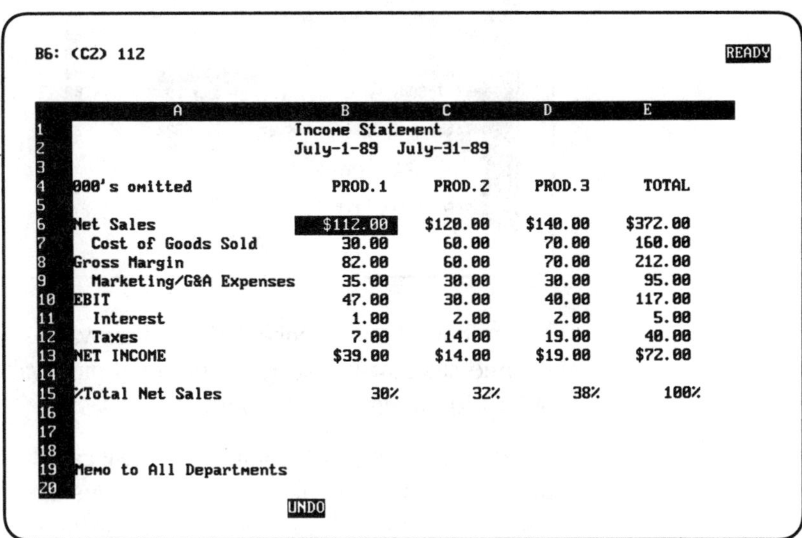

B6: (C2) 112 READY

	A	B	C	D	E
1		Income Statement			
2		July-1-89	July-31-89		
3					
4	000's omitted	PROD.1	PROD.2	PROD.3	TOTAL
5					
6	Net Sales	$112.00	$120.00	$140.00	$372.00
7	Cost of Goods Sold	30.00	60.00	70.00	160.00
8	Gross Margin	82.00	60.00	70.00	212.00
9	Marketing/G&A Expenses	35.00	30.00	30.00	95.00
10	EBIT	47.00	30.00	40.00	117.00
11	Interest	1.00	2.00	2.00	5.00
12	Taxes	7.00	14.00	19.00	40.00
13	NET INCOME	$39.00	$14.00	$19.00	$72.00
14					
15	%Total Net Sales	30%	32%	38%	100%
16					
17					
18					
19	Memo to All Departments				
20					

UNDO

Notice how all the values related to the contents of cell B6 are instantly updated to reflect the change you made. Net Income, in cell B13, has increased from $7 in the original to $39 in this scenario. Compare other values in the original against the new version.

2. What if Marketing/G&A expenses for Product 1 could be lowered by $2,000 and taxes decreased by 30%? What effect would this have on Net Income?

Move to: cell B9
Type: **33** [↵] (to lower the amount by $2,000)
Move to: cell B12
Type: **7*70%** [↵] (to lower the amount by 30%)

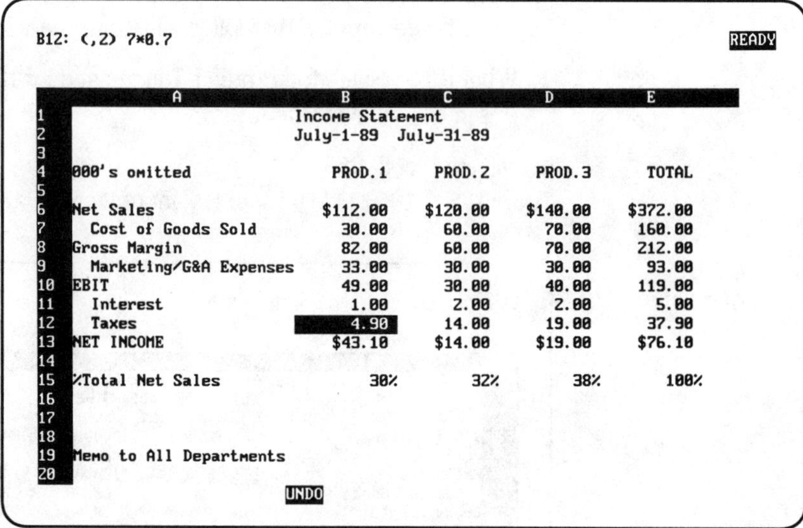
B12: (,2) 7*0.7 READY

	A	B	C	D	E
1		Income Statement			
2		July-1-89	July-31-89		
3					
4	000's omitted	PROD.1	PROD.2	PROD.3	TOTAL
5					
6	Net Sales	$112.00	$120.00	$140.00	$372.00
7	Cost of Goods Sold	30.00	60.00	70.00	160.00
8	Gross Margin	82.00	60.00	70.00	212.00
9	Marketing/G&A Expenses	33.00	30.00	30.00	93.00
10	EBIT	49.00	30.00	40.00	119.00
11	Interest	1.00	2.00	2.00	5.00
12	Taxes	4.90	14.00	19.00	37.90
13	NET INCOME	$43.10	$14.00	$19.00	$76.10
14					
15	%Total Net Sales	30%	32%	38%	100%
16					
17					
18					
19	Memo to All Departments				
20					

UNDO

Figure 3.62
More changes to the worksheet

Notice how these changes affect other values in the worksheet. Net Income has now increased from the original value of $7 to a new value of $43.10—a significant change.

When you perform these kinds of what-if calculations, 1–2–3 recalculates the worksheet very quickly because it uses a technique called **minimal recalculation.** 1–2–3 recalculates only formulas or cells that are affected by the change(s) you made. (Earlier releases of 1–2–3 recalculated all formulas and cells whether they were affected or not. In large worksheets, the recalculation time would be noticeable.)

Restoring Original Values

Before going on, restore the original values to the worksheet.

Move to: cell B6
Type: 100 [↵]
Move to: cell B9
Type: 35 [↵]
Move to: cell B12
Type: 7 [↵]

CREATING AND SAVING WORKSHEETS

Worksheets are often printed in reports and used in presentations. And a report or presentation might involve what-if scenarios. Thus, you could conceivably want different versions of the same worksheet.

This is easy with 1–2–3. Any time you change values in a worksheet, you can save the changed version of the worksheet under a new name (thereby creating a different file). For example, if you were to save the Income Statement with the changes entered above, you could use the name INCOME2 to differentiate it from the original version.

PRINTING THE WORKSHEET

Before you print a worksheet (or anything else), you should save the file so that all the latest changes are saved. Problems can occur because of the simplest errors or oversights and you might lose the final version of the worksheet.

Save the file.

Press: [/]
Select: File
Save
Press: [↵]
Select: Replace

The Print Settings

Printing the worksheet is a simple task. Before you print, however, you may want to change some of the 1–2–3 print settings. For example, your worksheet may be much wider than your paper. To take care of this, you could set wider margins or choose to print only a portion of the worksheet at a time. The Print menu determines these and other printing specifications for your worksheets.

> NOTE: If the data in the print range is wider than the paper you're printing on, 1–2–3 automatically prints the data that extends beyond the right margin on a separate page.

Before you start, be sure you installed a printer with the 1–2–3 Install program, and check that the printer is turned on and ready.

Press: [/]
Select: Print

1–2–3 offers you two choices at this point. You can send the output to the printer or to a print file. In this case, you want to send it to the printer. (A print file is an ASCII text file that can be saved and accessed later in DOS or other software programs.)

Select: Printer

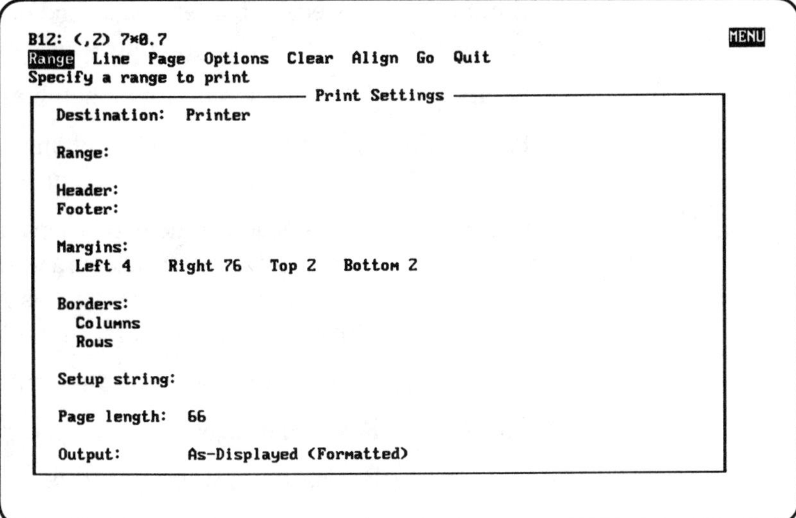

Figure 3.63 Print settings sheet

(2.2) The print settings sheet appears. As you may recall from changing the global column width setting earlier, a setting sheet is a new 1-2-3 Release 2.2 feature. It is a special screen that helps you keep track of the choices you are making so you can see them all at a glance. The print settings sheet offers you a number of choices about the appearance and format of the printout. The only option that you **must** specify is the range to be printed.

You change settings in a setting sheet by selecting commands from the menu that appears above the setting sheet.

Range — Specifies the range of the worksheet that will be printed. You must specify this even if you want to print all the data in the worksheet.

Line, Page — Each advances the paper one line or one page, respectively.

Options — Includes a number of choices about the appearance of the printout.

- Header, Footer — Specifies a header or footer to be printed on each page.
- Margins — Sets left, right, top, or bottom margins to fit the dimensions of the worksheet and the paper size.

Borders	Specifies border column and/or rows to appear on each page of the printout.
Setup	Establishes a printer setup string.
Pg-Length	Specifies the number of lines per page. This allows you to print on shorter or longer paper.
Other	This option includes two separate commands: you can opt to print the formulas in a worksheet; you can choose to ignore print settings such as top and bottom margins, page breaks, headers, and footers.

Clear	Resets some or all of the print settings.
Align	Resets the alignment of the paper to the top of the page.
Go	Begins the printing process.
Quit	Returns 1–2–3 to READY mode.

Now specify the range of the worksheet you want to print. You will be printing the entire Income Statement.

Select: Range
Move to: cell A1
Press: [.] (period)
Move to: cell E23

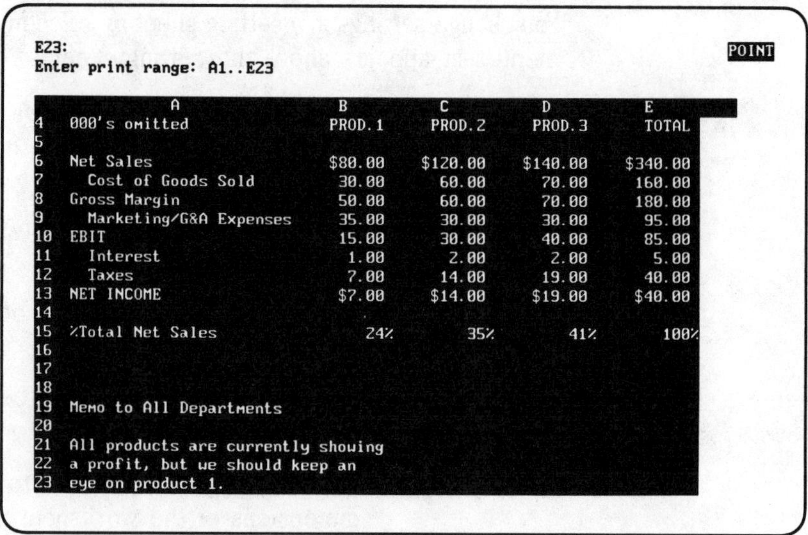

E23: POINT
Enter print range: A1..E23

	A	B	C	D	E
4	000's omitted	PROD.1	PROD.2	PROD.3	TOTAL
5					
6	Net Sales	$80.00	$120.00	$140.00	$340.00
7	Cost of Goods Sold	30.00	60.00	70.00	160.00
8	Gross Margin	50.00	60.00	70.00	180.00
9	Marketing/G&A Expenses	35.00	30.00	30.00	95.00
10	EBIT	15.00	30.00	40.00	85.00
11	Interest	1.00	2.00	2.00	5.00
12	Taxes	7.00	14.00	19.00	40.00
13	NET INCOME	$7.00	$14.00	$19.00	$40.00
14					
15	%Total Net Sales	24%	35%	41%	100%
16					
17					
18					
19	Memo to All Departments				
20					
21	All products are currently showing				
22	a profit, but we should keep an				
23	eye on product 1.				

Figure 3.64 Print range specified

Press: 
Select: Align
Go

The mode indicator flashes WAIT while the worksheet is printing. After the worksheet is printed, select Page to move the worksheet out of the printer and Quit to remove the **/Print** menu:

Select: Page
Quit

If you want to save the print settings you specified, save the file again.

2.2 NOTE: If you want to do some special formatting to your worksheet (add bold, shading, underlining, different fonts, for example), you can use the Allways program to both format and print your worksheet. See Chapter 6.

THE MAIN MENU COMMAND STRUCTURE

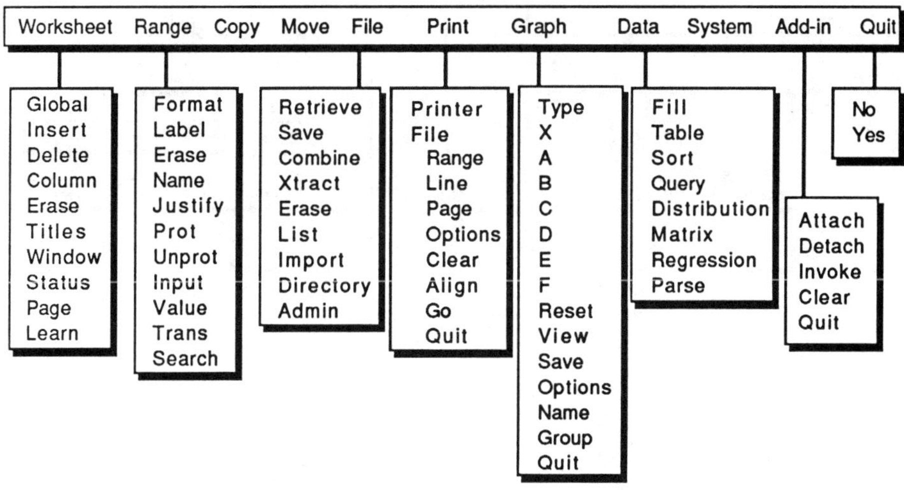

THE WORKSHEET COMMANDS

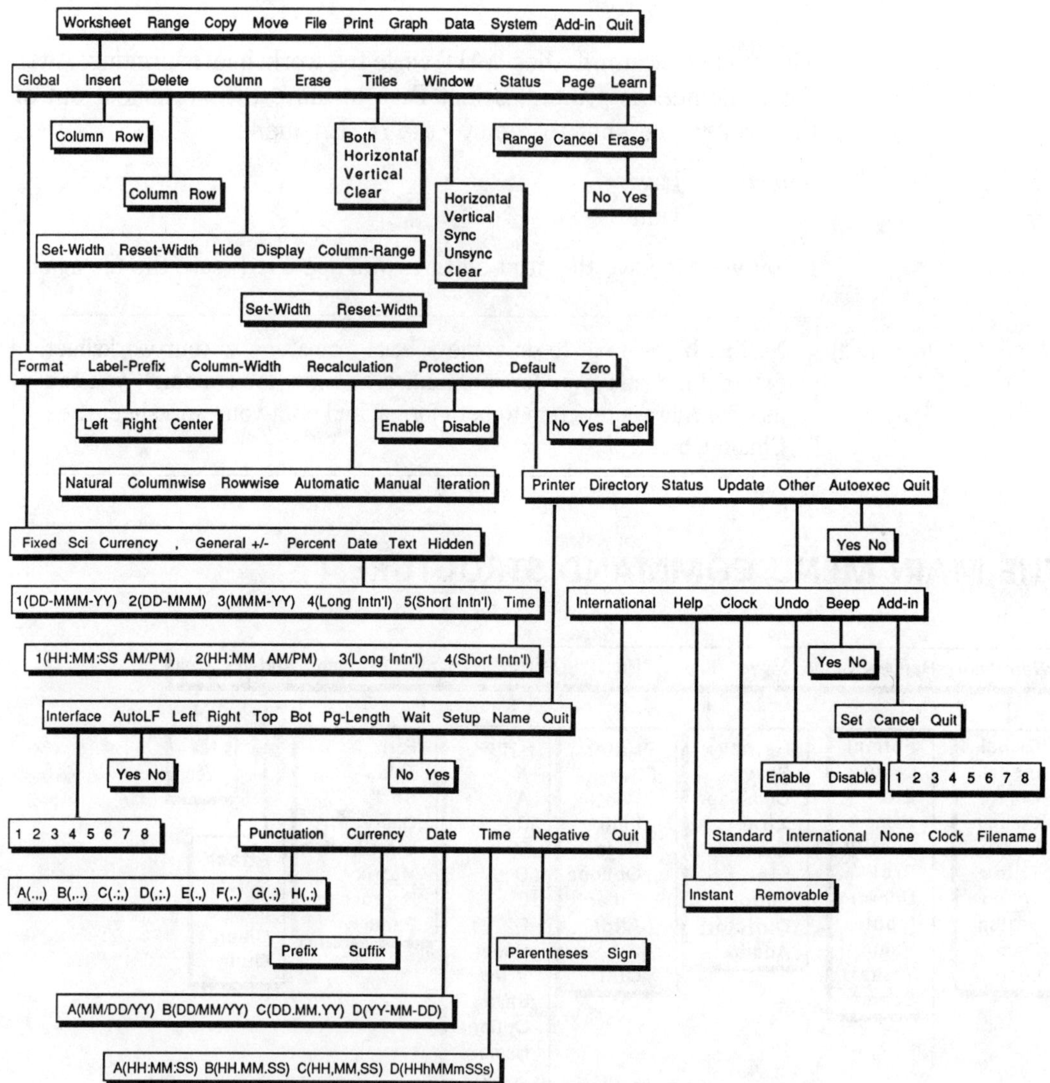

THE RANGE COMMANDS

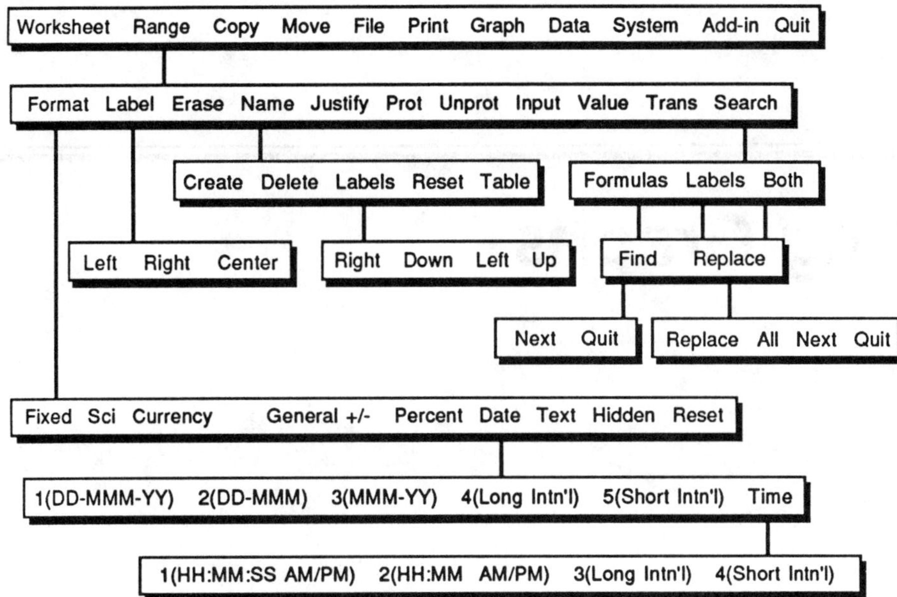

THE PRINT COMMANDS

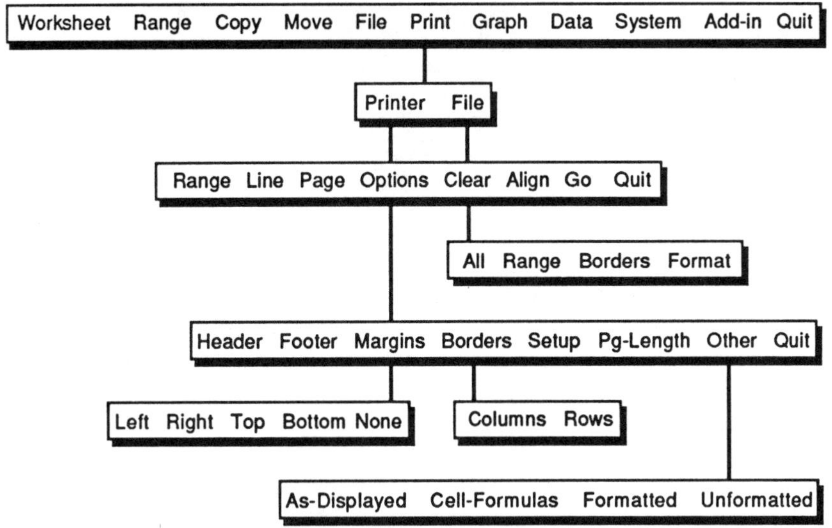

4

Creating Graphs

Business graphics are frequently used in presentations and reports. In many situations a graph can communicate worksheet data more clearly and effectively than the values themselves. A graph can reveal the patterns in rows and columns of values and can illustrate overall trends and projections.

1-2-3 lets you draw graphs directly from the data in a worksheet. What's more, the graph is dynamically connected to the worksheet data: change a number in the worksheet and the graph is instantly redrawn to reflect the change. You can view a graph on the screen as you create it, and you can change it or add to it as necessary. Once a graph is completed, you can print it out on a printer or plot it on a graphics plotter. You
2.2 can also use Allways to include a graph in a worksheet and print the worksheet data and the graph together. See Chapter 6 for details.

The graphics in 1-2-3 offer tremendous flexibility. You have the choice of five different types of graphs, and various shading and color options. For printing a graph, 1-2-3 provides a wide selection of colors for the graph and print styles for the titles and legends. You can enhance the graph even further with Allways.

In this chapter you will:

- Learn about different graph types
- 2.2 Produce a line graph quickly based on a small worksheet you'll create
- Create a bar graph and pie chart based on the income statement you created in Chapter 3
- Experiment with what-if graphics
- Print one of the graphs you created

Before You Start

For a two-diskette computer

- 1-2-3 should be set up to save files on a disk in drive B.
- The data disk should be in drive B.
- The Help Disk (5.25″ systems) or System, Help, and PrintGraph Disk (3.5″ systems) should be in drive A.

For a hard-disk computer

- 1-2-3 should be set up to save files in a subdirectory named TEMP.
- All the 1-2-3 disks should be copied in the root directory or in their own subdirectory on the hard disk.

GRAPH TYPES

1-2-3 offers five different types of graphs: line graphs, bar graphs, stacked bar graphs, pie charts, and XY graphs. All are drawn from the data in a worksheet, but each has a different purpose.

Line Graph

A line graph displays the values from a row or column in the worksheet as a continuous line. The graph has two axes: X (horizontal) and Y (vertical). The X axis defines a specific period of time. The Y axis is a numbered scale.

Line graphs show how much numeric values have changed over a period of time. They are particularly useful for identifying trends and making projections.

Figure 4.1
Line graph

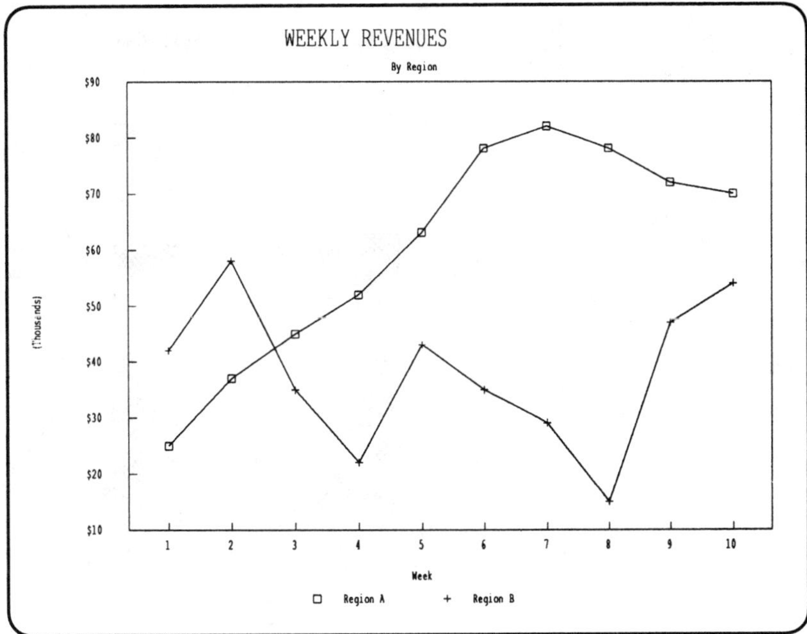

Bar Graph

A bar graph represents numeric values as vertical bars. Each bar reflects the value of a single worksheet cell. You can use bar graphs to compare related data at a given point in time.

The X axis of a bar graph has labels that identify what each bar represents. Each label can apply to as many as six bars. The Y axis is scaled numerically, according to the worksheet values being represented.

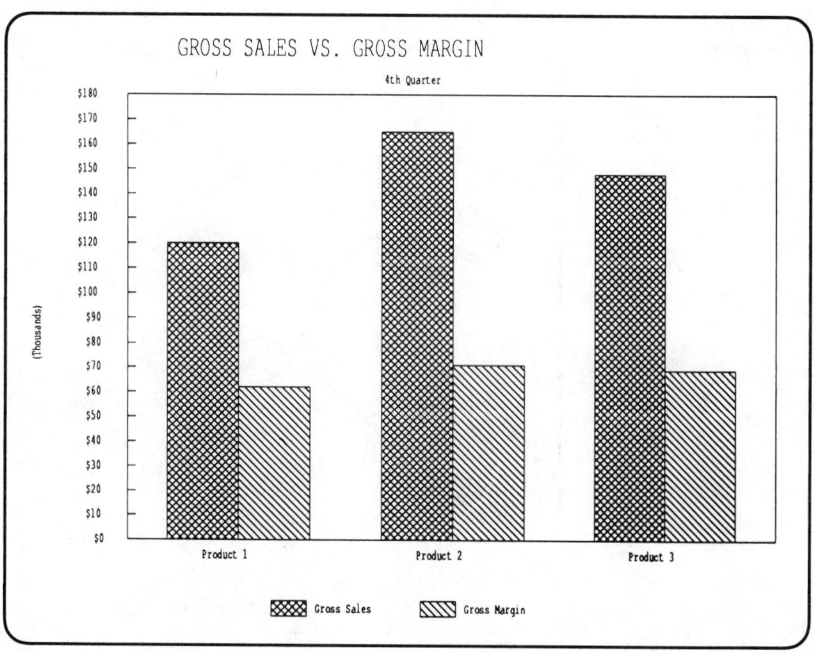

Figure 4.2
Bar graph

Stacked Bar Graph

A stacked bar graph is similar to a bar graph except that related bars are placed on top of each other (stacked) rather than side by side. Different hatch patterns or colors differentiate the parts of the bar, and up to six bars can be stacked. Each stacked bar has a label on the X axis, and each part of the stacked bar represents a cell value in the worksheet. A stacked bar graph often is used to compare totals for groups of bars.

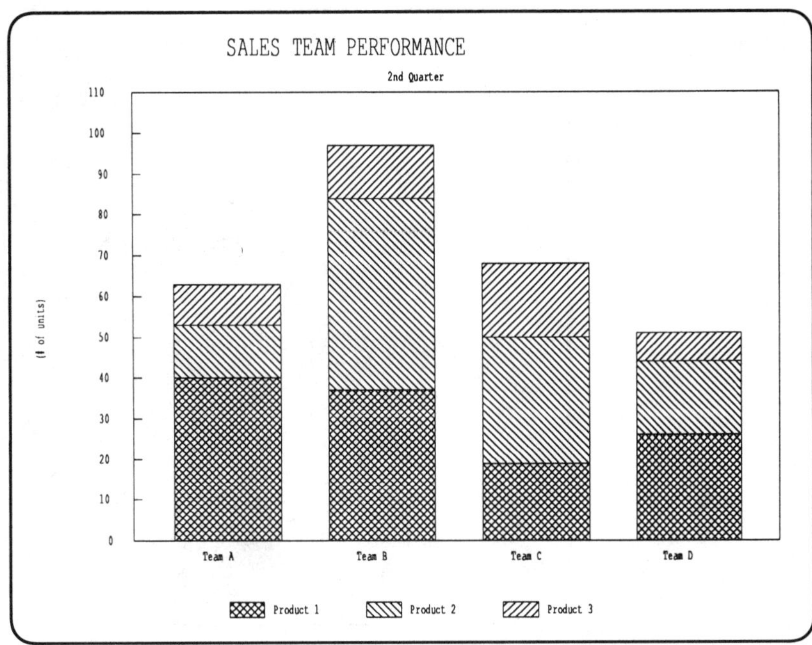

Figure 4.3 Stacked bar graph

Pie Chart

A pie chart, as its name implies, is a circle divided into slices. Each slice represents a cell value in the worksheet. If one value is twice as large as another, it gets a slice that is twice as large. A pie chart is used to compare parts to the whole. You can "explode" (separate and lift out) one or more slices of the pie for emphasis.

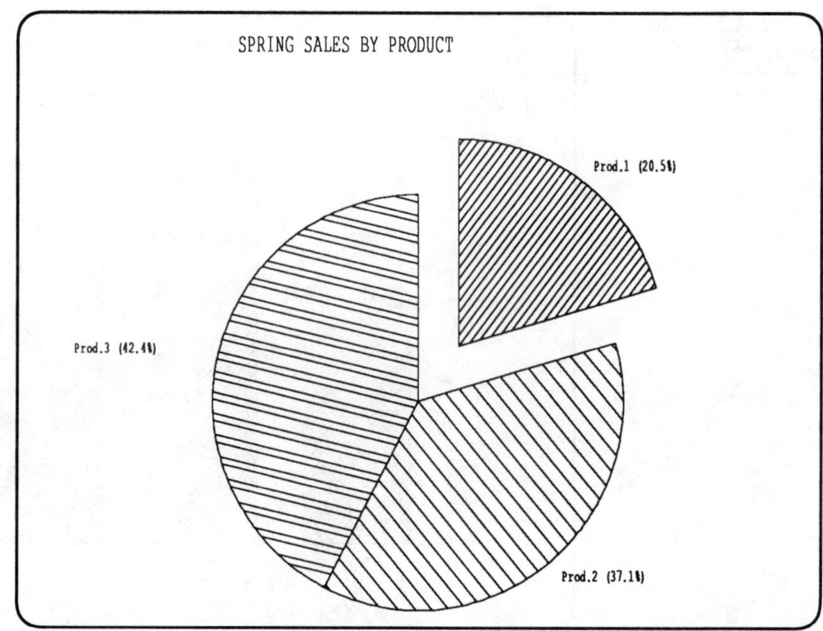

Figure 4.4
Pie chart

XY Graph

Each point on an XY graph depends on a value from both the X and Y axes. The X value determines how far left or right a point is placed on the graph. The Y value controls the vertical placement of a point. An XY graph is used to plot mathematical formulas and make statistical analyses.

Figure 4.5
XY graph

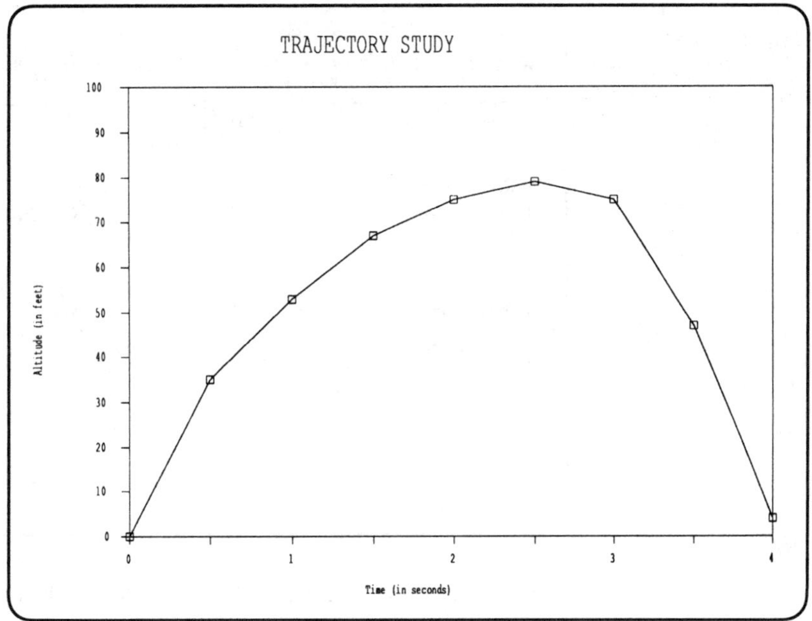

(2.2) GRAPH SETTINGS SHEET

You create a graph by using commands from the Graph menu to specify certain characteristics of the graph. Each graph has its own series of specifications, including its type and the worksheet data from which it is to be drawn.

When you first select **/Graph**, 1–2–3 displays a special screen called the graph settings sheet. Setting sheets are new to 1–2–3 Release 2.2. The graph setting sheet is particularly useful because graphs involve a number of settings. The settings sheet lets you see them all together so you don't have to try and remember what you specified.

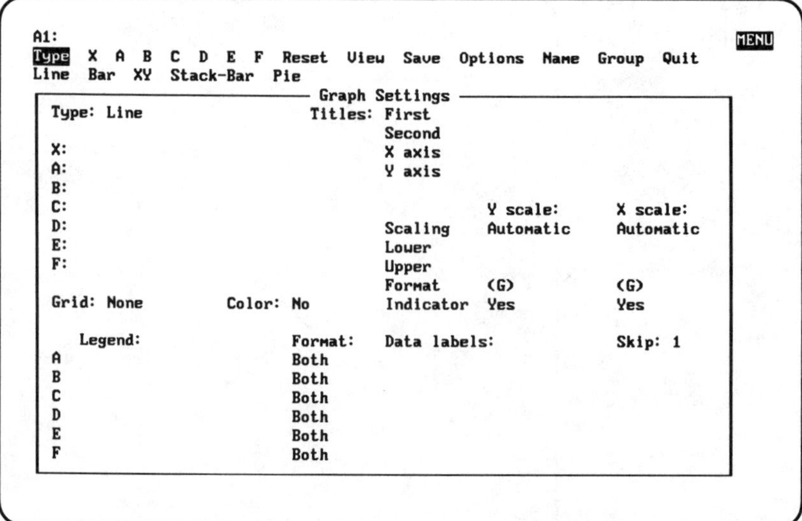

Figure 4.6 Graph settings sheet

You can change any of the settings on the graph settings sheet by selecting commands from the Graph menu displayed above the settings sheet (sometimes you will be selecting from submenus). As you select commands from the Graph menu, the settings sheet changes to reflect your choices.

To create a graph, you must define at least two settings: the type of the graph and the data ranges in the worksheet from which the graph is to be drawn. You can then embellish the graph in many ways. You can, for example, choose to add titles, change the numeric formatting for the X and Y axes, and perform other adjustments.

You can also choose to name the graph so you can call it up and view it at any time. This allows you to graph the same data from a worksheet in a number of different ways. All graphs are saved with the worksheet file from which they are drawn—so when you retrieve the file, you simply call up a graph by name.

If you want to print a graph, you must first save it in a special file called a graph (picture) file, identified by a .PIC extension.

(2.2) GRAPHING WITH /GRAPH GROUP

1–2–3 Release 2.2 has a convenient feature for quickly graphing the data in a group of consecutive rows or columns in the worksheet. Using the **Graph Group** command, you specify the group to be graphed, and 1–2–3 breaks up the group into the appropriate data ranges. (A **data range** is the range of values you're graphing.) Without /**Graph Group**, you have to specify each data range individually.

To see how /**Graph Group** works, you will first create a a simple worksheet that has sales figures for three European branch offices for a period of four years.

Creating the Worksheet

If you've been working with a different worksheet, save it and then start with a blank worksheet.

Press: [/]
Select: Worksheet
Erase
Yes

Enter the following labels in the worksheet:

Move to: cell B2
Type: 1986 [→]
1987 [→]
1988 [→]
1989 [↵]
Move to: cell A3
Type: Paris [↓]
Milan [↓]
London [↵]

Figure 4.7 Labels in worksheet

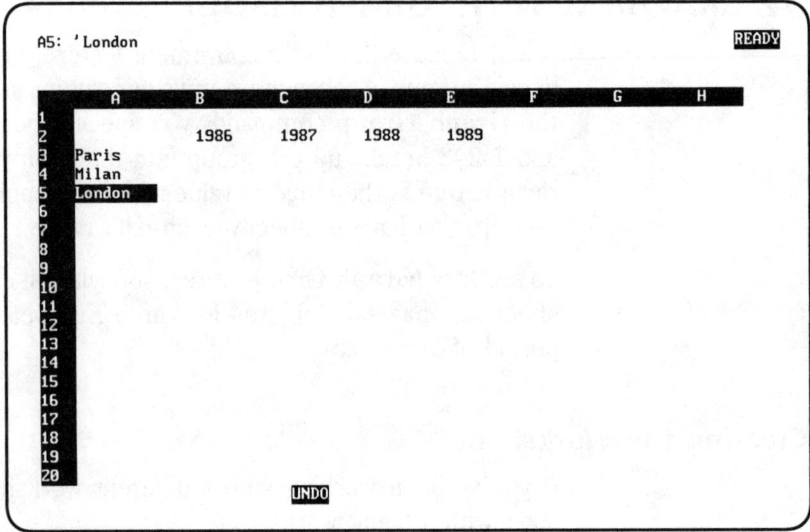

Now enter the sales figures.

Move to: cell B3

Type:
45678 [→]
34527 [→]
55112 [→]
62314 [↓]
56743 [←]
43244 [←]
51112 [←]
49998 [↓]
21334 [→]
23225 [→]
29988 [→]
32221 [↵]

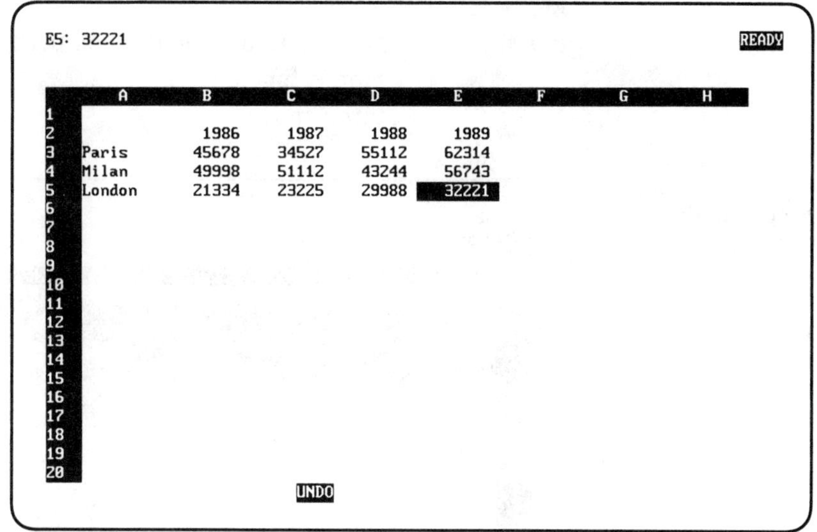

Figure 4.8
Completed worksheet

Your worksheet should look like the one in Figure 4.8.

Graphing a Group of Ranges

1–2–3 allows you to graph up to six data ranges. These ranges are named A to F and are graphed along the y axis. An additional range, the X range, provides labels for the x (horizontal) axis. When you graph a group of ranges in one step, 1–2–3 assumes that the first row or column in your group is the X range and the remaining rows or columns are the data ranges. When you specify the group to be graphed, you will therefore include the years in row 2 as part of the range so they serve as x-axis labels.

You will now create a line graph that shows the sales of the three European offices over four years.

Press: /
Select: Graph

Line is the default graph type, so you don't have to change it.

Select: Group

1–2–3 prompts you for the group range: the rows or columns you want to graph.

Move to: cell B2

Press: [•] (period) to anchor the cell pointer

[→] three times

[↓] three times

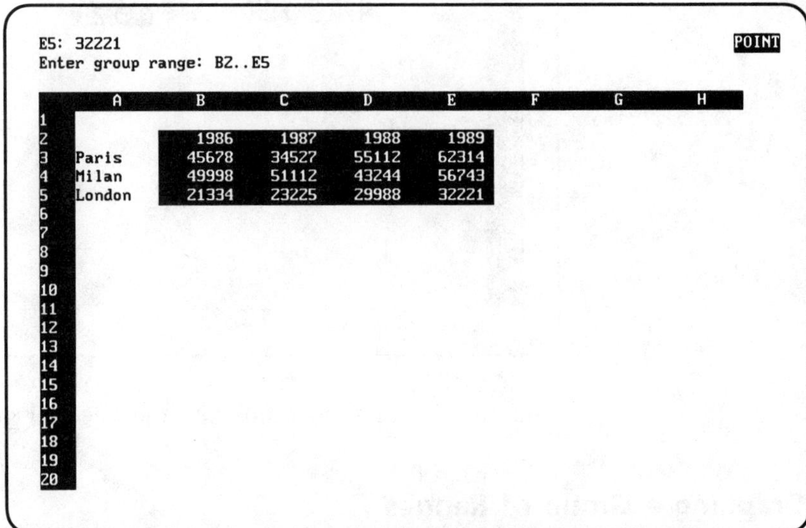
E5: 32221
Enter group range: B2..E5
POINT

	A	B	C	D	E	F	G	H
1								
2		1986	1987	1988	1989			
3	Paris	45678	34527	55112	62314			
4	Milan	49998	51112	43244	56743			
5	London	21334	23225	29988	32221			
6								
7								
8								
9								
10								
11								
12								
13								
14								
15								
16								
17								
18								
19								
20								

Figure 4.9 Group range highlighted

Press: [↵] to accept B2..E5 as the group range

1-2-3 now needs to know whether you want the range interpreted columnwise (so the group range is divided into data ranges by columns) or rowwise (so the group range is divided into data ranges by rows). The data in this worksheet is horizontal so you want the years in row 2 to be the X range, the numbers in row 3 to be the A range, and so on.

Select: Rowwise

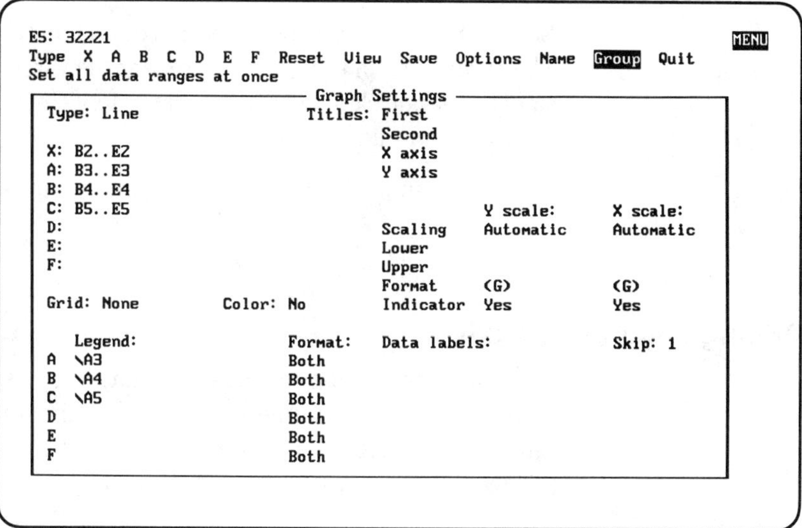

Figure 4.10
Graph settings

Notice that 1-2-3 automatically associated the correct ranges with the X, A, B, and C data ranges.

Now look at the graph on the screen (if you don't have a graphics monitor, you won't be able to do this, but you will be able to print the graph as described later in this chapter).

Select: View

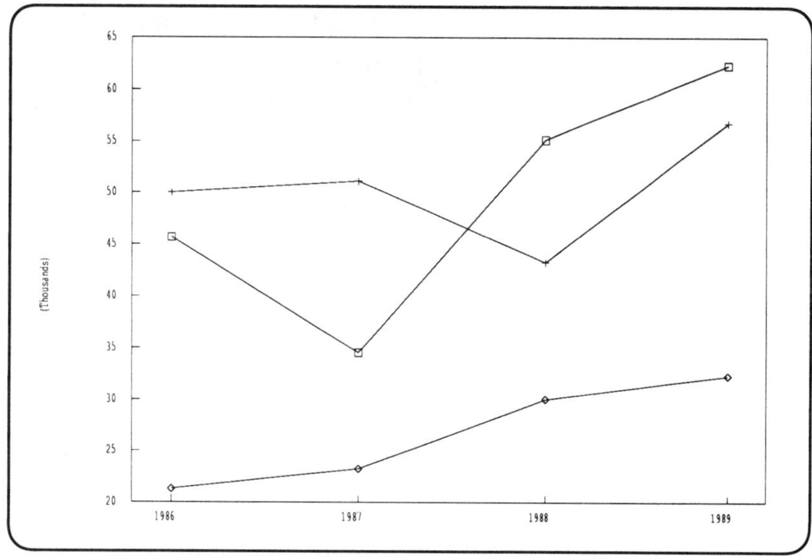

Figure 4.11
Line graph

Notice the years appear on the x axis to identify points on the graph. The three lines in the graph represent the three data ranges. Unfortunately, it's not clear which line represents which city, so you will go back now and add legends.

To clear a graph from the screen you can press any key.

Press: any key

Adding Legends Quickly

You can either define legends individually or as a group as with data ranges, if you have a row or column of labels in the worksheet that can serve as legends. You need to provide the names of the three cities as legends, so can use the labels in the range A3..A5.

Select: Options
Legend

At this point, you can choose to assign a legend to each data range individually or to assign several in one step by selecting Range. Your labels are in a range, so select Range and then highlight the range of labels:

Select: Range
Move to: cell A3
Press: [.] (period) to anchor the cell pointer
[↓] twice
[↵] to accept A3..A5 as the range
Select: Quit

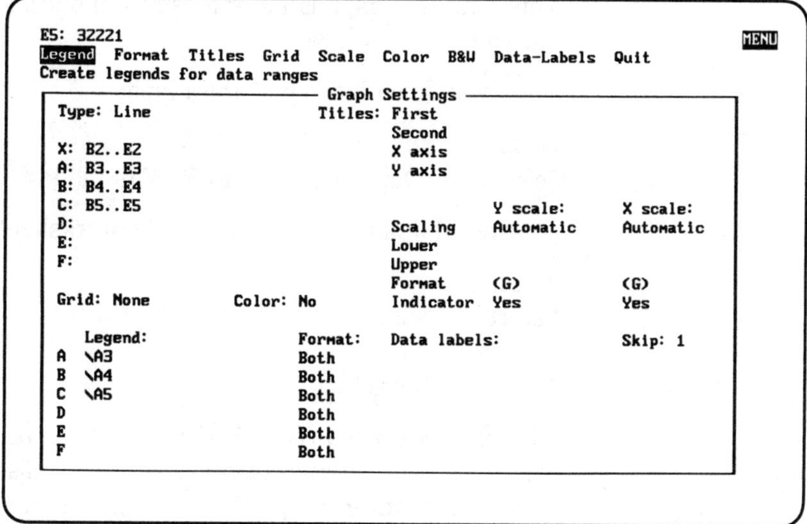

Figure 4.12 Graph settings sheet showing legends

Notice that 1-2-3 has correctly assigned the legends to the appropriate data range. For example, cell A3 (shown as \A3) is the legend for the A data range (the Paris numbers).

Now look at the graph again:

Select: View

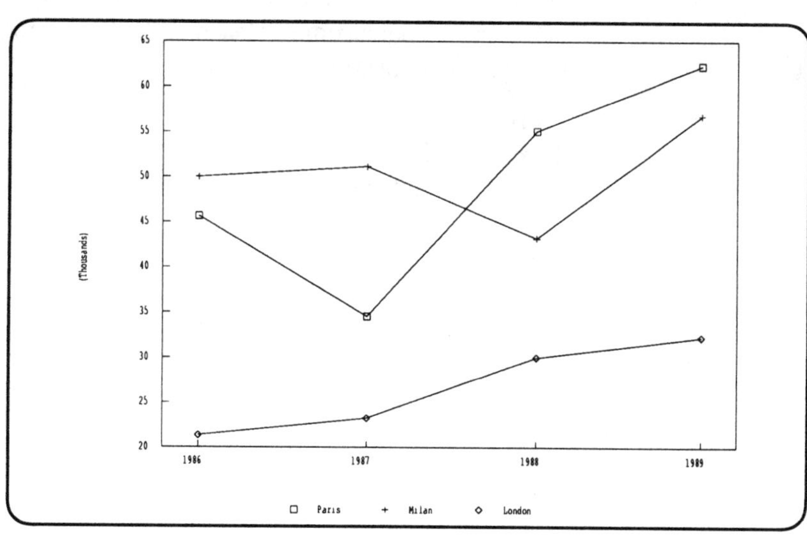

Figure 4.13 Line graph with legends

This time the graph is more meaningful because the legends explain the lines.

After you finish looking at the graph:

Press: any key
Select: Quit to return to READY mode

To save the graph, you must save the worksheet. Call the file SALES.

Press: /
Select: File
Save
Type: sales ↵

/Graph Group and **/Graph Options Legend Range** both provide convenient and fast ways of graphing data in adjacent columns or rows. At times, however, as you'll see in the rest of this chapter, you will want to graph data ranges that aren't next to each other in the worksheet, in which case you must specify the ranges individually.

CREATING A BAR GRAPH

The remaining exercises in this chapter use the Income Statement you created in Chapter 3. You will start by drawing a bar graph comparing net sales and net income for each of the three products. Start by retrieving the file INCOME.

Press: /
Select: File
Retrieve
INCOME.WK1
Press: ↵

Figure 4.14
Income statement

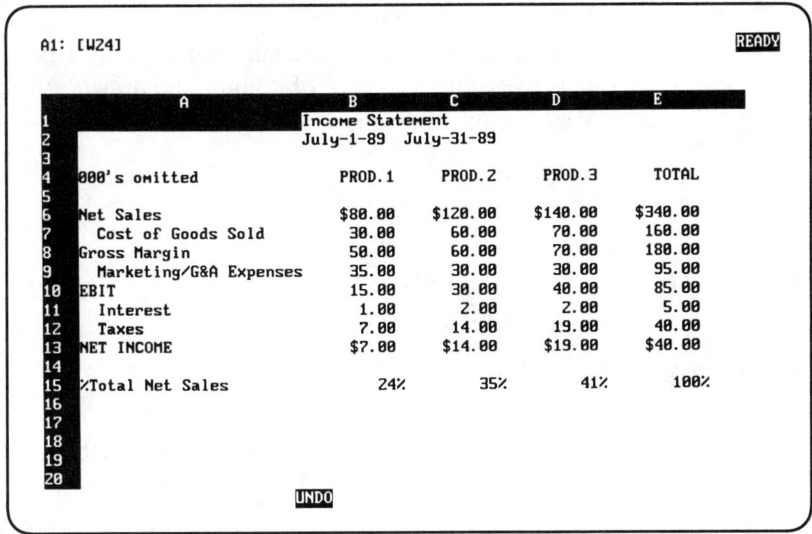

	A	B	C	D	E
1		Income Statement			
2		July-1-89	July-31-89		
3					
4	000's omitted	PROD.1	PROD.2	PROD.3	TOTAL
5					
6	Net Sales	$80.00	$120.00	$140.00	$340.00
7	Cost of Goods Sold	30.00	60.00	70.00	160.00
8	Gross Margin	50.00	60.00	70.00	180.00
9	Marketing/G&A Expenses	35.00	30.00	30.00	95.00
10	EBIT	15.00	30.00	40.00	85.00
11	Interest	1.00	2.00	2.00	5.00
12	Taxes	7.00	14.00	19.00	40.00
13	NET INCOME	$7.00	$14.00	$19.00	$40.00
14					
15	%Total Net Sales	24%	35%	41%	100%
16					
17					
18					
19					
20					

The Income Statement appears on the screen, and the mode indicator reads READY.

You will use the following Graph commands to create the bar graph:

/Graph menu

Type	Identifies which of the five types of graphs is to be drawn
X, A–F (Range)	Identify the ranges of the worksheet from which the graph is to be drawn and labeled
Name	Names and creates the graph in the worksheet file

/Graph Options menu

Legend	Adds a legend to identify the different worksheet ranges
Titles	Adds a title to the graph

Selecting the Graph Type

Because you're not drawing a line graph (the default), the first step is to specify the type of graph to be drawn. As soon as you make your selection, the graph settings sheet reflects your choice.

Press: /
Select: Graph
Type
Bar

Specifying Data and Labels

Use the range commands (X, A, B, C, D, E, F) to specify both the worksheet data to be graphed and the labels that describe that data. The commands refer to worksheet ranges.

X — This specifies a range of labels that appears along the X (horizontal) axis, or, for a pie chart, next to each slice. For a bar graph, each label identifies a bar or a related group of bars.

A to F — These specify ranges of data. You can specify up to six.

Figure 4.15 Graph x range labels

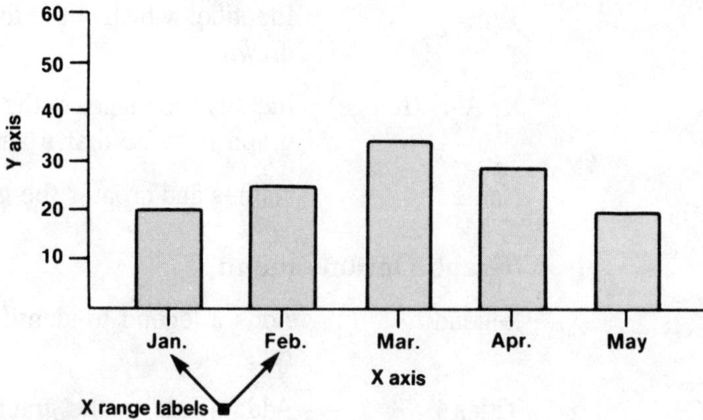

Because the bar graph will compare three products, use the names of the products to identify the bars. After you have invoked the command to select the ranges, you will point to the worksheet range that contains the product names.

Select: X
Move to: cell B4
Press: [·] to anchor the range
Move to: cell D4 to highlight the range B4..D4

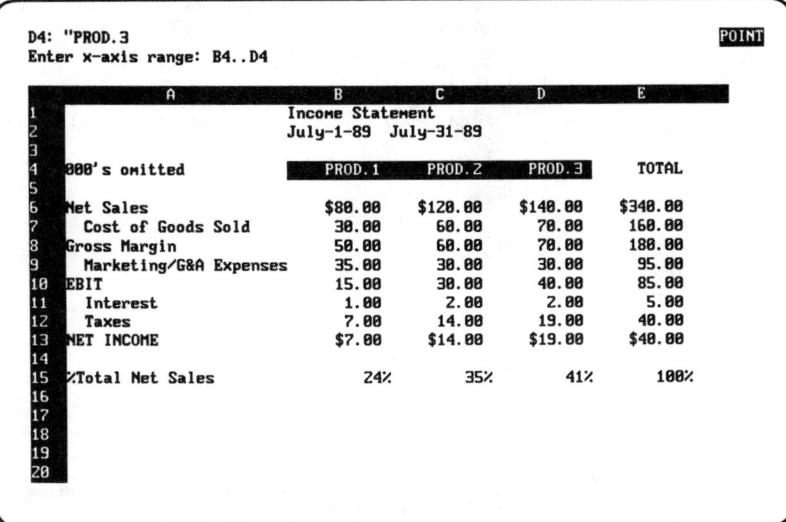

D4: "PROD.3 POINT
Enter x-axis range: B4..D4

	A	B	C	D	E
1		Income Statement			
2		July-1-89	July-31-89		
3					
4	000's omitted	PROD.1	PROD.2	PROD.3	TOTAL
5					
6	Net Sales	$80.00	$120.00	$140.00	$340.00
7	Cost of Goods Sold	30.00	60.00	70.00	160.00
8	Gross Margin	50.00	60.00	70.00	180.00
9	Marketing/G&A Expenses	35.00	30.00	30.00	95.00
10	EBIT	15.00	30.00	40.00	85.00
11	Interest	1.00	2.00	2.00	5.00
12	Taxes	7.00	14.00	19.00	40.00
13	NET INCOME	$7.00	$14.00	$19.00	$40.00
14					
15	%Total Net Sales	24%	35%	41%	100%
16					
17					
18					
19					
20					

Figure 4.16
X range highlighted

Press: [↵]

When you press Enter, the graph settings sheet reappears, showing the X range definition.

The letters A to F are used to specify up to six ranges of worksheet data to be graphed along the Y axis. Each new data range specified (A to F on the menu) adds another set of bars to the graph. You are going to use the A range to represent the first set of bars, showing net sales for each of the three products. Use the net sales row from the income statement.

When you created the income statement, you assigned the range name NET_SALES to the net sales figures so you can use this name instead of highlighting the range when 1-2-3 prompts you.

Select: A

Press: NAME (F3)

Figure 4.17 Selecting A range with Name (F3) key

```
A1: [W24]                                                        NAMES
Enter first data range:
GROSS_MARGIN   NET_INCOME   NET_SALES   PROD1       PROD2
               A              B       C       D          E
1                           Income Statement
2                           July-1-89  July-31-89
3
4  000's omitted               PROD.1   PROD.2   PROD.3     TOTAL
5
6  Net Sales                   $80.00  $120.00  $140.00   $340.00
7    Cost of Goods Sold         30.00    60.00    70.00    160.00
8  Gross Margin                 50.00    60.00    70.00    180.00
9    Marketing/G&A Expenses     35.00    30.00    30.00     95.00
10 EBIT                         15.00    30.00    40.00     85.00
11   Interest                    1.00     2.00     2.00      5.00
12   Taxes                       7.00    14.00    19.00     40.00
13 NET INCOME                   $7.00   $14.00   $19.00    $40.00
14
15 %Total Net Sales               24%      35%      41%      100%
16
17
18
19
20
```

Select: NET_SALES

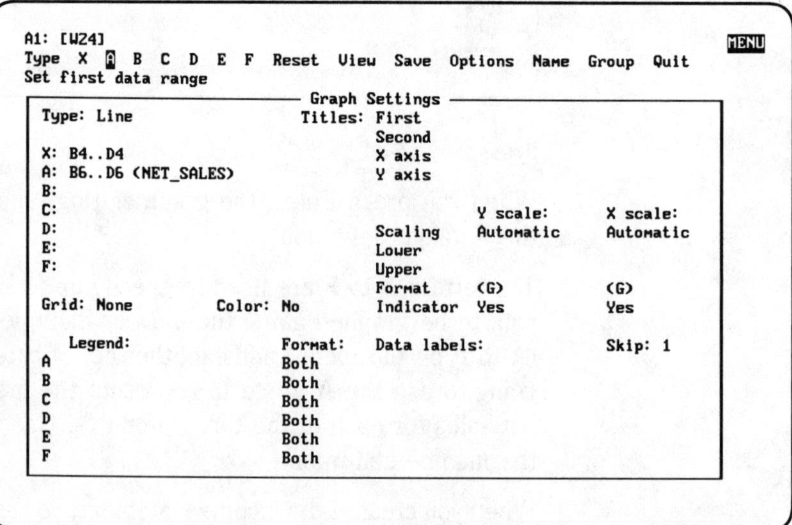

```
A1: [W24]                                                          MENU
Type  X  A  B  C  D  E  F  Reset  View  Save  Options  Name  Group  Quit
Set first data range
                        Graph Settings
Type: Line                     Titles: First
                                       Second
X: B4..D4                              X axis
A: B6..D6 (NET_SALES)                  Y axis
B:
C:                                              Y scale:    X scale:
D:                                     Scaling  Automatic   Automatic
E:                                     Lower
F:                                     Upper
                                       Format   (G)         (G)
Grid: None          Color: No          Indicator Yes        Yes

   Legend:                  Format:    Data labels:         Skip: 1
A                           Both
B                           Both
C                           Both
D                           Both
E                           Both
F                           Both
```

Figure 4.18 Graph settings sheet

Viewing the Graph

While creating a graph, you may often want to see what it looks like. The **Graph View** command lets you do just that. 1-2-3 temporarily replaces the worksheet with the graph. You can remove the graph and return to the worksheet by pressing any key. You've already entered enough specifications to create a bar graph. Use **/Graph View** to see how the graph looks.

Select: View

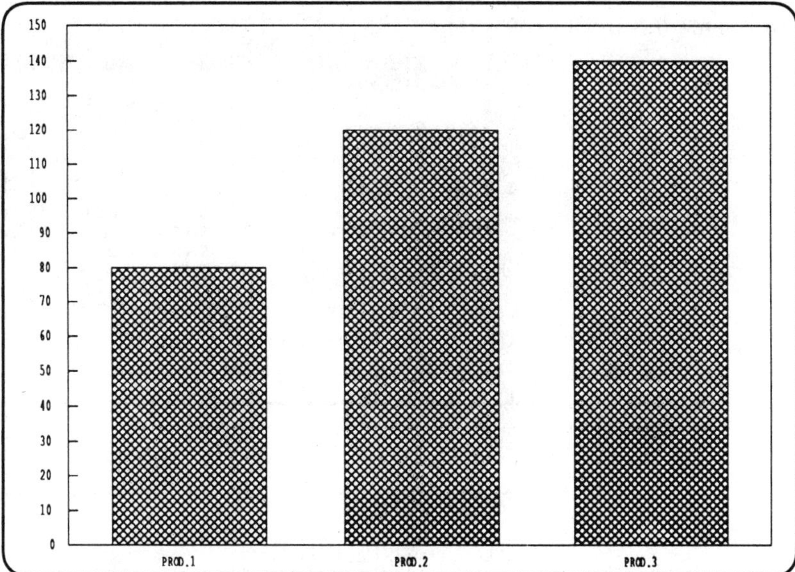

Figure 4.19
Displayed bar graph

1-2-3 automatically draws a scale on the Y axis. The tick marks are in increments of 10. The top of the scale is 140, the highest net sales value. Notice the shading pattern in each bar of the graph.

Remove the graph from the screen.

Press: any key

Graphing a Second Data Range

You are going to graph a second data range. To compare net sales to net income for each of the three products in the bar graph, you will designate the net income row on the income statement as the B range. You named this row NET_INCOME, so use this range name now.

Select: B
Press: NAME (F3)

Figure 4.20
Entering B range with Name (F3) key

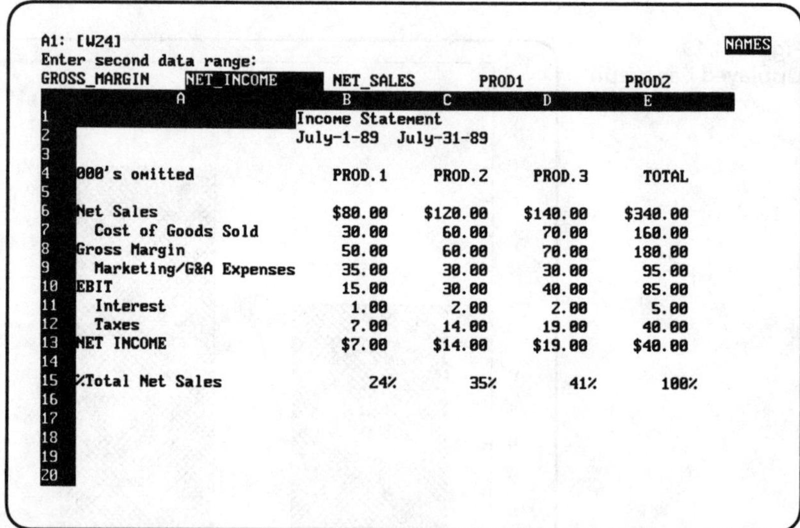

A1: [W24]
Enter second data range:
GROSS_MARGIN NET_INCOME NET_SALES PROD1 PROD2
NAMES

	A	B	C	D	E
1		Income Statement			
2		July-1-89	July-31-89		
3					
4	000's omitted	PROD.1	PROD.2	PROD.3	TOTAL
5					
6	Net Sales	$80.00	$120.00	$140.00	$340.00
7	Cost of Goods Sold	30.00	60.00	70.00	160.00
8	Gross Margin	50.00	60.00	70.00	180.00
9	Marketing/G&A Expenses	35.00	30.00	30.00	95.00
10	EBIT	15.00	30.00	40.00	85.00
11	Interest	1.00	2.00	2.00	5.00
12	Taxes	7.00	14.00	19.00	40.00
13	NET INCOME	$7.00	$14.00	$19.00	$40.00
14					
15	%Total Net Sales	24%	35%	41%	100%
16					
17					
18					
19					
20					

Select: NET_INCOME

Now view the graph again. You'll see one new bar for each label. Notice that 1-2-3 automatically gives each set of bars different shading patterns.

Select: View

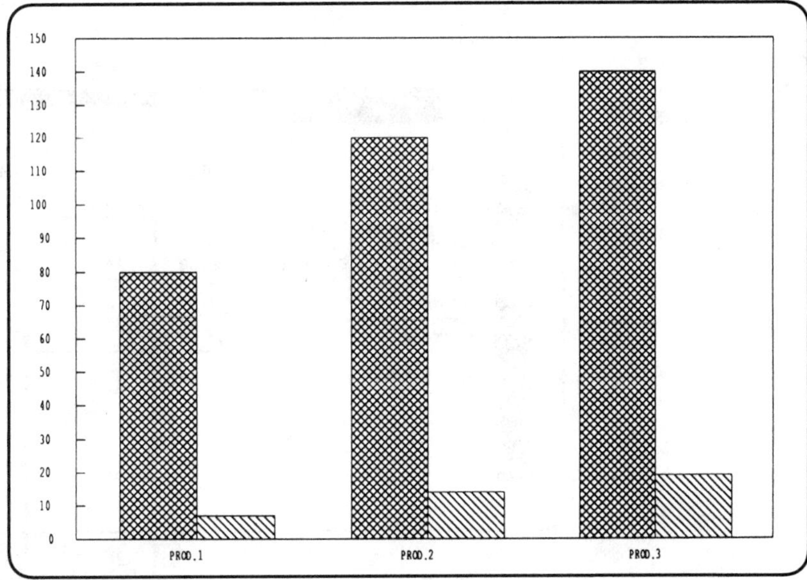

Figure 4.21 Viewed bar graph with two ranges

Figures 4.22 and 4.23 on the next page illustrate how data from the worksheet is transformed into a bar graph when the ranges are specified.

Figures 4.22 and 4.23 Correspondence between graph and worksheet

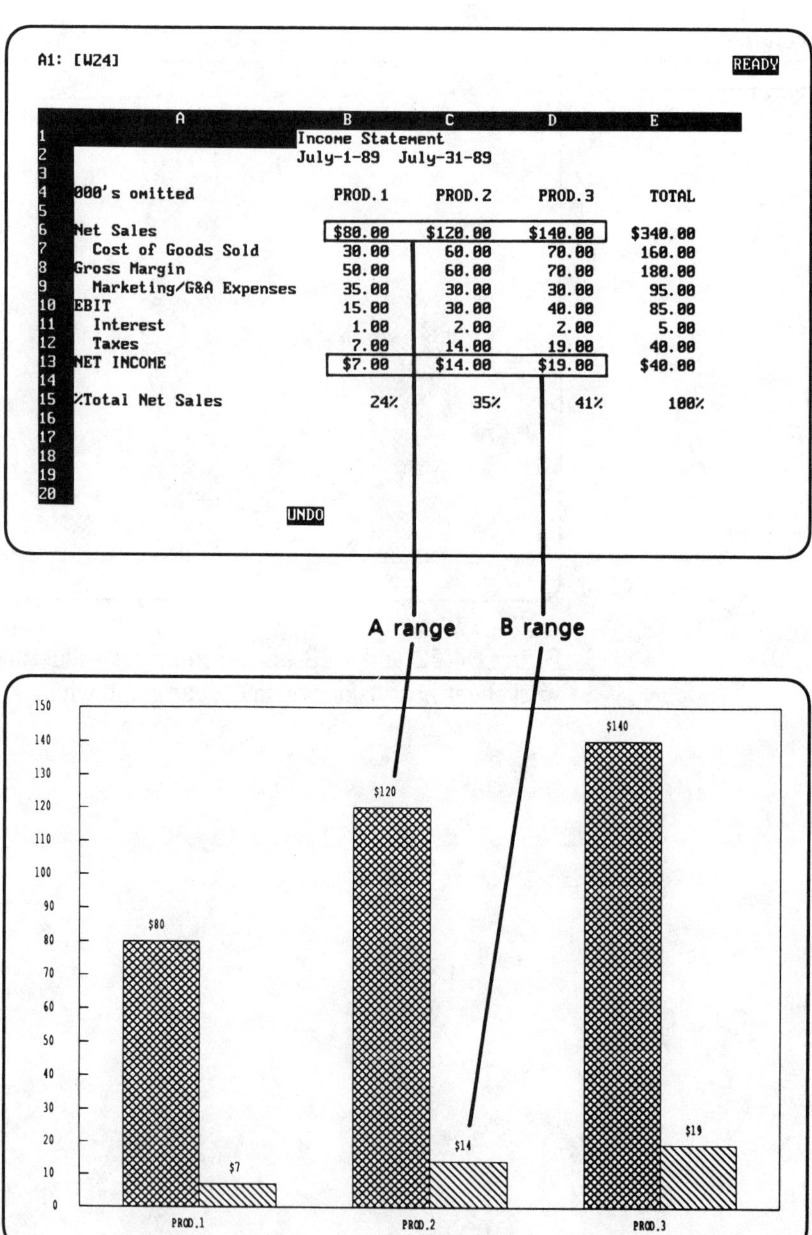

Legends

The Graph Options menu contains a number of commands that enhance the appearance of a graph and make it easier to understand. Legends are used to identify the A to F ranges. For example, it is not yet clear on the graph what the A and B ranges represent—that is, which is net sales and which is net income.

You are going to add legends to the graph. First you specify the range to be identified by a legend, and then type in the text of the legend. Name range A Net Sales and range B Net Income. Then view the graph and see how the legends look.

Press: any key to remove the graph from the screen
Select: Options
Legend
A
Type: Net Sales

Figure 4.24
Specifying a legend

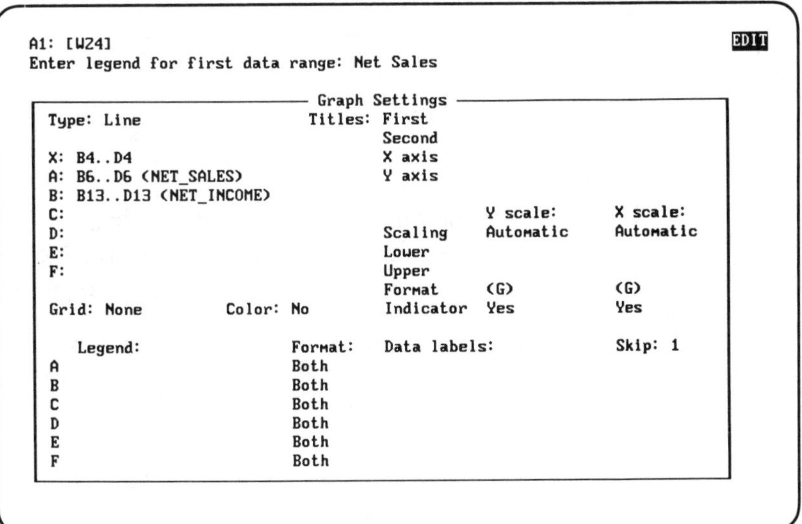

Press: ↵
Select: Legend
B

Type: Net Income [↵]
Select: Quit to leave the Graph Options menu
View

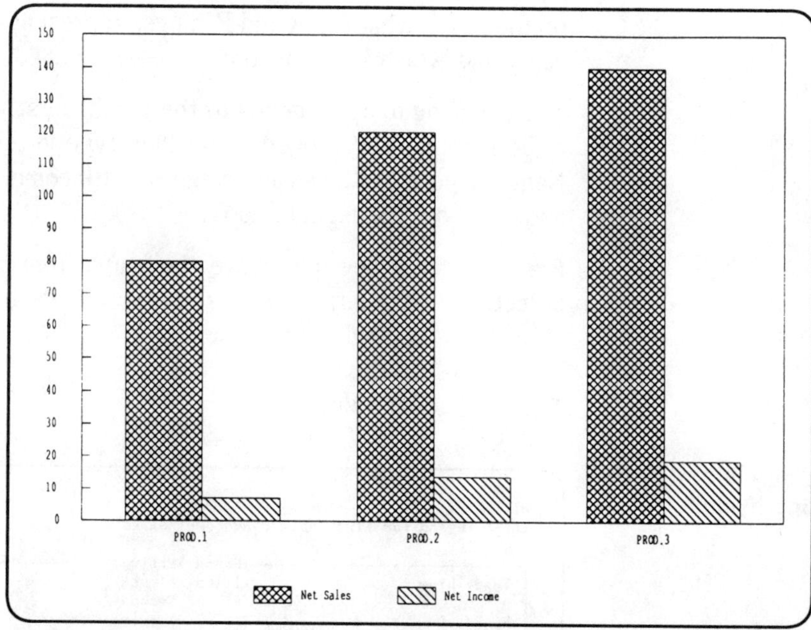

Figure 4.25 Viewed graph with legends

The legends appear at the bottom of the graph. Each legend represents a bar with a particular shading pattern. Notice that samples of the shading patterns appear next to each legend.

You can also enter the text of a legend in two other ways. First, Net Sales and Net Income are both row labels in the Income Statement. Instead of typing the legend, you can type the cell address of the matching label with a backslash (\) in front of it. Because Net Sales is in cell A8 of the Income Statement, you can type **\A8** at the prompt. The notation **\A8** appears on the graph settings sheet as the legend, but the words **Net Sales** appear on the bar graph. Second, as you saw
(2.2) in the section on using **/Graph Group**, if the labels you wish to use as legends appear in adjacent cells, you can select Range instead of A to F from the Graph Options menu. In this case, however, the labels aren't in adjacent cells, so you couldn't use the second method.

Titles

1-2-3 can print a two-line title at the top of a graph and one-line titles on the side and on the bottom. Selecting Titles from the **/Graph Options** menu calls up a new menu used to specify the location of the title: above the graph (First, Second), on the bottom (X axis), or along the side (Y axis). You are going to add the title Income Statement and place it above the graph by making it the first title.

Press: any key to remove the graph from the screen
Select: Options
Titles
First
Type: Income Statement

Figure 4.26 Enter first title

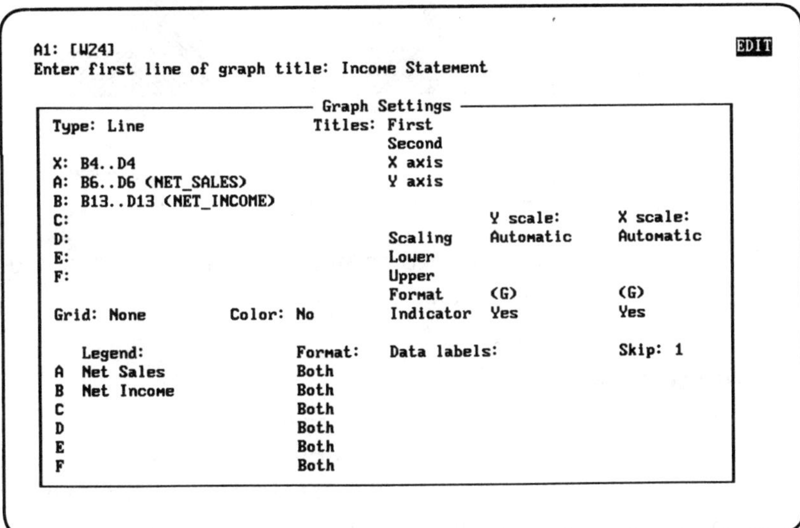

Press: ↵
Select: Quit
View

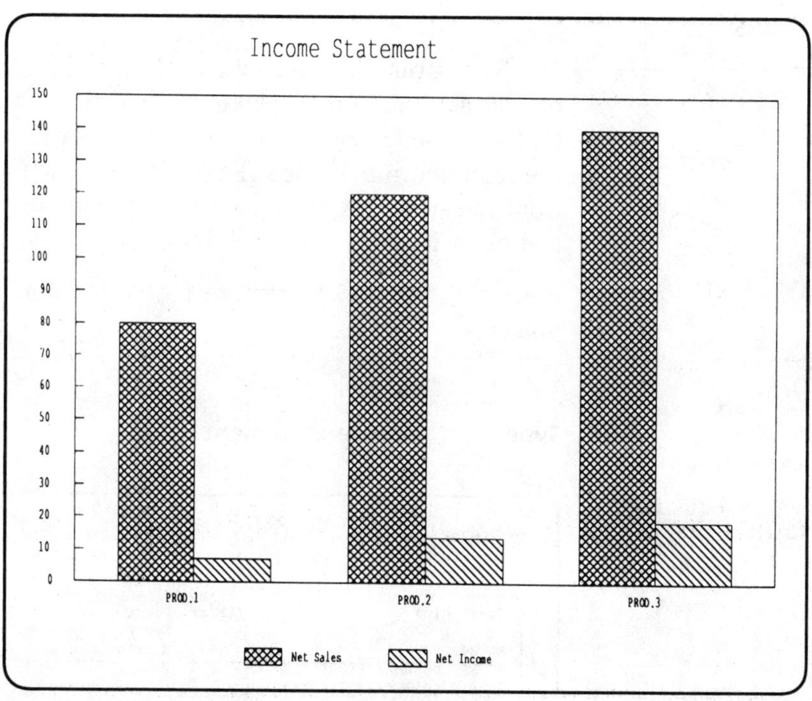

Figure 4.27 Viewed bar graph with title

The title **Income Statement** now appears at the top and the bar graph is complete.

Graphing in Color

If you have a color graphics display you have the choice of displaying either shading patterns (in black and white) or colors on the screen. Because the 1-2-3 initial setting is shading patterns, you must change the setting to Color. You can do this with **/Graph Options Color**.

> NOTE: If you do not have a color graphics display, skip to the next section.

Press: any key to remove the graph from the screen
Select: Options
Color
Quit
View

To change the display back to black and white, simply select **/Graph Options B&W.**

Naming the Graph

The graph is now complete—the ranges and options are in place. To save this graph and its settings, however, you must give it a name. You can then retrieve the graph at any time. This facility allows you to create and work with several graphs in one worksheet file.

When naming a graph, use a name that appropriately describes it. You're going to name this one BARGRAPH.

Press: any key to remove the graph from the screen
Select: Name
Create
Type: bargraph

Figure 4.28 Enter graph name

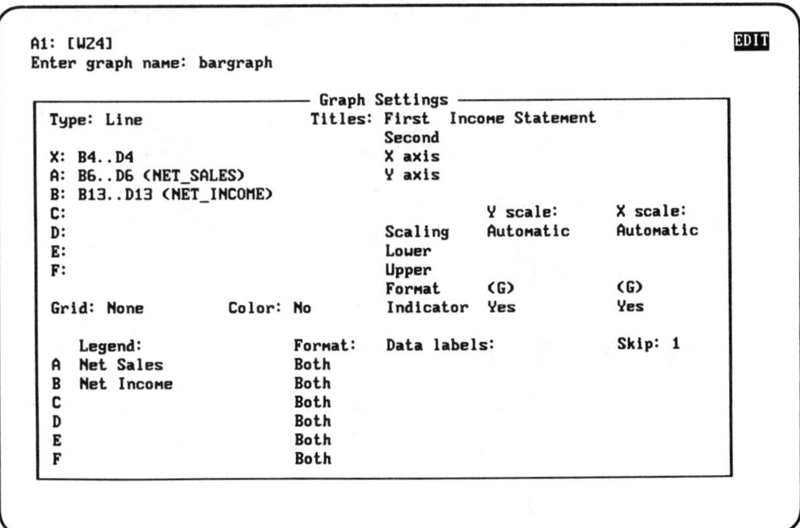

```
A1: [W24]                                                              EDIT
Enter graph name: bargraph

                              Graph Settings
 Type: Line                        Titles: First  Income Statement
                                           Second
 X: B4..D4                                 X axis
 A: B6..D6 (NET_SALES)                     Y axis
 B: B13..D13 (NET_INCOME)
 C:                                                 Y scale:      X scale:
 D:                                        Scaling  Automatic     Automatic
 E:                                        Lower
 F:                                        Upper
                                           Format   (G)           (G)
 Grid: None          Color: No             Indicator Yes          Yes

    Legend:                       Format:  Data labels:           Skip: 1
 A  Net Sales                     Both
 B  Net Income                    Both
 C                                Both
 D                                Both
 E                                Both
 F                                Both
```

Press: ↵

To retrieve a graph, select **/Graph Name Use.** To delete it, select **/Graph Name Delete.** You can also modify any graph and rename it using **/Graph Name Create** again.

Saving a Graph for Printing

The graph is saved along with the worksheet in a worksheet (.WK1) file. You cannot, however, use this file to print the graph. To print a graph (with PrintGraph or with Allways), you must save a ''picture'' of it in a 1-2-3 **graph file**. A graph file has a .PIC extension rather than the .WK1 extension used for worksheet files.

Save a picture of the bar graph. The process of saving is similar to that of saving a worksheet file. Type in a file name for the graph at the prompt. 1-2-3 automatically adds the .PIC extension.

Select: Save
Type: bargraph [↵]
Select: Quit

Saving the File

The graph named BARGRAPH is now part of the worksheet named INCOME. Save the file again so the graph will become part of the worksheet file on the disk.

Press: [/]
Select: File
Save
Press: [↵]
Select: Replace

CREATING A PIE CHART

In this section you'll create a pie chart comparing net sales for the three products in the income statement. The pie chart will be drawn from the same worksheet data as the bar graph. You'll also add shading patterns and ''explode'' a slice of the pie.

Changing the Type of Graph

You have two options when creating a new graph. Whenever you name and create a graph, you are actually saving a set of specifications as reflected on the graph settings sheet. If the new graph needs some of the same ranges and titles as the previous graph, you can simply alter the old settings until the new graph is complete, and then name those settings. If the new graph needs all new settings, however, you can use **/Graph Reset** to delete some or all of the old settings and start with a clean slate. In this case, you will use some of the settings from the bar graph.

The first step is to change the type of graph from Bar to Pie.

Press: [/]
Select: Graph
Type
Pie

Specifying Data

A pie chart uses only one range of data from a worksheet. Each slice of the pie represents one value in the data range. Leave the X range setting intact; it provides the labels for the slices of the pie. You'll use the same A range as in the bar graph, but delete the B range.

Select: Reset
B
Quit

Titling the Graph

Because the pie chart shows only one range of data, the bar graph title, "Income Statement," is not appropriate. Retitle the graph "Net Sales" to describe the single data range. Then view the graph.

Select: Options
Titles
First
Press: [ESC] to erase the old title
Type: Net Sales [↵]
Select: Quit

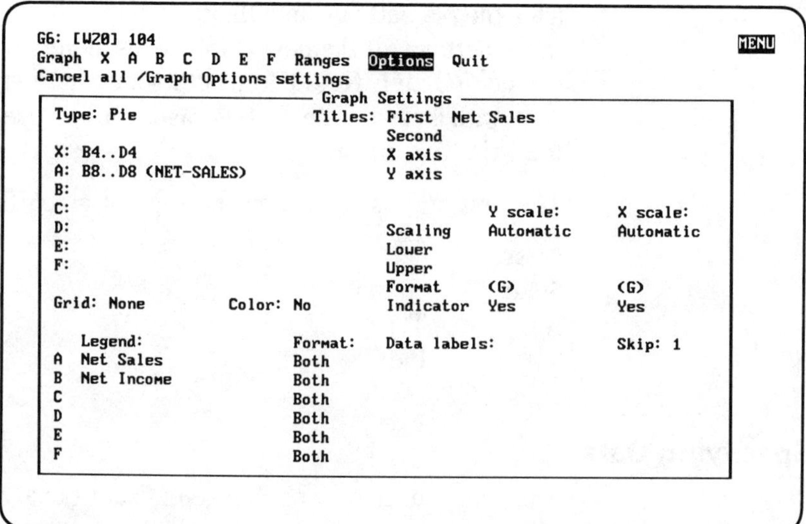

Figure 4.29
Settings for pie chart

Select: View

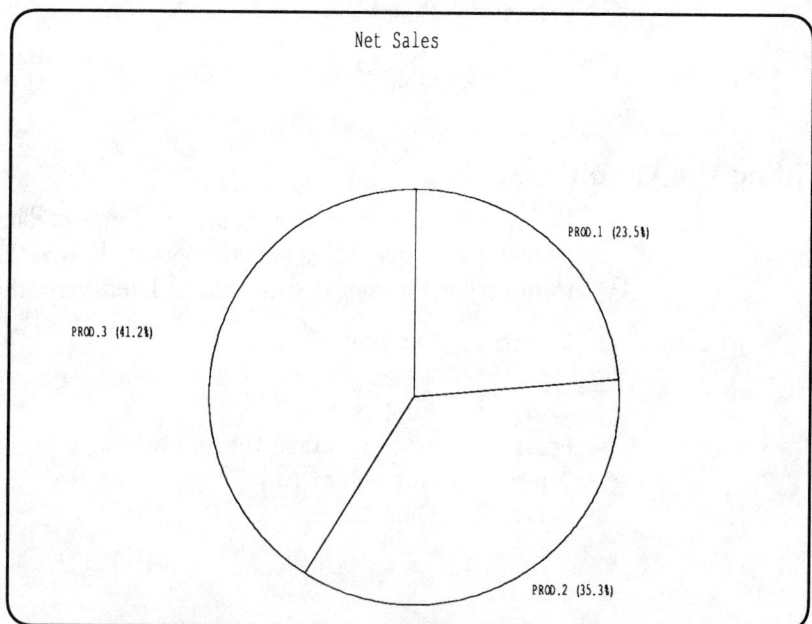

Figure 4.30
Pie chart

You now have a pie chart with three slices. Each slice represents a net sales value for one of the three products. 1-2-3 automatically calculates each slice's percentage of the whole and displays the percentage on the screen.

The X-range labels now serve to identify slices of the pie. Legends are unnecessary because only one numeric value can be associated with each label.

Pie Chart Shading Patterns

At this point the pie chart makes no distinction between the different slices of the pie. 1-2-3, however, offers a variety of shading patterns that you can assign to the slices. Shading patterns can improve the clarity and appearance of a graph.

1-2-3 offers seven different patterns; each corresponds to a number. See the illustration below for the assignment of the patterns. Notice that you can leave a slice of the pie blank by entering an 8 in the worksheet.

Figure 4.31
Shading patterns

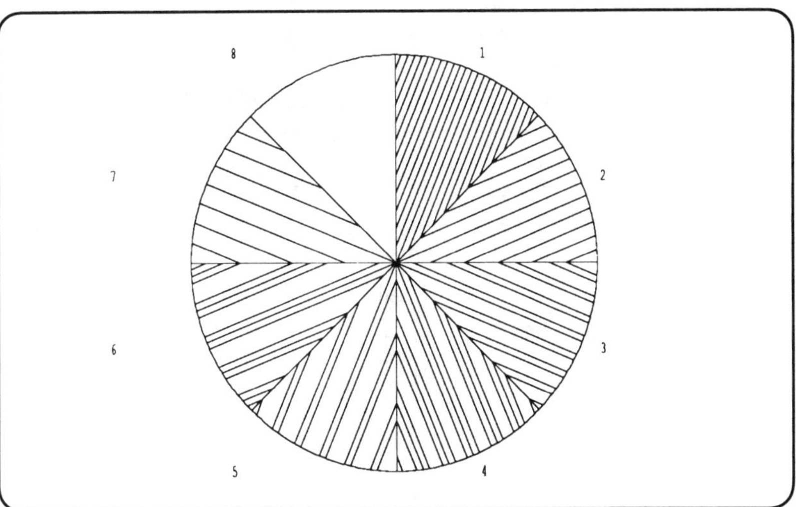

You have to create a new B range to add shading patterns to the slices. Because each slice represents one cell in a data range, you specify shading patterns for individual cells. Leave the Graph menu, return to the worksheet, and add values to create the B range.

Press: [ESC]
Select: Quit
Move to: cell G6
Type: 1 [↓]
2 [↓]
3 [↵]

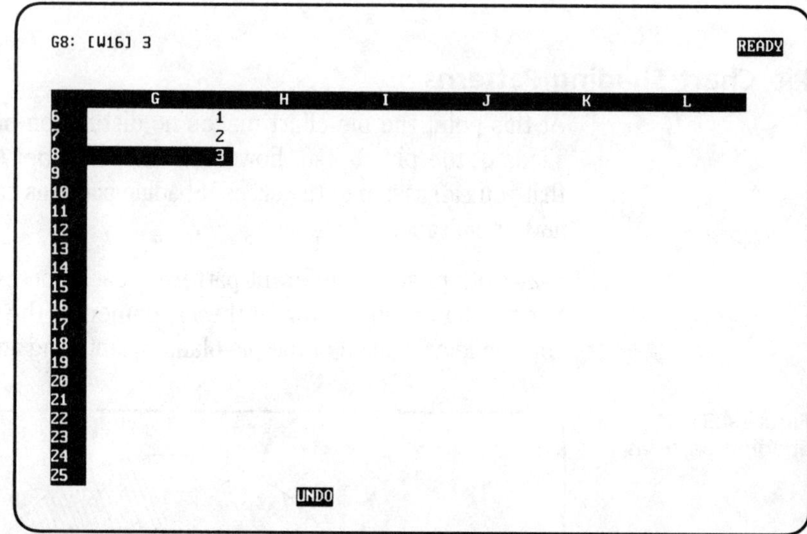

Figure 4.32 Shading codes entered

Press: [/]
Select: Graph
B
Move to: cell G6
Press: [.]
[↓] twice
[↵]
Select: View

Figure 4.33
Shaded pie chart

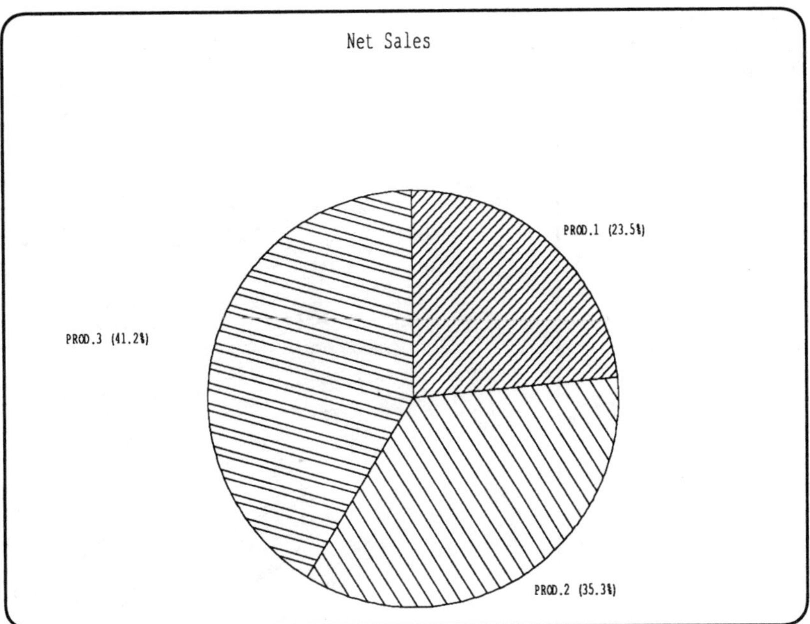

Now change the values in the worksheet and view the new patterns on the pie chart.

Press: any key
Select: Quit
Move to: cell G6)
Type: 4 [↓]
5 [↓]
6 [↵]
Press: [/]
Select: Graph
View

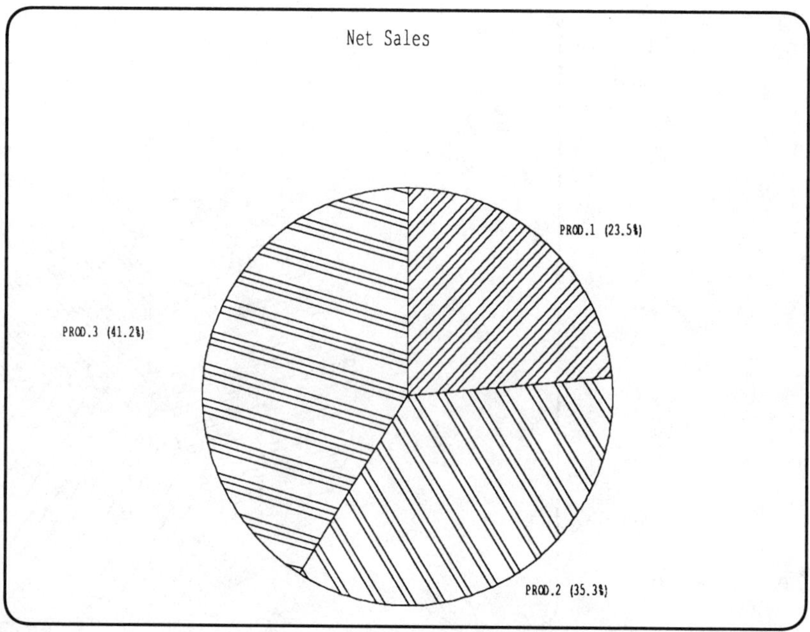

Figure 4.34
Changed shading in pie chart

Exploding a Slice of the Pie

You can make one or more slices of a pie chart **explode**, or break away, from the pie to emphasize a particular value or values. You do this by adding 100 to the shading pattern number entered in the worksheet. For example, to explode the slice defined by the shading pattern number 6, enter **106** on the worksheet. (Adding a value greater than 100 will not cause the slice to move farther away from the chart.)

Explode the pie slice representing Product 1. Then view the chart and return to the menu.

Press: any key
Select: Quit
Move to: cell G6
Type: 104 ↵

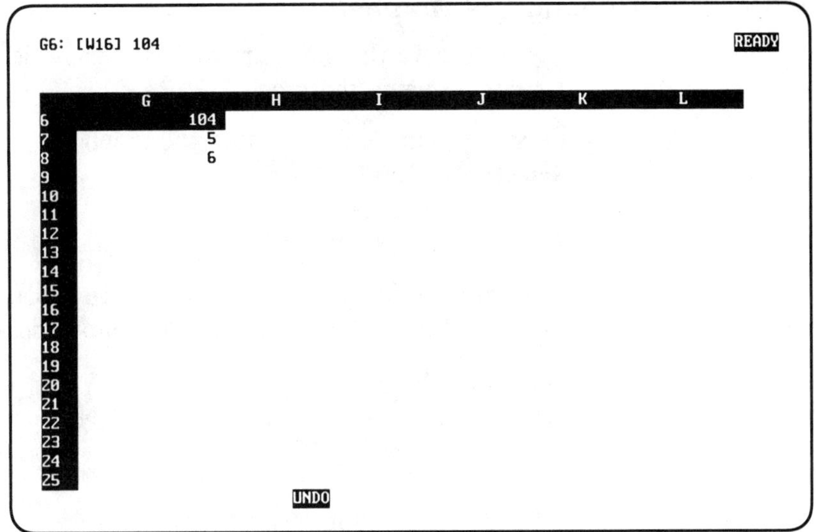

Figure 4.35
Exploded code entered

Press: /
Select: Graph
View

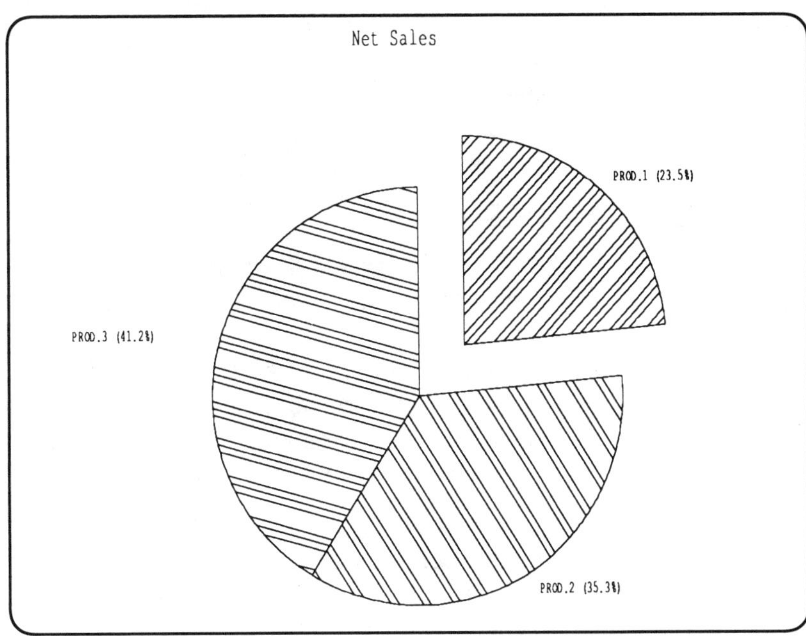

Figure 4.36
Exploded pie chart

Naming and Saving the Graph

Again, to save the pie chart you must name it. Use **/Graph Name Create** to name the graph PIECHART:

Press: any key to remove the graph
Select: Name
Create
Type: piechart [↵]

Now save the pie chart in a graph (.PIC) file for later printing. Remember that 1-2-3 adds the extension .PIC automatically.

Select: Save
Type: piechart [↵]
Select: Quit

Saving the File

Now that the pie chart has been created and named, save the INCOME file again.

Press: [/]
Select: File
Save
Press: [↵]
Select: Replace

WHAT-IF GRAPHICS

1-2-3 is an integrated program, and its automatic recalculation feature extends to graphs. If you change a value in the worksheet, a graph based on that value reflects the change the next time you draw it. This feature means that you can create and test what-if scenarios with graphs just as you can with worksheets. You can even save and print what-if graphics (by naming different versions of a graph) and incorporate them in a report or presentation using Allways.

To see how changing values in the worksheet affects graphs that have already been created, you are going to change a value in the income statement and display the two graphs. First change the net sales for product 1 from 80 to 60.

Move: cell B6
Type: 60 ↵

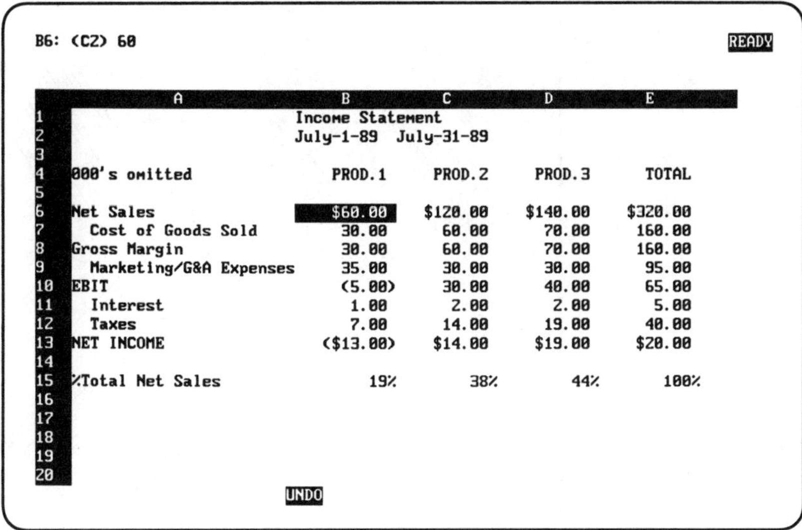

B6: (C2) 60 READY

	A	B	C	D	E
1		Income Statement			
2		July-1-89	July-31-89		
3					
4	000's omitted	PROD.1	PROD.2	PROD.3	TOTAL
5					
6	Net Sales	$60.00	$120.00	$140.00	$320.00
7	Cost of Goods Sold	30.00	60.00	70.00	160.00
8	Gross Margin	30.00	60.00	70.00	160.00
9	Marketing/G&A Expenses	35.00	30.00	30.00	95.00
10	EBIT	(5.00)	30.00	40.00	65.00
11	Interest	1.00	2.00	2.00	5.00
12	Taxes	7.00	14.00	19.00	40.00
13	NET INCOME	($13.00)	$14.00	$19.00	$20.00
14					
15	%Total Net Sales	19%	38%	44%	100%
16					
17					
18					
19					
20					

UNDO

Figure 4.37
What-if income

Notice that other values in the column for product 1 change. Gross margin changes from 50 to 30. Notice too that net income is now in parentheses: ($13). This means that it is a negative value.

When you display the pie chart, notice that the slice representing net sales for product 1 is smaller than before and that the others are proportionately larger.

Press: /
Select: Graph
View

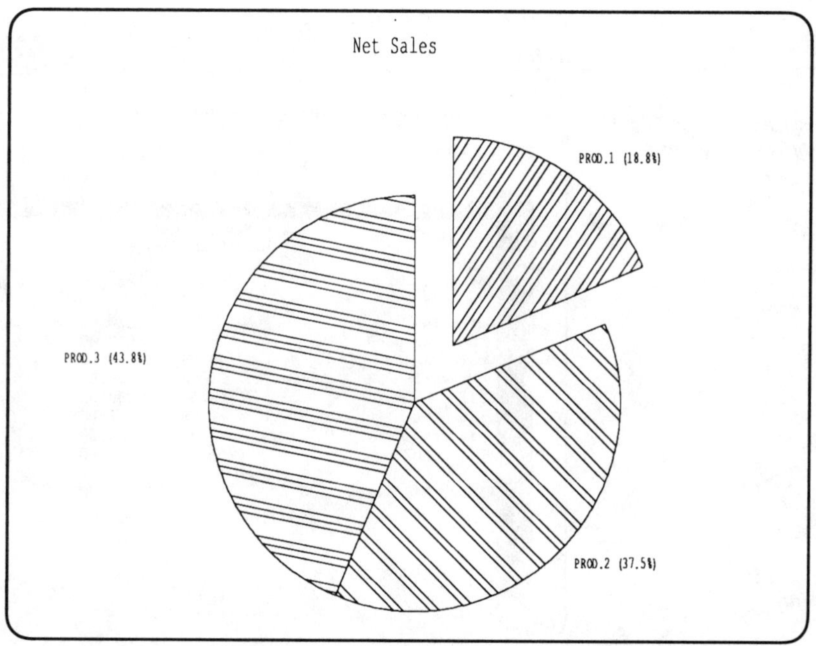

Figure 4.38
What-if pie chart

NOTE: You can also display the current graph another way. Pressing the Graph (F10) key calls up the graph most recently viewed—in this case, it would be the pie chart. (To see the bar graph you would have to select **/Graph Name Use** and specify BARGRAPH.)

Now display the bar graph to see how the changes made to the worksheet were reflected.

Press: any key
Select: Name
Use
BARGRAPH

Figure 4.39
What-if bar graph

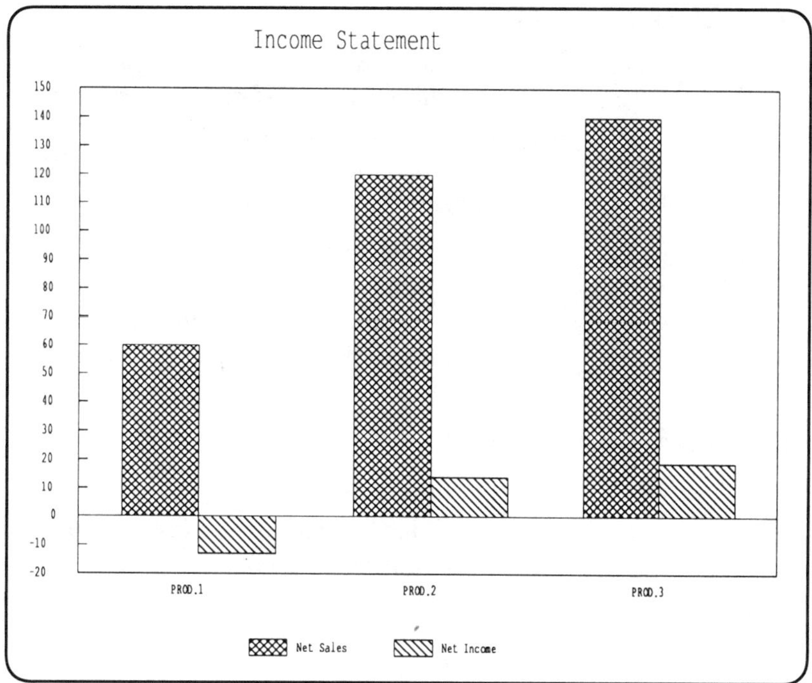

The bar graph shows both net sales and net income for each product. Both values for product 1 have been affected by the change in net sales.

Net income is a negative value; that is, when net sales dips below a certain value, the company loses money on this product. Notice that the bar representing net income for product 1 is below the X axis. 1-2-3 represents negative values on a bar graph in this way. The Y axis also expands to include the value −20.

Press: any key
Select: Quit

PRINTING A GRAPH

The following section discusses the basic steps for printing the bar graph created in this chapter. Before you start, be sure that your printer supports graphics and that you have run the 1-2-3 Install program to select a driver for the printer. Finally, check to see that the printer is properly connected to the computer and turned on.

If you want to incorporate a graph into a worksheet or enhance it further (perhaps by enclosing it in a shaded box and adding a striking title),
2.2 you can do so with Allways, as described in Chapter 6. In that case, you would also print the file using Allways.

The PrintGraph Program

The 1-2-3 PrintGraph program prints graphs created in 1-2-3. Several options in PrintGraph let you enhance the printed version of the graph. For example, PrintGraph offers eleven different type styles for titles and labels and a range of colors if you have a color printer. You can also alter the size and proportion of the graph. In addition, you can define and save hardware settings so that you can print the graph on a variety of printers.

The first step is to exit 1-2-3 (make sure you have saved the final version of the worksheet and graph files first). You start PrintGraph from DOS or from the 1-2-3 Access menu, depending how you started 1-2-3 originally.

Press:	/
Select:	Quit
	Yes

2.2 NOTE: If you select /**Quit** before saving your file, 1-2-3 warns you that you haven't saved it and gives you a chance to correct the situation.

The DOS prompt or the 1-2-3 Access menu should be on the screen now.

Starting PrintGraph

If you have a 5.25″ two-diskette computer, remove the Help Disk from drive A and insert the PrintGraph Disk. If you have a 3.5″ system, the correct disk (System, Help, and PrintGraph Disk) should already be in drive A. Leave the data disk with the .PIC files in drive B. If you have a hard-disk computer, you should have copied the PrintGraph files to the directory that contains your 1-2-3 program files.

If you started 1-2-3 from DOS:

Type: pgraph [↵]

> NOTE: With a hard-disk computer, you must be in the subdirectory that contains all the 1-2-3 disks.

If you started 1-2-3 from the Access menu:

Select: PrintGraph from the Access menu

Figure 4.40
PrintGraph screen

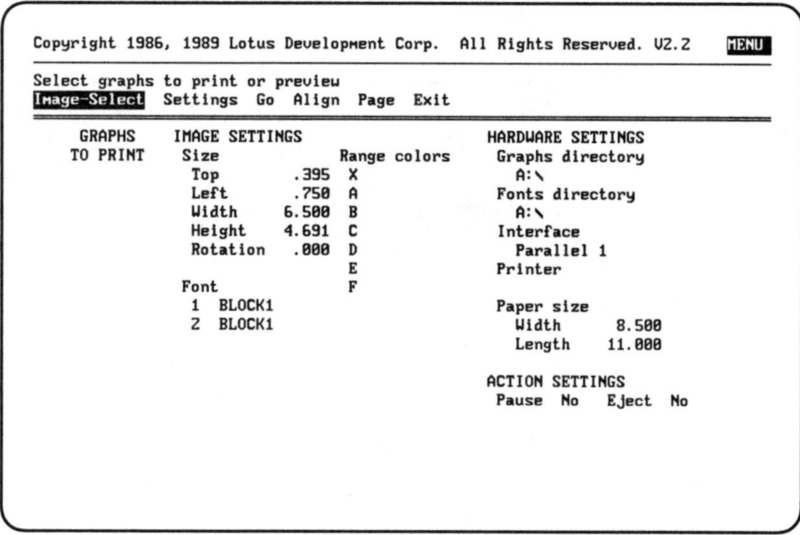

The PrintGraph screen appears. The top line of the screen contains copyright information; the next two lines contain the PrintGraph menu. The main part of the screen contains the current settings of the program.

Notice that some items have default settings. You are going to change the settings to those required to print the bar graph. Begin by calling up the Settings menu.

Select: Settings

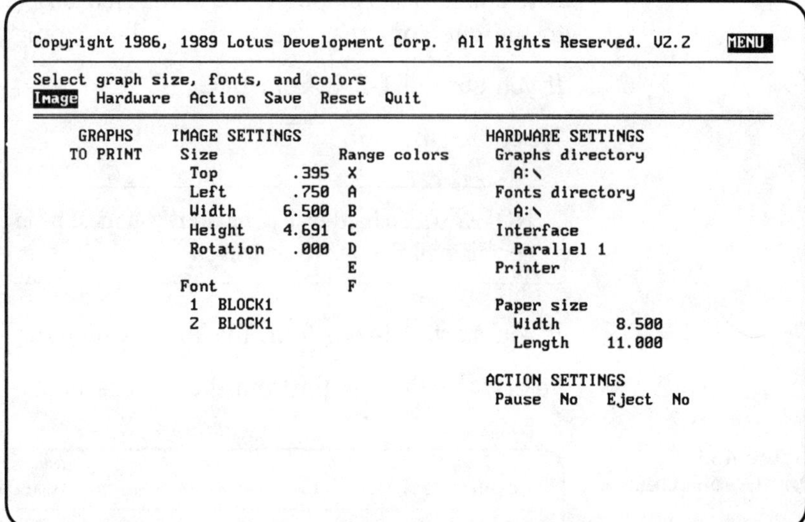

Figure 4.41
Settings menu

The Settings menu contains the commands that specify hardware requirements, colors, and print style fonts for the graph. First you will enter the hardware specifications.

Hardware Setup

Disk Drive

You have to tell PrintGraph which drive or directory contains the .PIC files you have created. Use the **Settings Hardware Graphs-Directory** command to indicate the drive containing the disk or directory containing the files. The initial setting is drive A. If you have a two-diskette system, the drive should be B; if you have a hard-disk system, the directory should be C:\TEMP (the directory where all your exercise files are being stored).

Select: Hardware
Graphs-Directory
Press: ESC
Type: b: (for a two-diskette computer)
or
c:\temp (for a hard-disk computer)
Press: ↵

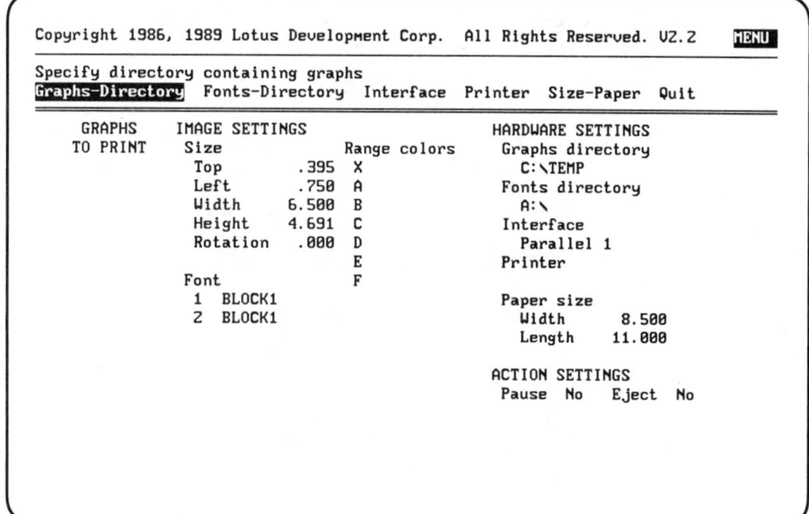

Figure 4.42 New graphs directory

Notice that the new setting appears on the right side of the screen under HARDWARE SETTINGS.

Printer

Use the **Settings Hardware Printer** command to specify the printer you're using. The name of the graphics printer defined in the driver set is on the screen. If you defined a number of printers and plotters during the Install procedure, they are also listed.

Along with the list of printers defined in the driver set, you are given a choice of densities. The density determines how many times the graph, titles, and legends are actually printed over. You should experiment with the densities until you are satisfied with the result. Remember that the higher the density, the longer the graph will take to print—but the graph will be darker and easier to read. Use the keys described on the right side of the screen to select the appropriate printer and density.

Select: Printer
the appropriate printer and density
Press: ↵

Font Directory

The **Settings Hardware Fonts-Directory** command tells PrintGraph where to look for the different font styles available for the titles and labels printed on the graph.

The initial setting is drive A. This is fine for a computer with two disk drives, because the PrintGraph Disk is in drive A. If, however, you have a hard-disk computer and have copied the 1–2–3 disks onto the hard disk, you will have to change the initial setting.

For a hard-disk computer only:

Select: Hardware
Fonts-Directory
Press: ESC
Type: c:\subdirectory name (where 1–2–3 is copied)
Press: ↵
Select: Quit to return to the Settings menu

Saving Hardware Specifications

Now that you have specified your hardware settings, save them for future use:

Select: Save

Graph Specifications

Selecting the Fonts

PrintGraph offers a variety of fonts for the labels and legends on the graph. The fonts differ in weight, size, and style. The **Settings Image Font** command selects the fonts. Font 1 specifies the style of the first title at the top of the graph. Font 2 specifies the style of any other text on the graph.

Select: Settings
Image
Font
1

A list of font styles appears on the screen. To select one for the title of the graph, use the special keys listed on the right of the screen.

Press: [↓] until the highlight rests on ROMAN1

[SPACE] to make the selection

Figure 4.43
Selecting a font

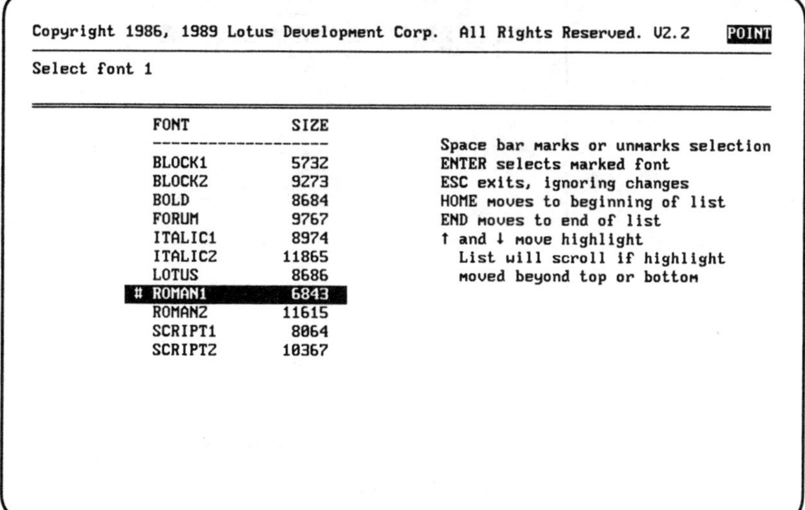

Notice that the number symbol (#) has moved to the highlighted font. This symbol indicates that the font has been selected.

Press: [↵]

Now select the print style for the labels on the graph:

Select: Font
2

Press: [↓] until the highlight rests on BLOCK2
[SPACE]
[↵]

Select: Quit
Quit

Selecting the Graph

Now that the settings have been specified, you are ready to print the graph. The last step is to select the specific graph you want to print. Use the **Image-Select** command to select one or more graphs for printing.

Select: Image-Select

Figure 4.44 Image-Select screen

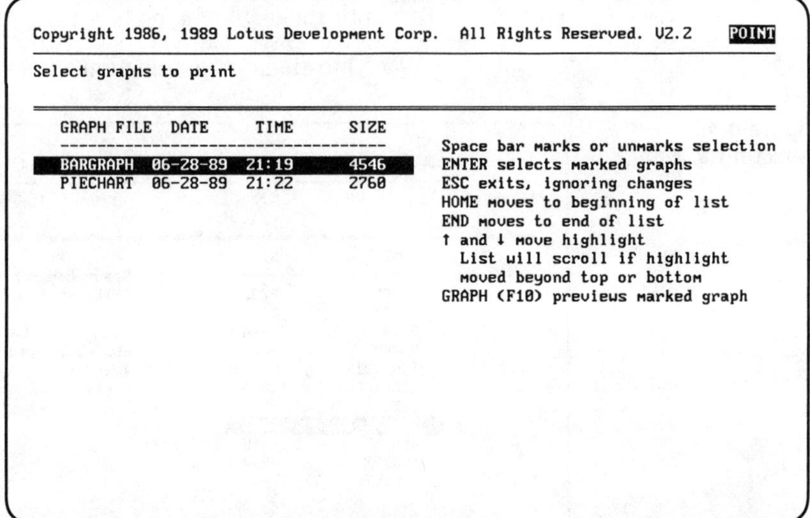

The files BARGRAPH and PIECHART are listed on the screen. PrintGraph also notes the date and time the graphs were saved, as well as the size of each file.

Move to: BARGRAPH
Press: SPACE

To get a preview of how the graph will look when printed, press the Graph (F10) key. The graph appears on the screen exactly as it will appear when printed—the increments on the Y axis will be the same, the titles will be in the correct proportion, and so on. Press any key to remove the graph from the screen.

Press: ↵

Figure 4.45
Image selected

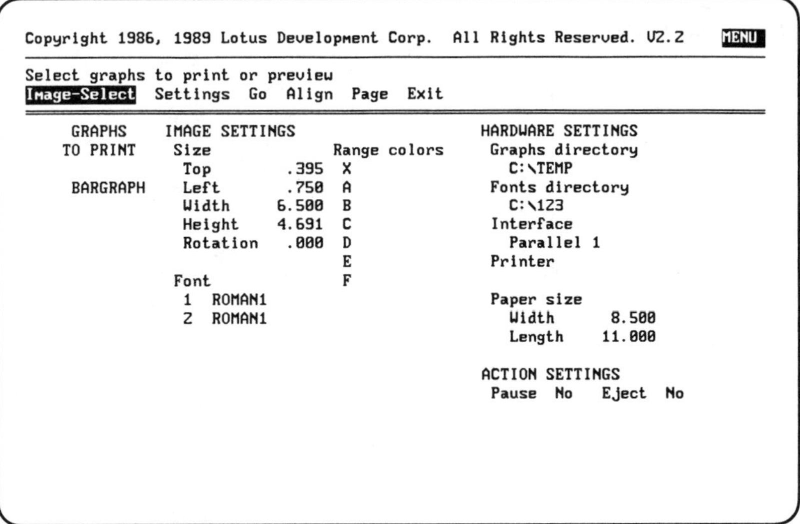

```
Copyright 1986, 1989 Lotus Development Corp.  All Rights Reserved. V2.2   MENU
Select graphs to print or preview
Image-Select  Settings  Go  Align  Page  Exit
     GRAPHS    IMAGE SETTINGS                    HARDWARE SETTINGS
    TO PRINT    Size             Range colors      Graphs directory
                 Top       .395  X                   C:\TEMP
     BARGRAPH    Left      .750  A                 Fonts directory
                 Width    6.500  B                   C:\123
                 Height   4.691  C                 Interface
                 Rotation  .000  D                   Parallel 1
                                 E                 Printer
                Font             F
                 1   ROMAN1                        Paper size
                 2   ROMAN1                          Width      8.500
                                                     Length    11.000

                                                  ACTION SETTINGS
                                                   Pause  No   Eject  No
```

Printing the Graph

Now you can print the graph. Before you start, make sure the printer is turned on and the paper is aligned at the top of the page. Select Align before printing to tell 1-2-3 where the top edge of the paper starts.

Select: Align
Go

The WAIT mode indicator flashes; it takes a few moments for 1-2-3 to print the graph.

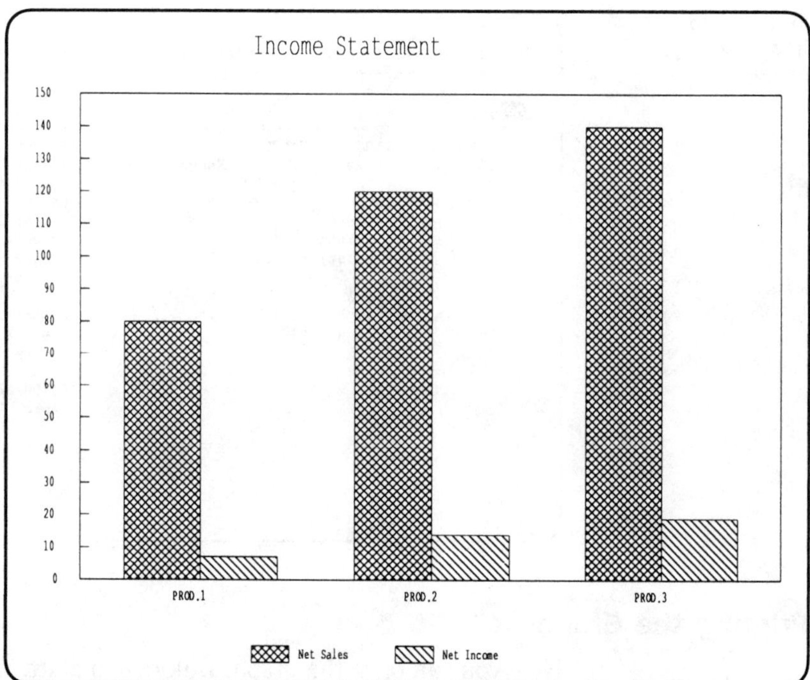

Figure 4.46
Printed bar graph

THE GRAPH COMMANDS

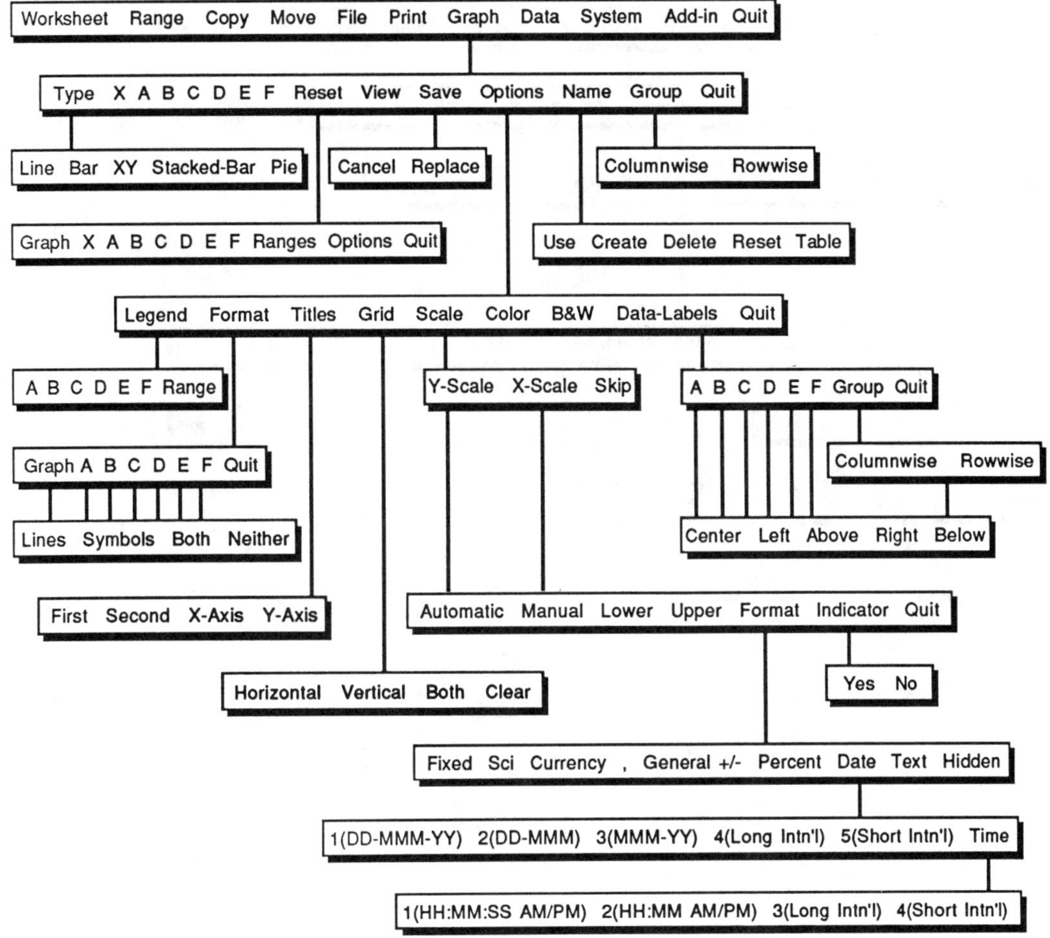

THE PRINTGRAPH MENU TREE

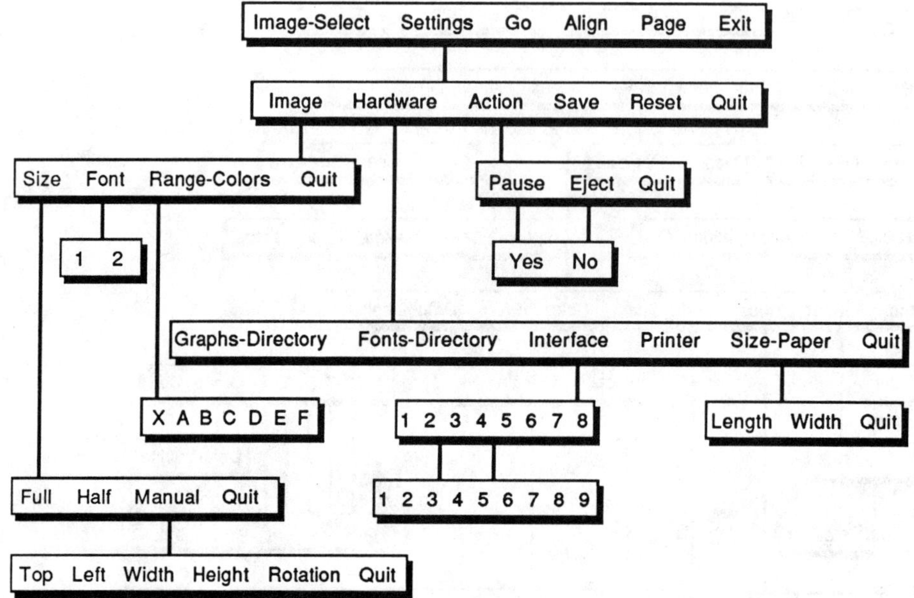

5

Creating a Database

A database is a collection of the same types of information about a group of people, places, or things. The information is divided into categories with the same format for each entry. A telephone book is an example of a simple database. It has separate categories for the same information for each person listed: name, address, and telephone number.

The most useful aspect of a database is its ability to hold and organize large amounts of information, or data, and to make any item of information immediately accessible. A database can expand or contract as necessary. The advantages of the electronic database for maintaining and manipulating data are immediately obvious. New entries can be added or old ones removed with instantaneous adjustment. The basic form itself can be adapted to let you add or remove specific categories of information.

The individual categories of information in the 1-2-3 database are called **fields**. The complete set of information contained in the fields for one entry constitutes a **record**. In the phone-book database, for example, the name, address, and number categories are the fields; each set for each person listed is a record.

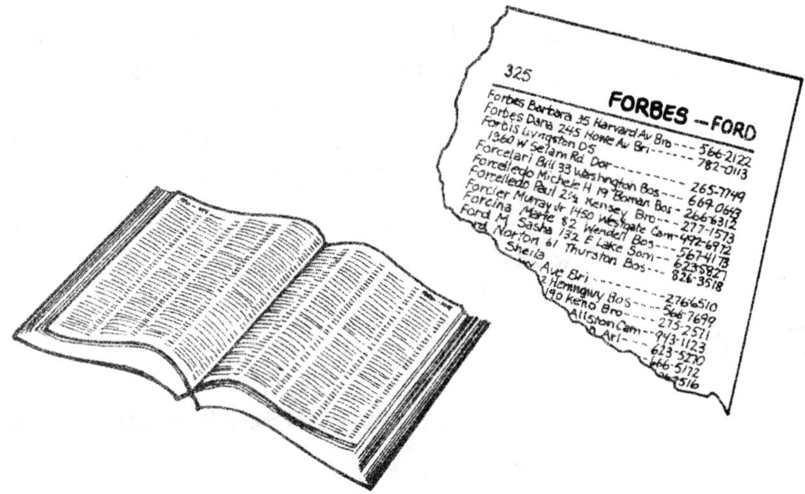

Figure 5.1 Freehand phone book

This chapter teaches you how to:

- Set up a 1–2–3 database
- Sort records in a database so they appear in a particular order
- Locate records in a database and extract information from a database (these operations are known as **querying** a database)
- 2.2 Replace information quickly in a database.

The 1–2–3 Database

The 1–2–3 database is a collection, or file, of records. Because it is entered in the worksheet, however, it offers many advantages over the traditional database. You can perform mathematical calculations with data records and manipulate the records with the following operations:

Sort Rearranges the order of records by any one of the fields, in alphabetical, numeric, or chronological order. This increases your ability to find a record. For example, if the phone book were a computerized database, you could sort the list according to name, address, and/or phone number. This flexibility would allow you to find a record based on information from only one of those fields.

Query Locates specific records in the database by matching criteria that you set up. This saves time and effort. You can ask 1–2–3 to find and extract all the records for those people who live on Hickory Lane, for example, and 1–2–3 will instantly copy those records to a designated area on the worksheet.

The following illustration shows how a phone book looks in the 1–2–3 worksheet.

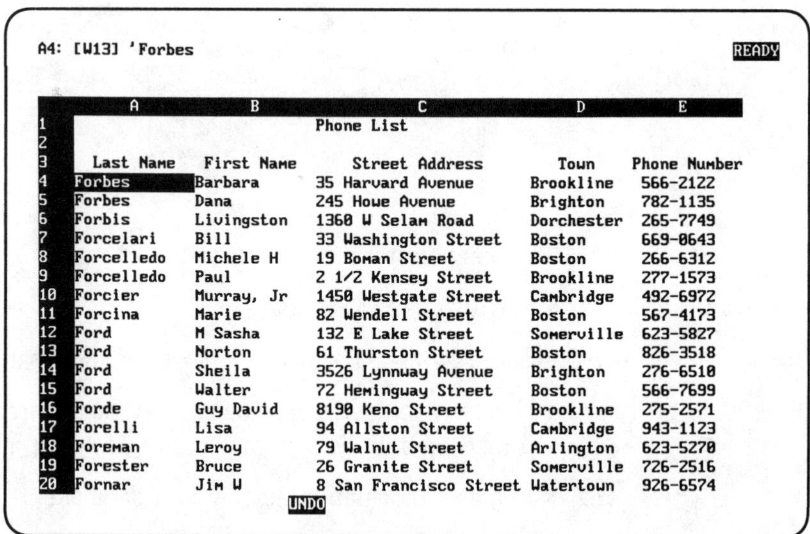
A4: [W13] 'Forbes READY

	A	B	C	D	E
1			Phone List		
2					
3	Last Name	First Name	Street Address	Town	Phone Number
4	Forbes	Barbara	35 Harvard Avenue	Brookline	566-2122
5	Forbes	Dana	245 Howe Avenue	Brighton	782-1135
6	Forbis	Livingston	1360 W Selam Road	Dorchester	265-7749
7	Forcelari	Bill	33 Washington Street	Boston	669-0643
8	Forcelledo	Michele H	19 Boman Street	Boston	266-6312
9	Forcelledo	Paul	2 1/2 Kensey Street	Brookline	277-1573
10	Forcier	Murray, Jr	1450 Westgate Street	Cambridge	492-6972
11	Forcina	Marie	82 Wendell Street	Boston	567-4173
12	Ford	M Sasha	132 E Lake Street	Somerville	623-5827
13	Ford	Norton	61 Thurston Street	Boston	826-3518
14	Ford	Sheila	3526 Lynnway Avenue	Brighton	276-6510
15	Ford	Walter	72 Hemingway Street	Boston	566-7699
16	Forde	Guy David	8190 Keno Street	Brookline	275-2571
17	Forelli	Lisa	94 Allston Street	Cambridge	943-1123
18	Foreman	Leroy	79 Walnut Street	Arlington	623-5270
19	Forester	Bruce	26 Granite Street	Somerville	726-2516
20	Fornar	Jim W	8 San Francisco Street	Watertown	926-6574

UNDO

Figure 5.2 Database from phone book

Before You Start

For a two-diskette computer

- 1–2–3 should be set up to save files on a disk in drive B
- The data disk should be in drive B
- The Help Disk (5.25″ systems) or System, Help, and PrintGraph Disk (3.5″ systems) should be in drive A.

For a hard-disk computer

- 1–2–3 should be set up to save files in a subdirectory named TEMP
- All the 1–2–3 disks should be copied in their own subdirectory on the hard disk.

SETTING UP A DATABASE

A 1-2-3 database uses the column-row structure of the worksheet to store information. When creating a database, you use the pointer-movement keys to move around and enter data, just as you do when creating a worksheet. Labels, or text entries, and values are treated the same way they are in the worksheet. (Refer to Chapters 2 and 3 for basic information on pointer-movement keys and cell entries.)

A 1-2-3 database contains one or more columns and at least two rows. The columns are called **fields**; they contain separate types of information for each entry. The first row contains **field names**. They identify the kind of information stored in each column. The subsequent rows are called **records** and contain the actual data. All the information in one row is included in a single record; the cells are linked and processed together as a unit.

Figure 5.3
Database

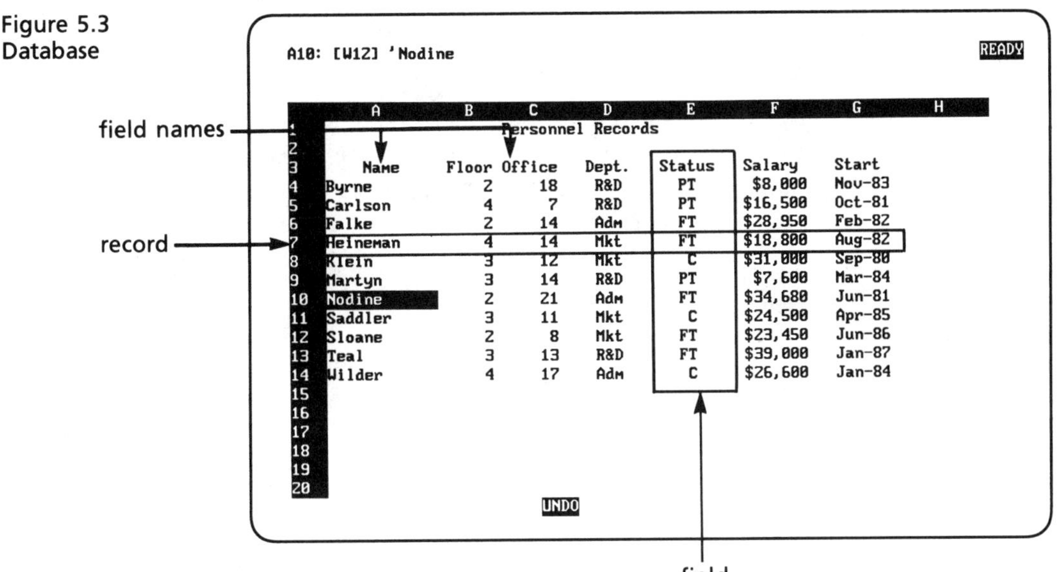

Name	Floor	Office	Dept.	Status	Salary	Start
Byrne	2	18	R&D	PT	$8,000	Nov-83
Carlson	4	7	R&D	PT	$16,500	Oct-81
Falke	2	14	Adm	FT	$28,950	Feb-82
Heineman	4	14	Mkt	FT	$18,800	Aug-82
Klein	3	12	Mkt	C	$31,000	Sep-80
Martyn	3	14	R&D	PT	$7,600	Mar-84
Nodine	2	21	Adm	FT	$34,680	Jun-81
Saddler	3	11	Mkt	C	$24,500	Apr-85
Sloane	2	8	Mkt	FT	$23,450	Jun-86
Teal	3	13	R&D	FT	$39,000	Jan-87
Wilder	4	17	Adm	C	$26,600	Jan-84

All database operations are carried out with the commands on the Data menu.

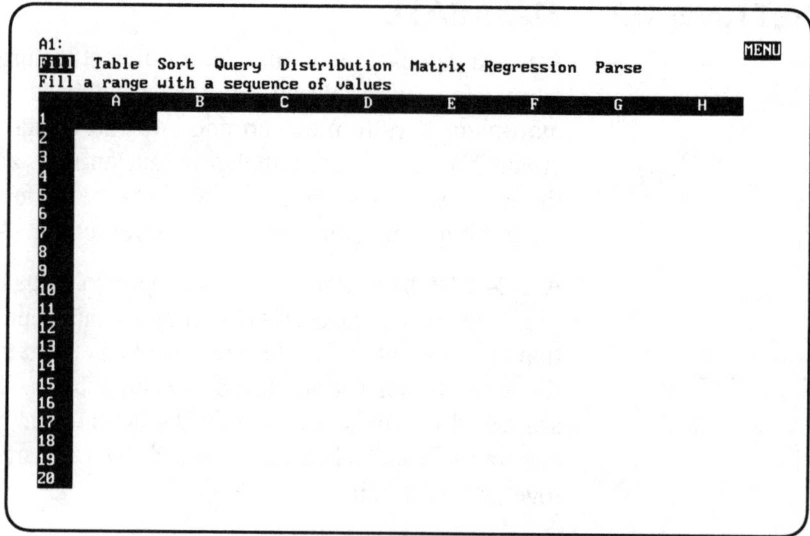

Figure 5.4
/Data menu

Clearing the Screen

Before you start, make sure the screen displays an empty worksheet. Take care to save any information on the screen that you might want later. When the blank worksheet appears, the mode indicator in the upper-right corner of the screen reads READY.

Press: [/]
Select: Worksheet
Erase
Yes

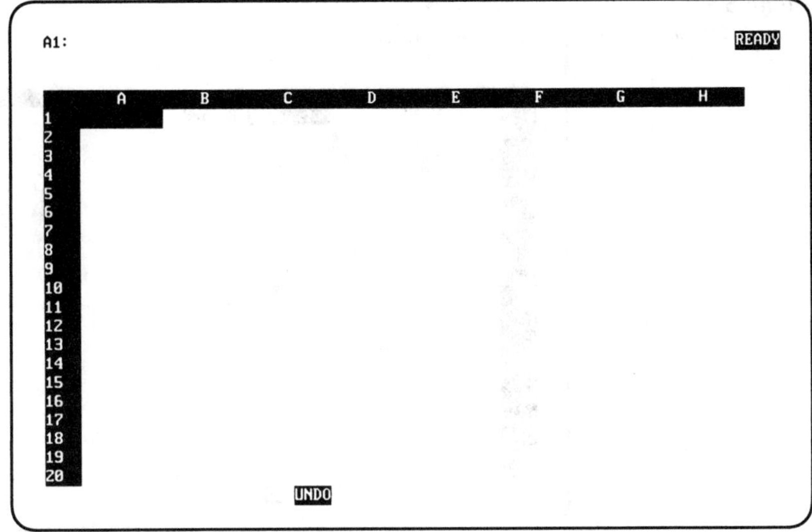

Figure 5.5
Empty screen

Entering Field Names

The first row of information in a 1-2-3 database always contains labels that serve as field names identifying the contents of each column. These field names are necessary for several of the database commands. There are two important rules concerning field names. First, no two fields can have the same name. Second, no blank spaces can be put at the beginning or end of a field name (1-2-3 reads the space as part of the name).

The first step is to enter the title of the database in the top row of the worksheet.

Move to: cell C1
Type: Personnel Records ↵

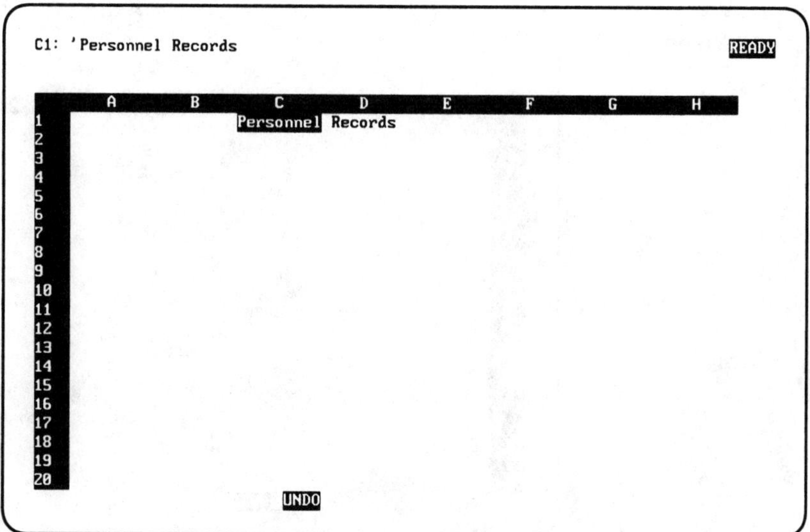

Figure 5.6
Title entered

Next you will enter the field names. This example includes seven fields, each containing a different piece of information about the personnel.

Move to: cell A3

Type: Name [→]
Floor [→]
Office [→]
Dept. [→]
Status [→]
Salary [→]
Start [↵]

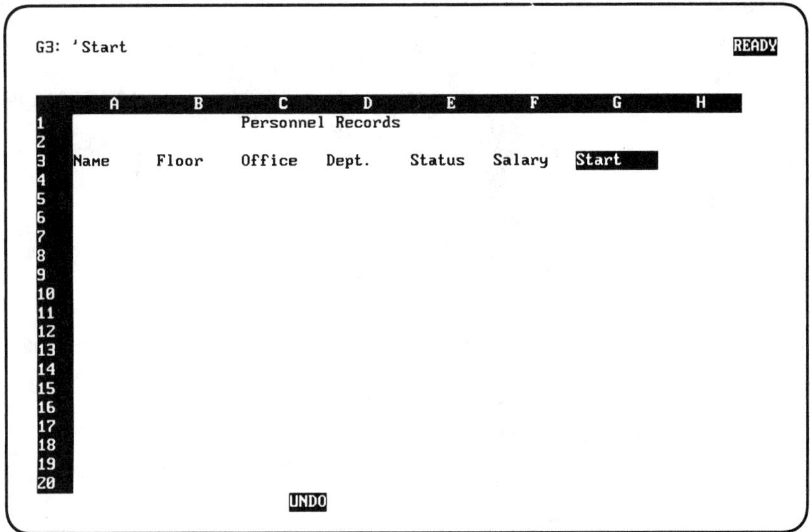

Figure 5.7 Field names entered

Entering Data Records

The first row of data in a database is always entered directly below the row containing the field names. Do not leave a blank line between the two rows because it can throw off certain operations. The 1–2–3 worksheet contains 256 columns, and all of them can be used in a database. Several of the database commands, however, can only address a maximum of 32 fields (columns).

All the entries across a data row are part of the record. 1–2–3 treats all the cells as part of the same unit: they are moved and manipulated as a single record. A field can contain any kind of information that can be entered in a worksheet (labels, values, and formulas).

Enter the first data record.

Move to: cell A4

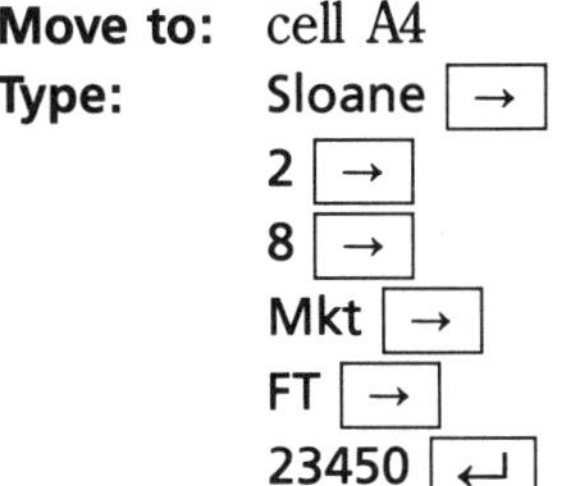

Type: Sloane [→]
2 [→]
8 [→]
Mkt [→]
FT [→]
23450 [↵]

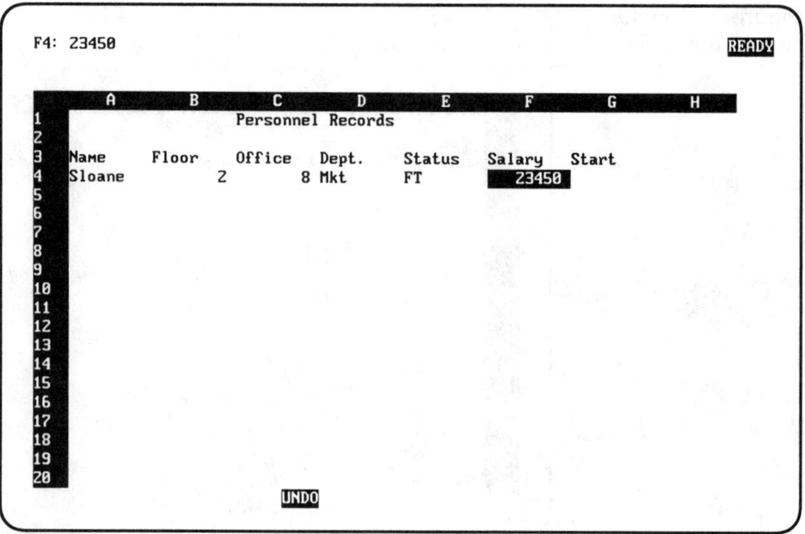

Figure 5.8 First record entered

The last figure you entered is a salary. Notice that it appears on the screen exactly as you type it. This is because the cell is unformatted and not in currency format. You are going to format the cell to display its contents as currency. 1-2-3 adds both a dollar sign and a comma between the thousands. Follow the prompts to specify no decimal places and to format only one cell.

Move to: cell F4
Press: [/]
Select: Range
Format
Currency
Type: 0 [↵] (to specify no decimal places)
Press: [↵] to format only this cell

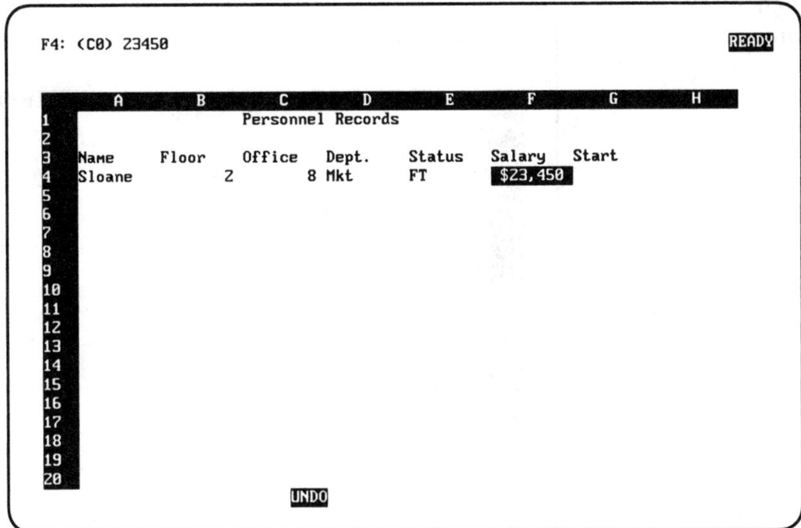

Figure 5.9
Formatted currency

Entering Dates

The final field in the data record contains a date. You enter a date using the @DATE function. 1-2-3 actually stores dates as values (based on the number of days since the beginning of the century). The date formats translate the value into any of five standard forms that can include the day, the month, and/or the year.

After specifying the @DATE function, you enter the date using numbers to refer to the year, month, and day. 1-2-3 translates the date into a value; you then format the value with one of 1-2-3's date formats so it appears as a date.

Enter the @DATE function for June 4, 1981.

Move to: cell G4
Type: @date(81,6,4) ↵

Figure 5.10
Unformatted date

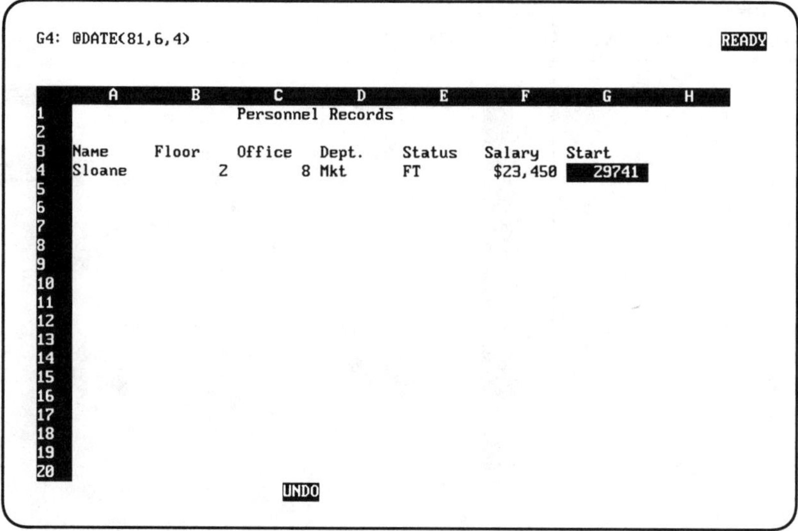

The value 29741 appears in the cell. Next use **/Range Format Date** to display the cell contents as a date.

Press: /
Select: Range
Format
Date

The five options for date formats appear in the third line of the control panel. You should choose a format based on the kind of information you want to include (year, month, and/or day). Some date formats are longer than others and will require you to adjust the column width. You are going to use the third format. The second line of the control panel reads **3 (MMM-YY)**; this means three letters for the month, a hyphen, and two numbers for the year (Jun-81).

Select: 3 (MMM-YY)
Press: ↵

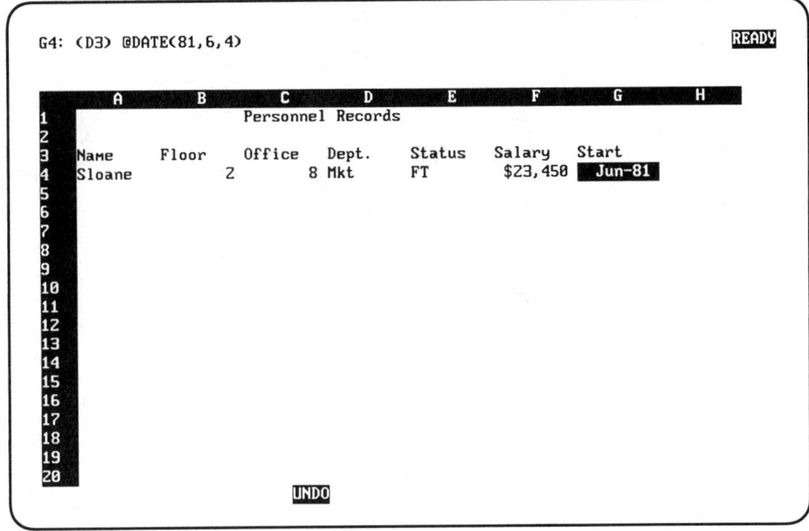

Figure 5.11
Formatted date

REFINING THE APPEARANCE OF THE DATABASE

The physical appearance of the database is important. It must be easy to read for you or for anyone else who might work with it. Now that you've built the basic structure and entered one record, refine the database so that it is easier to read.

Centering Field Names

The 1–2–3 default setting aligns labels entered in the worksheet on the left edge of the cell and values on the right. See how the appearance of the worksheet is improved by centering the field names.

Move to: cell A3
Press: /
Select: Range
Label
Center
Press: END → to highlight the range A3..G3
↵

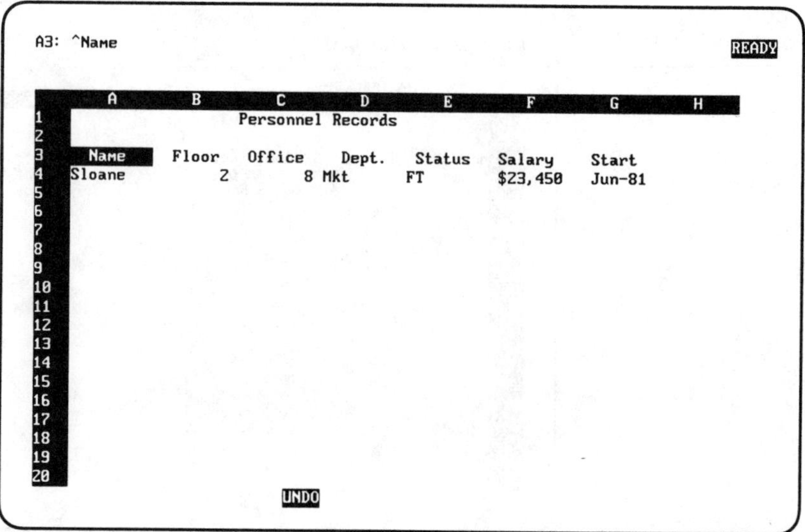

Figure 5.12
Centered field names

The field names are centered in the cells. If you place the pointer on a cell in the row and look at the first line of the control panel, you'll see that the labels are now preceded by a caret (^)—the centered label prefix.

Changing Column Widths

The 1–2–3 initial setting for column width is nine characters. While this has been sufficient to accommodate the data entered so far, it makes sense to alter some of the columns to fit the data better. The first step is to widen column A to accommodate the names.

Move to: cell A4
Press: [/]
Select: Worksheet
Column
Set-Width
Press: [→] three times to specify a width of 12

Figure 5.13
Widening column A

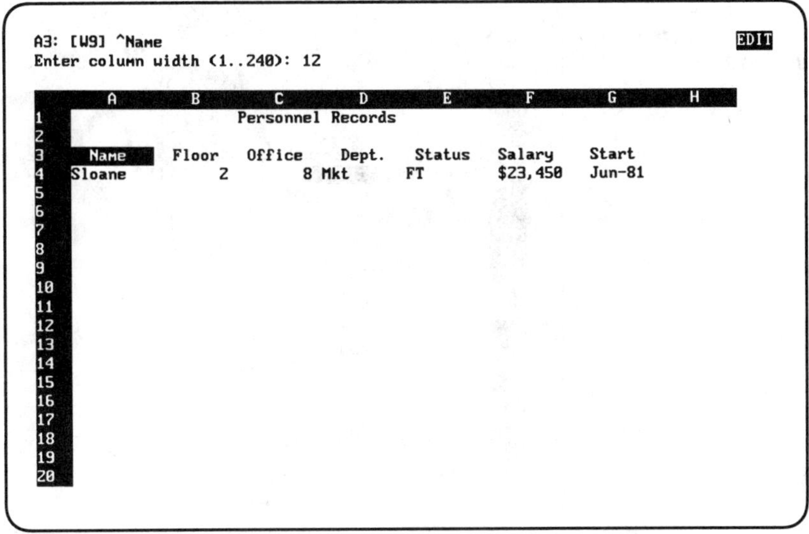

Press: ↵

2.2 Now you will decrease the width of columns B and C to seven characters. When you're changing the width of columns that are next to one another (adjacent) to the same width, 1-2-3 Release 2.2 lets you do all the columns together, instead of individually, using **/Worksheet Column Column-Range**:

Move to: cell B4
Press: /
Select: Worksheet
Column
Column-Range
Set-Width
Press: → to highlight column C as well as B
↵
Press: ← twice
↵

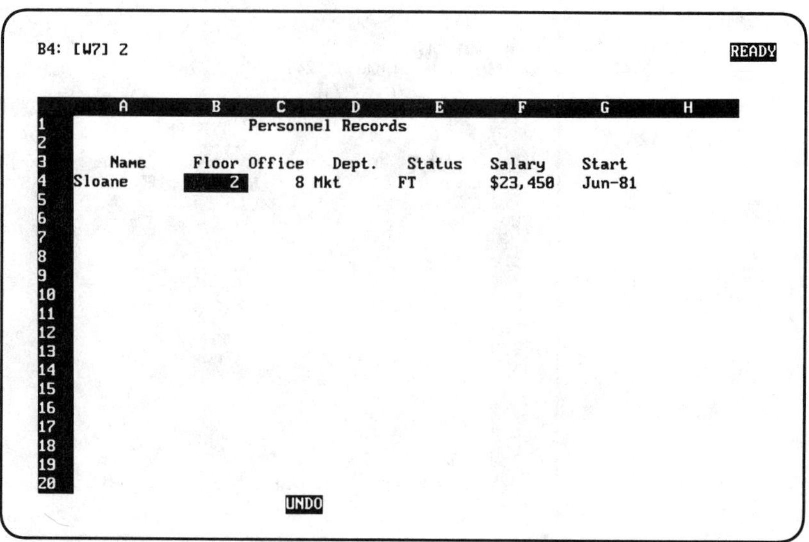

Figure 5.14
Columns decreased in width

Formatting Columns

You've entered and formatted data in columns F and G to display entries in currency and date format respectively. You can format both columns so that future entries will be formatted in the same way.

Move to: cell F4
Press: [/]
Select: Range
Format
Currency
Type: 0 [↵]
Press: [↓] ten times to highlight the range F4..F14

Figure 5.15
Currency format range

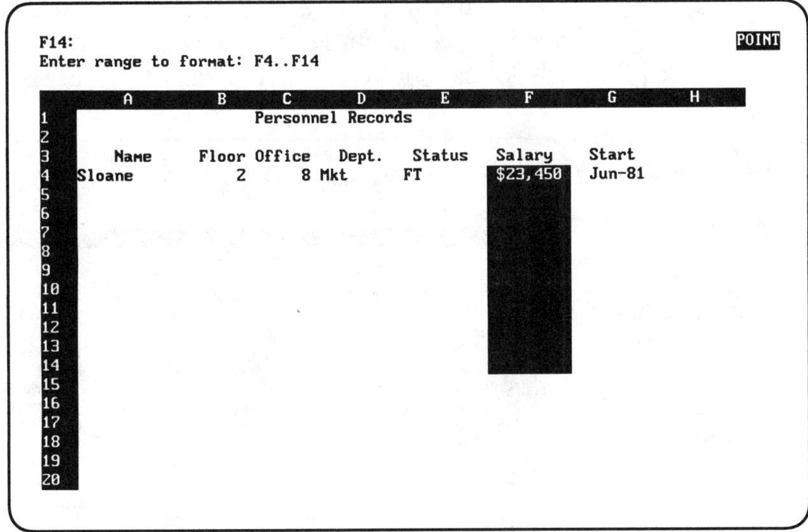

Press: ↵

Now format column G to display dates.

Move to: cell G4
Press: /
Select: Range
Format
Date
3 (MMM-YY)
Press: ↓ ten times to highlight the range G4..G14
↵

Columns F and G are formatted to display their contents as currency and dates, respectively. Now all entries made in either of those columns will appear in the appropriate format.

Entering Remaining Data Records

Now that the database has been set up, refined, and formatted, you can enter the remaining data records. Enter the data as shown in the screen illustrated below. Be careful to enter the dates in column G using the @DATE function: @DATE(YY,MM,DD). Notice that you must include a day of the month in the function even though it will not appear in the format you're using. Use any day you wish.

Figure 5.16
Entered data

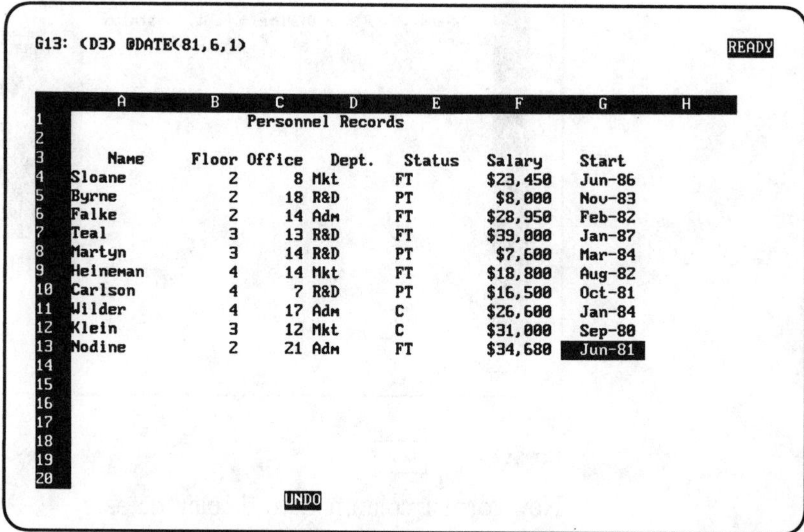

G13: (D3) @DATE(81,6,1) READY

	A	B	C	D	E	F	G	H
1			Personnel Records					
2								
3	Name	Floor	Office	Dept.	Status	Salary	Start	
4	Sloane	2	8	Mkt	FT	$23,450	Jun-86	
5	Byrne	2	18	R&D	PT	$8,000	Nov-83	
6	Falke	2	14	Adm	FT	$28,950	Feb-82	
7	Teal	3	13	R&D	FT	$39,000	Jan-87	
8	Martyn	3	14	R&D	PT	$7,600	Mar-84	
9	Heineman	4	14	Mkt	FT	$18,800	Aug-82	
10	Carlson	4	7	R&D	PT	$16,500	Oct-81	
11	Wilder	4	17	Adm	C	$26,600	Jan-84	
12	Klein	3	12	Mkt	C	$31,000	Sep-80	
13	Nodine	2	21	Adm	FT	$34,680	Jun-81	
14								
15								
16								
17								
18								
19								
20								

UNDO

Centering Labels

As a final step in refining the appearance of the database, you will center the labels in columns D and E. (You cannot format a range to center the labels until you have entered all the labels.)

Move to: cell D4
Press: /
Select: Range
Label
Center
Press: →
↓ nine times to highlight the range D4..E13
↵

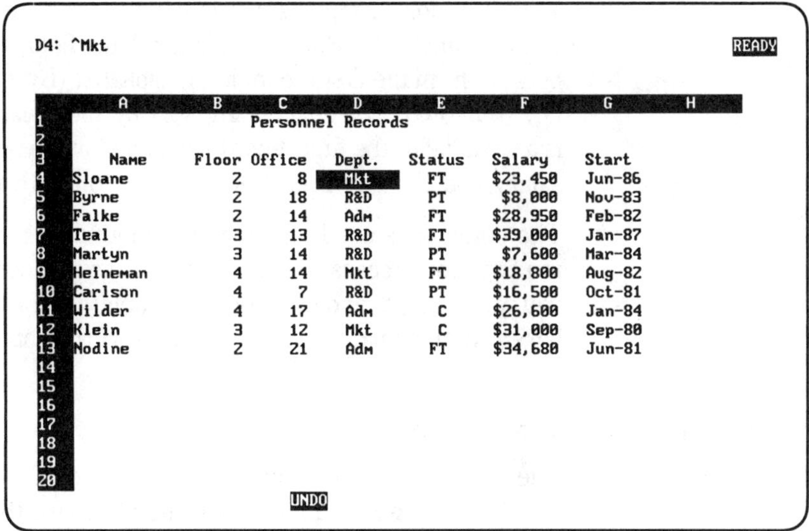

D4: ^Mkt READY

	A	B	C	D	E	F	G	H
1			Personnel	Records				
2								
3	Name	Floor	Office	Dept.	Status	Salary	Start	
4	Sloane	2	8	Mkt	FT	$23,450	Jun-86	
5	Byrne	2	18	R&D	PT	$8,000	Nov-83	
6	Falke	2	14	Adm	FT	$28,950	Feb-82	
7	Teal	3	13	R&D	FT	$39,000	Jan-87	
8	Martyn	3	14	R&D	PT	$7,600	Mar-84	
9	Heineman	4	14	Mkt	FT	$18,800	Aug-82	
10	Carlson	4	7	R&D	PT	$16,500	Oct-81	
11	Wilder	4	17	Adm	C	$26,600	Jan-84	
12	Klein	3	12	Mkt	C	$31,000	Sep-80	
13	Nodine	2	21	Adm	FT	$34,680	Jun-81	
14								
15								
16								
17								
18								
19								
20								

UNDO

Figure 5.17
Centered labels

SAVING THE FILE

Now that the database is complete, save the file. Because this is the first time you have saved the file, you will have to give it a name: name it DATABASE.

Press: [/]
Select: File
Save
Type: database [↵]

SORTING DATABASE RECORDS

When you first set up a database, records are listed in the order in which you enter them. 1-2-3's sorting feature lets you change the order. You can sort in three ways: alphabetically, numerically, and chronologically. Each sort is done according to one or two of the fields in the database. And each sort can be done in either ascending or descending order.

You could, for example, sort the database in ascending order according to the Name field. Because this is a label field, the sort will be alphabetical—from the first record in the alphabet (Byrne) to the last (Wilder). Or, you could do a descending sort by the Salary field. Because this is a value field, the first record would be for the person with the highest salary and the last record for the person with the lowest.

The commands used for sorting are found on the Data menu. Sorting is a two-step process: (1) specify the range that contains the data records you want sorted, and (2) choose the field(s) on which you want the sort based. In the next few steps you will sort the database you just created.

Identifying the Data Range

The range of cells containing the data records to be sorted is called the **data range**. You need to remember two things when specifying the data range. First, be sure to include only cells that contain data records. Be especially careful not to include the field name row. Second, you do not have to include the entire database in a sort. You can sort certain records if you prefer. Make sure, however, you always include all of the fields in a sort or your database will no longer have the correct information for each record.

Figure 5.18
Data range

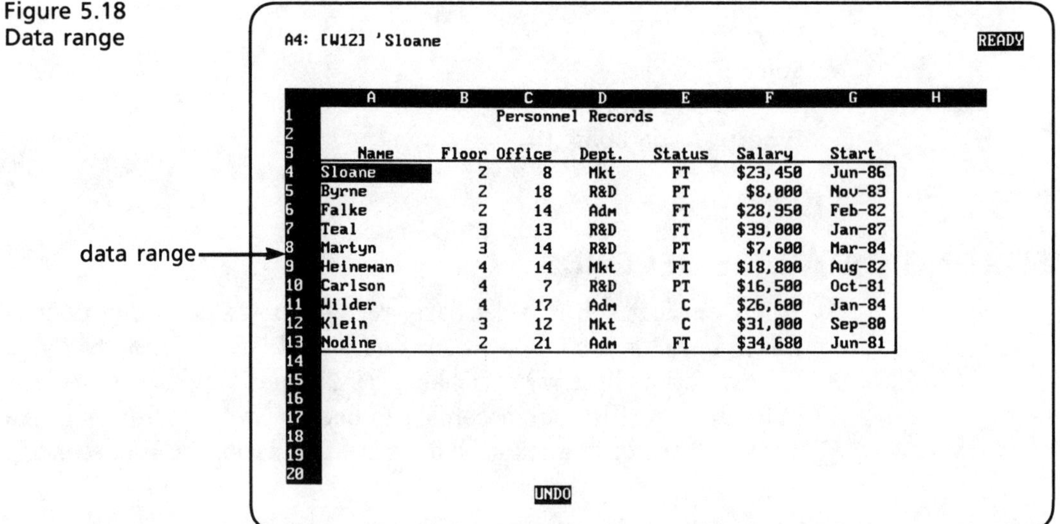

	A	B	C	D	E	F	G	H
1			Personnel Records					
2								
3	Name	Floor	Office	Dept.	Status	Salary	Start	
4	Sloane	2	8	Mkt	FT	$23,450	Jun-86	
5	Byrne	2	18	R&D	PT	$8,000	Nov-83	
6	Falke	2	14	Adm	FT	$28,950	Feb-82	
7	Teal	3	13	R&D	FT	$39,000	Jan-87	
8	Martyn	3	14	R&D	PT	$7,600	Mar-84	
9	Heineman	4	14	Mkt	FT	$18,800	Aug-82	
10	Carlson	4	7	R&D	PT	$16,500	Oct-81	
11	Wilder	4	17	Adm	C	$26,600	Jan-84	
12	Klein	3	12	Mkt	C	$31,000	Sep-80	
13	Nodine	2	21	Adm	FT	$34,680	Jun-81	
14								
15								
16								
17								
18								
19								
20								

All the database commands are on the Data menu. You are first going to identify the data range and include all the data records in rows 4 through 13.

Move to: cell A4
Press: [/]
Select: Data
Sort

Figure 5.19 Sort settings sheet

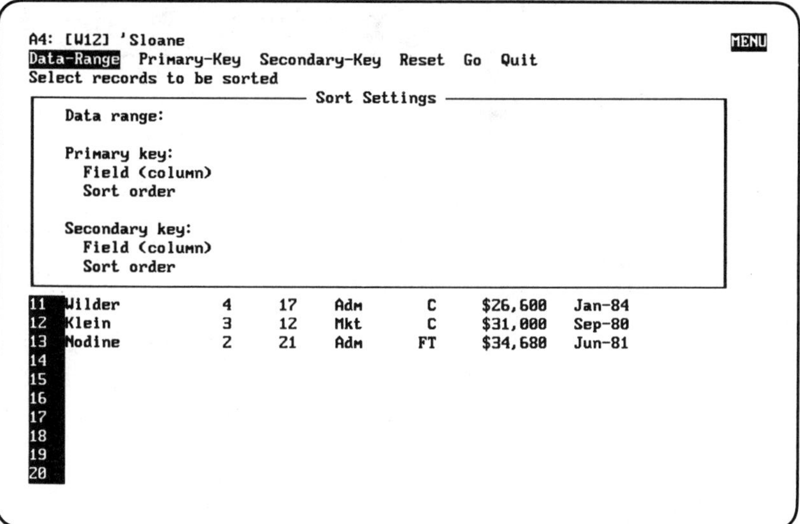

(2.2) When you select Sort, 1-2-3 displays the sort settings sheet, which shows you all the sort settings at a glance. Initially, the sort settings are blank. You will specify settings by selecting commands from the Data Sort menu that is above the setting sheet.

Select: Data-Range
Press: [.] (period)
[END] [↓] to expand the highlight to row 13
[END] [→] to highlight the range A4..G13

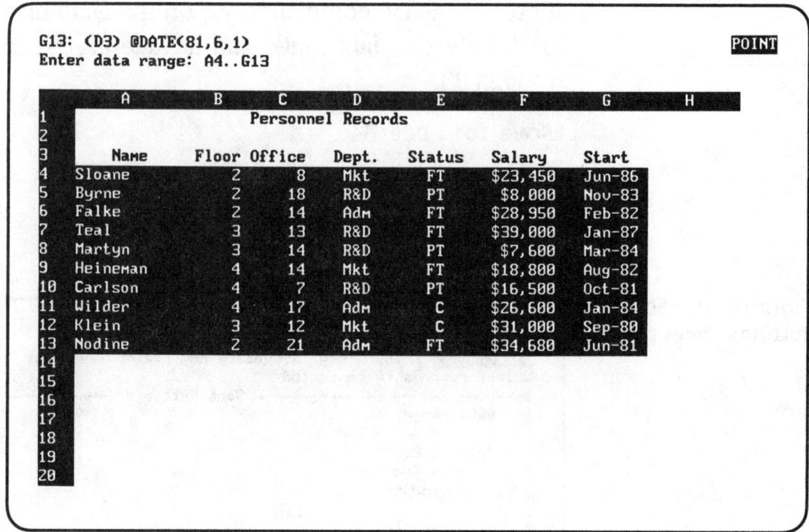
G13: (D3) @DATE(81,6,1)
Enter data range: A4..G13
POINT

	A	B	C	D	E	F	G	H
1			Personnel Records					
2								
3	Name	Floor	Office	Dept.	Status	Salary	Start	
4	Sloane	2	8	Mkt	FT	$23,450	Jun-86	
5	Byrne	2	18	R&D	PT	$8,000	Nov-83	
6	Falke	2	14	Adm	FT	$28,950	Feb-82	
7	Teal	3	13	R&D	FT	$39,000	Jan-87	
8	Martyn	3	14	R&D	PT	$7,600	Mar-84	
9	Heineman	4	14	Mkt	FT	$18,800	Aug-82	
10	Carlson	4	7	R&D	PT	$16,500	Oct-81	
11	Wilder	4	17	Adm	C	$26,600	Jan-84	
12	Klein	3	12	Mkt	C	$31,000	Sep-80	
13	Nodine	2	21	Adm	FT	$34,680	Jun-81	
14								
15								
16								
17								
18								
19								
20								

Figure 5.20 Highlighted data range

Press: ↵

The data range setting on the setting sheet should now read A4..G13. The sort settings sheet remains on the screen; you have to select Quit to leave the menu and return to the worksheet.

Sort Keys

When 1–2–3 sorts a database, it needs to know which field or fields to base the sort on. The sort keys specify this. Use the **Data Sort Primary-Key** command for the main sort; it sorts the entire database. For a secondary sort, use **/Data Sort Secondary-Key**; it serves as a tie-breaker for records that have the same data in the primary sort field.

For example, sorting the personnel records by Status groups them according to employment status. Those people who have the same status (such as those who work full-time and have FT in the Status field) require further differentiation. You can use **/Data Sort Secondary-Key** to sort them alphabetically.

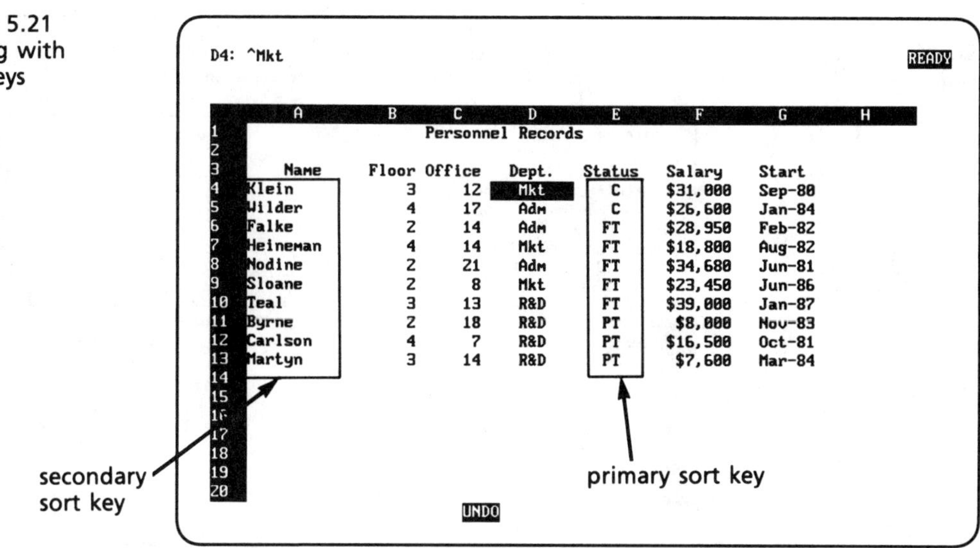

	A	B	C	D	E	F	G	H
1			Personnel	Records				
2								
3	Name	Floor	Office	Dept.	Status	Salary	Start	
4	Klein	3	12	Mkt	C	$31,000	Sep-80	
5	Wilder	4	17	Adm	C	$26,600	Jan-84	
6	Falke	2	14	Adm	FT	$28,950	Feb-82	
7	Heineman	4	14	Mkt	FT	$18,800	Aug-82	
8	Nodine	2	21	Adm	FT	$34,680	Jun-81	
9	Sloane	2	8	Mkt	FT	$23,450	Jun-86	
10	Teal	3	13	R&D	FT	$39,000	Jan-87	
11	Byrne	2	18	R&D	PT	$8,000	Nov-83	
12	Carlson	4	7	R&D	PT	$16,500	Oct-81	
13	Martyn	3	14	R&D	PT	$7,600	Mar-84	

Figure 5.21 Sorting with two keys

The database in this example is small enough to require only one sort key for most sorts. You are going to sort by the Name field in ascending alphabetical order.

When you select Primary-Key, a prompt in the control will read Primary sort key: A4. Locating the pointer in this cell tells 1-2-3 to sort by the Name field. A second prompt will then ask you to specify ascending or descending order. Finally, you will select Go to activate the sort.

Select: Primary-Key
Press: ↵ to accept A4
Type: a

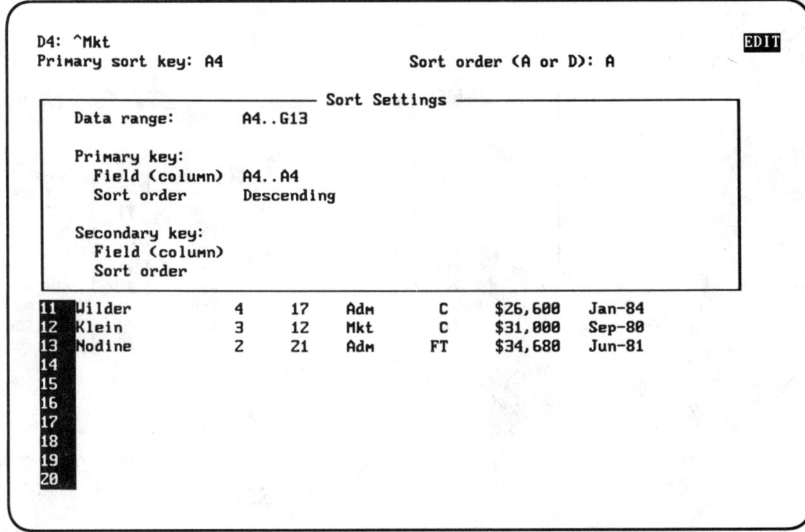

Figure 5.22 Entering sort order: A

Press: ↵

The sort settings sheet now reflects the primary sort key as well as the data range.

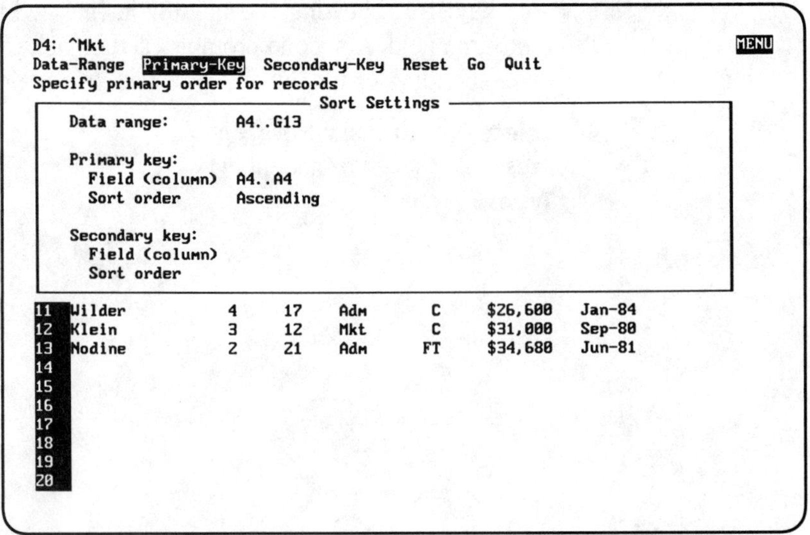

Figure 5.23 Updated setting sheet

Select: Go

The database is now in alphabetical order and the Data menu and sort settings sheet is gone from the screen.

Figure 5.24
Database sorted by name

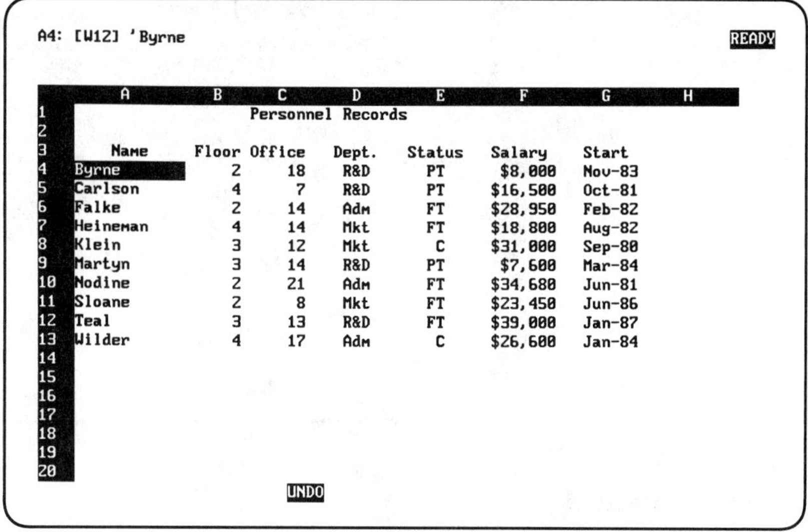

A4: [W12] 'Byrne READY

Personnel Records

Name	Floor	Office	Dept.	Status	Salary	Start
Byrne	2	18	R&D	PT	$8,000	Nov-83
Carlson	4	7	R&D	PT	$16,500	Oct-81
Falke	2	14	Adm	FT	$28,950	Feb-82
Heineman	4	14	Mkt	FT	$18,800	Aug-82
Klein	3	12	Mkt	C	$31,000	Sep-80
Martyn	3	14	R&D	PT	$7,600	Mar-84
Nodine	2	21	Adm	FT	$34,680	Jun-81
Sloane	2	8	Mkt	FT	$23,450	Jun-86
Teal	3	13	R&D	FT	$39,000	Jan-87
Wilder	4	17	Adm	C	$26,600	Jan-84

UNDO

Try sorting the database again, this time using Salary as the sort key. Notice that you do not need to specify the data range again; 1-2-3 remembers and offers the last range you specified. Put the list in descending order:

Press: [/]
Select: Data
Sort
Primary-Key
Move to: cell F4
Press: [↵]
Type: d [↵]
Select: Go

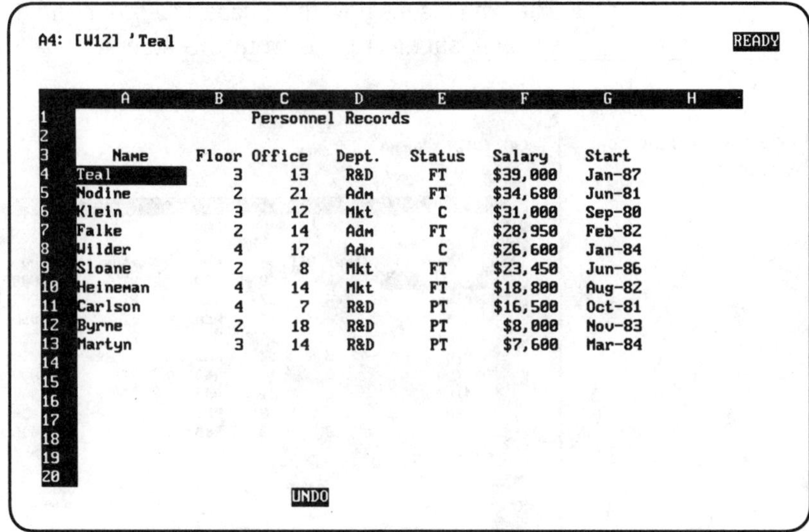

A4: [W12] 'Teal READY

A	B	C	D	E	F	G
		Personnel Records				
Name	Floor	Office	Dept.	Status	Salary	Start
Teal	3	13	R&D	FT	$39,000	Jan-87
Nodine	2	21	Adm	FT	$34,680	Jun-81
Klein	3	12	Mkt	C	$31,000	Sep-80
Falke	2	14	Adm	FT	$28,950	Feb-82
Wilder	4	17	Adm	C	$26,600	Jan-84
Sloane	2	8	Mkt	FT	$23,450	Jun-86
Heineman	4	14	Mkt	FT	$18,800	Aug-82
Carlson	4	7	R&D	PT	$16,500	Oct-81
Byrne	2	18	R&D	PT	$8,000	Nov-83
Martyn	3	14	R&D	PT	$7,600	Mar-84

UNDO

Figure 5.25
Database sorted by salary

Adding a Record

The entire database is now sorted according to the Salary field, in descending order. From now on, however, any new data record you add needs to be incorporated into the database in the proper location. You can do this easily with the 1-2-3 database. Simply enter the record at the end of the database, redefine the data range to include that row, and sort the list.

First, enter a new record in row 14.

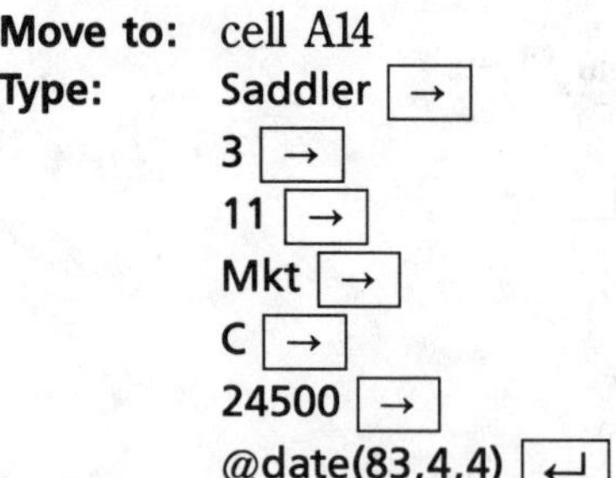

Move to: cell A14

Type: Saddler [→]
3 [→]
11 [→]
Mkt [→]
C [→]
24500 [→]
@date(83,4,4) [↵]

Center the labels in columns D and E. Because you earlier formatted F4..F14 as currency and G4..G14 as a date, the numbers you entered appear in the correct format.

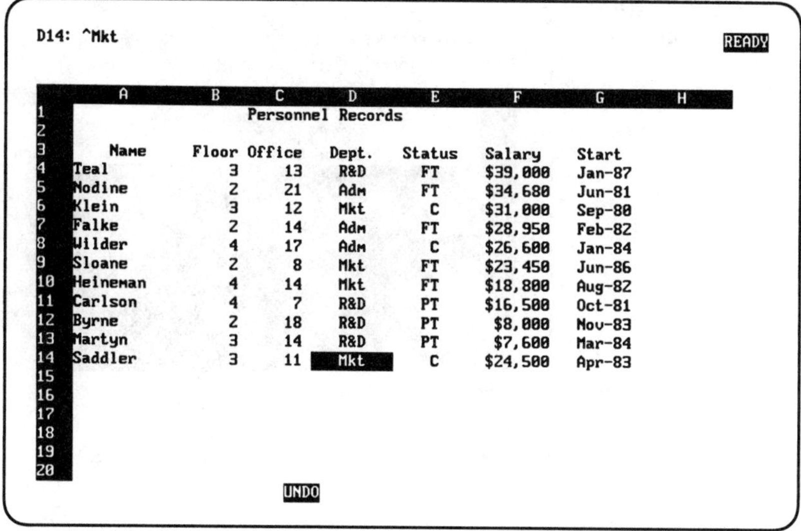
D14: ^Mkt READY

	A	B	C	D	E	F	G	H
1			Personnel	Records				
2								
3	Name	Floor	Office	Dept.	Status	Salary	Start	
4	Teal	3	13	R&D	FT	$39,000	Jan-87	
5	Nodine	2	21	Adm	FT	$34,680	Jun-81	
6	Klein	3	12	Mkt	C	$31,000	Sep-80	
7	Falke	2	14	Adm	FT	$28,950	Feb-82	
8	Wilder	4	17	Adm	C	$26,600	Jan-84	
9	Sloane	2	8	Mkt	FT	$23,450	Jun-86	
10	Heineman	4	14	Mkt	FT	$18,800	Aug-82	
11	Carlson	4	7	R&D	PT	$16,500	Oct-81	
12	Byrne	2	18	R&D	PT	$8,000	Nov-83	
13	Martyn	3	14	R&D	PT	$7,600	Mar-84	
14	Saddler	3	11	Mkt	C	$24,500	Apr-83	
15								
16								
17								
18								
19								
20								

UNDO

Figure 5.26 Record added and centered

Redefine the data range to include the new record. Again you'll notice that 1-2-3 offers the data range that you specified in the last sort. This time you'll amend it to extend the range down one row.

Press: [/]
Select: Data
Sort
Data-Range
Press: [↓]

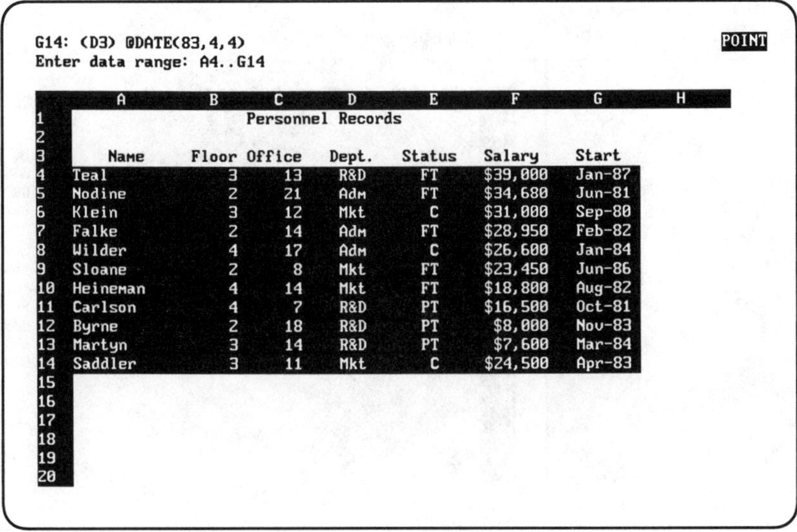

Figure 5.27 Setting new data range

Press: ↵

The sort settings sheet remains on the screen. Notice that 1-2-3 also remembers the most recent specification entered for the primary key. Because you are simply resorting according to the same sort key, you don't need to change any settings.

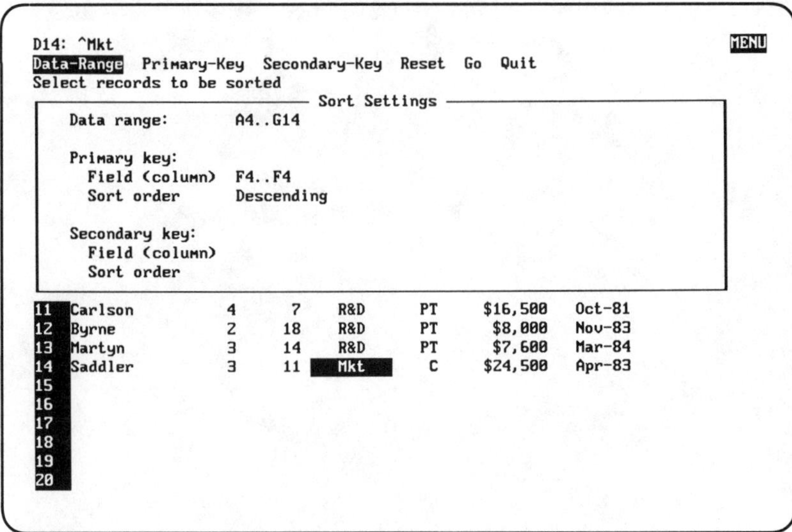

Figure 5.28 New sort settings

Select: Go

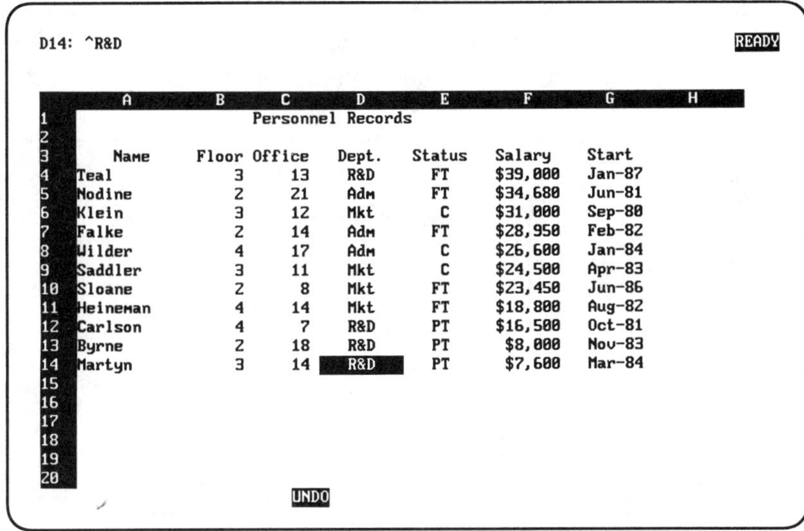
D14: ^R&D READY

	A	B	C	D	E	F	G	H
1			Personnel Records					
2								
3	Name	Floor	Office	Dept.	Status	Salary	Start	
4	Teal	3	13	R&D	FT	$39,000	Jan-87	
5	Nodine	2	21	Adm	FT	$34,680	Jun-81	
6	Klein	3	12	Mkt	C	$31,000	Sep-80	
7	Falke	2	14	Adm	FT	$28,950	Feb-82	
8	Wilder	4	17	Adm	C	$26,600	Jan-84	
9	Saddler	3	11	Mkt	C	$24,500	Apr-83	
10	Sloane	2	8	Mkt	FT	$23,450	Jun-86	
11	Heineman	4	14	Mkt	FT	$18,800	Aug-82	
12	Carlson	4	7	R&D	PT	$16,500	Oct-81	
13	Byrne	2	18	R&D	PT	$8,000	Nov-83	
14	Martyn	3	14	R&D	PT	$7,600	Mar-84	
15								
16								
17								
18								
19								
20								

UNDO

Figure 5.29 New record sorted

The new record is positioned correctly in the database (row 9, between Wilder and Sloane). You can add new records to the database up to the maximum of 8,192 rows in the 1-2-3 worksheet. You will always be able to resort the list and put new records in their proper places.

QUERYING THE DATABASE

One of the major advantages of an electronic database is the ease and speed with which you can find and select specific data records. You use the **Data Query** commands for this, specifying the criteria for the records you want to find. 1-2-3 queries the database and finds those records that match.

Assume, for example, that you want to know who works in the marketing department. The Dept. field contains the relevant information for each record. Simply specify the word Mkt in the Dept. field as the criterion.

You can set up a number of criteria. For example, you can query who works in marketing on a full-time basis and earns over $20,000 a year. 1-2-3 can search the database and select only those records that contain that particular information.

(2.2) When you select **/Data Query**, 1-2-3 displays the query settings sheet. This setting sheet includes all the ranges 1-2-3 uses when you use the **Data Query** commands to find records. Initially, the query settings are blank. You will specify query settings by selecting commands from the Data Query menu which is above the setting sheet.

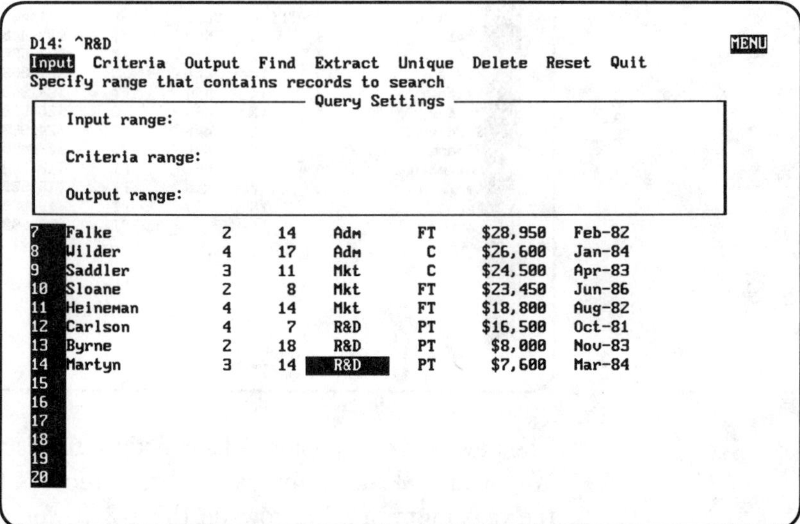

Figure 5.30 Query settings sheet

The Data Query menu includes a number of options, including four different query operations.

Find As you move the pointer down the rows in the database, 1-2-3 moves to and highlights the selected records.

Extract 1-2-3 finds the records that match the criteria and copies them to a designated place on the worksheet.

Unique 1-2-3 extracts records (as with Extract) but also makes sure that none of the records is the same. Only unique records are included.

Delete 1-2-3 finds and deletes the selected records. The other records shift to fill in the blank rows.

To use these **Data Query** commands, you must first set up a number of ranges.

Input Range

You must specify the area to be searched. This is called the **input range.** (It is similar to the data range that must be specified for the **/Data Sort** command.) The input range must include the row of field names. This is an important reference for 1-2-3 when it attempts to match the criteria. The input range does not necessarily have to include the entire database; sometimes you may want to search only part of it.

Figure 5.31
Input range

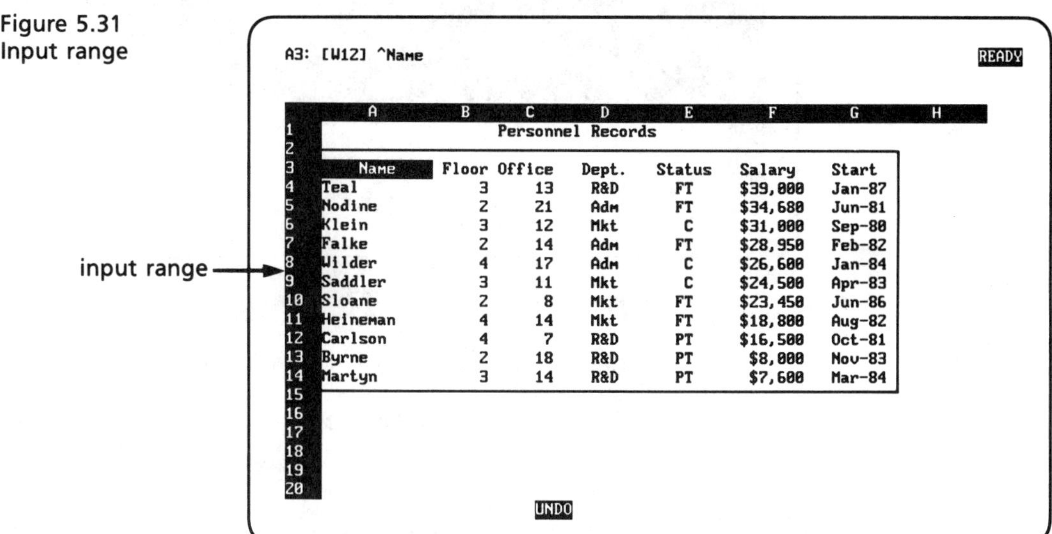

	A	B	C	D	E	F	G
3	Name	Floor	Office	Dept.	Status	Salary	Start
4	Teal	3	13	R&D	FT	$39,000	Jan-87
5	Nodine	2	21	Adm	FT	$34,680	Jun-81
6	Klein	3	12	Mkt	C	$31,000	Sep-80
7	Falke	2	14	Adm	FT	$28,950	Feb-82
8	Wilder	4	17	Adm	C	$26,600	Jan-84
9	Saddler	3	11	Mkt	C	$24,500	Apr-83
10	Sloane	2	8	Mkt	FT	$23,450	Jun-86
11	Heineman	4	14	Mkt	FT	$18,800	Aug-82
12	Carlson	4	7	R&D	PT	$16,500	Oct-81
13	Byrne	2	18	R&D	PT	$8,000	Nov-83
14	Martyn	3	14	R&D	PT	$7,600	Mar-84

Setting Up the Input Range

The first step in any **/Data Query** command is setting up the input range. 1-2-3 has to know what area of the database to search. Remember the input range must include the row of field names.

Move to: cell A3
Press: /
Select: Data
Query
Input
Press: .
END ↓ to expand the highlight to row 14
END → to specify the range A3..G14

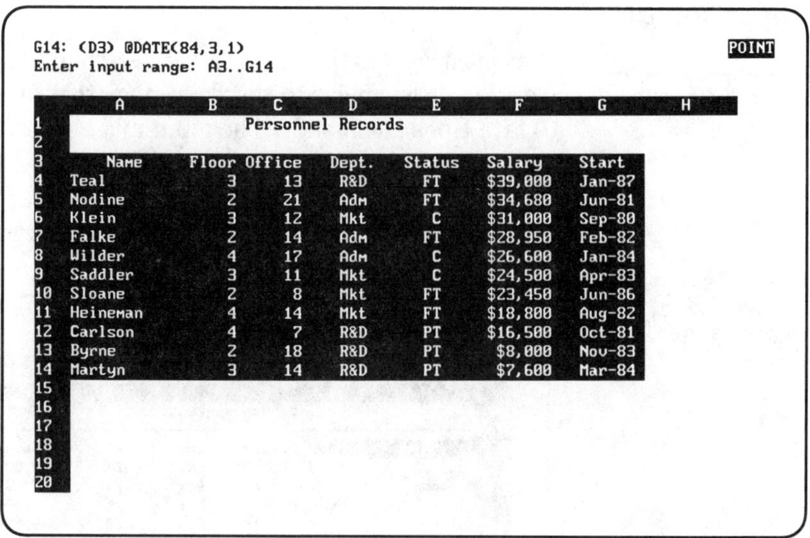
G14: (D3) @DATE(84,3,1)
Enter input range: A3..G14
POINT

Personnel Records

	Name	Floor	Office	Dept.	Status	Salary	Start
4	Teal	3	13	R&D	FT	$39,000	Jan-87
5	Nodine	2	21	Adm	FT	$34,680	Jun-81
6	Klein	3	12	Mkt	C	$31,000	Sep-80
7	Falke	2	14	Adm	FT	$28,950	Feb-82
8	Wilder	4	17	Adm	C	$26,600	Jan-84
9	Saddler	3	11	Mkt	C	$24,500	Apr-83
10	Sloane	2	8	Mkt	FT	$23,450	Jun-86
11	Heineman	4	14	Mkt	FT	$18,800	Aug-82
12	Carlson	4	7	R&D	PT	$16,500	Oct-81
13	Byrne	2	18	R&D	PT	$8,000	Nov-83
14	Martyn	3	14	R&D	PT	$7,600	Mar-84

Figure 5.32 Highlighted input range

Press: ↵

The query settings sheet now shows A3..G14 as the input range.

Select: Quit to leave the Data Query menu and query settings sheet

Criteria Range

The **criteria range** establishes the criteria that 1–2–3 uses in the search for matching records. The criteria range consists of two or more rows. The first row contains the field names from the input range. The field names in the criteria range must match those in the input range exactly because 1–2–3 uses both sets of field names as cross-references. The second row and any additional rows contain the actual criteria.

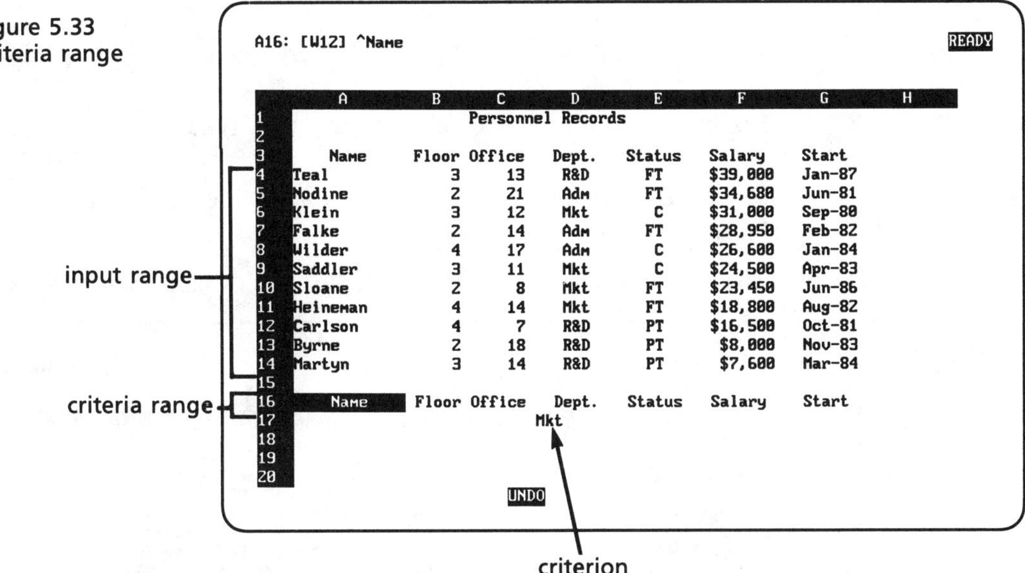

	A	B	C	D	E	F	G	H
1			Personnel Records					
2								
3	Name	Floor	Office	Dept.	Status	Salary	Start	
4	Teal	3	13	R&D	FT	$39,000	Jan-87	
5	Nodine	2	21	Adm	FT	$34,680	Jun-81	
6	Klein	3	12	Mkt	C	$31,000	Sep-80	
7	Falke	2	14	Adm	FT	$28,950	Feb-82	
8	Wilder	4	17	Adm	C	$26,600	Jan-84	
9	Saddler	3	11	Mkt	C	$24,500	Apr-83	
10	Sloane	2	8	Mkt	FT	$23,450	Jun-86	
11	Heineman	4	14	Mkt	FT	$18,800	Aug-82	
12	Carlson	4	7	R&D	PT	$16,500	Oct-81	
13	Byrne	2	18	R&D	PT	$8,000	Nov-83	
14	Martyn	3	14	R&D	PT	$7,600	Mar-84	
15								
16	Name	Floor	Office	Dept.	Status	Salary	Start	
17				Mkt				
18								
19								
20								

Figure 5.33
Criteria range

For example, if you want to find the personnel in the marketing department, you set up a criteria range with two rows. The first contains all the field names from the database, including the word Dept. for that field. The second contains the word Mkt, to correspond to the way that information is listed in the database. When 1-2-3 searches the database, it looks for records that contain the information listed in the criteria range; in this case, it looks for those that list the word Mkt in the Dept. field.

Setting Up the Criteria Range

To set up the criteria range, you have to leave the Data Query menu and return to the worksheet. Here you copy the row of field names to another location in the worksheet. This copy ensures that this row will be an exact duplicate of the original. (You do not have to use all the fields when you set up your criteria.)

Move to: cell A3
Press: /
Select: Copy
Press: END → to highlight the range A3..G3
↵
Move to: cell A16 where the names are to be copied to
Press: ↵

The row of field names appears in row 16, directly beneath the database.

Figure 5.34
Criteria range labels

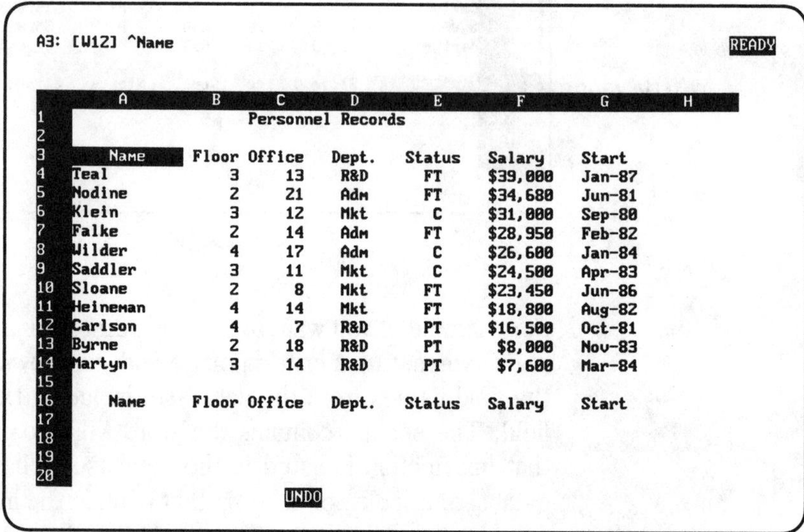

A3: [W12] ^Name READY

	A	B	C	D	E	F	G	H
1			Personnel	Records				
2								
3	Name	Floor	Office	Dept.	Status	Salary	Start	
4	Teal	3	13	R&D	FT	$39,000	Jan-87	
5	Nodine	2	21	Adm	FT	$34,680	Jun-81	
6	Klein	3	12	Mkt	C	$31,000	Sep-80	
7	Falke	2	14	Adm	FT	$28,950	Feb-82	
8	Wilder	4	17	Adm	C	$26,600	Jan-84	
9	Saddler	3	11	Mkt	C	$24,500	Apr-83	
10	Sloane	2	8	Mkt	FT	$23,450	Jun-86	
11	Heineman	4	14	Mkt	FT	$18,800	Aug-82	
12	Carlson	4	7	R&D	PT	$16,500	Oct-81	
13	Byrne	2	18	R&D	PT	$8,000	Nov-83	
14	Martyn	3	14	R&D	PT	$7,600	Mar-84	
15								
16	Name	Floor	Office	Dept.	Status	Salary	Start	
17								
18								
19								
20								

UNDO

Now you are going to select **/Data Query** again to establish the criteria range. The range includes the row directly below the row of field names. This is where you will enter the actual criteria.

Move to: cell A16
Press: /
Select: Data
Query
Criteria
Press: .
END →
↓ to highlight the range A16..G17

Figure 5.35
Highlighted
criteria range

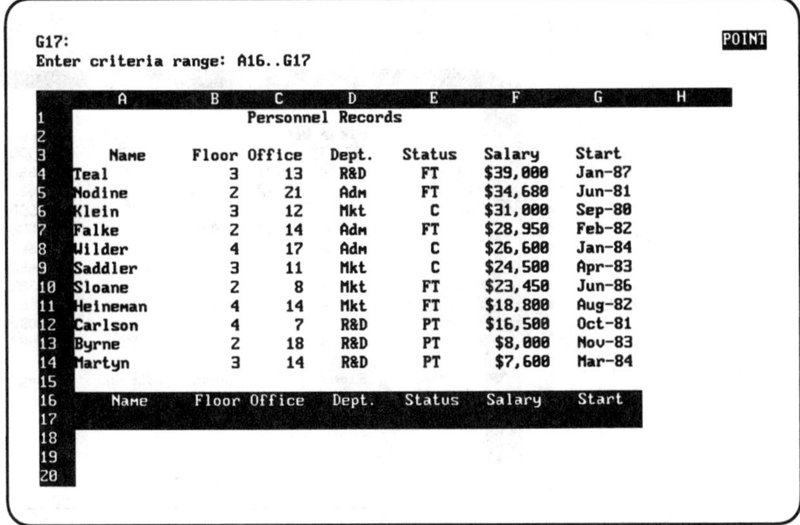
```
G17:                                                              POINT
Enter criteria range: A16..G17

      A           B     C       D        E        F         G       H
1                   Personnel Records
2
3      Name      Floor Office  Dept.   Status   Salary    Start
4  Teal             3     13    R&D      FT    $39,000   Jan-87
5  Nodine           2     21    Adm      FT    $34,680   Jun-81
6  Klein            3     12    Mkt       C    $31,000   Sep-80
7  Falke            2     14    Adm      FT    $28,950   Feb-82
8  Wilder           4     17    Adm       C    $26,600   Jan-84
9  Saddler          3     11    Mkt       C    $24,500   Apr-83
10 Sloane           2      8    Mkt      FT    $23,450   Jun-86
11 Heineman         4     14    Mkt      FT    $18,800   Aug-82
12 Carlson          4      7    R&D      PT    $16,500   Oct-81
13 Byrne            2     18    R&D      PT     $8,000   Nov-83
14 Martyn           3     14    R&D      PT     $7,600   Mar-84
15
16     Name      Floor Office  Dept.   Status   Salary    Start
17
18
19
20
```

Press: ↵
Select: Quit

FINDING DATA RECORDS

The **Data Query Find** command locates selected records. You'll notice that when you select **/Data Query Find**, the cell pointer moves to and highlights the first record that satisfies the selection criteria. You can then use the Up and Down keys to move the pointer among the selected records.

Now that you have established the input range and the criteria range, the final step before using **/Data Query Find** is to enter the actual criteria. In this example, you want to locate the records of those personnel who work in the marketing department. Specify this as the criterion by entering the word Mkt in the Dept. field of the criteria range.

Move to: cell D17
Type: Mkt ↵

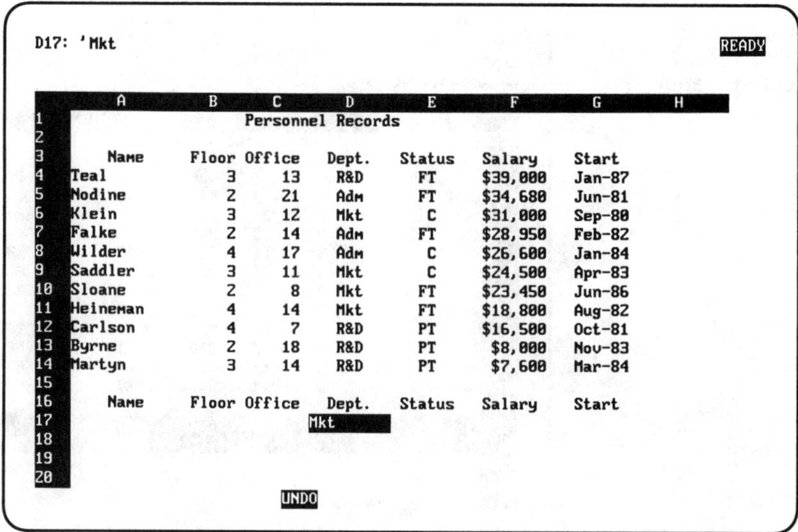

	A	B	C	D	E	F	G	H
1			Personnel Records					
2								
3	Name	Floor	Office	Dept.	Status	Salary	Start	
4	Teal	3	13	R&D	FT	$39,000	Jan-87	
5	Nodine	2	21	Adm	FT	$34,680	Jun-81	
6	Klein	3	12	Mkt	C	$31,000	Sep-80	
7	Falke	2	14	Adm	FT	$28,950	Feb-82	
8	Wilder	4	17	Adm	C	$26,600	Jan-84	
9	Saddler	3	11	Mkt	C	$24,500	Apr-83	
10	Sloane	2	8	Mkt	FT	$23,450	Jun-86	
11	Heineman	4	14	Mkt	FT	$18,800	Aug-82	
12	Carlson	4	7	R&D	PT	$16,500	Oct-81	
13	Byrne	2	18	R&D	PT	$8,000	Nov-83	
14	Martyn	3	14	R&D	PT	$7,600	Mar-84	
15								
16	Name	Floor	Office	Dept.	Status	Salary	Start	
17				Mkt				
18								
19								
20								

Figure 5.36
Entered criterion

You are now ready to return to the Data Query menu and select the **Find** command. As 1-2-3 starts the process, you'll see that the menu and the query settings sheet disappear, and that the mode indicator reads FIND. 1-2-3 stops when it finds the first record that matches the criterion (Klein). The entire record will be highlighted (from column A to column G).

Press: /
Select: Data
Query
Find

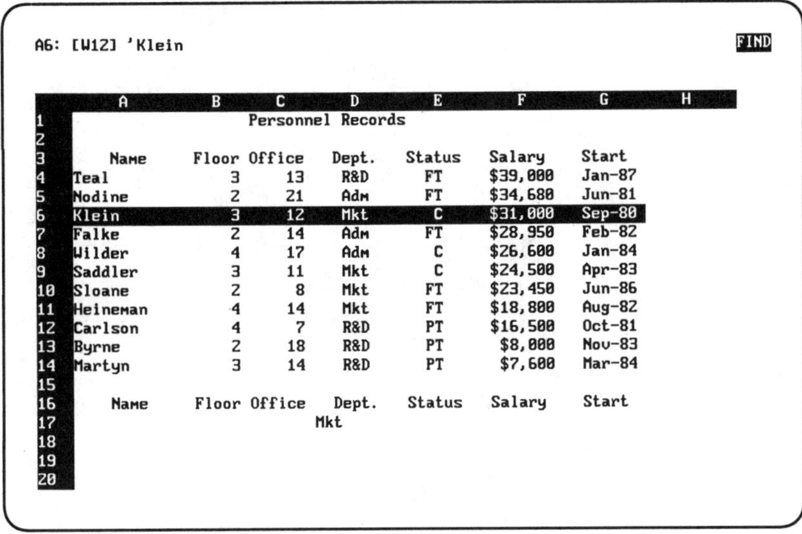

A6: [W12] 'Klein FIND

	A	B	C	D	E	F	G	H
1			Personnel Records					
2								
3	Name	Floor	Office	Dept.	Status	Salary	Start	
4	Teal	3	13	R&D	FT	$39,000	Jan-87	
5	Nodine	2	21	Adm	FT	$34,680	Jun-81	
6	Klein	3	12	Mkt	C	$31,000	Sep-80	
7	Falke	2	14	Adm	FT	$28,950	Feb-82	
8	Wilder	4	17	Adm	C	$26,600	Jan-84	
9	Saddler	3	11	Mkt	C	$24,500	Apr-83	
10	Sloane	2	8	Mkt	FT	$23,450	Jun-86	
11	Heineman	4	14	Mkt	FT	$18,800	Aug-82	
12	Carlson	4	7	R&D	PT	$16,500	Oct-81	
13	Byrne	2	18	R&D	PT	$8,000	Nov-83	
14	Martyn	3	14	R&D	PT	$7,600	Mar-84	
15								
16	Name	Floor	Office	Dept.	Status	Salary	Start	
17				Mkt				
18								
19								
20								

Figure 5.37 Finding first record

Now you will press the Down key to move to the next matching record.

Press: ↓

Figure 5.38 Finding second record

A9: [W12] 'Saddler FIND

	A	B	C	D	E	F	G	H
1			Personnel Records					
2								
3	Name	Floor	Office	Dept.	Status	Salary	Start	
4	Teal	3	13	R&D	FT	$39,000	Jan-87	
5	Nodine	2	21	Adm	FT	$34,680	Jun-81	
6	Klein	3	12	Mkt	C	$31,000	Sep-80	
7	Falke	2	14	Adm	FT	$28,950	Feb-82	
8	Wilder	4	17	Adm	C	$26,600	Jan-84	
9	Saddler	3	11	Mkt	C	$24,500	Apr-83	
10	Sloane	2	8	Mkt	FT	$23,450	Jun-86	
11	Heineman	4	14	Mkt	FT	$18,800	Aug-82	
12	Carlson	4	7	R&D	PT	$16,500	Oct-81	
13	Byrne	2	18	R&D	PT	$8,000	Nov-83	
14	Martyn	3	14	R&D	PT	$7,600	Mar-84	
15								
16	Name	Floor	Office	Dept.	Status	Salary	Start	
17				Mkt				
18								
19								
20								

The highlight moves down to the next record that lists Mkt (Saddler).

Press: ↓ twice to reach the last matching record

At this point, pressing the Down key again causes the computer to beep. Press the Up key to move the cursor up the list.

Press: [ESC] to return to the Data Query menu
Select: Quit

Try another query. You are going to search the database for those personnel who work full-time. The ranges can remain the same, but the criterion must be changed. The first step is to erase the old criterion, and then enter **FT** into the Status field.

Move to: cell D17
Press: [/]
Select: Range
Erase
Press: [↵] to accept the range D17..D17
Move to: cell E17
Type: FT [↵]

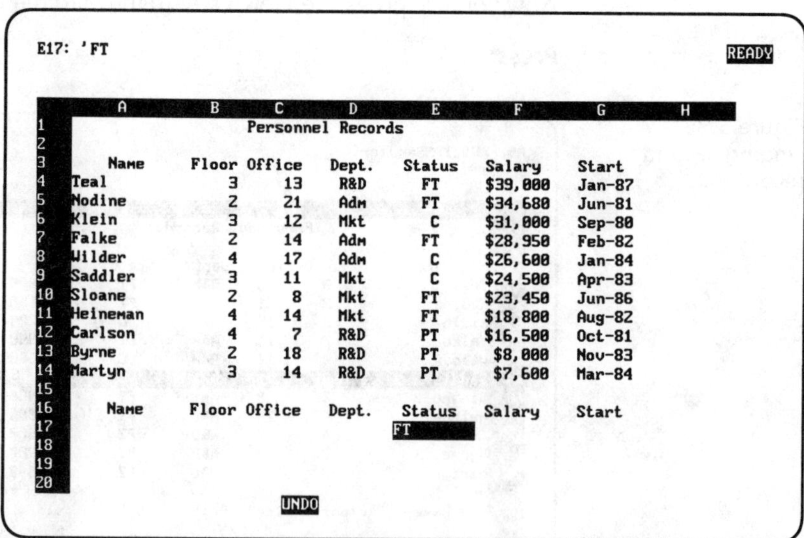
```
E17: 'FT                                                    READY

      A         B      C       D       E        F         G        H
1                    Personnel Records
2
3       Name    Floor Office  Dept.  Status   Salary     Start
4  Teal             3     13   R&D     FT    $39,000    Jan-87
5  Nodine           2     21   Adm     FT    $34,680    Jun-81
6  Klein            3     12   Mkt      C    $31,000    Sep-80
7  Falke            2     14   Adm     FT    $28,950    Feb-82
8  Wilder           4     17   Adm      C    $26,600    Jan-84
9  Saddler          3     11   Mkt      C    $24,500    Apr-83
10 Sloane           2      8   Mkt     FT    $23,450    Jun-86
11 Heineman         4     14   Mkt     FT    $18,800    Aug-82
12 Carlson          4      7   R&D     PT    $16,500    Oct-81
13 Byrne            2     18   R&D     PT     $8,000    Nov-83
14 Martyn           3     14   R&D     PT     $7,600    Mar-84
15
16      Name    Floor Office  Dept.  Status   Salary     Start
17                                   FT
18
19
20
                         UNDO
```

Figure 5.39 New criterion entered

Finally, select **/Data Query Find:**

Press: [/]
Select: Data
Query
Find

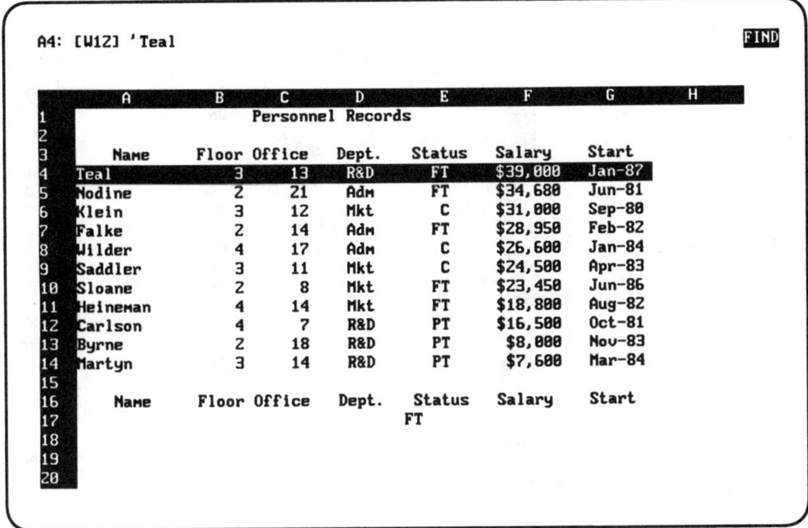

A4: [W12] 'Teal FIND

	A	B	C	D	E	F	G	H
1			Personnel Records					
2								
3	Name	Floor	Office	Dept.	Status	Salary	Start	
4	Teal	3	13	R&D	FT	$39,000	Jan-87	
5	Nodine	2	21	Adm	FT	$34,680	Jun-81	
6	Klein	3	12	Mkt	C	$31,000	Sep-80	
7	Falke	2	14	Adm	FT	$28,950	Feb-82	
8	Wilder	4	17	Adm	C	$26,600	Jan-84	
9	Saddler	3	11	Mkt	C	$24,500	Apr-83	
10	Sloane	2	8	Mkt	FT	$23,450	Jun-86	
11	Heineman	4	14	Mkt	FT	$18,800	Aug-82	
12	Carlson	4	7	R&D	PT	$16,500	Oct-81	
13	Byrne	2	18	R&D	PT	$8,000	Nov-83	
14	Martyn	3	14	R&D	PT	$7,600	Mar-84	
15								
16	Name	Floor	Office	Dept.	Status	Salary	Start	
17					FT			
18								
19								
20								

Figure 5.40
Finding first record

Use the Down and Up keys to move among the records that contain FT in the Status field.

Press: ESC
Select: Quit

EXTRACTING RECORDS

Often you will want to collect the queried data records in one place. The **Data Query Extract** command finds the data records that match the criteria and copies them to a designated area in the worksheet.

Output Range

An output range is necessary to use either the **Data Query Extract** or **Data Query Unique** commands. These commands locate selected records and copy them to a designated place in the worksheet. This place is called the **output range**. The first row of the output range must contain the field names from the database.

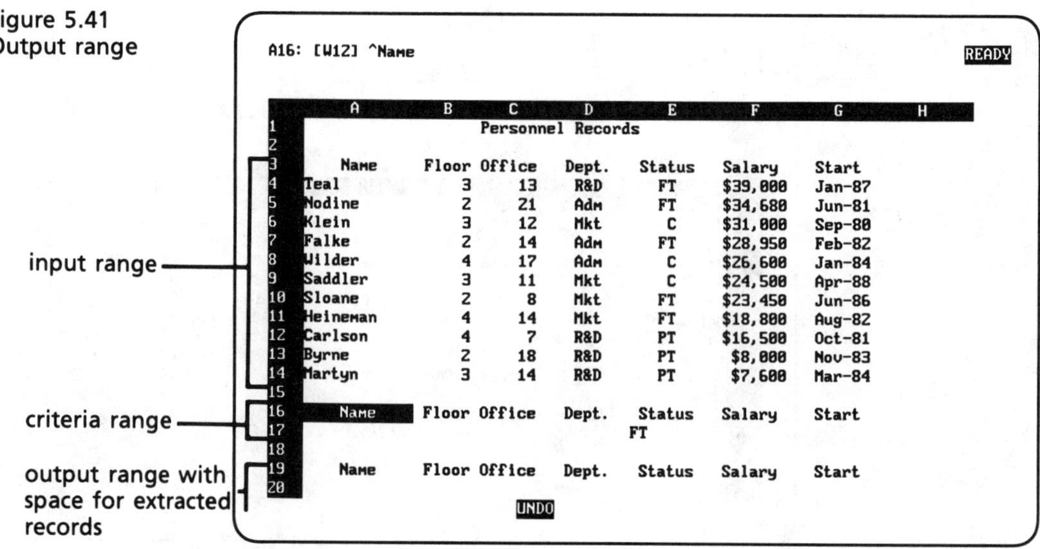

Figure 5.41
Output range

When specifying the output range, you may choose to designate a range that is just one row deep (the row of field names). 1-2-3 then uses the area below that row for the output range. (Remember that when 1-2-3 copies information to the output range, it erases the area first; make sure the rows below the output range don't contain any data you want.)

Setting Up the Output Range

You are going to set up the output range directly below the criteria range. In this example you will be able to see all the ranges on the same screen. The output range need be no more than the row of field names. 1-2-3 knows to copy the selected records to the area below that row.

The first step is to copy the row of field names to that area:

Move to: cell A3
Press: /
Select: Copy
Press: END → to highlight the range A3..G3
↵
Move to: cell A19
Press: ↵

The row of field names appears directly below the criteria range. Next you designate this row as the output range:

Move to: cell A19
Press: /
Select: Data
Query
Output
Press: .
END → to highlight the range A19..G19

Figure 5.42 Output range highlighted

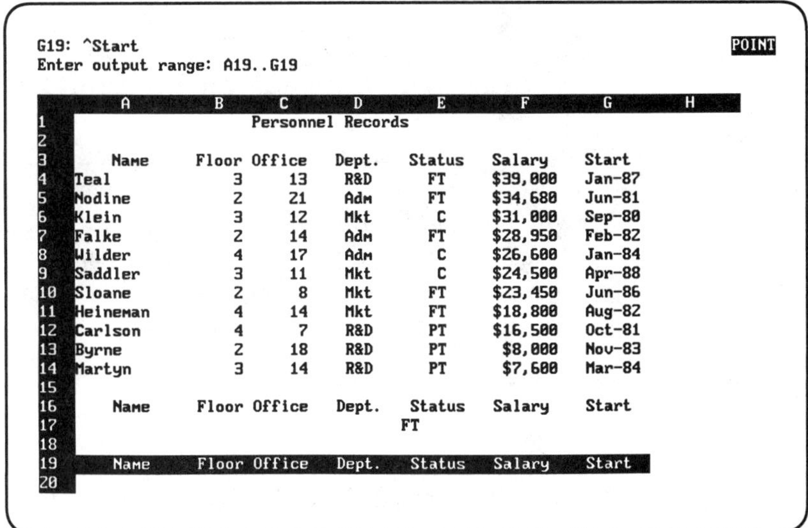

G19: ^Start
Enter output range: A19..G19
POINT

	A	B	C	D	E	F	G	H
1			Personnel Records					
2								
3	Name	Floor	Office	Dept.	Status	Salary	Start	
4	Teal	3	13	R&D	FT	$39,000	Jan-87	
5	Nodine	2	21	Adm	FT	$34,680	Jun-81	
6	Klein	3	12	Mkt	C	$31,000	Sep-80	
7	Falke	2	14	Adm	FT	$28,950	Feb-82	
8	Wilder	4	17	Adm	C	$26,600	Jan-84	
9	Saddler	3	11	Mkt	C	$24,500	Apr-88	
10	Sloane	2	8	Mkt	FT	$23,450	Jun-86	
11	Heineman	4	14	Mkt	FT	$18,800	Aug-82	
12	Carlson	4	7	R&D	PT	$16,500	Oct-81	
13	Byrne	2	18	R&D	PT	$8,000	Nov-83	
14	Martyn	3	14	R&D	PT	$7,600	Mar-84	
15								
16	Name	Floor	Office	Dept.	Status	Salary	Start	
17					FT			
18								
19	Name	Floor	Office	Dept.	Status	Salary	Start	
20								

Press: ↵

Extracting the Information

Now that you have set up the input range, the criteria range, and the output range, you can use the **Data Query Extract** command once you have established the criteria. The last criterion you specified was full-time personnel. Use that criterion again.

Figure 5.43 Query settings sheet

```
A19: [W12] ^Name                                                          MENU
Input  Criteria  Output  Find  Extract  Unique  Delete  Reset  Quit
Specify the range to which extracted records are copied
                          Query Settings
   Input range:        A3..G14

   Criteria range:     A16..G17

   Output range:       A19..G19

7  Falke           2    14   Adm     FT   $28,950   Feb-82
8  Wilder          4    17   Adm     C    $26,600   Jan-84
9  Saddler         3    11   Mkt     C    $24,500   Apr-88
10 Sloane          2     8   Mkt     FT   $23,450   Jun-86
11 Heineman        4    14   Mkt     FT   $18,800   Aug-82
12 Carlson         4     7   R&D     PT   $16,500   Oct-81
13 Byrne           2    18   R&D     PT    $8,000   Nov-83
14 Martyn          3    14   R&D     PT    $7,600   Mar-84
15
16     Name      Floor Office  Dept.  Status  Salary   Start
17                                    FT
18
19     Name      Floor Office  Dept.  Status  Salary   Start
20
```

When you used **/Data Query Find** in the last section, 1-2-3 moved to and highlighted the data records of personnel working full-time. When you use **/Data Query Extract**, 1-2-3 will find those same records and then copy them to the output range.

Select: Extract
Quit

After you select Extract, a number of records appear directly below the output range. They all contain FT in the Status field. Use the Down key to scroll the worksheet down and look at all the extracted records.

Figure 5.44
Extracted records

```
A25: [W12]                                                        READY

     A            B     C      D       E        F         G        H
6   Klein         3    12     Mkt      C     $31,000    Sep-80
7   Falke         2    14     Adm      FT    $28,950    Feb-82
8   Wilder        4    17     Adm      C     $26,600    Jan-84
9   Saddler       3    11     Mkt      C     $24,500    Apr-88
10  Sloane        2     8     Mkt      FT    $23,450    Jun-86
11  Heineman      4    14     Mkt      FT    $18,800    Aug-82
12  Carlson       4     7     R&D      PT    $16,500    Oct-81
13  Byrne         2    18     R&D      PT     $8,000    Nov-83
14  Martyn        3    14     R&D      PT     $7,600    Mar-84
15
16      Name     Floor Office  Dept.  Status  Salary    Start
17                                     FT
18
19      Name     Floor Office  Dept.  Status  Salary    Start
20  Teal          3    13     R&D      FT    $39,000    Jan-87
21  Nodine        2    21     Adm      FT    $34,680    Jun-81
22  Falke         2    14     Adm      FT    $28,950    Feb-82
23  Sloane        2     8     Mkt      FT    $23,450    Jun-86
24  Heineman      4    14     Mkt      FT    $18,800    Aug-82
25
                     UNDO
```

Using a Formula as Criterion

Now try extracting the data records of those personnel who work full-time and earn over $20,000. This selection requires two criteria. The first, the word FT in the Status field, is already set up. The second, specifying a salary over $20,000, must be in the form of a formula.

When creating a formula criterion, keep the following in mind: (1) write the formula as a test of the first record (second row) of the database; and (2) when specifying a cell address that refers to a database field, use a relative cell address; when specifying a cell address that refers to a value outside the database, use an absolute cell address.

You are going to enter a formula in the salary field of the criteria range (cell F17). The formula refers to cell F4 (the salary entry in the first record) and uses a relative reference: +F4>20000. This means that if the value in cell F4 is greater than 20,000, 1-2-3 should include it.

Move to: cell F17
Type: **+F4>20000** [↵] (don't forget the + sign to indicate a formula)

Figure 5.45
Formula entered

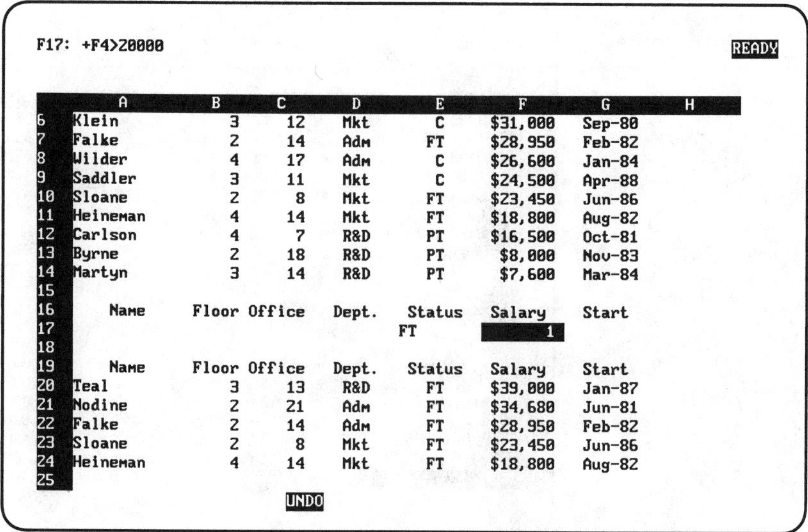

F17: +F4>20000 READY

	A	B	C	D	E	F	G	H
6	Klein	3	12	Mkt	C	$31,000	Sep-80	
7	Falke	2	14	Adm	FT	$28,950	Feb-82	
8	Wilder	4	17	Adm	C	$26,600	Jan-84	
9	Saddler	3	11	Mkt	C	$24,500	Apr-88	
10	Sloane	2	8	Mkt	FT	$23,450	Jun-86	
11	Heineman	4	14	Mkt	FT	$18,800	Aug-82	
12	Carlson	4	7	R&D	PT	$16,500	Oct-81	
13	Byrne	2	18	R&D	PT	$8,000	Nov-83	
14	Martyn	3	14	R&D	PT	$7,600	Mar-84	
15								
16	Name	Floor	Office	Dept.	Status	Salary	Start	
17					FT	1		
18								
19	Name	Floor	Office	Dept.	Status	Salary	Start	
20	Teal	3	13	R&D	FT	$39,000	Jan-87	
21	Nodine	2	21	Adm	FT	$34,680	Jun-81	
22	Falke	2	14	Adm	FT	$28,950	Feb-82	
23	Sloane	2	8	Mkt	FT	$23,450	Jun-86	
24	Heineman	4	14	Mkt	FT	$18,800	Aug-82	
25								

UNDO

The value 1 appears in the cell in the criteria range. This means that the value in the cell in the formula fulfills the condition. If it did not, the cell in the criteria range would display 0. Now use these criteria for the extraction.

Press: /
Select: Data
Query
Extract
Quit

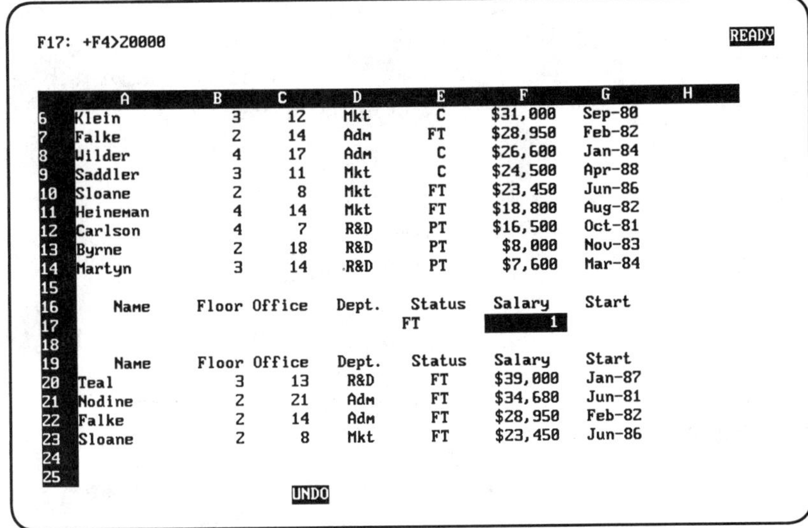

F17: +F4>20000 READY

	A	B	C	D	E	F	G	H
6	Klein	3	12	Mkt	C	$31,000	Sep-80	
7	Falke	2	14	Adm	FT	$28,950	Feb-82	
8	Wilder	4	17	Adm	C	$26,600	Jan-84	
9	Saddler	3	11	Mkt	C	$24,500	Apr-88	
10	Sloane	2	8	Mkt	FT	$23,450	Jun-86	
11	Heineman	4	14	Mkt	FT	$18,800	Aug-82	
12	Carlson	4	7	R&D	PT	$16,500	Oct-81	
13	Byrne	2	18	R&D	PT	$8,000	Nov-83	
14	Martyn	3	14	R&D	PT	$7,600	Mar-84	
15								
16	Name	Floor	Office	Dept.	Status	Salary	Start	
17					FT	1		
18								
19	Name	Floor	Office	Dept.	Status	Salary	Start	
20	Teal	3	13	R&D	FT	$39,000	Jan-87	
21	Nodine	2	21	Adm	FT	$34,680	Jun-81	
22	Falke	2	14	Adm	FT	$28,950	Feb-82	
23	Sloane	2	8	Mkt	FT	$23,450	Jun-86	
24								
25								

UNDO

Figure 5.46
Extract result

Notice that some of the records extracted in the previous query disappear. The records in the output range now match two criteria: they contain FT in the Status field and a value over $20,000 in the Salary field.

(2.2) REPLACING INFORMATION IN THE DATABASE

A database often contains repetitive information. A field such as Dept., for example, includes several instances of R&D. Let's suppose the company in the example you've been using reorganizes and decides that the R&D department should now be known as Engineering (Eng for short).

To save you from locating and changing each instance of R&D to Eng individually, 1-2-3 Release 2.2 has introduced the **Range Search** command that can both find the item you're looking for and (optionally) replace it with another item. In a large database, using **/Range Search** would save you a great deal of time, plus would ensure that you did in fact find every instance of a particular item. (You can also use **/Range Search** with a worksheet; the command lets you search for information in formulas, if you wish.)

You are going to search for all instances of R&D in column D of the database and replace each with Eng. When you select **/Range Search**, 1-2-3 prompts you for the range you wish to search. You will identify the Dept. field in the original database: D4..D14.

Move to: cell D4
Press: [/]
Select: Range
Search
Press: [.]
[END] [↓] highlight the range D4..D14

Figure 5.47 Search range highlighted

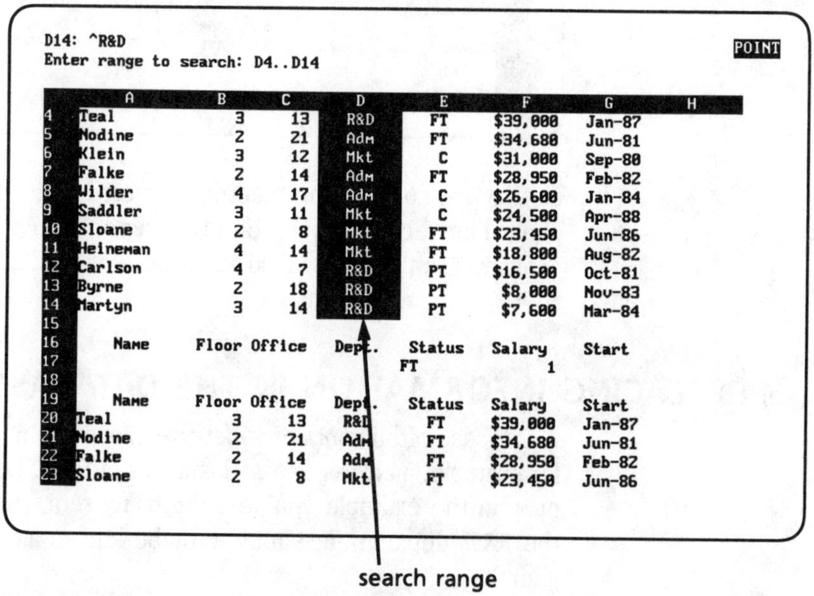

```
D14: ^R&D                                                          POINT
Enter range to search: D4..D14

     A              B      C      D      E        F         G        H
4   Teal            3     13    R&D     FT    $39,000   Jan-87
5   Nodine          2     21    Adm     FT    $34,680   Jun-81
6   Klein           3     12    Mkt     C     $31,000   Sep-80
7   Falke           2     14    Adm     FT    $28,950   Feb-82
8   Wilder          4     17    Adm     C     $26,600   Jan-84
9   Saddler         3     11    Mkt     C     $24,500   Apr-88
10  Sloane          2      8    Mkt     FT    $23,450   Jun-86
11  Heineman        4     14    Mkt     FT    $18,800   Aug-82
12  Carlson         4      7    R&D     PT    $16,500   Oct-81
13  Byrne           2     18    R&D     PT     $8,000   Nov-83
14  Martyn          3     14    R&D     PT     $7,600   Mar-84
15
16      Name      Floor Office  Dept.  Status  Salary    Start
17                                     FT           1
18
19      Name      Floor Office  Dept.  Status  Salary    Start
20  Teal            3     13    R&D     FT    $39,000   Jan-87
21  Nodine          2     21    Adm     FT    $34,680   Jun-81
22  Falke           2     14    Adm     FT    $28,950   Feb-82
23  Sloane          2      8    Mkt     FT    $23,450   Jun-86
```

search range

Press: [↵]

Next 1-2-3 asks for the string you want to search for. A **string** is simply text that can include both letters and numbers. The string you're looking for is R&D.

Type: R&D

Figure 5.48
Search string

```
D4: ^R&D                                                              EDIT
Enter string to search for: R&D

       A             B     C      D       E        F         G        H
4   Teal             3    13     R&D      FT    $39,000   Jan-87
5   Nodine           2    21     Adm      FT    $34,680   Jun-81
6   Klein            3    12     Mkt      C     $31,000   Sep-80
7   Falke            2    14     Adm      FT    $28,950   Feb-82
8   Wilder           4    17     Adm      C     $26,600   Jan-84
9   Saddler          3    11     Mkt      C     $24,500   Apr-88
10  Sloane           2     8     Mkt      FT    $23,450   Jun-86
11  Heineman         4    14     Mkt      FT    $18,800   Aug-82
12  Carlson          4     7     R&D      PT    $16,500   Oct-81
13  Byrne            2    18     R&D      PT     $8,000   Nov-83
14  Martyn           3    14     R&D      PT     $7,600   Mar-84
15
16      Name      Floor Office  Dept.   Status   Salary    Start
17                                     FT              1
18
19      Name      Floor Office  Dept.   Status   Salary    Start
20  Teal             3    13     R&D      FT    $39,000   Jan-87
21  Nodine           2    21     Adm      FT    $34,680   Jun-81
22  Falke            2    14     Adm      FT    $28,950   Feb-82
23  Sloane           2     8     Mkt      FT    $23,450   Jun-86
```

Press: ↵

1-2-3 gives you a choice of searching for labels, formulas, or both. In this case, you're searching for a label that you want to replace with another label, Eng. This second label is known as the **replacement string**.

Select: Labels
Replace

Type: Eng

Figure 5.49
Replacement string

```
D4: ^R&D                                                                  EDIT
Enter replacement string: Eng

        A          B      C      D        E         F          G          H
4   Teal           3     13     R&D       FT     $39,000    Jan-87
5   Nodine         2     21     Adm       FT     $34,680    Jun-81
6   Klein          3     12     Mkt       C      $31,000    Sep-80
7   Falke          2     14     Adm       FT     $28,950    Feb-82
8   Wilder         4     17     Adm       C      $26,600    Jan-84
9   Saddler        3     11     Mkt       C      $24,500    Apr-88
10  Sloane         2      8     Mkt       FT     $23,450    Jun-86
11  Heineman       4     14     Mkt       FT     $18,800    Aug-82
12  Carlson        4      7     R&D       PT     $16,500    Oct-81
13  Byrne          2     18     R&D       PT      $8,000    Nov-83
14  Martyn         3     14     R&D       PT      $7,600    Mar-84
15
16      Name       Floor Office  Dept.   Status   Salary     Start
17                                       FT             1
18
19      Name       Floor Office  Dept.   Status   Salary     Start
20  Teal           3     13     R&D       FT     $39,000    Jan-87
21  Nodine         2     21     Adm       FT     $34,680    Jun-81
22  Falke          2     14     Adm       FT     $28,950    Feb-82
23  Sloane         2      8     Mkt       FT     $23,450    Jun-86
```

Press: ↵

1–2–3 finds the first instance of R&D and offers four choices. If you select Replace, 1–2–3 replaces this instance of R&D with Eng and goes on to the next instance so you can decide again. If you select All, 1–2–3 replaces all instances of R&D with Eng without asking for confirmation. If you select Next, 1–2–3 doesn't replace the current instance and searches for the next. (This would allow you to leave R&D unchanged in some records if you wanted.) If you select Quit, 1–2–3 makes no further changes and returns to READY mode. In this case, you want every instance of R&D changed to Eng so you should select All:

Select: All

Figure 5.50
Database with Eng instead of R&D

D14: ^Eng READY

	A	B	C	D	E	F	G	H
4	Teal	3	13	Eng	FT	$39,000	Jan-87	
5	Nodine	2	21	Adm	FT	$34,680	Jun-81	
6	Klein	3	12	Mkt	C	$31,000	Sep-80	
7	Falke	2	14	Adm	FT	$28,950	Feb-82	
8	Wilder	4	17	Adm	C	$26,600	Jan-84	
9	Saddler	3	11	Mkt	C	$24,500	Apr-88	
10	Sloane	2	8	Mkt	FT	$23,450	Jun-86	
11	Heineman	4	14	Mkt	FT	$18,800	Aug-82	
12	Carlson	4	7	Eng	PT	$16,500	Oct-81	
13	Byrne	2	18	Eng	PT	$8,000	Nov-83	
14	Martyn	3	14	Eng	PT	$7,600	Mar-84	
15								
16	Name	Floor	Office	Dept.	Status	Salary	Start	
17					FT	1		
18								
19	Name	Floor	Office	Dept.	Status	Salary	Start	
20	Teal	3	13	R&D	FT	$39,000	Jan-87	
21	Nodine	2	21	Adm	FT	$34,680	Jun-81	
22	Falke	2	14	Adm	FT	$28,950	Feb-82	
23	Sloane	2	8	Mkt	FT	$23,450	Jun-86	

UNDO

The database now includes Eng instead of R&D in the Dept. field.

To correct the information in the output range (which still includes R&D in the Dept. field), use **/Data Query Extract** to repeat the extract on the corrected database.

SAVING THE FILE

Now that you have set up the various ranges and changed the name of one department, save the database again.

Press: [/]
Select: File
Save
Press: [↵]
Select: Replace

THE DATA COMMANDS

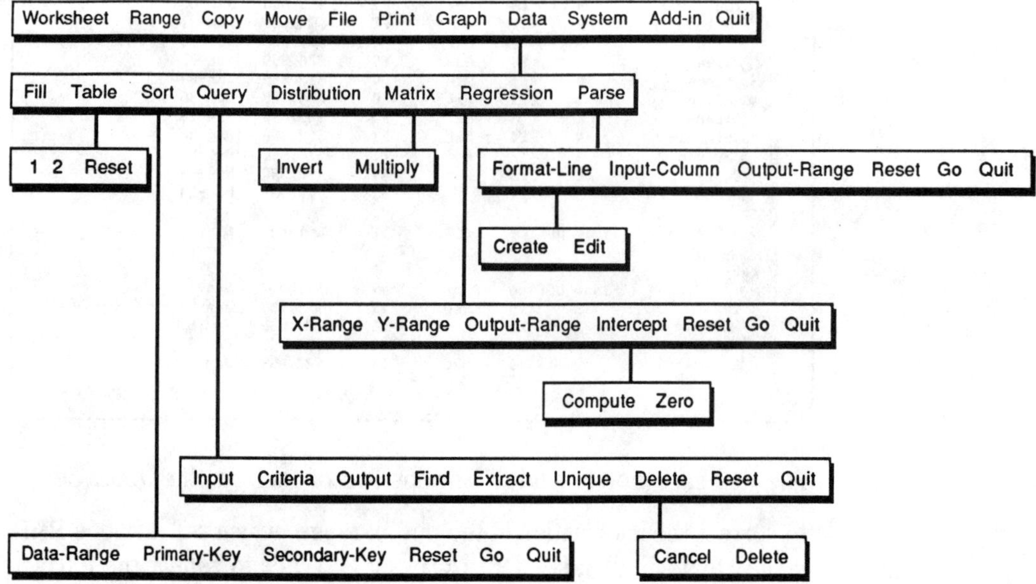

6

(2.2) Formatting and Printing with Allways

Financial reports and presentations frequently include spreadsheets as well as graphs that are based on spreadsheet data. To help you make your spreadsheets and graphs as visually effective as possible, 1-2-3 Release 2.2 includes a special program called Allways. Allways lets you format and print your 1-2-3 worksheets so they are of presentation quality.

Using Allways, you can:

- Use up to eight fonts in any printout
- Make text bold or underlined
- Shade areas of the worksheet
- Outline ranges or enclose cells in boxes
- Draw horizontal and vertical lines
- Adjust the height of rows and width of columns
- Include 1-2-3 graphs in the same printout as your worksheet.

Allways is a 1-2-3 **add-in**, which means it runs with the main 1-2-3 program. You can start Allways with a single keystroke, and return to 1-2-3 just as easily.

This chapter teaches you about:

- Starting Allways and returning to 1-2-3
- The Allways screen and menus
- Formatting a worksheet by changing fonts, adding boldface, underlining, and shading
- Including graphs in the worksheet and embellishing them
- Printing the formatted worksheet.

The exercises in this chapter use the income statement in the file named INCOME that you created in Chapter 3. They also include the bar graph in the file named BARGRAPH.PIC that you created in the Chapter 4. If you haven't gone through those chapters yet, do so now; you need to know how to create a worksheet and a graph to make use of Allways.

Before You Start

Allways requires a hard-disk system with a minimum of 512K of conventional memory. You cannot use Allways on a two-diskette system.

Allways has its own installation procedure during which you copy the Allways disks onto your hard disk and tell Allways what kind of printer and screen display you have. Be sure you go through this procedure as described in *Setting Up 1-2-3* before you try the exercises in this chapter.

Before you start:

- Allways must be installed and copied onto your hard disk
- 1-2-3 should be set up to save files in a subdirectory named TEMP
- All the 1-2-3 disks should be copied in their own subdirectory on the hard disk.

STARTING ALLWAYS

Starting Allways involves two steps: attaching and invoking. **Attaching** is the process of loading Allways into memory so it's ready to be used. **Invoking** is the process of activating Allways once it is attached so you can use the Allways commands to format and print your worksheet. You both attach and invoke Allways by using the 1-2-3 Add-In commands. These commands are new to 1-2-3 Release 2.2 and make it easy to run add-in programs (like Allways) right from 1-2-3. (All of the Add-In commands are described in Appendix A.)

Before starting Allways, you are going to retrieve INCOME, the file you'll format and print with Allways.

Press: /
Select: File
Retrieve
INCOME.WK1
Press: ↵

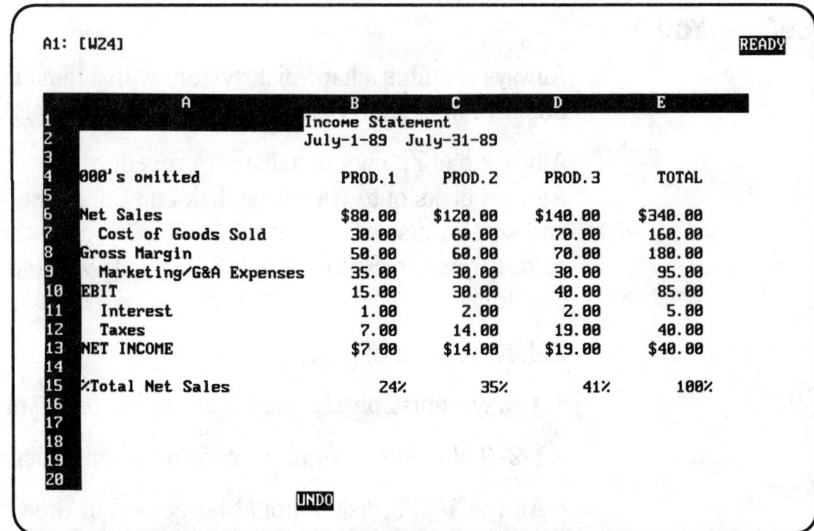
A1: [W24] READY

	A	B	C	D	E
1		Income Statement			
2		July-1-89	July-31-89		
3					
4	000's omitted	PROD.1	PROD.2	PROD.3	TOTAL
5					
6	Net Sales	$80.00	$120.00	$140.00	$340.00
7	Cost of Goods Sold	30.00	60.00	70.00	160.00
8	Gross Margin	50.00	60.00	70.00	180.00
9	Marketing/G&A Expenses	35.00	30.00	30.00	95.00
10	EBIT	15.00	30.00	40.00	85.00
11	Interest	1.00	2.00	2.00	5.00
12	Taxes	7.00	14.00	19.00	40.00
13	NET INCOME	$7.00	$14.00	$19.00	$40.00
14					
15	%Total Net Sales	24%	35%	41%	100%
16					
17					
18					
19					
20					

UNDO

Figure 6.1
Income statement

Attaching Allways

Before you can use Allways, you must attach or load it into your computer's memory. When you attach Allways, you will be asked to assign it to a function key or to select No-Key. Appl (Alt-F7), App2 (Alt-F8), App3 (Alt-F9), and App4 (Alt-F10) are all keys you can use to invoke add-in programs (like Allways) while you are working in 1-2-3.

If you select No-Key, you will not be able to invoke Allways with a function key. You will, however, be able to activate Allways using **/Add-In Invoke**.

Press: /
Select: Add-In
Attach

Figure 6.2
Attaching Allways

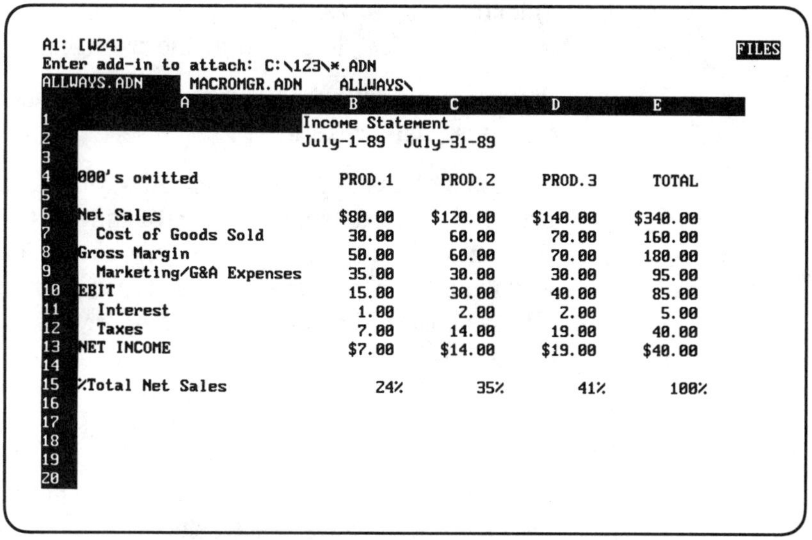

```
A1: [W24]                                                        FILES
Enter add-in to attach: C:\123\*.ADN
ALLWAYS.ADN    MACROMGR.ADN    ALLWAYS\
                A                B         C         D         E
1                              Income Statement
2                              July-1-89  July-31-89
3
4   000's omitted                PROD.1    PROD.2    PROD.3     TOTAL
5
6   Net Sales                    $80.00   $120.00   $140.00   $340.00
7     Cost of Goods Sold          30.00     60.00     70.00    160.00
8   Gross Margin                  50.00     60.00     70.00    180.00
9     Marketing/G&A Expenses      35.00     30.00     30.00     95.00
10  EBIT                          15.00     30.00     40.00     85.00
11    Interest                     1.00      2.00      2.00      5.00
12    Taxes                        7.00     14.00     19.00     40.00
13  NET INCOME                    $7.00    $14.00    $19.00    $40.00
14
15  %Total Net Sales                24%       35%       41%      100%
16
17
18
19
20
```

Select: ALLWAYS.ADN

You are going to assign Allways to Appl (Alt-F7). (If by any chance you've already assigned another add-in to this key, choose one of the other function keys for Allways.)

Figure 6.3
Selecting a function key for Allways

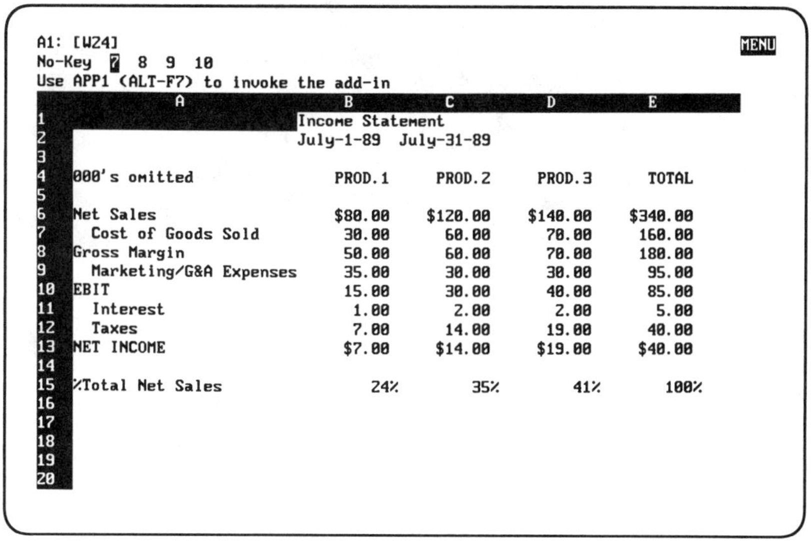

```
A1: [W24]                                                        MENU
No-Key  7  8  9  10
Use APP1 (ALT-F7) to invoke the add-in
                A                B         C         D         E
1                              Income Statement
2                              July-1-89  July-31-89
3
4   000's omitted                PROD.1    PROD.2    PROD.3     TOTAL
5
6   Net Sales                    $80.00   $120.00   $140.00   $340.00
7     Cost of Goods Sold          30.00     60.00     70.00    160.00
8   Gross Margin                  50.00     60.00     70.00    180.00
9     Marketing/G&A Expenses      35.00     30.00     30.00     95.00
10  EBIT                          15.00     30.00     40.00     85.00
11    Interest                     1.00      2.00      2.00      5.00
12    Taxes                        7.00     14.00     19.00     40.00
13  NET INCOME                    $7.00    $14.00    $19.00    $40.00
14
15  %Total Net Sales                24%       35%       41%      100%
16
17
18
19
20
```

Select: 7 to assign Allways to Appl (Alt-F7)
Quit to return to the worksheet

Allways is now attached, or in memory. To use the add-in, however, you must still invoke it.

You can also ask 1–2–3 to attach Allways automatically whenever you start 1–2–3. To do so, use the **Worksheet Global Default Other Add-In** command and specify Allways as an add-in to attach automatically. You must then update the 1–2–3 configuration file with **/Worksheet Global Default Update** so that Allways is attached at the start of every 1–2–3 session.

Invoking Allways

Whenever you want to use Allways, you must invoke it. You can do this in one of two ways. If you selected a function key when you attached Allways, you just press that key. For example, you chose 7 so you would press Appl (Alt-F7) to invoke Allways.

If you selected No-Key when attaching Allways, you select **/Add-In Invoke** and then select ALLWAYS from the menu of attached add-ins that appears.

Press: [APP1] (Alt-F7)

Allways is now activated, and you should see some changes on the screen.

THE ALLWAYS SCREEN

Figure 6.4
Allways screen

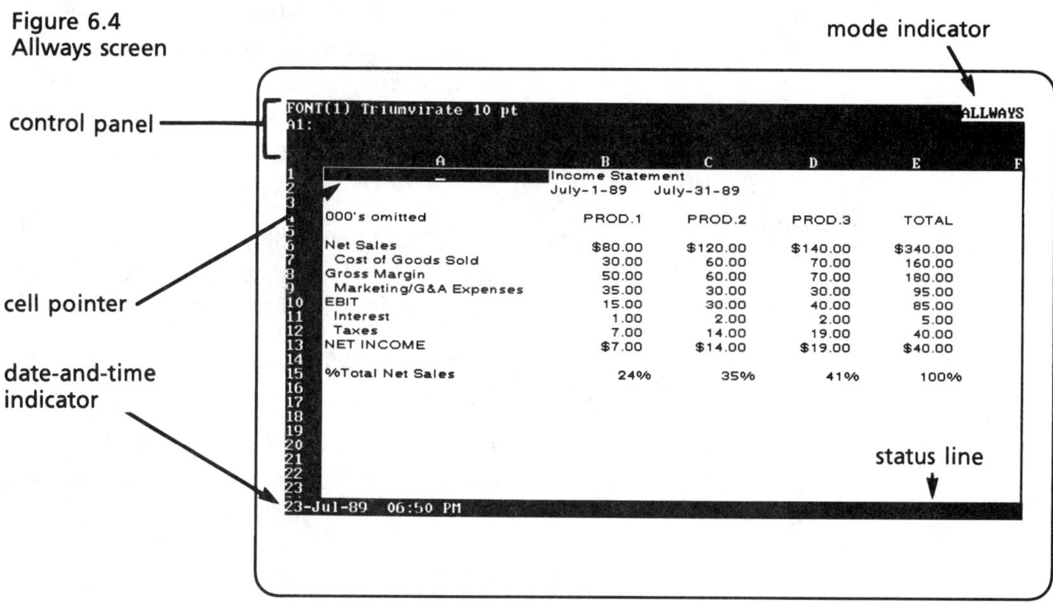

The Allways screen will remind you of 1–2–3. Just as in 1–2–3, the screen is divided into three areas: the worksheet area, the control panel, and the status line. If you have a graphics monitor, your screen should look something like Figure 6.4. If you have a text monitor, your screen will look very much like a 1–2–3 screen except the mode indicator will read ALLWAYS instead of READY and the control panel will include information about the format of the current cell.

> NOTE: The illustrations in this chapter all show the worksheet as it appears on a graphics monitor.

The **worksheet area** is where you will see formatting changes to your worksheet. Just as in 1–2–3, you see row numbers in the left border of the worksheet and column letters in the top border. The current cell is identified by the cell pointer.

The **control panel** displays information about what Allways is doing. It contains three lines of information about the current cell or about Allways commands.

The first line of the control panel displays the format of the current cell, for example, Font (1) Triumvirate 10 pt. At the far right of the control panel, Allways displays the mode indicator. When you invoke Allways, you are in ALLWAYS mode (which is equivalent to 1–2–3 READY mode); you can move about the worksheet freely with the pointer-movement keys. As you perform different operations, the mode could be MENU, POINT, WAIT, and so on.

The second line of the control panel shows the address and contents of the current cell. When you press / (slash) to display the Allways menu, however, the menu appears in the second line.

The third line of the control panel displays information about the command highlighted by the menu pointer.

The status line is the last line of the screen. Allways uses the status line to display the date-and-time indicator and status indicators that appear when you use certain keys (such as CAPS LOCK or NUM LOCK).

THE ALLWAYS MENU

Just as in 1–2–3, pressing / (slash) displays the main menu of Allways commands.

Figure 6.5 Allways main menu

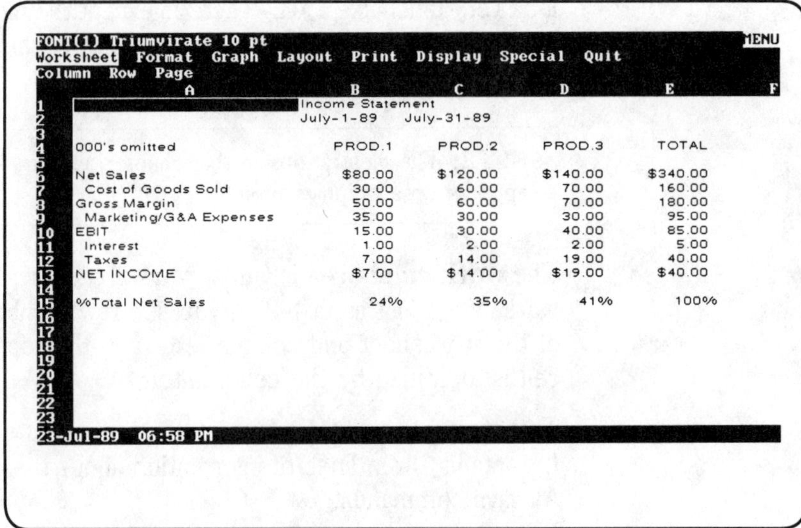

Notice that the mode indicator now reads MENU. Move the pointer along the list of commands and look at the different descriptions.

You select a command the same way as in 1-2-3: either highlight the command by moving the pointer to it and pressing Enter or type the first letter of the command. To complete a command, Allways may require you to select a further command from a submenu, respond to a prompt (such as a prompt for a range), or select an item from a list. You will learn how to select from a list as you try particular commands later in this chapter.

To leave an Allways menu, press Esc.

ALLWAYS FUNCTION KEYS

Allways uses some of the function keys that you use in 1-2-3, plus some additional ones. The keys are as follows:

DISPLAY (F6)	Switches screen between graphics mode and text mode.
ENLARGE (Alt-F4)	Enlarges the display of the worksheet.
GOTO (F5)	Moves the cell pointer to a cell or named range you specify.
GRAPH (F10)	Displays graphs on the screen or displays cross-hatched boxes in their place.
HELP (F1)	Displays an Allways Help screen.
NAME (F3)	In POINT mode, displays a menu of named ranges in the worksheet.
REDUCE (F4)	Reduces the display of the worksheet.

GETTING HELP

Allways includes a series of Help screens that you can view anytime while using Allways by pressing Help (F1). When you press Help (F1), Allways displays a Help screen that describes what you are currently doing.

The Allways Help system works just like the 1–2–3 Help system: each Help screen includes additional Help topics. Use the pointer-movement keys to highlight the topic about which you want additional help and press Enter. To return to Allways, press Esc.

RETURNING TO 1–2–3

During a typical session with Allways, you may find yourself going back and forth between Allways and 1–2–3. You will continue to use 1–2–3 for most worksheet operations. For example, you will use 1–2–3 to enter or edit data, or to move, copy, or erase it. Likewise, if you want to change the format of numbers or the alignment of labels, you will use **/Range Format** and **/Range Label**, respectively.

You are now going to return to 1–2–3 to make a few changes before starting to format the income statement with Allways.

Press: ESC

> NOTE: You can also return to 1–2–3 by pressing the same function key that you used to invoke Allways, for example, Appl (Alt-F7), or pressing / (slash) to bring up the Allways menu and selecting Quit.

Although you are no longer using it, Allways remains attached (in memory) until you end the 1–2–3 session or select **/Add-In Detach** or **/Add-In Clear** in 1–2–3. (For more information about /Add-In commands, see Appendix A.) As long as Allways is attached, you can invoke it at any point.

Turning Off Undo

The undo feature, which you learned about in Chapter 2, is automatically enabled (on) when you start 1–2–3. Unless you have expanded memory (additional memory for which you've purchased both hardware and software), however, you should turn off the undo feature before using Allways. (You can quickly check to see if you have expanded memory by selecting **/Worksheet Status**. If the entry next to Expanded Memory reads (None), you have no expanded memory.) Together, undo and Allways use a lot of memory so you can quickly start to run out.

To turn off, or disable, undo:

Press: [/]
Select: Worksheet
Global
Default
Other
Undo
Disable
Quit

After you finish working with Allways and are ready to work in 1-2-3, you can turn on, or enable, undo by going through the above steps and selecting Enable instead of Disable. Because of the way 1-2-3 uses memory, enable undo before retrieving a file, however.

Adding Rows and Columns

To make the income statement easier to read, you are going to add some white space above and to the left of it. You will do so by inserting two rows above the title and one column to the left of the labels currently in column A. When you insert a row or column, existing data shifts either down or to the right. First insert two rows at the top of the worksheet.

Move to: cell A1
Press: [/]
Select: Worksheet
Insert
Row
Press: [↓] to highlight rows 1 and 2

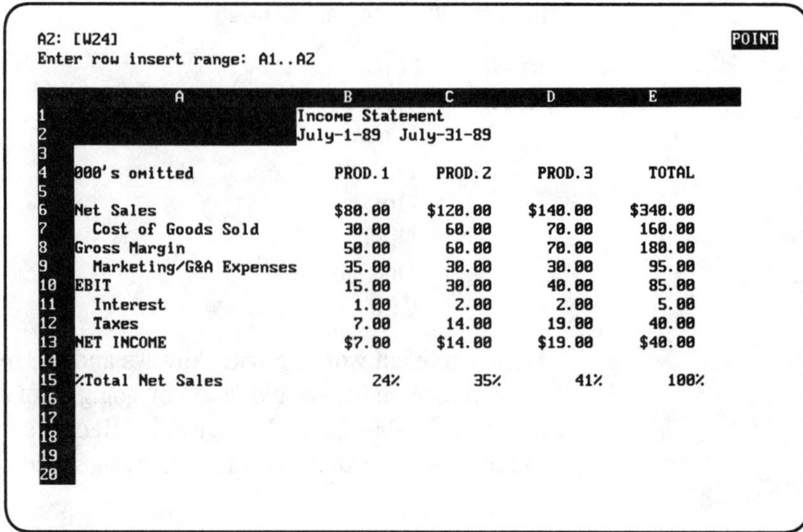

A2: [W24] POINT
Enter row insert range: A1..A2

	A	B	C	D	E
1		Income Statement			
2		July-1-89	July-31-89		
3					
4	000's omitted	PROD.1	PROD.2	PROD.3	TOTAL
5					
6	Net Sales	$80.00	$120.00	$140.00	$340.00
7	Cost of Goods Sold	30.00	60.00	70.00	160.00
8	Gross Margin	50.00	60.00	70.00	180.00
9	Marketing/G&A Expenses	35.00	30.00	30.00	95.00
10	EBIT	15.00	30.00	40.00	85.00
11	Interest	1.00	2.00	2.00	5.00
12	Taxes	7.00	14.00	19.00	40.00
13	NET INCOME	$7.00	$14.00	$19.00	$40.00
14					
15	%Total Net Sales	24%	35%	41%	100%
16					
17					
18					
19					
20					

Figure 6.6
Inserting two rows

Press: ↵

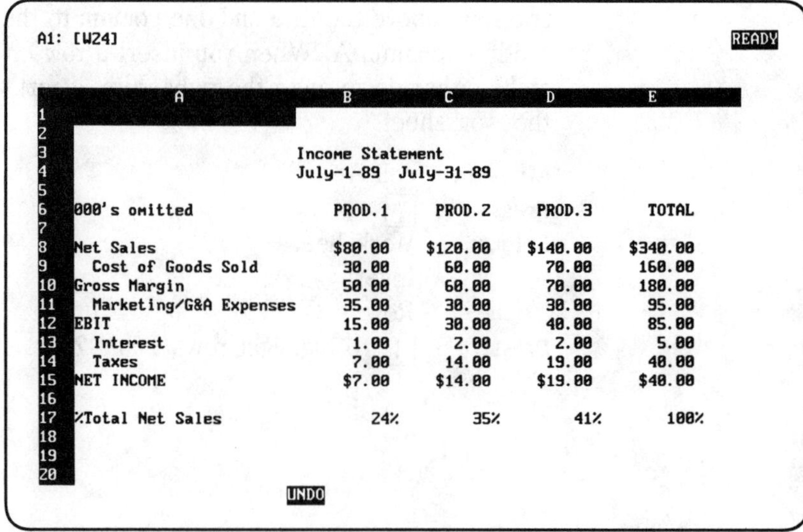

A1: [W24] READY

	A	B	C	D	E
1					
2					
3		Income Statement			
4		July-1-89	July-31-89		
5					
6	000's omitted	PROD.1	PROD.2	PROD.3	TOTAL
7					
8	Net Sales	$80.00	$120.00	$140.00	$340.00
9	Cost of Goods Sold	30.00	60.00	70.00	160.00
10	Gross Margin	50.00	60.00	70.00	180.00
11	Marketing/G&A Expenses	35.00	30.00	30.00	95.00
12	EBIT	15.00	30.00	40.00	85.00
13	Interest	1.00	2.00	2.00	5.00
14	Taxes	7.00	14.00	19.00	40.00
15	NET INCOME	$7.00	$14.00	$19.00	$40.00
16					
17	%Total Net Sales	24%	35%	41%	100%
18					
19					
20					

UNDO

Figure 6.7 Two rows inserted

Now insert a blank column in column A.

Press: /
Select: Worksheet
Insert
Column
Press: ↵ to indicate column A

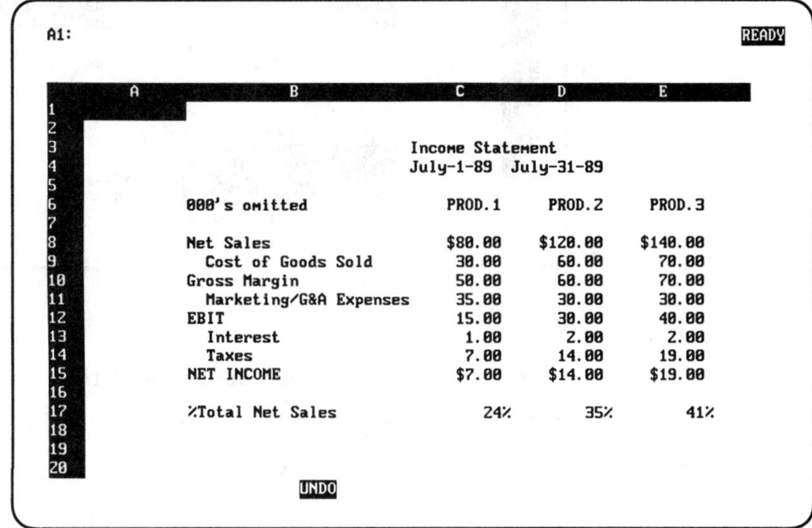

Figure 6.8
Inserted column

Erasing Data

In the worksheet chapter, you entered a short memo below the Income Statement. Because you just want to concentrate on formatting the spreadsheet itself, you're now going to erase this memo.

Move to: cell B21
Press: /
Select: Range
Erase
Press: ↓ four times

Figure 6.9
Erase range

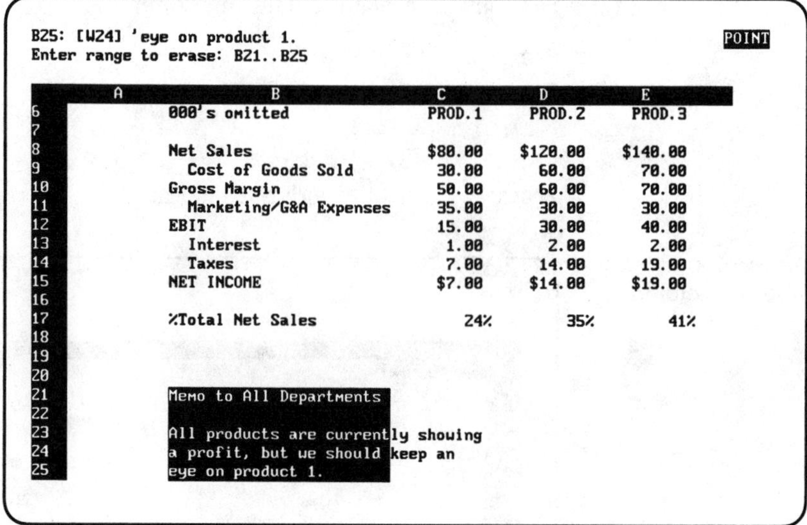

Press: ↵

To see the complete worksheet, move the cell pointer to F1.

Press: HOME
→ five times

Keeping Allways Attached

If your work involves switching between Allways and 1–2–3, keep Allways attached so that it can keep its formats synchronized with changes that you make to the worksheet with 1–2–3. This is especially important if you use 1–2–3 to move data or insert rows or columns. If Allways is not attached when you make these kinds of changes, the wrong cells will be formatted.

FORMATTING WITH ALLWAYS

You're already familiar with the process of formatting cells with 1–2–3 to change their appearance. For example, you know how to use **/Range Format** to display values as currency or percentages. You also know how to use the label prefixes (', ", and **^**) or **/Range Label** to center labels or line them up at the left or right edges of cells. Any formatting that you perform in 1-2-3 will carry through to Allways. For example, if you set a cell to Currency format with 0 decimal places, it will appear that way in Allways as well.

Allways offers a number of additional formats that you can apply to cells or ranges of cells in your worksheet. They include: fonts; boldface; underlining; text color; lines along the top, bottom left, or right edge of a cell; double-underlining; and light, dark, or solid black shade.

As you move the cell pointer from cell to cell, the format of the current cell appears in line 1 of the control panel.

You are now going to invoke Allways again and start formatting the income statement.

Press: APP1 (Alt-F7)

Figure 6.10 Worksheet in Allways

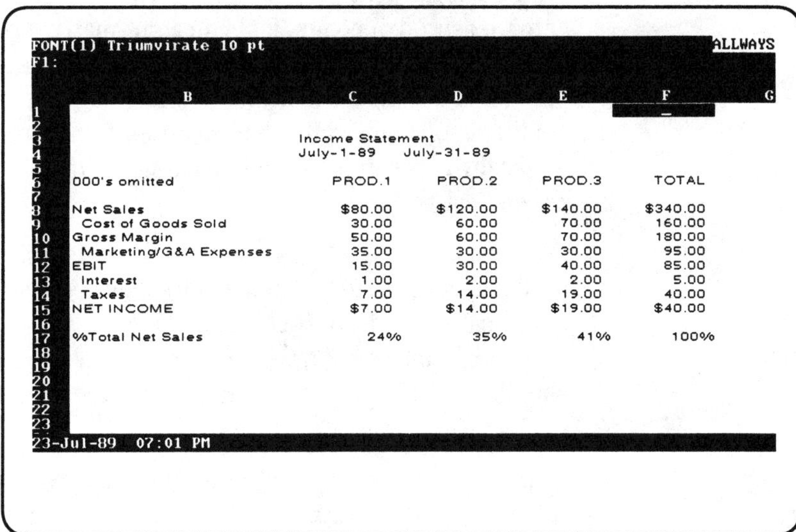

Notice that the changes you just made in 1-2-3 are reflected in Allways.

Changing Fonts

One of the first things you may want to change in the worksheet with Allways is the font used for data in the worksheet. A font has two elements: typeface and size.

The **typeface** is the overall design of the printed characters, and all the characters within the typeface share common design characteristics. Allways provides three typefaces for you to use: Courier, Times, and Triumvirate. Your printer will often provide additional typefaces such as Palatino or Pica.

The **size** of a font is normally measured in terms of the height of the typeface in points. A point is approximately $\frac{1}{72}$ of an inch. Times 12 point is a font whose characters are roughly $\frac{1}{6}$ of an inch high, whereas Times 24 point is a font that is twice as big, with characters roughly $\frac{1}{3}$ of an inch high.

As a general rule, you will use a 10- or 12-point font for normal text, a font between 14 and 24 points for headings, and a font between 5 and 8 points for fine print.

Although the fonts supplied with Allways and fonts on a laser printer are measured in points, fonts on a dot-matrix printer are usually measured in **pitch**, or characters per inch. Because fonts on a dot-matrix printer are all the same height (typically 10 points), their size is measured in terms of their width, which varies from font to font. Pitch choices typically range from 17 pitch (narrow) to 5 pitch (wide). Ten or 12 pitch is normal type.

Allways allows you to use up to eight fonts in any printout. Whenever you select a font to use in the worksheet, you select from a list of eight fonts called the **font set**. The fonts in the set are numbered 1 to 8, and each font consists of a typeface and a style. For example, Font 1 might be Times 10 point, Font 2 might be Times Italic 12 point, and so on.

When you first use Allways, the font set contains Times and Triumvirate typefaces in various point sizes, but you can replace any one (or all) of these fonts with a font supported by your printer. The particular selection of fonts in the font set is up to you, and it's easy to experiment with different combinations.

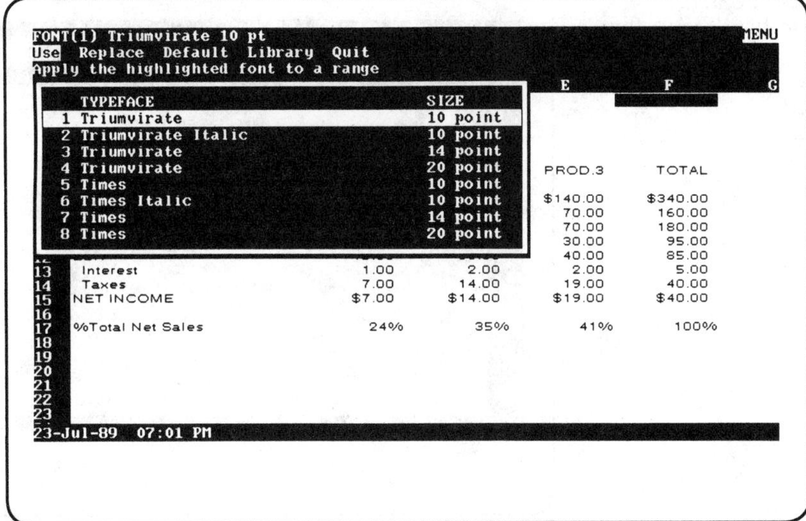

Figure 6.11
Initial font set

The font set makes it easy to make overall changes to the worksheet. Suppose you have set Font 5 to Times 12 point and have formatted a number of cells in that font. If you then decide you'd like Times 10 point instead, you don't have to reformat every cell individually. All you have to do is replace Font 5 with Times 10 point, and all the cells formatted in Font 5 change automatically from 12 to 10 point.

The fonts supplied by Allways are called **soft fonts** because they're provided through software and not built into your printer. Your printer can, however, reproduce them. To distinguish its soft fonts from the fonts your printer provides, Allways refers to your printer's fonts as **printer fonts**.

Changing the Default Font

The **default font** is the font that is used throughout the worksheet, except in cells that you explicitly format with another font. The default font is always Font 1 in the font set. Initially, Font 1 is set to Triumvirate 10 point, as you can see in the first line of the control panel. If Triumvirate 10 point is not to your liking, be sure to set Font 1 to a font that you will want to use for most of the text and data in the worksheet.

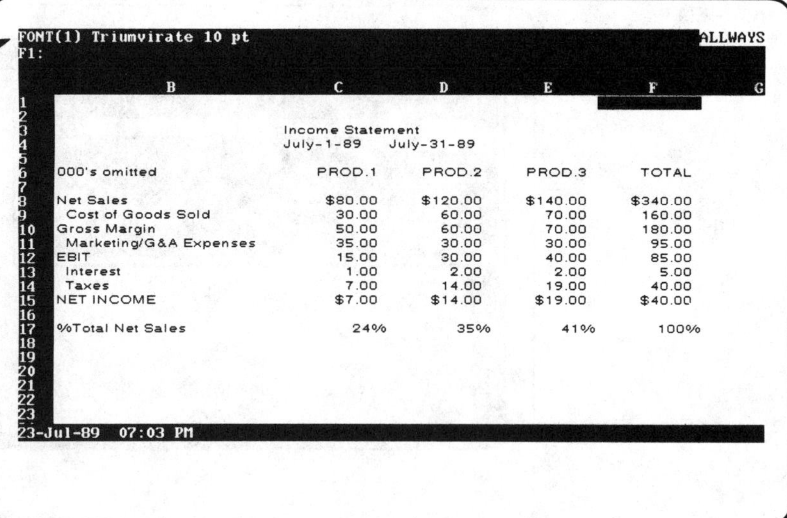

Figure 6.12
Initial default font

default font

You will now change the default font for the income statement to a different typeface (Times) and point size (12). Just as in 1–2–3, you call up the menu by pressing / (slash).

Press: /
Select: Format
Font

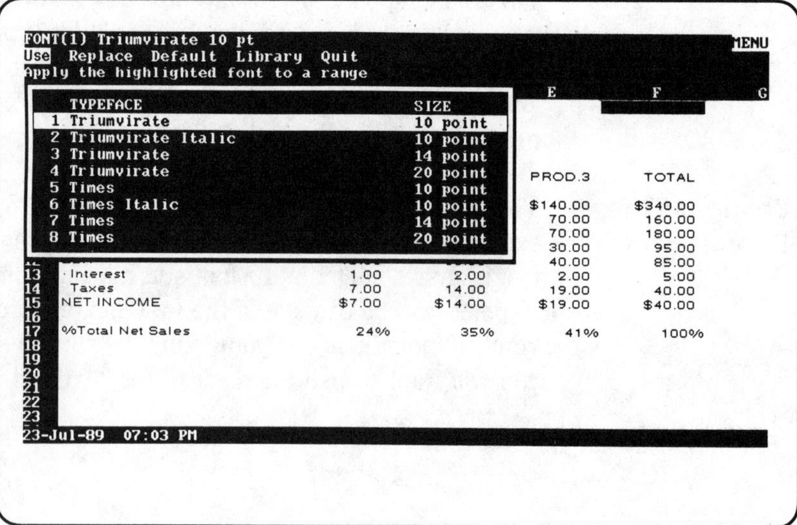

Figure 6.13
Font set

The font set appears on the screen and includes the fonts that Allways initially provides. The menu above the list of fonts allows you to work with the font set. Font 1 (the default font) should be highlighted; this is the font you will now replace.

Select: Replace

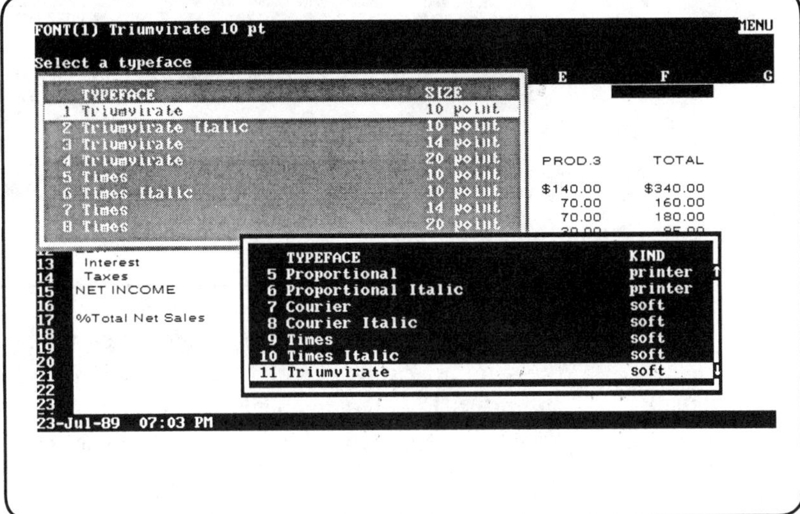

Figure 6.14 List of possible font replacements

The list of typefaces that now appears includes typefaces provided by Allways (identified by the word soft) and typefaces provided by your printer (identified by the word printer). The printer fonts that appear depend on the kind of printer you have, so the list that you see will differ from the illustration above.

You are going to choose one of the soft typefaces: Times. To select a typeface, you can either type the number next to it and press Enter, or highlight the typeface (by pressing Up or Down) and press Enter.

Select: Times

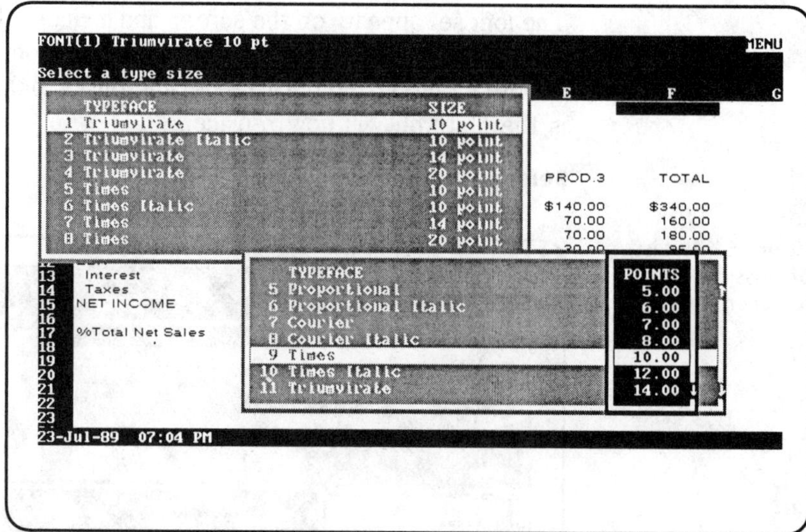

Figure 6.15 List of possible sizes

Allways displays a list of sizes from which to choose. You select a size the same way you select a typeface. Either type the number you want and press Enter, or highlight the size (using Up or Down) and press Enter. Because you want Times 12 point, you need to select 12.

Select: 12

Quit to see the change in the worksheet

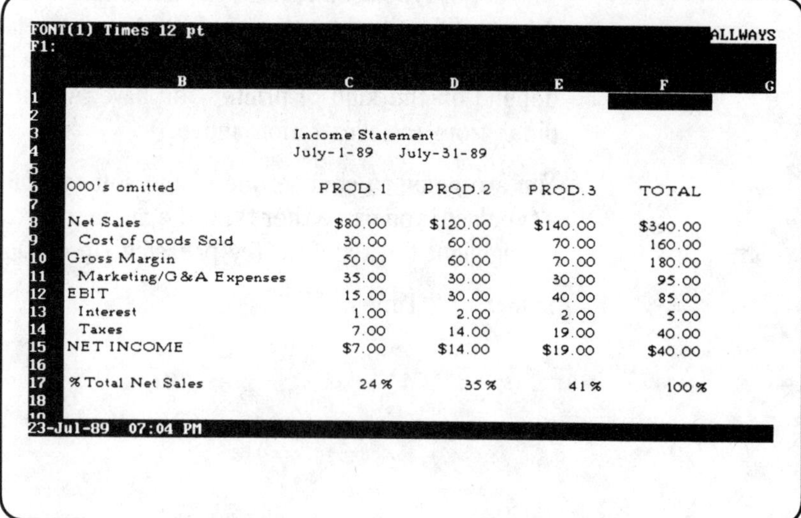

Figure 6.16 Worksheet in Times 12 point

Notice that the first line of the control panel now reads **Times 12 pt** and the Income Statement no longer all fits on the screen because of the larger characters.

Changing the Font for the Title and Dates

Now that you've changed the default font, you are going to change the font of some individual cells and ranges so they contrast with the rest of the worksheet.

If the font you want to use is in the font set, you simply tell Allways to use it in a particular cell or range. If it is not in the font set, you replace a font (other than Font 1) in the font set with the font you want to use. You follow the same procedure that you followed to change the default font.

To make the title of the spreadsheet stand out more, you are going to change its point size to 14, but keep the typeface as Times. Times 14 point happens to be in the font set, so you can just go ahead and use it.

Move to: cell C3
Press: /
Select: Format
Font

Times 14 point should be Font 7 in the font set. Highlight it by typing 7 or moving the pointer with Up or Down. Do not press Enter.

Type: 7

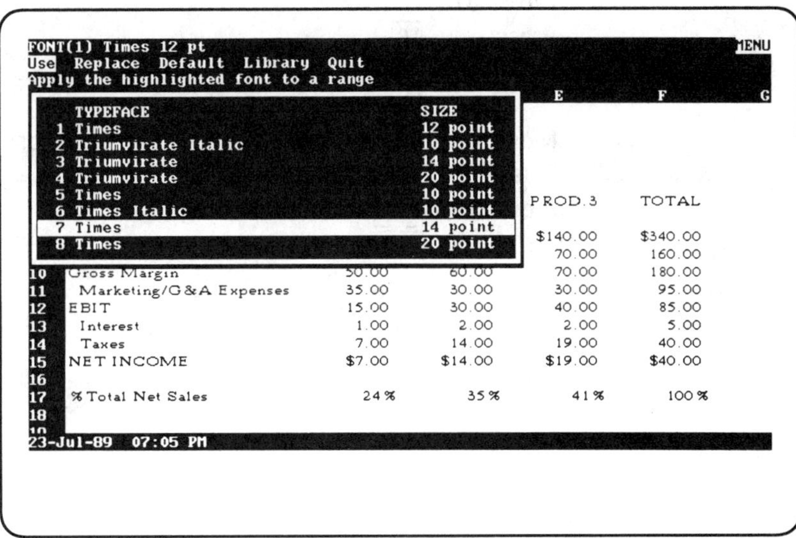

Figure 6.17 Times 14 highlighted

Select: Use

Press: [↵] to indicate C3 as the cell to change

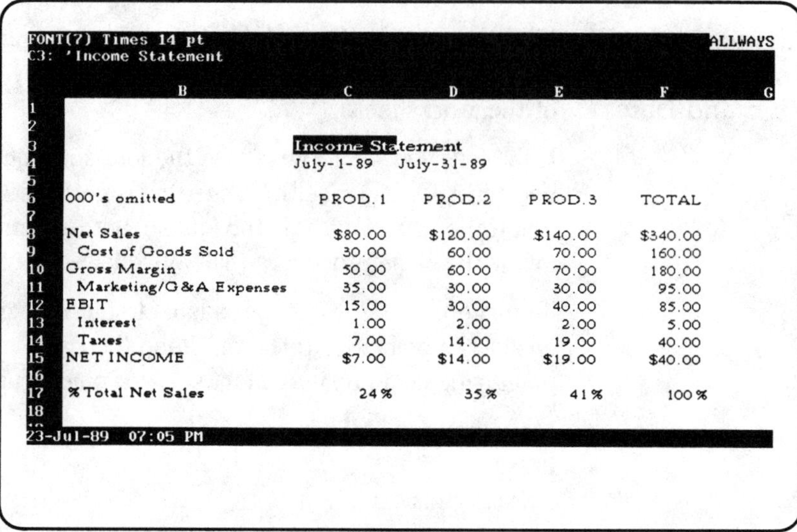

FONT(7) Times 14 pt
C3: 'Income Statement
ALLWAYS

	B	C	D	E	F
1					
2					
3		Income Statement			
4		July-1-89	July-31-89		
5					
6	000's omitted	PROD.1	PROD.2	PROD.3	TOTAL
7					
8	Net Sales	$80.00	$120.00	$140.00	$340.00
9	Cost of Goods Sold	30.00	60.00	70.00	160.00
10	Gross Margin	50.00	60.00	70.00	180.00
11	Marketing/G&A Expenses	35.00	30.00	30.00	95.00
12	EBIT	15.00	30.00	40.00	85.00
13	Interest	1.00	2.00	2.00	5.00
14	Taxes	7.00	14.00	19.00	40.00
15	NET INCOME	$7.00	$14.00	$19.00	$40.00
16					
17	% Total Net Sales	24%	35%	41%	100%
18					

23-Jul-89 07:05 PM

Figure 6.18 Title in Times 14 point

You want the dates below the title to look a little different, so you are going to format them in Times Italic 10 point. This font is also in the font set, so you can just use it.

Move to: cell C4

Press: [/]

Select: Format

Font

Move to: Times Italic 10 point. Do not press Enter

Select: Use

Press: [→] to indicate range C4..D4

[↵]

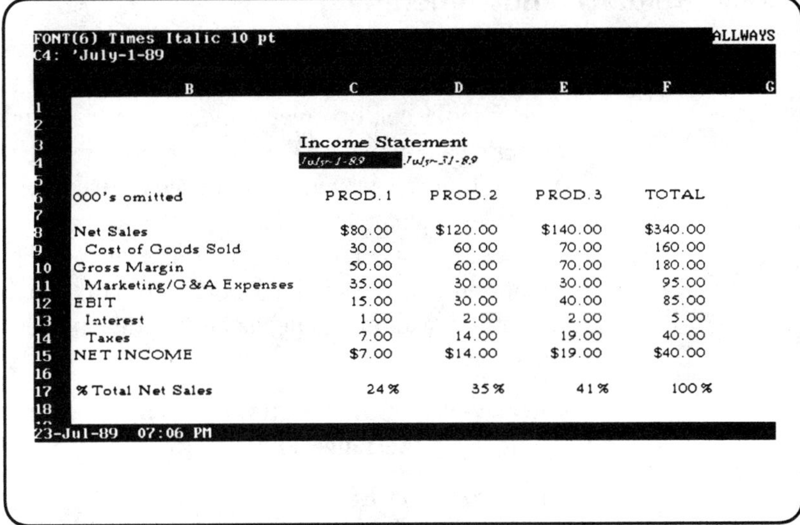

	B	C	D	E	F
3		Income Statement			
4		July-1-89	July-31-89		
6	000's omitted	PROD.1	PROD.2	PROD.3	TOTAL
8	Net Sales	$80.00	$120.00	$140.00	$340.00
9	Cost of Goods Sold	30.00	60.00	70.00	160.00
10	Gross Margin	50.00	60.00	70.00	180.00
11	Marketing/G&A Expenses	35.00	30.00	30.00	95.00
12	EBIT	15.00	30.00	40.00	85.00
13	Interest	1.00	2.00	2.00	5.00
14	Taxes	7.00	14.00	19.00	40.00
15	NET INCOME	$7.00	$14.00	$19.00	$40.00
17	% Total Net Sales	24%	35%	41%	100%

Figure 6.19 Dates in Times Italic 10 point

Saving the File

Having made these changes to the income statement, it's a good idea to save the worksheet now. You save the worksheet as usual in 1–2–3; when you do so, your Allways changes are also saved in a file that has the same name as your worksheet file, but a .ALL extension instead of .WK1.

When you retrieve the worksheet next time with the 1–2–3 **File Retrieve** command, you don't have to do anything special; once you attach and invoke Allways, your Allways formats will appear. (Remember to keep Allways attached as you change the worksheet with 1–2–3 so Allways can keep its formats synchronized with the changes you make.)

Return to 1–2–3 and save the worksheet.

Press: ESC
/
Select: File
Save
Press: ↵
Select: Replace

Adding Boldface and Underlining

You will now make the column titles stand out more by making them boldface and by double-underlining them. Up to now, you have been specifying a cell or range to format by responding to a prompt after selecting a command. This is the way you specify ranges in 1–2–3, too. With Allways, however, you have the choice of highlighting a range *before* you select a command. This is particularly useful if you want to perform a sequence of operations on the same range or if you just want to experiment and see the effects of different commands on the same range. The range will remain highlighted until you press Esc or move the cell pointer.

Because you want to do two things to the column titles, you are going to highlight the range first.

Move to: cell B6
Press: [.] to anchor the range
[END] [→] to highlight the range B6..F6

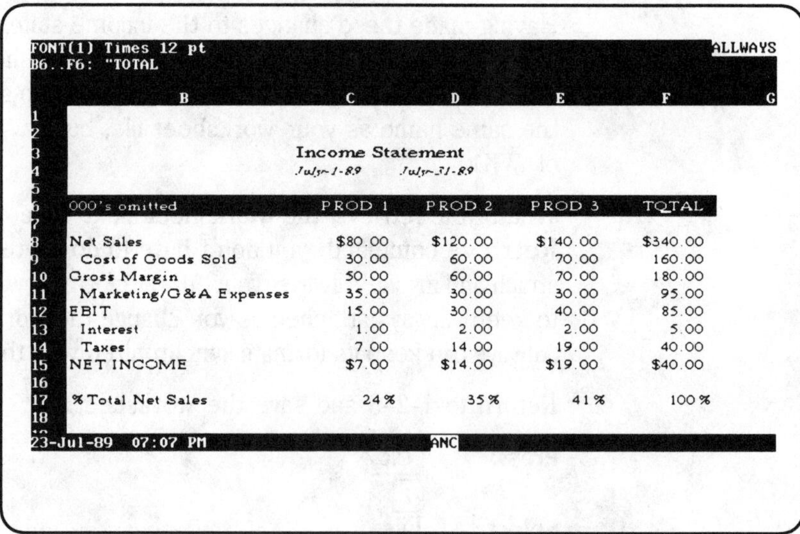

FONT(1) Times 12 pt ALLWAYS
B6..F6: "TOTAL

	B	C	D	E	F
1					
2					
3		Income Statement			
4		July-1-89	July-31-89		
5					
6	000's omitted	PROD 1	PROD 2	PROD 3	TOTAL
7					
8	Net Sales	$80.00	$120.00	$140.00	$340.00
9	Cost of Goods Sold	30.00	60.00	70.00	160.00
10	Gross Margin	50.00	60.00	70.00	180.00
11	Marketing/G&A Expenses	35.00	30.00	30.00	95.00
12	EBIT	15.00	30.00	40.00	85.00
13	Interest	1.00	2.00	2.00	5.00
14	Taxes	7.00	14.00	19.00	40.00
15	NET INCOME	$7.00	$14.00	$19.00	$40.00
16					
17	% Total Net Sales	24%	35%	41%	100%
18					

23-Jul-89 07:07 PM ANC

Figure 6.20 Range highlighted before command

Notice the ANC indicator at the bottom of the screen to remind you that the pointer is anchored and you have highlighted a range.

Press: [/]
Select: Format
Bold
Set

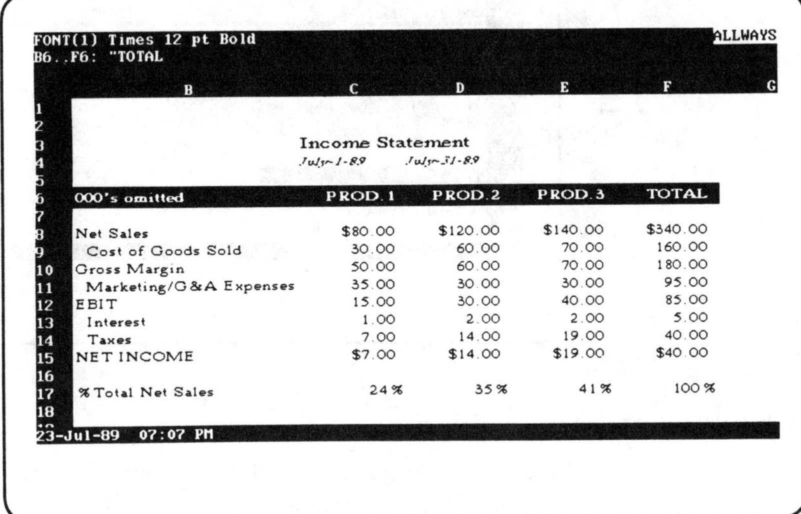
FONT(1) Times 12 pt Bold
B6..F6: "TOTAL
ALLWAYS

	B	C	D	E	F
1					
2					
3		Income Statement			
4		July-1-89	July-31-89		
5					
6	000's omitted	PROD.1	PROD.2	PROD.3	TOTAL
7					
8	Net Sales	$80.00	$120.00	$140.00	$340.00
9	Cost of Goods Sold	30.00	60.00	70.00	160.00
10	Gross Margin	50.00	60.00	70.00	180.00
11	Marketing/G&A Expenses	35.00	30.00	30.00	95.00
12	EBIT	15.00	30.00	40.00	85.00
13	Interest	1.00	2.00	2.00	5.00
14	Taxes	7.00	14.00	19.00	40.00
15	NET INCOME	$7.00	$14.00	$19.00	$40.00
16					
17	% Total Net Sales	24%	35%	41%	100%
18					

23-Jul-89 07:07 PM

Figure 6.21
Highlighted range now in bold

Notice that the range is now in boldface, but remains highlighted so you can perform another operation.

Press: [/]
Select: Format
Underline
Double
Move to: cell B15 where you will be doing more formatting

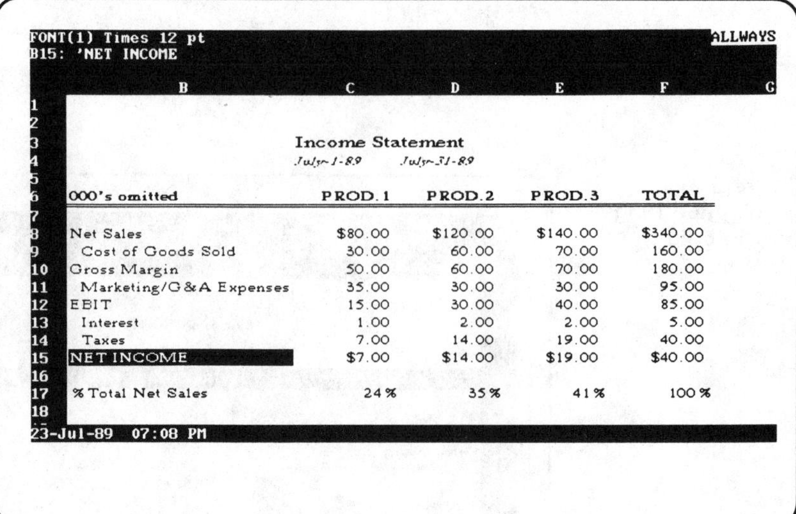

Figure 6.22
Boldface and double-underlining added

Adding Lines

Your are now going to add a horizontal line above and below the net income figures to make them stand out more. You add lines with the **Format Lines** command. When you add a line to the worksheet, you indicate which side of a cell or range you want to draw it on: left or right side for a vertical line and top or bottom side for a horizontal line. In this case, you need to add a line to both the top and bottom of row 15.

Because you'll be performing two operations (adding two lines) to the same range, you will highlight the range before selecting the commands. The cell pointer should be in cell B15.

Press: [.] to anchor the cell pointer
[END] [→] to highlight the net income figures
[/]

Select: Format
Lines
Top

Repeat the steps for the bottom line, but select Bottom:

Press: [/]
Select: Format
Lines
Bottom
Press: [ESC] to remove the highlight so you can see the lines

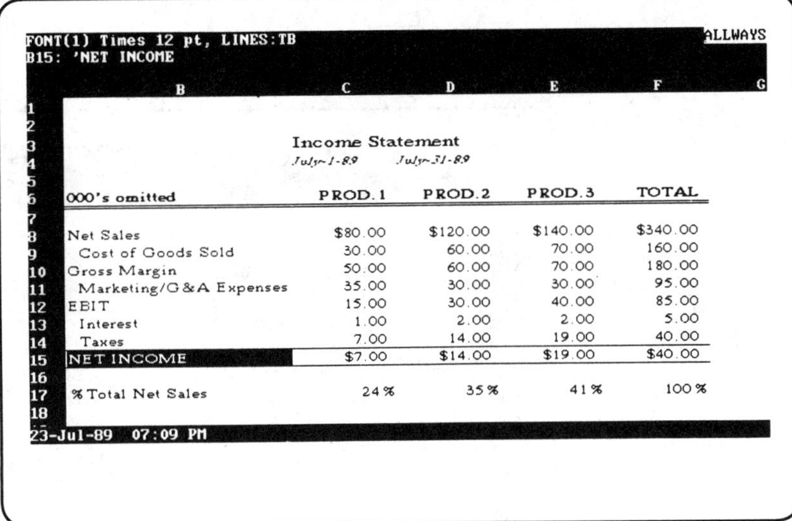

FONT(1) Times 12 pt, LINES:TB ALLWAYS
B15: 'NET INCOME

	B	C	D	E	F
1					
2					
3		Income Statement			
4					
5					
6	000's omitted	PROD.1	PROD.2	PROD.3	TOTAL
7					
8	Net Sales	$80.00	$120.00	$140.00	$340.00
9	Cost of Goods Sold	30.00	60.00	70.00	160.00
10	Gross Margin	50.00	60.00	70.00	180.00
11	Marketing/G&A Expenses	35.00	30.00	30.00	95.00
12	EBIT	15.00	30.00	40.00	85.00
13	Interest	1.00	2.00	2.00	5.00
14	Taxes	7.00	14.00	19.00	40.00
15	NET INCOME	$7.00	$14.00	$19.00	$40.00
16					
17	% Total Net Sales	24%	35%	41%	100%
18					

23-Jul-89 07:09 PM

Figure 6.23 Lines added above and below net income figures

Shading

You want to draw further attention to net income and net sales, so you are going to shade those rows lightly. You can either highlight the range first or wait for Allways to prompt you. This time you'll wait for the prompt.

Move to: cell B15
Press: [/]
Select: Format
Shade
Light
Press: [END] [→] highlight the range B15..F15
[↵]

Repeat the shading process for net sales.

Move to: cell B8
Press: /
Select: Format
Shade
Light
Press: END →
↵
↓ to see the shading better

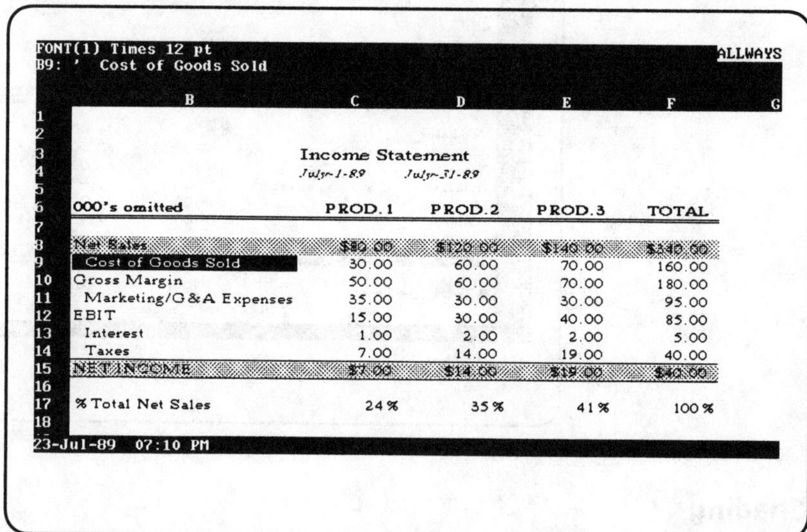

Figure 6.24
Shaded rows

Save the file again. This time, return to 1-2-3 through the Allways menu.

Press: /
Select: Quit
Press: /
Select: File
Save
Press: ↵
Select: Replace

INCLUDING GRAPHS

In Chapter 4, you learned how to create a graph in 1–2–3, save it in a graph (.PIC) file, and print it using the PrintGraph program. To print a graph with worksheet data, however, you would have to paste in the graph by hand.

With Allways, you can place graphs in the worksheet right alongside your spreadsheet data, view them on the screen together, and then print the worksheet and the graphs together.

The graphs that you use with Allways must be saved in .PIC files. You must create the graph in 1–2–3 and then save it with **/Graph Save** before you can use Allways to include it in the worksheet.

The bar graph you created in Chapter 4 contrasted net sales and net income, the same ranges you just shaded with Allways. You will place this graph (which you saved in a file named BARGRAPH.PIC) below the income statement to help emphasize the shaded ranges.

Adding a Graph to the Worksheet

When you add a graph to the worksheet, you must first have created the graph in 1–2–3 and used **/Graph Save** to save it in a graph (.PIC) file. During the process of adding the graph, Allways will ask you to specify a range for the graph. Once you do so, Allways will automatically size the graph so it fits within the range you specified.

You will now add the bar graph that you previously saved as BARGRAPH.PIC.

Move to: cell C21
Press: [/]
Select: Graph
Add
BARGRAPH.PIC
Press: [→] three times
[↓] eight times to highlight the range C21..F29

Figure 6.25
Range for graph

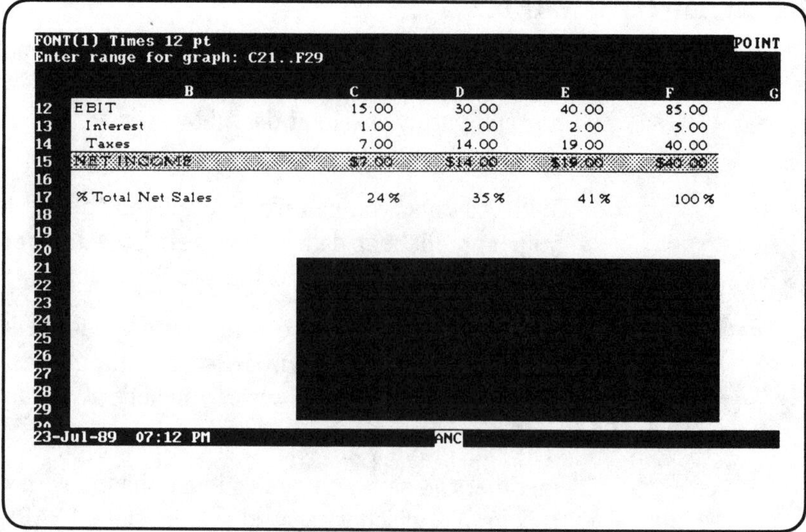

Press: ↵
Select: Quit

Figure 6.26
Graph on screen

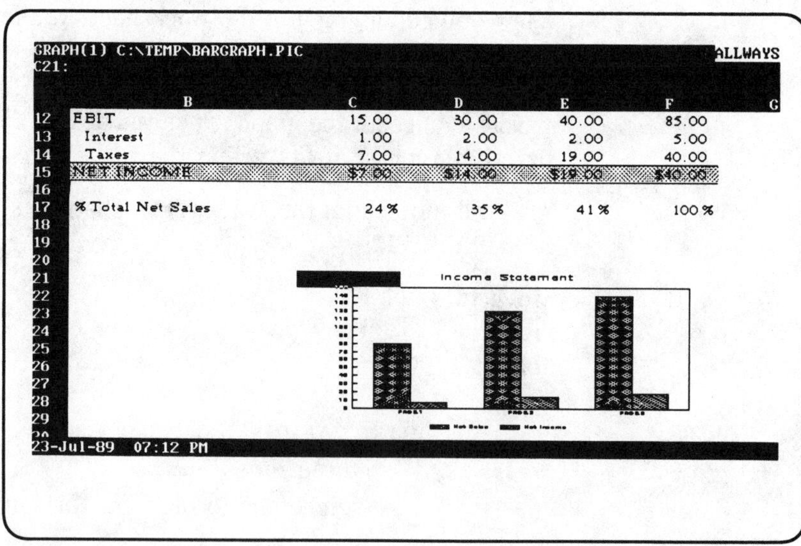

The graph appears on the screen if you have a graphics monitor. The name of the graph is in the first line of the control panel.

NOTE: If you have a text monitor, you will see a series of G characters throughout the range of the graph.

Suppressing the Display of Graphs

By default, Allways displays graphs on the screen. If you have many graphs in a worksheet, you may not want to display them all the time because not displaying graphs gives you faster response time as you work. The **Display Graphs** command lets you turn the display of graphs on and off. Even if you turn off the display of graphs initially, it's always a good idea to look at a graph on the screen before printing to make sure it looks the way you want it to.

You will now see what happens if you turn off the display of graphs.

Press: [/]
Select: Display

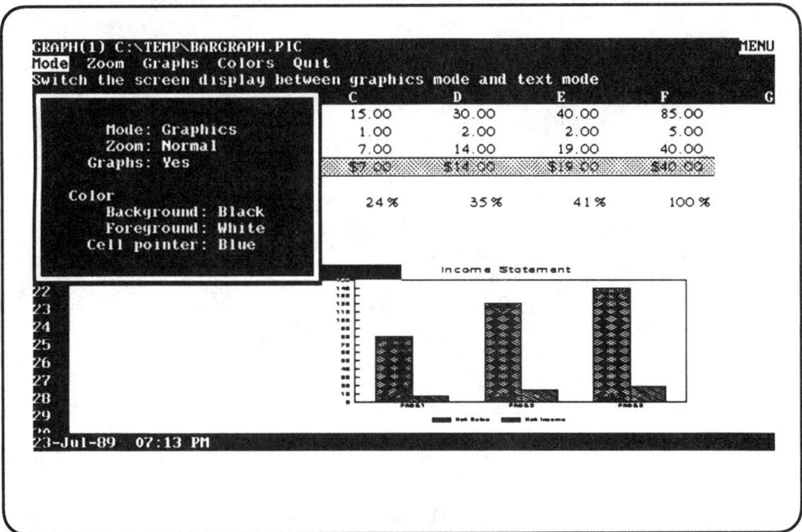

Figure 6.27
Display settings

Allways displays a setting sheet for all of the display settings. The display settings control whether you are in graphics or text mode, whether the display of the worksheet is magnified or reduced, which colors are used for the display (if you have a color monitor), and whether graphs are shown or not. Currently the setting for showing graphs is set to Yes. As with 1–2–3 setting sheets, you change settings on the sheet by selecting commands from the menu above the setting sheet.

Select: Graphs
No
Quit

Figure 6.28
Cross-hatched box representing graph

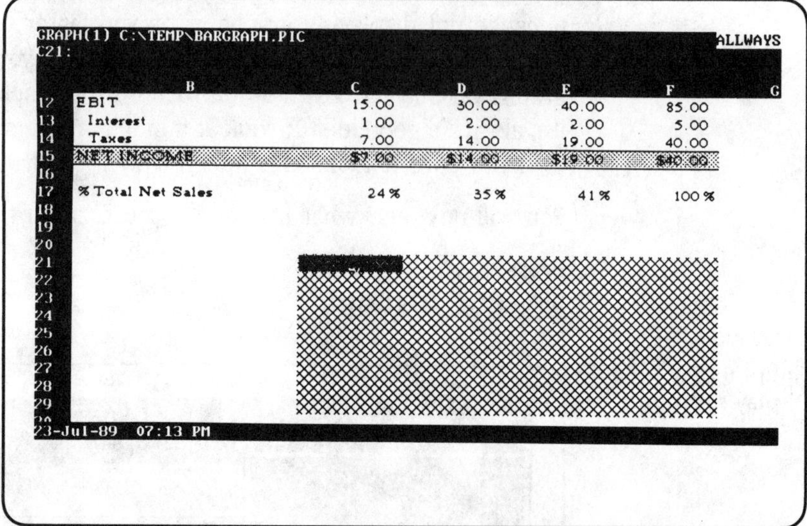

You can also switch between displaying graphs and displaying cross-hatched boxes with Graph (F10). Redisplay the graph now:

Press: GRAPH (F10)

Changing the Graph's Size

Compared to the spreadsheet on the screen, the graph looks small, so you are going to enlarge it. You do so by changing the graph's range with **/Graph Settings Range**; Allways will adjust the size of the graph accordingly. You can also use this command to move the graph to another position in the worksheet.

Press: /
Select: Graph
Settings

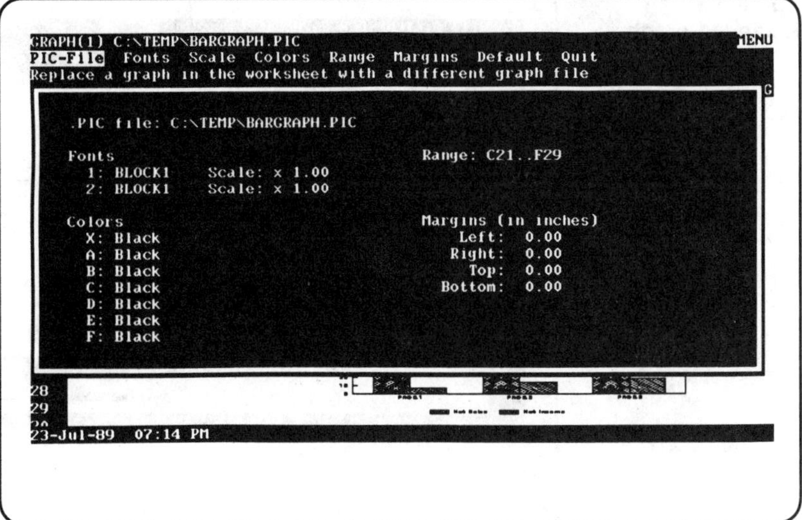

Figure 6.29
Graph settings

The Allways graph settings sheet appears, reflecting the current graph's settings. The settings include the fonts, colors, and margins used in the graph, as well as positioning information. The current range of the graph is C21..F29. You are going to lengthen the range by four rows.

Select: Range
Press: ↓ four times
↵
Select: Quit

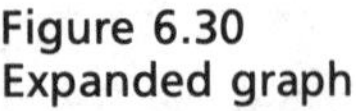

Figure 6.30
Expanded graph

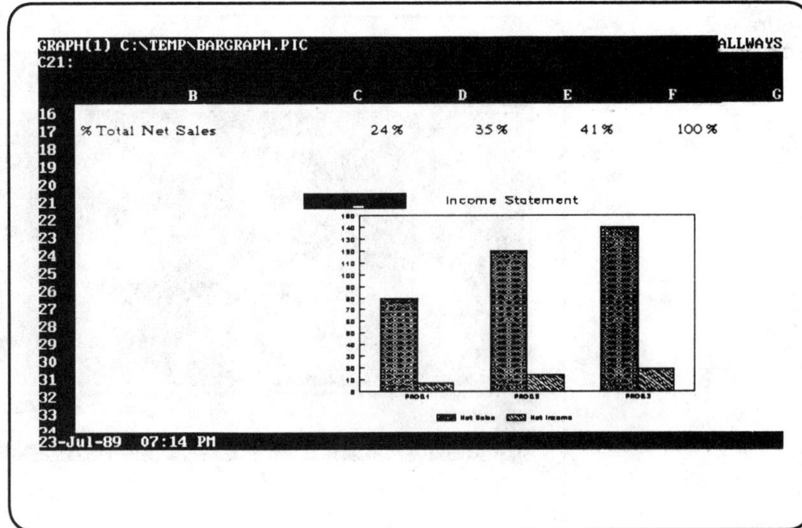

Changing the Size of Text on the Graph

Some of the text on the graph, especially the legends and labels on the axes, is quite small. Allways gives you the choice of enlarging it to make it more readable. You enlarge the text by changing the scale of the graph fonts with **/Graph Settings Scale**.

The fonts that you use with graphs in Allways are identical to those available with the 1-2-3 PrintGraph program: BLOCK1, BLOCK2, FORUM, and so on. Just as with PrintGraph, you can use two fonts per graph. Font 1 applies to the graph's first title line (Income Statement in the bar graph); Font 2 applies to all the other text on the graph.

By default, both graph fonts are BLOCK1. You are going to leave the fonts as they are and just change the scaling of Font 2. The normal scale for a graph is 1.00, but you can scale either down or up to make the font smaller or larger, respectively. You will try a scale of 1.25 on the bar graph.

Press: [/]
Select: Graph
Settings
Scale
2
Type: 1.25

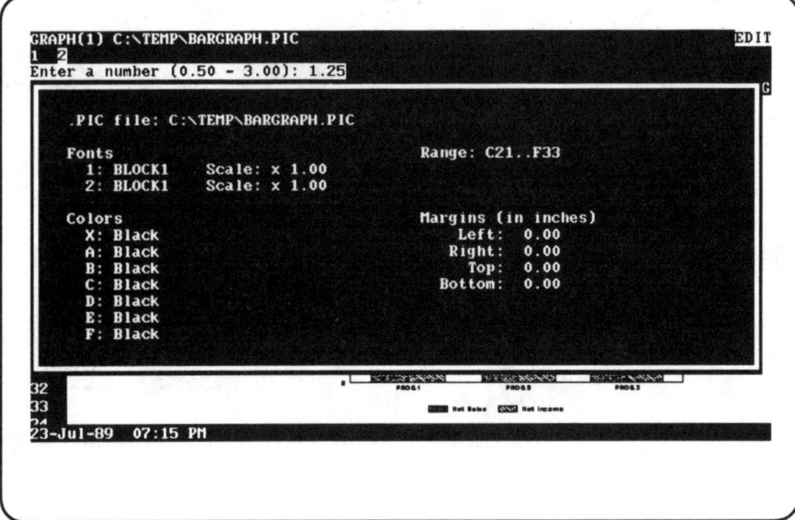

Figure 6.31
Changing the scale of text on a graph

Press: ↵
Select: Quit

The text on the graph should now be more readable.

Enclosing the Graph in a Box

You will next enhance the graph by including it in a box and adding a striking title below it. You can add a box (outline) around a range with the **Format Lines** command. The **Format Lines** command also lets you create horizontal and vertical lines in the worksheet (as you did with the net income row) and place boxes around individual cells in a range.

Move to: cell C20
Press: /
Select: Format
Lines
Outline
Press: → 3 times
↓ 14 times to highlight the range C20..F34
↵

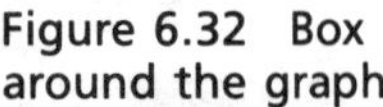

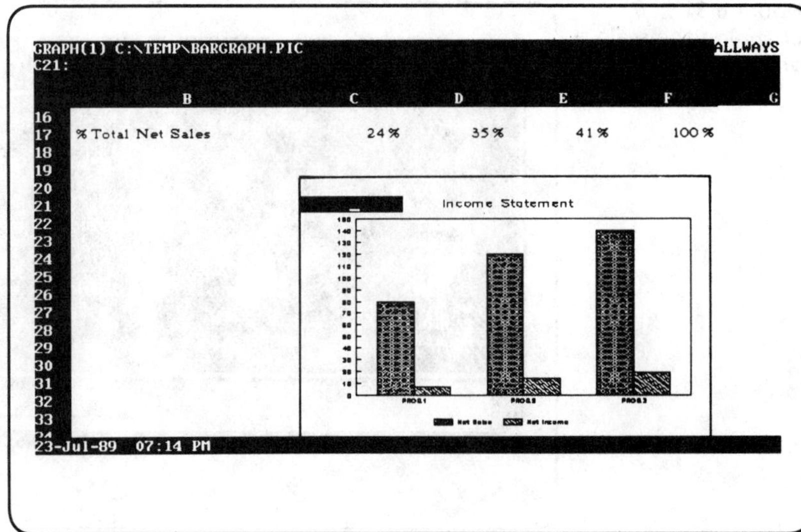

Figure 6.32 Box around the graph

Adding a Title

Now you will add the title **Top Selling Products** below the graph. To enter the text of the title, you must return to 1-2-3 (you cannot enter data in Allways). You will then come back to Allways to make the title bold and increase its size.

Because the graph you included with Allways will not appear in the worksheet when you return to 1-2-3, position the cell pointer where you want the title before leaving Allways to avoid having to guess where to put the title.

Move to: cell D36
Press: ESC to return to 1-2-3

Notice that in 1-2-3 the screen is blank where the graph was in Allways.

Type: Top Selling Products
Press: ↵
APP1 (Alt-F7) to return to Allways

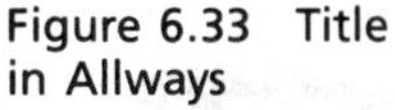

Figure 6.33 Title in Allways

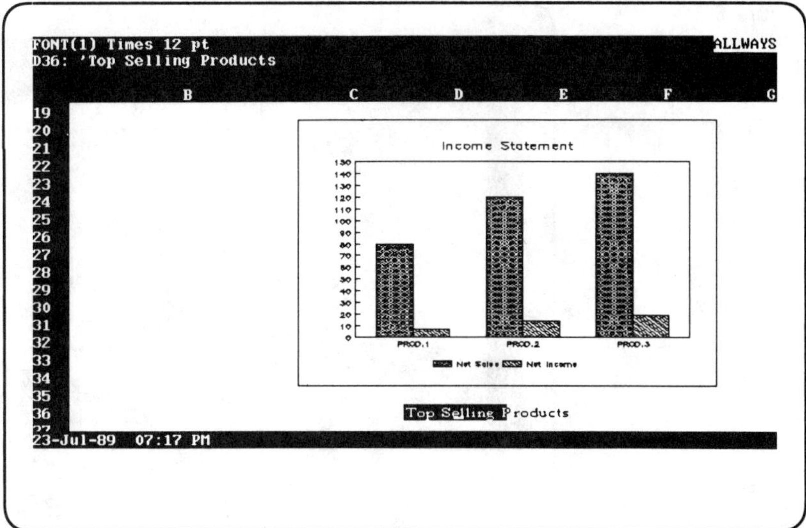

First make the title bold and then increase its size to 14 points (leave the typeface as Times).

Press: [/]
Select: Format
Bold
Set
Press: [↵] to select D36
[/]
Select: Format
Font
Move to: Times 14 point
Select: Use
Press: [↵] to select D36
[↓] so you can see the title more clearly

Figure 6.34
Enlarged and bolded title

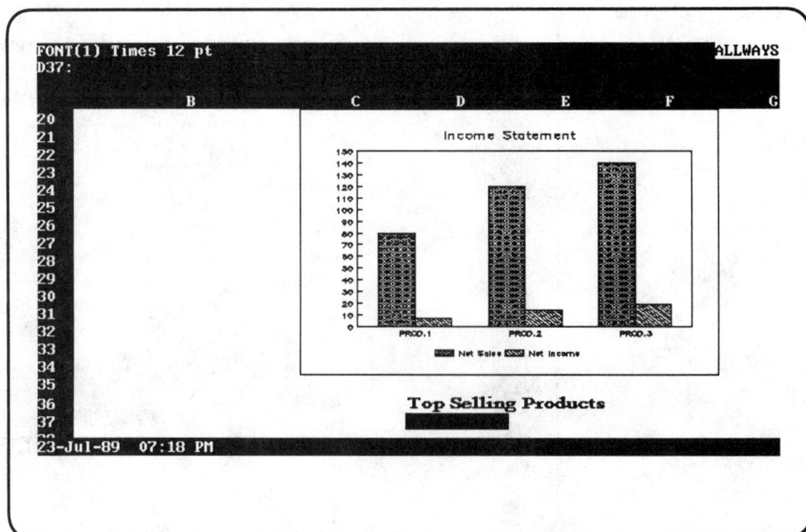

Save the file.

Press: ESC
/
Select: File
Save
Press: ↵
Select: Replace

PRINTING WITH ALLWAYS

Allways offers a number of features that allow you to control the appearance of the printed page and the printing process. The Layout commands, for example, let you define headers and footers (**/Layout Titles**), indicate which rows or columns should appear on each page of a multiple-page printout (**/Layout Borders**), set margins (**/Layout Margins**), and indicate paper dimensions (**/Layout Page-Size**).

In addition, the Print commands let you define the printer you are using, as well as print settings such as number of copies and page numbering.

Before You Begin

When you installed Allways, you should have selected a printer driver. If you did not, refer to *Setting Up 1-2-3* and install a printer now. If you selected more than one printer driver, you may want to choose a particular printer now with the Allways **Print Configuration Printer** command. (Installing a printer for 1-2-3 is *not* the same as installing one for Allways; you must go through two separate procedures.)

In addition, use **/Print Configuration Interface** to check that your printer interface is correct. The **interface**, or port, refers to the way your printer is connected to the computer. The interface may be parallel or serial, and your computer may have more than one interface of either type. Initially, the interface is set to Parallel 1, which is the most common setting.

Defining the Print Range

Printing with Allways is very similar to printing with 1-2-3. Before you can print you must specify the range you want to print. You are going to print the Income Statement with its accompanying graph.

Press: [APP1] (Alt-F7) to return to Allways
Move to: cell B3
[/]
Select: Print
Range
Set
Press: [→] four times
[PGDN] twice to highlight the range B3..F37

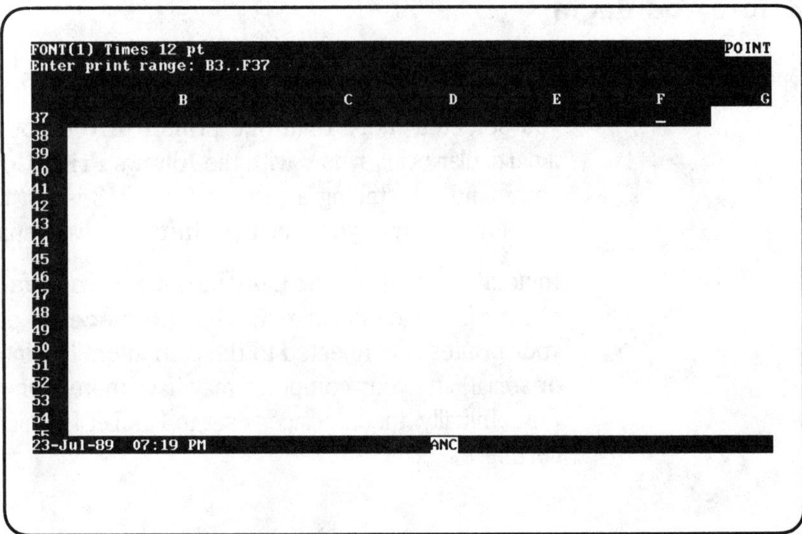

Figure 6.35
Highlighting the print range

Press: ↵ to select B3..F37 as the print range

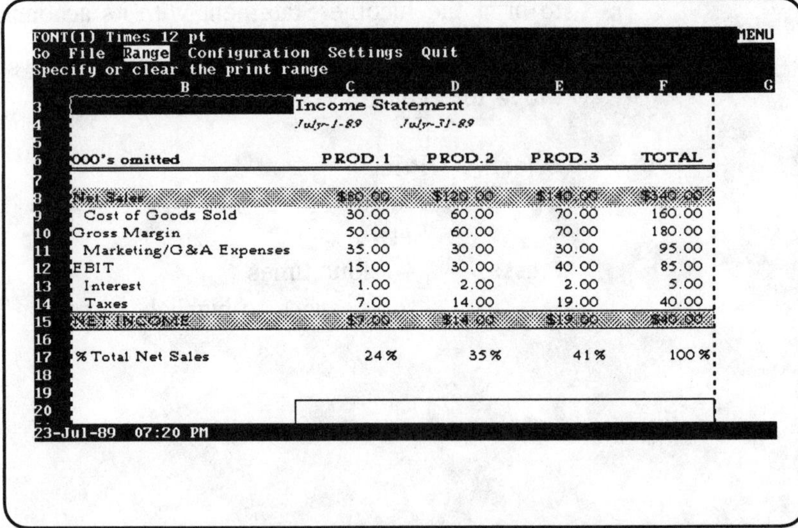

Figure 6.36
Print range

Allways shows the print range by using dashed lines along its edges. These dashed lines remain on the screen even after you print the range. To clear them, you must explicitly delete the print range with **/Print Range Clear**.

Printing the Worksheet

Now the print range is defined, you can print it. Make sure your printer is turned on and on line.

Select: Go

Allways starts printing and, in line 2 of the control panel, tells you which row of the worksheet it is currently printing. To stop printing at any point, press Ctrl-Break.

If you wish, save your file again.

Figure 6.37
Printout

Income Statement

July-1-89 *July-31-89*

000's omitted	PROD.1	PROD.2	PROD.3	TOTAL
Net Sales	$80.00	$120.00	$140.00	$340.00
Cost of Goods Sold	30.00	60.00	70.00	160.00
Gross Margin	50.00	60.00	70.00	180.00
Marketing/G&A Expenses	35.00	30.00	30.00	95.00
EBIT	15.00	30.00	40.00	85.00
Interest	1.00	2.00	2.00	5.00
Taxes	7.00	14.00	19.00	40.00
NET INCOME	$7.00	$14.00	$19.00	$40.00
%Total Net Sales	24%	35%	41%	100%

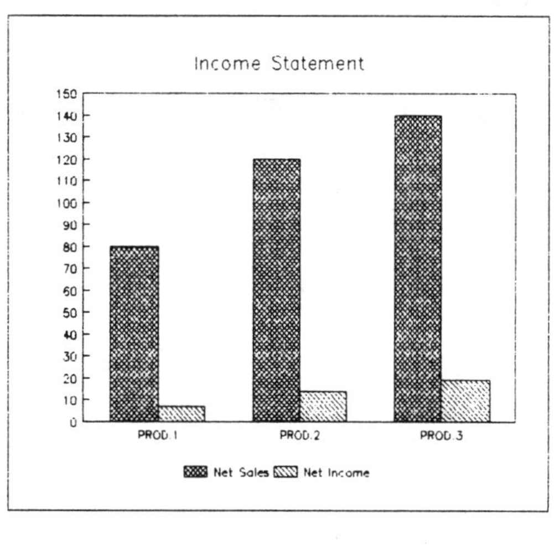

Top Selling Products

ALLWAYS MENU COMMAND STRUCTURE

THE ALLWAYS MAIN MENU COMMANDS

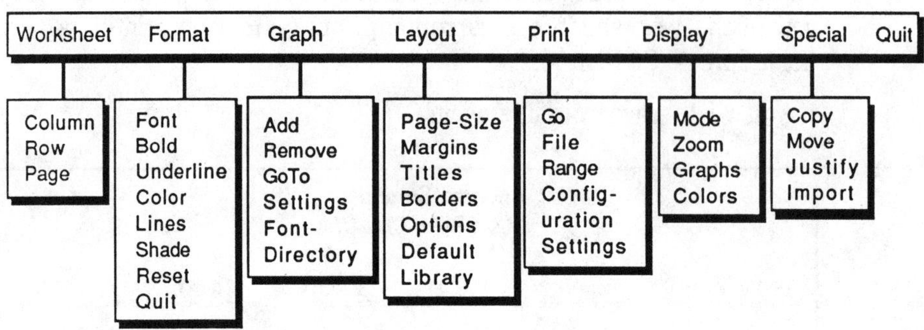

THE WORKSHEET COMMANDS

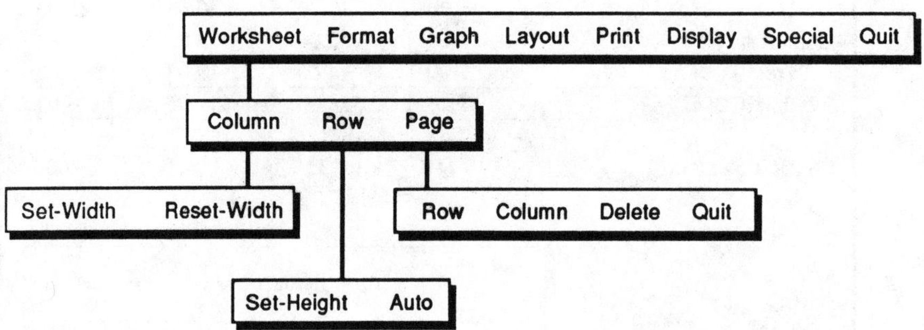

THE FORMAT COMMANDS

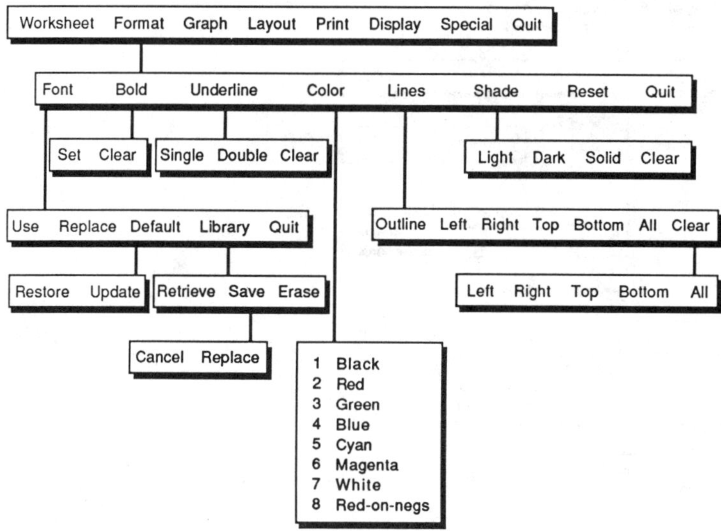

THE GRAPH COMMANDS

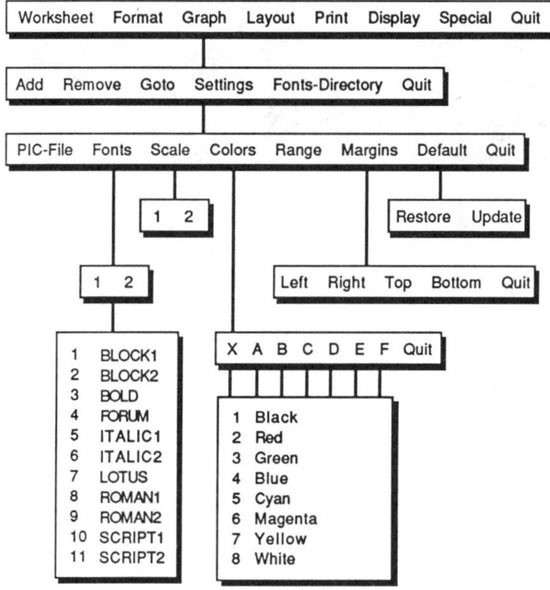

THE LAYOUT COMMANDS

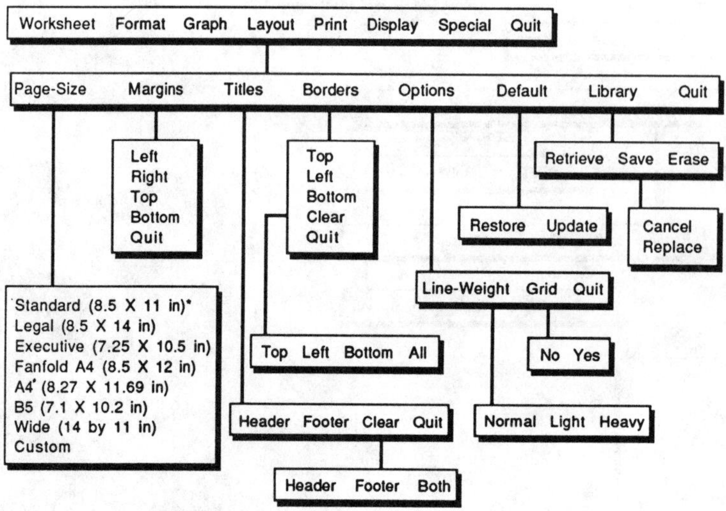

* Your available selections may be different depending on the type of printer you selected.

THE PRINT COMMANDS

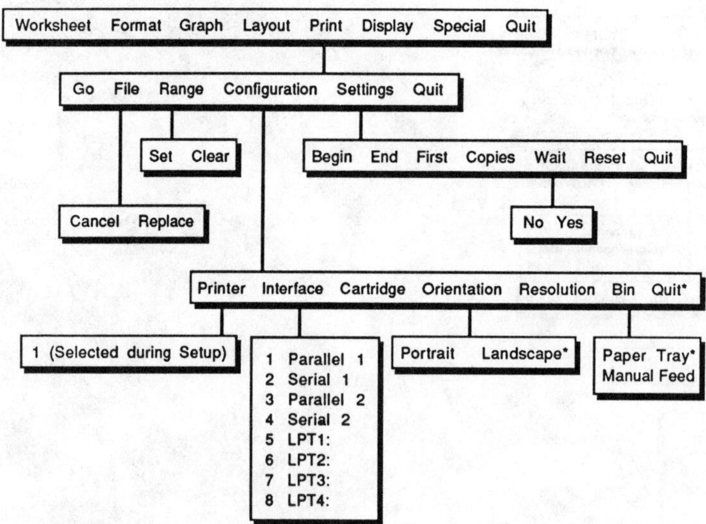

* Your available selections may be different depending on the type of printer you selected.

THE DISPLAY COMMANDS

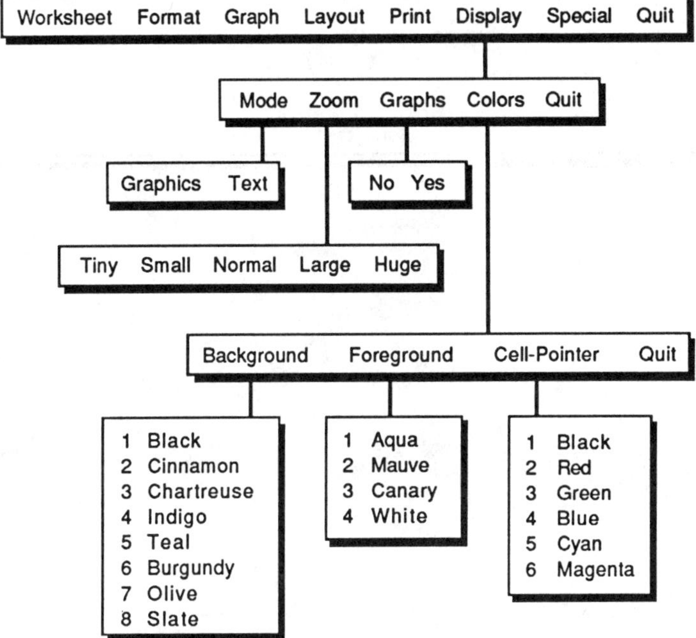

7

Tips

This chapter presents shortcuts and tips to some of the more advanced 1–2–3 operations. The tips are organized into six sections: Worksheet, @Functions and Formulas, Database, Printing, Graphics, and Allways. Feel free to read through the whole chapter at once, or simply refer to the individual tips as you need them. They should prove informative, and set you on the road toward mastering 1–2–3.

WORKSHEET

Recalculation of the Worksheet

1–2–3 has an initial setting for automatically recalculating the worksheet in a natural order. Automatic recalculation means that each time you change the contents of a cell, 1–2–3 recalculates any formulas that are affected by the change. A natural order of calculation means that before recalculating a particular formula, 1–2–3 recalculates any other formulas on which that formula depends. For example, if the formula in cell D6 depends on the formula in cell D28, 1–2–3 recalculates the formula in cell D28 before it recalculates the formula in cell D6.

(2.2) When the recalculation order is set to natural, 1–2–3 recalculates only those cells that have changed since the worksheet was last calculated. This feature is knows as **minimal recalculation** and makes recalculation of the worksheet very fast. Natural order of recalculation is suitable for most worksheet calculations.

You can, however, change the recalculation order from natural to columnwise or rowwise. If the recalculation order is set to columnwise, 1–2–3 starts in cell A1 and moves column by column through the worksheet, recalculating all formulas. If the recalculation order is set to rowwise, 1-2-3 starts in cell A1 and moves row by row through the worksheet, recalculating all formulas. If you set the order to either columnwise or rowwise, 1-2-3 no longer uses minimal recalculation and recalcuates all the formulas in the worksheet.

You also have the choice of switching from automatic recalculation to manual. If recalculation is set to manual and you enter a value or formula in the worksheet, you must press Calc (F9) each time you want 1-2-3 to recalculate the worksheet. 1-2-3 reminds you to do this by displaying the word CALC in the status line whenever you make a change to the worksheet.

Manual recalculation is useful when you're running macros because 1-2-3 performs automatic recalculation of the worksheet between macro instructions, thus slowing down the macro. If you use manual recalculation when running a macro use the advanced macro commands {CALC}, {RECALC}, and {RECALCCOL} in your macros to control when 1-2-3 recalculates formulas. For more information about macros, refer to Part II of this book.

To change any recalculation settings, use the **Worksheet Global Recalculation** command.

Figure 7.1
Worksheet with CALC indicator

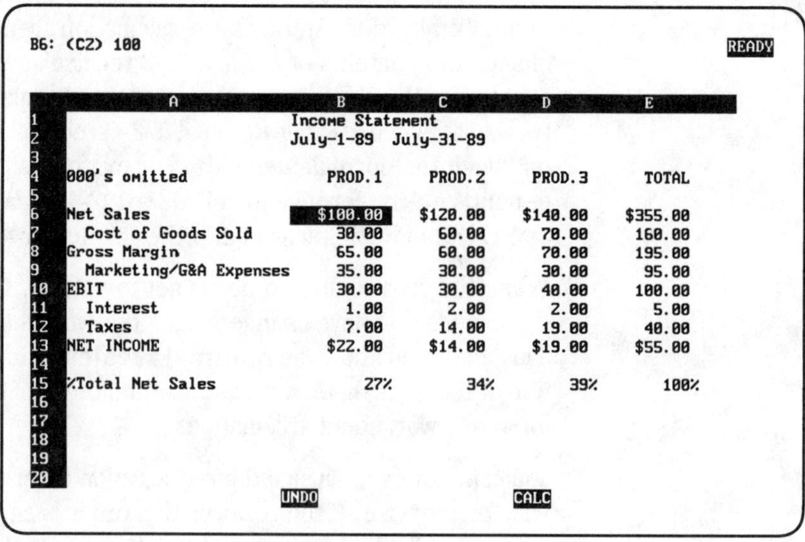

B6: (C2) 100 READY

	A	B	C	D	E
1		Income Statement			
2		July-1-89	July-31-89		
3					
4	000's omitted	PROD.1	PROD.2	PROD.3	TOTAL
5					
6	Net Sales	$100.00	$120.00	$140.00	$355.00
7	Cost of Goods Sold	30.00	60.00	70.00	160.00
8	Gross Margin	65.00	60.00	70.00	195.00
9	Marketing/G&A Expenses	35.00	30.00	30.00	95.00
10	EBIT	30.00	30.00	40.00	100.00
11	Interest	1.00	2.00	2.00	5.00
12	Taxes	7.00	14.00	19.00	40.00
13	NET INCOME	$22.00	$14.00	$19.00	$55.00
14					
15	%Total Net Sales	27%	34%	39%	100%
16					
17					
18					
19					
20					

UNDO CALC

In the worksheet in Figure 7.1, a new value has been entered in cell B6 but 1–2–3 has not recalculated the worksheet. Notice that the numbers do not add up correctly and that the status indicator reads CALC. Pressing Calc (F9) will cause 1–2–3 to recalculate the cells affected by the change in cell B6.

Setting Horizontal and Vertical Titles

Labels that identify columns and rows are often placed at the top or left edges of a worksheet and scroll off the screen as you move around the worksheet. As a result, it can be difficult to identify the kind of values you're looking at. The **Worksheet Titles** command lets you freeze the rows or columns (or both) of labels at the edges of the worksheet. The labels stay in place when you move around the worksheet. For example, in a worksheet with the months of the year entered as the top row of the worksheet, setting the top row as a title would keep the months visible no matter how far you moved down.

Before setting the titles, locate the cell pointer in a cell just to the right of the column you wish to set as a vertical title, or just below the row you wish to set as a horizontal title. If you want to set both horizontal and vertical titles, place the cell pointer in the cell to the right of the column and below the row to be set.

To freeze titles at the top or left edges of the worksheet:

Press: [/]
Select: Worksheet
Titles

The menu in the second line of the control panel gives the options Both Horizontal Vertical Clear. After you make your choice, the menu disappears and the titles are frozen.

Figure 7.2
Frozen titles

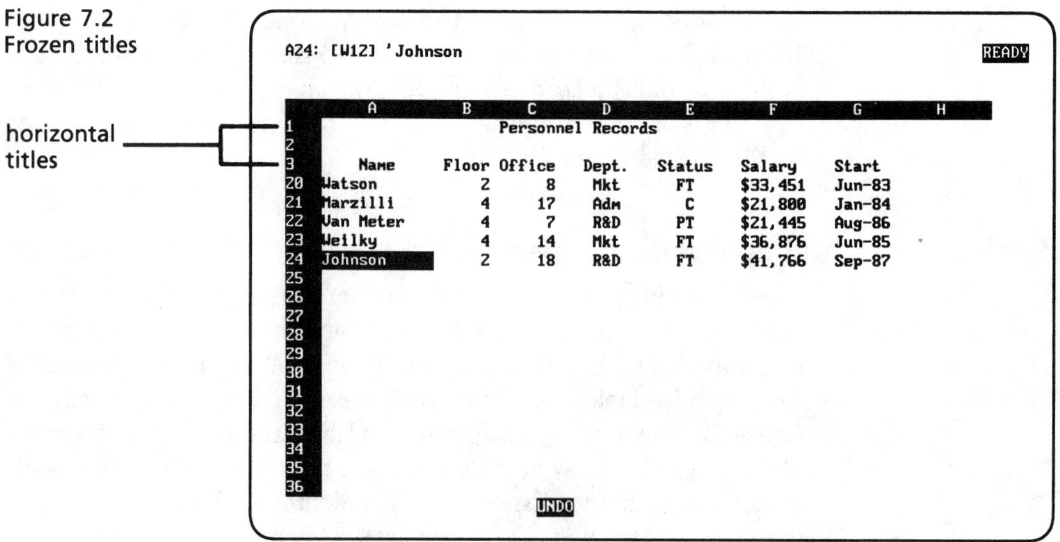

In the database illustrated above, the top three rows (containing the title of the database and the field names) have been made a horizontal title. Because these rows are frozen at the top of the screen, you can scroll down the worksheet (in this case to see the records in rows 20 through 24) and keep the field names in view at the same time.

> NOTE: Titles that you set affect only the display of the worksheet on the screen; they have no effect on a printout. If you want to print the same column or row titles on each page of a multiple-page printout, use **/Print Printer Options Borders**, as described in ''Printing Column and Row Borders'' later in this chapter.

To clear the set titles, select **/Worksheet Titles Clear**.

Global Settings

When you start up 1-2-3, many variable aspects of the worksheet's appearance and function are already determined. The worksheet format is set so all the columns are the same width, the cells have a specific format, and so on. These preset specifications are called the global settings because they affect the entire worksheet or 1-2-3 session.

You can change the global settings to settings that meet your needs. You can alter them in countless ways, and you can customize 1–2–3 to your hardware.

(2.2) Global and Default Settings Sheets

1–2–3 provides two setting sheets to help you keep track of global settings: the global settings sheet and the global default settings sheet. The global settings sheet reflects settings such as recalculation method and global column width, as well as information about available memory and circular references.

To see the global settings sheet:

Press: /
Select: Worksheet
Global

Figure 7.3 Global settings sheet

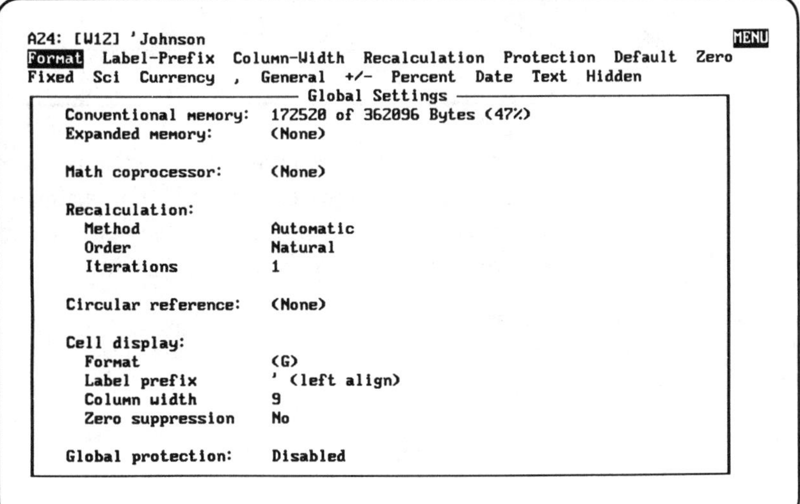

```
A24: [W12] 'Johnson                                                          MENU
Format  Label-Prefix  Column-Width  Recalculation  Protection  Default  Zero
Fixed  Sci  Currency  ,  General  +/-  Percent  Date  Text  Hidden
                         Global Settings
  Conventional memory:  172520 of 362096 Bytes (47%)
  Expanded memory:      (None)

  Math coprocessor:     (None)

  Recalculation:
    Method              Automatic
    Order               Natural
    Iterations          1

  Circular reference:   (None)

  Cell display:
    Format              (G)
    Label prefix        ' (left align)
    Column width        9
    Zero suppression    No

  Global protection:    Disabled
```

You change settings on this setting sheet by selecting **/Worksheet Global** commands.

The **Default** command on the Worksheet Global menu displays the default settings sheet and lets you change settings that determine how 1–2–3 is configured or set up. For example, the default settings indicate the current drive or directory for your data files, the kind of format to use for the date and time, the status of the undo feature, and so on. Figure 7.4 shows some sample default settings.

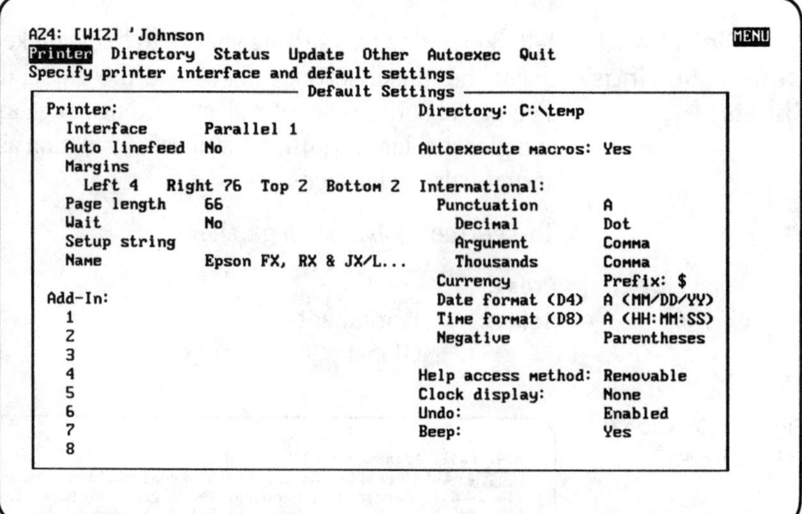

Figure 7.4 Sample default settings

You change settings on the default settings sheet by selecting **/Worksheet Global Default** commands. For example, if you find the beeping sound the computer makes when you make a mistake with 1-2-3 annoying, you can turn the sound off this way:

Press: /
Select: Worksheet
Global
Default
Other
Beep
No

The Beep setting on the default settings sheet is now set to No.

The default settings are stored in a **configuration file** called 123.CNF. 1-2-3 reads this file every time you start up a session, and the settings take effect automatically. If you change a default setting and want to save it for future sessions, you must select **/Worksheet Global Default Update**, which will save the change in the 123.CNF file.

Copying and Moving

Copying Cell Formats

When you copy the contents of one cell to another, you are also copying the format of the first cell to the second. The new format overrides any previous format of the second cell.

In general, this feature is helpful. If you formatted the first cell to display its contents as a percentage with two decimal places, it would be disconcerting to see the same value, when copied to another cell, displayed as an integer. You should, however, be careful to remember this feature when copying; you may want a different format in the new cell.

Specifying TO and FROM Ranges

When you are copying or moving one range of cells to another range, you should be careful about specifying the TO and FROM directions.

First, when copying or moving FROM a range, it's a good idea to specify only one cell as the TO range. 1-2-3 regards this single cell as the upper-left corner of the range to be copied or moved to, and fills in the range with the new cell contents.

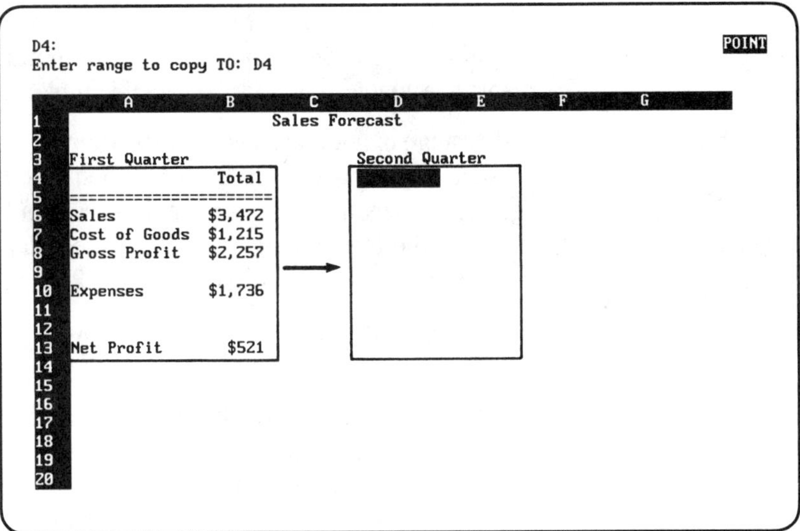

Figure 7.5 TO and FROM ranges

Second, make sure that the two ranges do not overlap at any point when copying. If they do, some of the original cell contents will be erased.

Writing Over Cell Contents

Finally, be aware that copying and moving data to a range of cells always erases the previous contents of the cells. If the undo feature is on and you press Undo (Alt-F4) right after you write over some cells, you will
2.2 recover their contents; otherwise, you will not be able to recover them. Formulas that refer to these cells will still be valid, but the calculated values may change to reflect the new contents.

Always check a range before copying or moving new data into it. If it contains information you want to keep, move the old data somewhere else before proceeding.

Highlighting a Range

As you know by now, you can indicate a range of cells when using 1–2–3 commands such as **/Copy** and **/Move** in four ways. You can type the cell addresses (for example, E3.F6), type a range name (for example, SALES), press Name (F3) and select a named range, or you can highlight the range in the worksheet.

When highlighting a range, keep a few points in mind:

- The range is anchored if the prompt in the control panel displays a range of cells, for example, E3..E3; it is not anchored if the prompt displays a single cell address, for example, E3.
- If the range is not anchored, press . (period) to anchor it. To release an anchored range, press Esc or Backspace. Esc removes the highlighting and unanchors the cell pointer without moving it; Backspace removes the highlighting, unanchors the cell pointer, and moves the cell pointer to where it was before 1–2–3 entered POINT mode.
- After you anchor the range, use the arrow keys to extend the highlight if necessary.
- You can change the free corner of the highlighted range, designated by the small blinking cursor in the lower-middle of the cell, by pressing . (period). Each time you press . (period), the free corner cell moves to a different corner of the range. You can then expand the highlight in the direction of the free corner.
- Use the End key along with the arrow keys to highlight various ranges in the active area of the worksheet. If the cell pointer is in a blank cell, it moves in the direction of the arrow either to the first filled

cell or to the edge of the worksheet. If the pointer is on a filled cell, it moves in the direction of the arrow either to the last filled cell before a blank cell or to the edge of the worksheet.

- To highlight the entire active area of the worksheet when specifying a range for a command:

Press: HOME
. (period)
END
HOME
↵ to enter the range

Planning and Documenting a Worksheet

Before you actually start to create a worksheet with 1-2-3, take the time to plan it out and write down all your assumptions.

First, think about what the worksheet will contain. Do you want to create separate sections for different groups of data? How will these sections relate to each other? For example, will formulas link them? How large do the areas need to be, and will they need room to expand?

Next, given the answers to the questions above, map out a worksheet on paper. You do not have to be exact in your allocation of rows and columns, but sketch out the general locations of groups of data and the size of the area each group will occupy.

Next, make a record of the assumptions involved in building the worksheet. You can do this either on the screen or on paper. Record such things as dates, numbers used in formulas, and so on.

Finally, after you have built the worksheet, print out a document that lists only the cell contents line by line. (See the Tip on ''Printing Cell Contents.'') This printout will give you information on all the material in each cell—formula, label, format, and so on—and will provide a reference for any questions you may have.

Protecting the Worksheet

When you create a new worksheet, all of the cells are unprotected; you can enter data into any of them. It's a good idea to protect the final version when you have finished building and modifying a worksheet.

This will prevent you from inadvertently modifying or erasing important cell contents (labels, formulas, or values).

The protection feature is global: it protects all the cells in the worksheet. Once global protection is instated, you can unprotect specific ranges of cells that you want to be able to access and change.

To protect the entire worksheet:

Press: /
Select: Worksheet
Global
Protection
Enable

After enabling global protection, you will not be able to change any of the cells in the worksheet. To alter specific cells, you must unprotect them:

Press: /
Select: Range
Unprot

The second line of the control panel reads **Enter range to unprotect:**. You can either type in the range address or name or highlight the range.

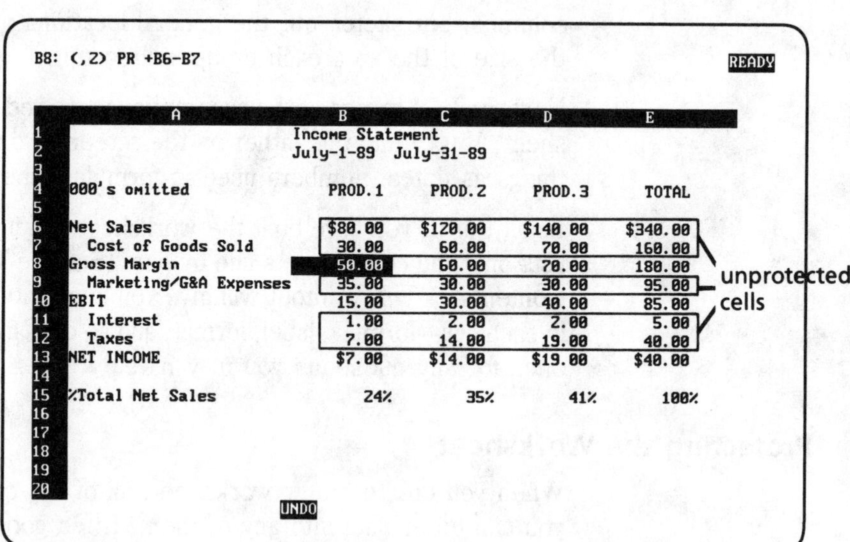

Figure 7.6
Protected and unprotected cells

In the worksheet illustrated in Figure 7.6, the unprotected cells have been highlighted; on the screen, the unprotected cells actually appear brighter than the others on the screen. In this worksheet, the cells containing labels and formulas have been protected; the cells containing numbers are unprotected, allowing you to enter data at any time. U appears in the first line of the control panel next to the contents of an unprotected cell; PR appears in the control panel next to the contents of a protected cell.

To re-protect a range of cells you have unprotected, use **/Range Protect**. (Note that you cannot simply use this command to protect a range on an unprotected worksheet. The 1-2-3 global protection feature applies to the entire worksheet; **/Range Protect** can be used only to re-protect ranges that have been unprotected.)

Range Names

The ability to name a range of cells is one of 1-2-3's most helpful features. With a little practice, you can easily learn to use range names in most commands that call for ranges. Referring to the names can save you the time and trouble of remembering and pointing to the actual cell addresses.

The Range Name menu gives you a number of choices, providing a great deal of flexibility in the creation and manipulation of the ranges. The following are some tips to keep in mind:

- When choosing a name for a range, use only one word. If you want to use two words, connect them with an underscore (_).
- To modify the named range, select **/Range Name Create** and then the name. The currently defined range of cells will be highlighted; use the arrow keys and the period key to change the range and then press Enter.

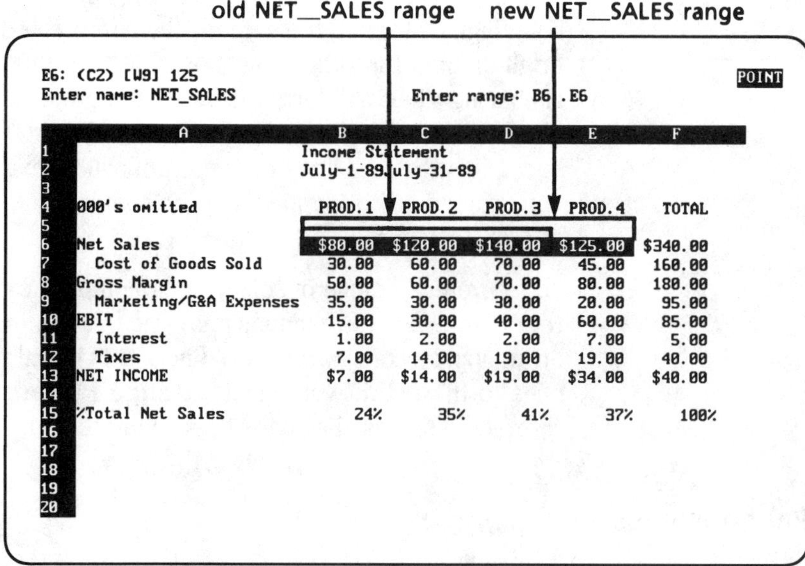

Figure 7.7 Redefined named range

- When you change the range of cells assigned to a name, any references to the original range are transformed into references to the new range. For example, if you change a range that is named and used in a formula, the formula will now refer to the new range assigned to the name. In addition, if you name a range that is already used in a formula, that formula will display the range name—instead of the range itself—in the control panel. The references are modified whether they were originally made by cell addresses or by name.
- You can delete all the range names in the worksheet by selecting **/Range Name Reset**. You can delete single names by selecting **/Range Name Delete**.
- Using **/Range Name Delete** or **/Range Name Reset** to eliminate range names does not cancel references to the range. The range name simply ceases to be associated with the range. Formulas that previously referred to the range name now refer to the range itself.
- To rename a range, select **/Range Name Create** and then the name. Press Edit (F2); the highlighted range is frozen, and you can now edit the range name itself. When you have changed the name and pressed Enter, the old name will be deleted and the new name will define the original range.

The Name (F3) Key

You've already learned that when retrieving files you can press Name (F3) to see a full-screen list of the files in the current directory or on the current disk (on a two-diskette system). You can view lists of other types of files as well. To see the list of .PIC files, for example, select **/File List Graph** and then press Name (F3). The list appears on a similar screen.

You can also use Name (F3) to see the range names in the worksheet. This is particularly useful in any command that prompts you for a range. For example, if you want to move a named range, you can proceed as follows:

Press: /
Select: Move
Press: NAME (F3)

A screen appears listing all the range names in the worksheet. The third line of the control panel now displays the name and address of the currently highlighted range. Highlight the range you want to move and press Enter. Continue with the **Move** command as usual.

(2.2) 1-2-3 Release 2.2 also lets you press Name (F3) when you're entering a formula to allow you to select a range name for inclusion in the formula. Type the formula as usual. When you're ready to include a reference to a range, press Name (F3). 1-2-3 will display a list of all the range names in the worksheet. Highlight the one you want and press Enter. The name will appear as part of the formula.

In FILES and NAMES modes, Name (F3) works as a toggle key: pressing it once displays a menu of names in the third line of the control panel, pressing it twice displays a full-screen menu of names, and pressing it three times displays a menu of names in the control panel again.

Hiding Columns

1-2-3 includes commands that hide (and display) one or more columns in a worksheet. This allows you to view otherwise separated columns next to each other, and to print otherwise non-adjacent ranges next to each other. It makes it easier to compare certain ranges of values.

To hide columns in a worksheet:

Press: [/]
Select: Worksheet
Column
Hide

1-2-3 now prompts you for the column to hide; the mode indicator reads POINT. You can either type in the cell addresses of the range of columns you wish to hide, or you can press . (period) and use the arrow keys to extend the highlight to the right or left. You can include as many columns as you like. When you have highlighted the range, press Enter. The selected columns disappear and the cell pointer rests on the column to the right of the hidden range.

You can use **/Worksheet Column Hide** as many times as you like on different areas of the worksheet.

Figure 7.8
Hidden columns

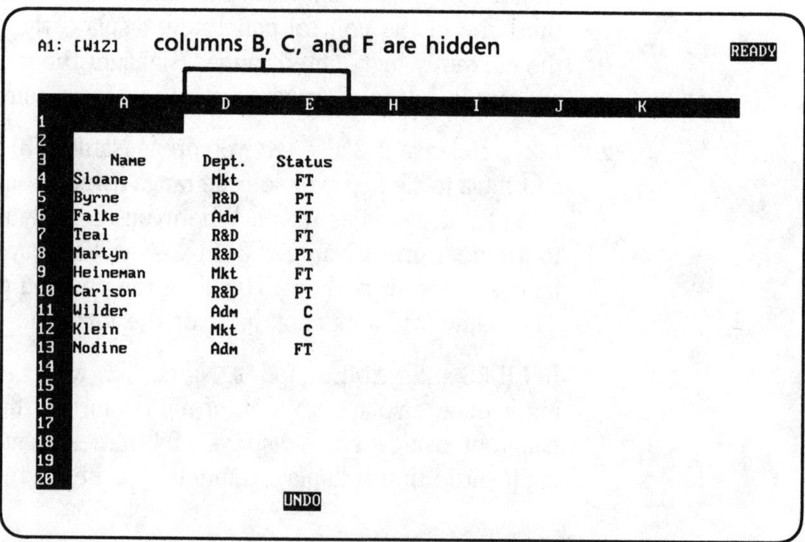

In the database illustrated above, columns B, C, F, and G are hidden. The column containing the Dept. listings is now directly adjacent to the column containing the names, thus making it easier to compare those two fields.

Hidden columns are not displayed in READY mode, nor are they accessible—you cannot enter data in them. The existing contents of the columns still figure in the worksheet, however; for example, formulas that refer to the cell contents calculate correctly.

Hidden columns are displayed whenever you are in POINT mode. Therefore you can see those columns when you select commands that call for a range, or when you're entering a formula and pointing to the cells. Hidden columns are identified by an asterisk placed after the column letter in the top border of the worksheet.

To redisplay hidden columns:

Press: /
Select: Worksheet
Column
Display

Again, you can type the cell addresses of the range or highlight the columns you wish to redisplay. Note that you can expand the highlight over displayed columns to reach non-adjacent ranges if you like. Once you have specified the range, press Enter.

The Ins Key

When you press Edit (F2) to begin editing cell contents, you are automatically in insert mode. This mode allows you to add new characters without displacing the old ones in the cell. You can switch to overstrike mode while editing by pressing the Ins key. Overstrike mode allows you to write over the current cell contents.

When you press the Ins key while in EDIT mode, the status indicator reads OVR. You can write over the contents of the cell—value, formula, label. Pressing Enter enters the edited cell contents and turns off overstrike mode.

(2.2) Displaying Negative Values

If you've formatted cells in either currency or , (comma) format, any negative numbers automatically appear in parentheses. 1-2-3 Release 2.2 gives you the choice, however, of displaying negative numbers with a minus sign preceding them.

To display negative numbers with a minus sign:

Press: [/]
Select: Worksheet
Global
Default
Other
International
Negative
Sign

If you want this setting to apply to all worksheets (not just the current one), be sure to select **/Worksheet Global Default Update** to change the 1-2-3 configuration file (123.CNF).

Listing Information About Files

You can obtain information about files in the current directory or drive in two ways while in 1-2-3: (1) you can view a temporary list with **/File List** or (2) you can create a table of files in the worksheet with **/File Admin Table.**

To create a temporary list that overlays the current worksheet:

Press: [/]
Select: File
List

1-2-3 now gives you a choice of displaying worksheet files, print (.PRN) files, graph (.PIC) files, linked files, or all files. Once you make your choice, the list appears on the screen.

Figure 7.9 File list of worksheet files

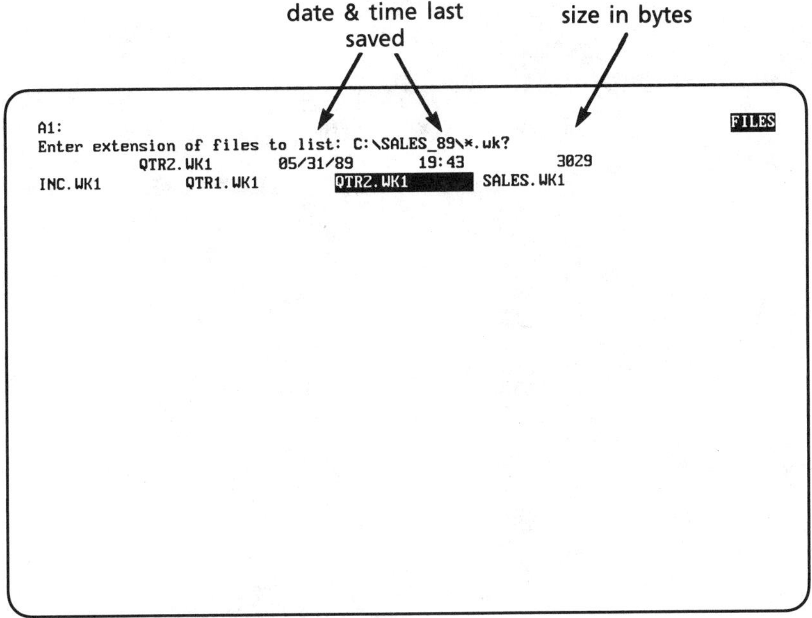

If you highlight a name in the list, 1–2–3 displays additional information about the file above the list.

When you're ready to return to the worksheet, press Enter.

(2.2) To create a permanent table of files in the worksheet:

Press: /
Select: File
Admin
Table

Just as with **/File List**, 1–2–3 gives you a choice of listing worksheet files, print (.PRN) files, graph (.PIC) files, linked files, or all files.

Once you make your choice, 1–2–3 prompts you for a range for the table. Choose an empty area of the worksheet or 1–2–3 will write over any data in the range. The table will occupy four columns and as many rows as the files you are listing plus one row. If you make a mistake when creating the table and the undo feature is on, press Undo (Alt-F4) right away to restore the worksheet to its original state.

Figure 7.10 File table of graph files

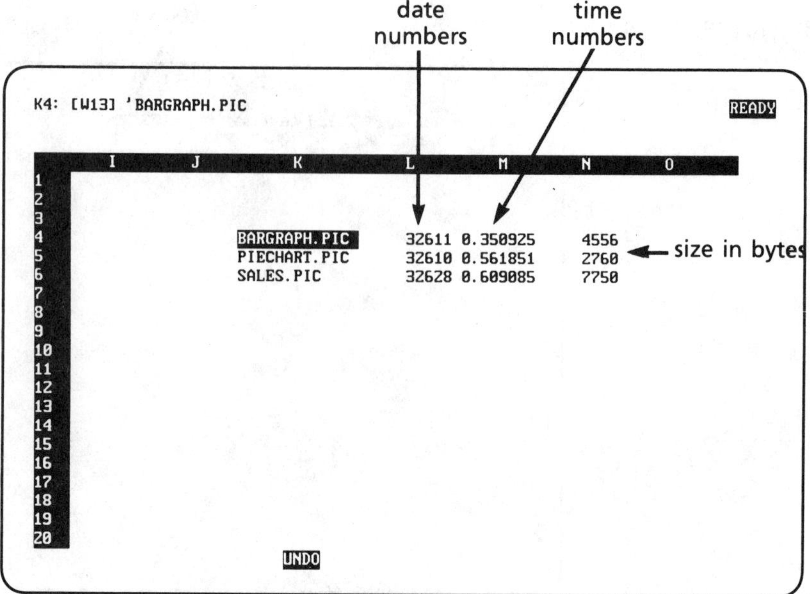

The second and third columns of the table contain date and time numbers, respectively. To show these as dates and times, use **/Range Format** to format them.

Figure 7.11 File table with formatted dates and times

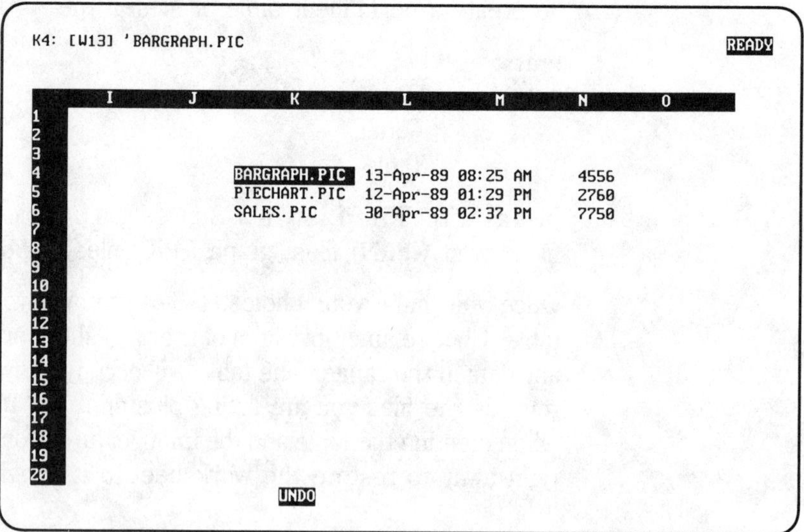

FUNCTIONS AND FORMULAS

Rounding Off Numbers

You can control the number of decimal places displayed in the worksheet in three ways: with the **Range Format Fixed** command, the @INT function, or the @ROUND function. Each of these procedures, however, affects the values displayed in the worksheet in a different way.

/Range Format Fixed determines how a number is displayed, but it does **not** affect the actual value of the number. No matter how many decimal places are displayed on the screen, the number is stored at its full value in the cell. The @INT function, on the other hand, actually deletes all decimal places from 1–2–3's memory and leaves only an integer (a positive or negative whole number). The @ROUND function rounds a value up or down to the specified number of decimal places.

You can see the different effect of each of these procedures by entering the same numbers in all three ways. See the table below.

Column A Shows the values exactly as they are entered on the keyboard.

Column B Contains the values from column A, but the cells have been formatted with /**Range Format Fixed** to display 0 decimal places.

Column C Contains the values from column A, entered with the @INT function (for example, @INT(2.33)=2), which deletes any decimal places.

Column D Contains the values from column A, entered with the @ROUND function (for example, @ROUND(2.33,0)=2), which rounds the value up or down to the specified number of decimal places.

	A	B	C	D
	Values	/RFFO	@INT(value)	@ROUND(value)
	2.33	2	2	2
	55.111	55	55	55
	12.66	13	12	13
TOTAL	70.101	70.101	69	70

Notice that the totals for columns A and B are exactly the same; this is because **/Range Format Fixed** does not change the actual values of the numbers. The @functions do change the values, however, so the totals for columns C and D are different.

The Abs (F4) Key

Pressing the Abs (F4) key changes the nature of a cell address in a formula. You can control whether the cell address will be mixed, absolute, or relative by pressing the key a specific number of times. Abs (F4) works both when you point to a cell or a range while you create a formula, or when you enter the cell address directly.

When entering or editing a formula, press Abs (F4) when the cursor is on or immediately to the right of a cell address or range name.

Press Abs (F4)	**Result**
First time	\$A\$1 (absolute cell address)
Second time	A\$1 (relative column address, absolute row address)
Third time	\$A1 (absolute column address, relative row address)
Fourth time	A1 (relative cell address)

Figure 7.12
Relative and absolute addresses

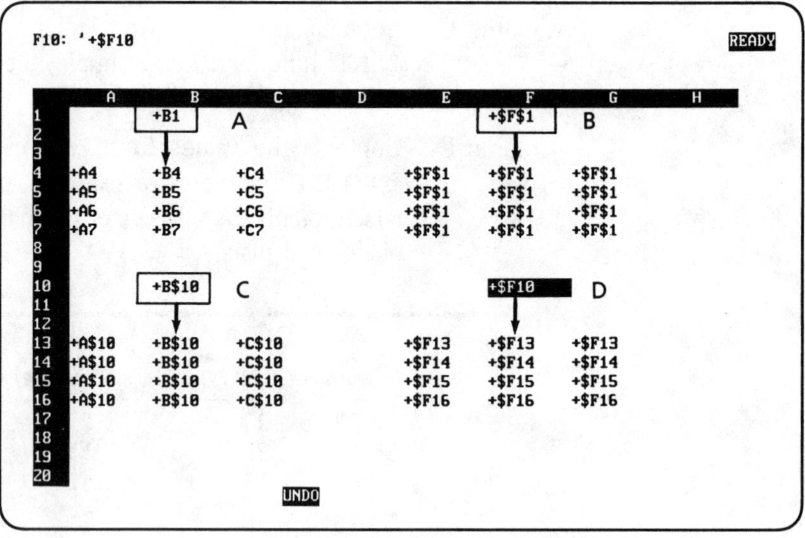

Figure 7.12 shows the four different combinations for relative and absolute cell addresses. When the cell address in cell B1 (A) is copied, both the row number and the column letter change because the address is relative. Because the cell address in cell F1 (B) is absolute, neither the row number nor column letter change when the cell address is copied. The cell address in cell B10 (C) has a relative column address and an absolute row address; only the column letter changes when the cell address is copied. And because the cell address in cell F10 (D) has an absolute column address and a relative row address, only the row number changes when that cell address is copied.

Editing Formulas

Sometimes after entering a formula in a cell, you find that the formula is not working as it should, especially in the case of long and complex formulas. Rather than retyping the entire formula, you can use a simple process to debug it.

You want to take a look at the formula, and try different combinations of cell addresses and operators—but you want to leave the original entry intact to avoid forgetting it. To do this, convert the formula to a label, copy the formula to another cell, and then test the various options. By converting the formula to a label, you preserve the cell addresses, which, being relative cell addresses, would change if the formula were copied to another cell.

To convert the formula to a label:

Move to: the cell containing the formula
Press: EDIT (F2)
HOME to move to the beginning of the entry
Type: ' (apostrophe)
Press: ↵

If the new label is longer than the width of the column and if there is data in the cell to the right, only a portion of the label will appear in the cell. If you need to see the entire label, widen the column.

Now copy the label to another cell in the worksheet. Then, after editing the label, convert it back to a formula: press Edit (F2), Home, Del, and Enter to eliminate the label prefix. Check the resulting calculation from the formula, and, if necessary, repeat the editing process until the formula works.

Figure 7.13
Formula converted to label

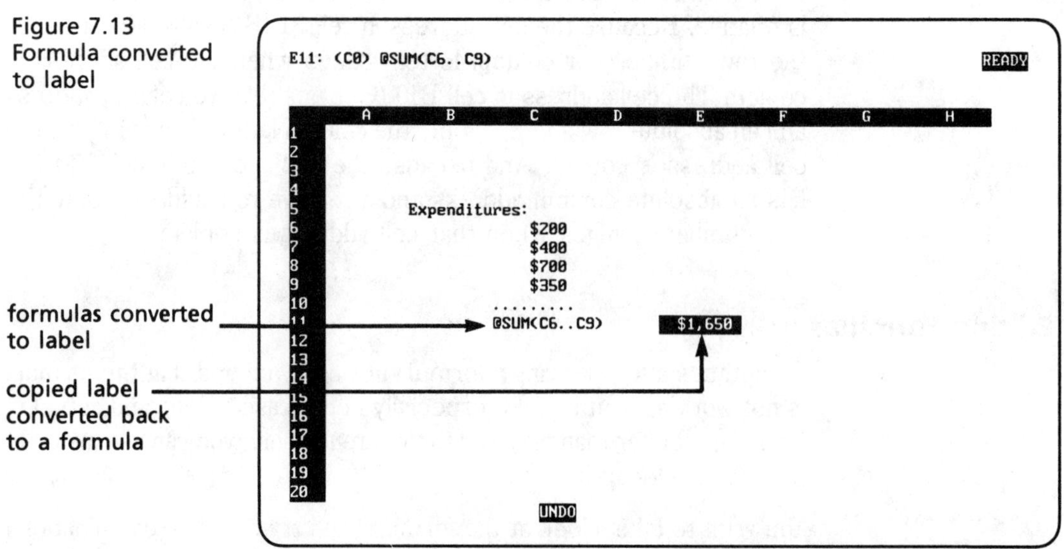

In the worksheet in Figure 7.13, a simple formula was converted into a label and copied to another cell, where it was converted back to a formula and then tested. This process enables you to keep all the cell addresses the same in the original and the copied versions. (In the example the formula is actually correct, but you can see the value of this method for longer formulas.)

When your copied formula is correct, you may convert it into a label and copy it into the original cell, replacing the label there.

To convert the original entry back to a formula, move back to the cell, press Edit (F2), Home, Del, and Enter to get rid of the label prefix.

Dates for the Years 1900 to 2099

When you use the @DATE function, 1-2-3 assigns a value to a date that represents the number of days from the beginning of this century (January 1, 1900) to the date. For example, the entry @DATE(1,2,4) stands for February 4, 1901; 1-2-3 assigns it the value 401, which stands for 401 days from January 1, 1900. (The value appears in the cell until you format the cell to display its contents as a date.)

1-2-3 can display dates for any year from 1900 to 2099. For years after 1999, you simply identify the year as a number between 100 and 199—this just means adding 100 to the last two digits of the year. For example, to enter the date October 31, 2042, you type @DATE(142,10,31).

Figure 7.14
Year 2042

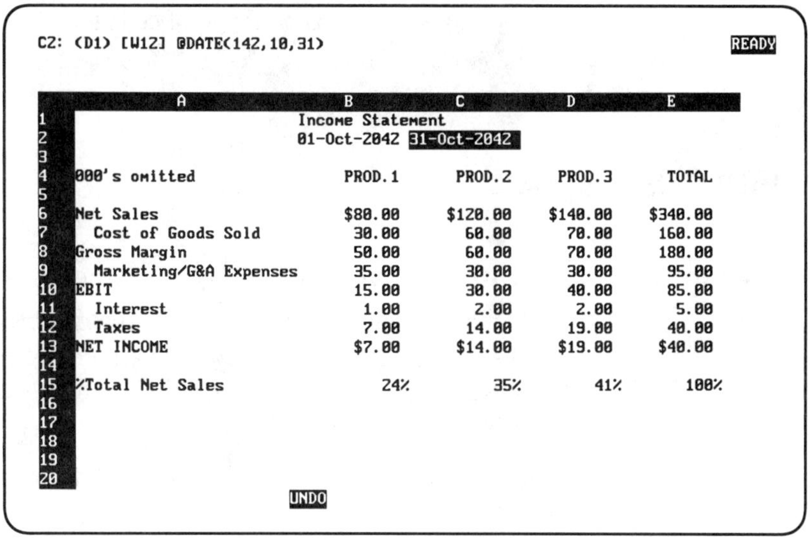

```
C2: (D1) [W12] @DATE(142,10,31)                                        READY

             A                     B            C          D          E
1                            Income Statement
2                            01-Oct-2042  31-Oct-2042
3
4   000's omitted                  PROD.1      PROD.2      PROD.3     TOTAL
5
6   Net Sales                      $80.00     $120.00     $140.00   $340.00
7     Cost of Goods Sold            30.00       60.00       70.00    160.00
8   Gross Margin                    50.00       60.00       70.00    180.00
9     Marketing/G&A Expenses        35.00       30.00       30.00     95.00
10  EBIT                            15.00       30.00       40.00     85.00
11    Interest                       1.00        2.00        2.00      5.00
12    Taxes                          7.00       14.00       19.00     40.00
13  NET INCOME                      $7.00      $14.00      $19.00    $40.00
14
15  %Total Net Sales                  24%         35%         41%      100%
16
17
18
19
20
                         UNDO
```

Years from 2000 to 2099 appear as four digits when the cell is formatted to display dates, so be sure the cell is wide enough to accommodate the longer entry.

Changing Formulas to Values

It's possible to change a formula in a cell to a value. This prevents the value from changing when the worksheet is recalculated. The **Range Value** command converts formulas into values, and then gives you the option of copying the converted value to another part of the worksheet (thus preserving the original formula) or replacing the formula permanently).

To change a formula into a value:

Move to: the cell containing the formula
Press: /
Select: Range
Value

You will be asked for the FROM range and the TO range. If you want to preserve the original formula or formulas, specify a TO range in another area of the worksheet; the values appear in that area and you can then decide whether to leave them there or to copy them over the original range. If you simply want to replace the formulas with the values, specify the same range of cells for both the FROM and the TO ranges.

DATABASE

Wildcard Characters in Criteria Range

When setting up the criteria range in a database, you usually have to make sure that the word or words in the range match exactly the word or words you are trying to find in the database. Any incorrect characters will throw off the search.

Three wildcard characters let you search for records that do not match exactly. The characters ?, *, and ~ tell 1-2-3 to look for more than one specific label.

? Matches any single character; ''t?p'' will match ''tap'' and ''tip'' (but not ''tips''). You can use more than one ? in a label; ''s??r'' will match ''sear'' and ''sour'' (but not ''soul'').

* Matches all characters to the end of the label; ''dum*'' will match ''dumpling'' and ''dumb'' (but not ''drum'').

~ The tilde at the beginning of a label is the equivalent of ''not equal'': it instructs 1-2-3 to accept any label **except** the one following the tilde. For example, ~Milne will select all records that do not have Milne in that field. You can place labels beginning with tildes in several fields of the database at once.

Figure 7.15 Criteria

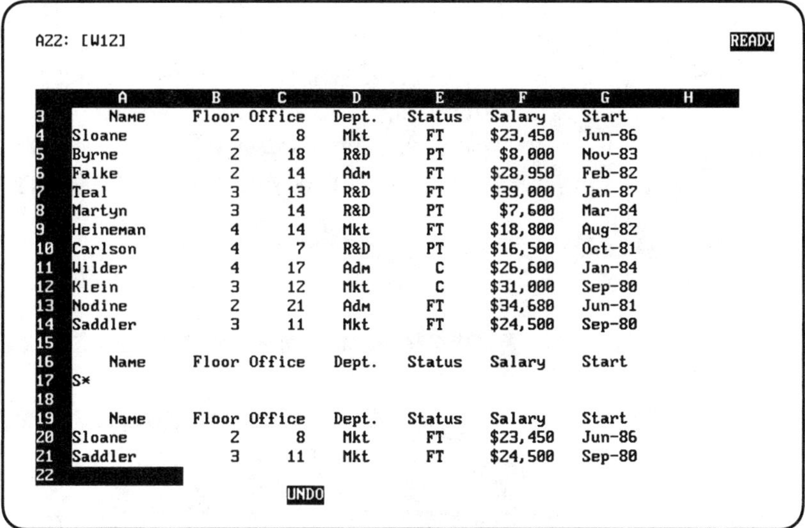
A22: [W12] READY

	A	B	C	D	E	F	G	H
3	Name	Floor	Office	Dept.	Status	Salary	Start	
4	Sloane	2	8	Mkt	FT	$23,450	Jun-86	
5	Byrne	2	18	R&D	PT	$8,000	Nov-83	
6	Falke	2	14	Adm	FT	$28,950	Feb-82	
7	Teal	3	13	R&D	FT	$39,000	Jan-87	
8	Martyn	3	14	R&D	PT	$7,600	Mar-84	
9	Heineman	4	14	Mkt	FT	$18,800	Aug-82	
10	Carlson	4	7	R&D	PT	$16,500	Oct-81	
11	Wilder	4	17	Adm	C	$26,600	Jan-84	
12	Klein	3	12	Mkt	C	$31,000	Sep-80	
13	Nodine	2	21	Adm	FT	$34,680	Jun-81	
14	Saddler	3	11	Mkt	FT	$24,500	Sep-80	
15								
16	Name	Floor	Office	Dept.	Status	Salary	Start	
17	S*							
18								
19	Name	Floor	Office	Dept.	Status	Salary	Start	
20	Sloane	2	8	Mkt	FT	$23,450	Jun-86	
21	Saddler	3	11	Mkt	FT	$24,500	Sep-80	
22								

UNDO

In the database in Figure 7.15, an entry has been made in the Name field of the criterion range using the letter S and an asterisk. This criterion matches all entries that begin with the letter S (it does not matter what follows the first letter), so the data records for all those personnel whose names begin with S have been extracted to the output range.

Editing During a Find Operation

The Find operation allows you to locate in a database those data records that match specified criteria. In addition, you can edit those records once you have found them.

When in FIND mode, 1-2-3 highlights each data record that matches the conditions in the criteria range. The cells in the row containing the record are highlighted. Within the highlight, the current cell is identified by a blinking cursor; the current cell contents are displayed in the first line of the control panel. If you simply want to locate the other records that match the criteria range, you use the Up and Down keys to move the highlight to the next matching record.

If you want to edit one of the cells in the highlighted record, you can do so. First, use the Right and Left keys to move the blinking cursor along the cells in the record; notice that the cell contents in the first line of the control panel change.

Second, during the Find operation 1–2–3 treats the current cell as it does in READY mode. You can either type in new data and press Enter; or you can press Edit (F2), modify the cell contents, and press Enter. In both cases, 1–2–3 returns to FIND mode and the highlight remains where it was. Simply pressing Enter while in FIND mode exits the Find operation and returns you to the Data Query menu.

Figure 7.16 Editing in FIND mode

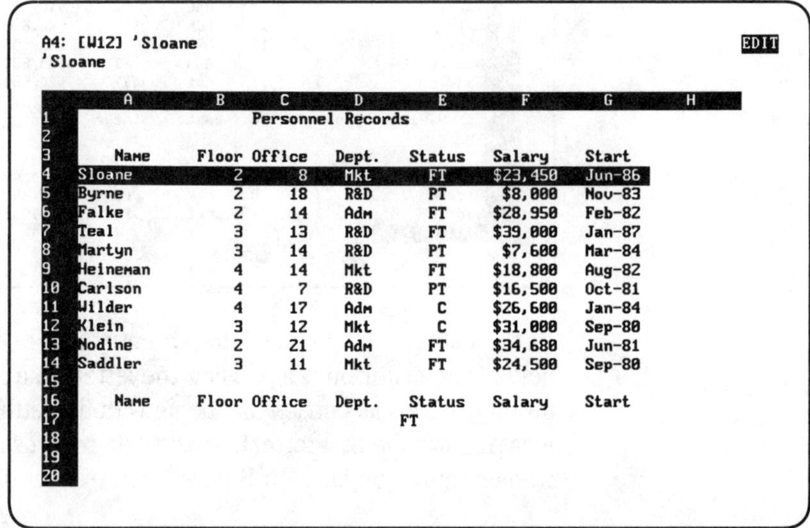

A4: [W12] 'Sloane
'Sloane
EDIT

	A	B	C	D	E	F	G	H
1			Personnel Records					
2								
3	Name	Floor	Office	Dept.	Status	Salary	Start	
4	Sloane	2	8	Mkt	FT	$23,450	Jun-86	
5	Byrne	2	18	R&D	PT	$8,000	Nov-83	
6	Falke	2	14	Adm	FT	$28,950	Feb-82	
7	Teal	3	13	R&D	FT	$39,000	Jan-87	
8	Martyn	3	14	R&D	PT	$7,600	Mar-84	
9	Heineman	4	14	Mkt	FT	$18,800	Aug-82	
10	Carlson	4	7	R&D	PT	$16,500	Oct-81	
11	Wilder	4	17	Adm	C	$26,600	Jan-84	
12	Klein	3	12	Mkt	C	$31,000	Sep-80	
13	Modine	2	21	Adm	FT	$34,680	Jun-81	
14	Saddler	3	11	Mkt	FT	$24,500	Sep-80	
15								
16	Name	Floor	Office	Dept.	Status	Salary	Start	
17					FT			
18								
19								
20								

The database illustrated in Figure 7.16 shows the highlight on the first record located by the Find operation, in this case, the first record containing FT in the Status field. The first cell in that record is cell A4, and its cell contents are listed in the first line of the control panel. Pressing Edit (F2) has moved the contents of that cell to the second line of the control panel; you can now modify its contents. Then press Enter to complete the step and return to FIND mode.

PRINTING

Printing Today's Date in Headers and Footers

You can instruct 1-2-3 to print today's date in the header or footer of a printout. Assuming either that your computer has an internal clock or that you entered the date correctly at the operating system prompt, the @ character specifies today's date in the header or footer.

After you have specified the range to be printed, follow these steps to print today's date in a header.

Press: [/]
Select: Print
Printer
Options
Header
Type: @ [↵]
Select: Quit
Align to align the top of the page
Go

Today's date will be printed as a header. 1-2-3's initial setting justifies the date with the left edge of the page. If you prefer to center the date, type ¦@; to align the date with the right edge, type ¦¦@.

Follow the same steps to print the date as a footer. (For more details on printing footers, see the next Tip.)

Printing the Footer on the Last Page

When you are printing a document of more than one page, you will notice that the footer is not automatically printed on the last page. You can, however, after the document has finished printing, select the **Page** command: this feeds the last page down to the bottom so that the footer does print.

To print the footer on the last page of a document, wait until the document has finished printing, then select Page from the Print menu. 1-2-3 will feed the paper down to the bottom of the page and print the footer.

(2.2) Using Data from a Cell in a Header or Footer

You can enter the text of a header or footer in one of two ways: by typing the text and pressing Enter or by typing a \ (backslash) followed by the the address or range name of the cell that contains the text for the header or footer.

Suppose cell B3 contains the label Income Statement and you want to use this as your footer. You would proceed as follows:

Press: [/]
Select: Print
Printer
Options
Footer
Type: \B3 [↵]

1-2-3 will automatically enter the contents of cell B3 when printing your footers.

Including a Filename in Headers or Footers

Sometimes it's useful to include the name of the current file in a header or footer so the printout identifies the file for you. Including a file name in a header or footer involves two steps: (1) you must enter the @CELLPOINTER function in a cell and (2) you must provide a reference to this cell in the text of the header or footer.

@CELLPOINTER is a function that provides information about the current cell. It can provide many kinds of information, depending on the argument you include with the @function. The *filename* argument results in 1-2-3 giving you information about the current file.

(2.2) Release 2.2 lets you include a reference to a cell in a header or footer by preceding the name of the cell with a backslash (\). For example, \G3 is a reference to cell G3. When 1-2-3 enounters such a cell reference in a header or footer, it substitutes the contents of the cell in the text of the header or footer. If, therefore, the cell you referenced contained the @CELLPOINTER(''filename'') function, the header or footer would include the file name.

If, for example, you wanted to produce a footer consisting of the name of the current file and wanted to enter the @CELLPOINTER function in cell D20, you would proceed as follows.

Move to: cell D20
Type: @cellpointer("filename") [↵]
Press: [/]
Select: Print
Printer
Options
Footer
Type: \d20 [↵]
Select: Quit
Align
Go

The name of the current file (for example, C:\TEMP\INCOME) will be printed as a footer. 1-2-3's initial setting justifies the file name with the left edge of the page. If you prefer to center the file name, type ¦\D20; to align the file name with the right edge, type ¦¦\D20.

Printing Cell Contents

When attempting to identify and isolate problems in a worksheet, it's very helpful to see all the cell contents (especially formulas) listed in full. With the **Print Printer Options Other Cell-Formulas** command, you can get a printout of all the literal cell contents.

The printout lists one cell per line and runs down the left side of the page. Each line gives the cell address, the cell format and column width (if other than 1-2-3's initial settings), and the actual contents of the cell (label, value, or formula).

A portion of the cell contents printout of the Income Statement created in the worksheet chapter is illustrated below.

```
C9: (,2) 30
D9: (,2) 30
E9: (,2) @SUM(B9..D9)
A10: [W24] 'EBIT
B10: (,2) +B8-B9
C10: (,2) +C8-C9
D10: (,2) +D8-D9
E10: (,2) @SUM(B10..D10)
A11: [W24] 'Interest
B11: (,2) 1
```

To get a printout listing the cell contents of the worksheet:

Press: /
Select: Print
Printer
Options
Other
Cell-Formulas
Quit
Align
Go

Be aware that this version of the printout takes up many more lines than a regular version. Also notice that the Cell-Formulas setting remains in effect (as the print settings sheet indicates) until you change it back to As-Displayed.

Printing Column and Row Borders

Column and Row Borders

When 1–2–3 prints a large worksheet, it automatically breaks up the printout into smaller chunks to fit on separate pages. As a result, you may lose important row and column labels from the top and left borders of the worksheet on the second and all following pages.

You can use the **Print Printer Options Borders** command to print certain columns, rows, or both at the top and left edges of every page of the printout. So, for example, if the labels for the months of the year are located at the top of the worksheet, you can print that row at the top of every page of the printout in order to keep track of related data more easily.

To print column and row borders on every page of the printout:

Press: /
Select: Print
Printer
Options
Borders

Make your choice and specify the rows and/or columns that you want printed. Note that you can choose any rows or columns from the worksheet—they do not have to be from the top or left edge. Do **not** include the rows and/or columns that you specified as borders in the print range, or 1-2-3 will print those rows and/or columns twice.

Column Letters and Row Numbers

Using the commands mentioned above, you can set up a situation where the printed row and column borders actually label the worksheet with column letters and row numbers. This process requires a little work, but it's very helpful to be able to refer to specific cells when looking at a printed worksheet.

Essentially, you create a row and a column that look similar to the top and left borders on the 1-2-3 screen, and then specify them as the borders to print out. The first step is to number the rows. Use the **Data Fill** command to create a column of consecutive numbers that match the left border.

As you follow the steps below, 1-2-3 asks you first for the fill range; specify the column and use the arrow keys to extend the highlight until it reaches the bottom of the active area of the worksheet. Then you will be asked for the start, step, and stop values; 1-2-3 offers initial settings that start at 0 and fill the range in steps of 1. You want to start at 1 and step by 1.

Move to: a cell in row 1 in a column to the right of the end of the active area of the worksheet

Press: [/]

Select: Data
Fill

Press: [.]
[↓] until the highlight reaches the bottom of the worksheet
[↵]

Type: 1 [↵]

Press: [↵]

Figure 7.17 Fill range prompt

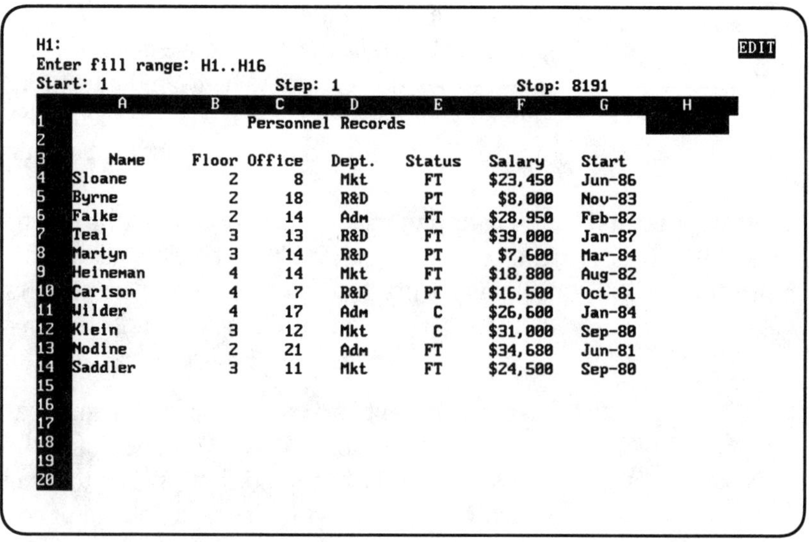

H1: EDIT
Enter fill range: H1..H16
Start: 1 Step: 1 Stop: 8191

	A	B	C	D	E	F	G	H
1			Personnel Records					
2								
3	Name	Floor	Office	Dept.	Status	Salary	Start	
4	Sloane	2	8	Mkt	FT	$23,450	Jun-86	
5	Byrne	2	18	R&D	PT	$8,000	Nov-83	
6	Falke	2	14	Adm	FT	$28,950	Feb-82	
7	Teal	3	13	R&D	FT	$39,000	Jan-87	
8	Martyn	3	14	R&D	PT	$7,600	Mar-84	
9	Heineman	4	14	Mkt	FT	$18,800	Aug-82	
10	Carlson	4	7	R&D	PT	$16,500	Oct-81	
11	Wilder	4	17	Adm	C	$26,600	Jan-84	
12	Klein	3	12	Mkt	C	$31,000	Sep-80	
13	Nodine	2	21	Adm	FT	$34,680	Jun-81	
14	Saddler	3	11	Mkt	FT	$24,500	Sep-80	
15								
16								
17								
18								
19								
20								

Press: ↵

When you have specified the range and all the values, numbers from 1 to the number of the last row of the active area appear in the column.

Now change the width of the column to be as narrow as the left border (the column prints out as it appears, so if there are spaces around the numbers, the spaces appear on the printout).

Press: /
Select: Worksheet
Column
Set-Width
Type: 4 ↵

The next step is to create a row of letters that will match the top border. Choose a row below the active area of the worksheet, and type in letters to correspond to the letters in the top border. The letters in the row must be centered in their cells.

Move to: a cell in column A in a row below the end of the active area of the worksheet
Type: ^A
Press: →

Type: ^B
Press: [→]

Continue labeling the columns across the row until you have covered all the columns containing data. The worksheet illustrated below shows the border column and row in place.

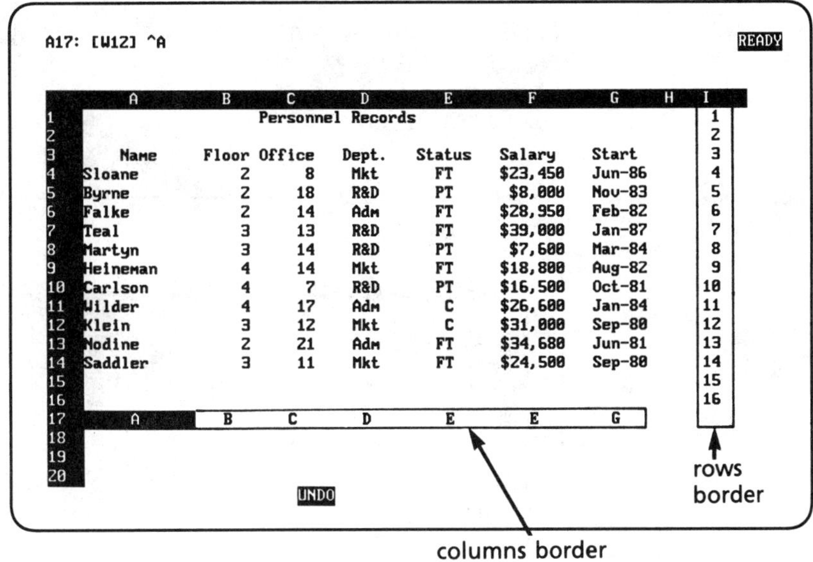

Name	Floor	Office	Dept.	Status	Salary	Start	I
Sloane	2	8	Mkt	FT	$23,450	Jun-86	4
Byrne	2	18	R&D	PT	$8,000	Nov-83	5
Falke	2	14	Adm	FT	$28,950	Feb-82	6
Teal	3	13	R&D	FT	$39,000	Jan-87	7
Martyn	3	14	R&D	PT	$7,600	Mar-84	8
Heineman	4	14	Mkt	FT	$18,800	Aug-82	9
Carlson	4	7	R&D	PT	$16,500	Oct-81	10
Wilder	4	17	Adm	C	$26,600	Jan-84	11
Klein	3	12	Mkt	C	$31,000	Sep-80	12
Nodine	2	21	Adm	FT	$34,680	Jun-81	13
Saddler	3	11	Mkt	FT	$24,500	Sep-80	14

Figure 7.18 Column and row labels

Set up the row and column you just created as the borders of the printout.

Press: [/]
Select: Print
Printer
Options
Borders

Specify the row and then the column containing the labels you just created.

Inserting Page Breaks

1-2-3 prints documents in a continuous flow. The printout breaks only to fit the document onto separate pages. You can, however, choose to break the printout at specific points. You might, for example, want to start a new page after the end of a section or the beginning of a memo.

The procedure to insert a page break is very simple:

Move to: the row where you want the new page to start
Press: /
Select: Worksheet
Page

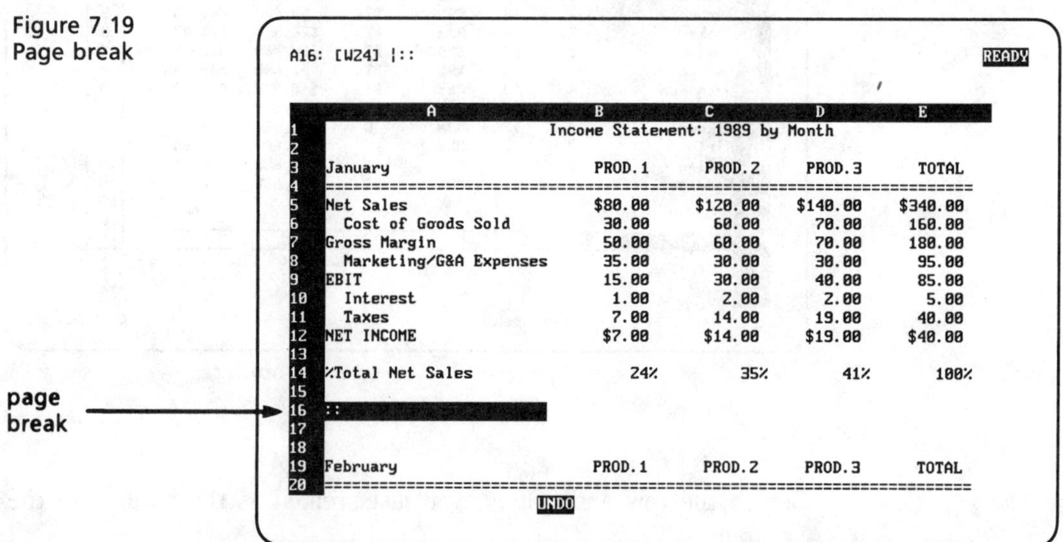

	A	B	C	D	E
1		Income Statement: 1989 by Month			
2					
3	January	PROD.1	PROD.2	PROD.3	TOTAL
4	=========================	==========	==========	==========	==========
5	Net Sales	$80.00	$120.00	$140.00	$340.00
6	Cost of Goods Sold	30.00	60.00	70.00	160.00
7	Gross Margin	50.00	60.00	70.00	180.00
8	Marketing/G&A Expenses	35.00	30.00	30.00	95.00
9	EBIT	15.00	30.00	40.00	85.00
10	Interest	1.00	2.00	2.00	5.00
11	Taxes	7.00	14.00	19.00	40.00
12	NET INCOME	$7.00	$14.00	$19.00	$40.00
13					
14	%Total Net Sales	24%	35%	41%	100%
15					
16	::				
17					
18					
19	February	PROD.1	PROD.2	PROD.3	TOTAL
20	=========================	==========	==========	==========	==========

Figure 7.19
Page break

1-2-3 inserts a new row above the pointer; it contains the label ::. If you look at the cell contents in the first line of the control panel, you will see that the cell actually contains |::. When 1-2-3 encounters this series of characters while printing, it automatically advances to the next page and continues printing.

To clear a page break, locate the cell pointer in the row containing the page break, and select **/Worksheet Delete Row**. Alternatively, use **/Range Erase** to erase the cell with the page break.

GRAPHICS

Graphing in Color

To view graphs in color, you need a color monitor. You select **/Graph Options Color**, and the current graph appears in color. To view a graph in black and white again, select **/Graph Options B&W**.

You can choose the color option even if you have a monochrome monitor. The graph will still appear, and, depending on your hardware, may have a variety of different shadings to distinguish the ranges (or it may make all the ranges look the same).

The only way to change the colors that 1–2–3 uses to draw the graphs is to reassign the data ranges to different ranges on the graph. You can modify the colors on a color printer or color plotter.

When you save a graph, 1–2–3 assigns a different color to each data range. PrintGraph can then draw the graph in color, even if the graph was created with the B&W option.

Skipping Labels on the X Axis

If the x axis of a graph contains several labels, you may find that the labels look crowded. This often happens if the X data range contains long labels.

You can solve this problem by using **/Graph Options Scale Skip**. You instruct 1–2–3 to skip labels at a certain interval.

To skip labels on the x axis of a graph:

Press: [/]
Select: Graph
Options
Scale
Skip

The second line in the control panel reads Enter skip factor (1..2048): 1. The number you enter, up to 2048, will determine which labels are printed. For example, an entry of 5 means that every fifth label will be printed. The entry 1 is the initial setting, and means that all labels are included. To print every other label, enter 2.

Type: 2 ↵
Select: Quit
View

Figure 7.20
Skipped labels on x axis

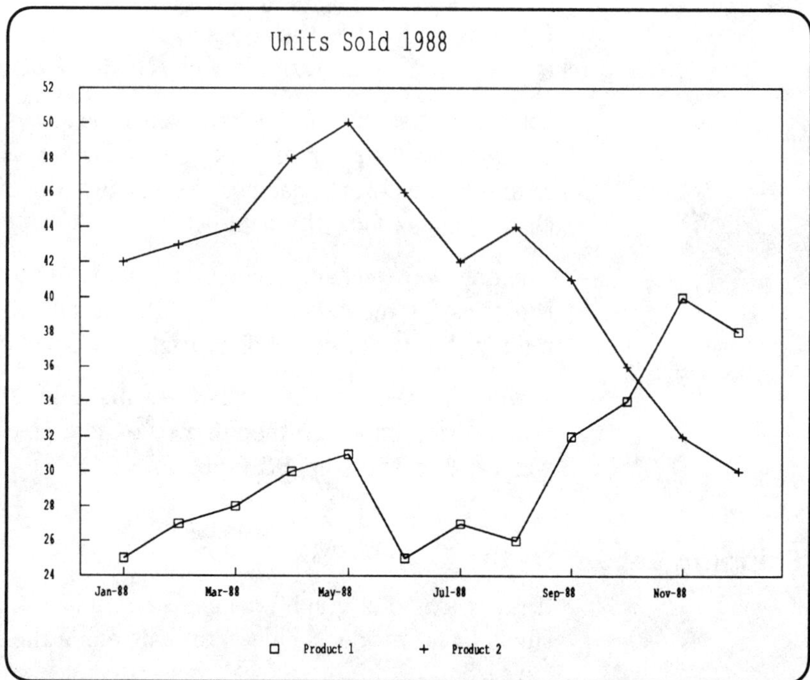

In the graph illustrated in Figure 7.20, only every other label is included on the X axis (a skip factor of 2). The best time to use this option is when the labels are sequential (as with months) and you can easily determine what the missing labels are.

Suppressing the Scale Indicator

When applicable, 1–2–3 automatically places a label next to the y axis that indicates the scale of the numbers shown. The label is shown in parentheses and reads **Thousands**, **Millions**, and so on.

Figure 7.21 Y axis scale indicator

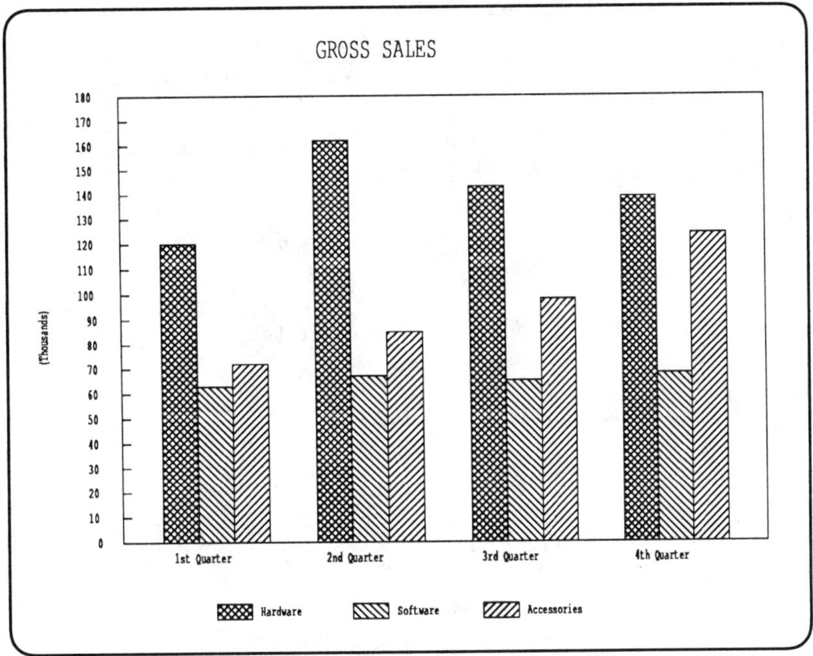

In the graph illustrated above, the indicator informs you that the y axis is actually graphing numbers in the hundreds of thousands ($100 stands for $100,000, and so on).

You can change the initial setting and suppress the scale indicator. To suppress it:

Press: [/]
Select: Graph
Options
Scale
Y-Scale
Indicator
No
Quit
Quit
View

The scale indicator is suppressed, but the actual scale of the y axis does not change—the numbers look the same.

Adding Data Labels to Graphs

1-2-3 has a feature that allows you to add data labels to a graph. The labels appear on the graph itself, next to the data points.

Data labels are drawn from a range on the worksheet. A range of data labels is matched against a range of data being graphed; each label corresponds to a value in the data range. You can specify a different range of labels for each range of data being graphed. The labels can be values or words.

To add data labels to a graph:

Press: /
Select: Graph
Options
Data-Labels

You are prompted to choose the data range against which to place the labels (range A through F). Once you have made your choice, the second line of the control panel reads **Enter label range for A range data:**. Use the arrow keys to point to the range you wish to use as labels. Note that if you select a range that has more or fewer cells than the data range, only the first corresponding labels will be used.

After you have specified the range of cells to be used as labels, the command menu reads **Center Left Above Right Below**. For line and XY graphs, 1-2-3 lets you determine where the labels are placed in relation to the data points. For bar and stacked bar graphs, the labels are automatically placed above the bars. Once you have selected the position of the labels, view the graph.

Select: Quit
Quit
View

Figure 7.22
Data labels

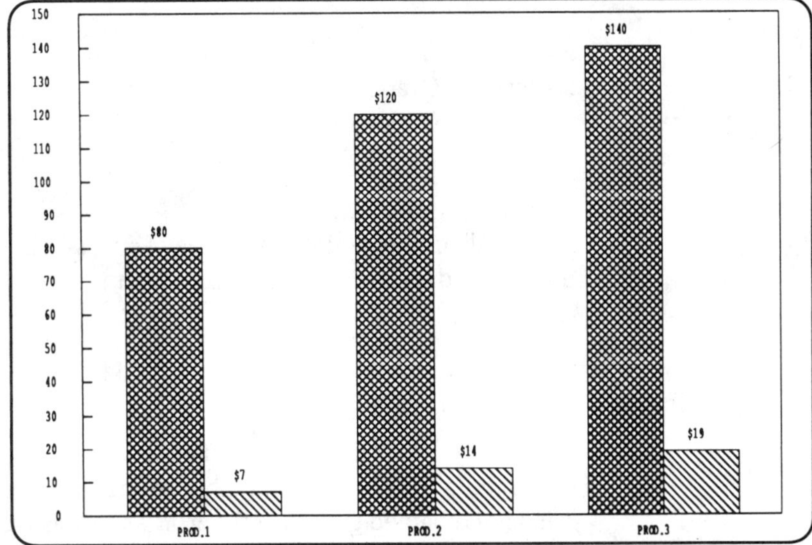

In the graph illustrated in Figure 7.22, the ranges used for the data labels are the same as the ranges used for the data points themselves. You can see the actual values being graphed above the bars.

Pie charts do not accept data labels because they plot only one data range. Note, however, that the data in the cells specified as the X range is used as labels next to the pie slices. Simply specify an X range that contains the labels you want for the slices (again, you can label the slices with the numeric quantities they represent by specifying the same cells for the X and A data ranges).

(2.2) Adding Data Labels Quickly

If the labels you want to use as data labels are in consecutive cells of the worksheet, you can assign them to data ranges as a group instead of individually. For example, suppose you have three data ranges and three labels (in cells F5..F7) you want to use as labels for those ranges. You can then use **/Graph Options Data-Labels Group** to assign the labels to the ranges.

To assign data labels as a group:

Press: /
Select: Graph
Options
Data-Labels
Group

1-2-3 will prompt you for the range of data labels and then for the position of the data labels. Figure 7.22 illustrates what data labels look like on a bar graph.

(2.2) Creating a Table of Graphs

If you have several graphs in one worksheet, you may find it useful to list them in the form of a table. A graph name table alphabetically lists all the named graphs in the worksheet, as well as their types and titles. A graph name table is like a range name table which lets you see all the named ranges in the worksheet.

To create a table of graph names:

Press: /
Select: Graph
Name
Table

1-2-3 will prompt you for a range for the table. Make sure you choose an empty location of the worksheet, or the table will write over data in the location. A graph name table takes up three columns and as many rows as there are named graphs, plus one blank row. If you make a mistake when placing the table and the undo feature is on, press Undo (Alt-F4) right away to restore the worksheet to its original state.

Figure 7.23
Graph name table

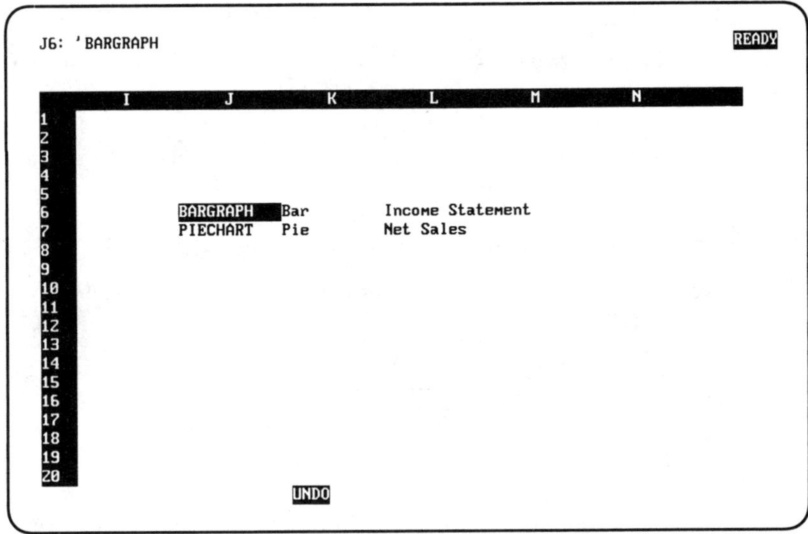

(2.2) ALLWAYS

Adjusting Row Heights

When you use Allways with a worksheet that you haven't yet formatted, all the rows are the same height, just as in 1–2–3. As you begin to select fonts of different sizes, rows that contain larger fonts become taller than rows that contain smaller fonts.

Initially, the height of each row is set to Auto. This means that Allways will adjust the height of the row automatically to accommodate the largest font in that row.

Allways measures the height of rows in points. Typically, the automatic row height is one or two points higher than the font height.

You also have the choice of setting a row height manually. You may want to fine tune the spacing between lines of text, or create special effects like shade or black bars of varying heights. If you have text in a row, you will usually want to keep the row set to Auto so you do not accidentally leave insufficient space for characters.

To create a black bar, for example, you would take the following steps:

Move to: a blank row where you want the bar
Press: /
Select: Format
Shade
Solid

Indicate the range for the bar when prompted. The solid shading will fill the entire range you specified. Next you need to shorten the row to produce a bar.

Press: /
Select: Worksheet
Row
Set-Height

Either type a number of points and press Enter, or use the Up and Down keys till the bar is the height you want.

Figure 7.24
Black bar

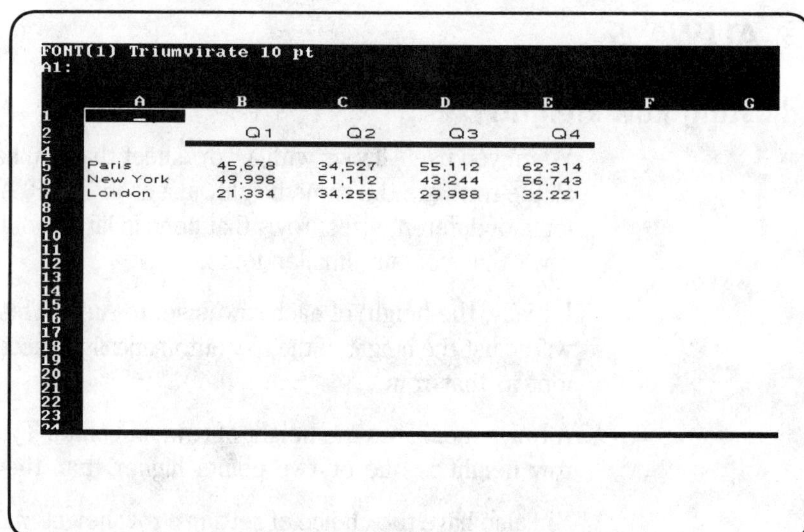

Adjusting Column Widths

You can make columns wider or narrower right from Allways, using a command very much like the **/Worksheet Column** in 1-2-3.

In Allways, column width is measured in terms of the number of characters that will fit in a column, but you can adjust the column's width more finely than you can in 1-2-3. For example, you can set a column to 9.6 characters of 12.53 characters. As in 1-2-3, you set the column width by entering or number or using the arrow keys to adjust the column's width visually.

Initially, each column in Allways is set to the same width that it is set to in 1-2-3. When you adjust a column width in Allways, you will not be affecting its 1-2-3 width; when you return to 1-2-3, the column will be the same width as when you left it.

Because you can have many fonts in Allways and the character widths can vary widely, Allways uses a standard measure for the width of a character. For the purpose of column widths, the width of one character equals the width of a numeric digit in Font 1.

Taking Advantage of Your Printer's Fonts

Initially, Allways provides a default font set consisting of soft fonts that are part of the Allways program. Allways, however, lets you use any font that your printer supports.

If, for example, you have a font in which you generally like to print your worksheets, you can do so very easily with Allways. Make this font the default font (Font 1) as follows:

Press: [/]
Select: Format
Font
Font 1
Replace
the typeface you want
the size you want
Quit

The worksheet now appears in the font you chose as Font 1. You can use the same procedure to replace any of the other initial fonts in the font set with a font that your printer supports; the mix of fonts is up to you.

> NOTE: If you have the choice of the same font in a soft and printer version, you're best off choosing the printer version because it's faster to print and is unlikely to get clipped (cut off) if a row is too short or column too narrow.

When you change fonts in the font set, the font set is saved as part of the worksheet. When you start work on a new worksheet, you will start with the default font set of soft fonts that Allways provides. If you've created a particular font set that you would prefer as the default font set (for use with all new worksheets), take the following steps after creating the font set.

Press: /
Select: Format
Font
Default
Update

The current font set is now the default font set, and will be in effect for all new worksheets.

Accelerator Keys

Accelerator keys are command shortcuts. They are combinations of Alt and a letter or number key, for example, Alt-B. When pressed, they execute a commonly used command. Accelerator keys reduce the number of keystrokes required for a number of tasks, saving you time.

You don't need to know the accelerator keys; anything you can do with an accelerator key you can also do with a command. Once you're familiar with Allways, however, you'll probably find it faster and more convenient to use them.

The accelerator keys do **not** prompt you for a range; you must select the cell or range **before** pressing an accelerator key. To format a single cell, just position the cell pointer in that cell. To format a range of cells, type . (period) to anchor the cell pointer, highlight the range, and press Enter.

To use an accelerator key, press and hold down Alt and then press the letter or number key for the task you want to perform (letters can be lowercase or uppercase).

Some accelerator keys cycle among two or more formats. For example, Alt-S cycles among light, dark, solid, and no shade. Keep pressing the accelerator key till the choice you want appears.

Accelerator Key	Description
Alt-B	Boldface: Set/Clear
Alt-G	Print grid lines: On/Off
Alt-L	Lines: Outline/All/None
Alt-S	Shade: Light/Dark/Solid/None
Alt-U	Underline: Single/Double/None
Alt-1	Set Font 1
Alt-2	Set Font 2
Alt-3	Set Font 3
Alt-4	Set Font 4
Alt-5	Set Font 5
Alt-6	Set Font 6
Alt-7	Set Font 7
Alt-8	Set Font 8

Keeping Allways and 1–2–3 Synchronized

Whenever you make changes to the worksheet with 1–2–3 that affect the location of cells, Allways keeps its formats synchronized with the cells to which they apply. If, for example, you use 1–2–3 to move cells or to insert or delete columns or rows, Allways makes sure that its formats follow the cells that are affected.

To be able to track cell movement, Allways **must** be attached. If you detach Allways while you are making a change to a worksheet formatted with Allways, a mismatch may result between the cells of the worksheet and their Allways formats, and the formats you applied in one place will appear somewhere else.

For this reason, if you go back and forth between Allways and 1-2-3 a lot, you might seriously consider having 1-2-3 automatically attach Allways at the start of each 1-2-3 session to prevent potential mismatching of formats. To attach Allways automatically, select **/Worksheet Global Default Other Add-In** and specify ALLWAYS.ADN as the add-in to attach automatically. Then update the 1-2-3 configuration file with **/Worksheet Global Default Update**.

Part II: 1–2–3 Macros

Macros can automate almost any task you can do with 1–2–3—from typing a simple sequence of keystrokes to creating complex applications.

(2.2) 1–2–3 Release 2.2 Macro Enhancements

1–2–3 Release 2.2 has added a number of features to make macros more useful:

- A **learn feature** records your keystrokes automatically as a macro. This gives you a quick way to create macros and minimize typing errors in the macros.
- The **Macro Library Manager** add-in allows you to use macros with more than one worksheet. In previous releases of 1–2–3, a macro was restricted to the worksheet in which you created it, unless you re-entered or copied the macro to another worksheet. With the Macro Library Manager, you can save macros in a library for use with any worksheet.
- Several new or enhanced **advanced macro commands** extend what you can do with 1–2–3 macros.
- A new **naming convention** for macros so you can give macros any range name (up to 15 characters long), not just a name consisting of a \ (backslash) and a single character as before.

- No restrictions about the number of macros in a single worksheet.
- Improved debugging of macros through enhancements to **STEP mode**.

How to Use this Part of the Guide

- If you've had some experience with macros, skim through Chapter 8 or review the information in "A Summary of Macro Basics." Then go on either to Chapter 9 which teaches the learn feature or to Chapter 10 which discusses advanced macro commands.
- If you're new to macros, go through Chapters 8 and 9 to learn the basics of creating macros with 1–2–3. Then go on to Chapter 10.
- Chapters 11 and 12 are for everyone because they teach you how to create a number of utility macros and how to save them in a library so you can use them with any worksheet. You will find a use for many of these macros in your own work. You will also find them useful in creating the more complex applications described in Chapters 13 and 14.
- Chapters 13 and 14 describe more complex applications, such as doing a graph presentation and setting up your own set of menus. The macros in these chapters will give you many ideas for automating your own work.

8

Getting Started with Macros

Macros can automate almost any task you can do with 1-2-3. Macros can enter numbers and text, choose commands from menus, move around the worksheet—in short, a macro can do almost anything you can do with 1-2-3. No matter how many steps the task involves, however, you activate a macro with a single command.

This chapter teaches you how to:

- Create simple macros
- Name and run macros
- Edit macros
- Refer to special keys in macros
- Troubleshoot macros

BASIC INFORMATION ABOUT MACROS

Macros consist of keystroke sequences and special commands needed for 1-2-3 to perform a certain task. For example, suppose you frequently instruct 1-2-3 to move to a certain location in the worksheet so you can refer to information there and then you move the cell pointer back to the previous location. Instead of pressing Goto (F5) and typing a cell address twice—to move and then to return—you can accomplish the same movement with a macro that is activated by only two keystrokes. This macro would include the very keystrokes and commands that you use to perform the task manually.

Macros can include any of the following components, individually or in combination:

- **Key names.** Commands that represent the keys on the keyboard. Such keys include the pointer-movement keys, the Enter key, and the function keys. For example, a macro that contains the key name {RIGHT} will move the pointer one cell to the right. Key names within a macro are always enclosed in braces ({ }).
- **Keystrokes that select menu items.** A series of keystrokes that selects menu items always begins with a / (slash). The menu commands themselves are abbreviated to the first letter of the command.
- **Keystrokes that represent labels or values.** These keystrokes will cause the macro to enter a label or a value in a particular location in the worksheet.
- **Formulas and @functions.** The formula +85+86 in a macro will add the contents of these two cells as the macro runs.
- **1–2–3 advanced macro commands.** Pre-programmed commands perform certain operations specific to macros. For example, the advanced macro command {GET} followed by a cell address stops the macro until you type a single keystroke and then stores the keystroke in the cell address you specified.

When you enter and run macros, you must follow a number of important rules and guidelines:

- All macro commands—keystroke sequences, key names, and advanced macro commands—must be entered as labels. If the macro begins with a character that 1-2-3 interprets as a value, you must type a label prefix before entering the macro. Macros that begin with a / (slash), a + (plus sign), an @ (at sign), or any other non-alphabetic character must be preceded with a label prefix, generally an ' (apostrophe). Advanced macro commands and key names entered in braces (for example, {GOTO}) are interpreted as labels, so 1-2-3 adds the label prefix automatically.
- Macros are stored in ranges in the worksheet and are identified with names. You name a macro by naming the range. You can give a macro any range name (up to 15 characters long) or you can name it with
2.2 a \ (backslash) and a single letter. You can run (execute) any macro by pressing Run (Alt-F3) and selecting the macro's name from the list that appears. If the macro's name consists of a \ (backslash) and

single letter, you can run it by pressing and holding Alt and then typing the letter. For example, to run a macro named \A, you would hold down Alt and type A. When you run a macro either with Run (Alt-F3) or Alt, 1-2-3 moves to the range in the worksheet that you specified and starts executing the commands it finds there. As a macro is running, the CMD indicator appears in the status line at the bottom of the screen.

KEYSTROKE MACROS

The simplest kind of macro is a stored sequence of the keystrokes you type to perform a task. Such a macro might include the keystrokes that erase a cell, name a range, create a window, or display a graph—the same keystrokes that you would type on the keyboard. The advantages of using macros that store keystrokes are substantial. A macro can:

- Take the drudgery out of a repetitive task by repeating the same keystrokes as many times as necessary
- Eliminate typing mistakes in a complex sequence of keystrokes; once you enter the macro correctly, there's no chance of pressing the wrong key
- Save time by automatically typing a long sequence of keystrokes

THE ADVANCED MACRO COMMANDS

A macro can do many tasks in addition to just typing keystrokes. A more sophisticated kind of macro uses the advanced macro commands of 1-2-3, which are a powerful built-in programming language. The advanced macro commands let you automate tasks that can't be done with keystrokes alone. For example, macros let you:

- Create your own menus that offer only the choices you specify
- Create custom prompt lines
- Use sophisticated programming features, such as looping and branching

Advanced macro commands add tremendous power and sophistication to 1–2–3's macro capability. In fact, macro programs can perform almost any task that can be done with a programming language such as BASIC or COBOL. Chapter 10 contains descriptions of each of the advanced macro commands.

ENTERING MACROS

Macros are entered in the worksheet. Like any other type of entry, macros occupy a cell or range of cells. If a macro occupies more than one cell, all the cells must be in a single column. Figure 8.1 shows one macro entered in a single cell and two other macros entered in consecutive cells down a column. (The macro names appear in the cells to the left of the top cell of each macro.)

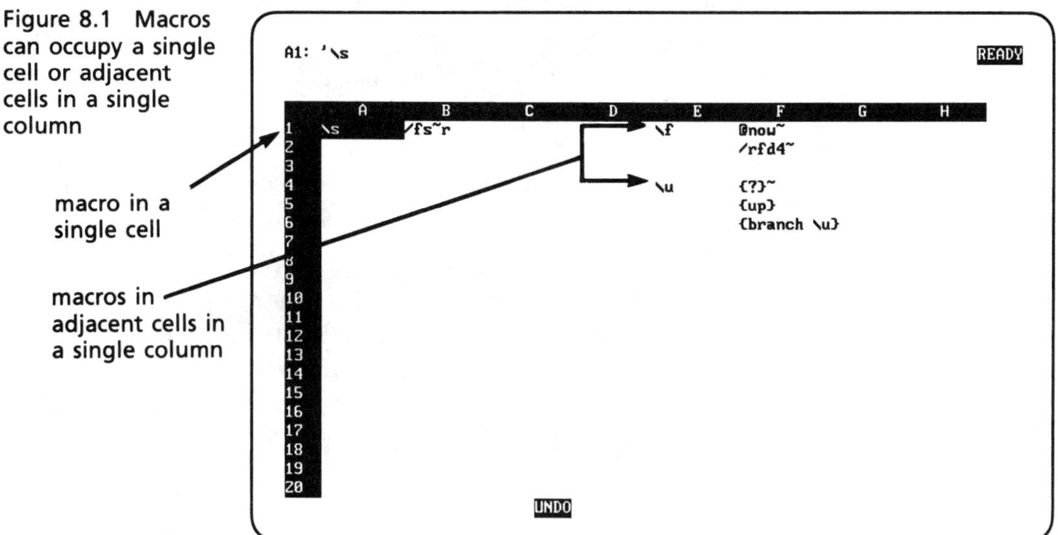

Figure 8.1 Macros can occupy a single cell or adjacent cells in a single column

Macro Cell Entries

1–2–3 carries out the instructions in a macro, or **executes** the macro, by reading down a column. It stops executing the macro when it reaches a blank cell, a cell that contains a numeric value, or a cell that contains the advanced macro command {QUIT}. Therefore, a multiple-cell macro can't contain blank cells or numeric cell entries. If it does, 1-2-3 can't complete the macro procedure.

1-2-3 automatically distinguishes between a numeric value and a label (a text entry). Even though macros can contain both numeric and text characters, you must always enter macro instructions as labels. This means that each cell in a macro begins with a label prefix, usually an apostrophe (').

When a cell entry in a macro begins with a digit or one of the numeric characters (+ . # (@ – or $), you must begin the entry by typing a label prefix.

For example, if you want a macro to type the number 100 automatically, you must type an apostrophe before the number:

```
'100
```

If, however, the macro starts with a letter or any other character that 1-2-3 recognizes as text, you don't have to type a label prefix because 1-2-3 automatically adds it. For example, to enter a macro that types the word Hello, simply type

```
Hello
```

As with any cell entry, the label prefix appears in the control panel, but not in the cell.

You can use any label prefix with a macro entry, but the apostrophe has several advantages. It is the default label prefix (the one 1-2-3 uses automatically), and it aligns the label at the left edge of the cell. This makes a macro easier to type and easier to read. The macro instructions in this book use the apostrophe label prefix.

Many macros include special key indicators (special key and function key instructions) and/or advanced macro commands. These two types of macro instructions are always enclosed in braces (for example, {HOME} and {QUIT}). 1-2-3 reads the opening brace as a text character, so when a macro cell entry begins with one of these instructions you do not need to type a label prefix.

To determine whether you need to type a label prefix for a macro cell entry, start typing the macro and look at the mode indicator in the upper right corner of the screen. It should always read LABEL when you're typing a macro. If it reads VALUE instead of LABEL, you need to type a label prefix before the first character in the entry. Press Edit (F2) and then Home, and insert an apostrophe at the beginning of the entry.

Macro Instructions

A macro is made up of a series of instructions. The macro above that types Hello consists of five instructions; each keystroke is a separate instruction. Anything enclosed in braces, such as {HOME}, is a single instruction. When you enter a macro in more than one cell, you cannot break up an instruction; that is, anything enclosed in one set of braces must be in a single cell (other instructions, of course, can also be in that cell).

A single macro cell may contain several instructions. Only the first character matters in determining if the cell entry is a label. The following macro enters a number in a cell, moves the pointer to the cell to the right, and enters another number. You must use a label prefix because the first character is numeric:

'1{right}2{right}

In the following macro, you don't need to use a label prefix because the macro begins with a brace:

{right}1{right}2{right}

PROTECTING DATA

To avoid problems when macros are in a worksheet that contains other data, always enter the macros in an out-of-the-way location, an area that you don't plan to use for anything else. The best location for macros is an area that is diagonally opposite your work. Some people put macros below and to the right of data in the worksheet. Others put macros at the top of the worksheet and build spreadsheets below and to the right of macros.

Separating macros from other worksheet information also minimizes the risk of accidentally damaging a macro. For example, when you keep macros in an area that is diagonally opposite other worksheet data, you won't accidentally delete part or all of the macro if you decide to delete a row or column. Likewise, you won't insert a blank row in the middle of a macro if you insert a row.

If you need to add information to a worksheet that contains macros, it's a good idea to insert rows or columns to hold the new information. This ensures that the macros remain separated from the other information in the worksheet.

USING MACROS

You can use a macro at almost any point in a 1–2–3 session. For example, you can use a macro that types a word when you're creating an entry, when you're editing an entry, or in response to a prompt during a command.

Macros don't have to complete an entire procedure. You can use a macro to start a command and then complete the command yourself. For example, a macro might begin the **Range Name Create** command (/rnc). The macro ends at the point where you must enter the range name, so you complete the procedure yourself.

Some macros are interactive. **Interactive macros** perform tasks automatically, but they also pause for you to enter information and then continue processing. These macros use advanced macro commands. Chapter 10 discusses them in more detail.

SIMPLE MACROS

The simplest kind of macro stores a sequence of keystrokes. The sequence can include any letter, number, or symbol that you can type at the keyboard, as well as most of the 1–2–3 special keys.

The only keys that you can't include in a macro are 1–2–3's Compose (Alt-F1), Learn (Alt-F5), Run (Alt-F3), Step (Alt-F2), and Undo (Alt-F4) keys and the computer's Caps Lock, Num Lock, Print Screen, Scroll, Shift, Sys Req, F11, and F12 keys.

A simple macro can:

- Type any combination of letters, numbers, and symbols
- Enter formulas and @functions
- Press keys such as Esc, Tab, Enter, Ins, and Del
- Move the cell pointer around the worksheet or use the cell pointer to highlight a range
- Select menu items from a menu
- Select a file name or range name
- Activate most of 1-2-3's function keys, including Edit (F2), Window (F6), and Calc (F9)

To include a letter, number, or other character in a macro, just type the actual keystroke. For example, the following macro types the word Lotus in the control panel.

```
Lotus
```

To include a special key in a macro, you type the key name in braces. For example, to include the End key, you type {END}; to include Calc (F9), you type {CALC}. The key name can be in lowercase or uppercase.

The following macro moves the cell pointer to the home position and types Lotus in the control panel.

```
{HOME}Lotus
```

The one key name that is not identical to the key it represents is the ~ (tilde), which is the name for the Enter key. The tilde is a single character and is not enclosed in braces.

Enter is one of the most frequently used keys in any work session. Most procedures that can be automated as macros include at least one instance of Enter. Be sure to type one tilde for each time you would press Enter if you were performing the task manually. Forgetting tildes in a macro is probably the most common reason for a macro not running correctly.

Many macros include instructions to move to a specific cell, such as A1. You can type either lowercase or uppercase letters: a1 or A1. The same is true of range addresses. 1-2-3 displays a range address by separating cell addresses with two periods: A1..D5. You can use this format when you specify a range address in a macro, but you can also type only one period and lowercase letters: a1.d5.

Many of the examples of macros in this book use range names to refer to worksheet locations rather than cell or range addresses. Range names ensure that a macro always uses the correct cell or range, even if you move data to other locations in the worksheet. If you reorganize a worksheet, ranges names still refer to the same ranges even if the ranges no longer occupy the same cells. 1–2–3 does not distinguish between uppercase and lowercase range names.

Examples

Here are some examples of simple macros:

1. This macro automatically types the word Lotus and enters it in the current cell. You must position the cell pointer before you use this macro.

   ```
   Lotus~
   ```

   The ~ (tilde) represents the Enter key. This macro uses Enter once to enter the word in the cell.

   To move to another cell after entering Lotus, replace the tilde with a pointer-movement instruction. For example:

   ```
   Lotus{RIGHT}
   ```

   enters Lotus in the current cell and moves the pointer to the next cell to the right.

2. This macro automatically changes the column width to 10 characters. To do this without a macro, you must press the following keys:

Keystroke	Effect
/	Calls up the menu
W	Selects Worksheet
C	Selects Column
S	Selects Set-Width
10	Types the new column width of 10 characters
Enter	Completes the command

The macro consists of exactly the same keystrokes:

```
'/wcs10~
```

The first five keystrokes in the macro are exactly the same as the keystrokes you type manually; the tilde represents Enter. Because 1–2–3 displays the menu when you press /, you must include a label prefix at the beginning of this macro. (1–2–3 ignores the label prefix when you run the macro.)

3. This macro moves the cell pointer to cell A3 and enters the formula +A1–A2. The macro is entered in two cells, one directly above the other.

```
{GOTO}A3~
'+A2-A1~
```

The first line of the macro presses Goto (F5), types A3, and presses Enter to complete the instruction; the second line types the formula and presses Enter to enter it. Because the second line starts with a numeric character (a + sign), you must type a label prefix first.

Even though this macro can easily fit in one cell, it is entered in two cells because it consists of two steps. Most macros perform tasks that are made up of a number of discrete steps. Entering the instructions for each step in separate cells makes it easier to follow the macro if you or anyone else needs to edit it.

Remember that anything enclosed in braces is a single instruction, so you can't break it into two cells. You must complete each individual instruction within a single cell.

Creating a Simple Macro

Now you are going to enter a macro in the worksheet. This macro types a company name automatically, which saves time if you have to type the name frequently.

If you need the information in the worksheet, save it before you continue.

Press: [/]
Select: File
Save

Press: ↵
Select: Replace

Then start with a blank worksheet.

Press: /
Select: Worksheet
Erase
Yes

Planning the Macro

Before you enter a macro in the worksheet, decide exactly what you want the macro to do. Then plan the macro so it accomplishes the task in the easiest way.

Entering the Macro

Always enter the macro in an out-of-the-way area of the worksheet so you don't change or erase it accidentally. The best location for a macro is an area that is diagonally opposite your other work: below and to the right of other work, or above and to the left. You'll test the macros you create in this chapter in columns A though H, so enter this macro in cell K1.

Move to: cell K1
Type: Lotus Development Corporation
Press: ↵

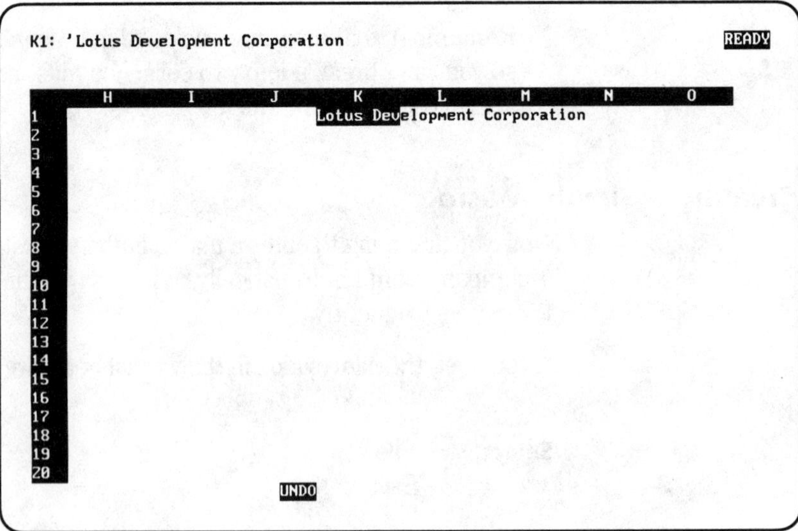

Figure 8.2
Macro in cell K1

Naming the Macro

Before you use a macro, you have to assign it a range name, which you later use to activate, or run, the macro. Without a range name, a macro is nothing more than one or more label entries in the worksheet.

Macro range names can take two forms:

- A \ (backslash) followed by a single letter, for example, \B
- (2.2) Any combination of up to 15 characters, for example, COMP_NAME

Using \ (backslash) followed by a letter is the simplest way to name a macro, but a full name can be more descriptive and help you to remember the macro's function.

(2.2) If you use a full name for a macro, follow the rules for range names. Like a regular range name, a macro range name should not duplicate cell addresses, @function names, advanced macro commands, or 1-2-3 key names. It also should not include any spaces, commas, periods, semicolons, or math operators.

Name this macro \C. The cell pointer should still be in cell K1.

Press: [/]
Select: Range
Name
Create
Type: \c
Press: [↵]

1-2-3 now prompts you for the range and offers the current cell address (the pointer's current location). You assign a range name only to the top cell of macro, so pressing Enter to accept K1 as the range is all that's required to finish naming the range.

Press: [↵]

Documenting the Macro

In a cell to the left of the one that contains the macro, enter a label to remind you that the name of the macro is \C. This step labels the macro and documents its name. Labeling a macro with its name is especially important if a worksheet contains a number of macros or if other people are going to use the worksheet.

Because this macro name begins with a backslash, you must first type a label prefix when you enter the name in the cell. If you don't, the character that follows the backslash repeats across the width of the cell.

Move to: cell J1
Type: '\c
Press: ↵

Figure 8.3
Labeled macro

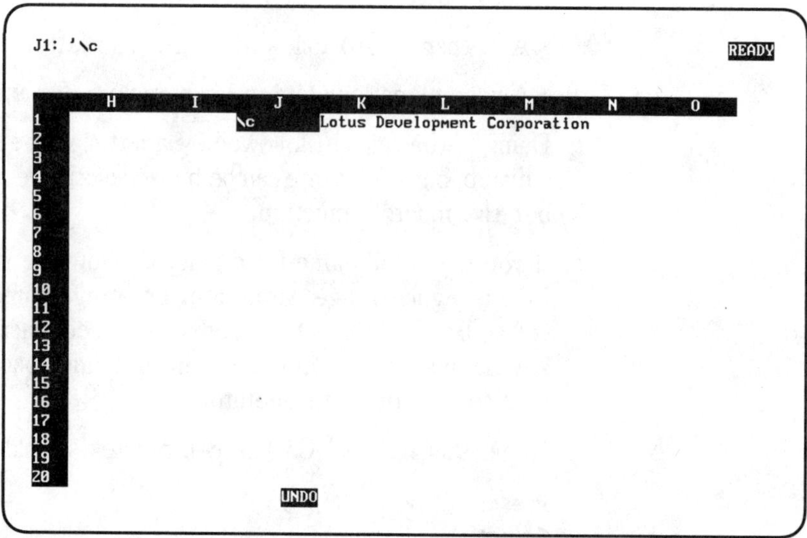

Running a Macro

You run (activate) a macro in one of two ways: with the Alt key or with the Run (Alt-F3) key. The method you use depends on the macro's name.

Running a Macro with Alt

If the macro's name consists of a backslash and a single letter (for example, \N), you can use Alt and the letter to run the macro. Just hold down Alt and then press the letter you assigned the macro. For example, to run a macro named \N, press Alt-N.

(2.2) Running a Macro with Run (Alt-F3)

If the macro's name consists of any other combination of characters (for example, COMP_NAME), you must use Run (Alt-F3) to run the macro. (You can also use Run (Alt-F3) to run macros named with a backslash and single character.)

To run a macro with Run (Alt-F3):

- Press Run (Alt-F3).

  1-2-3 will display a list of range names. If you have a lot of range names, press Name (F3) to see a full-screen list.

- Highlight the macro you want and press Enter.

You will now use the Alt key method to run the \C macro and enter the company name in cell G3.

Move to: cell G3
Press: ALT – C

Figure 8.4
Company name in control panel

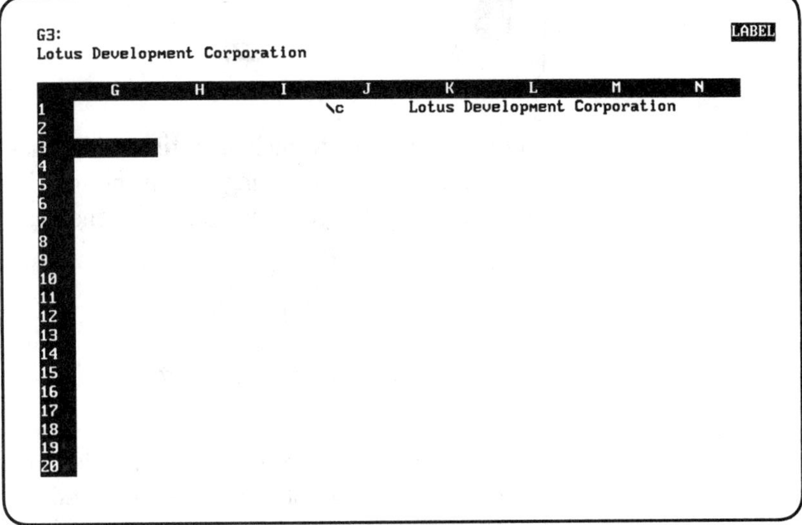

Look at the screen. The words **Lotus Development Corporation** appear in the control panel, but not in cell G3. This is because the macro doesn't include a tilde, the special key name for Enter. Whenever you type information in 1-2-3, you need to press Enter or a pointer-movement key to enter the information in a cell.

Press: ↵

Figure 8.5
Name in cell G3

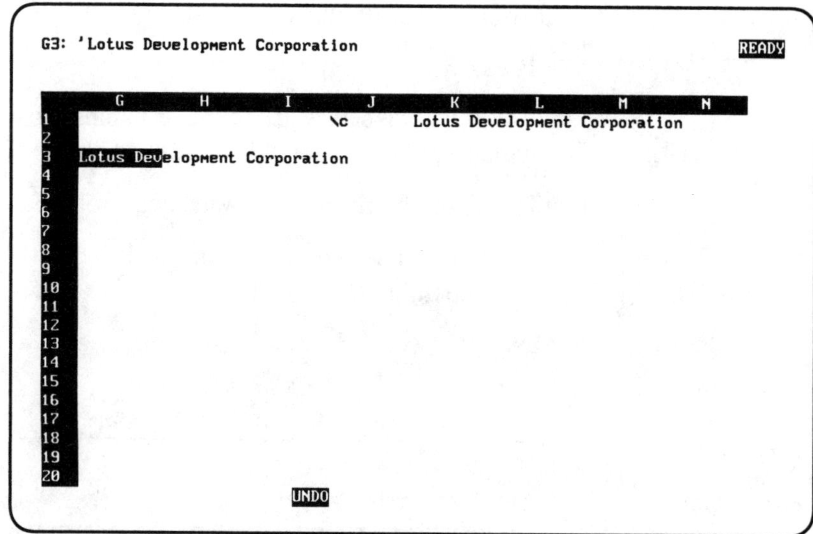

You may not want to include a tilde in a macro that enters text. For example, if you are planning to use the text in this macro only as part of a longer entry, you shouldn't end the macro with a tilde.

Move to: cell G4
Press: ALT – C
SPACE
Type: Statement of Earnings
Press: ↵

Because the macro doesn't include a tilde, you can add more text after the macro is finished. The text isn't entered into the cell until you press Enter.

Editing a Macro

After you enter a macro, you may want to change it, or you may notice a mistake in it that you need to fix. To correct mistakes or make changes in a macro, you edit the macro just as you edit any cell entry. For example, to make the macro above complete the cell entry, edit it so it includes a tilde.

Move to: cell K1
Press: [EDIT] (F2)
Type: ~
Press: [↵]

When you use the macro again, you won't need to press Enter. The macro will type the company name and enter it into the cell. Try it in cell G5.

Move to: cell G5
Press: [ALT]–[C]

Saving a Macro

You save a macro by saving the worksheet as usual. When you next retrieve the worksheet file, the macro will be available for your use.

Save the macro you've created in a file named MACROS1.

Press: [/]
Select: File
Save
Type: macros1
Press: [↵]

(2.2) If you create a macro that could be useful with more than one worksheet, perhaps a macro to save a file, you can save it in a macro library. A macro in a macro libary can be used with any worksheet. Saving macros in a macro library saves you from copying a macro from one worksheet to another; you just create the macro once and save it in a library. For details of macro libraries, see Chapter 12.

1–2–3 SPECIAL KEYS

In macros, the 1–2–3 special keys (function keys and pointer-movement keys) are represented by key names enclosed in braces. Some key names have optional abbreviations, such as {D} for {DOWN}.

Macro Key Names

You can type macro key names in either uppercase or lowercase letters. Uppercase letters are used in the examples in this book.

1–2–3 Key	Macro Key Name
ABS (F4)	{ABS}
APP1 (Alt-F7)	{APP1}
APP2 (Alt-F8)	{APP2}
APP3 (Alt-F9)	{APP3}
APP4 (Alt-F10)	{APP4}
BACKSPACE	{BACKSPACE} or {BS}
BIG LEFT (Ctrl-Left) or BACKTAB (Shift-Tab)	{BIGLEFT}
BIG RIGHT (Ctrl-Right) or TAB	{BIGRIGHT}
CALC (F9)	{CALC}
DEL	{DELETE} or {DEL}
↓	{DOWN} or {D}
EDIT (F2)	{EDIT}
END	{END}
↵	~ (tilde)
ESC	{ESC}
GOTO (F5)	{GOTO}
GRAPH (F10)	{GRAPH}
(2.2) HELP (F1)	{HELP}
HOME	{HOME}
INS	{INSERT} or {INS}
←	{LEFT} or {L}

NAME (F3)	{NAME}
PGUP	{PGUP}
PGDN	{PGDN}
→	{RIGHT} or {R}
QUERY (F7)	{QUERY}
TABLE (F8)	{TABLE}
↑	{UP} or {U}
2.2 WINDOW (F6)	{WINDOW}
/ (slash) or < (less-than symbol)	/, <, or {MENU}
~ (tilde)	{~}
{ (open brace)	{{}
} (close brace)	{}}

Notice that because the tilde and braces have specific meanings in macros you must include them in braces if you want to use the characters themselves.

To repeat keystrokes in a macro, include a number (or the cell address or range name of a cell that contains a number) after the macro key name. For example, {RIGHT 7} presses the Right arrow key seven times.

Using Key Names in Macros

Some of the sample macros shown earlier included key names. This macro uses key names to display a list of range names. You can use this list to move to any named range in the worksheet.

Creating the Macro

This macro moves the cell pointer to a named range you choose from a menu. Enter this macro in the same worksheet you used earlier.

Move to: cell K7
Type: {goto}
Press: [↓]
Type: {name}
Press: [↵]

This macro would fit in one cell, but entering each instruction separately lets you read the macro more easily.

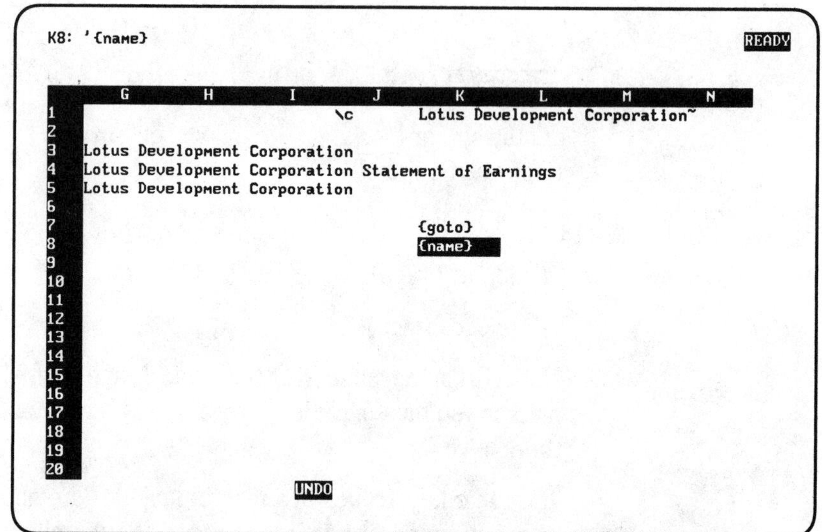

Figure 8.6 Macro with two keynames

Naming the Macro

You must assign the macro a name before you can use it. Although short macros like this one usually would be named with a backslash and single letter (because they're quicker to run), you will name this macro MOVE_TO so you can practice using the Run key (Alt-F3).

Press: [/]
Select: Range
Name
Create
Type: move_to
Press: [↵] to accept the name
[ESC] to cancel the range 1–2–3 offers
Move to: cell K7
Press: [↵] to accept K7 as the range

Now label the macro in cell J7:

Move to: cell J7
Type: move_to
Press: ↵

Using the Macro

After you name the macro, you can try it. You're going to use the macro to move to the range you earlier named \C, so move the cell pointer away before you run the macro:

Press: HOME

(2.2) Because this macro's name does not consist of a backslash and single letter, you're going to use Run (Alt-F3) to activate it.

Press: RUN (Alt-F3)

1-2-3 asks you for the name of the macro to run and lists the range names in the control panel. Unless you've created other range names in this worksheet, the list contains only two names: MOVE_TO and \C.

Select: MOVE_TO

The MOVE_TO macro now prompts you for the address to go to, and lists the range names in the worksheet.

Select: \C

The cell pointer moves to cell K1, which contains the \C macro.

After you finish practice using the two macros you've created, you may want to erase the data you entered in cells G3..G5.

Save the worksheet again as file MACROS1.

A SUMMARY OF MACRO BASICS

The following section summarizes basic points to keep in mind when you enter or use 1-2-3 macros.

Macro Review

- Macros can be very simple, consisting only of keystrokes and key names. Such macros are useful in many situations: if you must enter the same information often, for example, or if you use a particular command frequently. Simple macros can type keystrokes, activate function keys, or do almost any other task you can do from the keyboard.

- Macros can also consist of advanced macro commands or a combination of advanced macro commands and keystroke instructions. The advanced macro commands add a sophisticated programming ability to 1-2-3's ability to remember keystrokes in a macro. Chapter 10 discusses the advanced macro commands.

Entering Macros

- Macros can take up any number of adjoining cells in a column, although no blank cells are allowed within a macro. To separate different macros that occupy the same worksheet column, however, leave at least one blank cell between them.
- Each cell can hold up to 240 characters, so a macro can often fit in a single cell. Even if a macro contains fewer than 240 characters, however, you should probably enter separate instructions in separate cells. This makes the macro easier to read and edit.
- You enter a macro as a label or column of labels. If a macro instruction begins with a number or numeric character, type a label prefix before typing the macro. If the instruction begins with a letter, curly brace, or other text character, you don't need to type the label prefix.
- The mode indicator should read LABEL when you are typing a macro cell entry. If it reads VALUE, you must precede it with a label prefix.
- Before you enter a macro, run through the task. Note every keystroke you type, particularly Enter. This can save you editing time later.
- If a macro consists of keystroke instructions (no advanced macro commands) you can either type it in the worksheet yourself, as described  in this chapter, or use the learn feature to record keystrokes in macro format as you type. The learn feature is described in the next chapter.

Protecting Worksheet Data

- Enter macros in an out-of-the-way place in the worksheet. The best place is diagonally opposite other information in the worksheet—above and to the left, or below and to the right, for example. Keeping macros separate from other entries in the worksheet helps to ensure that you don't accidentally alter either the data or the macros. For example, if your macros are below and to the right of worksheet data, inserting or deleting a row or column will not affect your macros.

Naming Macros

- You assign a range name to a macro just as you assign any range name—with **/Range Name Create**. A macro name can take one of two forms: (1) a backslash (\) followed by a single letter or (2) a
(2.2) descriptive name up to 15 characters long. 1–2–3 does not distinguish between uppercase and lowercase characters in a range name. If you want to distinguish macro range names from other range names in the worksheet, you may want to start all macro range names with the same character, such as \.
- Keep track of macros by documenting their names. Enter the macro as a label in the cell to the left of the top cell of the macro.

Running Macros

- To run a macro, you use one of two keys—Alt or Run (Alt-F3)—depending how you named the macro. Use Alt to run any macro whose name consists of backslash and a single letter. If your macro is named \A, for example, you would run it by pressing Alt-A.

(2.2) Use Run (Alt-F3) to run any macro (including those named with a backslash and single letter). Press Run (Alt-F3), highlight the macro you want from the list of range names 1–2–3 displays, and press Enter. If you have a lot of range names in a worksheet, press Name (F3) after you press Run (Alt-F3) for a full-screen list of range names.

Saving Macros

- To save a macro for future use, save the worksheet as usual. The next time you retrieve the worksheet file, you'll be able to use the macros contained in the worksheet.
- (2.2) To save a macro for use with more than one worksheet, you can save it in a macro library. That way the macro will be in a central location, available whenever you want it, not just with a particular worksheet. Chapter 12 describes macro libraries.

MACRO TROUBLESHOOTING CHECKLIST

Typing errors are a common cause of macro failure. If you make a mistake typing a macro instruction, correct the mistake just as you would correct any other kind of entry.

If the screen displays an error message when you run a macro, press Esc or Enter to clear the error. Then move to the part of the worksheet that contains the macro and look for one of the following problems:

- Spelling mistakes
- Missing characters, such as omitted tildes (~), or incorrect characters, such as square brackets or parentheses instead of braces
- Spaces where there shouldn't be any, or missing spaces where you need them
- Missing steps in a command sequence, for example, /rf0~~ instead of /rfc0~~
- Incorrect cell or range addresses, or range names
- Range names that duplicate macro key names or advanced macro command keywords, for example, NAME or HELP

When you find the error, move the cell pointer to the cell, press Edit (F2), and correct the error.

To check a macro's range name, press Goto (F5), press Name (F3) twice, and scroll through the list of range names that appears. Press Enter when the name you want is highlighted. The cell pointer should move to the first cell of the macro; if it doesn't, use **/Range Name Create** to reassign the range name.

To move to the first cell in a macro, simply press Goto (F5), type the range name, and press Enter. You can use macro names in all the ways you can use ordinary range names.

9

(2.2) 1-2-3's Learn Feature

1-2-3 Release 2.2 includes a learn feature that offers a second way of creating keystroke macros. Instead of typing the macro instructions, you simply perform the task you want to automate. 1–2–3 "learns" your keystrokes and translates them into macro format in a worksheet range called the **learn range**. You then name and document the macro the regular way.

Using the learn feature to create macros has the following advantages:

- The learn feature lets you record a keystroke macro and test it at the same time. Because you are performing the procedure that will be automated in the macro, you can see on the screen exactly what will happen when the macro runs.
- The learn feature minimizes the possibility of errors because it records keystrokes in the learn range in the correct macro format. You simply press the keys and respond to the menus and prompt lines as they appear on the screen.

Learn is particularly useful for entering a long, complex keystroke macro because you don't need to figure out all the instructions in advance. For example, if you're using learn to create a macro that produces a bar graph, you simply type the keystrokes that specify the various graph settings you want—the keystrokes are saved automatically as a macro.

Although you can't use the learn feature directly to write macros that include advanced macro commands, you can later enter those commands manually in the learn range.

This chapter teaches you how to:

- Set up the learn range where 1-2-3 records your keystrokes
- Record the macro in the learn range

- Name and run the macro
- Correct mistakes
- Add to the learn range

While learning these aspects of the learn feature, you will create two macros: a cell formatting macro and a macro that creates a table of worksheet files in the current directory.

The Learn Range

When you create a macro with the learn feature, 1-2-3 stores the macro in a worksheet learn range. You must specify this range with **/Worksheet Learn Range** before you start to use the learn feature.

The learn range must be a single-column range. (If you specify a multiple-column range, 1-2-3 automatically redefines it to a single column.) When determining a size for the learn range, it's always better to make it larger than you think you might need so 1-2-3 doesn't run out of space when recording your keystrokes. As with any macro, the learn range should be in an out-of-the-way area of the worksheet.

After you activate the learn feature, you perform the task you want to record. As you do so, 1-2-3 records all your keystrokes in the learn range; you don't enter anything into the learn range directly. In fact, the learn range is often in a part of the worksheet that isn't visible as you perform the task.

Guidelines for Entering Macros with Learn

Because every keystroke you type while using the learn feature is recorded in the learn range, follow these guidelines to make your macros as efficient as possible.

- To select a command from a menu, type the first letter of the command instead of highlighting it with the menu pointer.
- To select a name from a list (such as range name), type the name and press Enter instead of highlighting the name.
- To specify a range, type the range address or name instead of highlighting it.

Using the arrow keys to highlight a command in a menu, a name, or a range involves additional macro instructions that take up space in the learn range and make the macro slower to run. The two macros in the illustration below were created with the learn feature. Both perform exactly the same task of creating a range name table. The macros press / to call up the menu, select **Range Name Table**, and specify cell N2 as the location for the table. The macro on the left was created using the guidelines above; the one on the right used arrow keys to make selections and specify cell N2. Notice that 1-2-3 records arrow keys such as Right and Up in abbreviated form: {R} and {U}.

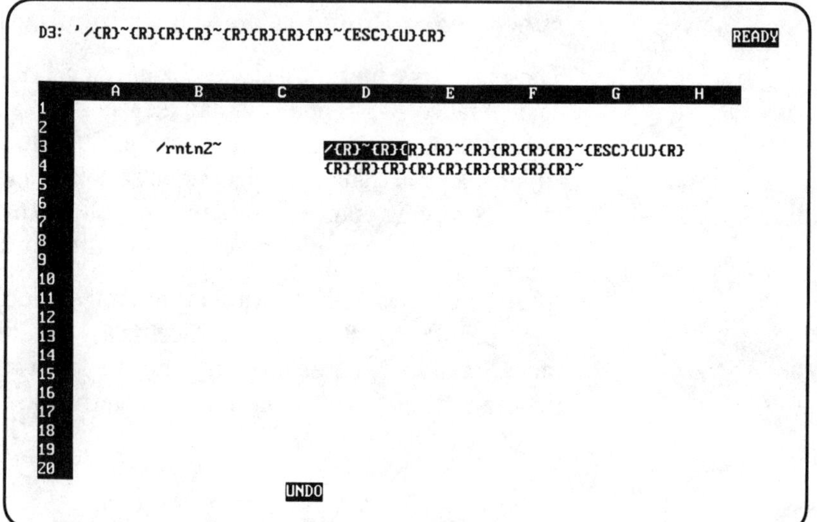

Figure 9.1 Two macros created with learn

Basic Procedure When Using Learn

To create a macro with the learn feature, you go through five main steps.

1. Specify a learn range for the macro and turn on the learn feature.
2. Perform the task you want to automate.
3. Turn off the learn feature.
4. Name the macro by assigning a range name to the first cell in the learn range.
5. Run the macro to see if it works, and, if necessary, edit it.

CELL-FORMATTING MACRO

This simple keystroke macro formats a cell in currency format with zero decimal places.

Specifying the Learn Range

The first step is to specify a learn range with **/Worksheet Learn Range**. The learn range is the worksheet area where 1-2-3 records the keystrokes as you type them. The cell-formatting macro needs only a one-cell range. Start with a blank worksheet and define cell F1 as the learn range.

Press: /
Select: Worksheet
Erase
Yes
Move to: cell F1
Press: /
Select: Worksheet
Learn
Range

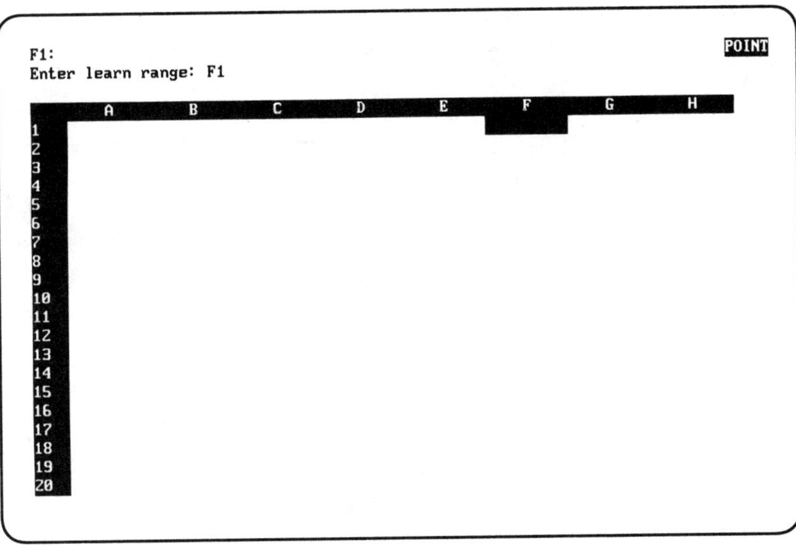

Figure 9.2 Specifying learn range

Press: ↵ to accept F1 as the range

Recording the Keystrokes

To have something to practice with, you are going to enter some values in the worksheet.

Move to: cell A1
Type: 45677
Press: ↓
Type: 2345.01
Press: ↵

Figure 9.3
Worksheet with two values

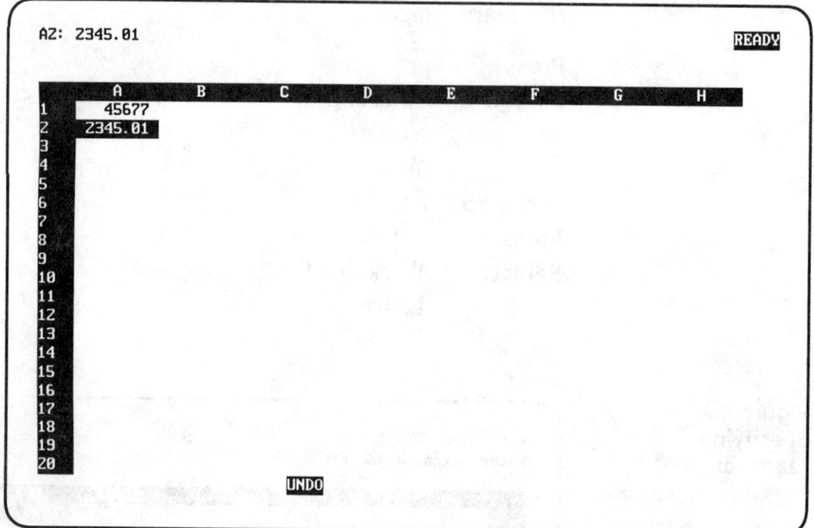

You will now use the learn feature to record the keystrokes for the cell-formatting macro. As soon as you turn the learn feature on, the LEARN indicator appears in the status line. You can then start performing the task of selecting the formatting commands. 1-2-3 will store the keystrokes in macro format in the learn range (if you make a mistake, correct it, and keep typing).

You are going to format the number in cell A1. As you do so, 1-2-3 will record your keystrokes in the learn range (cell F1). You turn the learn feature on by pressing Learn (Alt-F5).

Move to: cell A1
Press: LEARN (Alt-F5)
/
Select: Range
Format
Currency
Type: 0
Press: ↵
↵ to accept A1 as the cell to format

Now turn off the learn feature so that 1–2–3 stops recording keystrokes.

Press: LEARN (Alt-F5)

The LEARN indicator disappears from the status line, but the CALC indicator appears to tell you that you need to perform an additional step to enter the macro keystrokes into the learn range.

Press: ↵

Pressing Enter confirms that you've finished with the learn feature. The CALC indicator disappears. Now look at the learn range (cell F1).

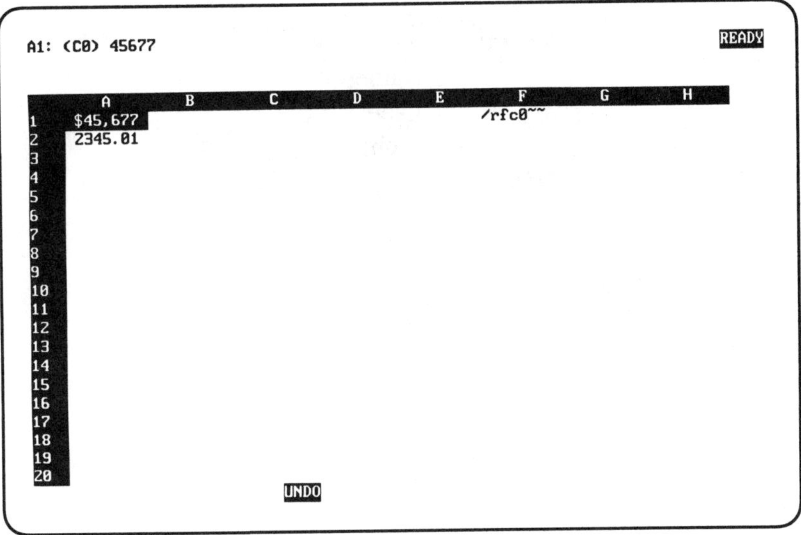

Figure 9.4
Macro stored in learn range

As you can see, pressing / caused / to appear in the learn range, selecting **Range Format Currency** resulted in the keystrokes rfc, typing 0 and pressing Enter twice resulted in 0~~.

> NOTE: If you made and corrected any errors while creating the macro, your macro will look different because 1-2-3 includes all the keystrokes you made.

Naming the Macro

As always, you need to name and document the macro. You will use a shortcut this time. If you document the name first, you can use **/Range Name Labels** to name the macro. This command names a range by using a label next to it for the name. For example, if you enter the name in a cell to the left of the macro, you indicate that you want to name the cell to the right. Name this macro \F.

Move to: cell E1
Type: '\f
Press: [↵]
[/]
Select: Range
Name
Labels
Right
Press: [↵]

Figure 9.5
Named macro

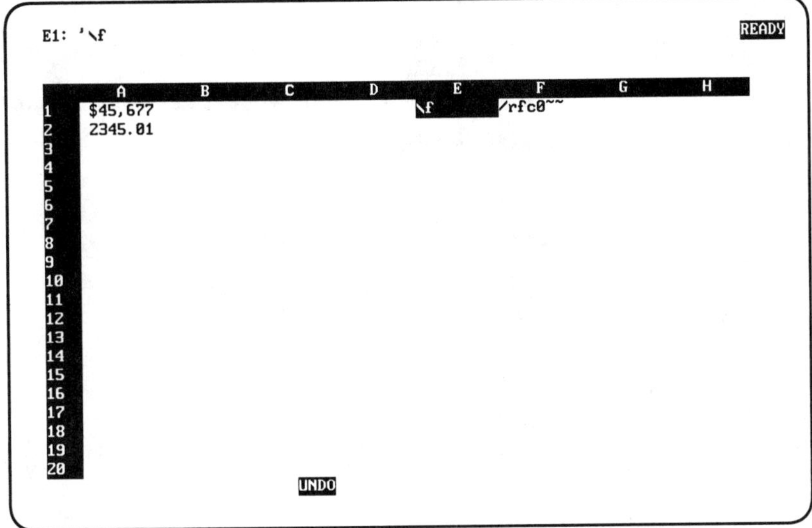

Running the Macro

Now make sure the macro works. Format the value in cell A2.

Move to: cell A2
Press: ALT — F

The value in cell A2 is formatted as currency, with a leading dollar sign, a comma, and no decimal places.

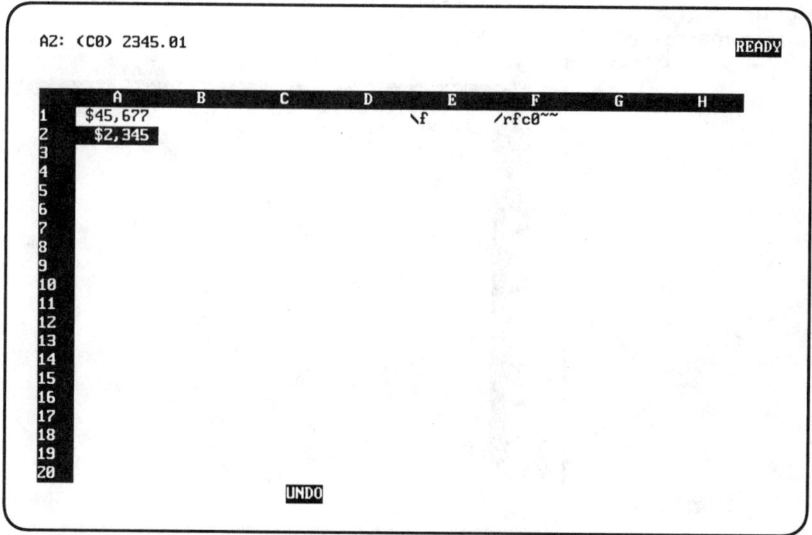

Figure 9.6 Cells A1 and A2 formatted

Now save your work in a file named MACROS2.

Press: [/]
Select: File
Save
Type: macros2
Press: [↵]

FILE TABLE MACRO

This longer macro moves to a specific cell in the worksheet and creates a table of all the worksheet files in the current directory using the **File**
(2.2) **Admin Table** command. This command is new to Release 2.2 and lets you list the worksheet files, the graph (.PIC) files, the print (.PRN) files, the linked files, or all the files in a directory of your choice.

/File Admin Table produces a four-column table. The first column lists the file names alphabetically, the second lists the date the file was last saved, the third lists the time the file was last saved, and the fourth lists the size of the file in bytes. The dates and times appear as date and time numbers, respectively, so to see the actual dates and times, you need to format the numbers as dates and times.

This macro will create a table of all of the worksheet files in the current directory (C:\TEMP) or on the current disk (B:). You should therefore see all the worksheet files you've created while going through the exercises in this book. Once you use **/File Admin Table** to produce the initial table, you will widen the first three columns of the table to accommodate lengthier file names and the date and time formats you'll be using. You will then format the date numbers as dates and the time numbers as times.

Redefining the Learn Range

Before you begin to record keystrokes for this second macro, you need to cancel the current learn range (which now contains the formatting macro) and define a new learn range. Make F3..F13 the new range.

Press: [/]
Select: Worksheet
Learn
Cancel
Move to: cell F3
Press: [/]
Select: Worksheet
Learn
Range
Press: [.]
[↓] ten times
[↵]

Recording the Keystrokes

This macro will create a file table (using **/File Admin Table**) starting in cell A5.

Press: [LEARN] (Alt-F5)
[GOTO] (F5)
Type: a5
Press: [↵]
[/]

Select: File
Admin
Table
Worksheet

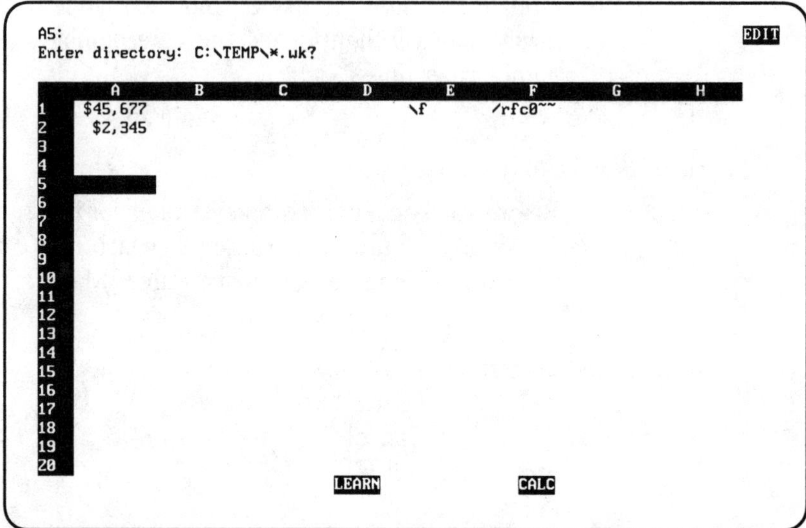

Figure 9.7 Selecting the directory

1-2-3 now prompts for a directory, offering the name of the current directory. If you have a hard-disk computer, you should see **C:\TEMP*.wk?**; on a two-diskette computer, you should see **B:*.wk?**. (If you see something different, press Esc and type the correct directory or drive name: **C:\TEMP** or **B:**.)

Press: ↵

1-2-3 asks for the range you want to use for the table and offers A5.

Press: ↵ to accept A5 as the top left cell of the table

Figure 9.8
Unformatted
file table

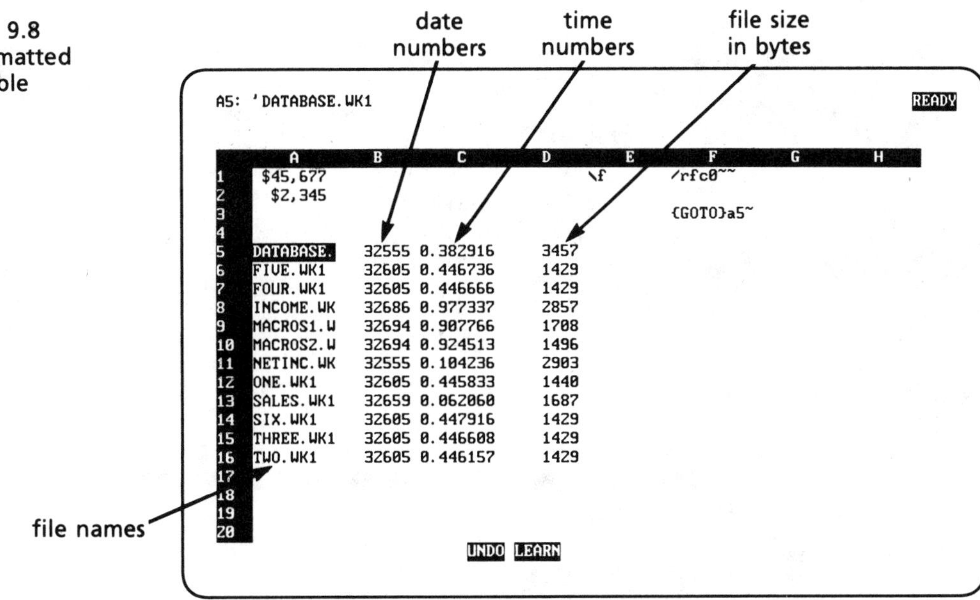

A four-column table appears. Notice the date and time number in columns B and C. Also notice that some file names in column A are cut off. To make room for them and for the date and time formats you will use in columns B and C, you need to widen columns A to C to 12 characters. To do so, you'll use **/Worksheet Column Column-Range** to avoid widening each of the columns individually. The Column-Range
(2.2) option is a Release 2.2 feature that lets you change the width of two or more adjacent columns in one step.

Press:	/
Select:	Worksheet
	Column
	Column-Range
	Set-Width
Press:	→ twice to highlight columns A to C
	↵
Type:	12 ↵

Columns A to C are now wider, so you can format columns B and C as dates and times, respectively.

Move to: cell B5
Press: /
Select: Range
Format
Date
1 (DD-MMM-YY)
Press: END ↓
↵

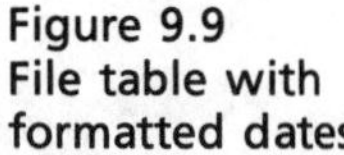

Figure 9.9
File table with formatted dates

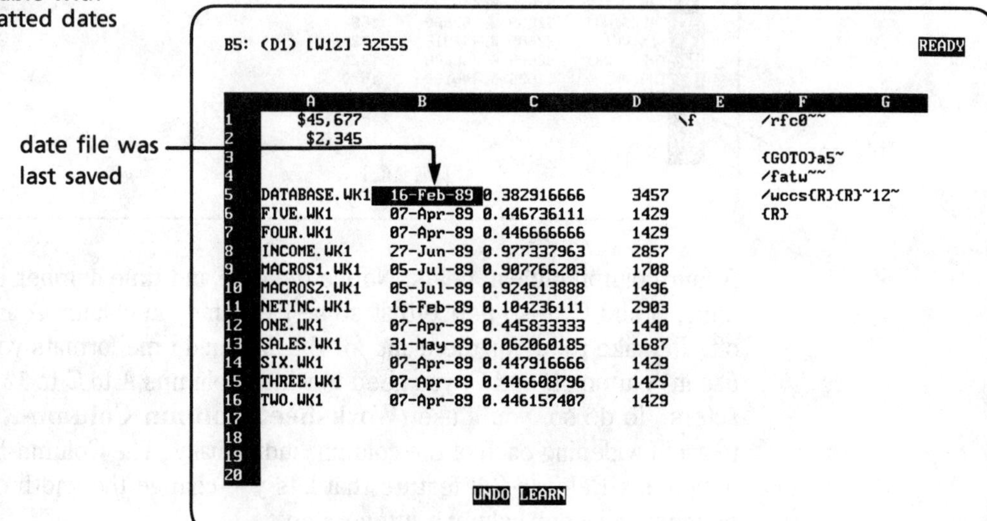

Move to: cell C5
Press: /
Select: Range
Format
Date
Time
1 (HH:MM:SS AM/PM)
Press: END ↓
↵

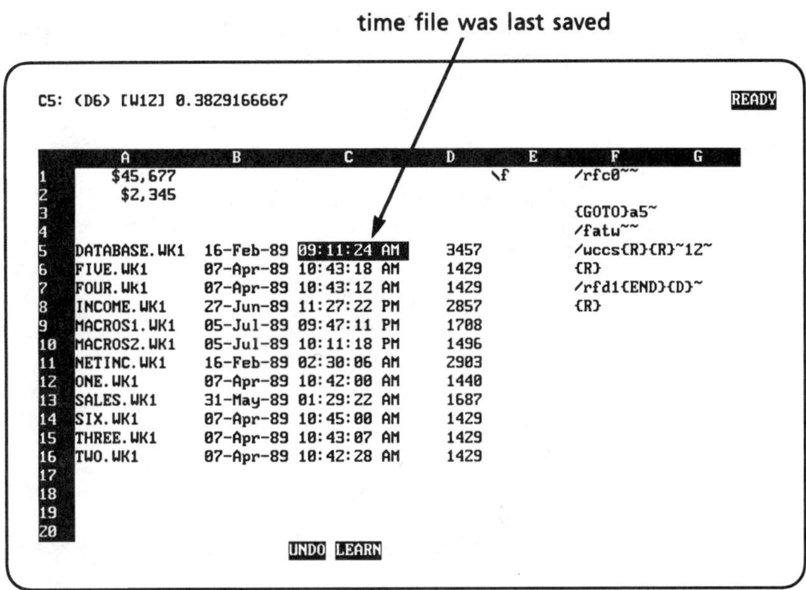

Figure 9.10
File table with formatted times

Now turn off the learn feature to stop recording keystrokes:

Press: LEARN (Alt-F5)
↵ to enter all the keystrokes in the learn range

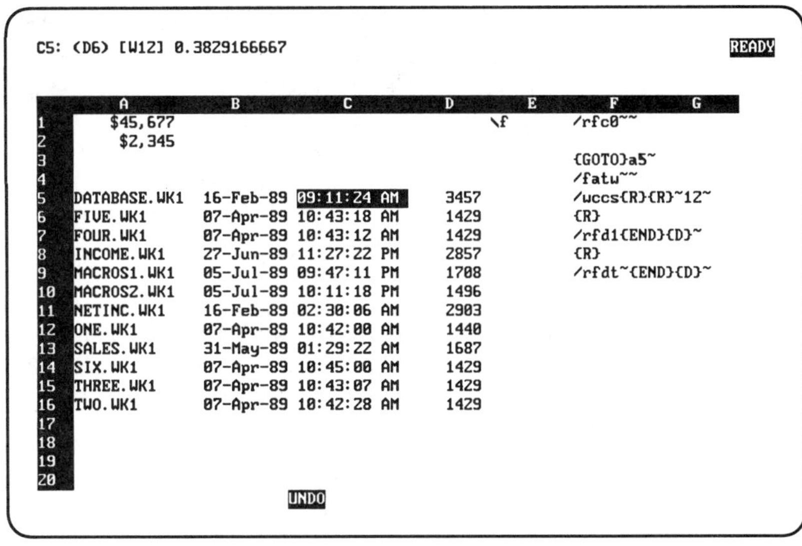

Figure 9.11
Macro for file table in learn range

Notice that when you pressed Goto (F5), 1-2-3 recorded the key in macro format: {GOTO}.

Naming the Macro

Name this macro F_TABLE.

Move to: cell F3
Press: [/]
Select: Range
Name
Create
Type: f_table
Press: [↵]
[↵] to accept F3 as the range

Now enter the macro's name in cell E3.

Move to: cell E3
Type: f_table [↵]

Running the Macro

The F_TABLE macro always starts the table in the same cell (A5), so erase the current table before testing the macro.

Move to: cell A5
Press: [/]
Select: Range
Erase
Press: [→] three times
[END] [↓]
[↵]

Because this macro moves the cell pointer for you, the cell pointer can be anywhere when you start the macro. You gave the macro a full name (rather than a backslash letter combination), so use Run (Alt-F3) to run the macro.

Press: [RUN] (Alt-F3)
Select: F_TABLE

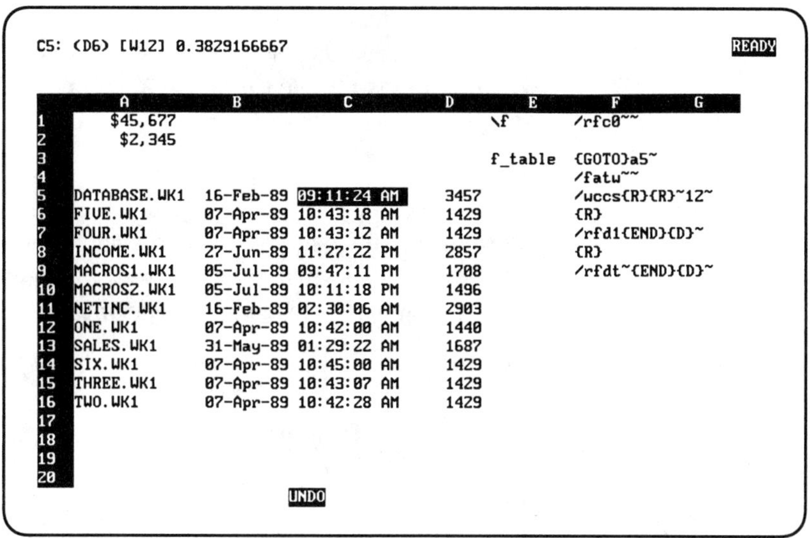

Figure 9.12 Table of worksheet files

The table of worksheet files appears starting in cell A5 with the dates and times formatted correctly.

To see an updated table of files after you create additional files, just use the F_TABLE macro again.

CORRECTING MISTAKES

If you make a mistake while storing keystrokes in the learn range, you can correct it in two ways.

- If the mistake is a minor one—you pressed the wrong key or made a typographical error—don't turn off the learn feature. Take whatever steps are necessary to correct the mistake. For instance, if you've typed the wrong character, press Backspace and type the correct character. If you've made the wrong choice from a menu, press Esc and select the correct command.

  After you finish the task and turn off the learn feature, move to the learn range, press Edit (F2) and make the necessary corrections. As you edit, be sure not to leave any blank cells in the middle of the macro, or 1-2-3 will interpret the blank cell as the end of the macro.

- If the mistake would take too long to fix by using Edit (F2), erase the learn range and start from scratch. Use **/Worksheet Learn Erase** to erase the learn range. You don't need to specify the learn range again, just press Learn (Alt-F5) to start recording keystrokes again.

You may also want to edit a macro if you want it to work differently. For example, suppose you want to change the \F macro you created so that instead of formatting in Currency with no decimal places, it formats in , (comma) format with two decimal places. Edit the macro now.

Move to: cell F1
Press: EDIT (F2)
← four times till the cursor is on 'c'
DEL twice
Type: ,2
Press: ↵

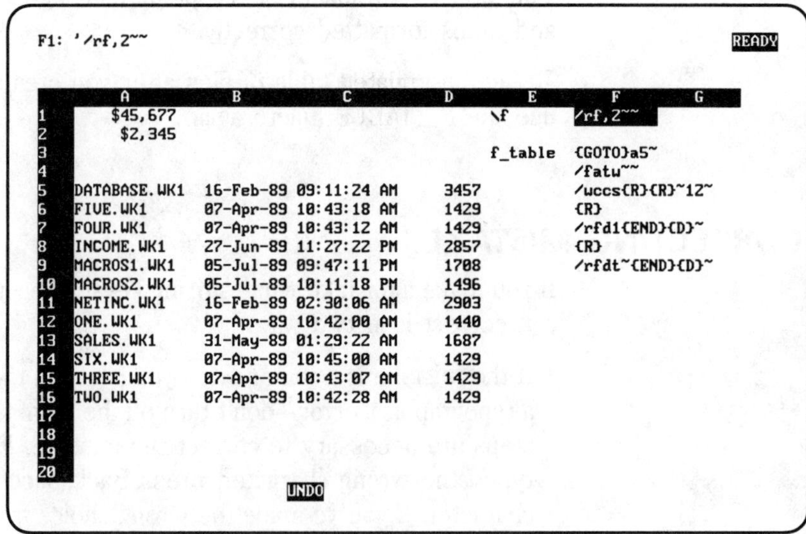

Figure 9.13
Edited macro

The macro now reads '/rf,2 ~ ~ .

Try the macro on the value in cell A1.

Move to: cell A1
Press: ALT – F

The value in cell A1 is now in , (comma) format with two decimal places. Repeat the macro in cell A2.

Figure 9.14
Reformatted values

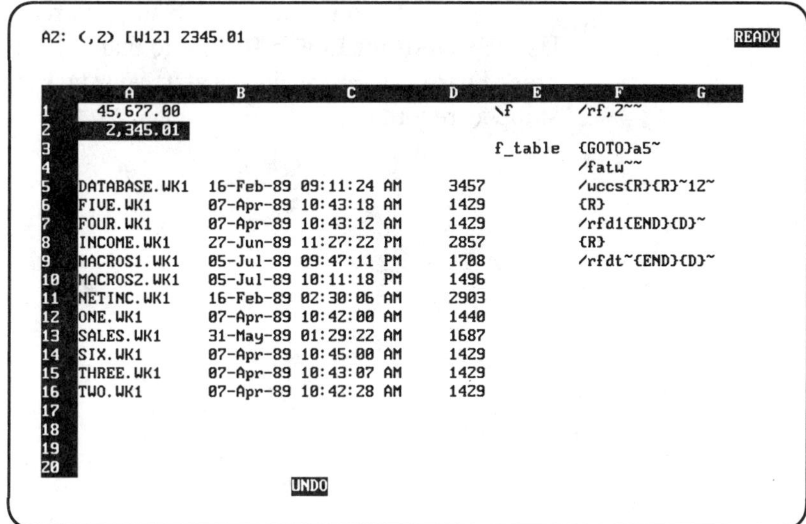

SAVING THE MACROS

Save your macros by saving the worksheet in file MACROS2.

Press: /
Select: File
Save
Press: ↵
Select: Replace

ADDING TO A LEARN RANGE

Once you've created a macro with the learn feature, you can add more keystrokes at the end of the current learn range. Turn learn mode on with Learn (Alt-F5) and add what you want. Any keystrokes you type will be appended to the contents of the learn range. Keep in mind, however, that the learn range must have enough room for what you want to enter. (If necessary, specify a larger range with /**Worksheet Learn Range**.)

If you're using the learn feature and 1–2–3 runs out of room in the learn range, you will get an error message telling you the learn range is full. The learn feature will be turned off automatically. Examine the learn range and note where 1–2–3 stopped recording your keystrokes. Use **/Worksheet Learn Range** to make the learn range larger. Then press Learn (Alt-F5) again and start your task at the point where 1–2–3 stopped recording.

10

Building Advanced Macros

The advanced macro commands are 1-2-3's built-in programming language. Some of the advanced macro commands duplicate tasks that you could automate with keystroke macros, but they save time and typing. Others automate tasks that cannot be accomplished with keystrokes, such as calling up menus you create.

Though the advanced macro commands are powerful, they don't necessarily make macros more complicated. You can use the advanced macro commands to create complex programs, or just to increase the ability of 1-2-3 to store keystrokes in a macro.

This chapter

- Explains the structure of advanced macro commands
- Steps you through the process of creating two macros that include advanced macro commands
- Teaches you how to use STEP mode to debug macros and explains what to look for in a macro when it doesn't work correctly
- Provides an alphabetical list of the 50 advanced macro commands

ADVANCED MACRO COMMAND STRUCTURE

The advanced macro commands consist of **keywords** and **arguments**. Each keyword represents the action 1-2-3 performs when it encounters the instruction. For example, the keyword {BEEP} causes the computer to beep.

Many keywords require arguments to complete the advanced macro command. Arguments tell 1-2-3 the object of the keyword's action. For example, the argument A1 in the advanced macro command {BLANK A1} tells the macro to erase the entry in cell A1.

The general format of an advanced macro command is shown in Figure 10.1.

Figure 10.1
Advanced macro command syntax

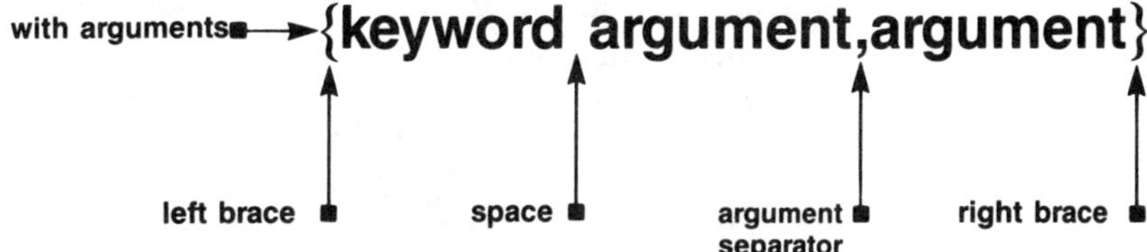

No matter how many arguments an advanced macro command includes, the entire command (both keyword and arguments) is enclosed in braces. Each command constitutes one instruction, so you must enter it in a single cell. In the illustration below, the advanced macro commands in column B are entered properly, but those in column E are not.

Figure 10.2
Advanced macro command must be in one cell

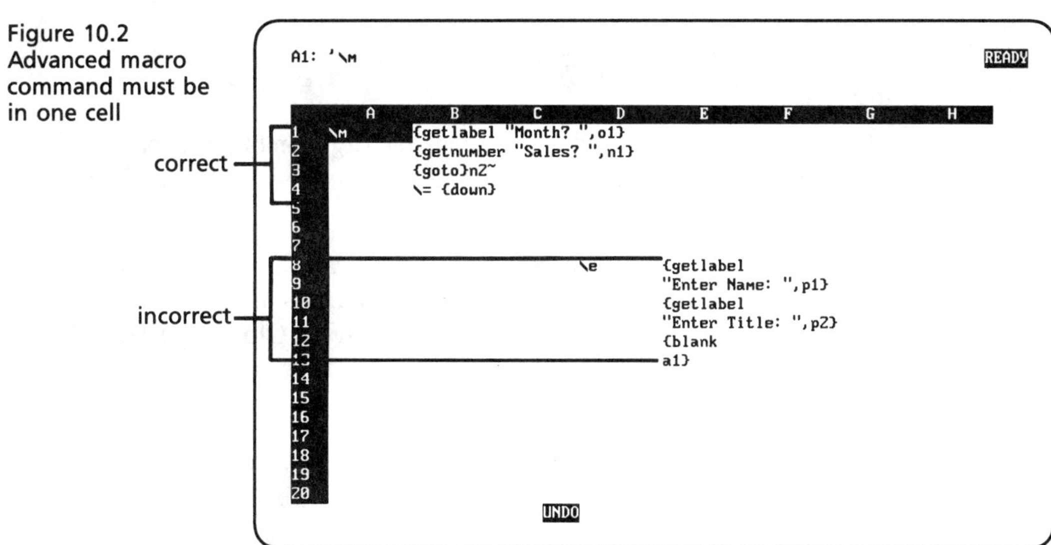

General descriptions of the advanced macro commands appear later in this chapter. Each command description lists the keyword and type of argument(s), if any, the command requires and then describes the action of the command.

Arguments

Some advanced macro commands include arguments, and some do not. Advanced macro commands that do not use arguments consist of keywords that produce one and only one result, regardless of when they are used. For instance, the {QUIT} command always ends a macro and the {FRAMEOFF} command always suppresses the worksheet frame (column letters and row numbers).

Most advanced macro commands, however, include one or more arguments along with the keyword. In these commands, the keyword is the general instruction and the arguments determine the exact result of the instruction. For example, in the command {BEEP 1}, the argument 1 specifies which tone the computer will sound. That command produces a tone that is different from the one {BEEP 2} produces.

Many advanced macro commands require more than one argument. For instance, the {LET} statement, which stores a specified entry in a specified location, needs both a cell location and a cell entry, such as {LET A1,100}.

Argument Separators

In an advanced macro command, the arguments are separated from the keyword by a space. Arguments are separated from each other by an argument separator.

By default, semicolons and commas are valid argument separators for advanced macro commands, and the examples in this book always use commas. You can, however, use /**Worksheet Global Default Other International Punctuation** to set a different argument separator.

Argument Types

The advanced macro commands use four types of information as arguments:

A **numeric argument** is a number, formula, @function, or the range name or address of a cell that contains a number, formula, or @function.

A **string argument** can be a literal string (any sequence of letters, numbers, and symbols enclosed in quotation marks), a string formula, or the range name or address of a cell that contains a label or string formula.

A **location argument** is a range name or address, or any formula that evaluates to a range name or address. Many advanced macro commands let you store a range name or address in a cell. You can then use that
2.2 cell (preceded by a + symbol) as the location argument, and 1-2-3 will interpret its contents as the true location. For example, if cell F4 is named INCOME and contains the string Z25, a statement such as {LET INCOME,10} would place 10 in cell INCOME (F4). If you preceded INCOME with a plus symbol (+), however, as in {LET +INCOME,10), 1-2-3 would place 10 in cell Z25 because the + indicates that INCOME contains a range name or address.

A **condition argument** is a logical formula or @function, or the range name or address of a cell that contains a logical formula.

2.2 NOTE: You can also use a link to data in another file as an argument to an advanced macro command, for example, {LET GROSS,+<<PARIS>>SALES}. For information about file linking, see Chapter 3.

You must supply the correct type of argument or arguments for the particular advanced macro command you use. If you supply the wrong argument type, or if you leave out an argument that's required, the macro won't execute correctly. Usually, an incorrect argument type or a missing argument results in an error: 1-2-3 stops executing the macro, displays an error message, and replaces the READY indicator with the ERROR indicator.

Examples

Most macros that use 1–2–3's advanced macro commands include both advanced macro commands and keystroke sequences. The following commands would typically be used in macros that also include keystroke sequences.

1. If you have a macro that prints a form letter automatically, the macro should pause before printing each letter while you fill in the name of the addressee and other variable information. One way to do this is with the {GETLABEL} command, which suspends the macro and asks you to type in a label:

   {GETLABEL "Enter name: ",A1}

   This command stops the macro and displays the prompt Enter name: at the top of the screen. (The space character after the word name in the macro is part of the prompt.) Your response to the prompt appears in the control panel as you type it. When you press Enter, 1–2–3 stores the name as a label in cell A1.

2. Instead of using a cell address in the {GETLABEL} command, you can also use a range name:

   {GETLABEL "Enter name: ",ADDRESSEE}

   This version of the macro stores the name in the cell named ADDRESSEE.

   Using {GETLABEL} makes a macro interactive because the macro requires you to enter information when it runs.

3. In some cases, you may want a macro to transfer control elsewhere. You can use a {BRANCH} command to do this. For example, the command

   {BRANCH TOTALS}

   transfers control to the location named TOTALS. If range TOTALS doesn't exist in the worksheet, the macro stops and 1–2–3 displays an error message telling you that the branch is invalid.

USING ADVANCED MACRO COMMANDS

In this section, you'll create two macros that use both keystroke instructions and advanced macro commands. Both these macros are interactive: they require you to enter information, and the result of each macro depends on the information you enter.

Macro 1: Entering Sales Figures

The first macro uses the {GETLABEL} and {GETNUMBER} commands and the keystroke instruction {CALC} (equivalent to pressing Calc (F9)) to enter a monthly sales figure in the worksheet.

The {GETNUMBER} command is just like the {GETLABEL} command, except that it enters a value instead of a label. The {CALC} instruction causes the month and sales figure to appear on the screen.

Unlike keystroke macros, many advanced macro commands do not automatically update the screen. In this macro, the {CALC} instruction tells 1-2-3 to update the screen. If you are using a {GETLABEL} or {GETNUMBER} command in a macro that also contains keystroke instructions, however, you may not need to follow the command with a {CALC} instruction. 1-2-3 updates the screen whenever it encounters a tilde or an instruction that moves the cell pointer.

Creating the Macro

If you need the information your current worksheet contains, save it before you continue. Start this macro with a blank worksheet:

Press: /
Select: Worksheet
Erase
Yes

Although all the macro instructions can fit in one cell, you will enter them in three cells (F1, F2, and F3). This will allow you to see all the instructions on the screen, which is helpful if you need to edit the macro.

As you type this macro, don't forget to leave spaces where they appear in the macro instructions. These spaces become important when you use the macro.

Macro instructions are like any other cell entry, so you can enter them with the pointer-movement keys as well as with Enter. You'll start the macro in cell F1.

Move to: cell F1
Type: {getlabel "Month? ",a1}
Press: [↓]

Figure 10.3 First line of macro in cell F1

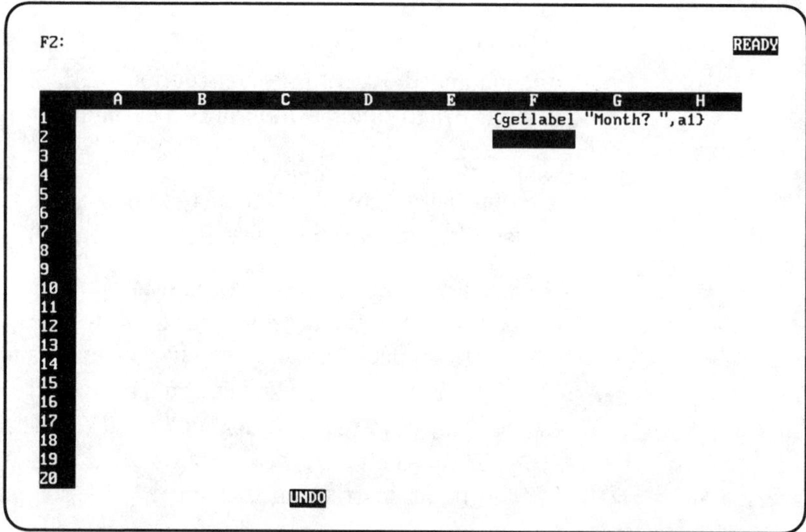

This instruction directs 1-2-3 to display **Month?** in the control panel to prompt you to enter the month. The macro then enters your response to the prompt in cell A1. Now enter the rest of the macro (the cell pointer should be in cell F2):

Type: {getnumber "Sales? ",b1}
Press: [↓]
Type: {calc}
Press: [↵]

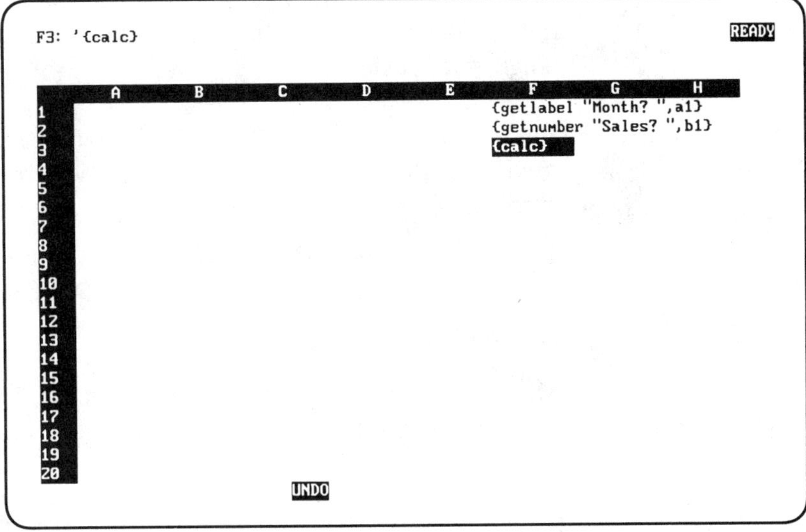

Figure 10.4 Macro in cells F1, F2, and F3

Labeling and Naming the Macro

Even when a macro takes up more than one cell, you assign a range name to the top cell only. In this example, you'll combine labeling the macro with naming it. First, enter the macro's name in cell E1; the macro's name is \S:

Move to: cell E1
Type: '\s (don't forget the label prefix)
Press: ↵

The **Range Name Labels** command uses a label entry as a range name for an adjoining cell (a cell that is above, below, to the right, or to the left of the cell that contains the label entry). You just documented the macro's name in cell E1, and now you'll use that label to name the macro that begins in cell F1, the cell to the right of the label. The cell pointer should still be in cell E1:

Press: /
Select: Range
Name
Labels
Right
Press: ↵ to accept the range that contains the label

/Range Name Labels names the range that begins in the cell to the right (the direction you specified) with the label in cell E1 (the label range you specified).

Invoking the Macro

You named the macro with a backslash and single letter, so you can run it with the Alt key. Hold down Alt and type the letter part of the macro name.

This macro enters data you supply in cells A1 and B1 no matter where the cell pointer is on the worksheet when you run the macro.

Press: ALT – S

The CMD indicator appears in the bottom of the screen when 1-2-3 is executing a macro.

Figure 10.5 First line of macro creates prompt

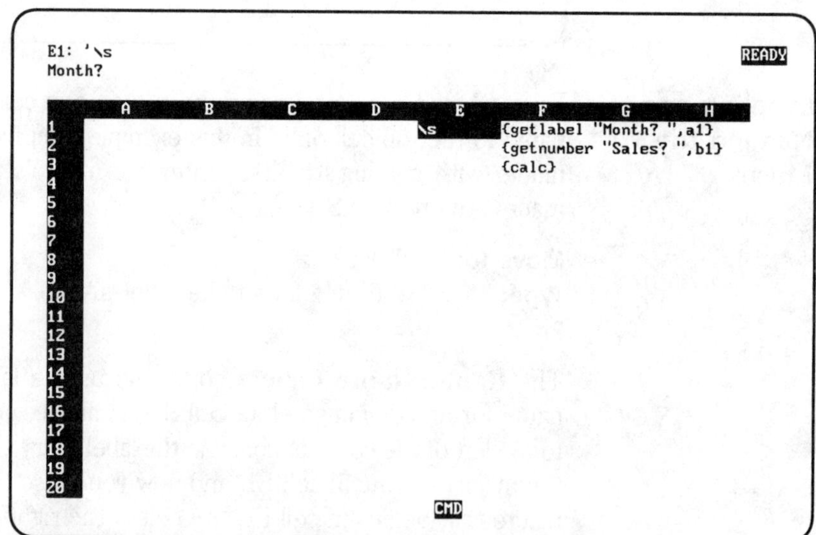

When you entered the macro, you left a space after the question mark following the prompts. Because of this space, your response begins one space away from the prompt instead of immediately after it. Type a response to the prompt:

Type: September
Press: ↵

The CALC indicator appears at the bottom of the screen and a new prompt that says **Sales?** appears in the control panel. Type a response to the prompt:

Type: 2000 ↵.

The month and sales figure appear in cells A1 and B1, respectively.

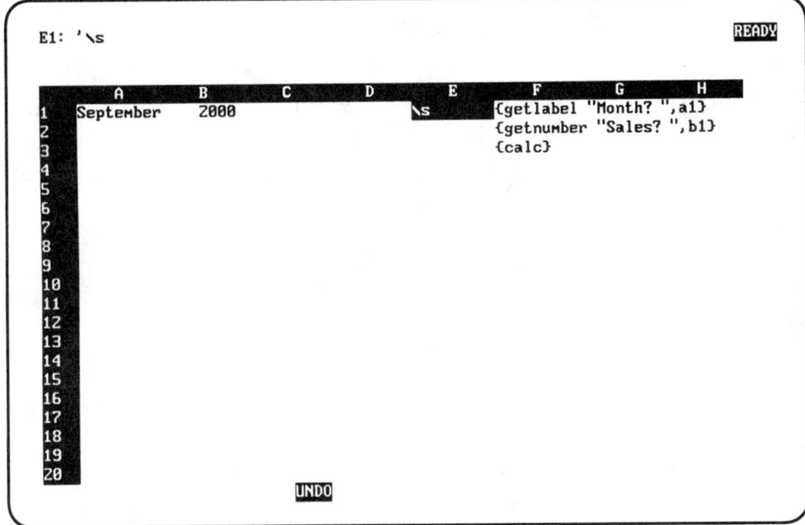

Figure 10.6 Macro enters your responses to prompts

Press the Down key a few times and run the macro again by pressing Alt-s. Use a different month and sales figure this time. The new data replaces that previously entered in cells A1 and B1.

If you're working on a large worksheet and want to change a sales figure to see the results of "what-if" calculations, this macro can be useful.

If you want to keep this macro, save the worksheet.

Macro 2: Entering and Formatting a Date

This macro also combines advanced macro commands and keystroke instructions. It uses a series of {GETNUMBER} commands, the @DATE function, and /**Range Format** to enter and format the date automatically.

A {CALC} instruction is not necessary in this macro because the {GETNUMBER} commands are followed by an @function, which causes 1-2-3 to update the screen.

Again, start with a new worksheet:

Press: [/]
Select: Worksheet
Erase
Yes

Creating the Macro

Once again, you'll enter each step in a separate cell, though you could enter the entire macro in one cell. Remember to leave spaces where they are indicated in the macro instructions. Start the macro in cell F1:

Move to: cell F1
Type: {home}
Press: [↓]
Type: {getnumber "Year? ",c6}
Press: [↓]
Type: {getnumber "Month? ",c7}
Press: [↓]
Type: {getnumber "Day? ",c8}
Press: [↓]
Type: '@date(c6,c7,c8)~
Press: [↓]
Type: '/rfd4~
Press: [↵]

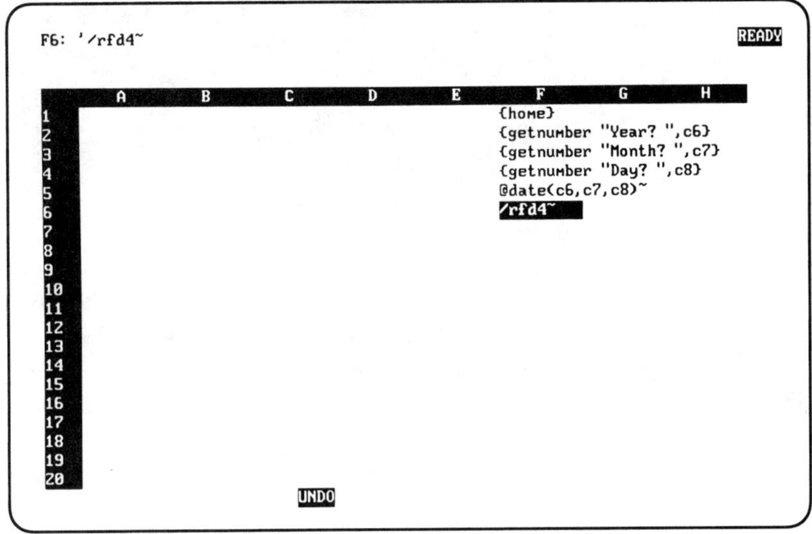

Figure 10.7 Date macro consists of six instructions

In this macro, the three {GETNUMBER} commands end with cell addresses. The macro stores the data you type in response to the **Year?**, **Month?**, and **Day?** prompts in cells C6, C7, and C8, respectively.

The @DATE function requires three arguments: the year number, the month number, and the day number. In the fifth line of the macro (cell F5) you used three cell addresses as arguments in the @function: cells C6, C7, and C8. The @DATE function uses the numbers the macro stored in those cells to produce the date.

Finally, the last line of the macro formats the date in Date Format 4 (MM-DD-YY).

Labeling and Naming the Macro

This macro will be named \D. Before you name the macro, document the name in cell E1:

Move to: cell E1
Type: '\d
Press: [→]

Now assign a range name to the first cell of the macro:

Move to: cell F1
Press: [/]
Select: Range
Name
Create
Type: \d
Press: [↵] to accept the name
[↵] to accept the range 1-2-3 offers

Running the Macro

Finally, try the macro. The first instruction in the macro moves the pointer to cell A1, so it doesn't matter where the pointer is when you run the macro:

Press: [ALT] – [D]

The cell pointer moves to cell A1, and the prompt **Year?** appears in the control panel. Type the last two digits of the year:

Type: 88
Press: [↵]

Next enter the month after the **Month?** prompt:

Type: 7
Press: [↵]

Finally, enter the day after the **Day?** prompt:

Type: 7
Press: [↵]

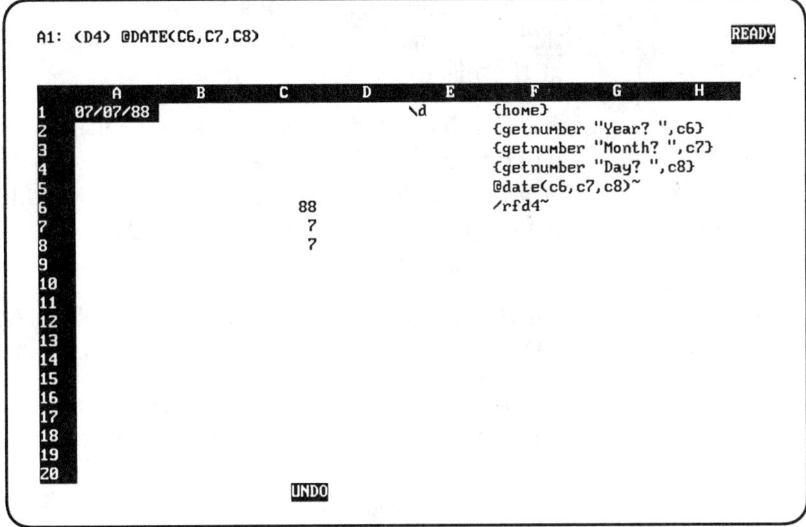

Figure 10.8 Cell A1 displays the formatted date

The macro enters the year, month, and day in cells C6, C7, and C8. It then enters the @DATE function in cell A1 (the pointer's location), with the cell addresses C6, C7, and C8 as arguments. The @DATE function uses the numbers in those cells (the numbers you typed in response to the prompts) to generate a date serial number. Finally, the macro automatically assigns the Date 4 format to the cell that holds the serial number. Date serial numbers and @functions are discussed in detail in the *1-2-3 Reference Manual*.

Don't erase this macro—you'll need it in the next section.

CORRECTING A MACRO WITH STEP MODE

STEP mode is a 1-2-3 feature that helps you correct, or **debug**, macros. All the macros you've entered so far are relatively simple. If one of them fails to work properly, you can usually find the place in the instructions where the macro stops working. This can be more difficult in a complex macro, however.

The likelihood of making a mistake in a macro increases with the complexity of the macro. Some mistakes cause a macro to stop running and display an error message. You can also write a macro incorrectly, so that it still runs but does not produce the correct result. It's often difficult to find the source of either of these mistakes just by looking at the macro.

1-2-3's STEP mode is ideal for isolating mistakes in a macro. With STEP mode turned on, 1-2-3 executes a macro step-by-step, one instruction at a time. After each instruction, 1-2-3 waits for you to press a key before proceeding to the next instruction. (You can press any key, but the space bar is most convenient.)

You turn STEP mode on or off by pressing Step (Alt-F2). Press the key once to turn on STEP mode, and press it again to turn off STEP mode.

When you turn on STEP mode, the STEP indicator appears at the bottom of the screen. When you run the macro you want to test, the STEP indicator changes to a blinking SST indicator; this indicates that 1-2-3 is waiting for you to press a key before it executes the first macro instruction. When the macro ends, the SST indicator disappears and the STEP indicator reappears. You then turn off STEP mode.

Although you can use STEP mode with any macro, there is normally no reason to use it with a very short macro. For convenience, however, try STEP mode with the date macro you created above ("Macro 2: Entering and Formatting a Date").

Check for the STEP indicator when you turn on STEP mode. When you run the macro, the indicator changes to a blinking SST indicator:

Press: [STEP] (ALT-F2)
[ALT] – [D]
[SPACE] twice

After you press the space bar the second time, the prompt **Year?** appears in the control panel and the SST indicator blinks in the status line.

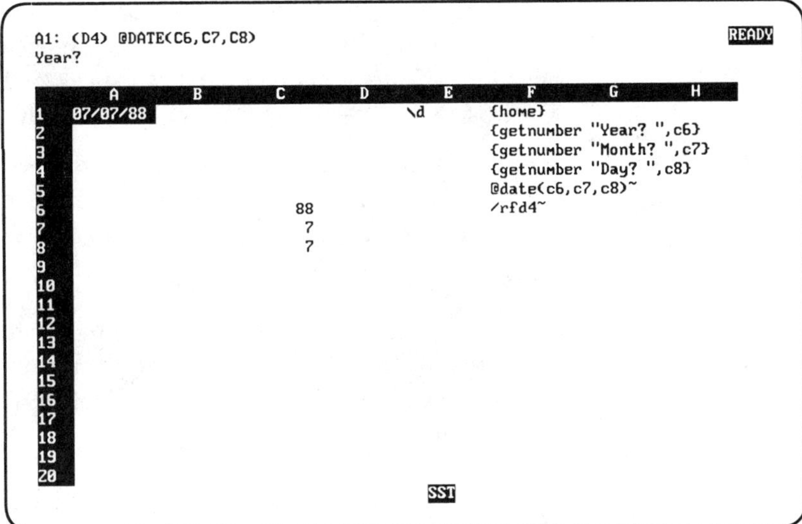

Figure 10.9
Year? prompt in STEP mode

Type in a response.

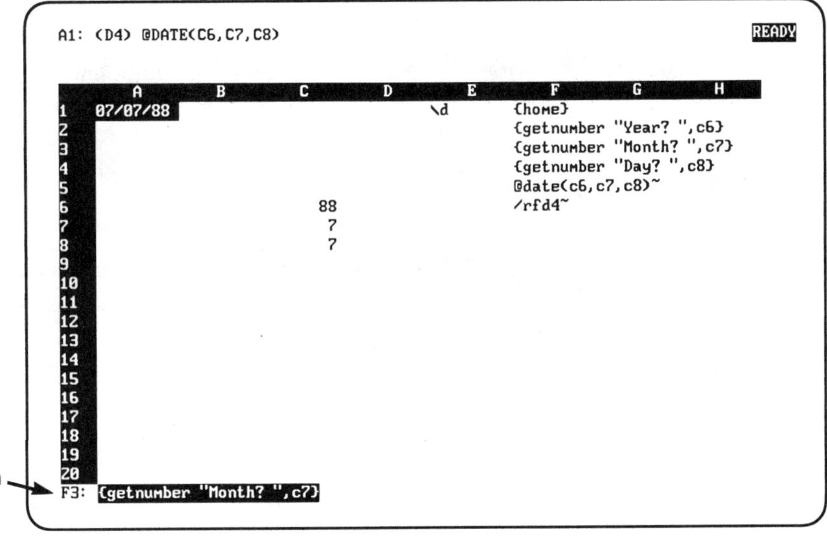

Figure 10.10
Instruction in cell F3 in STEP mode

(2.2) The status line now shows the cell address of the cell (F3) that contains the macro instructions being executed and the contents of that cell. Press the space bar and enter the month when prompted. The status line now shows the contents of cell F4.

Enter responses to the prompts and continue to press the space bar until the macro is finished. You must press the space bar (or any other key) once for each instruction in the macro—in other words, once for each keystroke, each special key indicator, and each advanced macro command.

When the macro ends, you'll notice that the SST indicator disappears but the STEP indicator tells you that STEP mode is still on. Turn off STEP mode.

Press: STEP (Alt-F2)

Now you'll change a macro instruction to create a typing mistake, as this is the most common type of error in a macro. The macro will still run, but it won't produce the correct result. Edit the @DATE function by deleting the 'd'.

Move to: cell F5
Press: EDIT (F2)
HOME
→ twice to move to the first letter of date
DEL to delete the d
↵ to accept the edited entry

Run the macro once to see what happens.

Press: ALT – D

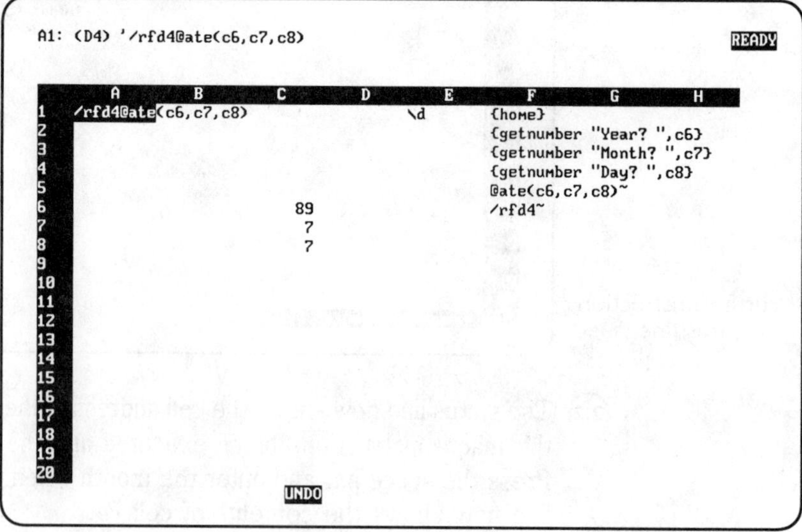

Figure 10.11
Entry in cell A1
is incorrect

1-2-3 beeped shortly before the macro ended, and cell A1 contains a label entry rather than the date. The label entry combines the last two lines of the macro. Running the macro in STEP mode will show you exactly what happened:

Press: [STEP] (Alt-F2)
[ALT]–[D]
[SPACE]

Enter responses to the prompts, press Enter, and press the space bar to go through the macro. When the macro gets to the @DATE function, it's clear what is wrong. 1-2-3 switches to EDIT mode and moves the cursor to the mistake, but the macro continues to execute. It adds the last line of the macro as text before the invalid @function.

Go back to the macro and correct the mistake:

Press: [STEP] (Alt-F2) to turn off STEP mode
Move to: cell F5
Press: [EDIT] (F2)
[HOME]
[→] twice to move the cursor to the first letter
Type: d
Press: [↵] to accept the new entry

If you run the macro again, it will work correctly.

SUMMARY OF ADVANCED MACROS

This section summarizes some of the points to keep in mind when you use 1-2-3 advanced macro commands.

Entering Advanced Macro Commands

- Enter advanced macro commands in braces. Both keywords and arguments go inside the braces.
- Most advanced macro commands require one or more arguments.
- You must enter an entire advanced macro command in a single cell. In other words, the entire command, including keyword and arguments, must be entered in the cell in which it begins. (The cell can also contain other information.)

- You can use uppercase or lowercase letters when you type advanced macro commands.

Keywords

- Advanced macro commands always include a keyword.
- Do not type a space after the keyword unless the keyword requires one or more arguments. Type a space between the keyword and the beginning of the first argument.

Arguments

- You must use an argument separator between arguments in an advanced macro command. The initial default separators are the semicolon and comma. (This book uses commas.)
- Type a space before the first argument, but don't type spaces between arguments.
- An argument may be one of four types: numeric, string, location, or condition. Some keywords require a particular type of argument, while others allow more than one type.
- You can use a cell address or range name as an argument if the cell or named range contains the required type of argument.
- You can usually use an @function or other formula as an argument.
- Location arguments can be **indirect**. You can store a range or a cell address in a cell and then use that cell (preceded by a + symbol) as the location argument. When 1-2-3 encounters a cell reference preceded by a + symbol, it interprets the contents of the cell as the true location.

TROUBLESHOOTING CHECKLIST

If a macro doesn't produce the result you intended or if 1-2-3 beeps and displays an error message during macro execution, go through the macro carefully to determine the cause of the error. Common sources of errors include the following:

- Typing or spelling errors in a macro key name, advanced macro command keyword, or range name
- Missing characters, such as omitted tildes (~), or missing spaces where you need them

- Square brackets or parentheses instead of braces around a key name or advanced macro command
- Unnecessary characters, such as spaces between arguments in an advanced macro command
- Missing arguments or arguments of the wrong type
- Misplaced or missing argument separators
- Incorrect cell or range references

Macro error messages include the location of the instruction 1-2-3 was executing at the time it encountered the error. Check this cell for the kinds of errors listed above. When you find the error, move the pointer to the cell, press Edit (F2), and correct the error.

THE ADVANCED MACRO COMMANDS

Each of the 50 advanced macro commands is listed below along with a short explanation of the command and the argument type(s) the command requires. Keywords appear in uppercase letters; arguments are in lowercase italics.

This list illustrates the variety of advanced macro commands available; for more detailed instruction on how to use each command, see the *1-2-3 Reference* Manual.

The examples in this book use many of the advanced macro commands. If a command is used in an example, the name of the example is listed after the description of the command. To find the example, refer to the List of Examples in the Table of Contents.

Many advanced macro commands require a *location* argument. Unless otherwise specified, *location* can be the address or range name of either a single cell or a range.

When an advanced macro command requires a numeric or string argument, you can also use the address of a cell that contains a numeric or text value.

Brackets around an argument mean it is optional. When an argument is italicized, it means you must substitute something else when you write the command. When an argument is not italicized, you must include that exact word as the argument in the command.

{subroutine} (subroutine call)

The structure of a subroutine call:

{*subroutine [arg1],[arg2],. . .[argn]*}

A subroutine call shifts macro execution to *subroutine*, a discrete unit of macro instructions. When the macro instructions at *subroutine* are completed, macro control automatically shifts back to the original macro instructions.

Subroutine is a range name assigned to one or more cells of macro instructions. The optional *arg1-argn* arguments specify data that is passed to the subroutine for processing.

Example

Chapter 13: Form Letter Macro

{?}

The structure of a {?} command:

{?}

The {?} command temporarily stops the macro until you press Enter. You can type any number of keystrokes (letters and numbers, special keys, pointer-movement keys, and function keys) before pressing Enter.

Examples

Chapter 11: Pointer-Movement Macros
Chapter 13: Sort Macro
Form Letter Macro

{BEEP}

The structure of a {BEEP} command:

{BEEP *[tone-number]*}

The {BEEP} command sounds one of 1-2-3's four tones. *Tone-number* is an optional argument that specifies which tone to sound: 1, 2, 3, or 4. (If you do not include an argument, the command produces a tone equivalent to that produced when you give 1 as the argument.)

{BLANK}

The structure of a {BLANK} command:

{BLANK *location*}

The {BLANK} command erases the contents of *location*. *Location* can be a cell or range.

Example

Chapter 13: Entering Records Macro

(2.2) **{BORDERSOFF}**

{BORDERSOFF} is identical in functionality to {FRAMEOFF}. For details, see the description of {FRAMEOFF}.

(2.2) **{BORDERSON}**

{BORDERSON} is identical in functionality to {FRAMEON}. For details, see the description of {FRAMEON}.

{BRANCH}

The structure of a {BRANCH} command:

{BRANCH *location*}

The {BRANCH} command shifts macro control permanently from the current cell to the specified *location*. Macro execution continues with the instructions in *location*. A subroutine call (see {subroutine}), on the other hand, does return control to the original macro instructions after performing the subroutine.

The *location* can be a cell or range.

Examples

Chapter 11: Pointer-Movement Macros
Looping Macro
Chapter 13: Form Macro
Entering Records Macro
Chapter 14: Macro Menu

(2.2) {BREAK}

The structure of a {BREAK} command:

{BREAK}

The {BREAK} command simulates pressing Esc one or more times to return to 1-2-3 READY mode; it will not interrupt a macro.

{BREAKOFF}

The structure of a {BREAKOFF} command:

{BREAKOFF}

The {BREAKOFF} command disables Ctrl-Break so that you cannot interrupt a macro. Normally, you can stop a macro at any time by pressing Ctrl-Break.

Use {BREAKOFF} with caution. Add it to a macro only after you have thoroughly tested it. With Ctrl-Break disabled, you may have to restart the computer to stop the macro. If a macro goes awry, it can damage data; if you shut your computer off, you lose any changes you have made to the worksheet since the last time you saved it.

{BREAKON}

The structure of a {BREAKON} command:

{BREAKON}

The {BREAKON} command restores the use of Ctrl-Break, undoing a {BREAKOFF} command.

> NOTE: {BREAKOFF} and {BREAKON} have no connection to the {BREAK} command, which works only to return you to READY mode.

{CLOSE}

The structure of a {CLOSE} command:

{CLOSE}

The {CLOSE} command closes the open text file, if one is currently open. This command reverses the {OPEN} command.

{CONTENTS}

The structure of a {CONTENTS} command:

{CONTENTS *target-location,source-location,[width],[cell-format]*}

The {CONTENTS} command copies the contents of *source-location* to *target-location* as a left-aligned label. This command lets you convert a value to a label so you can use it in a string formula. With the optional argument *width*, you can specify a width for the label. With *cell-format*, you can create a label that looks like a numeric cell in the specified format. For both *source-location* and *target-location*, you can specify a cell or a range.

{DEFINE}

The structure of a {DEFINE} command:

{DEFINE *location1,location2,...locationn*}

The {DEFINE} command is used in subroutines to make the arguments passed in a subroutine call available for processing. Each argument in the subroutine call must have a corresponding *location* argument. The {DEFINE} command stores *arg1* of the subroutine call ({*subroutine [arg1],[arg2],...[argn]*}) in *location1*, *arg2* in *location2*, and so on.

You must include {DEFINE} in any subroutine to which you pass arguments, and {DEFINE} must appear in the subroutine before any of the arguments are used.

Each *location* argument can be a cell or a range. You can optionally add one of two suffixes to each *location* argument. The suffix can be :s (for string) or :v (for value). The suffix specifies how 1-2-3 should process the corresponding argument in the {*subroutine*} command. Omitting the suffix is equivalent to specifying :s (string).

{DISPATCH}

The structure of a {DISPATCH} command:

{DISPATCH *location*}

The {DISPATCH} command transfers macro control to the cell whose name or address is entered in *location*. Use {DISPATCH} to have 1-2-3 branch to one of several possible macro routines, depending on the contents of *location* when 1-2-3 executes {DISPATCH}. *Location* must be a single cell.

{FILESIZE}

The structure of a {FILESIZE} command:

{FILESIZE *location*}

The {FILESIZE} command determines the number of bytes in the currently open text file and stores the number in *location*. *Location* can be a cell or range.

{FOR}

The structure of a {FOR} command:

{FOR *counter,start-number,stop-number,step,subroutine*}

The {FOR} command repeatedly executes the *subroutine* the number of times established by the *start-number*, *stop-number*, and *step* values. The macro keeps a running total in *counter* of the subroutine repetitions. When the value in *counter* exceeds the *stop-number*, macro execution shifts back to the macro instruction that follows the {FOR} command.

To use the {FOR} command, you must name a cell to serve as the *counter*. Choose a cell that is out of the way of the macro and any data in the worksheet.

Examples

Chapter 11: Looping Macro
Multiple-Copy Print Macro
Chapter 13: Entering Records Macro
Chapter 14: MEMOS Routine

{FORBREAK}

The structure of a {FORBREAK} command:

{FORBREAK}

The {FORBREAK} command ends a for loop created by a {FOR} command. Macro execution continues at the macro instruction immediately following the {FOR} command.

You should use {FORBREAK} only within a for loop. If you use it elsewhere in a macro, the macro will end with an error.

(2.2) {FRAMEOFF}

The structure of a {FRAMEOFF} command:

{FRAMEOFF}

The {FRAMEOFF} command suppresses the display of the worksheet frame (column letters and row numbers). The worksheet frame remains hidden until 1-2-3 reaches a {FRAMEON} command or the macro ends.

(2.2)
{FRAMEON}

The structure of a {FRAMEON} command:

{FRAMEON}

The {FRAMEON} command redisplays the worksheet frame, undoing the effect of a {FRAMEOFF} command.

{GET}

The structure of a {GET} command:

{GET *location*}

The {GET} command suspends macro execution until you press a key and then records the keystroke as a left-aligned label in *location*. You can specify a cell or range as *location*.

Example

Chapter 13: Form Letter Application

{GETLABEL}

The structure of a {GETLABEL} command:

{GETLABEL *prompt,location*}

The {GETLABEL} command temporarily stops the macro, displays *prompt* in the control panel, and waits for you to type a response. When you press Enter, 1-2-3 stores the response in *location* as a left-aligned label. You can specify a cell or range as *location*.

The *prompt* can include as many characters as fit within the control panel edit line.

Examples

Chapter 10: Macro 1
Chapter 13: Form Macro
Entering Records Macro
Form Letter Macro

{GETNUMBER}

The structure of a {GETNUMBER} command:

{GETNUMBER *prompt,location*}

The {GETNUMBER} command temporarily stops the macro, displays *prompt* in the control panel, and waits for you to type a response. When you press Enter, 1-2-3 stores the response in *location* as a value. You can specify a cell or range as *location*.

The *prompt* can include as many characters as fit within the control panel edit line.

If you type a label instead of a value, 1–2–3 stores it as ERR.

Examples

Chapter 10: Macro 1 and Macro 2
Chapter 14: NEW Routine

{GETPOS}

The structure of a {GETPOS} command:

{GETPOS *location*}

The {GETPOS} command determines the current position of the byte pointer in the open text file and stores the result as a number in *location*. You can specify a cell or range as *location*.

(2.2) {GRAPHOFF}

The structure of a {GRAPHOFF} command:

{GRAPHOFF}

The {GRAPHOFF} command removes a graph displayed by a {GRAPHON} command and redisplays the worksheet.

Example

Chapter 13: Graph Application

(2.2) {GRAPHON}

The structure of a {GRAPHON} command:

{GRAPHON *[named-graph]*,[nodisplay]}

The {GRAPHON} command with no arguments displays a full-screen view of the current graph while the macro continues to run. When 1–2–3 reaches a {GRAPHOFF} command, a command that displays a prompt or menu in the control panel, or the end of the macro, 1–2–3 removes the graph from the screen and redisplays the worksheet.

{GRAPHON} used with *named-graph* makes the *named-graph* settings the current graph settings and displays a full-screen view of the graph. Otherwise, it works just as {GRAPHON} used without any arguments.

{GRAPHON} used with *named-graph* and nodisplay makes the *named-graph* settings the current settings without displaying the graph.

Example

Chapter 13: Graph Application

{IF}

The structure of an {IF} command:

{IF *condition*}

The {IF} command evaluates *condition* to determine whether it is true or false. If *condition* is true, the macro continues at the next instruction in the same cell as the {IF} command. If *condition* is false, 1-2-3 ignores any further instructions in the same cell and the macro continues in the cell below the {IF} command.

Condition is usually a logical formula, or a reference to a cell that contains a logical formula.

Examples

Chapter 13: Form Macro
Entering Records Macro
Form Letter Macro

{INDICATE}

The structure of an {INDICATE} command:

{INDICATE *string*}

The {INDICATE} command displays *string* as the mode indicator. The indicator will remain on the screen until 1-2-3 reaches another {INDICATE} command or until you retrieve another file, select /**Worksheet Erase**, or end the 1-2-3 session.

(2.2) For *string* you can use any literal string, with as many chracters as fit within the first line of the control panel. You can also use a reference to a cell that contains the indicator string, or a string formula that evaluates to the indicator string.

An {INDICATE} command without an argument restores standard operation of the mode indicator in the control panel.

Examples

Chapter 13: Form Letter Applicaton
Chapter 14: Refining the Menu Macro

{LET}

The structure of a {LET} command:

{LET *location,entry*}

The {LET} command enters a number or left-aligned label in *location*. You can specify a cell or a range as *location*.

Entry can be a number, literal string, formula, or reference to a cell that contains a number, label, or formula.

{LOOK}

The structure of a {LOOK} command:

{LOOK *location*}

The {LOOK} command checks the keyboard buffer to see if you have typed anything since macro execution began. It records the first keystroke (if any) in the keyboard buffer in *location*. If you have not typed anything, {LOOK} stores an apostrophe label prefix in *location*.

{MENUBRANCH}

The structure of a {MENUBRANCH} command:

{MENUBRANCH *location*}

The {MENUBRANCH} command displays in the control panel the macro menu that starts in the first cell of *location*, waits for you to select an item from the menu, and then branches to the macro instructions associated with your menu selection. (A macro menu is a custom menu that you design and build. It looks and works like a standard 1-2-3 menu.)

The difference between {MENUBRANCH} and {MENUCALL} is the difference between a {BRANCH} command and a subroutine call ({*subroutine*}). The {MENUBRANCH} command transfers macro control to the cell address or range name specified in *location*. When 1-2-3 finishes executing the instructions that begin there, it does not automatically return to the macro that contained the {MENUBRANCH} command, as {MENUCALL} does.

Example

Chapter 14: Macro Menu

{MENUCALL}

The structure of a {MENUCALL} command:

{MENUCALL *location*}

The {MENUCALL} command displays in the control panel the macro menu found at *location*. After you select an item from the menu, 1-2-3 performs the associated macro instructions as a subroutine. (A macro menu is a custom menu that you design and build. It looks and works like a standard 1-2-3 menu.) When 1-2-3 completes the instructions, macro control returns to the statement in the original macro that follows {MENUCALL}.

The difference between {MENUBRANCH} and {MENUCALL} is the difference between a {BRANCH} command and a subroutine call ({*subroutine*}). The {MENUCALL} command switches execution to the cell address or range name specified in *location*. When 1-2-3 finishes executing the instructions that begin there, it automatically returns to the line after the {MENUCALL} instruction in the calling macro.

{ONERROR}

The structure of an {ONERROR} command:

{ONERROR *branch-location,[message-location]*}

The {ONERROR} command traps and handles errors that occur while a macro is running. If an {ONERROR} command is in effect when an error occurs, 1-2-3 returns to READY mode and branches to *branch-location* for further macro instructions instead of ending the macro. If you include the optional *message-location* argument, 1-2-3 records the error message in *message-location*.

For both *branch-location* and *message-location* you can specify either a cell or a range.

{OPEN}

The structure of an {OPEN} command:

{OPEN *filename,access-type*}

The {OPEN} command opens a text file named *filename* for processing. If the file is not in the current directory, *filename* should include the path and be enclosed in quotation marks. (*Filename* can also be the range name or address of a cell that contains a text file name.) *Access-type* is one of four characters that specifies the type of access you have to the file once it is opened: r (read access), w (write access), m (modify access), and a (append access).

{PANELOFF}

The structure of a {PANELOFF} command:

{PANELOFF [clear]}

The {PANELOFF} command freezes the control panel and status line until 1-2-3 encounters a {PANELON} command or the macro ends.
2.2 If you include the optional argument, clear, 1-2-3 clears the control panel and status line before freezing them.

Examples

Chapter 13: Graph Presentation Macro
Chapter 14: Refining the Menu Macro

{PANELON}

The structure of a {PANELON} command:

{PANELON}

The {PANELON} command unfreezes the control panel and status line, reversing the effect of a {PANELOFF} command.

Examples

Chapter 13: Graph Presentation Macro
Chapter 14: Refining the Menu Macro

{PUT}

The structure of a {PUT} command:

{PUT *location,column-offset,row-offset,entry*}

The {PUT} command enters a number or left-aligned label in *location*. *Column-offset* and *row-offset* are numbers that identify the column and row position of the data entry cell within *location*, which can be a two-dimensional range of any size as long as it contains the cell in which
2.2 you are entering data. You can precede *location*, *column-offset*, and *row-offset* with a + if they contain a reference to another cell.

{QUIT}

The structure of a {QUIT} command:

{QUIT}

The {QUIT} command ends a macro.

Examples

Chapter 13: Entering Records Macro
Chapter 14: EXIT Routine

{READ}

The structure of a {READ} command:

{READ *byte-count,location*}

The {READ} command starts at the current byte pointer position in the open text file, copies the specified number of bytes (*byte-count*) to *location*, and advances the byte pointer *byte-count* bytes.

Byte-count is a number (or an expression that results in a number) between 0 and 240. You can specify a cell or range as *location*.

{READLN}

The structure of a {READLN} command:

{READLN *location*}

The {READLN} command starts at the current byte pointer position in the open text file, copies the remainder of the current line to *location*, and advances the byte pointer to the beginning of the next line in the file.

{RECALC}

The structure of a {RECALC} command:

{RECALC *location,[condition],[iterations]*}

The {RECALC} command recalculates the values in *location*, proceeding row by row. Use {RECALC} to recalculate formulas located below and to the left of cells on which they depend.

The optional *condition* argument tells 1-2-3 to repeat the calculation until *condition* is true. The optional *iterations* argument tells 1-2-3 to perform a specific number of recalculation passes. You cannot use the *iterations* argument without the *condition* argument.

{RECALCCOL}

The structure of a {RECALCCOL} command:

{RECALCCOL *location,[condition],[iterations]*}

The {RECALCCOL} command recalculates the formulas in *location*, proceeding column by column. Use {RECALCCOL} to recalculate formulas located above and to the right of cells on which they depend.

The optional *condition* argument tells 1-2-3 to repeat the calculation until *condition* is true. The optional *iterations* argument tells 1-2-3 to perform a specific number of recalculation passes. You cannot use the *iterations* argument without the *condition* argument.

{RESTART}

The structure of a {RESTART} command:

{RESTART}

The {RESTART} command is used in subroutines to clear the subroutine stack. When 1-2-3 encounters a {RESTART} command, it continues to the end of the current subroutine, but ends the macro after it completes the subroutine instead of returning to the original macro.

{RETURN}

The structure of a {RETURN} command:

{RETURN}

The {RETURN} command is used in a subroutine. In a subroutine called by {*subroutine*} or {MENUCALL}, {RETURN} returns macro control from the subroutine to the location from which the {*subroutine*} or {MENUCALL} command was issued. In a subroutine called by a {FOR} command, {RETURN} ends the current iteration in the subroutine and immediately starts the next iteration.

Example

Chapter 13: The Justify Subroutine (Form Letter Macro)

{SETPOS}

The structure of a {SETPOS} command:

{SETPOS *offset-number*}

The {SETPOS} command positions the byte pointer in the open text file *offset-number* of bytes from the first byte in the file, which is at position 0.

{SYSTEM}

The structure of a {SYSTEM} command:

{SYSTEM *command*}

The {SYSTEM} command temporarily suspends the 1-2-3 session and returns you to DOS so you can execute a DOS *command*. When the command is completed, the 1-2-3 session automatically resumes and the macro continues.

Command can be any operating system command, including batch commands or commands to run another program such as an editor. To avoid problems, Lotus recommends that you enclose *command* in quotation marks.

{WAIT}

The structure of a {WAIT} command:

{WAIT *time-number*}

The {WAIT} command suspends macro execution and displays WAIT as the mode indicator until the time specified by *time-number.* During a {WAIT} command, the only keystroke 1-2-3 responds to is Ctrl-Break. At the specified time, 1-2-3 removes the WAIT indicator and continues the macro.

Time-number must be a time serial number. You can enter a number, numeric formula, or reference to a cell that contains a number or numeric formula. In most cases, you will use date and time @functions to specify *time-number.*

{WINDOWSOFF}

The structure of a {WINDOWSOFF} command:

{WINDOWSOFF}

The {WINDOWSOFF} command freezes the worksheet area of the screen (including worksheet borders) while a macro is running and suppresses the display of setting sheets. The area remains frozen until 1-2-3 encounters a {WINDOWSON} command or the macro ends. The {WINDOWSOFF} command does not affect the control panel and status line (see {PANELOFF}).

Examples

Chapter 14: MEMOS Routine
Refining the Menu Macro

{WINDOWSON}

The structure of a {WINDOWSON} command:

{WINDOWSON}

The {WINDOWSON} command restores normal updating of the worksheet area, undoing a {WINDOWSOFF} command.

By default, setting sheets do not appear while a macro is running. To display setting sheets in a macro, use {WINDOWSON}. If you've used {WINDOWSOFF} to turn off the display of the worksheet area, use {WINDOWSON} *twice*: once to redisplay the worksheet and the second time to redisplay setting sheets.

Examples

Chapter 14: MEMOS Routine
Refining the Menu Macro

{WRITE}

The structure of a {WRITE} command:

{WRITE *string*}

The {WRITE} command copies *string* to the open text file, starting at the current byte pointer position. *String* can be a literal string, string formula, or reference to a cell that contains a label or string formula.

{WRITELN}

The structure of a {WRITELN} command:

{WRITELN *string*}

The {WRITELN} command works the same way as {WRITE} does, except that it adds an end-of-line sequence (a carriage return and line feed) to the string it writes to the file. *String* can be a literal string, string formula, or reference to a cell that contains a label or string formula.

11

A Collection of Utility Macros

In this chapter, you'll get more experience working with 1-2-3's macro facility by creating a collection of utility macros. These macros automate frequently performed tasks such as assigning range names, entering ruled lines, and printing worksheets.

Utility macros save time and minimize chances of error. By entering procedures you perform frequently, you eliminate the need to repeat the tasks manually. 1-2-3 carries out the task correctly every time you use the macro.

The utility macros in this chapter include:

- Range naming macros that speed up the process of assigning range names to macros and ranges of data
- A file saving macro that saves the worksheet automatically
- Date and time macros that enter the current date and time automatically
- Single and double line macros that enter lines in a worksheet
- Pointer-movement macros that simplify the task of entering data in a worksheet
- A looping macro that converts a number into a label as many times as you specify
- Form letter macros that add standard paragraphs to a form letter
- Print macros that print worksheets automatically

ENTERING THE MACROS

You are going to enter the utility macros in a single worksheet named MACROS3.WK1. After you complete the chapter, you'll have a collection of utility macros stored in a single file. If you want to use any of these
2.2 macros with other worksheets, you can then copy them to a macro library. Chapter 12 explains this procedure in detail.

The directions in this chapter tell you to enter the macros in the upper left corner of the worksheet (you'll enter the macros in column B and document them in column A). This placement for macros is unusual. In worksheets that contain data as well as macros, you enter macros out of the way of other entries in the worksheet. In this chapter, however, you're creating a macro worksheet file that won't contain other data. Thus, you can enter the macros in the most convenient location, the upper left corner.

Unlike the last three chapters, this chapter does not give step-by-step instructions for entering the macros. Rather, it specifies the cell(s) to use for the macro name and the macro and then presents the macro instructions.

Enter each macro exactly as it appears on the page. If the macro instructions are printed on two or more lines and the instructions specify more than one cell, enter each line of the macro in a single cell. (You must enter a multiple-cell macro in adjoining cells in the same column.) For each macro:

- Label the macro by entering its name in the specified cell in column A
- Enter the macro in the specified cell(s) in column B
- Assign a range name to the top cell of the macro

The macro range names used in this chapter are suggested names. You can use whatever names you like, but remember that two or more macros in a single worksheet cannot have the same name.

If the current worksheet contains information you'll need later, save it before you continue. Then start with a new worksheet.

Press: [/]
Select: Worksheet
Erase
Yes

Now save the new worksheet, naming it MACROS3.

Press: [/]
Select: File
Save
Type: macros3
Press: [↵]

As you go through this chapter, save the worksheet periodically. You should save the worksheet after you enter each macro.

RANGE NAMING MACROS

Although naming ranges manually isn't very time-consuming, it does involve a number of repetitive keystrokes. When you enter and name a number of macros (as in this chapter) or assign a series of range names for any other reason, using a macro saves time.

/Range Name Labels Macro

In Chapter 10, you used the **Range Name Labels** command to assign the macro name for the Entering Sales Figures macro (Macro 1). This command is the most efficient way of assigning macro range names because it combines naming and labeling the macro (as long as you document the macro's name first in the cell to the left of the starting cell of the macro).

The following macro automates the **Range Name Labels** command. It uses the entry in the current cell as the name for the cell to the right.

Name the macro \N. Document the macro name in cell A1 and enter the macro in cell B1:

\N: '/rnlr~ (don't forget the apostrophe)

Figure 11.1 /Range Name Labels macro

The macro calls up the menu (/), selects **Range Name Labels** (rnl), and chooses Right (r) to indicate that the range you are naming is to the right of the cell that contains the range name label. The tilde at the end of the macro is equivalent to pressing Enter, which accepts the current cell as the cell that contains the range name.

You can use this macro to name the macros you create in the rest of this chapter. Remember, however, to label the macro you are naming before you run this macro.

Save the worksheet before you continue.

Range Naming Macro for a Multiple Cell Range

Ranges are used for many different purposes in 1-2-3, and most ranges consist of more than one cell. This macro lets you enter the range name and then specify a range of any size.

Name this macro \M. Document the macro name in cell A3 and enter the macro in cell B3:

```
\M:   '/rnc
```

Use the \N macro you created earlier to name this macro. Move the cell pointer to A3 if necessary. Then hold down Alt and type **N**; 1-2-3 will assign the name in cell A3 to cell B3.

Figure 11.2
Macro for naming a multiple-cell range

This macro stops after it selects **/Range Name Create**. You perform the rest of the naming manually. When the macro ends, you must type the range name and press Enter, then specify the range and press Enter again. You can either type the range address after the prompt (for example, a1.f8), or highlight the range using the period key to anchor the highlight and the pointer-movement keys to expand the highlight.

Save the worksheet before you continue.

FILE SAVING MACRO

To protect your data, save your work frequently, at least every 10 or 15 minutes. You can automate this process with a macro.

This macro saves an existing worksheet. When you create a new worksheet, you must save it manually the first time so you can assign it a file name. Once you do that, you can use this macro to save the worksheet under the file name you assigned.

Name this macro \S. Document the macro name in cell A5 and enter the macro in cell B5.

\S: '/fs~r

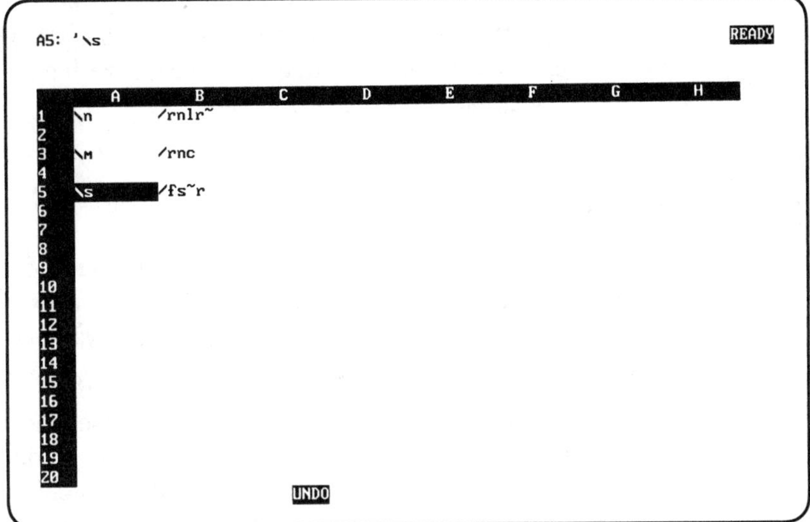

Figure 11.3 File saving macro

The macro presses the / key, selects **File Save**, presses Enter to accept the file name, and then types **r** to select Replace (to write over the existing file). To use this macro, hold down Alt and type **S** whenever you want to save the worksheet.

> CAUTION: Do not use this macro unless you have already saved the worksheet at least once. When you save a worksheet you've already saved once, 1–2–3 offers the name you used the last time you saved the worksheet. If you haven't saved the worksheet before, however, 1–2–3 doesn't enter a name in response to the prompt. Instead, it displays a list of the worksheet files on the disk. Using this macro in that situation will destroy a file on your disk because the tilde accepts the first name in the list of worksheet files 1–2–3 displays and the current worksheet will replace that file.

(2.2) A variation of this macro could select Backup instead of Replace. Backup is a Release 2.2 feature that saves the previous version of the file with a .BAK extension instead of .WK1. The current version of the worksheet is saved in a file with a .WK1 extension as usual. Using Backup instead of Replace, the macro would read '/fs~b.

Use the file saving macro to save the MACROS3 worksheet from now on. Before you use the macro (\S), save the MACROS3 file manually if you haven't already done so.

DATE AND TIME MACROS

When you build or revise a worksheet, you'll often want to include the current date or time. You may want to know exactly when you printed a copy of the worksheet, for example, or you may want to use the current date in calculations.

In Chapter 10, you created a macro that uses the advanced macro command {GETNUMBER} and the @DATE function to enter a date. The macros in this section use the @NOW function to enter the current date and time. These macros also format the date and time.

1-2-3 updates the date or time created by the @NOW function whenever it recalculates the worksheet—for example, when you make an entry in another cell, or when you press Calc (F9). It also uses the current date and time whenever you retrieve the worksheet. If you need a permanent record of the date or time, you must convert the @NOW function to its current value. The third macro in this section does this.

To use these macros, you must enter the correct time and date when you start the computer, unless your computer has a built-in clock. Otherwise, the date or time the @NOW function displays will be incorrect (for example, 01/01/80).

Date Macro

This macro enters the current date in the worksheet and then formats it in the Date 4 format (MM/DD/YY). The advantage of using this macro is that the date in the worksheet is always current. If you save the worksheet and then retrieve it a few days later, 1-2-3 recalculates the

@NOW function and displays the current date instead of the date when you last saved the worksheet. This means that you never have to change or edit the date when you revise a worksheet.

(2.2) Name this macro DATING. Document the macro name in cell A7. Enter the macro in cells B7 and B8:

DATING: '@now~ (don't forget the apostrophe)
'/rfd4~

Figure 11.4
DATING macro

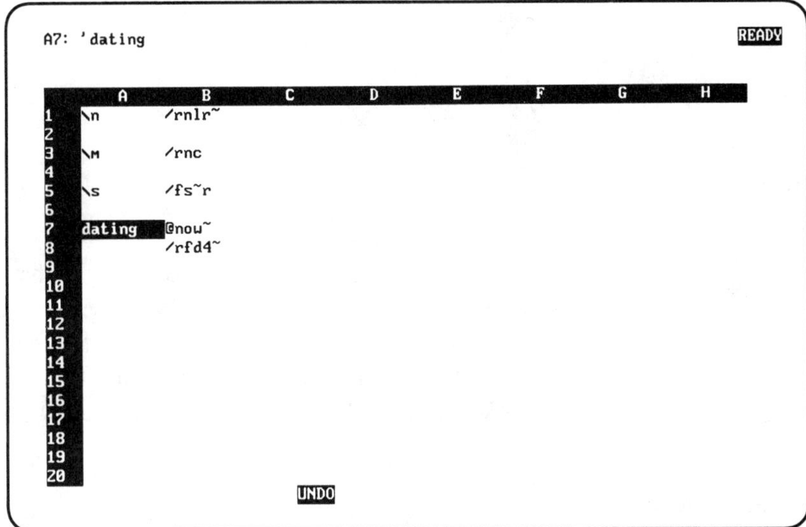

After entering the @NOW function in the current cell, this macro displays the menu, selects **Range Format Date**, and chooses the Date 4, or Long International, format.

(2.2) To use the macro, move the pointer to the cell where you want the date to appear. Because the macro's name is a full name (rather than backslash and single letter combination), you will use the Run (Alt-F3) key to run the macro. Press Run (Alt-F3) and select DATING from the list of range names that appears. The result is the current day's date formatted in the Date 4 format (for example, 10/25/88).

Test the macro now. Position the pointer in cell E7, press Run (Alt-F3), and select DATING.

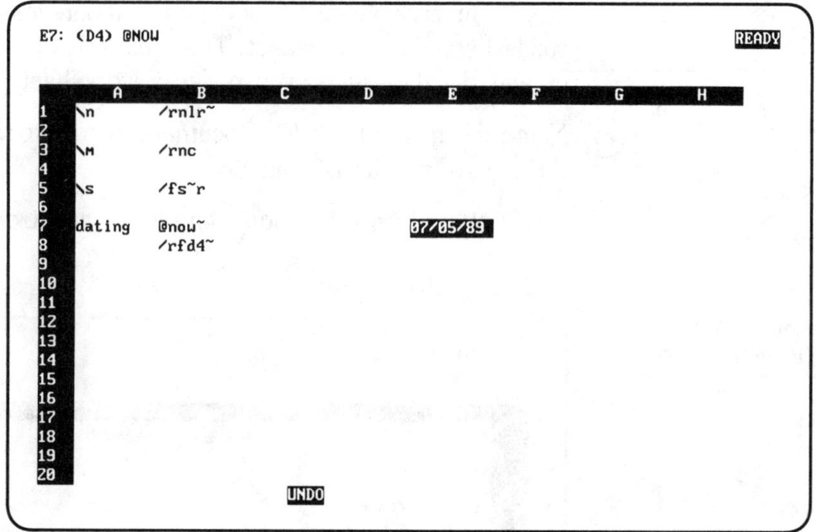

Figure 11.5
DATING macro enters current date

You can use any Date format you like. Bear in mind, however, that some Date formats may produce a date that is wider than the current column width. Any numeric entry that is too wide for the column width appears as a row of asterisks in the cell. To make the entry appear in the cell, use **/Worksheet Column Width-Set** to widen the column.

Time Macro

The following macro enters the current time in a worksheet. This macro is like the date macro above, but it uses one of the time formats in conjunction with the @NOW function.

(2.2) Name the macro TIMING. Document the name in cell A10 and enter the macro in cells B10 and B11:

```
TIMING:  '@now~
         '/rfdt2~
```

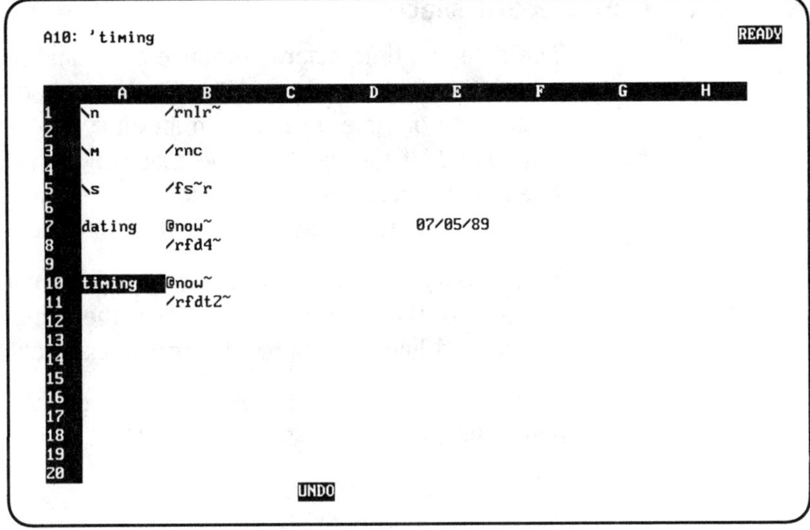

Figure 11.6
TIMING macro

(2.2) Test the macro now. Move the cell pointer to cell E10, press Run (Alt-F3), and select TIMING.

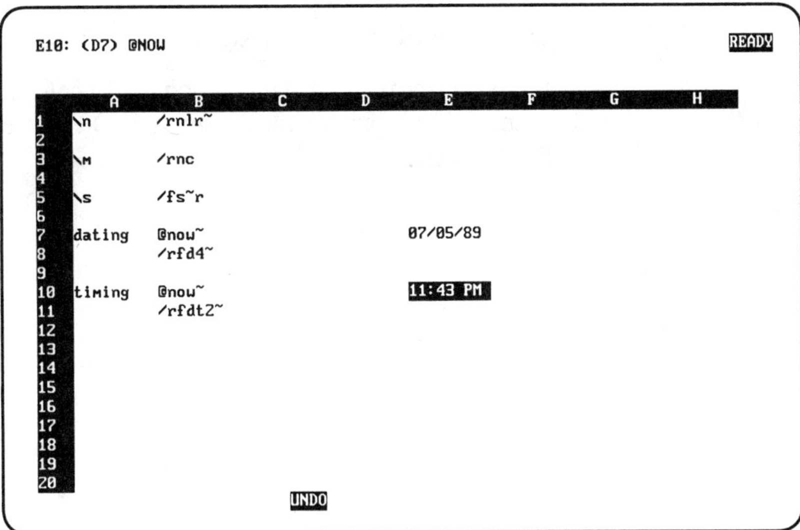

Figure 11.7
Time entered with TIMING macro

A Date or Time Record Macro

The date and time macros produce dates and times that change each time 1-2-3 updates the worksheet. If you need a permanent record of the date or time, rather than an entry that's constantly changing, you can adapt the date or time macro by adding another command. The new command is the instruction that converts the @NOW function to its current value: the current date or time.

This macro creates a permanent record of the current time. If you want a record of the date instead, replace the Time format instruction in the second line with the Date format instruction.

(2.2) Name this macro TIME_REC. Document the name in cell A13 and enter the macro in cells B13 and B14:

```
TIME_REC:  '@now{calc}~
           '/rfdt2~
```

The first instruction is the same as the first instruction in the time macro. The second instruction in the first line is new; it presses Calc (F9) to change the @function to its current value—the time when you invoke the macro. 1-2-3 will not update this value. The second line of the macro is unchanged; it assigns the time format to the cell.

(2.2) Try the macro. Move the cell pointer to cell F10. (Unless you erased it, cell E10 still displays the current time.) Press Run (Alt-F3) and select TIME_REC.

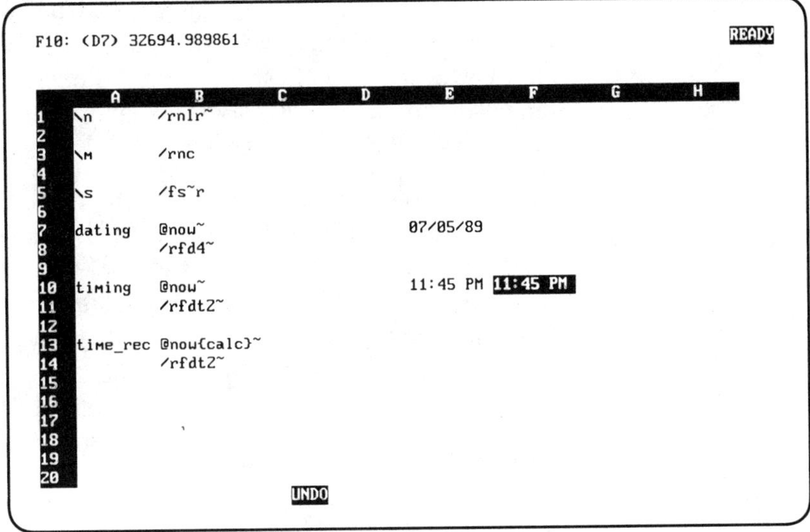

Figure 11.8 Two times are identical

Cells E10 and F10 display the same time. If you wait a minute and then press Calc (F9), however, you'll see that the contents of the two cells are different.

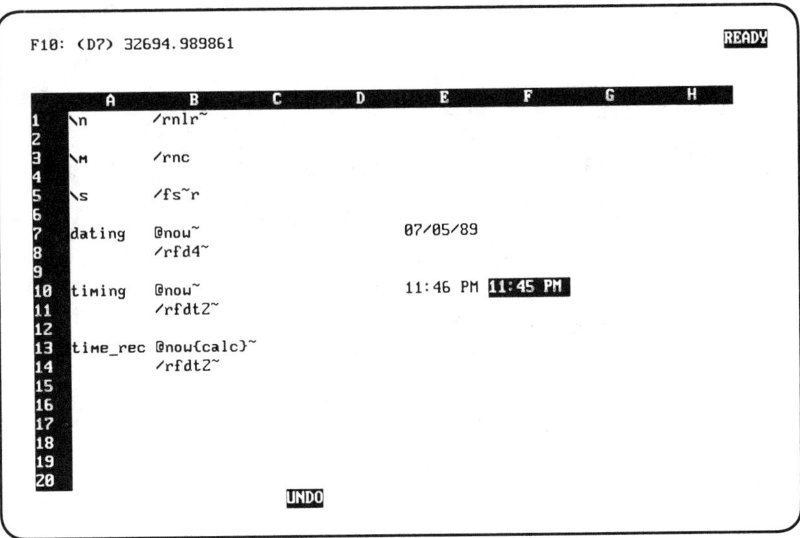

Figure 11.9 Cell E10 displays current time but cell F10 hasn't changed

Making a permanent record of the time can be useful in many situations. For example, you might want to measure the time you spent working on a particular project. To do this, you need to record your starting time with the TIME_REC macro. When you finish, subtract the starting time from the current time.

Now erase the date and times you entered by deleting the contents of columns E and F. Although you have to be careful when deleting columns or rows because 1-2-3 will delete *everything* in a column or row, deleting is useful because it deletes formatting information that takes up memory. **/Range Erase**, on the other hand, erases data but preserves the formats of cells (which can be useful, but not in this situation where you won't be re-entering data in the cells).

Move to: any cell in column E
Press: /
Select: Worksheet
Delete
Column
Press: → to specify columns E and F
↵

Use the file saving macro (\S) to save the worksheet before you continue. Hold down Alt and type **S**.

SINGLE AND DOUBLE LINE MACROS

When you create a financial spreadsheet, you often need to insert single or double lines to set off areas of the worksheet. You use hyphens to
(2.2) draw single lines and equal signs to draw double lines. (You can also produce professional-looking single and double lines by formatting and printing your worksheet with Allways, as described in Chapter 6.)

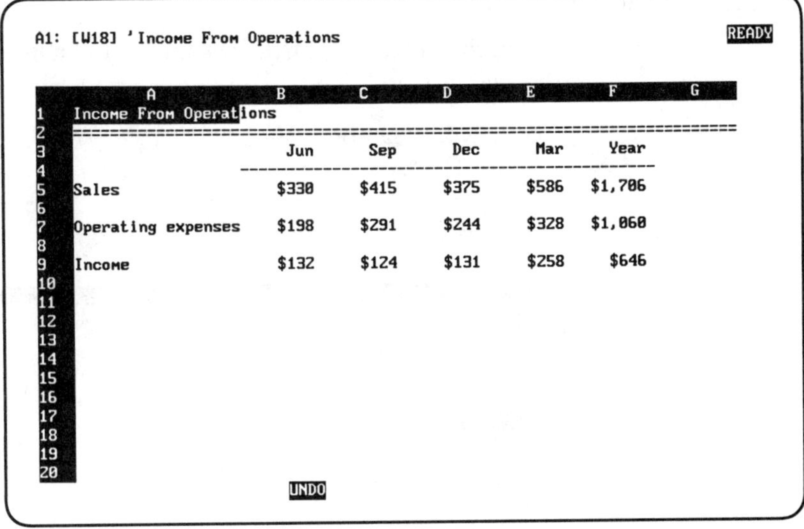

Figure 11.10 Double and single lines

One way to create a ruled line is to move to the leftmost cell in the row where you want the line to appear and enter a backslash (the label prefix that makes text repeat across a cell) followed by either a hyphen or an equal sign. This fills the cell with a series of hyphens or equal signs. To complete the ruled line, however, you must copy the cell entry to as many cells as necessary.

You can also use the @REPEAT function to create ruled lines. @REPEAT repeats a character (or a word or phrase) as many times as you specify. For example, @REPEAT("-",72) repeats a hyphen 72 times to create a single line 72 characters wide. The following macro automates the procedure. The macro uses a width of 72 characters because that is the number of characters on a single screen.

Using @REPEAT isn't the same as copying a repeating character to several cells. @REPEAT produces a long text entry in a single cell. 1-2-3 displays only as much of the entry as will fit before the next cell that contains an entry. If you make a new entry in one of the cells to the right of the @REPEAT function, 1-2-3 ends the line at the cell to the left of the new entry.

Single Line Macro

Name this macro S_LINE. Document the name in cell A16 and enter the macro in cell B16:

S_LINE: '@repeat("–",72)~

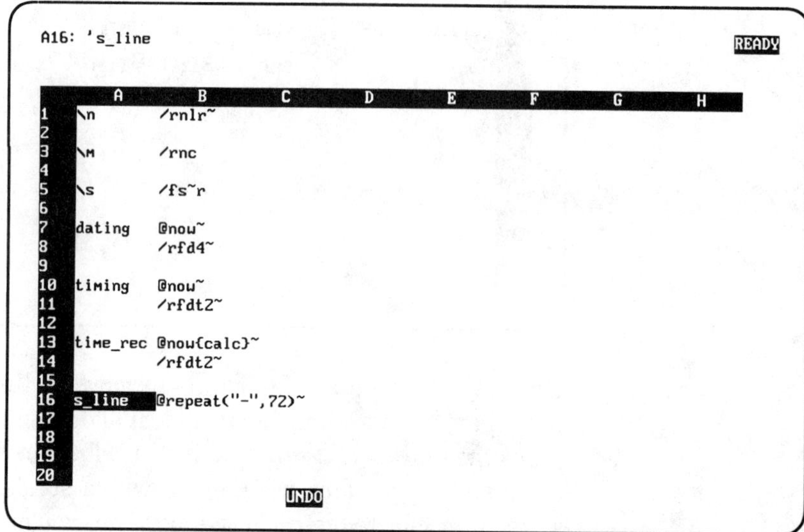

Figure 11.11
Single line macro

Double Line Macro

Name this macro D_LINE. Document the name in cell A18 and enter the macro in cell B18:

D_LINE: '@repeat("=",72)~

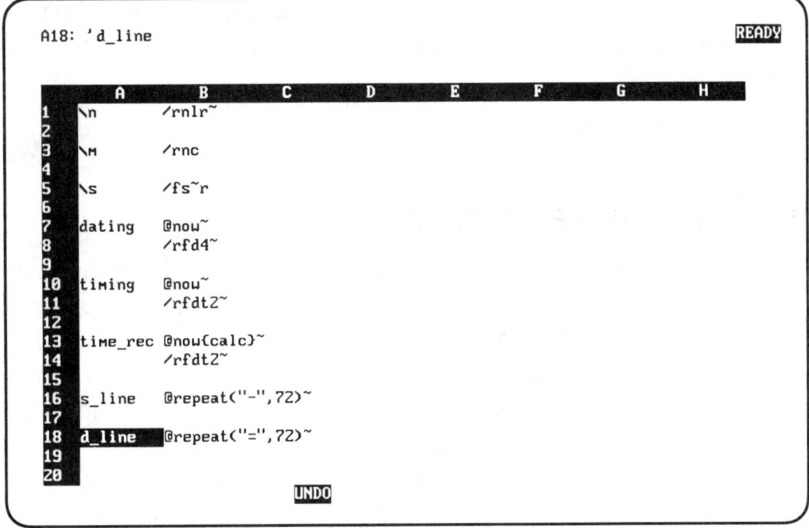

Figure 11.12 Double line macro

Whenever you need to enter a ruled line, move the cell pointer to the first cell in the row where you want the line to appear. Press Run (Alt-F3) and select either S_LINE or D_LINE.

Test both these macros now. Position the cell pointer in cell A20 and try the single line macro. Then move the cell pointer to cell A21 and try the double line macro.

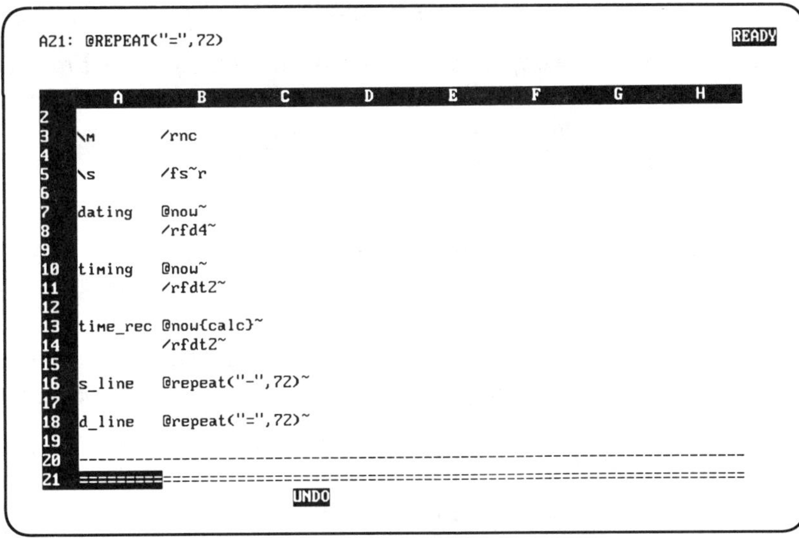

Figure 11.13 Lines created with macros

Erase both lines before continuing. With the pointer in cell A21, press /, select **Range Erase**, press Up, and then press Enter.

Save the file before you go on. You can use the \S (file saving) macro.

POINTER-MOVEMENT MACROS

If you enter lots of numbers, you may prefer to use the computer's numeric keypad, which looks like a calculator or adding machine keypad. On some keyboards, the pointer-movement keys and the numeric keys are separate. On others, however, the pointer-movement keys are on the numeric keypad. Pressing NumLock lets you use the numeric keypad, but you can't use any of the pointer-movement keys unless you hold down Shift while you press the key.

The pointer-movement macros are interactive macros that speed up the data-entry process. When you run one of these macros, 1-2-3 pauses for you to make an entry. After you type an entry and press Enter, the macro automatically moves the cell pointer to the next cell. These macros work even after you press NumLock.

These macros use the advanced macro command {BRANCH}. Instead of branching to another macro, however, they branch back to themselves. This makes them looping macros. Looping macros execute a task a given number of times or until you stop them by pressing Ctrl-Break.

Looping macros are useful when you want to perform a particular task many times. A looping macro can repeat until you stop it, or it can include a counter that tells the macro when to stop (see the looping macro in the next section).

(2.2) In these macros, to save you from unnecessary typing, you will use the abbreviated forms of {UP}, {DOWN}, {LEFT}, and {RIGHT}: {U}, {D}, {L}, and {R}. These abbreviations are new to Release 2.2.

Up Macro

Name this macro \U. Document the macro name in cell A20 and enter the macro in cells B20 to B22:

```
\U:  {?}~
     {u}
     {branch \u}
```

Down Macro

Name this macro \D. Document the macro name in cell A24 and enter the macro in cells B24 to B26:

```
\D:  {?}~
     {d}
     {branch \d}
```

Right Macro

Name this macro \R. Document the macro name in cell A28 and enter the macro in cells B28 to B30:

```
\R:  {?}~
     {r}
     {branch \r}
```

Left Macro

Name this macro \L. Document the macro name in cell A32 and enter the macro in cells B32 to B34:

```
\L:  {?}~
     {l}
     {branch \l}
```

Figure 11.14
Pointer-movement macros

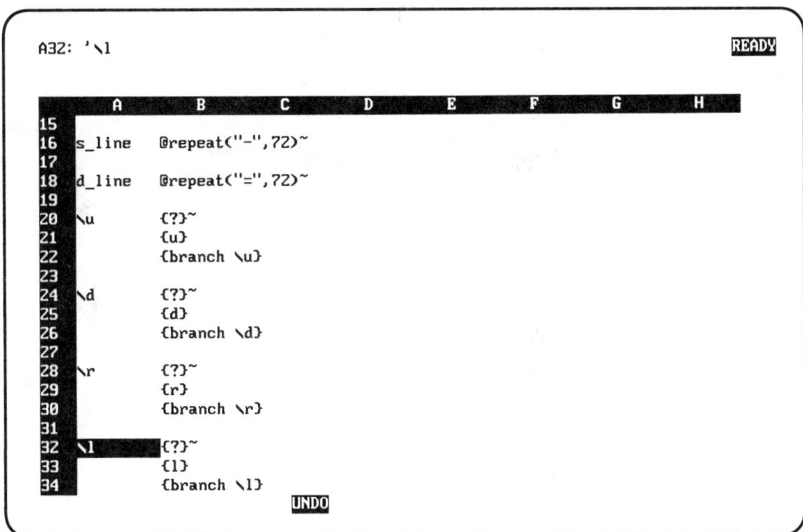

The {?} advanced macro command makes the macro pause temporarily so you can type an entry in the current cell. When you press Enter, the macro enters the data in the cell and moves the cell pointer one cell up, down, right, or left. The {BRANCH} command sends the macro back to the first instruction, the {?} command, which again makes the macro pause. This continues until you press Ctrl-Break. You must then press Esc to cancel the error that results from pressing Ctrl-Break.

To use any of these macros, move the cell pointer to the first cell in the row or column where you want to enter the data. Invoke the macro by holding down Alt and then typing the appropriate letter.

You're going to test two of these macros now. Remember that you have to press Ctrl-Break to interrupt the macros and then Esc to cancel the resulting error.

Move to: cell E28
Press: ALT – R

The CMD indicator appears in the status line.

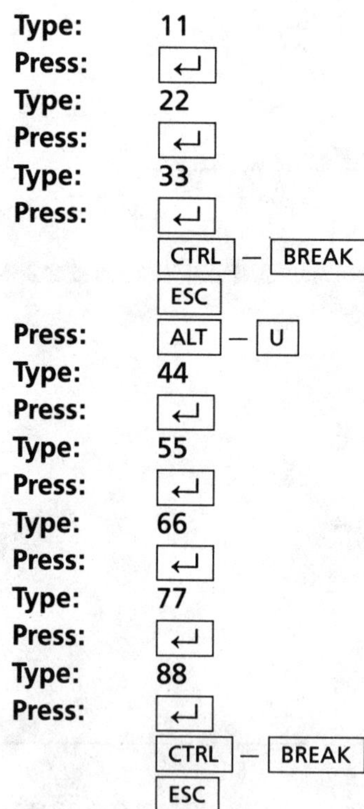

Type: 11
Press: ↵
Type: 22
Press: ↵
Type: 33
Press: ↵
CTRL – BREAK
ESC
Press: ALT – U
Type: 44
Press: ↵
Type: 55
Press: ↵
Type: 66
Press: ↵
Type: 77
Press: ↵
Type: 88
Press: ↵
CTRL – BREAK
ESC

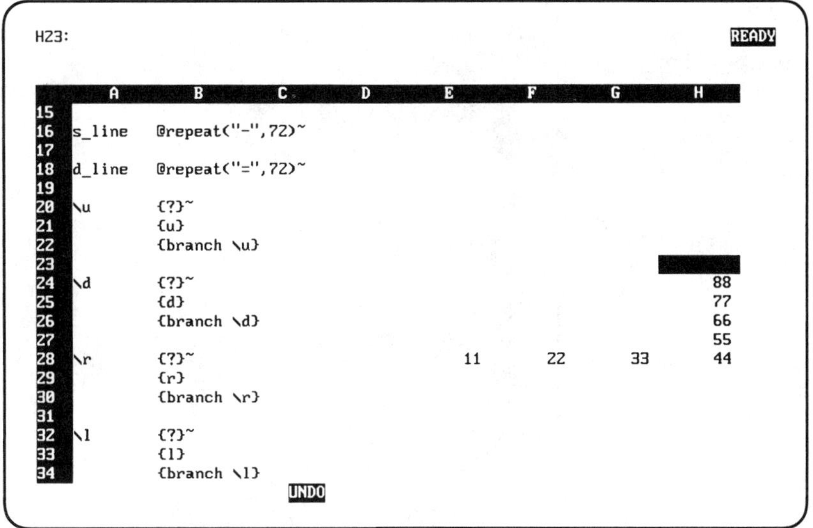

Figure 11.15
Data entered with pointer-movement macros

Erase the numbers you just entered. With the cell pointer in cell H23, press /, select **Range Erase**, press Down five times and Left three times, and then press Enter.

Before you continue to the next macro, save the worksheet.

LOOPING MACRO

In the last section, you created four macros that repeat (or loop) indefinitely, until you stop them with Ctrl-Break.

A looping macro can also repeat itself a specified number of times, rather than indefinitely. One use for this type of macro is to alter all the cells in a row or column. For example, you might want to change all the numbers in a worksheet column to labels so the numbers will appear on the left side of the cell instead of the right side. Changing numbers to labels also lets you use the numbers in string formulas, which require label entries.

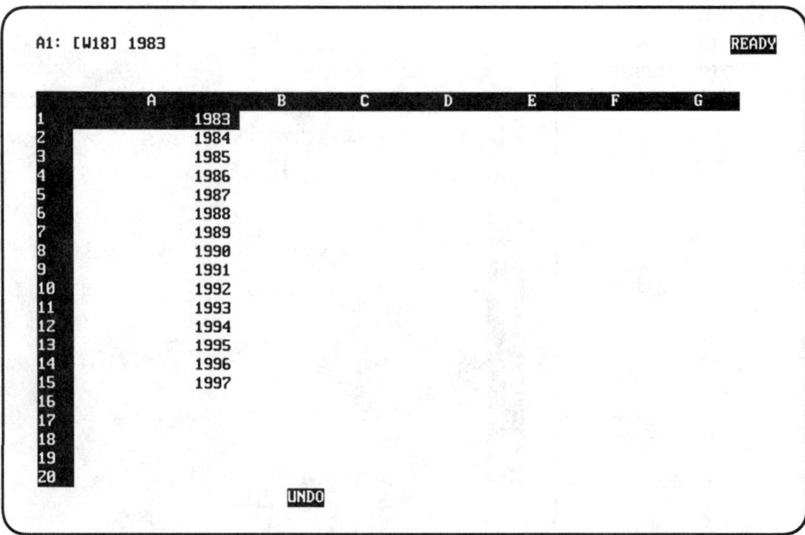

Figure 11.16 Years entered as numbers are right-aligned

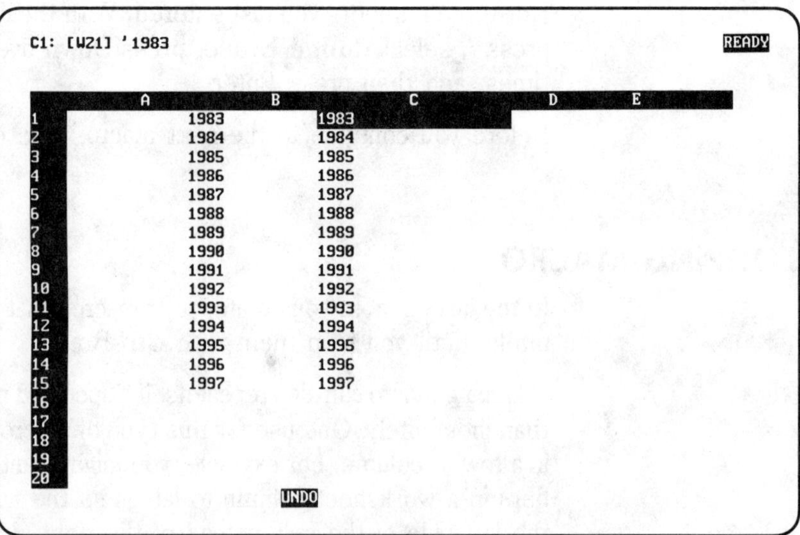

Figure 11.17 Years entered as labels are left-aligned

The looping macro you are going to enter converts numbers to labels a specific number of times and then stops automatically. The macro actually consists of two separate routines: one that controls the repetition cycle (the control routine, called \C) and one that contains the actual procedure to be executed (the procedure routine, called CONVERT).

The two routines must be separated in the worksheet by at least one blank cell, and they must be assigned different range names.

Name the procedure routine CONVERT. Document the name in cell A36 and enter the routine in cells B36 to B37:

```
CONVERT:  {edit}{home}'~
          {d}
```

Name the control routine \C. Document the name in cell A39 and enter the routine in cell B39:

```
\C:  {for times,1,6,1,convert}
```

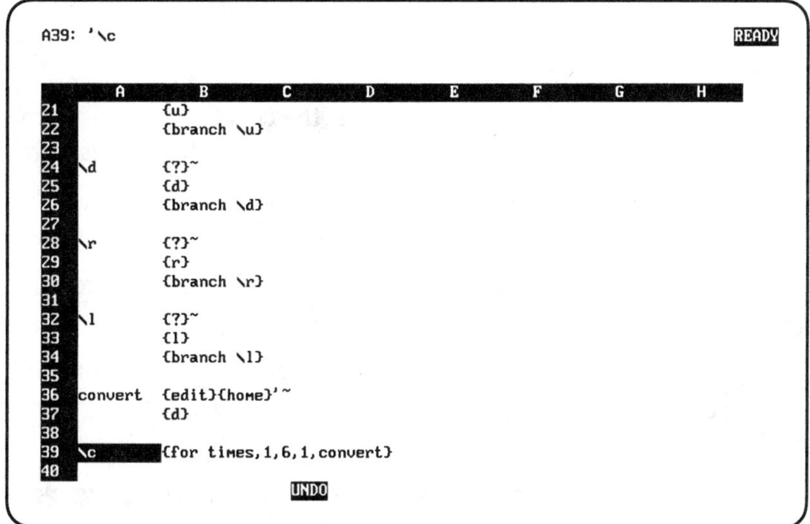

Figure 11.18
Looping macro

The procedure routine consists of a series of keystroke instructions, and the control routine consists of the advanced macro command {FOR}. The {FOR} command takes five separate arguments:

{FOR *counter,start-number,stop-number,step,subroutine*}

Each argument controls a different part of the command:

- *Counter* is the address or range name of a cell in the worksheet that the {FOR} command uses to determine when the procedure has been performed the correct number of times. In this macro, *counter* is a cell named TIMES.

- *Start-number* is the number at which to start counting (1 in this macro).
- *Stop-number* is the number at which to stop counting (6 in this macro).
- *Step* is the increment to add each time the procedure is repeated (1 in this macro).
- *Subroutine* is the cell address or range name of the subroutine to invoke (in this case, CONVERT, the procedure routine).

The {FOR} command uses the start, stop, and step values to determine the number of times to perform the task. In the counter cell, the {FOR} command keeps track of how many times the task has been performed. When the number in the counter cell exceeds the stop number, the macro stops repeating the task.

To make the {FOR} command work, you must choose a cell to be the *counter* cell. Choose an empty cell in the worksheet, in an area that you don't plan to use, as the counter location. Naming the *counter* cell and using the name is usually easier than trying to remember a cell address.

In this worksheet, you'll use cell D41 as the counter and name it TIMES. Document the name in cell C41 to the left of the TIMES cell.

Before you test the macro, enter the six numbers (1980 to 1985) in cells A41 to A46.

Figure 11.19 Six numbers for testing looping macro

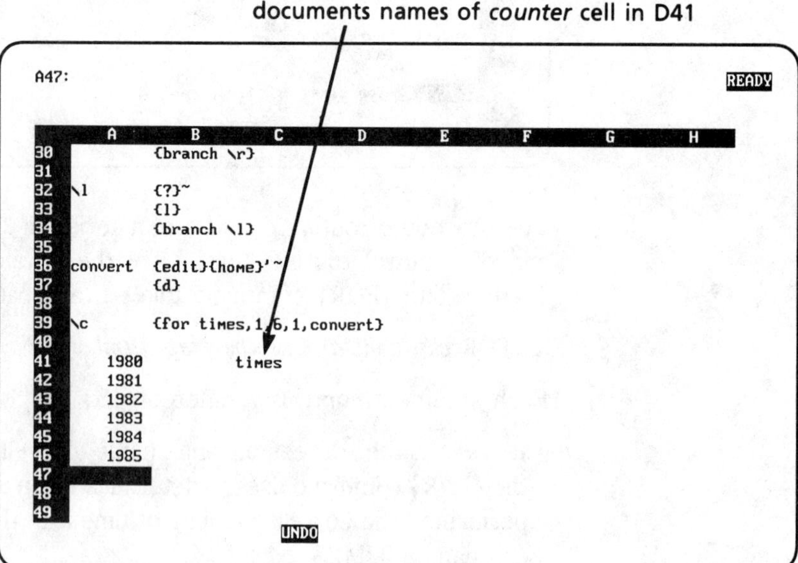

Now try the macro:

Move to: cell A41
Press: ALT – C

Figure 11.20
Converted numbers

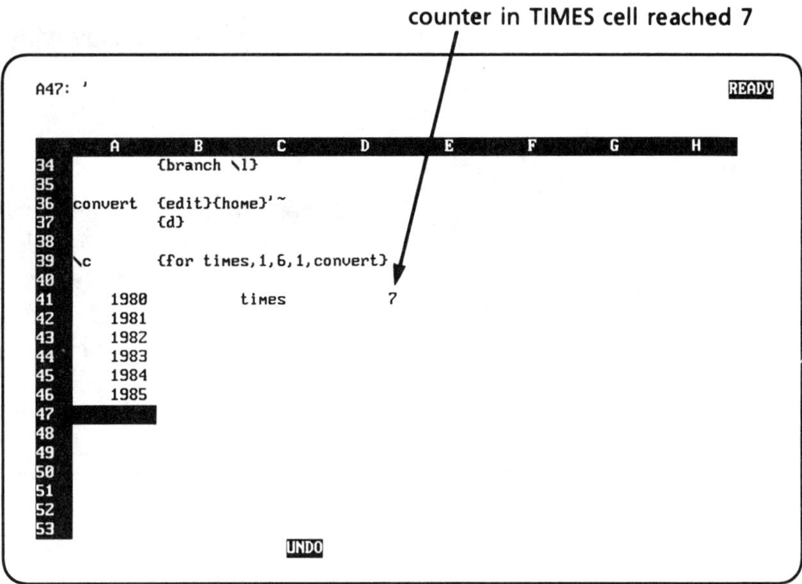

Holding Alt and typing C starts the looping macro. The macro inserts an apostrophe before each of the dates and stops automatically when it reaches row 47, the first blank row.

Look at the cell named TIMES (cell D41). The value in it is 7. The macro stopped because the value in TIMES exceeded the *stop-number.*

Before you continue, erase the numbers you just entered and erase the contents of the cell named TIMES.

To make the macro loop a different number of times, you would change the *stop-number* in the {FOR} command. To make this easier, you can use a range name instead of an actual number. For example, you might name a cell STOP and then change the macro to read:

```
{FOR TIMES,1,STOP,1,CONVERT}
```

To use the macro, enter the *stop-number* in the cell named STOP. Whenever you need to change the number of times the macro repeats the procedure, you can just change the value in STOP.

You can substitute any repetitive task for the procedure macro. To convert a column of formulas to their current values, for example, the procedure routine could consist of the **Range Value** command with the current cell serving as both the FROM and TO range.

Save the worksheet before you continue with the next macro.

FORM LETTER MACRO

Although 1–2–3 doesn't have a built-in word processing feature, it can produce simple documents such as business letters. If you type many letters that contain standard paragraphs, you may find it helpful to store standard paragraphs as macros. Once the macro enters the stored text in the worksheet, you use **/Range Justify** to make the entries look like a letter. (**/Range Justify** lets you format cell entries into paragraphs of the correct width.)

This example consists of four macros. The first three macros produce two standard paragraphs and a closing for a form letter. The fourth macro in this example is a macro that selects **/Range Justify** to create paragraphs that are 65 characters wide. When you create a macro for your own use, you can substitute your own standard paragraphs, add more paragraphs, and change the width.

The macros in this example simply enter standard information, but you can combine standard text with information you supply using advanced macro commands such as {?}, {GETLABEL}, and {GETNUMBER}. See the form letter macro in Chapter 13 for an example of an interactive macro that creates a form letter.

Paragraph Macros

You'll enter each of the following macros in more than one cell for convenience (each one would fit in a single cell, but you wouldn't be able to see the entire macro). The directions tell you to press the space bar once or twice after the final word in the cell so that 1–2–3 will insert a space between the end of the last word in one cell and the beginning of the first word in the next.

Name the first macro \X. Document the name in cell A41 and enter the macro in cells B41 to B43:

\X: Thank you for your interest in Wind4Sail, the latest [space bar]
product from Swensen Sail Technologies, Inc. [space bar]
I am enclosing a brochure and our list of dealers.~ {d 2}

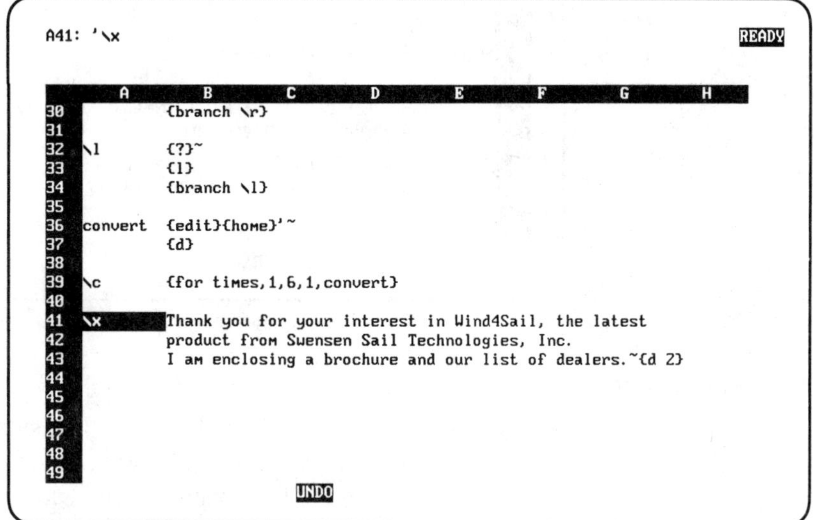

```
A41: '\x                                                    READY

     A        B        C        D        E        F        G        H
30            {branch \r}
31
32   \l       {?}~
33            {l}
34            {branch \l}
35
36   convert  {edit}{home}'~
37            {d}
38
39   \c       {for times,1,6,1,convert}
40
41   \x       Thank you for your interest in Wind4Sail, the latest
42            product from Swensen Sail Technologies, Inc.
43            I am enclosing a brochure and our list of dealers.~{d 2}
44
45
46
47
48
49
                         UNDO
```

Figure 11.21 First paragraph macro

Name the second macro \Y. Document the name in cell A45 and enter the macro in cells B45 and B46:

\Y: Please call me if you have further [space bar]
questions about any of our products.~

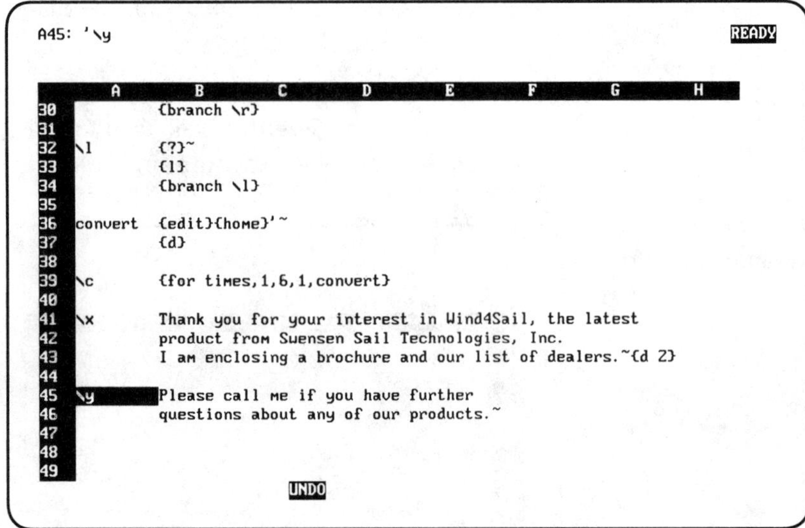

Figure 11.22
Second paragraph macro

Closing Macro

This macro enters a standard closing for a business letter. Enter it as a separate macro because you may want to use it with other letters in addition to this one. The macro begins with an instruction to move the cell pointer down three rows. This lets you run the macro as soon as you type the last word in the body of the letter.

Name the closing macro \Z. Document the name in cell A48 and enter the macro in cells B48 to B51:

```
\Z:  {d 3}Sincerely,{d 4}
     Joshua Typrowicz-Cohen{d}
     Sales Representative{d 4}
     JTC/at~
```

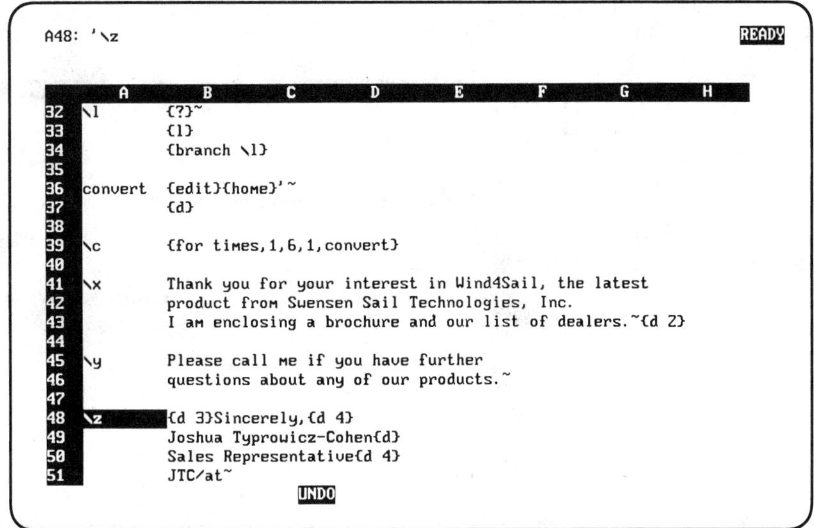

Figure 11.23
Closing macro

Test these macros now:

Move to: cell I41
Press: ALT – X

The macro enters the paragraph as a long text entry in cell I41 and moves the cell pointer down two rows. Enter the next paragraph with the second macro or type a paragraph of your own:

Press: ALT – Y

Now add the closing to the letter. The closing macro includes an instruction that moves the pointer down the correct number of rows, so you can leave the cell pointer where it is:

Press: ALT – Z

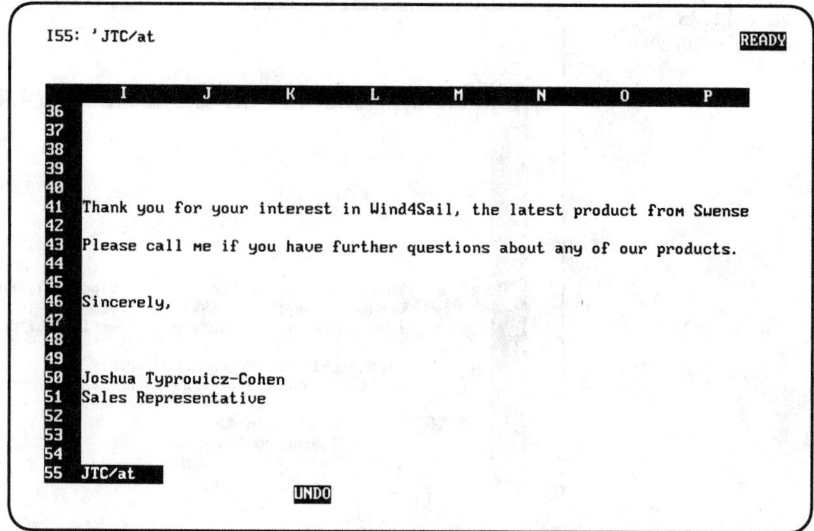

Figure 11.24 Letter produced by macro

/Range Justify Macro

At this point, the letter is difficult to read because the macros entered each of the paragraphs as a single cell entry. This means you can only read as much of each paragraph as 1-2-3 can fit across the screen.

/Range Justify breaks a long text entry, or a column of entries, into a column of cell entries of approximately the same length. You tell 1-2-3 what line length to use during **/Range Justify** by setting the column width to the length you want. This example uses 65 characters as the column width, or line length, but you can use any width you want.

Name the **/Range Justify** macro \J. Document the name in cell A53 and enter the macro in cells B53 and B54:

```
\J:  '/wcs65~~
     '/rj~
```

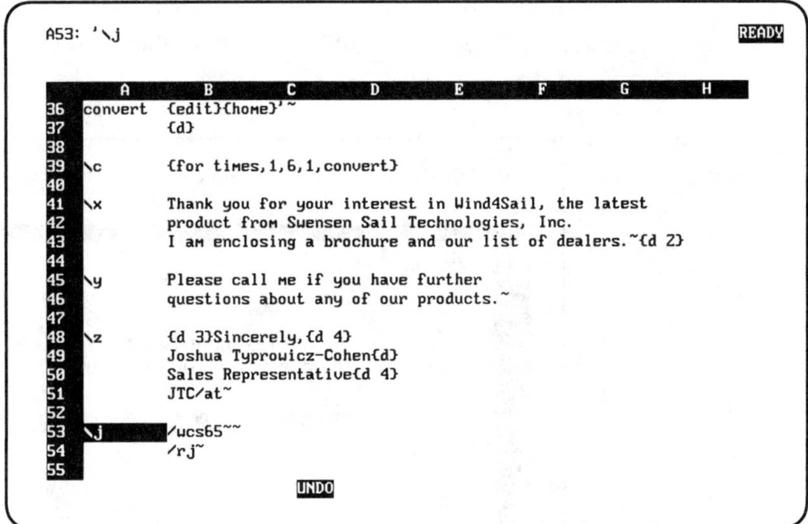

Figure 11.25
Justifying macro

The first line of this macro changes the column width to 65 (or the width you specified). The second line selects **/Range Justify**.

Now try this macro on the paragraphs you entered before. You must invoke the macro once for each paragraph. Before you invoke the macro, move the cell pointer to the cell that contains the text you want to justify:

Move to: cell I41
Press: ALT – J

The macro broke the long cell entry in cell I41 into three shorter cell entries. These entries aren't exactly 65 characters long, however, because 1–2–3 won't break a line in the middle of a word.

The \J macro specifies a single row as the range 1–2–3 will use for the justified paragraph. Specifying a single row allows 1–2–3 to use as many cells as necessary to create the paragraph. If you specify a range with more than one cell, 1–2–3 uses only the area you specify to hold the justified paragraph.

Notice that 1–2–3 shifted other entries further down the worksheet to make room for the extra entries. When you specify a single-row range, 1–2–3 shifts entries below the new range.

Now use the \J macro on the second paragraph:

Move to: cell I45 or the cell that contains the second paragraph if you used a different column width

Press: ALT – J

Figure 11.26
The letter

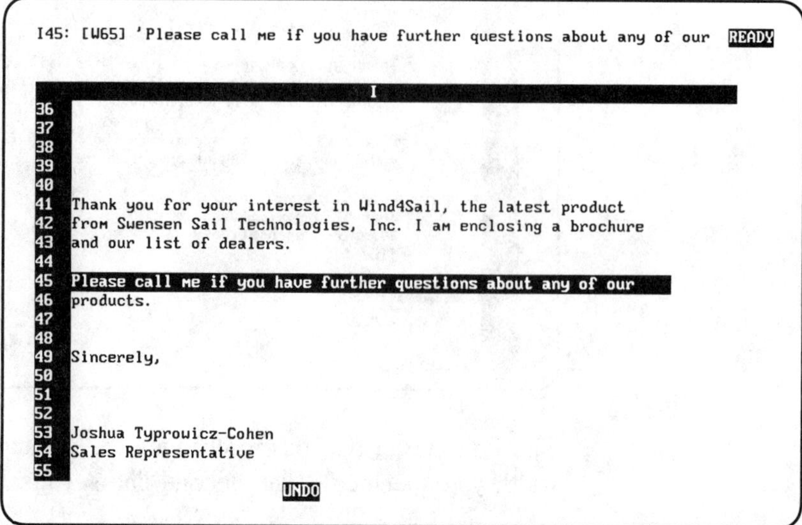

The letter looks like a letter now—the lines are of fairly even lengths. You don't need to use the \J macro on the closing because none of the lines is long enough to justify.

This example uses **/Range Justify** on two very long single text entries. **/Range Justify** isn't limited to single cell entries, however. You can use it to create cell entries of equal length out of any column of labels, as long as the range contains no blank rows or numeric entries.

Erase the letter and reset the column width before you continue. With the pointer in cell I41, press / and select **Range Erase**. Highlight the range that contains the letter and press Enter. Then press / again and select **Worksheet Column Reset-Width** to reset column I to 9 characters.

Save the worksheet before you continue.

PRINT MACROS

Probably the single most time-consuming task you can use a macro for is printing a copy of your work. A simple macro can specify the range you want to print and then activate the printer. After it prints the range, the macro advances the paper and leaves the /Print menu.

To print a worksheet manually, you would type the following keystrokes:

Keystroke	Effect
/	Calls up the menu
P	Select Print from the menu
P	Selects Printer
C	Selects Clear
R	Selects Range
R	Selects Range
HOME	Moves the cell pointer to cell A1
. (period)	Anchors the highlighted range
END HOME	Highlights the worksheet down to the lower right corner of the active area
↵	Enters the range to print
A	Selects Align to align the paper in the printer
G	Selects Go to start printing
P	Selects Page to advance the paper
Q	Selects Quit to return to the worksheet

You can translate this procedure into a macro.

Single-Copy Print Macro

Name this macro \P. Document the macro's name in cell A56 and enter the macro in cells B56 to B58:

```
\P:  '/ppccr
     {home}.{end}{home}~ (don't forget the period)
     agpq
```

Figure 11.27
Single-copy print macro

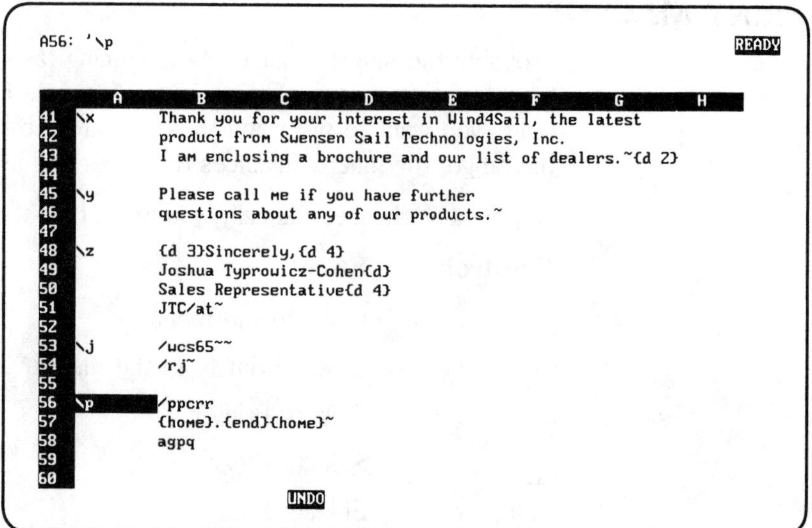

```
A56: '\p                                                READY

     A        B      C      D      E      F      G      H
41  \x        Thank you for your interest in Wind4Sail, the latest
42            product from Swensen Sail Technologies, Inc.
43            I am enclosing a brochure and our list of dealers.~{d 2}
44
45  \y        Please call me if you have further
46            questions about any of our products.~
47
48  \z        {d 3}Sincerely,{d 4}
49            Joshua Typrowicz-Cohen{d}
50            Sales Representative{d 4}
51            JTC/at~
52
53  \j        /wcs65~~
54            /rj~
55
56  \p        /ppcrr
57            {home}.{end}{home}~
58            agpq
59
60
                            UNDO
```

If you have a printer, you can test this macro now. It will print everything the MACROS3 worksheet contains. The cell pointer's location doesn't matter:

Press: ALT — P

This macro prints everything in the worksheet—including the print macro itself. If you don't want the print macro to appear in your printed copy, the best thing to do is to save it in a macro library, as described in Chapter 12.

Multiple-Copy Print Macro

This variation of the \P macro lets you print more than one copy of a document. Like the looping macro you created earlier, this macro actually consists of two separate routines. The first, \Q, is similar to the print macro you just created, but it also contains a {FOR} command that repeats the procedure in the second routine. The second routine, PRINTIT, selects the Align, Go, and Page commands.

Name the first routine \Q. Document the name in cell A60 and enter the routine in cells B60 to B63:

```
\Q: '/ppr{backspace}
    {home}.{end}{home}~
    {for counter,1,3,1,PRINTIT}
    q
```

Name the second routine PRINTIT. Document the macro in cell A65 and enter the routine in cell B65:

```
PRINTIT:  agp
```

Before you can use this macro, name a cell NUM to serve as the *counter*. Move to cell F64 now and name it NUM. Document the name in cell E64, to the left of the NUM cell.

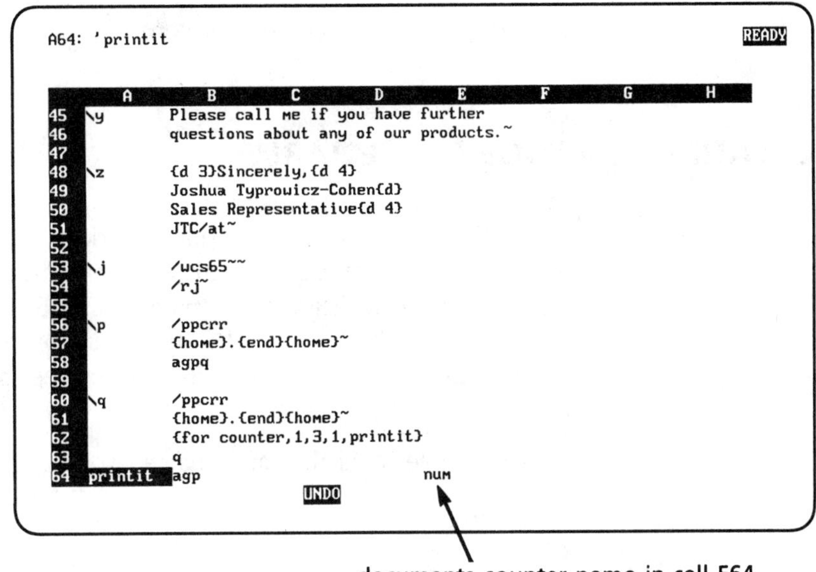

documents counter name in cell F64

Figure 11.28 Multiple-copy print macro

The first two lines of the \Q routine are the same as the single-copy print macro. The {FOR} command in the third line is like the one you used in the looping macro. The cell named NUM serves as the *counter* argument. The next three arguments (1,3,1) represent the *start-number*, *stop-number*, and *step*, respectively. PRINTIT is the *subroutine*, which causes 1-2-3 to transfer control to the second routine, PRINTIT.

The second routine selects the Align, Go, and Page commands. After 1-2-3 executes this macro, control reverts to \Q. Depending on the number in NUM, the macro either repeats the second routine to print another copy, or selects Quit and stops.

Test the macro now by holding down Alt and typing **Q**.

The macro prints three copies of the worksheet. You can write the macro to print as many copies as you like. To change the number of copies, change the *stop-number* to the number you want.

The looping macro section explained how to use a cell named STOP to hold the *stop-number* value. Using a range name in the {FOR} command makes it easier to change the *stop-number.*

Save the worksheet before you continue.

CREATING A RANGE NAME TABLE

You just entered 21 macros, each with its own range name. When you create this many macros in a single worksheet, it can be difficult to remember the range names when you haven't used the macros recently. 1-2-3 has a simple facility that creates a table that gives both the range name and the cell address of the first cell in the named range. Because macro names are range names, 1-2-3 includes them in a range name table.

Create a table of all the range names you assigned in this chapter.

Move to: cell G1
Press: [/]
Select: Range
Name
Table
Press: [↵]

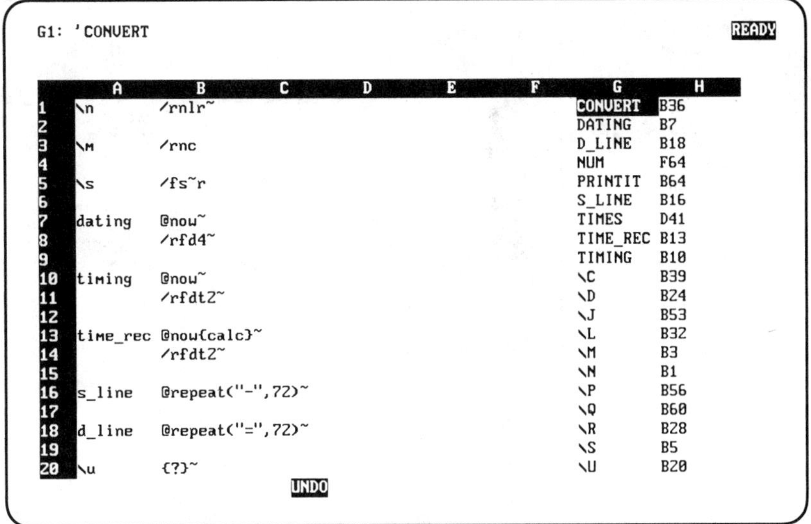

Figure 11.29 Table of range names

You may want to create a table of range names as a permanent fixture in a worksheet. If you do so, keep the following in mind:

- As with macros, you should position the table of range names in an out-of-the-way area of the worksheet.
- If you add more range names after creating the table, you must recreate the table so that it includes the new names. Position the cell pointer on the first cell of the table and select **/Range Name Table** again. The new table will replace the old one.
- You can assign a range name to the first cell in the table itself. Then you can go directly to the table at any time by pressing Goto (F5), typing the table's range name, and pressing Enter.

(2.2) Notice the advantage of giving macros descriptive names: it's easier to tell what their function is.

If you keep the MACROS3 file on a diskette, you may want to print a copy of the table of range names and attach it to the disk's protective envelope. That way, you'll be able to tell what macros are in the file without retrieving the worksheet. It is even more convenient if you enter a brief (one- or two-word) description of each macro next to the table of range names.

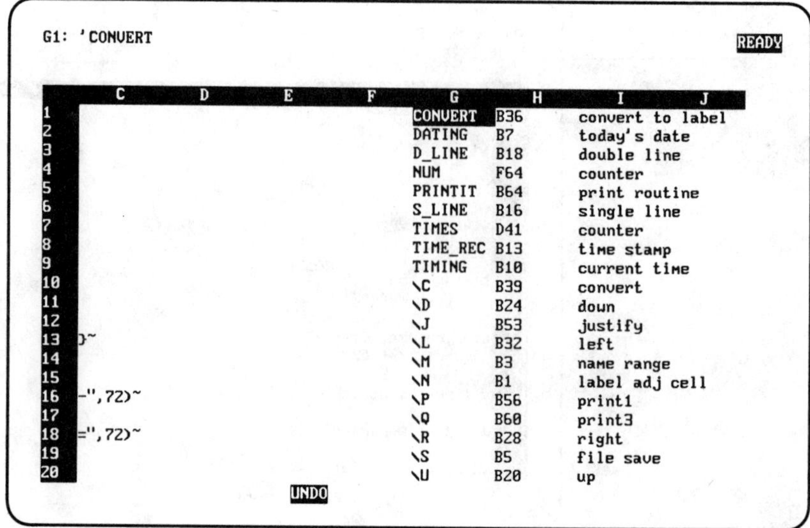
G1: 'CONVERT READY

	C	D	E	F	G	H	I
1					CONVERT	B36	convert to label
2					DATING	B7	today's date
3					D_LINE	B18	double line
4					NUM	F64	counter
5					PRINTIT	B64	print routine
6					S_LINE	B16	single line
7					TIMES	D41	counter
8					TIME_REC	B13	time stamp
9					TIMING	B10	current time
10					\C	B39	convert
11					\D	B24	down
12					\J	B53	justify
13	)~				\L	B32	left
14					\M	B3	name range
15					\N	B1	label adj cell
16	-",72)~				\P	B56	print1
17					\Q	B60	print3
18	=",72)~				\R	B28	right
19					\S	B5	file save
20					\U	B20	up

UNDO

Figure 11.30
Range name table with descriptions

Be sure to save the MACROS3 worksheet before you go on to the next chapter.

12

(2.2) Creating a Macro Library

There are many macros that you'll use often, such as utility macros that automate frequently performed tasks and more specialized macros designed for your particular job (perhaps database update procedures). To save you from having to enter these macros in every worksheet, 1-2-3 Release 2.2 lets you store the macros in a macro library and use them with any worksheet. The Macro Library Manager add-in is a program that you use with 1-2-3 to save macros in a library and retrieve them as you need them.

This chapter teaches you:

- What you can do with the Macro Library Manager
- How to start the Macro Library Manager, use its commands, and return to 1-2-3
- How to create and use a macro library of the utility macros you created in Chapter 11
- How to store and use frequently used data in a macro library
- How to edit the contents of a macro library

THE MACRO LIBRARY MANAGER

The Macro Library Manager add-in lets you create macro libraries and work with them. As a 1-2-3 add-in, the Macro Library Manager (like Allways) runs with 1-2-3 to extend its power and versatility.

Essentially, the Macro Library Manager lets you organize commonly used macros in one central location in memory, separate from the worksheet. (A copy of a library is also stored in a special library file with a .MLB extension.) The purpose of a library is to store macros that are useful with more than one worksheet. If you had a specialized macro that was designed to work with one particular worksheet, there'd be no point in saving the macro in a library.

A macro library can also be used to store just data (and no macros). For example, if you frequently use a tax or amortization table, you could enter it once, save it in a library, and then have it available with any worksheet to save you from re-entering the table.

To create a macro library, you begin by entering information in a worksheet that you want to put in the library. The information can consist of one or more macros, a combination of macros and data, or data alone. You then use the Macro Library Manager to name the library and indicate the range you want it to contain. The Macro Library Manager moves the range to the library, removing it from the worksheet. The library is now stored in memory (in an area that is separate from the worksheet) and in a library file (identified by a .MLB extension) on disk. You run the macros that are stored in a library just as you would run them if they were still in the worksheet.

Once you create a library, its contents have no relationship to a particular worksheet. If you retrieve a new file, the contents of the library remain undisturbed. You can now use the same macro with any number of different worksheet files. During future 1-2-3 sessions, you can use the library again by using the Macro Library Manager to move a copy of it from the library file on disk into memory.

STARTING THE MACRO LIBRARY MANAGER

Starting the Macro Library Manager involves two steps: attaching and invoking. **Attaching** is the process of loading the Macro Library Manager into memory so it's ready to be used. **Invoking** is the process of activating the Macro Library Manager once it is attached so you can use the Macro Library Manager commands to save and use macro libraries. You both attach and invoke the Macro Library Manager by using the 1-2-3 Add-In commands. These commands are new to 1-2-3 Release 2.2, and make it easy to run add-in programs like the Macro Library Manager and Allways right from 1-2-3. (All the Add-In commands are described in Appendix A.)

Before starting the Macro Library Manager, you are going to retrieve MACROS3, the file containing the utility macros you created in Chapter 11. You will save these macros in a library.

Press: [/]
Select: File
Retrieve
MACROS3.WK1
Press: [↵]
Move to: cell A1

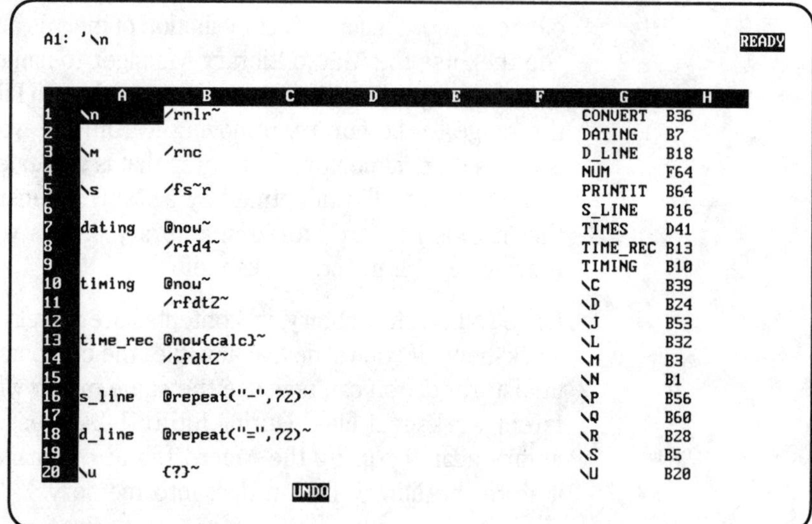

Figure 12.1
MACROS3 worksheet

Attaching the Macro Library Manager

Before you can use the Macro Library Manager, you must attach or load it into your computer's memory. When you attach the Macro Library Manager, you will be asked to assign it to a function key or to select No-Key. Appl (Alt-F7), App2 (Alt-F8), App3 (Alt-F9), and App4 (Alt-F10) are all keys you can use to invoke add-in programs (like the Macro Library Manager and Allways) while you are working in 1–2–3.

If you select No-Key, you will not be able to invoke the Macro Library Manager with a function key. You will, however, be able to activate the Macro Library Manager using **/Add-In Invoke**.

If you have a hard-disk computer, the Macro Library Manager (MACROMGR.ADN) should be in the subdirectory that contains your 1-2-3 files.

If you have a two-diskette computer, place the Install Disk in one of the diskette drives.

Press: /
Select: Add-In
Attach

Figure 12.2 Attaching the Macro Library Manager

```
A1: '\n                                                          FILES
Enter add-in to attach: C:\123\*.ADN
ALLWAYS.ADN      MACROMGR.ADN     ALLWAYS\
        A          B        C        D        E        F        G          H
1   \n         /rnlr~                                        CONVERT    B36
2                                                            DATING     B7
3   \m         /rnc                                          D_LINE     B18
4                                                            NUM        F64
5   \s         /fs~r                                         PRINTIT    B64
6                                                            S_LINE     B16
7   dating     @now~                                         TIMES      D41
8              /rfd4~                                        TIME_REC   B13
9                                                            TIMING     B10
10  timing     @now~                                         \C         B39
11             /rfdt2~                                       \D         B24
12                                                           \J         B53
13  time_rec   @now{calc}~                                   \L         B32
14             /rfdt2~                                       \M         B3
15                                                           \N         B1
16  s_line     @repeat("-",72)~                              \P         B56
17                                                           \Q         B60
18  d_line     @repeat("=",72)~                              \R         B28
19                                                           \S         B5
20  \u         {?}~                                          \U         B20
```

Select: MACROMGR.ADN

You are going to assign the Macro Library Manager to App2 (Alt-F8). (If you've already assigned another add-in to this key, choose one of the other function keys for the Macro Library Manager.)

Figure 12.3
Selecting function key for the Macro Library Manager

```
A1: '\n                                                              MENU
No-Key  7  8  9  10
Use APP2 (ALT-F8) to invoke the add-in
       A         B         C         D         E         F         G         H
1   \n         /rnlr~                                          CONVERT   B36
2                                                              DATING    B7
3   \m         /rnc                                            D_LINE    B18
4                                                              NUM       F64
5   \s         /fs~r                                           PRINTIT   B64
6                                                              S_LINE    B16
7   dating     @now~                                           TIMES     D41
8              /rfd4~                                          TIME_REC  B13
9                                                              TIMING    B10
10  timing     @now~                                           \C        B39
11             /rfdt2~                                         \D        B24
12                                                             \J        B53
13  time_rec   @now{calc}~                                     \L        B32
14             /rfdt2~                                         \M        B3
15                                                             \N        B1
16  s_line     @repeat("-",72)~                                \P        B56
17                                                             \Q        B60
18  d_line     @repeat("=",72)~                                \R        B28
19                                                             \S        B5
20  \u         {?}~                                            \U        B20
```

Select: 8 to assign the Macro Library Manager to App2 (Alt-F8)
Quit to return to the worksheet

The Macro Library Manager is now attached, or in memory. To use the add-in, however, you must still invoke it.

You can also ask 1–2–3 to attach the Macro Library Manager automatically whenever you start 1–2–3. To do so, use the **Worksheet Global Default Other Add-In** command and specify the Macro Library Manager (MACROMGR.ADN) as an add-in to attach automatically. You must then update the 1–2–3 configuration file with **/Worksheet Global Default Update** so that the Macro Library Manager is attached at the start of every 1–2–3 session. Having the Macro Library Manager attached automatically is very useful if you find yourself using the add-in frequently during 1–2–3 sessions.

Invoking the Macro Library Manager

Whenever you want to use the Macro Library Manager, you must invoke it. You can do this in one of two ways. If you selected a function key when you attached the Macro Library Manager, you just press that key. For example, you chose 8 so you would press App2 (Alt-F8) to invoke the Macro Library Manager.

If you selected No-Key when attaching the Macro Library Manager, you select **/Add-In Invoke** and then select MACROMGR from the menu of attached add-ins that appears.

Press: APP2 (Alt-F8)

Figure 12.4 The Macro Library Manager menu

```
A1: '\n                                                              MENU
Load  Save  Edit  Remove  Name-List  Quit
Read a macro library from disk into memory
     A          B          C     D     E     F       G          H
1   \n         /rnlr~                               CONVERT    B36
2                                                   DATING     B7
3   \m         /rnc                                 D_LINE     B18
4                                                   NUM        F64
5   \s         /fs~r                                PRINTIT    B64
6                                                   S_LINE     B16
7   dating     @now~                                TIMES      D41
8              /rfd4~                               TIME_REC   B13
9                                                   TIMING     B10
10  timing     @now~                                \C         B39
11             /rfdt2~                              \D         B24
12                                                  \J         B53
13  time_rec   @now{calc}~                          \L         B32
14             /rfdt2~                              \M         B3
15                                                  \N         B1
16  s_line     @repeat("-",72)~                     \P         B56
17                                                  \Q         B60
18  d_line     @repeat("=",72)~                     \R         B28
19                                                  \S         B5
20  \u         {?}~                                 \U         B20
```

As soon as you invoke the Macro Library Manager, the Macro Library Manager menu appears.

THE MACRO LIBRARY MANAGER MENU

The Macro Library Manager menu appears automatically whenever you invoke the add-in. The Macro Library Manager commands do the following:

Load	Copies the contents of a library (.MLB) file into memory so you can use the library
Save	Moves the contents of a range into a macro library in memory and saves a copy in a library (.MLB) file on disk
Edit	Copies the contents of a macro library in memory to a range in the worksheet so you can make changes to the library

Remove	Erases a macro library from memory (but not from disk)
Name-List	Enters a list in the worksheet of the range names contained in a macro library
Quit	Leaves the Macro Library Manager menu and returns you to 1-2-3

You select the Macro Library Manager commands just as you select 1-2-3 commands: either type the first letter of a command or highlight the command and press Enter.

SAVING MACROS IN A LIBRARY

You're now going to save the utility macros in a library. These macros already exist, so you can just go ahead and save them. If they didn't exist, you'd first enter them in a worksheet as usual and then invoke the Macro Library Manager so you could save them in a library.

The Macro Library Manager menu is already on the screen so you can go ahead and select the Save command:

Select: Save

The Macro Library Manager prompts you for a library name. You will name this library UTILS. You don't need to enter a file extension because the Macro Library Manager automatically adds .MLB to the file name you enter:

Type: utils

Figure 12.5
Entering library name

```
A1: '\n                                                                EDIT
Enter name of macro library to save: C:\TEMP\utils

       A         B         C      D      E      F      G         H
1   \n        /rnlr~                                   CONVERT   B36
2                                                      DATING    B7
3   \m        /rnc                                     D_LINE    B18
4                                                      NUM       F64
5   \s        /fs~r                                    PRINTIT   B64
6                                                      S_LINE    B16
7   dating    @now~                                    TIMES     D41
8             /rfd4~                                   TIME_REC  B13
9                                                      TIMING    B10
10  timing    @now~                                    \C        B39
11            /rfdt2~                                  \D        B24
12                                                     \J        B53
13  time_rec  @now{calc}~                              \L        B32
14            /rfdt2~                                  \M        B3
15                                                     \N        B1
16  s_line    @repeat("-",72)~                         \P        B56
17                                                     \Q        B60
18  d_line    @repeat("=",72)~                         \R        B28
19                                                     \S        B5
20  \u        {?}~                                     \U        B20
```

Press: ↵

You can save any part of the worksheet in the library. In this case, you will include the macros themselves, but not the descriptive information in columns G, H, and I. The range you want to specify is A1..B64. You can either type the range address or highlight it when the Macro Library Manager prompts you to enter the range you want to save in the library. Type the range address:

Type: a1.b64

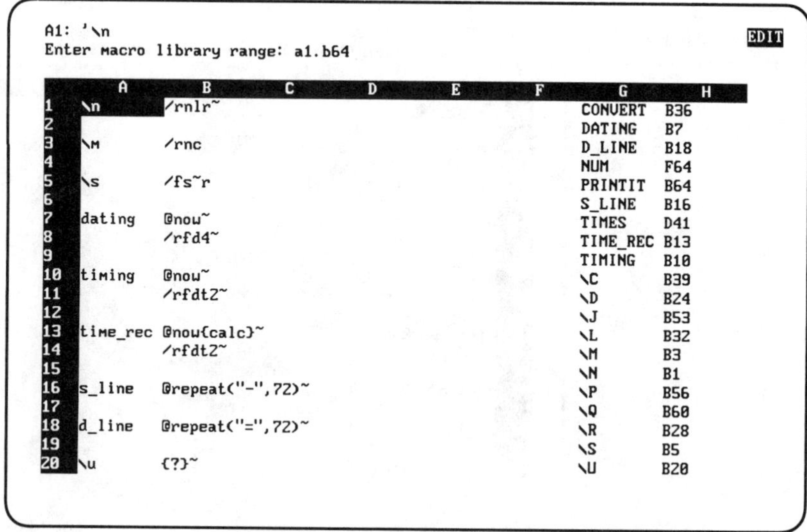

Figure 12.6 Range to be saved in library

Press: ↵

The Macro Library Manager now gives you the choice of using a password with the library. This prevents other users from editing the macro library.

Select: No

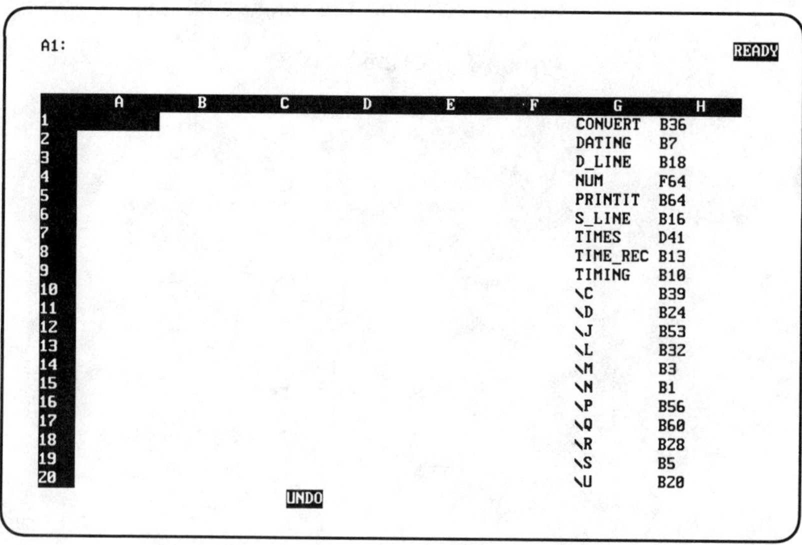

Figure 12.7 Macros erased after saving

The macros disappear from the worksheet. They are now in a library called UTILS in memory and in a disk file called UTILS.MLB. The Macro Library Manager menu is no longer on the screen and you're back in 1-2-3 READY mode.

USING MACROS IN A LIBRARY

Before trying the macros in the UTILS library, start with a blank worksheet (the MACROS3 worksheet file will still contain all the utility macros):

Press: [/]
Select: Worksheet
Erase
Yes

The UTILS macro library is in memory and you can run any of the macros it contains as you would normally run macros.

First try the date macro named DATING:

Move to: cell A1
Press: [RUN] (Alt-F3)
Select: DATING

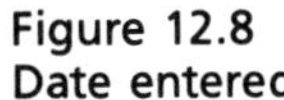

Figure 12.8
Date entered

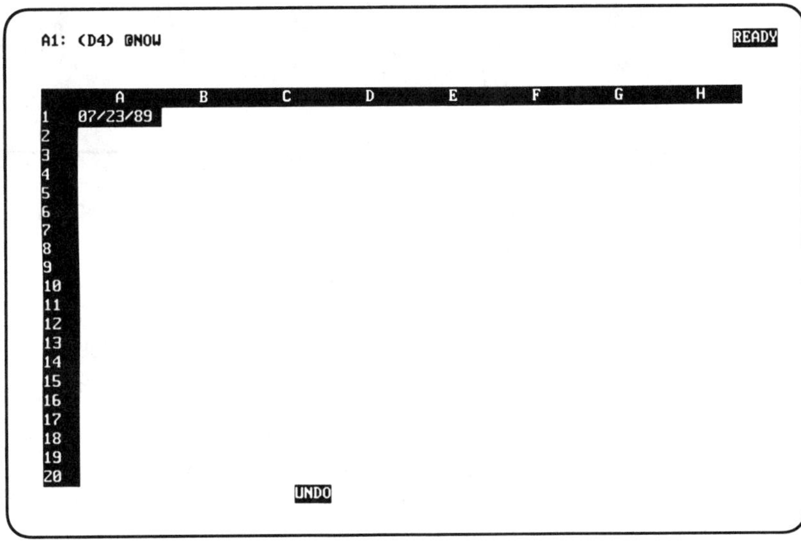

Save the worksheet in a file named TEST so you can later try the file save (\S) macro:

Press: [/]
Select: File
Save
Type: test [↵]

Now try the single line macro named S_LINE:

Move to: cell A2
Press: [RUN] (Alt-F3)
Select: S_LINE

Figure 12.9 Single line entered

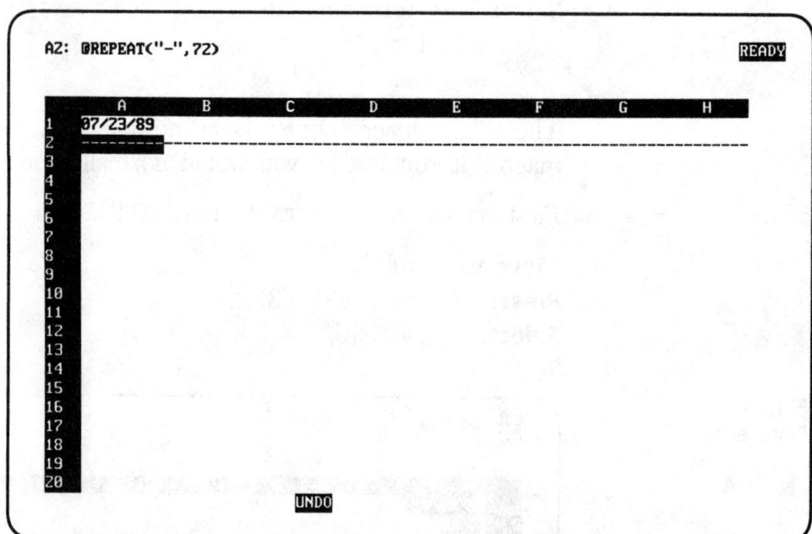

Last, try the file save (\S) macro (do this only if you've already saved the file once):

Press: [ALT] – [S]

As you can see, you run macros with Alt or Run (Alt-F3) just as you do when you're not working with a library.

Once you save macros in a library, they no longer appear in the worksheet. To see or edit the macros, you would use the **Macro Library Manager Edit** command. This command copies the contents of the library to a range in the worksheet so you can examine or change the contents of the library. If you change the contents and want to incorporate the changes in the library, you would then have to save the range again with the Save command.

REMOVING A LIBRARY FROM MEMORY

For now, you've finished working with the UTILS library, so you can remove it from memory to avoid using memory unnecessarily. When you use the **Macro Library Manager Remove** command, the library is removed from memory, but still remains in the library disk file. To use the library again, use the **Macro Library Manager Load** command.

Remove the library now:

Press: APP2 (Alt-F8) to invoke the Macro Library Manager
Select: Remove
UTILS

USING A LIBRARY FOR STORING DATA

Despite its name, the Macro Library Manager doesn't just let you store macros in libraries. You can store a combination of macros and data, or just data. Saving data in a library can be very useful, for example, if you find yourself constantly typing the months of the year into many worksheets; if you use large tables (such as tax tables) in many worksheets; or if there's a particular structure, or template, for worksheets that you use over and over again.

With the Macro Library Manager, you can enter the data once, use the **Save** command to store it in a library and then use the **Edit** command to place the data in another worksheet.

Creating and Saving a Template

In this section, you'll create a simple template for tracking monthly expenses, save it in a library, and then retrieve it into a worksheet. In your own work, you could enter and then save any data you use over and over again.

Start with a blank worksheet and widen column A to 12 characters:

Press: [/]
Select: Worksheet
Erase
Yes
Press: [/]
Select: Worksheet
Column
Set-Width
Type: 12 [↵]

Now enter the labels shown in Figure 12.10.

Figure 12.10
Monthly expenses template

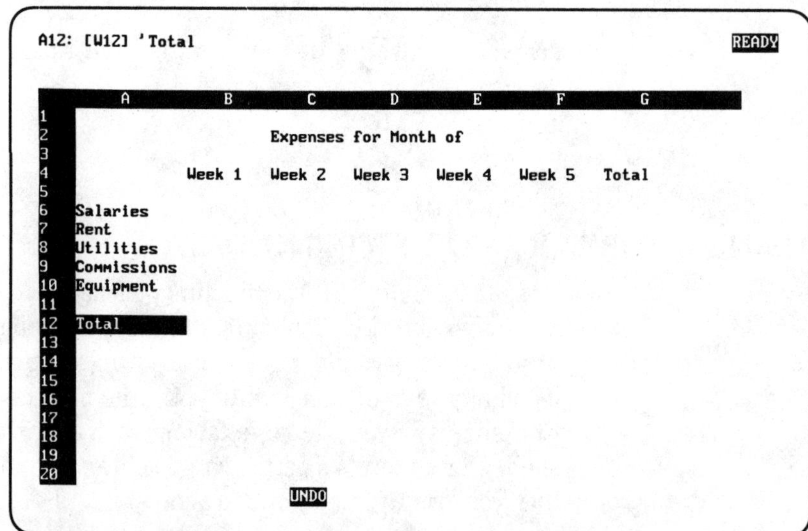

To make the template more useful, you will enter some formulas to total each type of expense and each week of expenses:

Move to: cell B12
Type: @sum(b6.b10)
Press: [↵]

Now copy the formula across the row to cells C12..G12:

Press: [/]
Select: Copy
Press: [↵] to accept B12 as the FROM range
[→]
[·] (to anchor the cell pointer)
[END] [→]
[↵] to accept C12..G12 as the TO range

Enter a second formula in cell G6 and copy it to cells G7..G10:

Move to: cell G6
Type: @sum(b6.f6) [↵]
Press: [/]
Select: Copy
Press: [↵] to accept G6 as the FROM range
[↓]
[·]
[↓] three times
[↵] to accept G7..G10 as the TO range

To make the worksheet more readable, line up the column headings in row 4 at the right edges of their cells:

Move to: cell B4
Press: [/]
Select: Range
Label
Right
Press: [END] [→]
[↵]

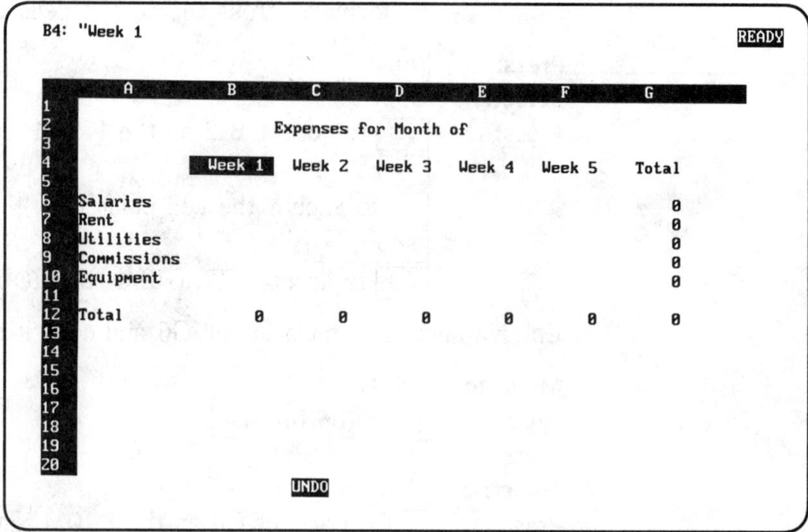

Figure 12.11
Completed template

Notice the zeros in the cells that contain formulas. Once you enter data in the worksheet, they will be replaced with values.

Now save the data in a library named TEMPLATE.

Press: APP2 (Alt-F8) to invoke the Macro Library Manager
Select: Save
Type: template ↵

The Macro Library Manager will prompt you for the range to save in the library. You need to save the range A2..G12.

Type: a2.g12
Press: ↵
Select: No

The worksheet clears. Your template is now in a library named TEMPLATE and a file named TEMPLATE.MLB.

Using the Template

You can retrieve your template into any worksheet with the Edit command. Start with a blank worksheet and position the cell pointer where you want the template you saved to begin.

Move to: cell A4
Press: [APP2] (Alt-F8) to invoke the Macro Library Manager
Select: Edit

The Macro Library Manager will list all the libraries currently in memory. In this case, you should just see TEMPLATE (you removed UTILS earlier).

Select: TEMPLATE

The Macro Library Manager now gives you a choice abou. how range names are handled if it finds the same range names in both the current worksheet and the library. If you select Ignore, the Macro Library Manager uses the range names in the worksheet over those in the library. If you select Overwrite, it uses the range names in the library over those in the worksheet. In this particular case, you don't have range names in either place, so the choice doesn't matter. Select Ignore:

Select: Ignore

The Macro Library Manager now prompts for a range for the contents of the library. If you were doing this with a worksheet that contained data, you would need to specify an empty part of the worksheet, or the contents of the library would replace data in the worksheet. You just need to indicate the upper left corner of the range.

Press: [↵] to accept cell A4 as the left corner of the range

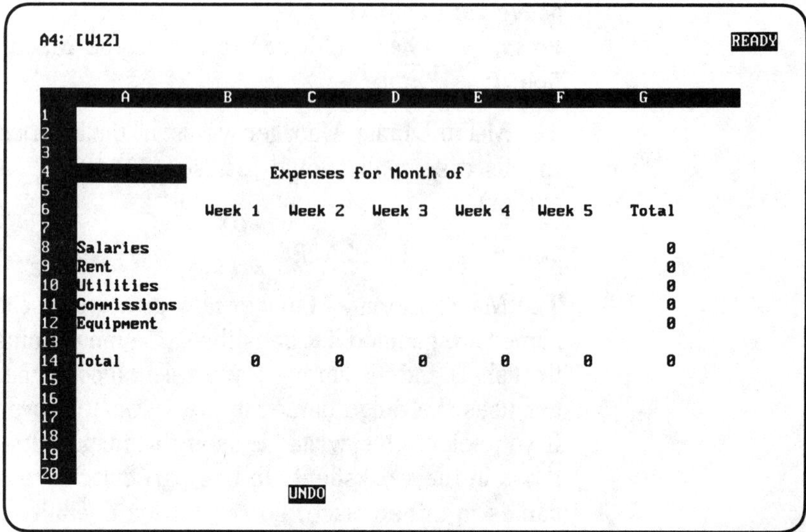

Figure 12.12
Template appears in worksheet

The contents of the library—the template—appear in the worksheet. The template is ready to be filled in. Add a month to the title and enter some numbers in the worksheet to see how the template works:

Move to: cell C4
Press: EDIT (F2)
SPACE
Type: July ↵
Move to: cell B6
Type: 555623
Press: ↓
Type: 1266 ↵

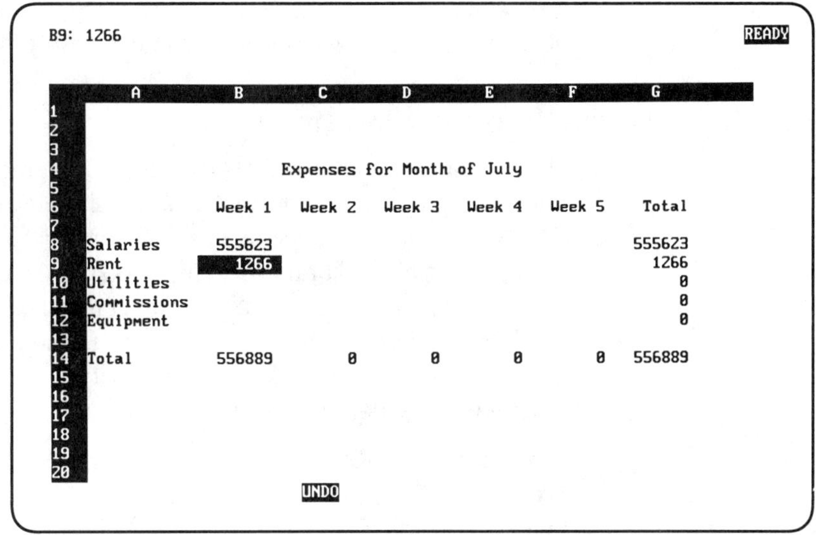

Figure 12.13
Template with some data

Notice that the some of the total cells in column G and row 14 now contain values.

As you can see, by entering the template once and saving it in a library, you can copy it into a worksheet with the **Macro Library Manager Edit** command and fill it in whenever you need to. You don't need to re-enter it each time.

EDITING A LIBRARY

You just saw how to use the **Macro Library Manager Edit** command to "paste in" data from a library. The more common use for the **Edit** command is, however, to make changes to the contents of a library. You will change one of the macros in the UTILS library.

Loading a Library into Memory

The UTILS library is not currently in memory, so you must first load it in:

Press: APP2 (Alt-F8) to invoke the Macro Library Manager
Select: Load
UTILS
Quit

You won't see any differences on the screen, but the UTILS macro library is now in memory so you can use any of the macros it contains.

Copying a Library into the Worksheet

One of the macros in the UTILS library entered the current date in one of the 1-2-3 date formats. You will change this macro (named DATING) so the date appears in a different format. First you must copy the contents of the library into the worksheet with the **Edit** command so you can make changes. When you copy a library into a worksheet, the library still remains in memory and in the library (.MLB) file. Be sure to copy the library to an empty part of the worksheet or it will write over any data in the worksheet.

Move to: cell A20
Press: APP2 (Alt-F8)
Select: Edit
UTILS

The library you're going to edit contains several range names (representing macro names), but you don't have any range names in the worksheet, so there's no conflict.

Select: Ignore
Press: ↵ to accept cell A20 as the upper left corner of the library

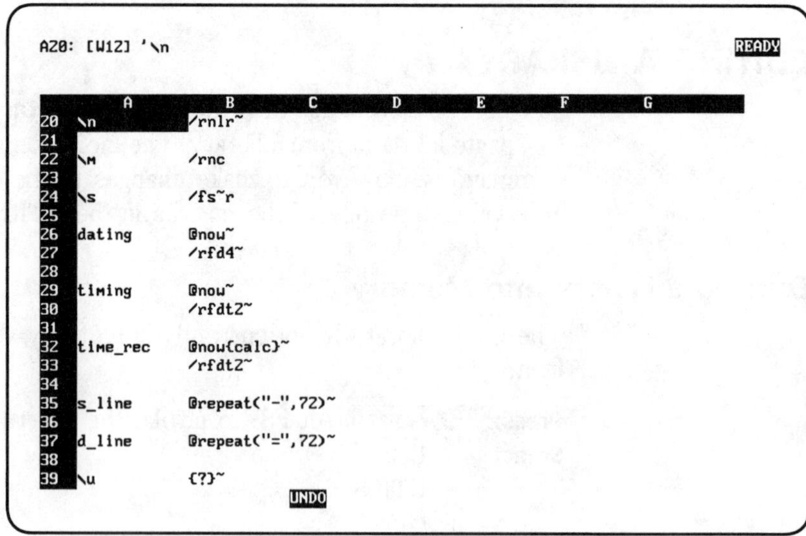

Figure 12.14 Library appears in worksheet

Changing a Macro in a Library

The library is in the worksheet, so you can make changes to its contents just as you would to any data in a 1–2–3 worksheet. You will change the DATING macro so the date appears in date 1 format (07-Jul-89) instead of date 4 format (07/07/89). Because the new date format takes up more space, however, you will also change the macro to increase the column width to 10 characters.

Move to: cell B27
Press: EDIT (F2)
← twice
DEL
Type: 1 ↵
Press: ↓
Type: '/wcs10~ ↵

Figure 12.15
Edited macro

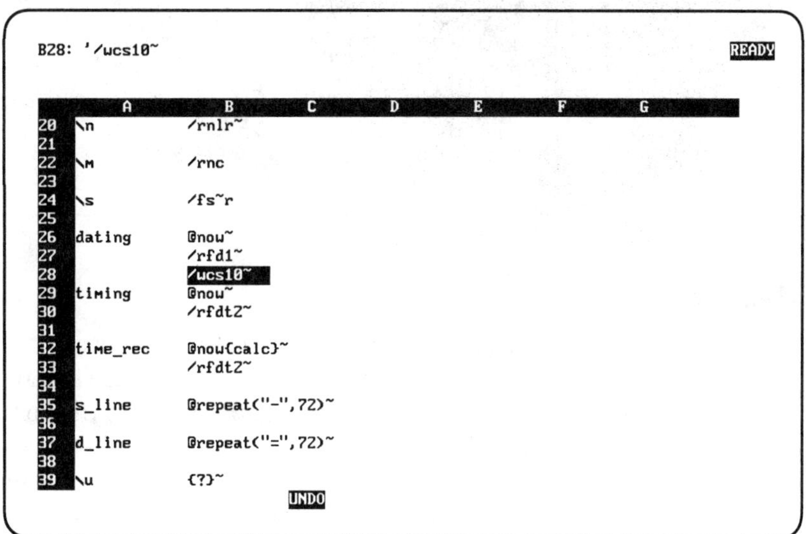

The DATING macro is no longer separated from the next macro (TIMING) by a blank cell to tell 1–2–3 that the instruction for widening the column marks the end of the macro. This means that instead of stopping after widening the column, 1–2–3 would execute the TIMING macro. To avoid this, insert a blank row between the two macros:

Move to: any cell in row 29
Press: /
Select: Worksheet
Insert
Row
Press: ↵ to accept row 29 as the row to insert

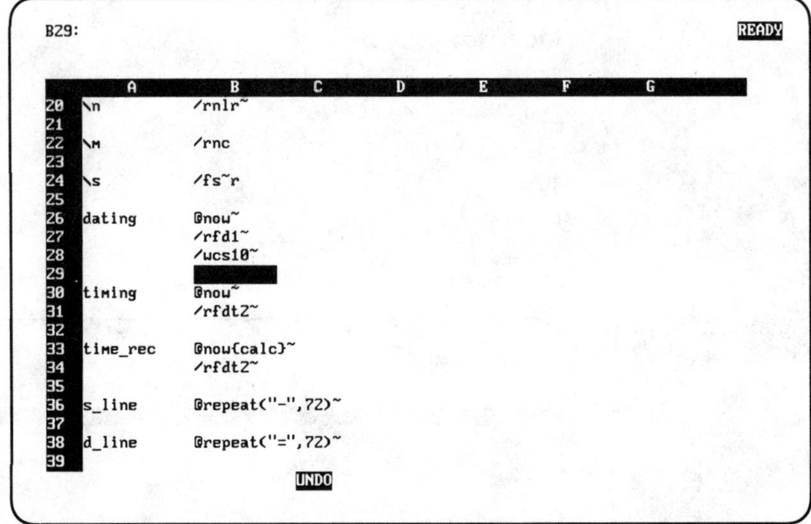

Figure 12.16
Inserted row separating macros

Updating the Library with Changes

Although you've changed the DATING macro in the current worksheet, the UTILS library in memory and the UTILS.MLB file still contain the original version of the macro. To update the library and the library file, you must save the range of macros in the library again. Before saving the macros, however, make sure the DATING macro works as you expected (it's always a good idea to test your macros before saving them in a library):

Move to: cell E26
Press: RUN (Alt-F3)
Select: DATING

> NOTE: If you press Name (F3) after pressing Run (Alt-F3) to see a full-screen list of range names, you'll see two DATING range names. The first is the one in the current worksheet (this is the one you want); the second is the UTILS library (which hasn't been updated yet). You can tell which macro is which by highlighting each instance of DATING. The DATING macro in the worksheet will be followed by its range address; the one in the library will be followed by the library name. See Figure 12.18 for an illustration.

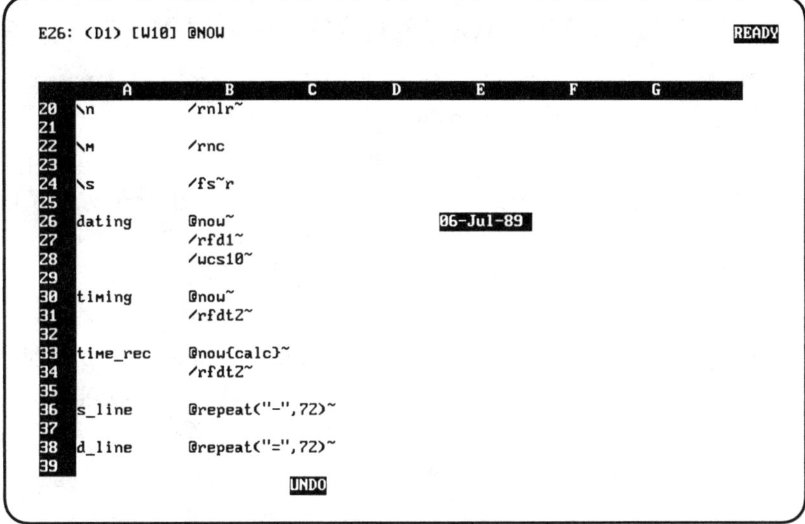

Figure 12.17 Date inserted with updated DATING macro

Now update the library:

Press: APP2 (Alt-F8)
Select: Save
Select: UTILS

The Macro Library Manager asks whether you want to write over the version of UTILS.MLB in memory.

Select: Yes

The range you want to save is A20..B84:

Type: a20.b84
Press: ↵
Select: No

The macros disappear from the worksheet. The UTILS library and UTILS.MLB file now include the updated DATING macro. You will find the UTILS library useful in the next two chapters.

WORKING WITH THE MACRO LIBRARY MANAGER

As you start using the Macro Library Manager in your own work, keep the following guidelines in mind:

- The Macro Library Manager must be attached (in memory) before you can invoke it. If you detach the Macro Library Manager (with **/Add-in Detach**), any macro libraries that were in memory will no longer be there.

- You run a macro in a library the same way you run a macro in the worksheet. Either press Alt and a letter if you named the macro with a \ (backslash) and a single letter or press Run (Alt-F3) and select the macro from the list that appears.

  If you press Run (Alt-F3) and then press Name (F3) to see a full-screen list of macro range names, 1-2-3 first lists all the range names in the worksheet. It then lists all the range names in each macro library that is currently in memory. You can tell where the highlighted range is located by looking at the top of the menu. If the range is in the worksheet, it is followed by its coordinates (for example, C3.G3). If the range is in a macro library, it is followed by the name of the library that contains it (for example, UTILS.MLB).

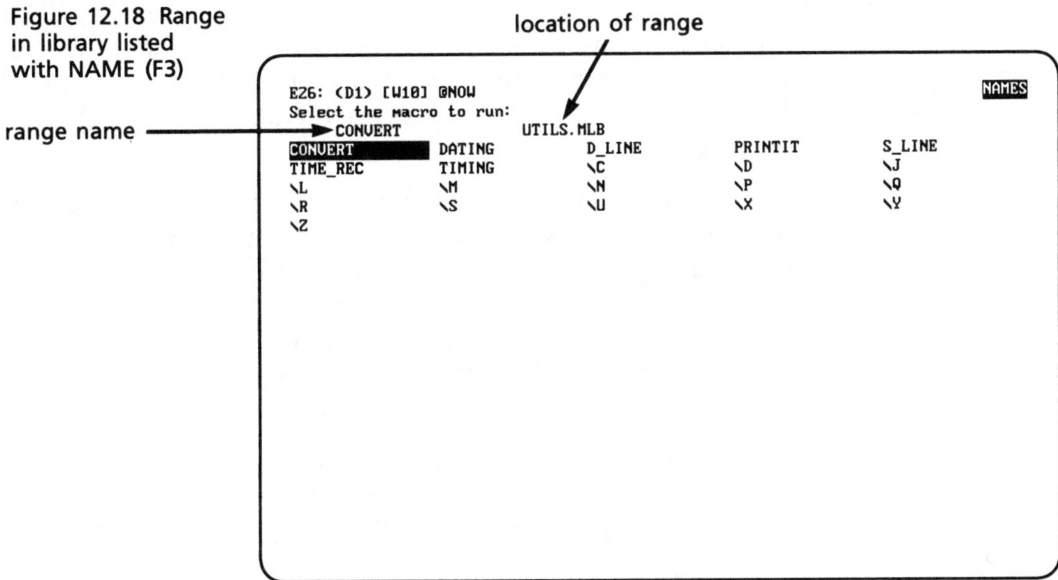

Figure 12.18 Range in library listed with NAME (F3)

- You can erase a worksheet (/**Worksheet Erase**) or retrieve another worksheet (/**File Retrieve**) without affecting any macro libraries in memory.
- The Macro Library Manager places a library in memory whenever you use the **Load** or **Save** commands. You can have up to 10 libraries in memory at the same time.
- To save on memory, load only the libraries you need into memory and remove them when you finish using them. This will give you more memory for creating worksheets.
- If you want to prevent others from either editing a macro library or viewing it in STEP mode, you can protect the library with a password when you use the **Macro Library Manager Save** command. Others can still load the library into memory and use its contents, however.
- Libraries in memory must have unique names. If you try to save a library using the name of a library that already exists, the Macro Library Manager will ask you whether you want to replace the existing library or not. When naming libraries, try to use descriptive names for them so you know what they contain.

- Avoid using the same range names in different libraries. If you've loaded more than one library into memory and duplicate range names exist, you may not get the macro you want when you try to run it. (1–2–3 searches the libraries in memory in the order in which they were loaded or saved.)

- You can access data in a macro library with a formula or a macro in the worksheet. A macro library has no cell coordinates, however, so if you want to refer to data in a library, you cannot use a cell or range address such as A3 or F11.F15. (Cell coordinates apply only to the worksheet.) The data in the library must be contained in a named range (for example, NET_INC) and you must refer to it with the range name.

- The Macro Library Manager will not let you save a range that includes a link to data in another file. An error message will appear if you try this. (File linking is discussed in Chapter 3.)

- If you're planning to use advanced macro commands in the macros you save in libraries, refer to the *1–2–3 Reference* Manual for further rules about working with the Macro Library Manager.

13

Application Macros

The short utility macros in Chapter 11 automate tasks you perform frequently when you use 1-2-3. These macros are useful in almost any 1-2-3 worksheet. For example, you can use the file saving macro with any worksheet, whether you are working on a financial spreadsheet, creating a graph, or entering new records in a database.

You can also create macros for more particular applications. Application macros can be as short as utility macros. Unlike utility macros, however, you use them only for a particular type of work. Application macros can be completely automatic, or they can be interactive, requiring you to supply information.

An application macro automates a particular process that you perform with 1-2-3. A single application macro often consists of a group of macros that automate the individual steps required to complete a specific task. For example, an application macro could automate many of the steps involved in creating and using a database, such as naming fields, entering records, and sorting the database.

In this chapter, you'll create three macro applications:

- The graph application produces a slide show presentation that alternates between the worksheet and a series of named graphs.
- The database application automates the process of creating a database form, entering records in the database, and sorting the database records.
- The form letter application automates the process of addressing, writing, and printing form letters.

Each of these applications simplifies a time-consuming process. The graph application involves a single macro that works with data and graphs you create before you run the macro. The database application is a group of macros, each of which automates a different database function. The form letter application consists of a single macro that uses subroutines to produce variations of a form letter.

Entering the application macros may seem difficult at first. You may leave out braces and tildes and make other typing mistakes when you enter the macros. As you become familiar with the way macros look and how they work, however, entering the commands becomes easier.

(2.2) Using the Utility Macros

In this chapter, you'll create three worksheets (one for each of the applications). Some of the utility macros you created in the Chapter 11 and saved in the UTILS library in Chapter 12 will be useful when you create these worksheets. Throughout the chapter, you'll see reminders of utility macros that you can use when creating a particular application.

To use any of the utility macros, you must first attach and invoke the Macro Library Manager and then load the UTILS library into memory.

Press: /

Select: Add-In
Attach
MACROMGR.ADN
Invoke
MACROMGR
Load
UTILS
Quit

You can now use any of the utility macros either by pressing Alt and a letter (for macros named with a backslash and single letter) or by pressing Run (Alt-F3) and selecting the macro from the list that 1-2-3 displays.

THE GRAPH APPLICATION

Graphs illustrate numeric data. A graph is often an effective way to present information because it shows trends and comparisons visually. Each of 1–2–3's five graph types illustrates a particular kind of comparison. A line graph, for example, shows change over time, whereas a pie chart compares parts to the whole.

In this section, you'll create a presentation that includes three separate graphs. Each graph illustrates a particular aspect of a simplified financial report. You might use such a series of graphs as part of a financial presentation.

To use the graph application macro, you must be able to display graphs on your monitor.

Before you create the graph presentation macro, you must set up the worksheet and create the graphs. Getting ready to use this application macro is time-consuming because you must enter the data the graphs illustrate and then create and name the graphs.

When you make a presentation of your own work, however, you use information in worksheets that already exist. The setup process doesn't require as much time because you have already entered the information, and you may have already created the graphs. You can use this presentation with any worksheet and any series of graphs you use in your own work. Just substitute the graph names and range names from the worksheet you are using.

Once you set up the worksheet and the graphs, you can use the presentation as often as necessary. If your numbers change, you don't need to create a new presentation; just change the figures in the existing worksheet, and 1–2–3 changes the graphs automatically. For example, you might need to make a presentation such as this at the end of every quarter, using the most recent sales figures. If the worksheet already exists, you need only enter the new sales figures. The macro can display the new graphs as soon as you revise the data.

Setting up the Worksheet

This application macro uses simplified data to track a company's financial performance. The first graph illustrates net income over a one-year period, the second compares net revenues by division for the same period, and the third follows the high and low stock prices for six quarters.

The rest of this section provides detailed instructions for entering the information in the worksheet and then creating and naming the graphs. If you don't need step-by-step instruction, copy the information from the screen illustrations and create and name the graphs yourself. Then go on to the next section, "Creating the Presentation Macro."

You're going to start with a blank worksheet, so save your current worksheet if you need the information it contains. Then erase the worksheet:

Press: [/]
Select: Worksheet
Erase
Yes

Several of the macros in the UTILS library are useful in this section, so remember to use them to save yourself time and keystrokes.

Macro	**Name**
Naming a multiple-cell range	\M
File saving	\S
Single Line	S_LINE
Double Line	D_LINE
Down	\D
Right	\R

For instructions about loading the UTILS library, see "Using the Utility Macros" earlier in this chapter.

Before you continue, save the worksheet, but do not use the file saving macro yet. You must save the worksheet manually the first time to name it.

Press: [/]
Select: File
Save
Type: graph
Press: [↵]

As you enter information, save the worksheet periodically to avoid losing data. Use the file saving macro (\S) from now on (hold down Alt and type s).

You'll now enter the numbers in the worksheet. You're going to create the financial spreadsheets in the upper left corner of the worksheet, starting with cell A1. The first set of figures you'll enter shows the company's sales, operating expenses, and income from operations. (If you don't need step-by-step instructions, copy the information from the screen illustration.)

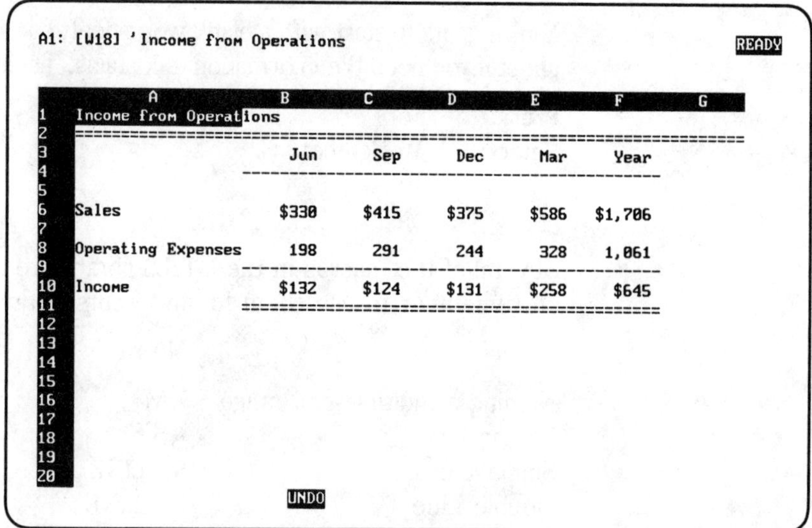

Figure 13.1 Income from Operations spreadsheet

First widen column A so the titles don't get cut off:

Press: HOME

/

Select: Worksheet

Column

Set-Width

Type: 18

Press: ↵

When you make the entries in this section, you may want to use two of the pointer-movement macros (\R and \D). Review the descriptions of these macros in Chapter 11. You will need to press Ctrl-Break to end the pointer-movement macros and Esc to cancel the resulting error.

You can also use the single line (S_LINE) and double line (D_LINE) macros in the next two sets of instructions instead of typing the @REPEAT function.

Next, enter the column headings, titles, and lines:

Type: Income from Operations
Press: [↓]
Type: @repeat("=",72) (to create a 72-character double line, or use the D_LINE macro)
Press: [↵]
Move to: cell B3

If you want to use the right (\R) macro to enter the labels, just press Enter after typing each one.

Type: "Jun [→]
"Sep [→]
"Dec [→]
"Mar [→]
"Year [↵]

If you're using the right macro (\R), press Ctrl-Break and Esc now to stop it. Then continue the headings:

Move to: cell B4
Type: @repeat("–",45) (to create a 45-character single line)
Press: [↵]
Move to: cell A6
Type: Sales [↓] [↓]
Operating Expenses [↓] [↓]
Income [↵]

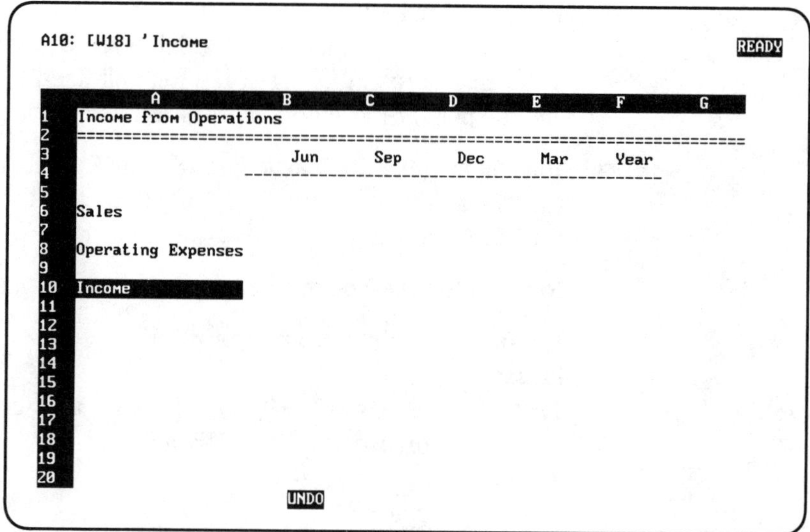

Figure 13.2 Spreadsheet headings

Now enter the numbers.

Move to: cell B6

Type: 330 [→] (you can use the right macro (\R) here)

415 [→]

375 [→]

586 [→]

If you're using the \R macro, press Ctrl-Break and Esc now to stop it.

The cell pointer should be in cell F6. Enter the @SUM function to add up the numbers in the row:

Type: @sum(b6.e6)

Press: [↵]

The sum of the sales figures appears in cell F6, though the control panel displays the @function.

Now enter the next row of figures. You'll use @SUM again at the end of this row; the directions tell you to type it in cell F8, but you can also copy the @function from cell F6. Start this row in cell B8:

Move to: cell B8
Type: 198 [→] (you can use the right macro (\R) here)
291 [→]
244 [→]
328 [→]
@sum(b8.e8) [↵]

If you're using the \R macro, press Ctrl-Break and Esc now to stop it.

The final row of figures is actually a row of formulas that subtract the value in row 8 from the value in row 6. You'll enter the formula once, in cell B10, and then copy it to the other cells in the row:

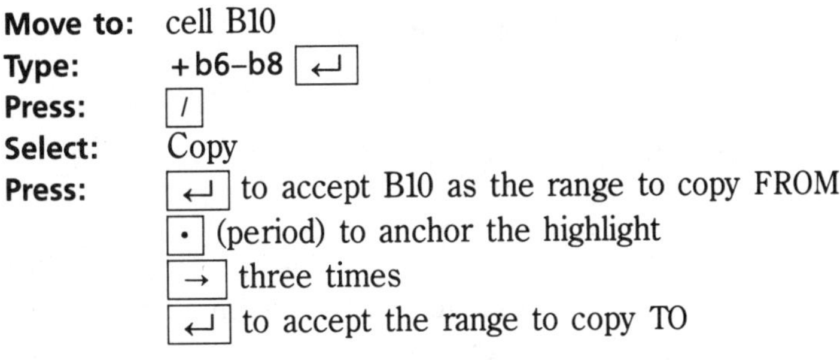

Move to: cell B10
Type: +b6–b8 [↵]
Press: [/]
Select: Copy
Press: [↵] to accept B10 as the range to copy FROM
[·] (period) to anchor the highlight
[→] three times
[↵] to accept the range to copy TO

1-2-3 displays the values in the cells.

You will now format and underline the numbers in the worksheet. The sales and income figures are going to be formatted as currency and the operating expenses will appear in comma (,) format.

Start by formatting the sales and income figures as currency.

Move to: cell B6
Press: [/]
Select: Range
Format
Currency
Type: 0 (to specify no decimal places)
Press: [↵]
[END] [→] to highlight B6..F6
[↵]
Move to: cell B10
Press: [/]

Select: Range
Format
Currency
Type: 0
Press: ↵
END →
↵

Now format the operating expense figures in comma (,) format.

Move to: cell B8
Press: /
Select: Range
Format
,
Type: 0 ↵
Press: END →
↵

As a final step, enter a single line under the operating expense figures and double line under the income figures. (To use the S_LINE and D_LINE macros, you would need to modify them so they entered 45 characters instead of 72.)

Move to: cell B9
Type: @repeat("–",45) ↵
Move to: cell B11
Type: @repeat("=",45) ↵

> NOTE: Entering single and double lines with @REPEAT can use extra memory in certain situations. If you're concerned about memory usage, use **/Range Value** to convert the lines to labels after you've entered the lines with @REPEAT.

Your worksheet should look like the one illustrated in Figure 13.1.

Use the file saving (\S) macro to save the worksheet before you continue.

Now you'll enter the information that compares revenues by division.

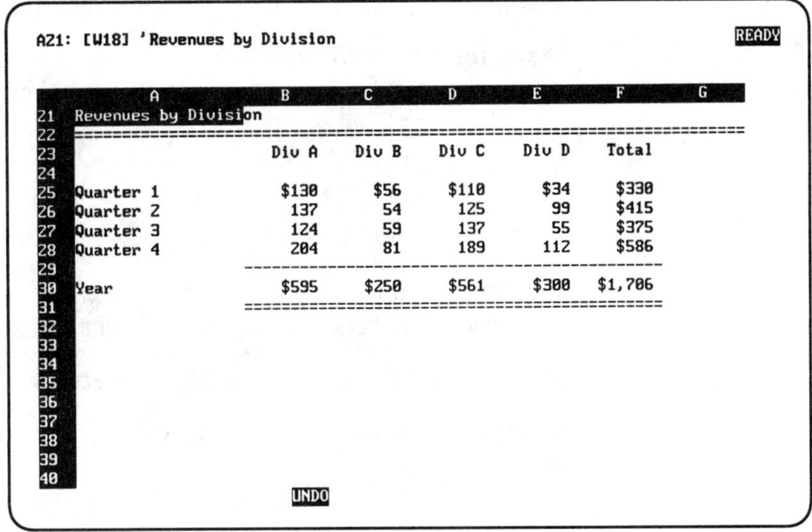

Figure 13.3
Revenues by Division spreadsheet

First enter the column headings. Precede them with the " label prefix so that they are right-aligned. Start in cell A21:

Move to: cell A21
Type: Revenues by Division [↓]
@repeat("=",72) [↓]
Press: [→]
Type: "Div A [→] (you can use the right macro (\R) here)
"Div B [→]
"Div C [→]
"Div D [→]
"Total [↵]

If you're using the \R macro, press Ctrl-Break and Esc now to stop it.

Move to: cell A25
Type: Quarter 1 [↓]
Quarter 2 [↓]
Quarter 3 [↓]
Quarter 4
Press: [↓] twice
Type: Year
Press: [↵]

When you finish, enter the figures for Quarter 1.

Move to: cell B25
Type: 130 [→] (you can use the right macro \R here)
56 [→]
110 [→]
34 [→]
@sum(b25.e25) [↵]

You don't need to stop the \R macro yet; you can use it to enter the next row of numbers. Moving the cell pointer doesn't affect the macro.

Enter the numbers for the other quarters.

Move to: cell B26
Type: 137 [→]
54 [→]
125 [→]
99 [→]
@sum(b26.e27) [↵] (you can copy from cell F25)
Move to: cell B27
Type: 124 [→]
59 [→]
137 [→]
55 [→]
@sum(b27.e27) [↵] (you can copy from cell F25)
Move to: cell B28
Type: 204 [→]
81 [→]
189 [→]
112 [→]
@sum(b28.e28) [↵] (you can copy from cell F25)

If you are using the \R macro, press Ctrl-Break and Esc to stop it.

To complete the Revenues by Division spreadsheet, enter an @SUM function to add up the figures in each column.

Move to: cell B30
Type: @sum(b25.b28)
Press: [↵]

Copy the @SUM function to cell C30, D30, E30, and F30. Follow the copying instruction above if you're not sure how to copy.

Now do some formatting and underlining. The top (Quarter 1) and bottom (Year) figures and Total column need to be in currency format; the rest need to be in comma (,) format. Use /**Range Format** as you did earlier in the chapter. Then add a single line under the Quarter 4 figures and a double line under the Year figures. Your worksheet should look like the one in Figure 13.3

When you finish, use the \S macro to save the worksheet.

Finally, enter the stock price information.

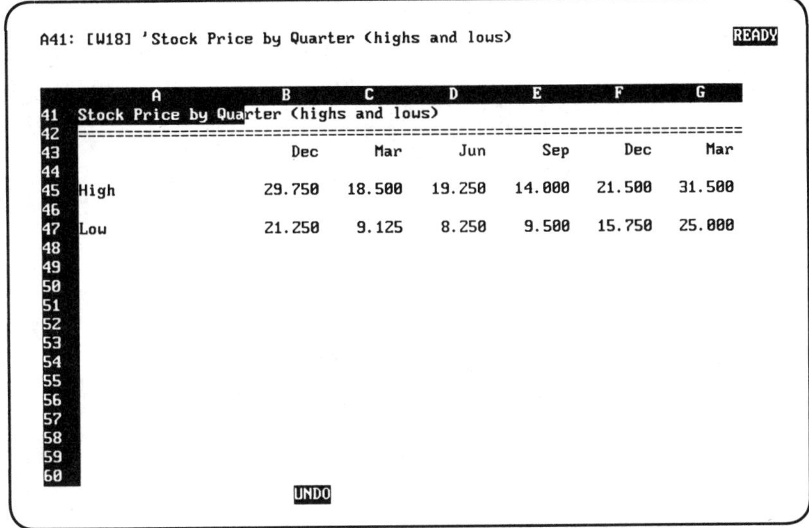

Figure 13.4 Stock Price spreadsheet

Start the heading in cell A41:

Move to: cell A41
Type: Stock Price by Quarter (highs and lows) ↵

To save retyping data, you will copy the double line and some of the month headings from the Income from Operations spreadsheet:

Move to: cell A2
Press: [/]
Select: Copy
Press: [↵] to accept A2 as the range to copy FROM
Move to: cell A42
Press: [↵]
Move to: cell B3
Press: [/]
Select: Copy
Press: [→] three times
[↵]
Move to: cell D43
Press: [↵]

Enter the remaining two months:

Move to: cell B43
Type: "Dec [→]
"Mar [↵]

Now enter the stock prices:

Move to: cell A45
Type: High [→]
29.75 [→]
18.5 [→]
19.25 [→]
14 [→]
21.5 [→]
31.5 [↵]
Move to: cell A47
Type: Low [→]
21.25 [→]
9.125 [→]
8.25 [→]
9.5 [→]
15.75 [→]
25 [↵]

If you're using the \R macro, press Ctrl-Break and Esc to stop it.

Change the format so the stock prices appear with three decimal places:

Move to: cell B45
Press: [/]
Select: Range
Format
Fixed
Type: **3** (to specify three decimal places)
Press: [↵]
[END] [→]
[↓] twice to highlight B45..G47
[↵]

Your worksheet should look like Figure 13.4 above.

Before you continue, save the worksheet.

Creating the Graphs

Now you'll create three graphs based on the information you just entered in the worksheet. You'll also name each graph; the graph presentation macro uses the graph names.

Create and name the income graph first. This graph uses the data in the Income from Operations spreadsheet. The graph compares figures, so you'll create a bar graph.

Press: [/]
Select: Graph
Type
Bar

Now specify the range to graph:

Select: A
Move to: cell B10
Press: [.] (period)
[→] three times
[↵]

Use the months in the third row as labels for the points along the graph's x-axis:

Select: X
Move to: cell B3
Press: [.]
[→] three times
[↵]

When you view the graph, 1-2-3 displays these labels along the graph's x-axis.

The graph is ready to name at this point, but titles make it easier to understand.

Select: Options
Titles
First
Type: Income from Operations
Press: [↵]
Select: Titles
X-Axis
Type: Quarter Ending
Press: [↵]
Select: Titles
Y-Axis
Type: Thousands of Dollars
Press: [↵]
Select: Quit

Now name the graph:

Select: Name
Create
Type: Income
Press: [↵]

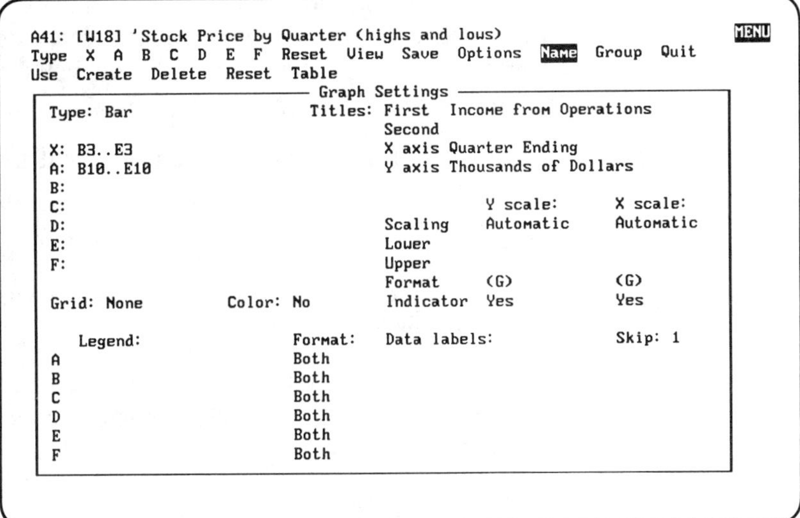

Figure 13.5 Graph settings for income graph

Select: View

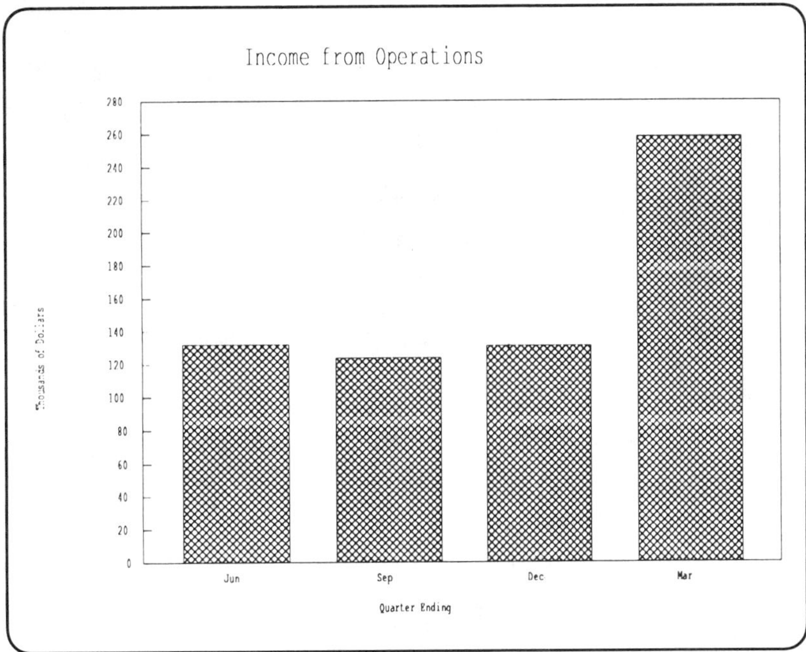

Figure 13.6 Income bar graph

The graph that appears on your screen should look like the one in Figure 13.6 above. If it doesn't, check the figures in your worksheet and check your graph settings. If no graph appears, you may be unable to display graphs on your monitor.

When you finish viewing the graph, clear it from the screen:

Press: any key
Select: Quit

Save the worksheet before you continue. Saving the worksheet also saves the graph you just named.

The next graph illustrates revenues by division. For this graph, you'll use a pie chart. A pie chart illustrates percentages. Each slice of this pie chart represents the percentage of total income contributed by one division.

1-2-3 offers seven possible shadings or colors you can use with a pie chart. Pie charts appear with no shading and color in the slices, however, unless you use codes to indicate the shadings or colors to use. The numbers 1 to 7 each represent a different shading or color; 0 and 8 both produce no shading or color. To use different shadings or colors in the slices of a pie chart, you must enter different codes in a range in the worksheet. In this graph, you'll use a different shading or color for each division.

Enter the codes in row 40:

Move to: cell B40
Type: 1 [→]
2 [→]
3 [→]
4 [↵]

Now you'll create the graph. The first step is to clear the settings from the first graph (you won't lose the first graph because you named it):

Press: [/]
Select: Graph
Reset
Graph

Now choose the graph type:

Select: Type
Pie

Set the graph ranges:

Select: A
Move to: cell B30
Press: [.]
[→] three times
[↵]
Select: X
Move to: cell B23
Press: [.]
[→] three times
[↵]
Select: B
Move to: cell B40
Press: [.]
[→] three times
[↵]

Finally, create a graph title and then name the graph:

Select: Options
Titles
First
Type: Revenues by Division [↵]
Select: Quit
Name
Create
Type: divrev [↵]

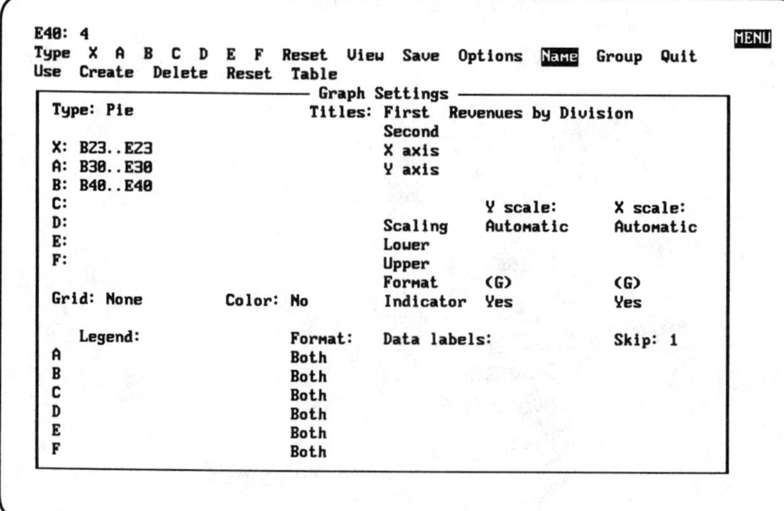

(2.2) Figure 13.7 Settings for pie chart

Select: View

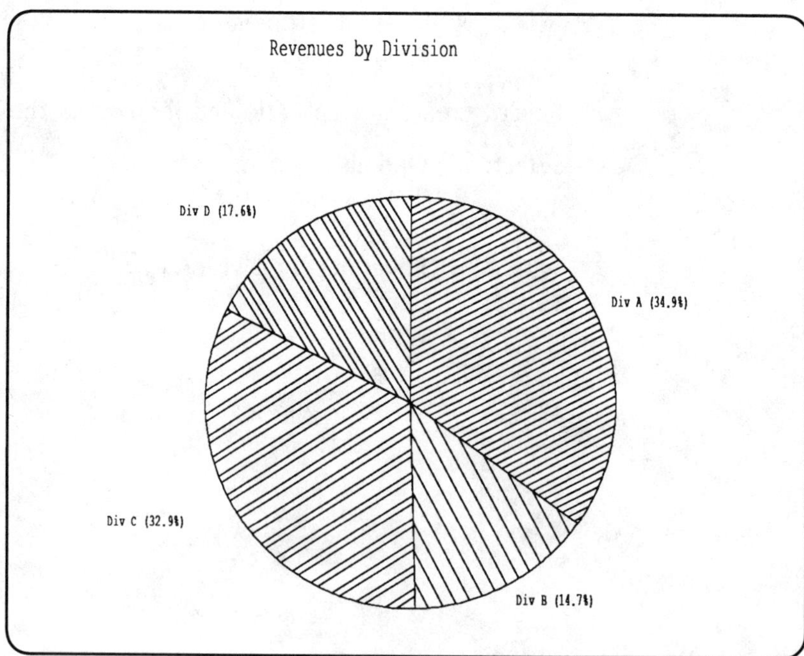

Figure 13.8 Pie chart for division revenues

When you finish viewing the graph, clear it from the screen:

Press: any key
Select: Quit

Save the worksheet before you continue.

The last graph shows changes in the high and low stock prices over time. For this graph, you'll use a line graph with two lines, representing two different ranges:

Press: [/]
Select: Graph
Reset
Graph to clear old settings
Select: A
Move to: cell B45
Press: [.]
[END] [→]
[↵]
Select: B
Move to: cell B47
Press: [.]
[END] [→]
[↵]
Select: X
Move to: cell B43
Press: [.]
[END] [→]
[↵]

Now specify the line format, the titles, and a legend to explain what the symbols on the lines mean:

Select: Options
Format
Graph
Both
Quit
Titles
First

Type: Stock Price by Quarter ↵
Select: Titles
Second
Type: (highs and lows) ↵
Select: Legend
A
Type: High ↵
Select: Legend
B
Type: Low ↵
Select: Quit

Now name the graph:

Select: Name
Create
Type: stock ↵

(2.2) Figure 13.9 Settings for line graph

```
A41: [W18] 'Stock Price by Quarter (highs and lows)                        MENU
Type  X  A  B  C  D  E  F  Reset  View  Save  Options  Name  Group  Quit
Use  Create  Delete  Reset  Table
 ----------------------------------------- Graph Settings -----------------
 Type: Line                          Titles: First   Stock Price by Quarter
                                             Second (highs and lows)
 X: B43..G43                                 X axis
 A: B45..G45                                 Y axis
 B: B47..G47
 C:                                                Y scale:       X scale:
 D:                                          Scaling  Automatic   Automatic
 E:                                          Lower
 F:                                          Upper
                                             Format    (G)          (G)
 Grid: None          Color: No               Indicator Yes          Yes

    Legend:                      Format:  Data labels:             Skip: 1
 A  High                         Both
 B  Low                          Both
 C                               Both
 D                               Both
 E                               Both
 F                               Both
```

Select: View

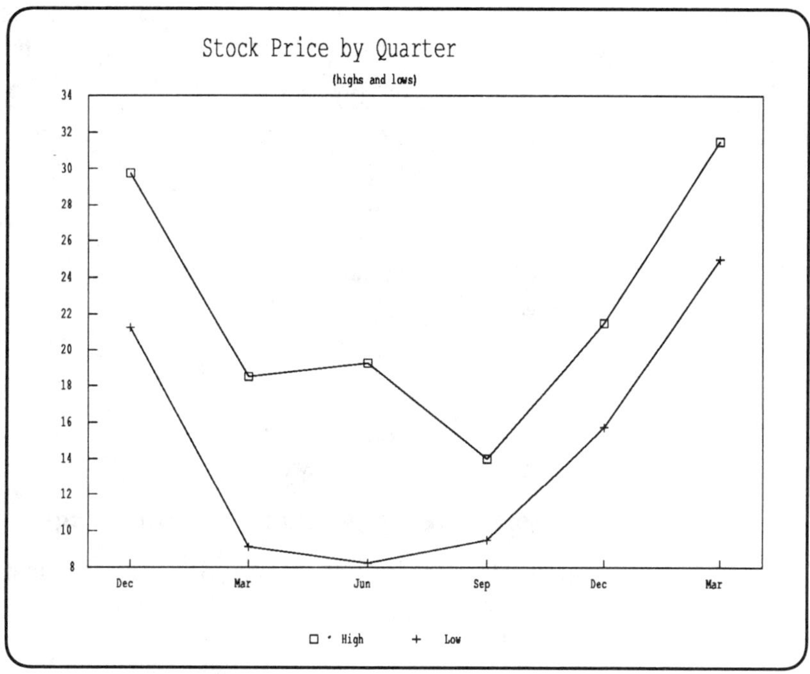

Figure 13.10
Line graph for stock prices

When you finish viewing the graph, clear it from the screen:

Press: any key
Select: Quit

Save the worksheet before you continue.

Creating the Graph Presentation Macro

Once you create the worksheet and the graphs, the graph presentation macro is fairly simple. The macro moves to each area of the worksheet, highlights the figures the graph represents, waits for a specified number of seconds, and then displays the graph for a specified number of seconds.

Before the macro displays each graph, it highlights the range of numbers the graph is based on. To do this, it reassigns range names to those ranges. Before you use the macro, you must assign these range names. You can use the naming macro for a multiple-cell range (\M) if you wish.

Assign the first range now. Move to the first cell of the range to be sure it contains the information you want to highlight:

Move to: cell B10
Press: [/] or you can use the \M macro
Select: Range
Name
Create
Type: income
Press: [↵]
[→] three times
[↵]

Now assign the rest of the range names using the names and range addresses in the following table:

Assign the range name	To this range
INCOME	B10..E10 (you just named this range)
DIVISION	B30..E30
HIGH	B45..G45
LOW	B47..G47

The active area of the worksheet starts in cell A1 and extends to cell G47. To avoid accidentally damaging data or the macro, you'll enter the macro below and to the right of information in the worksheet. Name the macro GRAPHING and document the name in cell O61. Start the macro in cell P61:

```
GRAPHING   {PANELOFF}{HOME}
           '/rncINCOME~
           {WAIT @NOW+@TIME(0,0,5)}~
           {GRAPHON "INCOME"}
           {WAIT @NOW+@TIME(0,0,10)}
           {GRAPHOFF}
           {PGDN}
           '/rncDIVISION~
           {WAIT @NOW+@TIME(0,0,5)}~
           {GRAPHON "DIVREV"}
           {WAIT @NOW+@TIME(0,0,10)}
           {GRAPHOFF}
           {PGDN}
```

```
'/rncHIGH~
{WAIT @NOW+@TIME(0,0,5)}~
'/rncLOW~
{WAIT @NOW+@TIME(0,0,5)}~
{GRAPHON "STOCK"}
{WAIT @NOW+@TIME(0,0,10)}
{GRAPHOFF}
{PANELON}
```

Figure 13.11
GRAPHING macro

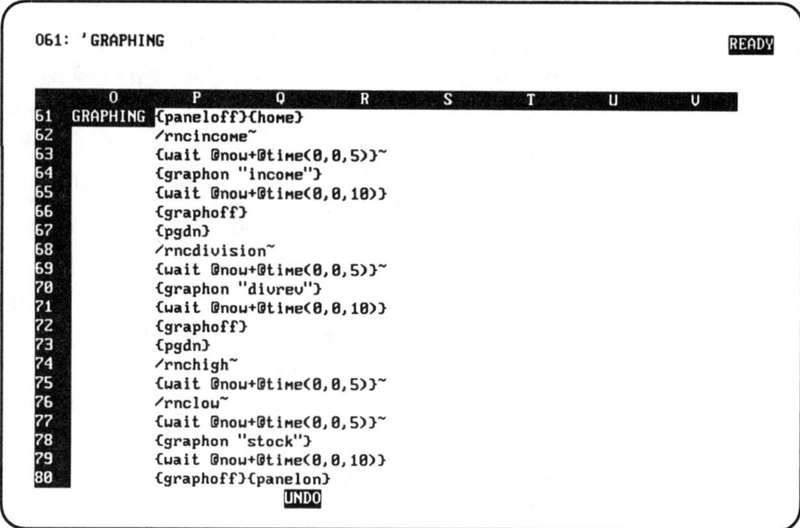

The {PANELOFF} command in the first line of the macro turns off the control panel while the macro is running. The macro then moves the cell pointer to cell A1 and begins to reassign the range name INCOME to the range that contains the income figures.

Before the range name reassignment is complete, however, the {WAIT} command stops the macro temporarily. The macro then highlights the range for a specified period of time before displaying the graph that is based on that range.

Two @functions tell 1-2-3 when to resume macro execution. The first, @NOW, results in the current time. The second, @TIME, has a value of 5 or 10 seconds in the {WAIT} commands depending on what is being displayed. (The arguments in the @TIME function represent hours, minutes, and seconds.) In these {WAIT} commands, 1-2-3 adds 5 or 10 seconds to the current time to determine what time to start the macro again.

Once the macro starts again, the tilde completes the range name assignment by accepting the current range as the range to name. The next
2.2 line of the macro uses a new advanced macro command, {GRAPHON}, to display the graph named INCOME. The graph remains on the screen for 10 seconds, as specified with the {WAIT} command. The {GRAPHOFF} command removes the graph from the screen.

The macro then moves the cell pointer to the next area of the worksheet and repeats the process of highlighting the named range and displaying the graph. In each segment of this macro, the instructions are the same; only the range names, the graph names, and the timing of the {WAIT} command vary. The last command in the macro, {PANELON}, restores the display of the control panel.

2.2 Now try the macro. Press Run (Alt-F3) and select GRAPHING. (It doesn't matter where the cell pointer is when you start the macro.) The cell pointer moves to the income figures, highlights the figures for 10 seconds, and then displays the first graph. The macro then highlights the second set of figures and displays the second graph. Finally, the macro highlights two sets of figures—the stock highs and lows—for 5 seconds each and then displays the third graph. The macro ends after 10 seconds.

If the macro doesn't work correctly, compare it with Figure 13.11 above. Check the macro carefully for typing mistakes, extra spaces, and missing tildes.

If you can't find the problem by reading the macro, use STEP mode to determine where the error is occurring. Press Step (Alt-F2) and then run the macro (press Run (Alt-F3) and select GRAPHING). Remember that you must press a key once for each step in the macro. It's easiest to use the same key repeatedly, such as the space bar.

THE DATABASE APPLICATION

A 1-2-3 database is a collection of related information, such as a collection of employee records. These records store information about each employee—for example, first name, last name, employee number, department, and date of hire.

A database consists of fields and records. Each field contains one kind of information (in the employee database, the first name field contains the first names of all the employees). Each record contains one set of all the different kinds of information (in the employee database, each record contains information about a single employee). A 1-2-3 database uses the columns and rows of the worksheet to store database information. Each record occupies a single row, and each field occupies a single column.

The database application consists of three macros that automate some of the tasks involved in creating and using a database: setting up the database, entering records in the database, and sorting the records after you enter them. Two of the macros, the FORM macro and the entering records macro, use a **data entry form**—a fill-in-the-blanks form that simplifies the process of entering information in the database.

The FORM macro performs the first task of creating a database. This is an interactive macro that requests field names for the data entry form and branches to the setup routine automatically after you finish typing field names. The setup routine sets up the form and the structure of the database. It uses the field names you typed to set up column headings in the area of the worksheet where you will store the database.

The entering records macro lets you enter records using the data entry form. This macro consists of three routines:

- The COUNTING routine determines how many times the values routine executes, depending on the number of fields in the database.
- The VALUES routine requests information to enter in the database.
- The TRANSFER routine stores information you enter in a row in the database.

The SORTING macro automates the third task of sorting the database. This macro reorganizes the records in the database so that they appear in the order that's most convenient to you—in numerical order by part number, for example, or in alphabetical order by last name.

Once you create the database application macros, you can use them to create and work with a variety of databases. You may use several different databases in your work—an employee database, an inventory database, and a customer database are a few examples. Each database has its own fields and records.

The data entry form is particularly useful if you're setting up a database that other people will use. The form allows people who are unfamiliar with 1-2-3 or with the database to enter information easily.

Using the data entry form is like using any fill-in-the-blanks form—you enter information in the spaces provided. You see only the record you're currently entering, instead of seeing the entire database. When you finish entering information, the macro automatically transfers the information to the database range—the range of the worksheet that contains all the records.

The {IF} Command

The database application uses the {IF} command to test a condition to see if it is true or false. The result of the test determines what instruction 1-2-3 executes next. 1-2-3 evaluates an {IF} command in much the same way a driver decides what to do at a traffic light. If the light is red, the driver stops. If it is green, he or she goes on.

When 1-2-3 encounters an {IF} command in a macro, it evaluates the condition in the command. When the condition is true, 1-2-3 continues executing the macro at the instruction immediately following the {IF} command *in the same cell*. When the condition is false, 1-2-3 skips to the next cell (line).

The {IF} command takes one argument: the condition. In addition, the instructions you want 1-2-3 to execute if the condition is true must follow the {IF} command in the same cell. This is one instance where the cell in which you place an instruction can affect the outcome of the macro.

The following table illustrates some possible uses of the {IF} command.

Command	Meaning
{IF A1=0}{QUIT}	If cell A1 contains the value 0, end the macro.
{IF A1< >0}{BRANCH \P}	If cell A1 contains any value other than 0, branch to the routine named \P.
{IF LIGHT="RED"}{HOME}STOP~{QUIT} {BRANCH\P}	If the cell named LIGHT contains the value RED, move the cell pointer to cell A1, enter *stop*, and end the macro. Otherwise, branch to the routine named \P.
{IF LIGHT=RED}{HOME}STOP~ {BRANCH \P}	If the cell named LIGHT equals the value of the cell named RED, move the pointer to cell A1, enter *stop*, and branch to the routine named \P. Otherwise, branch to the routine named \P.

Branching to a Named Range

When you use a {BRANCH} command you can use any valid range name or cell address. 1-2-3 executes the first instruction in the cell named by the {BRANCH} command whether you use a range name or a cell address. The cell the {BRANCH} command names can be a cell in another area of the worksheet, or it can be a cell within the macro itself.

(2.2) You can also use the name or address of a cell or range that contains another cell address or name. In that case, you must precede the argument with a + symbol. For example, if you want the macro to branch to a cell named SALES, you would enter the command {BRANCH

SALES}. If, on the other hand, a cell named INCOME contained the cell address B55, and you wanted to branch to cell B55, you would enter the command {BRANCH +INCOME}. The + tells 1-2-3 that the cell in question contains a further cell reference.

If you want to use a routine that a {BRANCH} command invokes as an independent macro, you must name the first cell with a macro name.

Setting Up the Worksheet

Before you start entering the macros, you need to erase the worksheet.

Erasing the Worksheet

If you need the information the current worksheet contains, save it now. Then start with a new worksheet:

Press: [/]
Select: Worksheet
Erase
Yes

Now save the new worksheet:

Press: [/]
Select: File
Save
Type: datamac [↵]

Save the worksheet frequently as you create the database application. If you use the file saving macro (\S) you created in Chapter 11, don't use it until you've saved the worksheet at least once.

Utility Macros

Several of the macros in the UTILS library are useful in this section, so remember to use them to save yourself time and keystrokes:

Macro	Name
Naming a single cell with **/Range Name Labels Right**	\N
File saving	\S

Range Names in the Database Application

Several ranges are required to set up both the form and the database. You must name three single-cell ranges before you use the form macro. In addition, the macros in the database application assign three range names. Though you could use cell addresses in the macro rather than range names, named ranges allow you to use the database application macro in any worksheet, regardless of the location of existing data.

The table below lists all the range names the database application macros use and describes the purpose of each range.

Range Name	**Purpose**
TEMP	A single cell that temporarily holds each value you enter. Several {IF} commands evaluate the contents of this cell in the macros that make up the database application. You must name a cell TEMP before you use the macros.
FIRSTFIELD	The cell where you begin to create the form. You must name a cell FIRSTFIELD before you use the form macro.
NEXTRECORD	The location where the macro enters the current record in the database. You must name a cell NEXTRECORD before you use the form macro. The macro reassigns this range name every time you enter a record.
FIELDNAMES	The part of the form that contains the field names. The FORM macro names this range.
FIELDVALUES	The part of the form where the macro enters values for each field. The FORM macro names this range.

The FORM macro requires you to name three cells: TEMP, the temporary holding cell; FIRSTFIELD, the first cell of the range that will contain the form; and NEXTRECORD, the first cell of the database (NEXT-RECORD is used in the setup routine).

When you use the FORM macro with your own work, you will choose the cells to name. Be sure there is enough space between FIRSTFIELD and NEXTRECORD so that the form and the database won't overlap. For example, if your form will have 10 lines, or fields, you must leave at least 11 blank rows between FIRSTFIELD and NEXTRECORD. Always put FIRSTFIELD above NEXTRECORD; that way, there is no danger of losing the form as the database grows.

Name these cells now, using the information in the table below. Follow these instructions to name TEMP:

Move to: cell E21
Press: [/]
Select: Range
Name
Create
Type: temp
Press: [↵]
[↵] to accept the current range

Now name the other cells, using the names and cell addresses from the following table:

Assign the name	To cell
TEMP	E21
FIRSTFIELD	A21
NEXTRECORD	A101

You can use the naming a single cell macro (\N) if you wish.

The FORM macro

The FORM macro lets you create a form that simplifies entering records in a database. It also sets up the database structure by entering field names as column headings at the top of the range where you will store records; the setup routine contains these instructions.

Entering the FORM macro

The FORM macro creates the data entry form.

In this worksheet, the form starts in cell A21 and the database starts in cell I01. You should always enter macros out of the way of other information in the worksheet, so you'll start the FORM macro in cell AA1, which is above and to the right of the other data the worksheet contains. If you use this macro to create a database that contains more than 26 fields, however, you'll need to put the macro even further to the right.

The FORM macro begins by moving to FIRSTFIELD and widening the column. It then asks you to type a field name, which it stores in the cell named TEMP. The macro then copies the field name from TEMP to the appropriate line of the form and loops back to the range of the macro named LOOP1 to ask for the next field name.

During each loop, the macro tests the field name to see if you simply pressed Enter. If this is the case, the macro branches to the setup routine. The instructions in the setup routine name the FIELDNAMES and FIELDVALUES ranges and set up the database range.

When you enter the macro, name the first cell of the loop LOOP1 (cell AB5). Do not leave a blank line before the cell named LOOP1, and enter the entire {GETLABEL} command in a single cell (it won't fit on one line in this book, but it will fit in a single 1-2-3 cell).

Name the FORM macro FORM. Document the name in cell AA1 and start the macro in cell AB1:

```
FORM    {GOTO}FIRSTFIELD~/wcs20~
LOOP1   {GETLABEL "Type field name and press ENTER
        (ENTER alone to stop): ",TEMP} enter in one cell
        {IF TEMP=""}{BRANCH SETUP} use two quotation marks
        '/cTEMP~~
        {D}
        {BRANCH LOOP1}
```

Figure 13.12
FORM macro

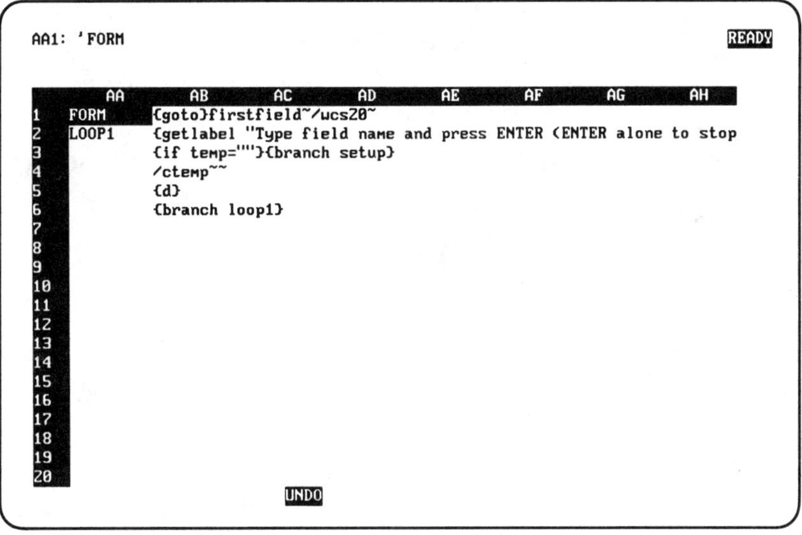

If you haven't already done so, assign the three range names (TEMP, FIRSTFIELD, and NEXTRECORD) the FORM macro uses. Follow the instructions in "Range Names in the Database Application" earlier in this chapter.

In the macro above, the first line widens the FIRSTFIELD column (column A) to 20 characters. If you use field names that are wider than 20 characters, change the width accordingly.

The macro contains two {BRANCH} commands. The first {BRANCH} command (in the sixth line of the macro) is conditional. It depends on the {IF} command, which checks to see if you typed an entry or simply pressed Enter. Pressing Enter without typing anything ends the field naming process, and the macro branches to the cell named SETUP. (SETUP is the first cell of the setup routine, which you'll create next.) If you typed another field name before pressing Enter, the macro copies the entry from the holding cell, TEMP, to the current cell in the form and then moves the cell pointer to the next row.

The last line of the macro contains the second {BRANCH} command. The {BRANCH LOOP1} command is an internal branch: it returns control to the cell named LOOP1 *within the macro* (cell AB2). 1-2-3 executes the last five lines of the macro until the condition in the {IF} command (cell AB3) is met, that is, until you press Enter without typing anything.

At this point, the macro branches to the setup routine, which contains the final set of instructions.

Before you go on, save the worksheet. Use the file saving macro (\S) if you have saved the worksheet at least once.

Creating the SETUP Routine

The instructions that begin in the cell named SETUP create range names for the form and enter column headings in the top row of the database.

You'll create the setup routine now. One line is indented; these instructions belong in the same cell as the instructions in the line above (cell AB10). Name cell AB8 SETUP. Document the name in cell AA8, and enter instructions starting in cell AB8:

```
SETUP   {GOTO}FIRSTFIELD~
        '/rncFIELDNAMES~{BS}.{END}{D}~
        '/rncFIELDVALUES~{BS}.{END}{D}{R}..{R}~
        '/rtFIELDNAMES~NEXTRECORD~
```

Notice the SETUP routine uses {BS}, the abbreviated form of {BACKSPACE}, as well as the abbreviated forms of {DOWN} and {RIGHT}.

Figure 13.13
SETUP routine

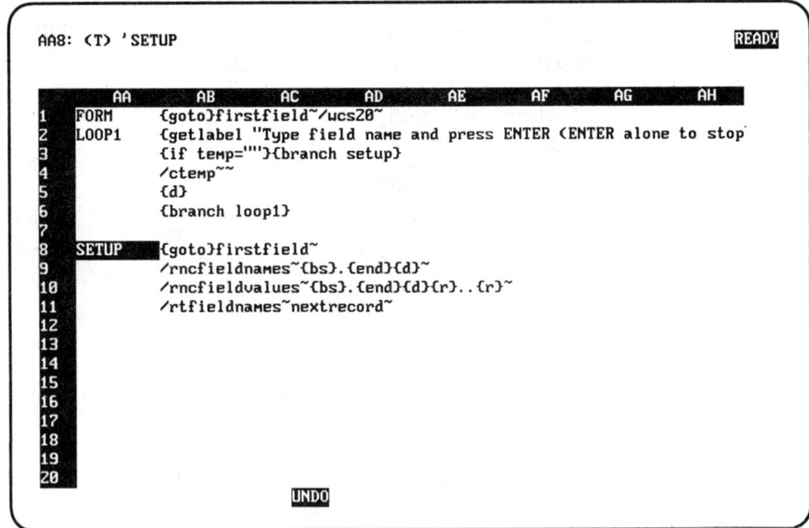

These instructions name the ranges that hold the field names and the field values. The last line uses the **Range Trans** command to create the database column headings by transposing the field names, which you typed in a column, to a row starting at the cell named NEXTRECORD (cell A101 in this worksheet).

You'll test this macro and the FORM macro later, after you create the entering records macro in the next section.

You're ready to begin the next macro. Save the worksheet first.

Entering Records Macro

This part of the database application consists of three routines that automate the process of entering records in the database. The first is the COUNTING routine, which erases the entries in the FIELDVALUES range (if any) and branches to the VALUES routine once for each field name. The second is the VALUES routine, which asks for field entries.

The third routine, the TRANSFER routine, assigns the range name NEXTRECORD to the next row of the database and then copies the information from the form to the database. Depending on your response to a prompt, the routine then returns to the counter routine or ends, leaving the pointer in the first row of the database (the row that contains the field names).

Before you can use this macro, you must name a cell to serve as the *counter.* You will call this cell COUNTER. Do this now:

Move to: cell AU1
Press: /
Select: Range
Name
Create
Type: counter ↵
Press: ↵ to accept the current range

The COUNTING Routine

Name the next routine COUNTING. Document the name in cell AQ1 and start the macro in cell AR1:

```
COUNTING    {GOTO}FIRSTFIELD~{R}
            {BLANK FIELDVALUES}~
            {FOR COUNTER,1,@ROWS(FIELDNAMES),1,VALUES}
            {BRANCH TRANSFER}
```

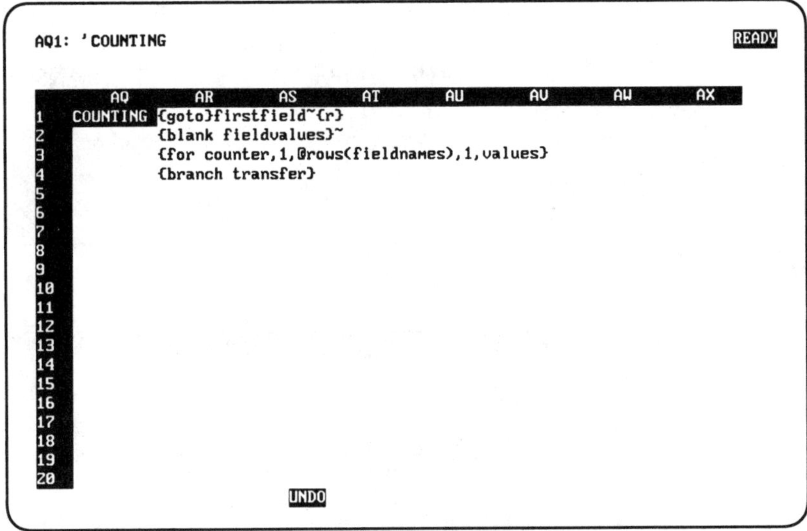

Figure 13.14
COUNTING routine

This routine moves to the first field in the form and then moves right, to the cell where you'll enter the first field value. Moving to the range named FIRSTFIELD rather than the FIELDVALUES range ensures that you can always see the field names while you enter information.

Before you enter field values, the macro erases any values the FIELDVALUES range already contains with the advanced macro command {BLANK}.

The next instruction in the counter routine is a {FOR} command that tells 1-2-3 how many times to branch to the VALUES routine. 1-2-3 determines the stop value in the {FOR} command by counting the number of rows in the field names range with the @ROWS function.

The last instruction in the routine branches to the TRANSFER routine. 1-2-3 performs this step only when it has executed the values routine the number of times required by the {FOR} command.

The VALUES Routine

Name the next routine VALUES. Document the name in cell AQ6 and start the routine in cell AR6. Be sure to enter the {GETLABEL} command in a single cell:

VALUES {GETLABEL "Enter field value (Enter x to skip remaining fields): ",TEMP} enter in one cell
{IF TEMP="x"}{BRANCH TRANSFER} don't forget the quotation marks
'/cTEMP~~
{D}

Figure 13.15
VALUES routine

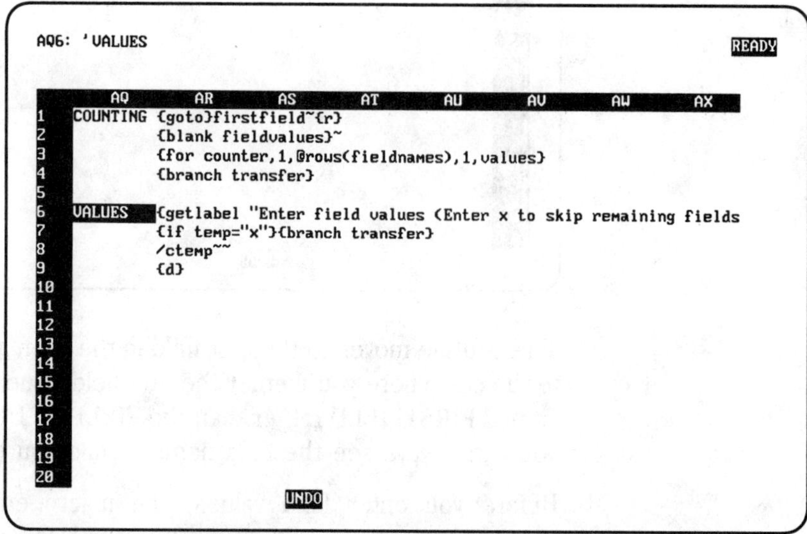

The first line of this routine requests the field value and places it in the temporary holding cell TEMP. To skip the remaining fields, you can type X and press Enter. The {IF} command checks the value you type. If you enter X, the macro immediately branches to the TRANSFER routine, which enters the values in the database and asks if you want to enter another record.

If the entry is anything but X, the macro enters the value you typed in the form and moves down a line. The COUNTING routine then branches to the VALUES routine. If the COUNTING routine has branched to the VALUES routine the number of times specified in the {FOR} command, it branches to the TRANSFER routine.

> NOTE: This macro assumes you can type either an uppercase X or a lowercase x. If, however, you've installed the ASCII collating order driver, 1-2-3 will be case sensitive. In that situation, the case of the x you enter must match the one in the VALUES routine.

The TRANSFER Routine

In the TRANSFER routine, name the fourth line (cell AR14) QUEST. Type the entire {GETLABEL} command in the cell named QUEST. It appears on two lines in this book, but you must enter it in a single 1-2-3 cell, or the macro will not work.

Document the name of the TRANSFER routine in cell AQ11 and start the routine in cell AR11:

TRANSFER	{GOTO}NEXTRECORD~
	'/rncNEXTRECORD~{D}~ don't forget the second tilde
	'/rtFIELDVALUES~NEXTRECORD~{D}
QUEST	{GETLABEL "Enter another record? Type Y or N and press ENTER: ",TEMP} enter in one cell
	{IF TEMP="y"}{BRANCH COUNTING} type the quotation marks
	{IF TEMP="n"}{END}{U}{QUIT}
	{BEEP}{BRANCH QUEST}

Figure 13.16
TRANSFER routine

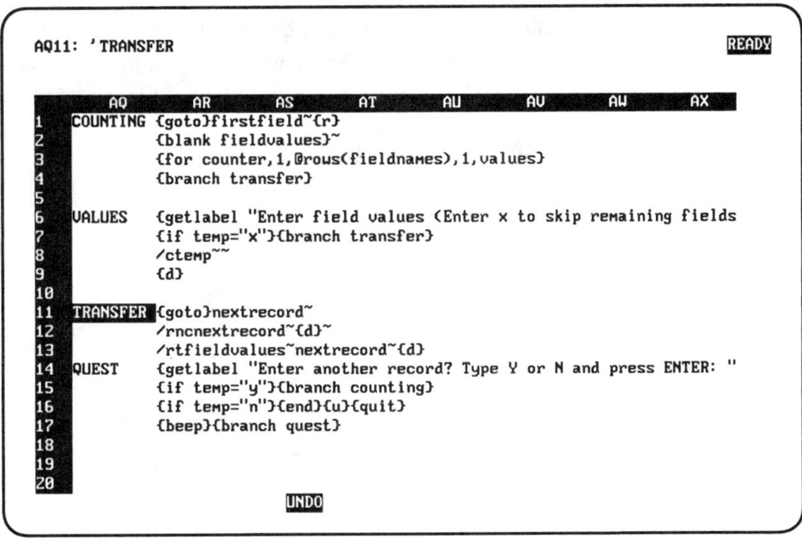

This routine moves to the cell named NEXTRECORD, which currently contains the last entry in the database. (The first time you enter records after creating the form, NEXTRECORD contains the field names.) The routine reassigns the name NEXTRECORD to the cell below the cell currently named NEXTRECORD. Finally, it moves the pointer to the first cell of the new record.

The instruction in the cell named QUEST asks if you want to enter another record. Two {IF} commands follow. The first checks to see if you typed Y and branches to the COUNTING routine if you did. The second checks to see if you typed N. In that case, the routine moves the pointer to the top of the database (the row that contains the field names) and ends the macro.

1-2-3 executes the final line of this routine only if you don't type Y or N in response to the prompt. If you type any other character, or type nothing at all but press Enter, 1-2-3 executes the final line by beeping and repeating the prompt. To end the macro, you must type N. 1-2-3 doesn't distinguish between n and N unless the ASCII collating driver is installed.

Save the worksheet before you continue.

Testing the FORM and Entering Records Macros

You must create a form before you can use the entering records macro.
(2.2) Use the FORM macro now to create a form. Press Run (Alt-F3) and select FORM. Then type the following field names in response to the prompt:

Type: Last Name ↵
First Name ↵
Address ↵
City ↵
State ↵
Zip Code ↵

Press: ↵

When you press Enter without typing anything, the macro stops requesting field names and sets up the form and the database.

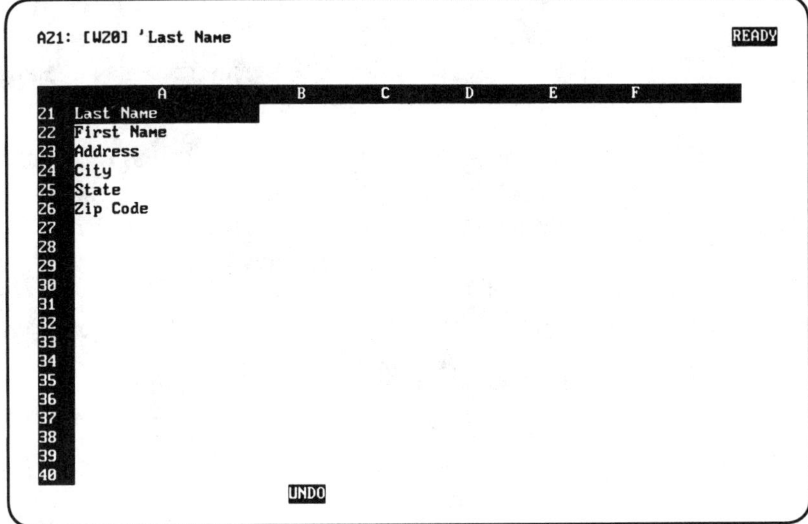
A21: [W20] 'Last Name READY

	A	B	C	D	E	F
21	Last Name					
22	First Name					
23	Address					
24	City					
25	State					
26	Zip Code					
27						
28						
29						
30						
31						
32						
33						
34						
35						
36						
37						
38						
39						
40						

UNDO

Figure 13.17
The form

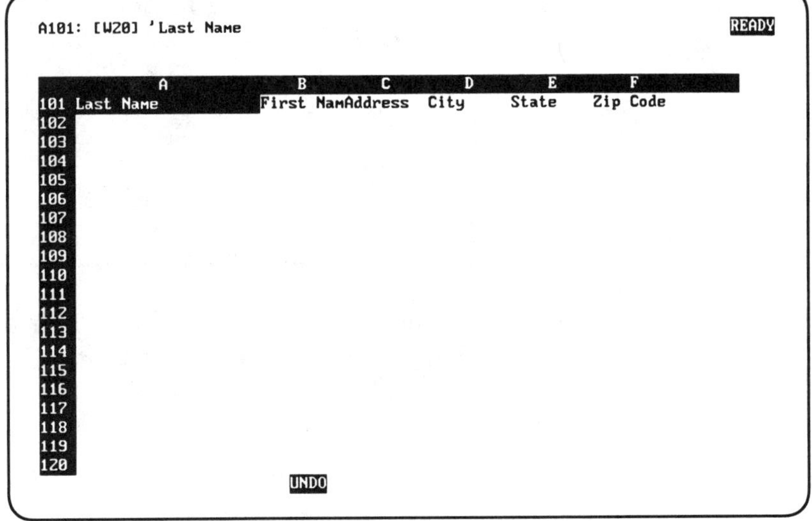
A101: [W20] 'Last Name READY

	A	B	C	D	E	F
101	Last Name	First Nam	Address	City	State	Zip Code
102						
103						
104						
105						
106						
107						
108						
109						
110						
111						
112						
113						
114						
115						
116						
117						
118						
119						
120						

UNDO

Figure 13.18
Database column headings

If the FORM macro didn't work correctly, read through it to see that it doesn't contain typing mistakes, extra spaces, or missing tildes.

Then check the range names to see if they are correct. The FORM macro won't work if you didn't create the ranges TEMP, FIRSTFIELD, and NEXTRECORD; see the instructions in "Range Names in the Database Application" if you haven't named these ranges.

To check the range names, press Goto (F5) and then press Name (F3) twice. A list of all the range names in the worksheet appears. Read through the names to be sure they are correct. You can use the pointer to select one of the names to go to.

Figure 13.19 List of range names

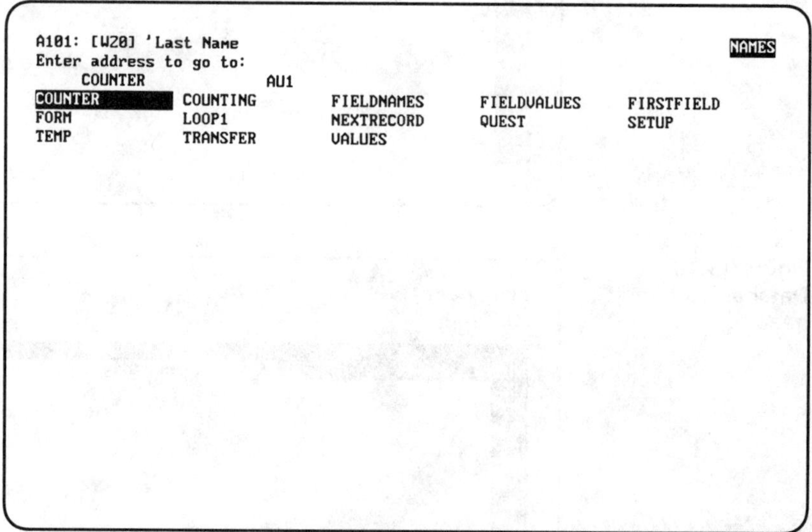

If you still can't find the problem, use STEP mode to go through the macro step-by-step. To use STEP mode, press Step (Alt-F2), press Run (Alt-F3), and select FORM. Press a key (the space bar is best) once for each step in the macro.

If the FORM macro worked properly, you're ready to try the entering records macro. To start the macro, press Run (Alt-F3) and select COUNTING. The macro erases the FIELDVALUES range (even though it is empty) and then requests a field value:

Type: Typrowicz-Cohen [↵]

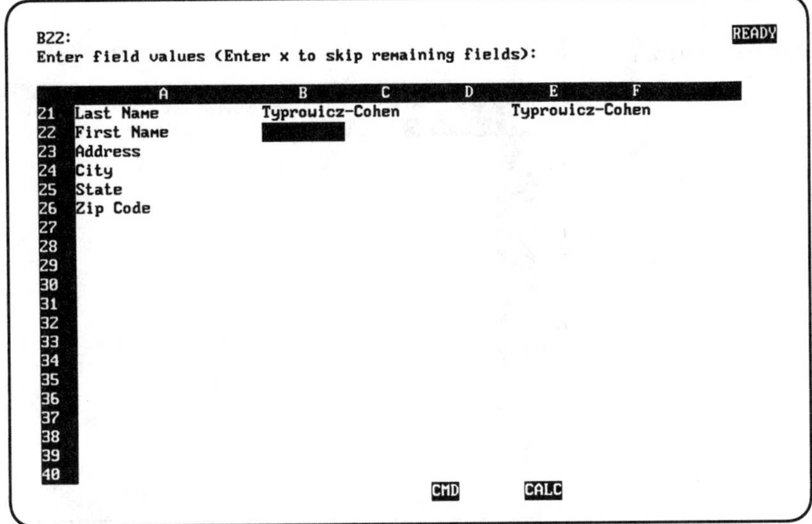

Figure 13.20
Prompt for field value

Cell E21, the TEMP cell, contains the entry Typrowicz-Cohen, as does cell B21, the first line of the form. When you enter field values with the form, carefully read each entry you type *before* you press Enter to enter it in the form. You can't correct entries once you press Enter until after you finish using the macro. Now enter the rest of the field values:

Type: Joshua ↵
123 Lotus St ↵
Cambridge ↵
MA ↵
02142 ↵

Figure 13.21
Completed
database entry

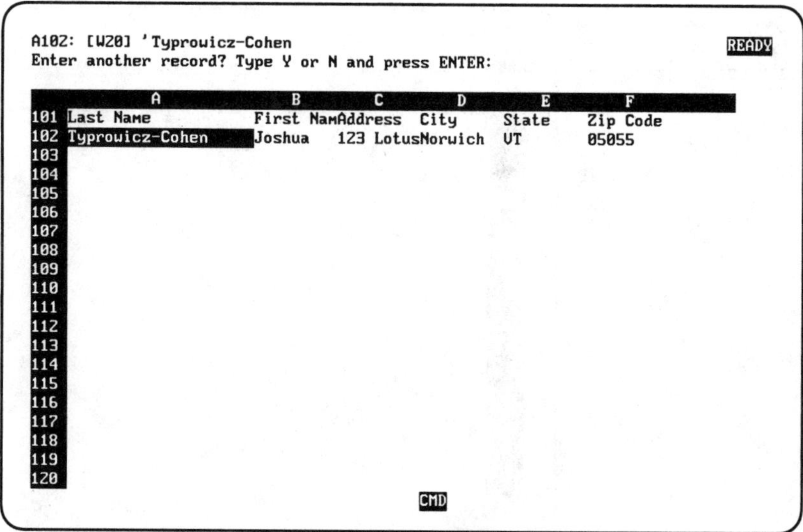

Each time you press Enter after typing an entry, 1-2-3 places the new entry in the temporary holding cell TEMP, checks to see if you entered X (which stops the field-entering process early), and places the entry in the current line of the form. (To skip a field but enter values in subsequent fields, you can press Enter without typing anything.)

When you type the last entry (or X), 1-2-3 automatically copies all the entries to a row in the database. The counter in the {FOR} command dictates how many entries the macro will accept. You'll use X later in this example.

If you've used 1-2-3 to store addresses before, you may have had problems with zip codes that begin with zero and with street addresses that contain both numbers and letters. This is because 1-2-3 treats entries that start with numbers as numeric. It automaticaly removes zeroes that do not affect the value of a number, such as those at the beginning of an integer. It also does not allow you to mix numbers and letters in a numeric entry. In this macro, however, the zip codes appear correctly and the street addresses do not cause an error because a {GETLABEL} command makes only label entries.

If the entering records macro doesn't work properly, read through it to see if you can determine what's causing the problem. You may have left out an argument or made a typing mistake when you entered one of the range names. Extra spaces and missing tildes are a common source of errors.

The {FOR} command in the COUNTING routine requires a cell named COUNTER. If you didn't name this cell earlier, the entering records macro won't work. Cell AU1 should be named COUNTER.

If you can't find the mistake, try running the macro in STEP mode. Press Step (Alt-F2), press Run (Alt-F3), and select COUNTING. Press a key (space bar works best) once for each step in the macro.

After the macro transfers the record to the database, it asks if you want to enter another record. You can respond Y (for yes) or N (for no). If you type any other character, the macro beeps and displays the prompt again:

Type: 1 ↵

The macro contains two {IF} commands that test to see if you type Y or N. It also includes instructions that loop back to the prompt if you do not respond to the prompt correctly. If you typed N above, start the entering records macro again by pressing Run (Alt-F3) and selecting COUNTING (typing N or n ends the macro). If the Enter another record? prompt still appears in the control panel, type Y and press Enter (Y and y are equivalent). Then enter two more records:

Type: Nelson ↵
Mark ↵
19 Symphony Rd ↵
Boxford ↵
MA ↵
01921 ↵
y ↵ (to enter another record)
Cohen ↵
Richard ↵
99 Metro Ave ↵
Norwich ↵
VT ↵
05055 ↵

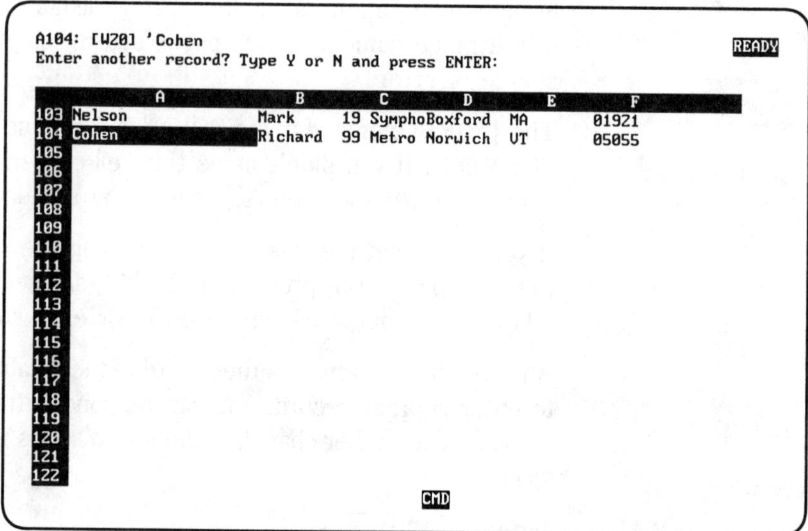
A104: [W20] 'Cohen
Enter another record? Type Y or N and press ENTER:

	A	B	C	D	E	F
103	Nelson	Mark	19 Sympho	Boxford	MA	01921
104	Cohen	Richard	99 Metro	Norwich	VT	05055

Figure 13.22 Three entries in database

1-2-3 copies the first record to the database and asks if you want to enter another record. It then adds the next record to the database and repeats the prompt.

Now type x before you enter the full number of field values:

Type: y (to enter another record)
Cohen ↵
Andrew ↵
1221 Advertising Way ↵
New York ↵
x ↵

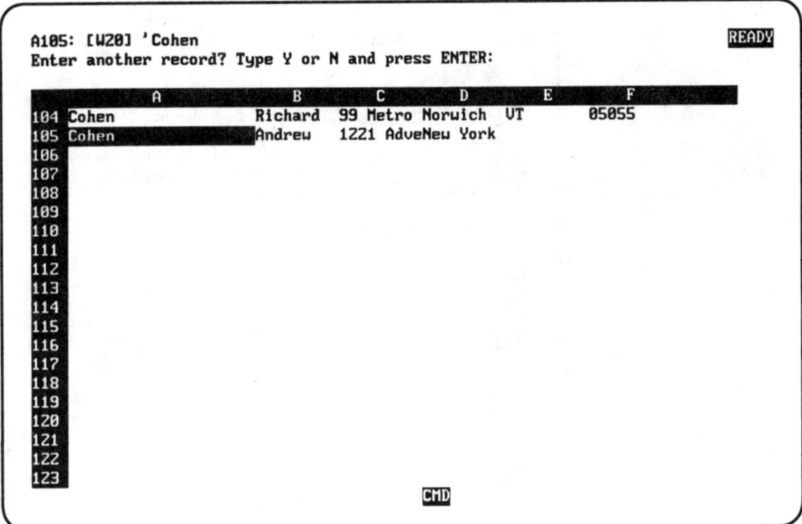

Figure 13.23 Blank fields in database

Even though the two fields are empty, typing **x** causes the macro to transfer this record to the database and ask if you want to enter another record.

Type: n [↵]

The pointer moves to the top row of the database (cell A101), allowing you to see the entire database. Some of the entries are too long for the whole entry to appear in the cell, and the columns in the database appear to overlap. Changing the column widths allows complete entries to appear.

Figure 13.24
Entire database

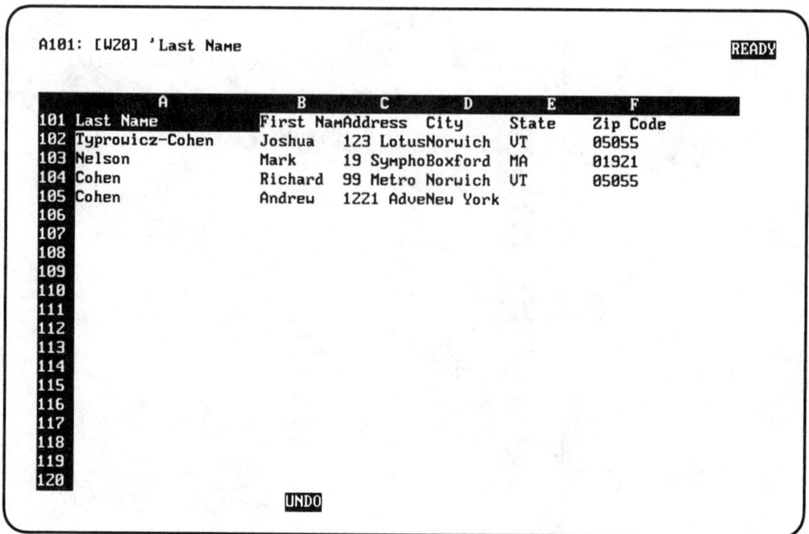

Save the worksheet before you continue to the next macro. Do not erase the form or the database. You'll use this database to test the sort macro.

The SORTING Macro

Once you enter records in a database, you can reorganize them by sorting them. For example, you might want the entries you just made to appear in alphabetical order by last name, or in the order of the zip codes.

To sort a database manually, you must perform several steps before actually sorting the records. This macro performs one of these steps automatically—specifying the range that contains the records. The other two steps, however, require information from you. In these two steps, you must identify what fields to use as the primary and secondary sort keys.

Sort keys tell 1-2-3 what fields to use to reorganize the database. For example, if you want to arrange the database alphabetically by last name, use the last name field as the primary sort key. After you specify the primary sort field, you must also specify the order in which you want 1-2-3 to arrange the records. If you choose A (for ascending) 1-2-3 organizes records from A to Z or from lowest to highest number. If you choose D (for descending), the order is reversed: records that begin with Z appear first whereas those that begin with A appear last, and higher numbers appear before lower ones.

The secondary sort key tells 1-2-3 what to do if two values in the primary sort key are identical. For example, if you use the first name field and ascending order for the secondary sort key, 1-2-3 would arrange a database so that Andrew Cohen comes before Richard Cohen.

Document the name of the SORTING macro in cell BG1. Start the macro in cell BH1:

```
SORTING   {GOTO}NEXTRECORD~
          '/dsrd.{END}{U}{END}{R}{D}~
          p{?}~{?}~s{?}~{?}~
          g{END}{U}
```

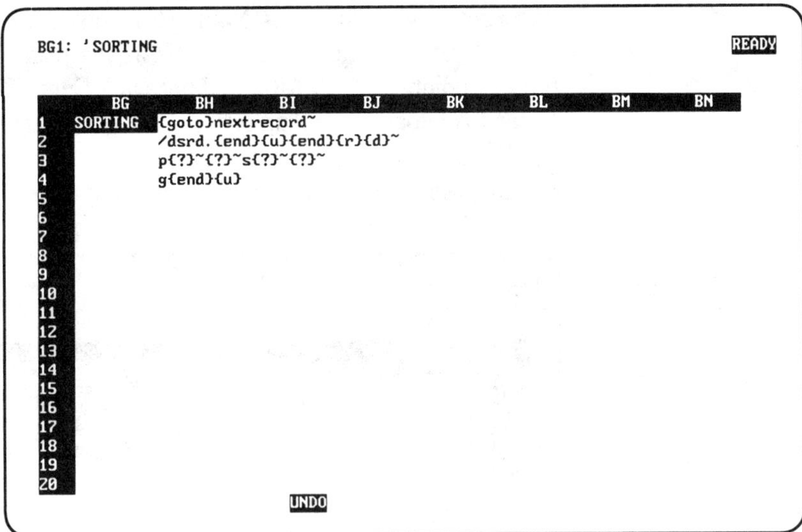

Figure 13.25
SORTING macro

The first line moves the cell pointer to the last record in the database. The next line first resets the range to sort and then specifies the sort range.

The four {?} commands in the third line pause the macro temporarily at the points where you must specify sort keys and sort orders. To specify a sort key, you can type a cell address or move the pointer

(1–2–3 will display the area of the worksheet that contains the last primary sort key you specified). Moving the pointer to the first field value in the field you want to use is simplest—this ensures that you are choosing the field you want.

The sort begins in the last line of the macro. While 1–2–3 is sorting the database, the WAIT indicator flashes. Once the sort is complete, the cell pointer moves to the top row of the database.

> NOTE: The SORTING macro, as well as other parts of the database application, assumes that the first field contains a cell entry. If that won't always be the case, you need to modify the application accordingly.

Save the worksheet before you continue.

(2.2) Now try the SORTING macro. Press Run (Alt-F3) and select SORTING (remember you can press Name (F3) to see a full-screen list of range names). Specify the last name field as the primary sort key by moving the cell pointer to cell A102 and pressing Enter. Then type A and press Enter to choose ascending order. Move the pointer to cell B102 to specify the first name field as the second sort key and press Enter. Type A and press Enter to choose ascending order.

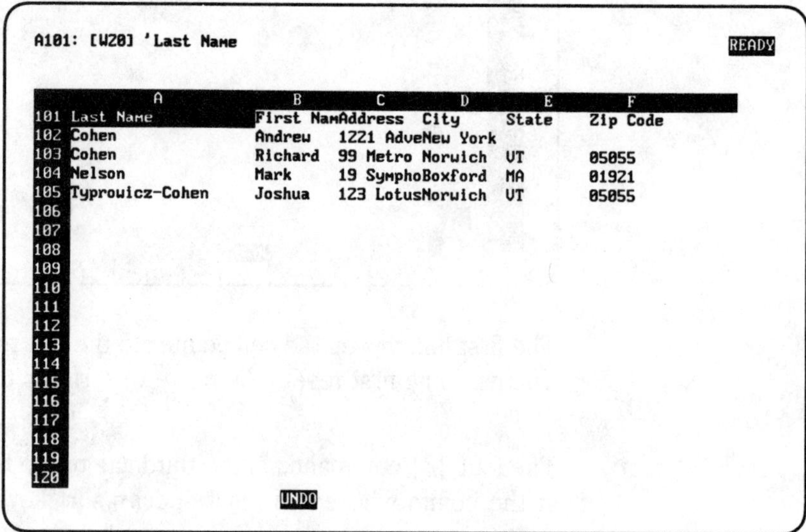

Figure 13.26
Sorted database

1-2-3 reorganized the records in alphabetical order by last name. With the two last names that are the same, it used the first names to determine the order.

If your macro didn't work correctly, read through it to check for mistakes such as typing errors, extra spaces, or misspelled range names. A missing curly brace or tilde can stop the macro from functioning. If you can't find the mistake easily, use STEP mode to go through the macro step-by-step until you determine where the problem lies.

THE FORM LETTER APPLICATION

One of the utility macros you created in Chapter 11 automates a simple form letter. The form letter macro you'll create in this section is more sophisticated—it asks for a name and address and then offers three types of form letters to choose from.

Two things make these choices possible: the {IF} command and subroutines. The {IF} command is discussed in the database application section of this chapter. Briefly, {IF} tests a statement, or condition, to see if it is true or false. In this macro, processing switches to one of the subroutines, depending on the results of the test.

The form letter macro application introduces subroutines. A subroutine is a separate macro that the original macro invokes.

Subroutines are similar to the routines you invoked with the {BRANCH} command. When you use a {BRANCH} command, however, the macro ends when the branch macro ends—the {BRANCH} command does not automatically return control to the original macro. You can use another {BRANCH} command to return to the original macro, but this returns you to the beginning of the macro. To use {BRANCH} to return to a specific line within a macro, you must name the line (as you did in the database application).

Subroutines function as part of the original macro (known as the **calling macro**). When 1-2-3 finishes executing a subroutine, it returns control to the calling macro. The macro resumes execution at the line *after* the line that called the subroutine and begins processing from that point.

Because a subroutine automatically returns to the next cell in the calling macro, the instruction that switches processing to the subroutine must be the last instruction in a cell. 1–2–3 will not execute any instructions that follow the subroutine call in the same cell.

To use a subroutine in a macro, you enter the subroutine name enclosed in braces. You must also use **/Range Name Create** to assign a name to the first cell of the subroutine. A subroutine name can be any valid range name. It's best to use names that document the subroutine's function where possible.

Avoid subroutine names that 1–2–3 might confuse with other kinds of instructions, especially key names or advanced macro commands. For example, don't name a subroutine {EDIT} or {DOWN}. 1–2–3 will assume these are special key indicators, not subroutine names.

The form letter macro also introduces two additional advanced macro commands: {GET} and {INDICATE}. The {GET} command stops a macro until you press a key. It then records this keystroke in a specified cell. A {GET} command is usually followed by an {IF} command that tests to see what the keystroke is and takes appropriate action. In the form letter macro, {GET} will let the user choose among three types of form letters by typing one of three characters.

The {INDICATE} command lets you replace the standard 1–2–3 mode indicator (READY, EDIT, VALUE, and so on) with an indicator or message of your choice (or with no indicator). In the form letter macro, you will use {INDICATE} to tell the user which key to press to produce a particular type of form letter. The {GET} command will then record this keystroke.

Setting Up the Worksheet

Before you continue, save the information in the current worksheet. Then erase the worksheet:

Press: [/]
Select: Worksheet
Erase
Yes

Utility Macros

Several of the macros in the UTILS library are useful in this section, so remember to use them to save yourself time and keystrokes:

Macro	Name
Naming a single cell with **/Range Name Labels Right**	\N
File saving	\S

Save the worksheet before you continue:

Press: /
Select: File
Save
Type: letter ↵

Don't use the file saving macro (\S) until you've saved the worksheet at least once.

Range Names in the Form Letter Application

The form letter application uses several named ranges. The table below explains these ranges and lists the cells you'll name for this macro.

Assign the name	To cell	Purpose
CHOICE	H1	Temporary holding cell for choices user will make
DATE	A1	Date line of letter
NAMES	A3	Name line of letter
ADDRESS	A4	Address line of letter
CITZIP	A5	City, state, zip code

When you create a form letter macro to use in your own work, you'll choose the cells to name. Be sure the cells you use are located in the same relative positions as the cells in the table above. In other words, DATE must be two rows above NAMES, which must be the cell above ADDRESS, and so on.

Name these cells now. Follow the instructions to name the first cell, and then repeat the procedure for the other cells using the names and cell addresses in the table above. You'll use cell H1 for the temporary holding cell CHOICE in this worksheet:

Move to: cell H1
Press: [/]
Select: Range
Name
Create
Type: choice [↵]
Press: [↵] to accept the current range

Now name the other cells as shown above. Save the worksheet when you finish.

Creating the Form Letter Macro

The form letter macro includes four subroutines. The first three produce text that is appropriate for a particular type of letter. Each time you use the macro, you choose one of the three options. 1-2-3 then uses that subroutine to produce the letter.

The final subroutine comes at the end of the macro, after 1-2-3 has entered the text of the letter. This subroutine uses **/Range Justify** to create paragraphs made up of lines of approximately the same length.

The Macro

In this section, you'll create the macro itself. In the sections that follow, you'll create the subroutines. You can't test this macro until you've completed all the subroutines because the macro requires the subroutines to run.

Some of the entries are too long to appear in full in the control panel. To read a long entry, press Edit (F2) and use the Right and Left keys to move through the entry.

When you enter the macro, name the seventh cell CHOOSE (cell S67). Do not leave a blank line before the cell named CHOOSE. The next line of the macro loops to this instruction.

You'll enter the macro in two parts. Name the macro LETTERS. Document the name in cell R61 and start the macro in cell S61. Remember that any line that appears indented must be entered in the same cell as the instruction above:

```
LETTERS   {GOTO}DATE~/re.{PGDN 3}~/wcr
          {GETLABEL "Enter Date: ",DATE}{D 2}
          {GETLABEL "Enter Name: ",NAMES}{D}
          {GETLABEL "Enter Address: ",ADDRESS}{D}
          {GETLABEL "Enter City, State, and Zip Code: ",CITZIP}{D 2}
          Dear {?},~{D 2}/rncFIRST~~
CHOOSE    {BEEP}
          {INDICATE "Type N for new customer, O for old, or P
            for prospective"}
          {GET CHOICE}
          {INDICATE}
          {IF CHOICE<>"N"}{IF CHOICE<>"O"}
            {IF CHOICE<>"P"}{BRANCH CHOOSE}
          {IF CHOICE="N"}{NEW}
          {IF CHOICE="O"}{OLD}
          {IF CHOICE="P"}{PROSPECT}
```

Figure 13.27 First part of LETTERS macro

```
R61: 'LETTERS                                                        READY

      R        S         T         U         V         W         X         Y
61 LETTERS {goto}date~/re.{pgdn 3}~/wcr
62         {getlabel "Enter Date: ",date}{d 2}
63         {getlabel "Enter Name: ",names}{d}
64         {getlabel "Enter Address: ",address}{d}
65         {getlabel "Enter City, State, and Zip Code: ",citzip}{d 2}
66         Dear {?},~{d 2}/rncfirst~~
67 CHOOSE  {beep}
68         {indicate "Type N for new customer, O for old, or P for prospec
69         {get choice}
70         {indicate}
71         {if choice<>"n"}{if choice<>"o"}{if choice<>"p"}{branch choose}
72         {if choice="n"}{new}
73         {if choice="o"}{old}
74         {if choice="p"}{prospect}
75
76
77
78
79
80
                         UNDO
```

The first line of the macro moves the pointer to the cell named DATE, erases the range that extends from DATE down 60 rows, and resets the column width to the default number of characters. These instructions aren't useful the first time you use the macro. When you use the macro subsequently, however, they erase the previous letter. If you need to save a copy of a letter, do so before you start the macro again.

The {GETLABEL} commands in the next four lines (cells S62 to S65) ask for the date, name, and address to use with the letter. The sixth line (cell S66) uses the {?} command to complete the salutation. The macro types **Dear** and pauses for a name. After you type a name and press Enter, the macro enters a comma and moves down two rows to where the first paragraph will begin and names the cell FIRST (in this example, this is cell A9).

The instruction in the seventh line (cell S67) is the {BEEP} command. The beep draws attention to the message created by the {INDICATE} command in cell S68, which asks you to choose the type of letter you want to write. The possibilities are N (to a new customer), O (to an old customer), and P (to a prospective customer). The {GET} command enters your response in the cell named CHOICE, which is a holding cell the {IF} command will test.

The {INDICATE} command in cell S70 restores the standard 1-2-3 mode indicator.

You must name cell S67 CHOOSE. The {BRANCH} command in the next line uses this name.

The {IF} commands in cell S71 evaluate the cell named CHOICE to see if it contains a value that is not one of the valid choices (N, O, or P). If you type anything but **n**, **o**, or **p** in response to the message produced by the first {INDICATE} command, the macro executes the {BRANCH} command that follows the {IF} commands. The {BRANCH} command transfers execution back to cell S67 (named CHOOSE) and the macro repeats the message that asks you to choose a type of letter. You must respond to this prompt by typing one of the choices the macro offers; if you type anything else, or if you just press Enter, the macro beeps and repeats the prompt.

> NOTE: You can type your response in either uppercase or lowercase. 1-2-3 is case insensitive unless you've installed the ASCII collating driver.

The next three {IF} commands (in cells S72 to S74) also evaluate the entry in the cell named CHOICE. If the condition in one of the {IF} commands is true (CHOICE contains the value n, o, or p), the macro calls the appropriate subroutine: NEW, OLD, or PROSPECT. The subroutines are discussed in more detail later in this chapter.

Save the worksheet before you continue.

In the form letter in Chapter 11 you entered the text of the letter as part of the macro; here you will enter the text of the letter separately from the macro. The macro will copy the text. By keeping the text of the letter separate from the macro, you'll find it much easier to read and modify the text should you need to change it.

The text of this form letter consists of two sections: standard text that concludes the letter to all recipients and either text for new customers, text for old customers, or text for prospective customers. You will enter each section of text in the worksheet, name the range that contains the text, and then copy the named range as part of the macro. The standard text will be copied by the main macro; the other text will be copied by the NEW, OLD, and PROSPECT subroutines.

You will enter the standard letter text starting in cell AA120. Because each paragraph of this section is quite short, you'll enter it in a separate cell. (You will not always be able to see all the text of a paragraph on the screen.)

Move to: cell AA120
Type: Creature Comforts offers a wide range of services, including: (enter in one cell)
Press: ↓ twice
Type: Complete meal service--and we deliver it ready to eat!!
Press: ↓ twice
Type: Alteration and tailoring free of charge--at your convenience and in your home or office! (enter in one cell)
Press: ↓ twice
Type: Complete dry cleaning and laundry--we pick it up, we bring it back! (enter in one cell)
Press: ↓ twice
Type: Phone shopping--call in your grocery order and we'll deliver it to your home! (enter in one cell)
Press: ↓ twice
Type: Gift shopping--give us your gift list, and we'll make sure those birthday presents arrive on time! (enter in one cell)
Press: ↓ twice

Type: These are just a few of the services that your Creature Comforts credit account provides. Come in to any of our 32 stores to find out about the rest.
Press: ↓ three times
Type: Sincerely,
Press: ↓ four times
Type: Rich Cohen
Press: ↓
Type: Account Manager
Press: ↓ three times
Type: RC/at

Now name the range containing this text STD:

Move to: cell AA120
Press: /
Select: Range
Name
Create
Type: std ↵
Press: PGDN
↓ three times
↵

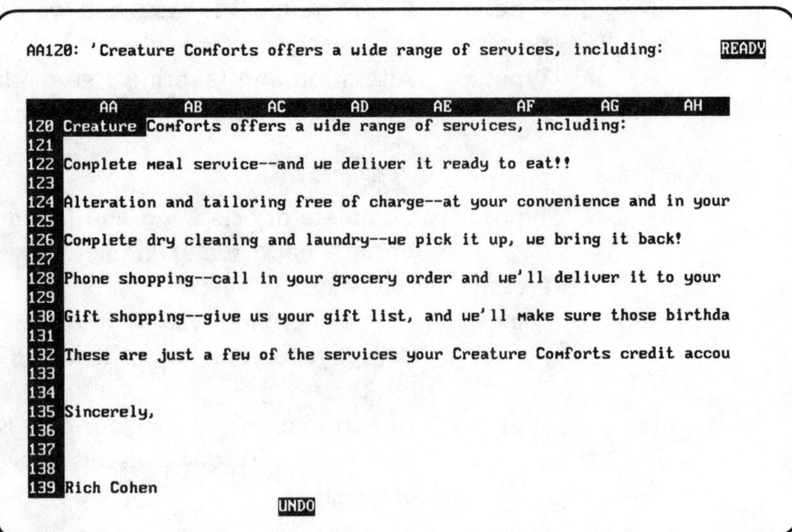

Figure 13.28 Standard text of letter

Now you've entered the text, enter the rest of the macro. This part of the macro will copy the standard text and then justify the letter. Don't leave a blank space between the part of the macro you entered earlier and what you are about to enter: the macro won't run properly if you do. Start this part of the macro in cell S75:

```
'/cstd~~
{GOTO}FIRST~/wcs65~~
{JUSTIFY}
{BEEP}
{GETLABEL "Print this letter? Type Y or N and press ENTER: ",CHOICE}
{IF CHOICE="N"}{QUIT}
'/pprLETTER~agpg
```

Figure 13.29
Second part of LETTERS macro

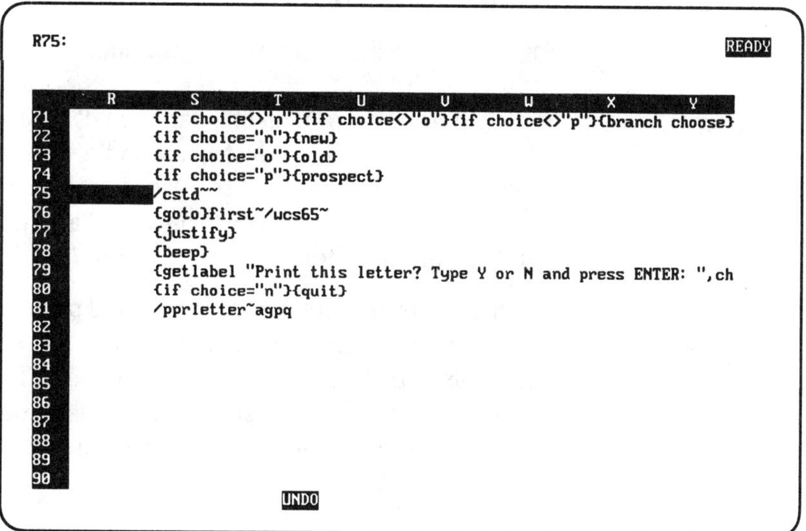

The instructions in cell S75 copy the range named STD to the current cell.

The first instruction in cell S76 moves the cell pointer to the first line of the text of the letter, after the date, address, and salutation. The second instruction changes the column width to 65. (You can use another column width, but 65 characters is a standard line length.)

In cell S77, the {JUSTIFY} instruction calls the JUSTIFY subroutine. This subroutine uses **/Range Justify** to set up the letter. It also names the range of cells that contains the letter. This subroutine is described more fully in ''The JUSTIFY Subroutine'' section.

When the JUSTIFY subroutine is complete, 1-2-3 returns to the next line of the calling macro (cell S78). The instructions in the next three lines ask if you want to print the letter and then, depending on your response to the prompt in the {GETLABEL} command in cell S79, either print a copy or end the subroutine. The {BEEP} instruction draws your attention to the prompt.

The **Print Printer Range** command in cell S81 accepts the range named LETTER as the print range. The JUSTIFY subroutine assigns this range name to the letter.

Save the worksheet before you continue.

The NEW, OLD, and PROSPECT Subroutines

You often need more than one variation of a form letter. For example, a new customer, an old customer, and a prospective customer each require slightly different letters. Much of this information is the same, but you also want to include information that is addressed to the particular type of customer.

The macro you just created copied several paragraphs of standard text—text that is the same no matter what type of letter you choose. These three subroutines copy text that is intended for particular customer types: new, old, and prospective. The subroutines are very short because once again you'll store the text in named ranges that the subroutines will copy.

Enter the text for new customers starting in cell AA150. Enter each paragraph in a separate cell.

Move to: cell AA150

Type: Thank you for opening a Creature Comforts credit account. You can use your credit account when you shop in one of our 32 stores, when you order by mail, or when you place a telephone order.

Press: [↓] twice

Type: You're undoubtedly familiar with the quality merchandise Creature Comforts is famous for, but are you aware of our other great services?

Press: [↵]

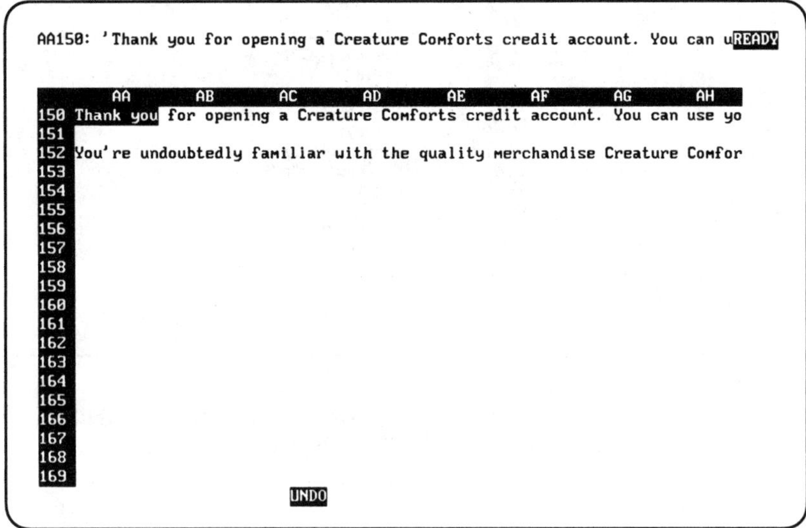

Figure 13.30 Text for new customers

Now name the range containing the text NEW_TEXT:

Move to: cell AA150
Press: [/]
Select: Range
Name
Create
Type: new_text [↵]
Press: [↓] twice
[↵]

Document the NEW subroutine name in cell R83 and start the NEW subroutine in cell S83:

```
NEW   '/cnew_text~~
      {END}{D 3}
```

Figure 13.31
NEW subroutine

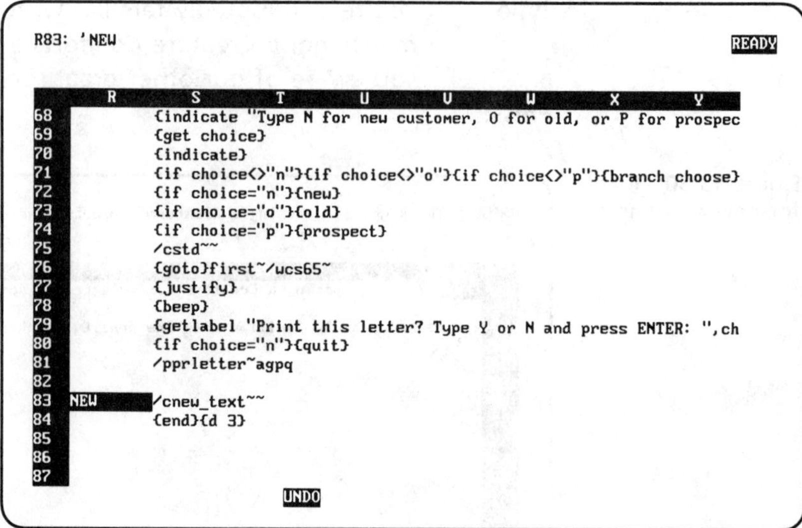

NEW first copies the text in the range named NEW_TEXT starting in the current cell. It then moves the cell pointer beyond the copied text so it's correctly positioned for the standard text the main macro copies.

Save the worksheet before you continue.

Next enter the text for old customers. Start entering it in cell AA160. Enter each paragraph in a separate cell:

Move to: cell AA160

Type: Because of valued customers like you, Creature Comforts has grown to 32 stores in the Metro area--and you can use your Creature Comforts credit account at every one of them.

Press: [↓] twice

Type: I know you love our quality merchandise, but are you aware of the other services Creature Comforts provides?

Press: [↵]

Figure 13.32 Text for old customers

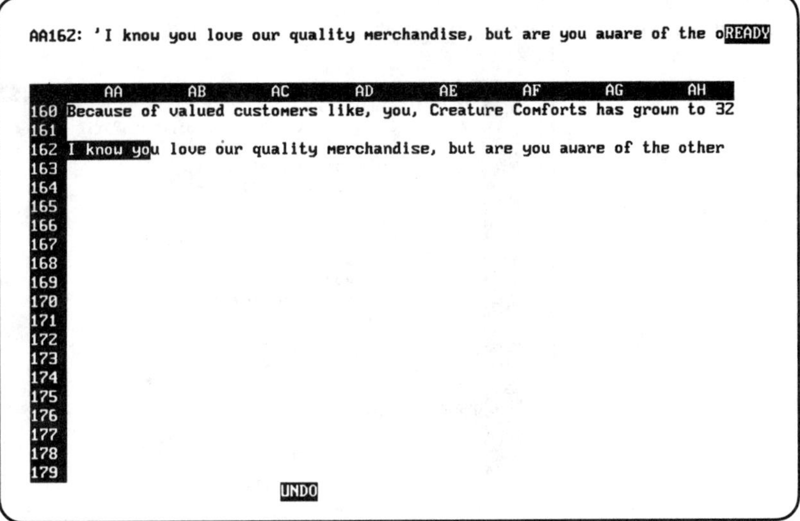

Name this range OLD_TEXT:

Move to: cell AA160

Press: [/]

Select: Range
Name
Create

Type: **old_text** [↵]

Press: [↓] twice
[↵]

Document the routine name in cell R86 and start the OLD subroutine in cell S86:

```
OLD   '/cOLD_TEXT~~
      {END}{D 3}
```

Figure 13.33
OLD subroutine

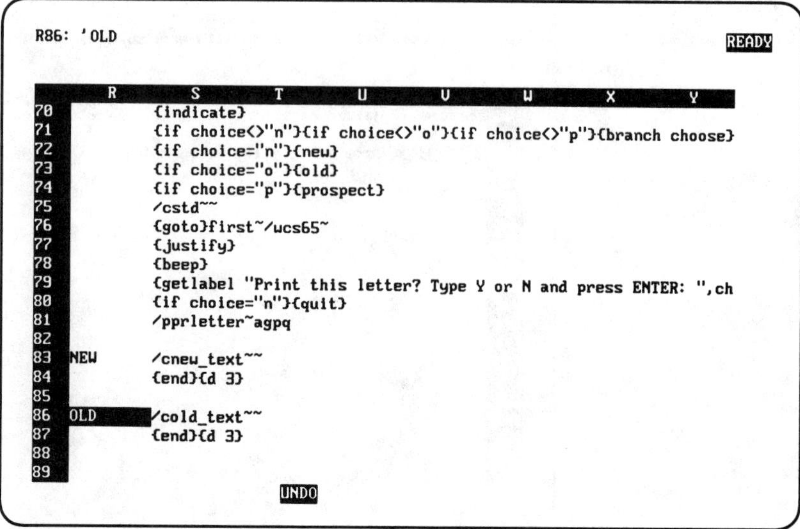

The OLD routine works just like the NEW routine except it copies text from the range named OLD_TEXT.

Save the worksheet before you continue.

Finally, enter the text for prospective customers starting in cell AA170:

Move to: cell AA170

Type: I'm sure you know about Creature Comforts. You've probably shopped in at least one of our 32 stores. But do you know how easy it is to shop with a Creature Comforts credit account?

Press: ↓ twice

Type: All you have to do is call 555-4321 and we'll set up an account immediately.

Press: ↓ twice

Type: Once you open an account, you'll realize how much more there is to Creature Comforts than the quality merchandise we're famous for.

Press: ↵

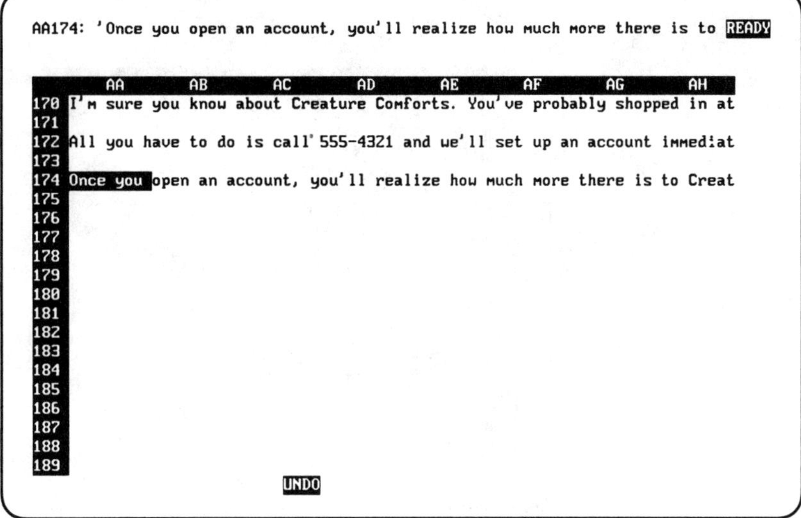

Figure 13.34
Text for prospective customers

Name this range PROSP_TEXT:

Move to: cell AA170
Press: /
Select: Range
Name
Create
Type: prosp_text ↵
Press: ↓ four times
↵

Document the routine name in cell R89 and start the PROSPECT subroutine in cell S89:

```
PROSPECT   '/cPROSP_TEXT~~
           {END}{D}{END}{D 3}
```

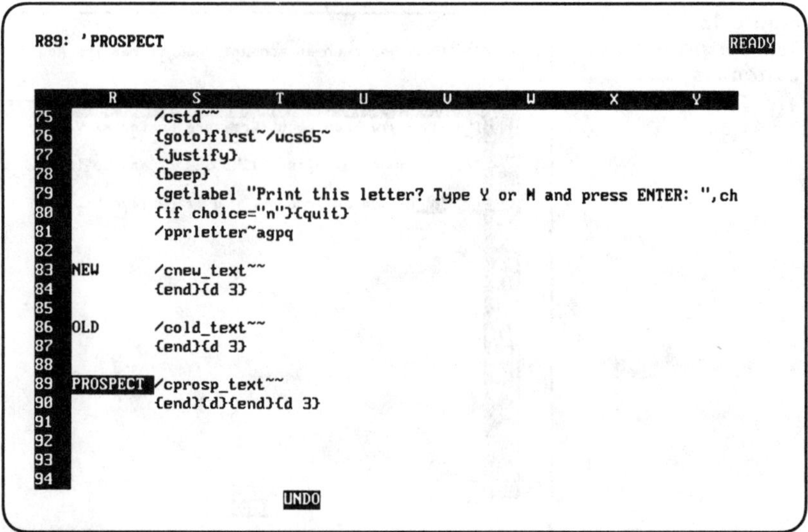

Figure 13.35 PROSPECT subroutine

Because the text for prospective customers has an extra paragraph, the instructions in cell S90 include an extra {END}{DOWN}.

Save the worksheet before you continue.

Each of these three subroutines enters text immediately after the salutation. 1-2-3 uses the subroutine that corresponds to your response to the prompt **Type N for new customer, O for old, or P for prospective** entered by the {GET} command in cell S69.

The final step before testing this macro is to enter the JUSTIFY subroutine.

The JUSTIFY Subroutine

In Chapter 11, you used **/Range Justify** with a simple form letter. The letter this macro creates is more complex. It contains several paragraphs, each separated by a blank cell. To justify the letter automatically, you need a looping macro that moves to each new block of text and uses **/Range Justify** on that block. To move from one block to the next, the JUSTIFY subroutine uses the End and Down keys. You don't need to use **/Range Justify** on the entries that follow the text of the letter (the closing and signature lines).

The JUSTIFY subroutine uses an {IF} command and an @function to evaluate the contents of the current cell. The {IF} command in this subroutine uses the @CELLPOINTER function.

The @CELLPOINTER function can provide many different kinds of information about the current cell (the cell pointer's current location). This @function requires an argument, which can be one of several different types; in this example, it is 'contents'. With this argument, @CELLPOINTER tests whether the contents of the current cell are 'Sincerely,'.

1-2-3 automatically recalculates @CELLPOINTER when you make an entry in the worksheet. The condition is true if the entry in the current cell is 'Sincerely' and false if it is not.

Now enter the JUSTIFY subroutine. Document the name in cell R92 and start the subroutine in cell S92. Make sure the {RETURN} command is in the same cell as the {IF} command.

```
JUSTIFY   '/rj~
          {END}{D}
          {IF @CELLPOINTER("CONTENTS")="Sincerely,"}{D 8}
            /rncLETTER~{BS}.{HOME}~ {HOME}{RETURN}
          {BRANCH JUSTIFY}
```

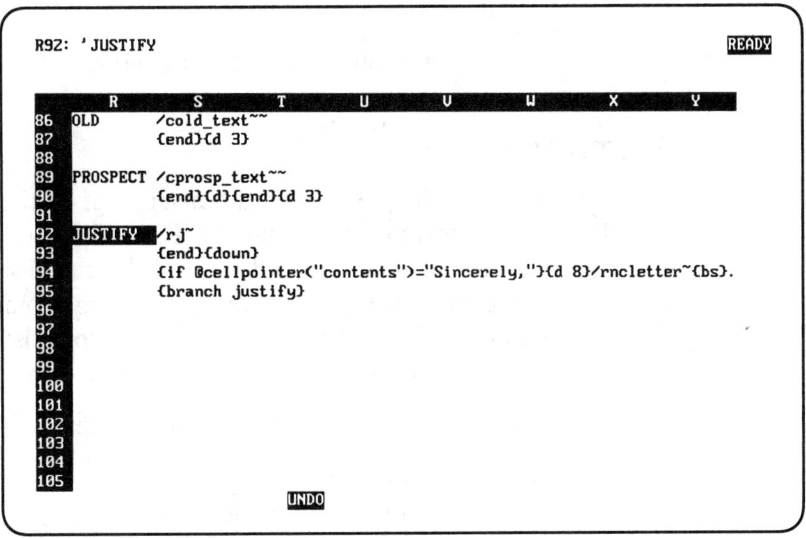

Figure 13.36
JUSTIFY subroutine

The first line of the subroutine selects **/Range Justify** and accepts the cell pointer's current location as the top of the range to justify. 1–2–3 includes every label entry in the range to be justified until it reaches a cell that is blank or contains a number.

In the next line (cell S93), the {END} and {HOME} instructions move the cell pointer to the next block of text.

The next instruction (in cell S94) is the {IF} command. The {IF} command evaluates the result of the @CELLPOINTER function. If it is true (the cell pointer is currently in the cell that contains the entry 'Sincerely,'), the subroutine executes the rest of the instructions in this cell. These instructions name the range that contains the letter and move the pointer to the top of the letter. The final instruction that 1–2–3 executes when the condition is true is the {RETURN} command. This command returns control to the calling macro even though the subroutine contains more instructions.

When the condition is not true, the {BRANCH} command returns to the first instruction in the JUSTIFY subroutine. The subroutine then repeats the process of justifying text until the entry in the current cell is 'Sincerely,'.

Save the worksheet before you continue.

Using the LETTERS Macro

Now that you've created the macro and all the subroutines, you can (2.2) try the macro. Press Run (Alt-F3) and select LETTERS (remember you can press Name (F3) to see a full-screen list of all the range names in the worksheet). Then respond to the prompts. Before you press Enter to enter your responses, check for mistakes. Once you press Enter, you must end the macro to correct a mistake.

First, create a letter for a new customer:

Type: May 19, 1989 ↵
Joshua Typrowicz-Cohen ↵
123 Lotus St ↵
Norwich, VT 05055 ↵
Mr. Typrowicz-Cohen ↵
N

Figure 13.37
Form letter for
new customer

```
May 19, 1989

Joshua Typrowicz-Cohen
123 Lotus St
Norwich, VT 05055

Dear Mr. Typrowicz-Cohen,

Thank you for opening a Creature Comforts credit account. You
can use your credit account when you shop in one of our 32
stores, when you order by mail, or when you place a telephone
order.

You're undoubtedly familiar with the quality merchandise
Creature Comforts is famous for, but are you aware of our other
great services?

Creature Comforts offers a wide range of services, including:

Complete meal service--and we deliver it ready to eat!!

Alteration and tailoring free of charge--at your convenience and
in your home or office!

Complete dry cleaning and laundry--we pick it up, we bring it
back!

Phone shopping--call in your grocery order and we'll deliver it
to your home!

Gift shopping--give us your gift list, and we'll make sure those
birthday presents arrive on time!

These are just a few of the services your Creature Comforts
credit account provides. Come in to any of our 32 stores to find
out about the rest.


Sincerely,



Rich Cohen
Accounts Manager


RC/at
```

The macro copies text and then justifies the ranges. (If the changing screen bothers you, you can add the {WINDOWSOFF} and {WINDOWSON} commands to the macro later.) When it finishes the letter, the macro beeps and displays a prompt in the control panel. The prompt asks if you want to print the letter. If your printer is ready and you want a copy of the letter, type Y and press Enter. Otherwise, type N and press Enter. (1–2–3 doesn't distinguish between uppercase and lowercase when you respond to the prompt unless you've installed the ASCII collating driver.)

If the macro failed to work properly, read through it to see if you can find the mistake. Misspelled command, missing or misplaced braces, extra spaces, and missing tildes are common causes of errors.

If you didn't name the ranges the form letter macro uses, it won't work. Name the DATE, NAMES, ADDRESS, and CITZIP ranges if you didn't do so earlier.

If the macro either doesn't justify the letter or doesn't stop justifying, check that the {IF} command with the @CELLPOINTER function is correct.

Check the other range names to be sure they are spelled correctly and that they are assigned to the correct cells. Press Goto (F5) and then press Name (F3) twice. A list of all the range names in the worksheet appears. Check all the names to be sure they are spelled correctly. To go to one of the named cells, select the name from the list.

If you can't find the mistake, use STEP mode to go through the macro step-by-step. Remember to press a key such as the space bar once for each step in the macro.

If you make a typing mistake when you are entering the name and address and don't find it until after you press Enter, type **N** when the prompt asks you to print the letter. This ends the macro. Correct the mistake by editing the cell that contains the entry. Then print the letter manually.

Try the macro using the other two letter types. Once you're familiar with how the macro operates, you can adapt it so that it creates letters you can use in your work.

If your form letter macro provides many different options or if many different people will use it, you may want to use a macro menu. Chapter 14 describes macro menus in detail.

14

A Macro Menu

In Chapter 11, you created utility macros that automate repetitive tasks. In Chapter 13, you created three application macros—macros that automate a specific task. Some of these were relatively short and simple, whereas others were substantially more sophisticated.

A macro can automate nearly any 1-2-3 task, regardless of its length or complexity. A sophisticated macro can automate an entire 1-2-3 work session. Such a macro might run the work session from beginning to end without stopping. It might also be interactive, pausing at times for the user to enter information and then processing that information as part of the macro routine.

Any business procedure that you regularly perform with 1-2-3 consists of a variety of tasks. For example, you might have a large worksheet in which you enter weekly sales figures. You might then perform many calculations based on those figures. In addition, you may want to draw graphs that track weekly sales trends and print a report that includes the graphs and sales figures to show the numbers behind the trend. You could easily automate the entire procedure with an interactive 1-2-3 macro.

An interactive macro that carries out all the tasks involved in a work session is helpful if you're setting up a worksheet that other people will use. Once you define the tasks in a macro, others can use the macro to perform the task without knowing anything about the worksheet or how it operates. Specific instructions and options that lead the user through the tasks are part of the macro itself.

A macro that a number of people will use is best set up as a macro menu. A macro menu links a number of routines that perform different tasks. It looks and works like a regular 1-2-3 menu: menu items appear in the control panel and each item has its own command description that appears when the menu pointer is on the item. Each item in a macro menu invokes a different macro routine. When the user selects a menu item, 1-2-3 executes the corresponding routine.

In this chapter, you'll create a macro that uses a menu to automate a worksheet procedure similar to the one described above. The macro works with a worksheet that details the quarterly budget and actual expenses of a group of managers. The macro draws a graph that shows the difference between the two figures for each manager and makes separate lists for those under and over budget. Another item prints individual memos to the managers telling them what they were budgeted, what they spent, and the percentage by which they are under or over budget.

You don't need to be an expert to create a macro menu. If you've gone through the preceding chapters successfully, you know enough about 1-2-3 macros to create a macro menu.

HOW THE MACRO MENU WORKS

Throughout this chapter, you'll create different routines for a macro that works with a sales expenses worksheet. A menu macro ties together all the routines; each menu item starts a different routine. The menu the macro produces is similar to any 1-2-3 menu—the menu appears in the control panel, and you select menu items as usual. Some of the menu items start a procedure as soon as you select them, whereas others have submenus that require you to make further choices.

The macro menu you'll create in this chapter is shown in the illustration in Figure 14.1.

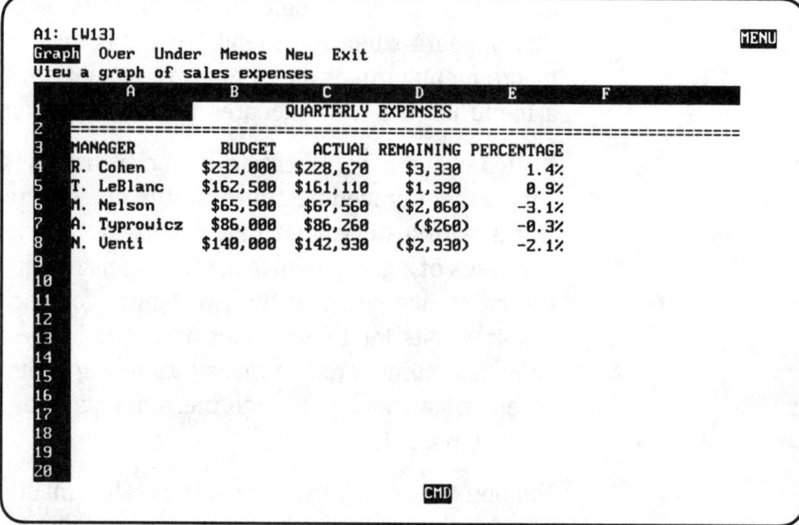

Figure 14.1 Macro menu and sales expenses worksheet

The items in this menu carry out the following tasks:

Graph	Draws a bar graph of budgeted and actual expenses for each manager
Over	Displays a list of all managers over budget
Under	Displays a list of all managers under budget
Memos	Creates and prints memos to managers
New	Lets you enter new figures in the worksheet or erase the current figures
Exit	Ends the macro

CREATING THE SALES EXPENSES WORKSHEET

Before you create the macro, you need to create the worksheet that goes with it. In your own work, you'll use much larger worksheets with macro menus, but this worksheet is large enough to illustrate how a macro menu works.

The worksheet you'll create in the following sections contains five rows of information. It also contains two ranges you'll use with two of the routines.

Setting Up the Worksheet

The sales expenses worksheet breaks down the quarterly sales expenses of a company's managers and compares budgeted amounts with the actual expenses.

Figure 14.2 Sales expenses worksheet

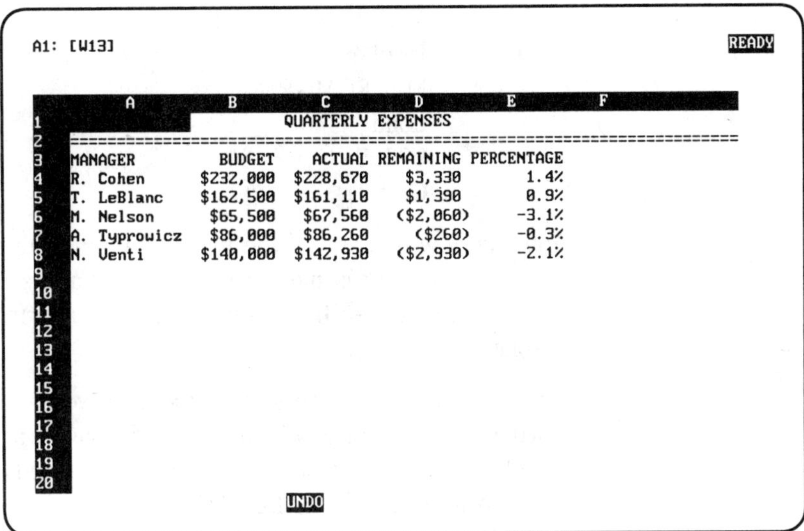

	A	B	C	D	E	F
1			QUARTERLY EXPENSES			
2	==========	==========	==========	==========	==========	==========
3	MANAGER	BUDGET	ACTUAL	REMAINING	PERCENTAGE	
4	R. Cohen	$232,000	$228,670	$3,330	1.4%	
5	T. LeBlanc	$162,500	$161,110	$1,390	0.9%	
6	M. Nelson	$65,500	$67,560	($2,060)	-3.1%	
7	A. Typrowicz	$86,000	$86,260	($260)	-0.3%	
8	N. Venti	$140,000	$142,930	($2,930)	-2.1%	

Save the current worksheet if you need the information it contains. Then start the sales expenses worksheet by erasing the worksheet with **/Worksheet Erase Yes.**

(2.2) Using the Utility Macros

Some of the utility macros you created in Chapter 11 and saved in the UTILS library in Chapter 12 will be useful when you enter the macros in this chapter. The utility macros you'll find useful are as follows:

Macro	**Name**
Naming a single cell with **/Range Name Labels Right**	\N
Naming a multiple-cell range	\M
File saving	\S
Double line	D_LINE
Right	\R

To use any of the utility macros, you must first attach and invoke the Macro Library Manager and then load the UTILS library into memory.

Press: [/]
Select: Add-In
Attach
MACROMGR.ADN
Invoke
MACROMGR
Load
UTILS
Quit

You can now use any of the utility macros either by pressing Alt and a letter (for macros named with a backslash and single letter) or by pressing Run (Alt-F3) and selecting the macro from the list that 1–2–3 displays.

You'll need to save the sales expenses worksheet frequently as you build it. The easiest way is to use the file saving macro (\S). The macro won't work correctly, however, until you've saved the worksheet at least once. Name this file SALESEXP.

Press: [/]
Select: File
Save
Type: salesexp [↵]

Use the \S macro frequently as you enter macros in this chapter.

Changing the Global Column Width

The sales expenses worksheet illustrated above contains several columns of numbers. With the default column width of 9 characters, the numbers would be difficult to read because they would be quite close together. Some of the numbers that are formatted as currency would also be too long to appear in the cell. To improve the worksheet's appearance, use **/Worksheet Global Column-Width** to change the default column width to 10.

Entering the Headings

The first two lines of the worksheet contain a title and a double line. Enter these now (you can use the D_LINE utility macro to enter the double line if you wish).

Move to: cell C1
Type: QUARTERLY EXPENSES [↵]
Move to: cell A2
Type: @repeat("=",72) [↵]

Next, enter the column headings. You can use the right (\R) macro to enter them. Type the column headings exactly as shown. This is important because you'll use them to name ranges later on, and many of the macros rely on these range names.

Move to: cell A3
Type: MANAGER
Press: [→]
Type: "BUDGET (the " aligns the entry at the right of the cell)
Press: [→]
Type: "ACTUAL
Press: [→]
Type: "REMAINING
Press: [→]
Type: "PERCENTAGE
Press: [↵]

Entering the Names of the Managers

Now enter the names of the five managers in column A as illustrated in Figure 14.3.

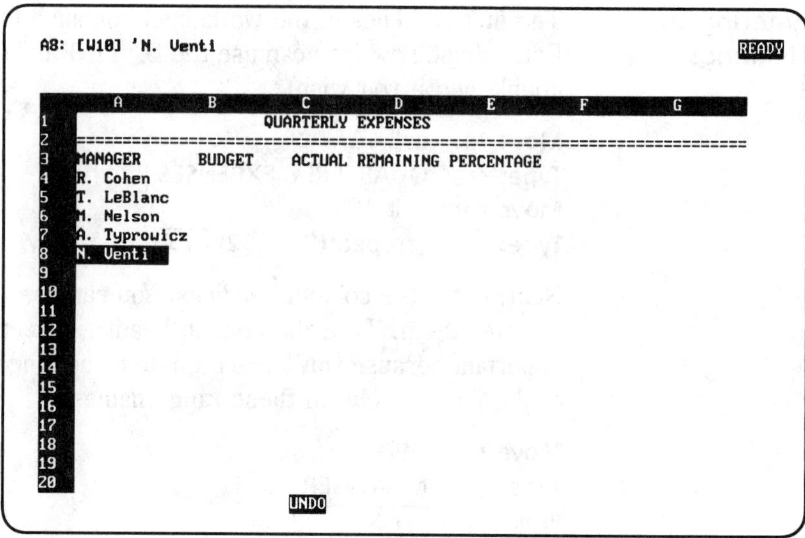

Figure 14.3
Names of managers in column A

Widen column A to 13 characters.

Press: [/]
Select: Worksheet
Column
Set-Width
Type 13 [↵]

Before you enter the numbers in columns B to E, change the global worksheet format to currency format with no decimal places. Then format the range of cells in column E as percentages with one decimal place.

Press: [/]
Select: Worksheet
Global
Format
Currency
Type: 0
Press: [↵]
Move to: cell E4
Press: [/]
Select: Range
Format
Percent

Type: 1
Press: ↵
↓ four times

Entering the Budgeted and Actual Figures

Column B contains the budgeted amount for each manager for the quarter, whereas column C lists the amount each manager has actually spent. Copy these figures from Figure 14.4. Don't type the dollar signs or commas as 1-2-3 inserts them automatically.

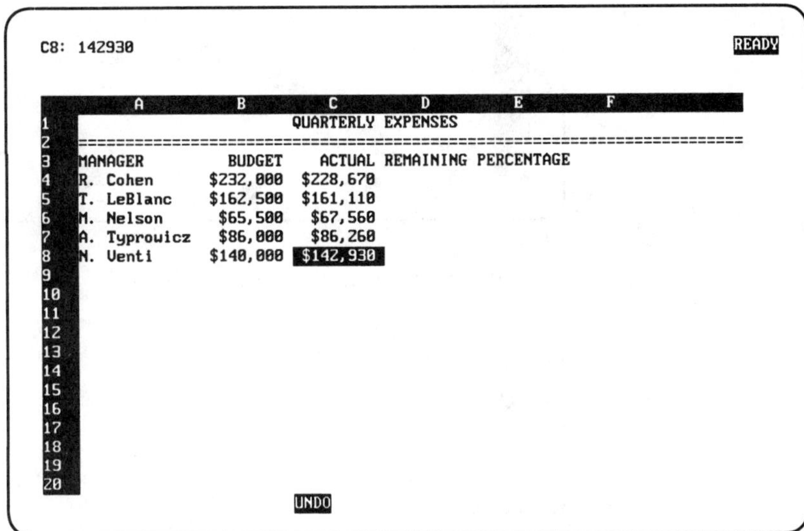
C8: 142930 READY

	A	B	C	D	E	F
1			QUARTERLY EXPENSES			
2	=======	=======	=======	=======	=======	=======
3	MANAGER	BUDGET	ACTUAL	REMAINING	PERCENTAGE	
4	R. Cohen	$232,000	$228,670			
5	T. LeBlanc	$162,500	$161,110			
6	M. Nelson	$65,500	$67,560			
7	A. Typrowicz	$86,000	$86,260			
8	N. Venti	$140,000	$142,930			
9						
10						
11						
12						
13						
14						
15						
16						
17						
18						
19						
20						

UNDO

Figure 14.4 BUDGET and ACTUAL figures

Entering the Formulas

Columns D and E contain formulas that calculate the difference between the budgeted and actual figures. 1-2-3 displays the results of each formula in the cells: column D displays the difference as a dollar amount and column E displays it as a percentage. You enter each formula once only; then copy the formulas to the other cells.

Move to: cell D4
Type: +b4−c4
Press: →
Type: +d4/b4
Press: ↵

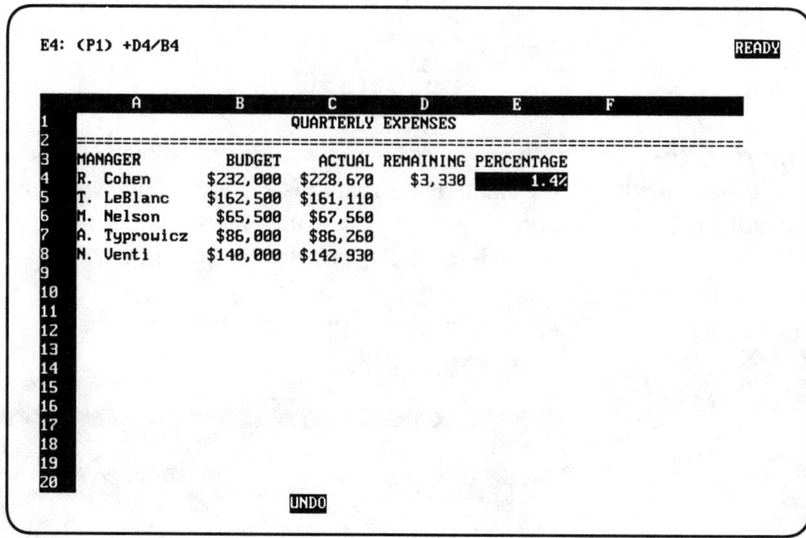

Figure 14.5
REMAINING and PERCENTAGE formulas

Now copy the formulas to rows 5 to 8.

Move to: cell D4
Press: [/]
Select: Copy
Press: [→]
[↵]
Move to: cell D5
Press: [.]
[→]
[↓] three times
[↵]

The figures in the worksheet should match those in Figure 14.6. If they don't, check the numbers in columns B and C against the illustration, and check to see that you've entered the formulas in columns D and E correctly. (The currency format displays negative numbers in parentheses.)

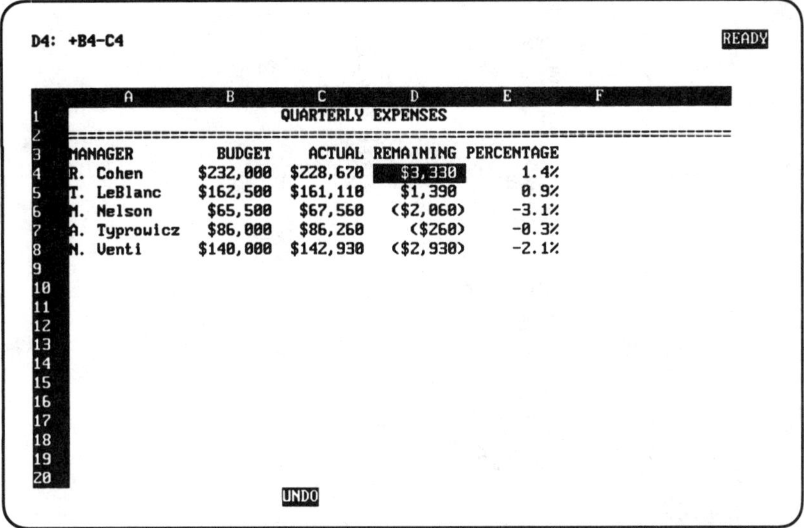

Figure 14.6 Values of formulas

Assigning Range Names to the Columns

Assign range names to the cells in row 4. Some of the routines will use these range names to extract information from the data you just entered. These routines use the **Data Query** command, and treat the entries you just made as a database.

Use **/Range Name Labels Down** to assign each entry in row 3 as a range name for the cell directly below.

Move to: cell A3
Press: [/]
Select: Range
Name
Labels
Down
Press: [END] [→] to highlight A3..E3
[↵]

The GRAPH routine uses three ranges to create the graph:

- The NAMES range contains all the managers' names.
- The PROJECTED range contains the numbers in the BUDGET column.
- The CURRENT range contains the numbers in the ACTUAL column.

Name these ranges now (you can use the naming a multiple-cell range macro (\M) if you wish).

Move to: cell A4
Press: [/]
Select: Range
Name
Create
Type: **names** [↵]
Press: [END] [↓]
[↵]
Move to: cell B4
Press: [/]
Select: Range
Name
Create
Type: **projected** [↵]
Press: [END] [↓]
[↵]
Move to: cell C4
Press: [/]
Select: Range
Name
Create
Type: **current** [↵]
Press: [END] [↓]
[↵]

Finally, name the range that contains the entries. You'll use this range in the next section and in the MEMOS routine. Use the range name BUDGET_DATA.

Move to: cell A3
Press: [/]
Select: Range
Name
Create
Type: **budget_data** [↵]
Press: [END] [→]
[END] [↓]
[↵]

Before you continue to the next section, save the worksheet. Use the file saving macro by holding down Alt and typing s.

Setting Up Ranges for the OVER and UNDER Routines

In the last section, you created the area of the worksheet that contains the data that the macro menu routines use. The OVER routine and the UNDER routine treat the information you just entered as a database. These routines use **/Data Query** to extract information from the database.

Before you can use **/Data Query** to choose database records, however, you must set up and identify several ranges; you'll do this next. These ranges are the following:

- The **input range** contains the database records and the field names. You created this range in the last section—it's the area of the worksheet you named BUDGET_DATA.
- The **criteria range** contains some or all of the column headings (called field names) that appear in the database. When you create a criteria range, it's easier to copy all the field names from the database. This also allows you more flexibility when you use the criteria range.

  The criteria range headings are followed by one or more blank rows. When you're using **/Data Query** to find or copy selected information from a database, you use these rows to indicate the criteria (kind of information) you want 1-2-3 to use when it searches the database. For example, if you want 1-2-3 to find records that have a negative value in the REMAINING column in the worksheet you just created, you enter the formula +REMAINING<0 in the REMAINING column of the criteria range before you use one of the **Data Query** commands. 1-2-3 then searches for any record that contains a value that is less than 0 in the cell in the REMAINING column.
- The **output range** is the area of the worksheet 1-2-3 uses to display records that meet the criteria you enter in the criteria range. The output range uses **/Data Query Extract**, which copies records that meet the criteria to the output range.

  You must be very careful when you set up an output range. If you specify a single row as an output range, 1-2-3 erases any entries below that row, down to the bottom of the worksheet. In this section, you'll create an output range that consists of 20 rows; if you specify more than one row, 1-2-3 doesn't erase entries below the output range. When you create an output range for your own work, be sure to allow enough rows to contain the highest possible number of records that meet the criteria or make sure you don't enter data below the output range.

In this section you will:

- Set up the criteria and output ranges used in the OVER and UNDER routines and
- Specify the input, criteria, and output ranges using **/Data Query**.

Setting Up the Criteria and Output Ranges

To set up the criteria and output ranges, you'll copy the column headings in row 3 down to rows 21 and 25. The criteria range will start in row 21 and the output range will start in row 25. Later, you'll use these ranges in the OVER and UNDER routines on the macro menu.

Move to: cell A3
Press: [/]
Select: Copy
Press: [END] [→]
[↵]
Move to: cell A21
Press: [↵]
[/]
Select: Copy
Press: [END] [→]
[↵]
Move to: cell A25
Press: [↵]

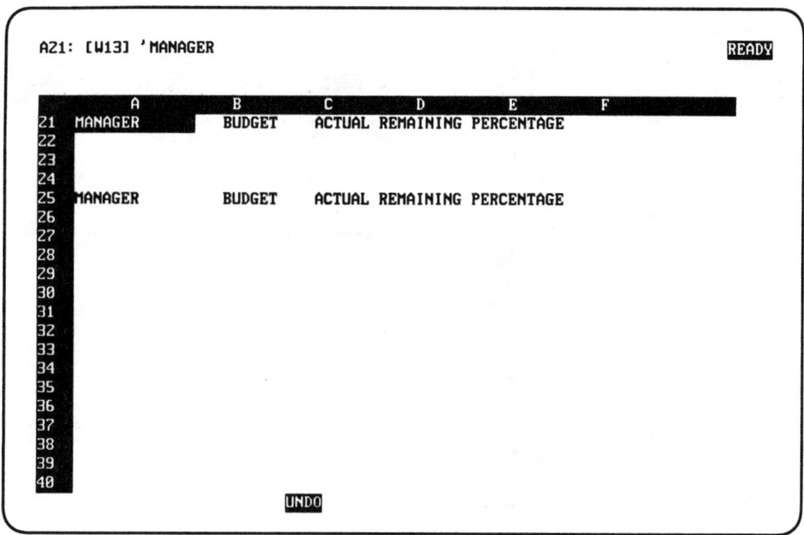

Figure 14.7 Copied column headings

Specifying the Ranges

Now you're ready to use **/Data Query** to tell 1–2–3 where the input, criteria, and output ranges are. Start by selecting **/Data Query**:

Press: [/]
Select: Data
Query

Now specify the ranges:

Select: Input
Press: [NAME] (F3)
Select: BUDGET_DATA
Criteria
Move to: cell A21
Press: [·]
[END] [→]
[↓]
[↵]
Select: Output
Move to: cell A25
Press: [·]
[END] [→]
[PGDN]
[↵]

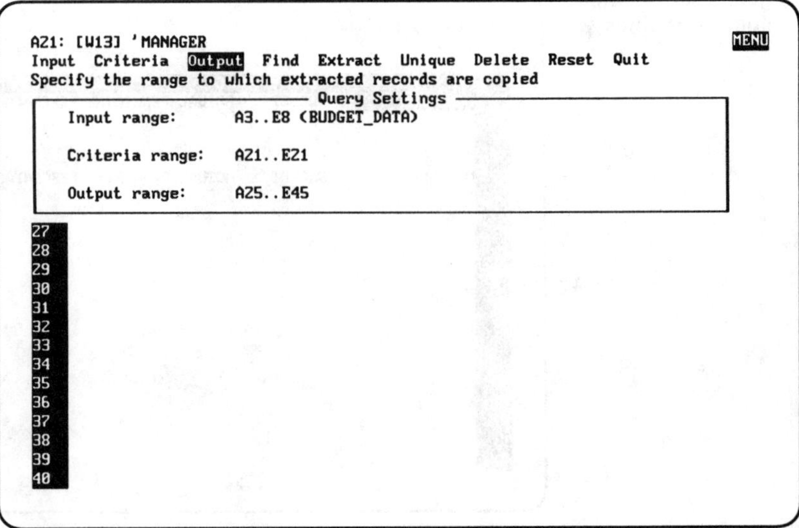

Figure 14.8
Database settings

Notice that all the ranges are now specified on the setting sheet.

Select: Quit

You can't see any changes in the worksheet, but 1-2-3 will use these ranges when you use **/Data Query** to find, extract, or delete information in the database. Try one of these commands now:

Move to: cell D22
Type: +remaining>0
Press: ↵
/
Select: Data
Query
Extract
Quit

Figure 14.9
Matched records in output range

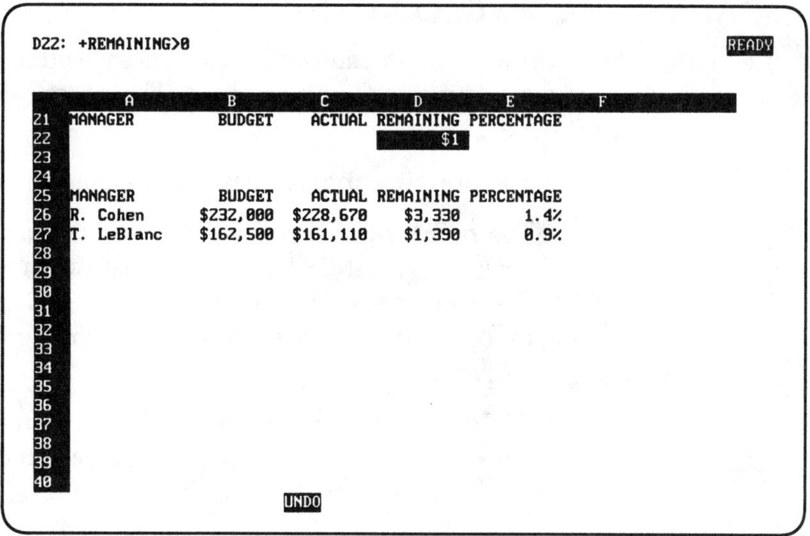

1-2-3 went through the input range and copied all the records in which the remaining balance was greater than 0 to the output range. Now erase the formula in cell D22 and the records in the output range.

Move to: cell D22
Press: [/]
Select: Range
Erase
Press: [↵]
Move to: cell A26
Press: [/]
Select: Range
Erase
Press: [END] [HOME]
[↵]

Before you go on, save the worksheet.

CREATING THE MACRO MENU

Once you finish entering information and setting up the ranges, you're ready to create the macro menu. The macro menu consists of several parts:

- The **starting macro** makes the menu appear.
- The **menu macro** contains the menu items, descriptions of each item, and {BRANCH} commands that switch control to the routines. The menu macro doesn't look like a regular macro—you enter the various parts of the menu macros across rows rather than down columns.
- The **routines** carry out the tasks: displaying the graph, displaying lists of managers over or under budget, creating and printing memos, and allowing you to enter new numbers or erase the current ones.

A macro menu can include up to eight items. This one has six. When you enter the names of the items, 1-2-3 automatically capitalizes the first letter of each item. (A menu name can also begin with a number or numeric character as long as you enter it with a label prefix.)

A macro menu works just like a regular 1-2-3 menu: You select an item by typing the first letter of the menu item or by highlighting the menu item and pressing Enter.

The macro menu instructions should go in an out-of-the-way area of the worksheet, diagonally opposite the other information that worksheet contains. You'll enter all the parts of the macro menu below and to the right of the sales expenses worksheet.

Remember to save the worksheet frequently as you go through this section.

Entering the Starting Macro

The starting macro is the macro that actually calls up the menu you're going to create. Name the starting macro \M. Document the name in cell AA40 and enter the starting macro in cell AB40.

\M {HOME}{MENUBRANCH MAIN_MENU} don't leave out the underscore between the two words

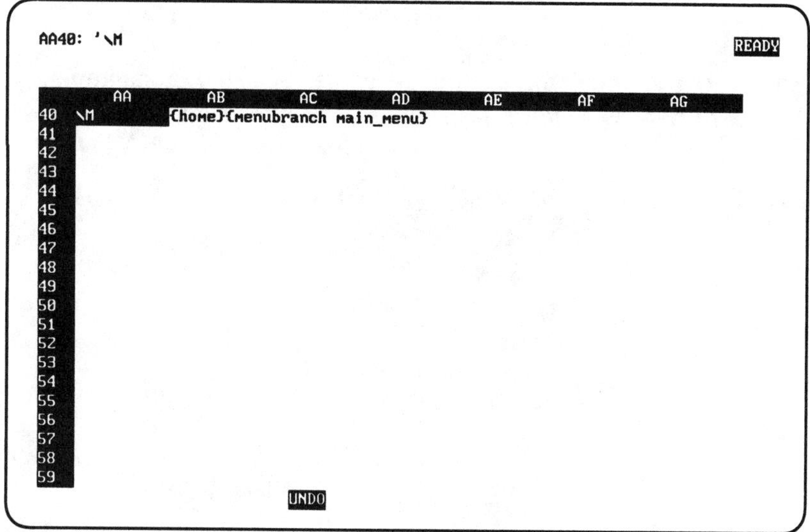

Figure 14.10
The starting macro

This macro moves the cell pointer to cell A1. It then uses the {MENUBRANCH} command to send control to the specified worksheet location, in this case, the range MAIN_MENU, and to invoke the menu entered there.

Entering the Menu Macro

The menu itself begins in another row of the worksheet, with at least one blank cell separating it from the starting macro. The cell to the right of the macro should also be blank.

Before going on, enter the name of the macro menu to the left of the first menu item and assign a range name to the first cell of the range where you'll enter the menu:

Move to: cell AA44
Type: MAIN_MENU don't forget the underscore
Press: ↵
/
Select: Range
Name
Labels
Right
Press: ↵

Now you can start entering the parts of the menu.

Entering the Menu Items

You'll enter the names of all the menu items first. You enter the menu items in separate cells in the same row. The right (\R) macro is useful here. Start the menu items in cell AB44.

Move to: cell AB44
Type: Graph
Press: →
Type: Over
Press: →
Type: Under
Press: →
Type: Memos
Press: →
Type: New
Press: →
Type: Exit
Press: ↵

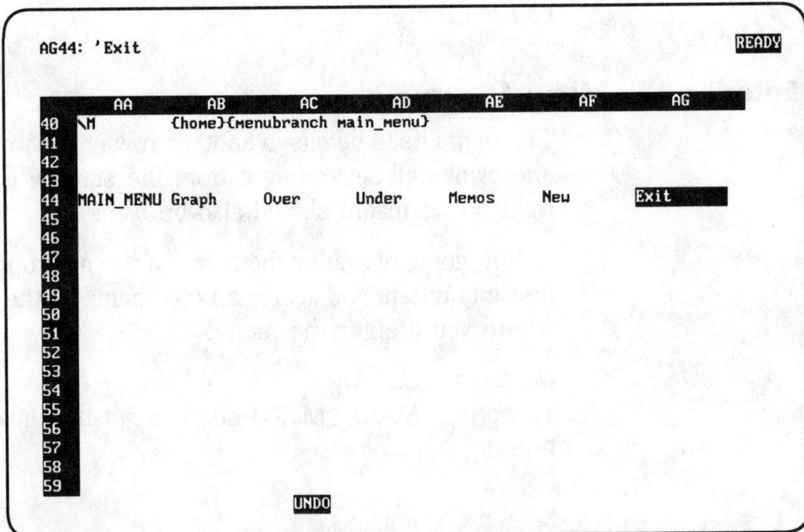

Figure 14.11 Menu items entered in a row

If you're using the right (\R) macro, you don't need to end it—it will be useful with the next set of entries, too.

Entering the Description Lines

The command descriptions explain what the menu items do, and are entered in the row below the menu items. Each description is in a separate cell. The columns in the worksheet are only 10 characters wide, so the descriptions overlap when you enter them. When you use the menu, however, the entire command description appears in the control panel when you highlight the corresponding menu item with the menu pointer.

Enter the command descriptions in the cells directly below the menu items.

Move to: cell AB45
Type: View a graph of sales expenses
Press: [→]
Type: View a list of managers over budget
Press: [→]
Type: View a list of managers under budget
Press: [→]
Type: Print memos to managers
Press: [→]
Type: Enter new figures in worksheet
Press: [→]
Type: Return to worksheet
Press: [↵]

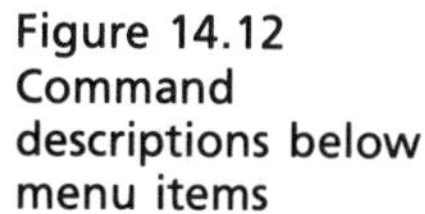

Figure 14.12
Command descriptions below menu items

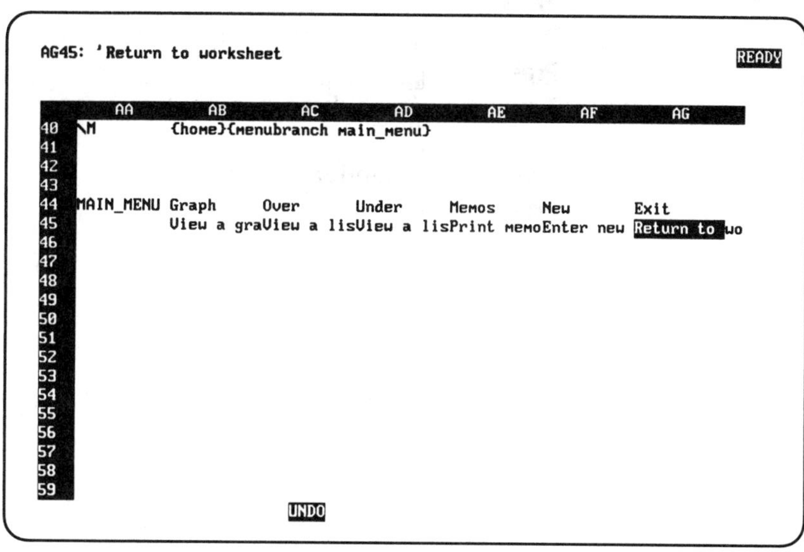

If you're using the right (\R) macro, you can continue to use it in the next set of instructions.

Entering the Macro Menu Branches

The actual instructions for each of the routines could begin in the third row of the macro menu. In this menu, however, {BRANCH} commands transfer control to the menu routines you'll enter in another part of the worksheet. This makes the routines easier to read and edit.

The first four options use {BRANCH} commands to transfer to the routines, and the last two use {MENUBRANCH} commands. Each of the {BRANCH} commands transfers macro execution to the corresponding routine (GRAPH, OVER, UNDER, or MEMOS). The NEW and EXIT routines, however, require another macro menu. The {MENUBRANCH} command allows you to transfer control to another menu.

Enter the {BRANCH} and {MENUBRANCH} commands in the row below the command descriptions.

Move to: cell AB46
Type: {branch graph}
Press: [→]
Type: {branch over}
Press: [→]
Type: {branch under}
Press: [→]
Type: {branch memos}
Press: [→]
Type: {menubranch new}
Press: [→]
Type: {menubranch exit}
Press: [↵]

Figure 14.13
Menu macro

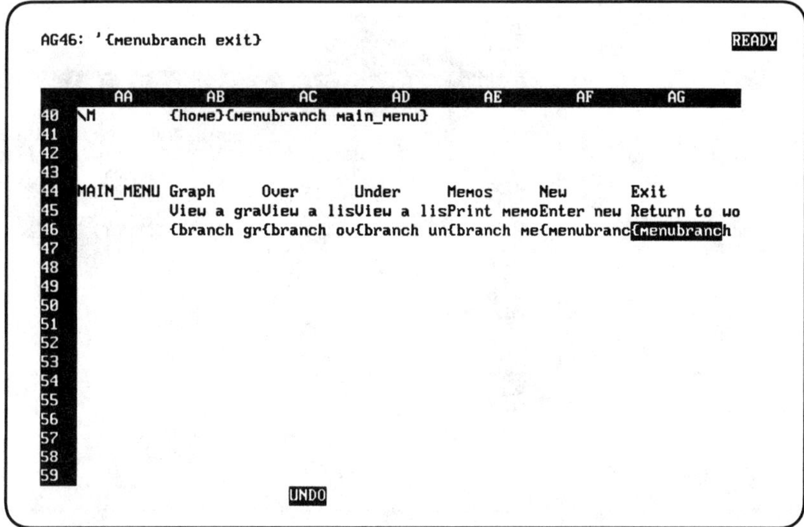

If you're using the right macro (\R), press Ctrl-Break now to end it. Then press Esc to cancel the error.

Before going on, check to see that you entered the {BRANCH} and {MENUBRANCH} commands correctly. Move the pointer to cell AB46 so you can see the entire cell entry in the control panel and check to see that it is correct. Do the same for the other entries in this row.

Save the worksheet before you continue.

Displaying the Macro Menu

You can see the macro menu now, although you can't use it yet because you haven't created any of the routines. Hold down Alt and type m.

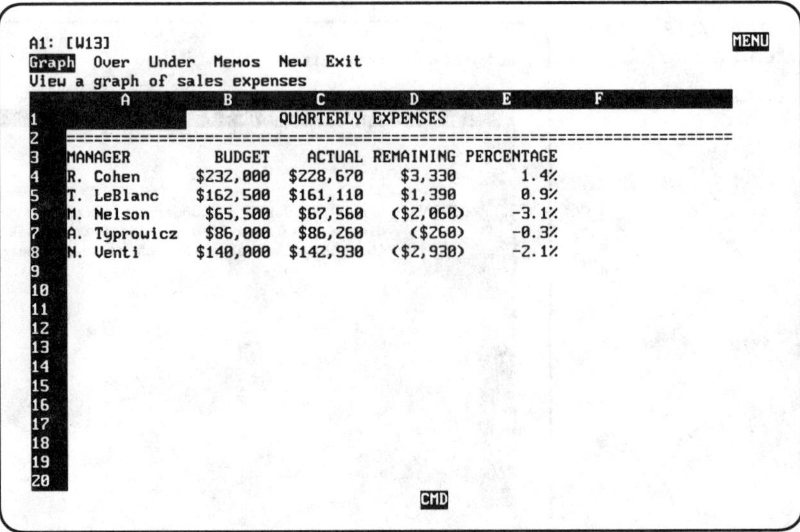

Figure 14.14 Menu appears in control panel

The menu items appear in the control panel, with the command descriptions below them. Now try moving around in the menu by pressing Right to move from one item to the next. All the pointer-movement keys work exactly as they do in a 1-2-3 menu. Use Home now to move to the first menu item.

Because none of the menu items works yet, you can't select Exit to leave the macro menu. Use Esc instead:

Press: ESC

CREATING THE MACRO MENU ROUTINES

The six macro menu routines are all named for their respective menu options: GRAPH, OVER, UNDER, MEMOS, NEW, and EXIT. The option that takes you out of the macro menu is not called QUIT (as it is in regular 1-2-3 menus) to avoid confusion with the {QUIT} advanced macro command.

In most of this section, the macros are presented as they were in earlier chapters. (The exceptions are the NEW and EXIT routines.) The entire macro appears, without step-by-step instructions. Enter each line of the macro in a single cell. Some lines of the MEMOS routine are too long to fit on one line in this book, though they fit in a single cell. Enter a line that is indented in the same cell as the line above.

The NEW and EXIT routines are presented step by step. These two routines displays submenus, so the menu items and menu routines must be entered side by side.

After you enter each routine, you should test it. If you've made typing errors or if the macro doesn't function properly, it may be easier to find the mistake when the routine is fresh in your mind. If you don't want to spend the time testing the routines individually, you will test the entire menu once you enter all the routines.

Entering the GRAPH Routine

You'll enter the GRAPH routine first. This routine draws a bar graph that compares the budgeted sales expenses and actual sales expenses for each manager.

Name the routine GRAPH and document the name in cell AA48. Start the macro in cell AB48. Be careful to type the instructions exactly as they appear.

```
GRAPH   '/gtbxNAMES~aPROJECTED~bCURRENT~
        olaBudget~lbActual~
        tfSales Expenses by Manager~
        qvrgq
        {MENUBRANCH MAIN_MENU}
```

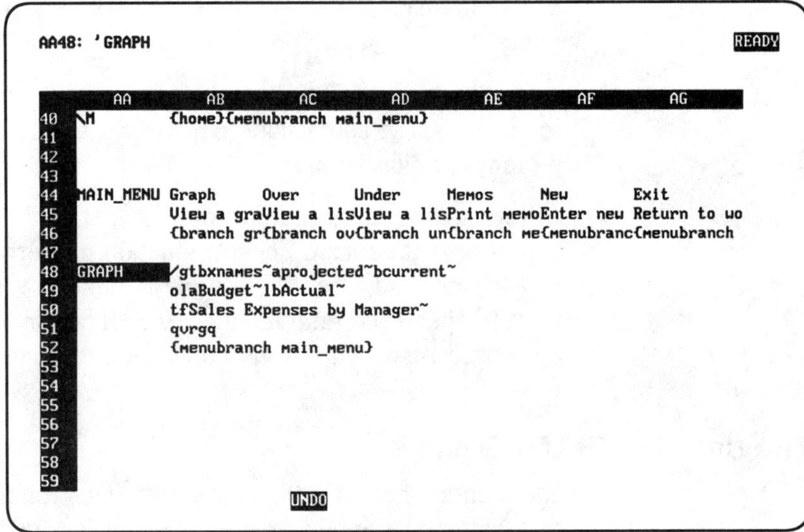

Figure 14.15
GRAPH routine

The first line of the macro calls up the menu and selects the **Graph** command. It then chooses **Bar** as the graph type and specifies the X, A, and B ranges. It uses the range names NAMES, PROJECTED, and CURRENT to specify these ranges: You assigned these range names earlier in this chapter when you created the sales expenses worksheet.

The next line of the macro chooses **Options** from the menu and types **Budget** as the legend for the A range and **Actual** as the legend for the B range. The third line types **Sales Expenses by Manager** as the first (and only) line of the graph title.

The final line of the macro chooses **Quit** to leave the Options menu and then chooses **View** to make the graph appear. The remaining instructions in the macro (rgq) take place after you press any key to clear the graph from the screen.

Once you finish viewing the graph and press a key, the macro chooses **Reset Graph** to clear the current graph settings in preparation for the next time you select the Graph item from the menu. The routine ends by returning to the main macro menu.

Save the worksheet before you continue. Then test the GRAPH routine. Even though you haven't entered all the routines yet, you can use this one:

Press: ALT – M
Select: Graph

The bar graph appears in a few seconds.

Figure 14.16
Bar graph

Clear the graph from the screen.

Press: any key

After you press a key, the GRAPH routine continues by clearing the graph settings and displaying the macro menu again in response to the {MENUBRANCH MAIN_MENU} command. Because you haven't created the EXIT routine yet, you must press Esc to clear the menu and return to the worksheet.

Press: ESC

NOTE: You can always use Esc to leave the macro menu.

If the graph that appears on the screen doesn't look like the one in Figure 14.16, or if an error message appears when you run the GRAPH routine, press Esc to stop the macro (you may have to press Esc twice). Then carefully compare the instructions you entered to those illustrated above. If they don't match exactly, edit the macro and correct the instructions. If you still can't find the source of the error, use STEP mode to go through the macro step by step until you locate the error.

Entering the OVER Routine

Now enter the OVER routine. This routine displays a list of managers who are over budget. The list appears in the output range you created in earlier in the chapter.

To avoid using cell addresses in the macro, name cell D22 CRIT and name cell A25 OUT. For instructions about naming ranges, see earlier in this chapter.

Name the routine OVER and document the name in cell AA55. Begin the OVER routine in cell AB55.

```
OVER   {GOTO}CRIT~ +REMAINING<0~
       '/dqeq{GOTO}OUT~
       {MENUBRANCH MAIN_MENU}
```

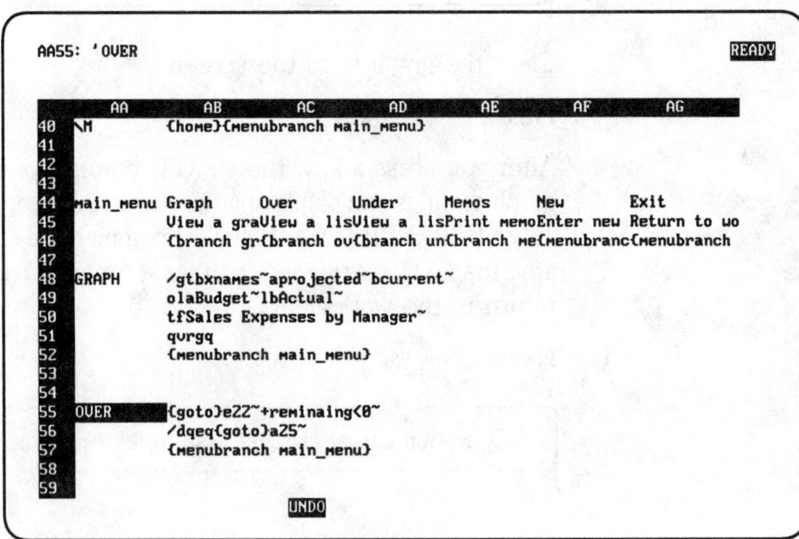

Figure 14.17
OVER routine

The OVER routine moves the cell pointer to the cell named CRIT (D22) in the criterion range. It then enters the formula +REMAINING<0 and selects **/Data Query Extract**. This command produces a list in the output range (starting in row 25) of all of the records with a figure of less than zero in the REMAINING column. When 1-2-3 finishes extracting records, it moves the pointer to the cell named OUT (A25) so you can see them. Finally, the routine returns control to the main macro menu.

Now test this routine. Remember to use Esc to leave the macro menu when you finish. (You'll test all the menu items again later, after you finish creating them.) To test the OVER routine, hold down Alt, type m, and select Over.

Entering the UNDER Routine

The UNDER routine is similar to the OVER routine. Instead of producing a list of managers who are over budget, however, it produces a list of those who are under budget.

Name this routine UNDER. Document the name in cell AA59. You can type this routine or copy and edit the OVER routine. To type the UNDER routine, start in cell AB59.

```
UNDER   {GOTO}CRIT~+REMAINING>=0~
        '/dqeq{GOTO}OUT~
        {MENUBRANCH MAIN_MENU}
```

This macro is the same as the OVER routine except for the formula in the first line. You can enter the routine by copying and then editing the OVER routine.

Move to: cell AB55
Press: [/]
Select: Copy
Press: [↓] twice
[↵]

Move to: cell AB59

Press: ↵

EDIT (F2)

← ← BACKSPACE

Type: >=

Press: ↵

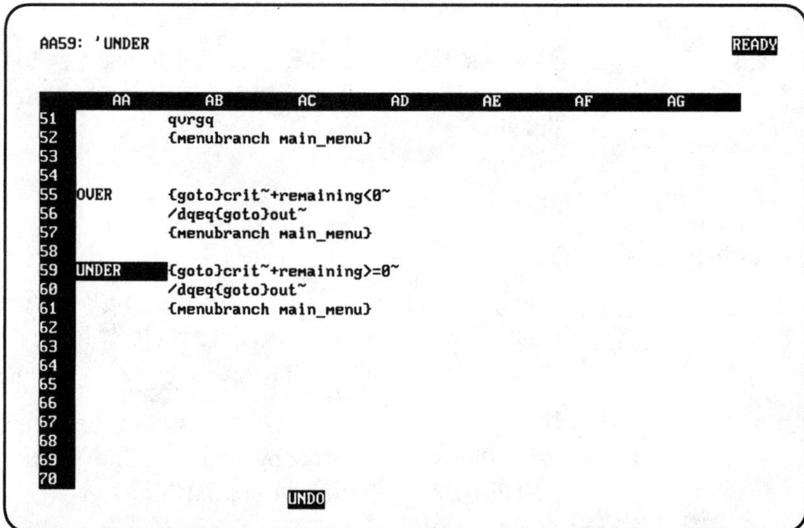

Figure 14.18
UNDER routine

No matter how you enter it, the UNDER routine functions in exactly the same way as the OVER routine, except that the final result is a list of managers who are under budget.

Save the worksheet before you continue.

Test the UNDER routine. Remember to use Esc to leave the macro menu when you finish. (You'll test all the menu items again later, after you finish creating them.)

Entering the MEMOS Routine

The MEMOS routine is more complex than the routines you've created so far. This routine creates and prints a memo that informs each manager of his or her budget for sales expenses, the actual outlay, and the percentage by which he or she is over or under budget.

The MEMOS routine consists of several kinds of macro instructions. You have encountered most of the special key names and advanced macro commands before. The routine also contains several instructions that enter the text of the macro.

The routine enters much of the text of the macro by entering string formulas. **String formulas** use the symbol "&" to combine text into one text entry. In this routine, many of the string formulas combine text the macro types in the formula with text the macro creates by converting numbers to text. This routine uses the @STRING function to convert numbers from the BUDGET, ACTUAL, and PERCENTAGE columns to text in the memo. It then uses {EDIT} and {CALC} instructions to convert the formulas to their values so that **/Range Justify** will function correctly. (**/Range Justify** interprets any formula as a numeric value, and it will not justify a cell that contains a numeric value.)

The routine also uses the @IF function, which is similar to the {IF} command: it tests a statement and then executes an instruction according to the results of the test. The @IF function takes three arguments. The first is the condition (in this case, PERCENTAGE>0). The second tells 1-2-3 what to do if the condition is true (in this case, type under). The third tells 1-2-3 what to do if the condition is false (in this case, type over).

Because the flickering of the screen is annoying while the macro is running, this routine uses the {PANELOFF}/{PANELON} and {WINDOWSOFF}/{WINDOWSON} commands to suppress the screen display. These commands are discussed in more detail in "Refining the Macro Menu" later in this chapter.

The MEMOS routine is actually two routines: the MEMOS routine begins the memo and then branches to the TEXT routine, which enters the text and prints the memo. The MEMOS routine contains a {FOR} command that switches to the TEXT routine once for each memo.

The MEMOS Routine

You'll create the MEMOS routine first. The first line of the MEMOS routine requires a cell named START. This is the first cell in the range that contains the letter. For this example, use cell A41. Go to cell A41 now and name it START with **/Range Name Create**. Do not document the range name; this cell is part of the letter. The {FOR} command in the sixth line also requires a named cell: name it COUNTER. Go to cell H47, name it COUNTER, and document the name in cell G47.

Name the routine MEMOS and document the name in cell AA63. Then start entering the routine in cell AB63:

```
MEMOS   {GOTO}START~{PANELOFF}{WINDOWSOFF}
        {R 6}TEMPMAN{R 2}
        TEMPBUD{R}TEMPACT{R}TEMPREM{R}TEMPERR~
        '/rnld{END}{L}{END}{L}~
        {GOTO}START~/rfd1~@NOW~
        {FOR COUNTER,1,@ROWS(BUDGET__DATA)-1,1,TEXT}
        {HOME}/wcr{MENUBRANCH MAIN__MENU}
```

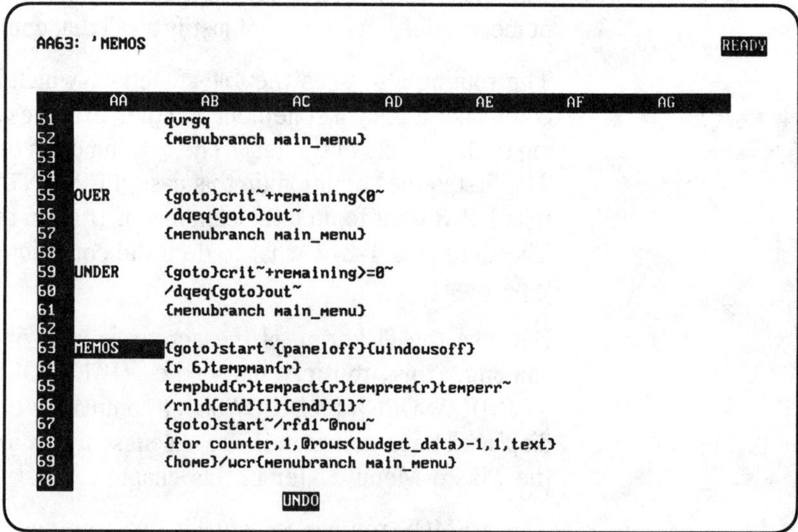

Figure 14.19
MEMOS routine

The first line of this routine moves the cell pointer to the cell named START and freezes the display of the screen (as long as the {WINDOWSOFF} and {PANELOFF} commands are in effect, 1-2-3 will not update the screen display).

The second line moves the cell pointer to the right. The macro then enters labels; the instructions in the fourth line assign these labels as range names for the cells below. (When the macro runs, it copies information to these named cells from the sales expenses records you created earlier.)

The fifth line (cell AB67) moves the cell pointer to the START cell and starts the letter by entering the current date with the @NOW function. (If you didn't set the date when you entered your computer, your memos will be dated incorrectly.)

The sixth line contains the {FOR} command. This command uses the @ROWS function to calculate the number of times to execute the TEXT routine. (The macro must subtract 1 from the value that @ROWS (WORKSHEET) produces because the WORKSHEET range contains an extra row for the column headings.) It then executes the TEXT routine once for each manager.

The final line of the macro moves the cell pointer to the home position (cell A1) and resets the column width to the default. The {MENUBRANCH} command returns to the main menu.

Before you continue, save the worksheet.

The TEXT Routine

The TEXT routine contains several formulas. As you enter the formulas in the routine, don't forget to type a label prefix before you type +. If you don't, 1-2-3 will enter the value of the formula in the cell, and the macro won't run correctly.

Enter each line in one cell. If a line in the macro is indented, enter it in the same cell as the line above. Do not type extra space characters; adding spaces will prevent the macro from running correctly.

Name this routine TEXT and document the name in cell AA71. Start the TEXT routine in cell AB71.

```
TEXT   {GOTO}START~{PANELOFF}{WINDOWSOFF}{D 2}
         /re{PGDN}~
       {GOTO}MANAGER~{D COUNTER-1}
       '/c{END}{R}~TEMPMAN~{GOTO}START~{D 2}
       '+"To: "&TEMPMAN{D}
       From: Loren Miller{D}
       '+"Subject: Sales Expenses for the quarter ending "
       &@STRING(@MONTH(@NOW),0)&"/"&@STRING
         (@YEAR(@NOW),0)
       {EDIT}{CALC}~{D 2}
       '+"Your budget for sales expenses for the last quarter was $"
       &@STRING(@ABS(TEMPBUD),0)&". "{EDIT}{CALC}~{D}
```

```
'+"Your actual outlay for the quarter was $"
&@STRING(@ABS(TEMPACT),0)&". "{EDIT}{CALC}~{D}
'+"You are "&@IF(TEMPERR>0,"under","over")
  &" budget by "
&@STRING(@ABS(TEMPERR)*100,1)&"%. "{EDIT}{CALC}~
  {D 2}
Please call the Finance Department to confirm these figures.
{D 2}Thank you.~
'/wcs65~{GOTO}START~{D 6}/rj~
{D 6}/rncLETTER~{BS}.{U 12}~{WINDOWSON}
  {PANELON}
'/pprLETTER~agpq
```

Figure 14.20
TEXT routine

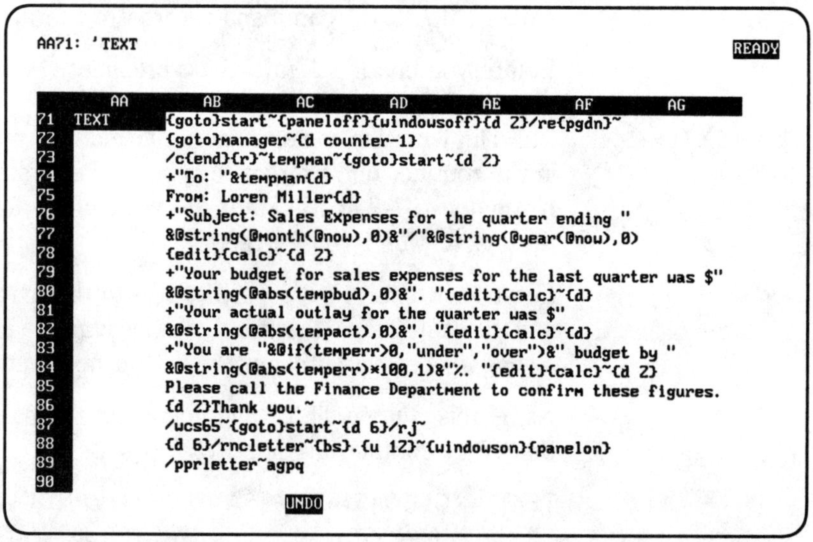

```
AA71: 'TEXT                                                         READY

        AA        AB        AC        AD        AE        AF        AG
71  TEXT       {goto}start~{paneloff}{windowsoff}{d 2}/re{pgdn}~
72             {goto}manager~{d counter-1}
73             /c{end}{r}~tempman~{goto}start~{d 2}
74             +"To: "&tempman{d}
75             From: Loren Miller{d}
76             +"Subject: Sales Expenses for the quarter ending "
77             &@string(@month(@now),0)&"/"&@string(@year(@now),0)
78             {edit}{calc}~{d 2}
79             +"Your budget for sales expenses for the last quarter was $"
80             &@string(@abs(tempbud),0)&". "{edit}{calc}~{d}
81             +"Your actual outlay for the quarter was $"
82             &@string(@abs(tempact),0)&". "{edit}{calc}~{d}
83             +"You are "&@if(temperr>0,"under","over")&" budget by "
84             &@string(@abs(temperr)*100,1)&"%. "{edit}{calc}~{d 2}
85             Please call the Finance Department to confirm these figures.
86             {d 2}Thank you.~
87             /wcs65~{goto}start~{d 6}/rj~
88             {d 6}/rncletter~{bs}.{u 12}~{windowson}{panelon}
89             /pprletter~agpq
90

                        UNDO
```

The first line of the TEXT routine moves the cell pointer to the cell named START, which lets you see the range that will contain the memo. The {WINDOWSOFF} and {PANELOFF} commands freeze the screen. The last instruction in the first line erases the previous memo, or the range that will contain the memo.

The second line (cell AB72) moves the cell pointer to the cell named MANAGER. The next instruction moves the cell pointer down the number of times indicated by the value in COUNTER minus one. Each time the macro executes the TEXT routine, it adds 1 to the value in the cell named COUNTER: the first time, the value of COUNTER is 1; the second time, its value is 2; and so on. To avoid skipping the first set of entries, the TEXT routine must subtract 1 from the value in COUNTER; the first time the macro runs the TEXT routine, it moves the pointer down 0 rows, the next time down 1, and so on.

The third line of the TEXT routine (cell AB73) copies information from the row the cell pointer is in to the range that begins with the cell named TEMPMAN. The named cells in this range act as temporary holding cells for the information the macro will use.

The next line (cell AB74) includes a string formula. This formula combines the text in quotation marks with the value in the cell named TEMPMAN to address the memo to one of the managers. For example, if TEMPMAN contains R. Cohen, the string formula produces the text "To: R. Cohen." The fifth line (cell AB75) simply enters the text that tells who the memo is from.

The sixth and seventh lines (cells AB76 and AB77) include a more complex string formula that enters text and then adds the current month and year to the end of it. The {EDIT} and {CALC} instructions in cell AB78 convert the string formula to its value.

Lines 9 through 12 (cells AB79 to AB82) also include string formulas. The @STRING functions in these lines convert values from the temporary holding cells TEMPBUD and TEMPACT to text (@ABS ensures that the values are positive before 1-2-3 converts them). The formula then enters the converted values in the memo along with the other text. For example, if TEMPACT contains $228,670, the formula in lines 11 and 12 (cells AB81 and AB82) produces a sentence that reads "Your actual outlay for the quarter was $228,670."

The next two lines (cells AB83 and AB84) also include a string formula. In addition to an @STRING function, this formula contains an @IF function. Both of these functions use the value in the temporary holding cell TEMPERR. The @IF function evaluates TEMPERR to see if the value it contains is greater than 0. If it is, the @function types under in the memo. Otherwise, it types over.

The @STRING function in cell AB84 converts the value in TEMPERR to text and enters it in the memo.

The instructions in the next two lines (cells AB85 and AB86) simply enter text, move the cell pointer, and enter more text. The next two lines (cells AB87 and AB88) widen the column to 65 characters, justify the only paragraph of the letters that contains more than one line, name the range that comprises the memo, and turn on the screen display. The final line (cell AB89) prints the contents of the LETTER range—the memo.

Save the worksheet before you continue.

You can try the MEMOS routine now or wait until the entire menu is complete. When you test the MEMOS routine, you'll notice that nothing seems to happen while the routine creates each memo. The routine is working, but the {WINDOWSOFF} and {PANELOFF} commands keep the worksheet from changing. Only the CMD indicator at the bottom of the screen tells you the macro is running. One way to make this less confusing is described below in "Refining the Macro Menu."

Entering the NEW Routine

The NEW routine lets you enter new information in the BUDGET and ACTUAL columns. Because you could lose data if you chose this option by mistake, the NEW routine displays a submenu with two choices: Menu and Type. Menu allows you to return to the main menu without entering new figures. Once you choose Type, however, the only way to avoid writing over the existing figures is to press Ctrl-Break to end the macro.

A submenu routine looks like any menu you create with a macro, such as the main macro menu you created at the beginning of this chapter. Because the NEW routine produces a submenu with two menu items, you enter instructions for each menu item. For each menu item, you must enter (in the same column) the name of the option (Menu or Type), the command description, and actual instructions for the routine.

You must enter the two parts of the NEW routine in adjacent columns. Document the routine's name (NEW) in cell AA91. Name cell AB91 NEW. Start the first part, which creates the Menu item on the submenu, in cell AB91. Type each line in a separate cell.

Move to: cell AB91
Type: Menu
Return to main menu
{menubranch main_menu}

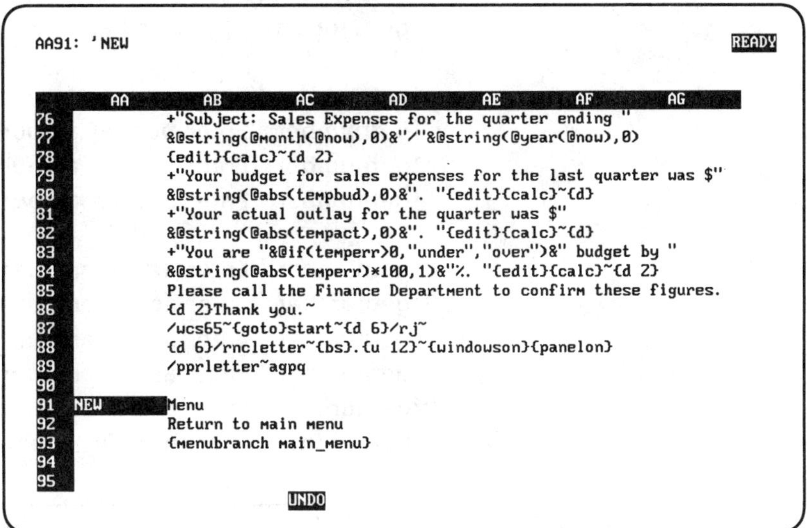

Figure 14.21 The NEW routine Menu option

Save the worksheet before you continue.

To avoid using cell addresses in the macro, name the cells in the BUDGET and ACTUAL columns as shown in the following table:

Cell Address	Range Name
B4	BUDG1
B5	BUDG2
B6	BUDG3
B7	BUDG4
B8	BUDG5
C4	ACT1
C5	ACT2
C6	ACT3
C7	ACT4
C8	ACT5

Once you name the cells, enter each line of this part of the NEW routine in a separate cell, beginning with cell AC91:

Move to: cell AC91

Type: Type
Enter new figures in BUDGET and ACTUAL columns
{goto}budg1~{getnumber "Enter budget amount: ",budg1}{d}
{getnumber "Enter budget amount: ",budg2}{d}
{getnumber "Enter budget amount: ",budg3}{d}
{getnumber "Enter budget amount: ",budg4}{d}
{getnumber "Enter budget amount: ",budg5}{goto}act1~
{getnumber "Enter actual amount: ",act1}{d}
{getnumber "Enter actual amount: ",act2}{d}
{getnumber "Enter actual amount: ",act3}{d}
{getnumber "Enter actual amount: ",act4}{d}
{getnumber "Enter actual amount: ",act5}{d}
{home}{menubranch main_menu}

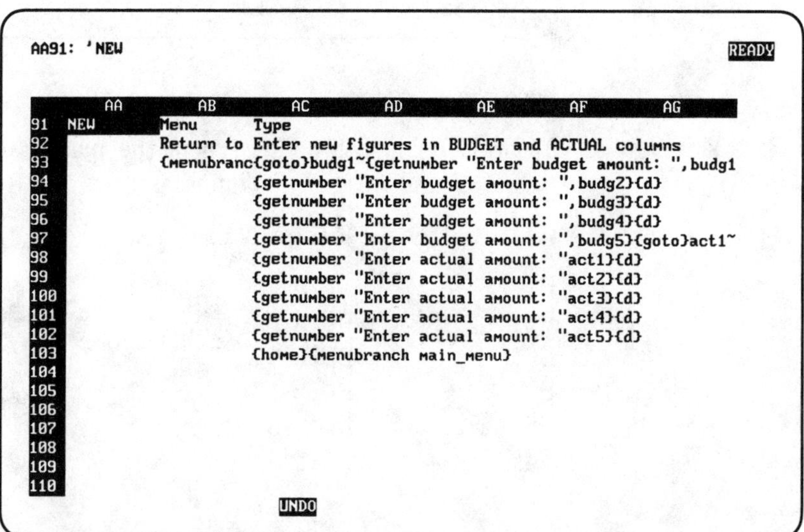

Figure 14.22 The NEW routine with both options

The instructions in column AC overlap some of the instructions in column AB. Even though you can't see the entire command description and {MENUBRANCH} command, they are stored in cells AB92 and AB93.

Save the worksheet before you continue.

When you choose New from the main macro menu, 1-2-3 displays a submenu with two items: Menu and Type. A command description appears under the menu item that is highlighted. Try it now.

Press: ALT – M
Select: New
Press: → ←

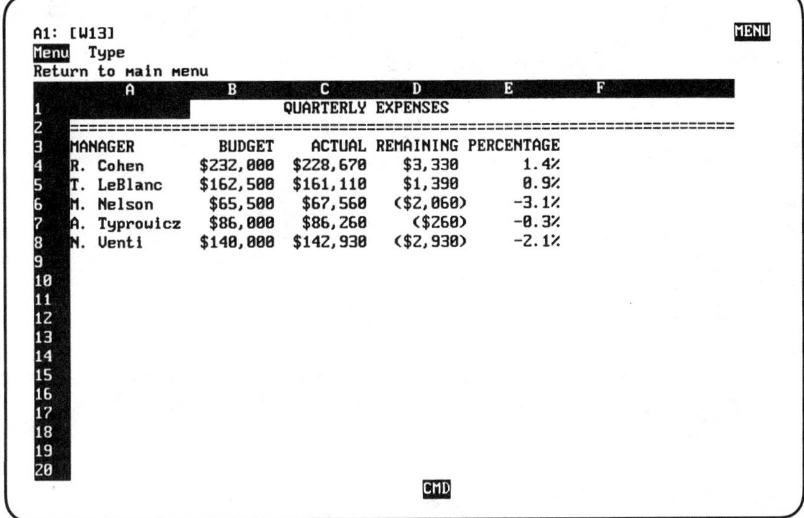

Figure 14.23
The NEW routine submenu

Leave the submenu and main menu.

Select: Menu
Press: ESC

When you choose Type from the New submenu, the routine moves the pointer to cell BUDG1 (C4) and asks for a budget amount. The routine repeats this process for all of the cells in the BUDGET and ACTUAL columns and then moves the pointer to cell A1 and returns to the main macro menu. Choosing Type always replaces existing entries in these cells. Even if you simply press Enter, the existing entries disappear and the cells are blank.

Entering the EXIT Routine

The EXIT routine lets you leave the main macro menu. Like the NEW routine, the EXIT routine displays a submenu so you can confirm your choice.

Document the name of the routine (EXIT) in cell AA105 and start the routine in cell AB105.

The EXIT routine displays a submenu that offers the choice of ending the macro (Yes) or returning to the main macro menu (No). Enter the No menu item first; enter each line in a separate cell.

Move to: cell AB105
Type: No
Do not end macro
{menubranch main_menu}

Save the worksheet before you continue.

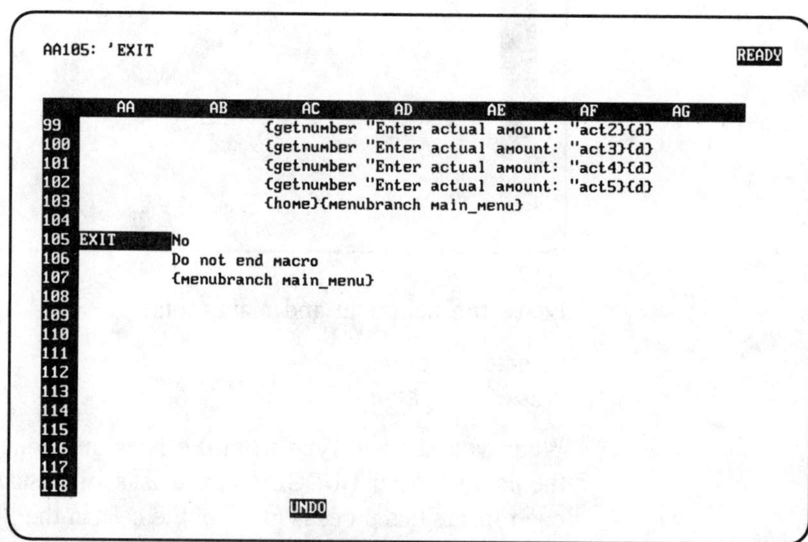

Figure 14.24
The EXIT routine
No option

The Yes submenu moves the pointer to cell A1 and then ends the macro with a {QUIT} command. Now enter the Yes option; enter each line in a separate cell in column AC.

Move to: cell AC105
Type: Yes
End macro
{home}{quit}

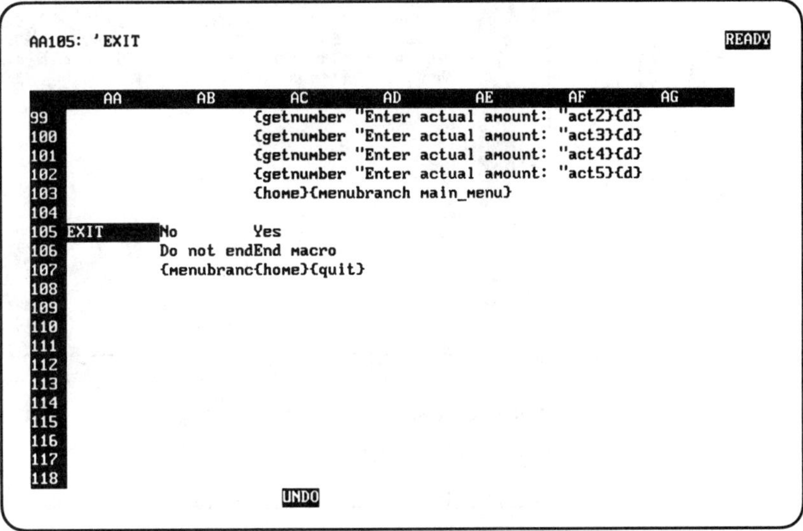

Figure 14.25
The EXIT routine

The EXIT submenu works like the main macro menu or the NEW routine: it is invoked with the advanced macro command {MENUBRANCH} and provides menu items, command descriptions, and instructions for each option.

Save the worksheet before you continue.

TESTING THE MACRO MENU

The macro menu is complex. If any of the routines fail to run properly when you test them, go back and check the routine you entered against the illustration.

Now that the macro menu is complete, you can try it.

Press: ALT – M

Figure 14.26
The macro menu

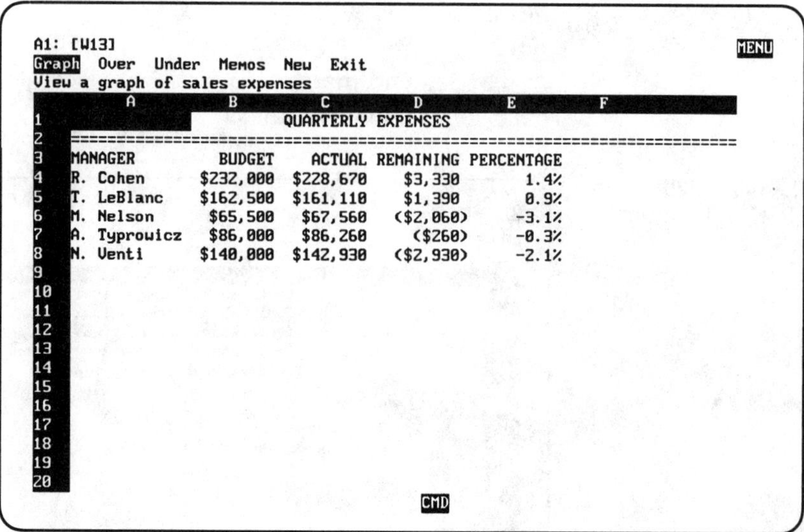

The menu appears at the top of the screen. (If the menu doesn't appear, check for errors in the starting macro.)

You may have tested some or all of the menu items already. Skip those you've already tested if you want to, but test each menu item at least once to be sure it's working properly.

Use Right to move the menu pointer through the menu items. Notice how the descriptions change as you move from item to item. Highlight each of the menu items in turn.

Press: → five times
Select: Graph

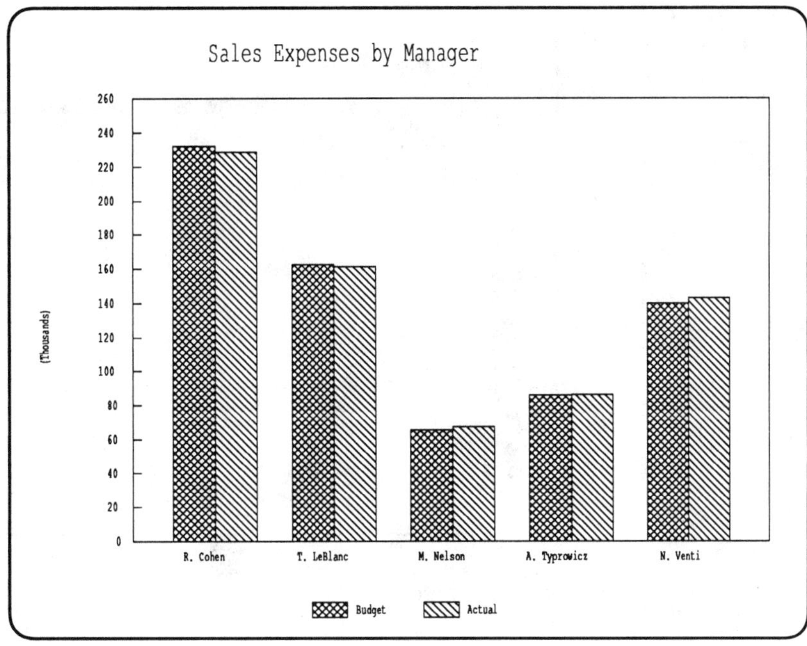

Figure 14.27 The bar graph appears

A bar graph that shows the budgeted and actual sales expenses for each manager should appear. To clear the graph, press any key.

Now try the next menu item.

Select: Over

The pointer moves to cell CRIT (D22) while the macro checks the REMAINING field for entries that are less than zero. The macro then displays a list of managers over budget, beginning in row 26.

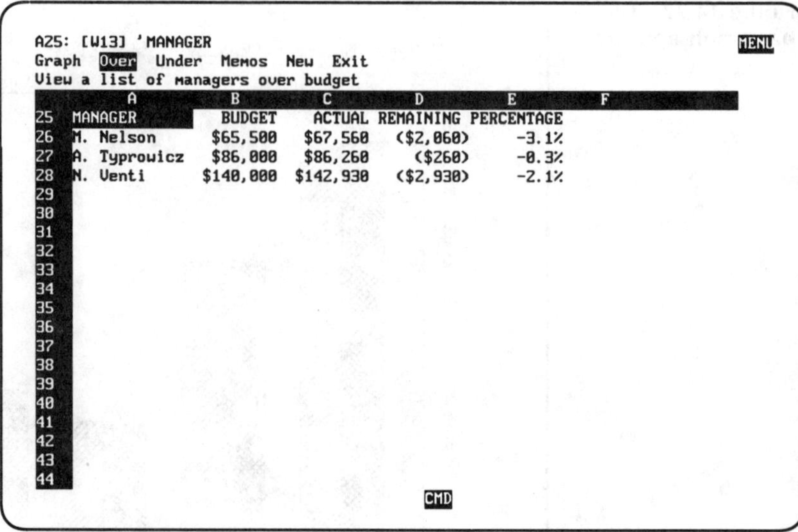

Figure 14.28 The over budget list

Try the next macro item:

Select: Under

Once again, the cell pointer moves to cell CRIT (D22) while the macro tests the REMAINING field entries. Then the macro displays a list of managers who are under budget, beginning in row 26.

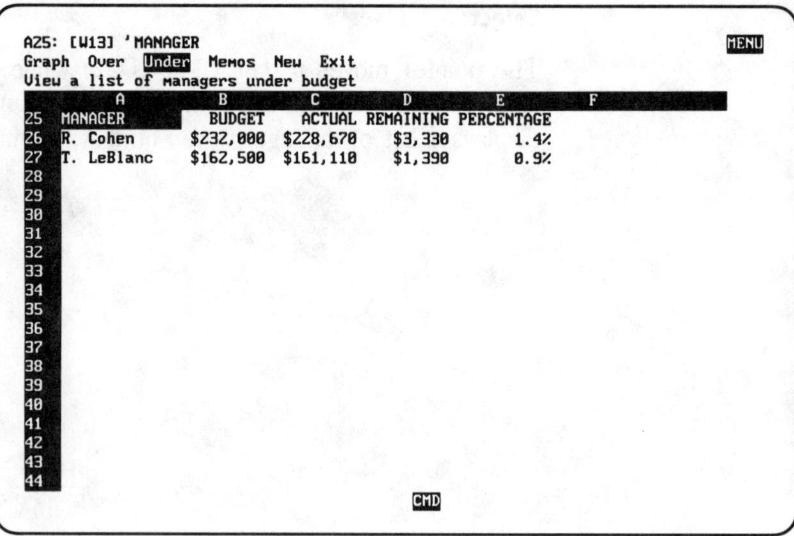

Figure 14.29 The under budget list

Before you select the Memos menu item, make sure your printer is turned on and ready.

Select: Memos

Figure 14.30 Five different memos produced by macro

```
                                                19-Jul-89
To: A. Typrowicz
From: Loren Miller
Sub    : Sales Expenses for the quarter ending 7/89
         les expenses for the last quarter was $86000.
          the quarter was $86260.  You are over
                                      irm these figures.
```

```
                                                19-Jul-89
To: R. Cohen
From: Loren Miller
Subject: Sales Expenses for the quarter ending 7/89

Your budget for sales expenses for the last quarter was
$232000.  Your actual outlay for the quarter was $2
are under budget by 1.4%.

Please call the Finance Depa

Thank you.
```

```
                                                19-Jul-89
To: N. Venti
From: Loren Miller
  bject: Sales Expenses for the quarter ending 7/89
             expenses for the last quarter was
                    the quarter was $142930.  You
```

```
                                                19-Jul-89
To: M. Nelson
From: Loren Miller
Subject: Sales Expenses for the quarter ending 7/89

Your budget for sales expenses for the last quarter was $65500.
Your actual outlay for the quarter was $67560.  You are over
budget by 3.1%.

Please call the Finance Department to confi

Thank you.
```

```
                                                19-Jul-89
To: T. LeBlanc
From: Loren Miller
Subject: Sales Expenses for the quarter ending 7/89

Your budget for sales expenses for the last quarter was
$162500.  Your actual outlay for the quarter was $161110.  You
are under budget by 0.9%.

Please call the Finance Department to confirm these figures.

Thank you.
```

After all the memos are printed, try the New menu item.

Select: New
Type

Type entries in response to the prompt. You saved the worksheet before you started testing the macro, so you have a copy of the original entries in a file.

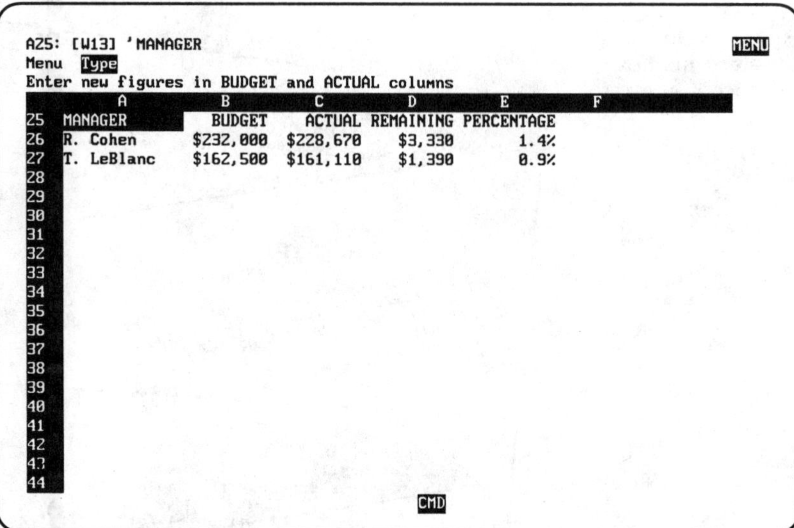

Figure 14.31
Choosing Type from the New menu

You can leave the macro menu at any time.

Select: Exit

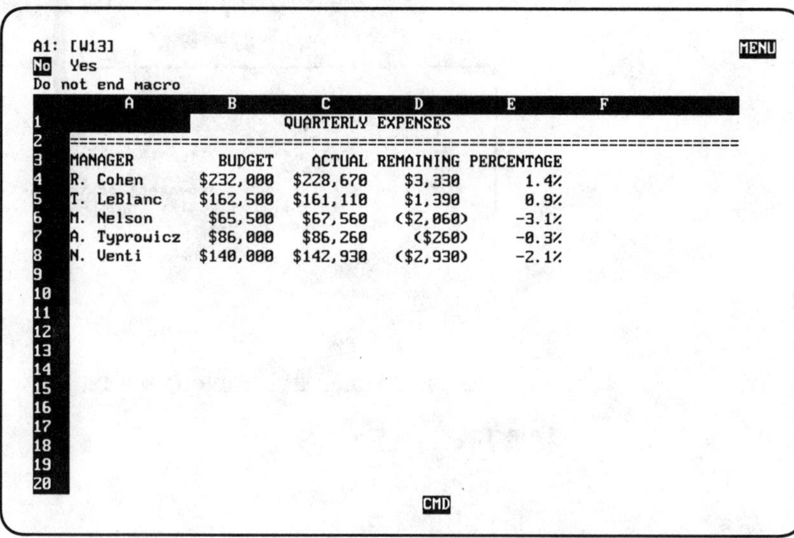

Figure 14.32
The Exit menu

Select Yes from the Exit submenu to end the macro, or select No to keep using the macro menu. As with any 1-2-3 menu, you can also back out of the macro menu by pressing Esc.

REFINING THE MACRO MENU

As the routines run, the screen changes constantly. To eliminate most of this activity, add {PANELOFF}/{PANELON} and {WINDOWSOFF}/{WINDOWSON} commands to each routine. (You already entered these commands in the MEMOS routine.)

These commands freeze the control panel and screen and keep them from changing while the macro runs. The "on" and "off" versions of these commands are used in tandem: you turn off the panel and/or window at one point in a macro and then turn it back on.

When the panel and window are off, the lack of activity on the screen may lead you to think that the macro isn't running. You can use the {INDICATE} command to change the mode indicator and avoid this confusion.

Freezing the Control Panel and Screen

Enter {PANELOFF}/{PANELON} and {WINDOWSOFF}/{WINDOWSON} commands in the GRAPH routine.

Move to: cell AB48
Press: EDIT (F2)
HOME
→
Type: {paneloff}{windowsoff}
Press: ↵

Figure 14.33 {PANELOFF} and {WINDOWSOFF} commands added to GRAPH routine

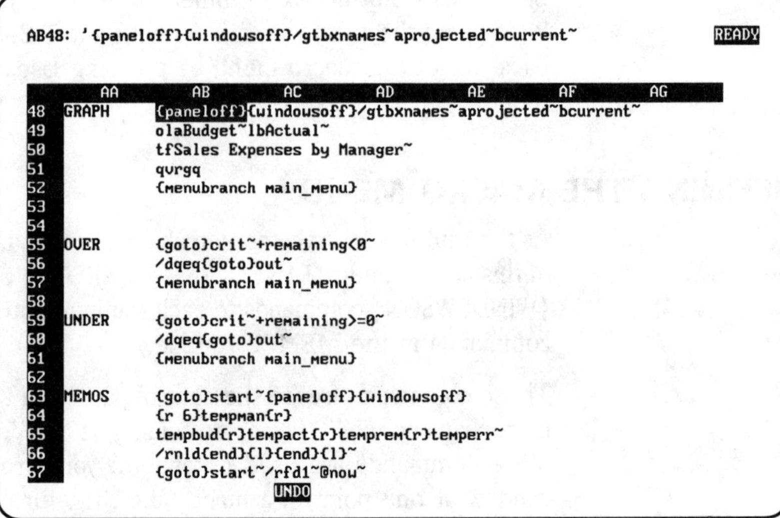

```
AB48: '{paneloff}{windowsoff}/gtbxnames~aprojected~bcurrent~          READY

      AA        AB        AC        AD        AE        AF        AG
48  GRAPH     {paneloff}{windowsoff}/gtbxnames~aprojected~bcurrent~
49            olaBudget~lbActual~
50            tfSales Expenses by Manager~
51            qvrgq
52            {menubranch main_menu}
53
54
55  OVER      {goto}crit~+remaining<0~
56            /dqeq{goto}out~
57            {menubranch main_menu}
58
59  UNDER     {goto}crit~+remaining>=0~
60            /dqeq{goto}out~
61            {menubranch main_menu}
62
63  MEMOS     {goto}start~{paneloff}{windowsoff}
64            {r 6}tempman{r}
65            tempbud{r}tempact{r}temprem{r}temperr~
66            /rnld{end}{l}{end}{l}~
67            {goto}start~/rfd1~@now~
                              UNDO
```

Move to: cell AB51
Press: EDIT (F2)
HOME
→ twice
Type: {windowson}
Press: END
Type: {panelon}
Press: ↵

Figure 14.34
The edited GRAPH routine

You must use the {WINDOWSON} command before the macro selects the **View** command, or you won't be able to see the graph.

Now hold down Alt and type m to invoke the menu macro. Select Graph. This time, the 1-2-3 graph settings sheet and menus do not appear on the screen; only the completed graph appears. Press Esc to clear the graph and return to the macro menu (it takes a few seconds for the menu to reappear) and select Exit followed by Yes to end the macro.

Next add the {PANELOFF}/{PANELON} and {WINDOWSOFF}/{WINDOWSON} commands to the OVER routine.

Move to: cell AB55
Press: EDIT (F2)
HOME
→
Type: {paneloff}{windowsoff}
Press: ↓
EDIT (F2)
Type: {panelon}{windowson}
Press: ↵

Figure 14.35
The edited OVER routine

Now add the {PANELOFF}/{PANELON} and {WINDOWSOFF}/{WINDOWSON} commands to the UNDER routine.

Move to: cell AB59
Press: EDIT (F2)
HOME
→
Type: {paneloff}{windowsoff}
Press: ↓
EDIT (F2)
Type: {panelon}{windowson}
Press: ↵

Figure 14.36
The edited UNDER routine

Before you continue, save the file.

Try the macro again. Hold down Alt and type m. Then select the Over and Under options. The names of the managers who are over or under budget appear without the cell pointer first moving to cell E22.

You don't need to add these commands to the MEMOS and NEW routines. You entered the {PANELOFF} and {WINDOWSOFF} commands in the MEMOS routine when you created it. In the NEW routine, you need to see the changes that take place on the screen.

Changing the Mode Indicator

When you use the GRAPH, OVER, and UNDER routines now that you have added {WINDOWSOFF} and {PANELOFF} commands, it may seem that nothing happens for a short time after you choose the menu item. (With the MEMOS routine, which also contains {WINDOWSOFF} and {PANELOFF} commands, it takes quite a while for the screen to change.)

The {WINDOWSOFF} and {PANELOFF} commands freeze the screen display so that it doesn't change—only the CMD indicator in the status line tells you that 1-2-3 is running a macro. When the screen isn't changing and the READY indicator is on, it may seem as if the macro isn't working.

One way to show that the routine is working is to use the {INDICATE} command. This command lets you change, remove, or restore the mode indicator in the upper right corner of the screen, depending on whether you use a text argument, a blank argument, or no argument. (In Chapter 13, you used {INDICATE} to display a message to the user.)

Command	**Action**
{INDICATE "MEMOS"}	Changes the mode indicator so it reads MEMOS.
{INDICATE " "}	Removes the mode indicator altogether.
{INDICATE}	Restores the indicator so it reflects the mode 1-2-3 is in (for example, READY, WAIT, EDIT, and so on).

Changing the mode indicator to the routine's name while the routine is running lets you know that 1-2-3 is carrying out the instructions. Add an {INDICATE} command with the routine name as the argument *before* every {PANELOFF} command and add an {INDICATE} command with no argument at the end of each routine.

Edit the GRAPH routine first.

Move to: cell AB48
Press: EDIT (F2)
HOME
→
Type: {indicate "GRAPH'}
Press: ↵

```
AB48: '{indicate "GRAPH"}{paneloff}{windowsoff}/gtbxnames~aprojected~bcurre READY

        AA        AB        AC        AD        AE        AF        AG
48 GRAPH     {indicate "GRAPH"}{paneloff}{windowsoff}/gtbxnames~aprojected~
49           olaBudget~lbActual~
50           tfSales Expenses by Manager~
51           q{windowson}vrgq{panelon}
52           {menubranch main_menu}
53
54
55 OVER      {paneloff}{windowsoff}{goto}crit~+remaining<0~
56           /dqeq{goto}out~{panelon}{windowson}
57           {menubranch main_menu}
58
59 UNDER     {paneloff}{windowsoff}{goto}crit~+remaining>=0~
60           /dqeq{goto}out~{panelon}{windowson}
61           {menubranch main_menu}
62
63 MEMOS     {goto}start~{paneloff}{windowsoff}
64           {r 6}tempman{r}
65           tempbud{r}tempact{r}temprem{r}temperr~
66           /rnld{end}{l}{end}{l}~
67           {goto}start~/rfd1~@now~
                         UNDO
```

Figure 14.37 The {INDICATE "GRAPH"} instruction precedes the {PANELOFF} command in cell AB48

Move to: cell AB51
Press: EDIT (F2)
Type: {indicate}
Press: ↵

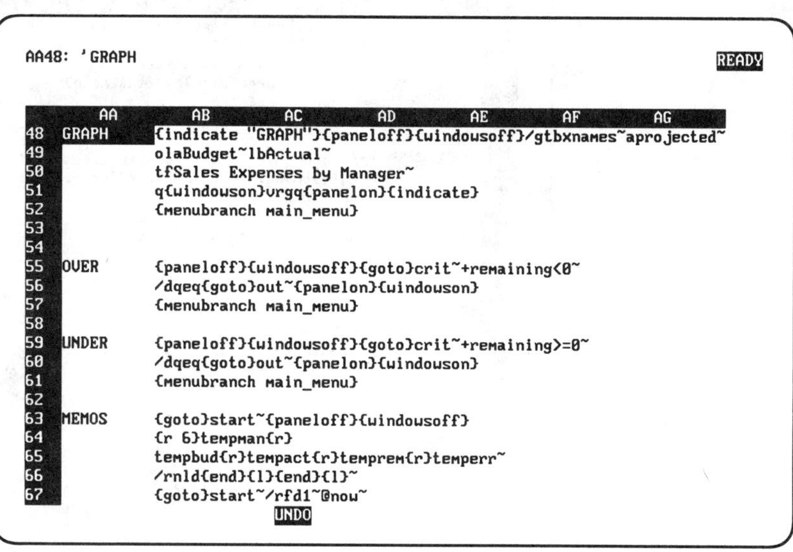
```
AA48: 'GRAPH                                                              READY

        AA        AB        AC        AD        AE        AF        AG
48 GRAPH     {indicate "GRAPH"}{paneloff}{windowsoff}/gtbxnames~aprojected~
49           olaBudget~lbActual~
50           tfSales Expenses by Manager~
51           q{windowson}vrgq{panelon}{indicate}
52           {menubranch main_menu}
53
54
55 OVER      {paneloff}{windowsoff}{goto}crit~+remaining<0~
56           /dqeq{goto}out~{panelon}{windowson}
57           {menubranch main_menu}
58
59 UNDER     {paneloff}{windowsoff}{goto}crit~+remaining>=0~
60           /dqeq{goto}out~{panelon}{windowson}
61           {menubranch main_menu}
62
63 MEMOS     {goto}start~{paneloff}{windowsoff}
64           {r 6}tempman{r}
65           tempbud{r}tempact{r}temprem{r}temperr~
66           /rnld{end}{l}{end}{l}~
67           {goto}start~/rfd1~@now~
                         UNDO
```

Figure 14.38 The final GRAPH routine

Now hold down Alt and type m to invoke the menu macro. Select Graph. The mode indicator changes to GRAPH. After the graph appears on the screen, press Esc to clear the graph and return to the macro menu (it takes a few seconds for the menu to reappear). The mode indicator reads MENU. Select Exit Yes to end the macro.

Save the worksheet before you continue.

Next add the {INDICATE} command to the OVER routine.

Move to: cell AB55
Press: EDIT (F2)
HOME
→
Type: {indicate "OVER"}
Press: ↓
EDIT (F2)
Type: {indicate}
Press: ↵

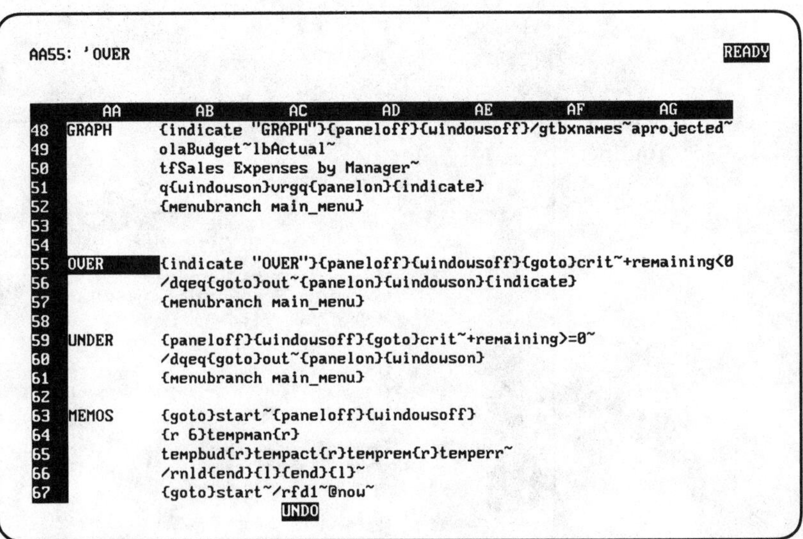

```
AA55: 'OVER                                                        READY

      AA        AB        AC        AD        AE        AF        AG
48  GRAPH     {indicate "GRAPH"}{paneloff}{windowsoff}/gtbxnames~aprojected~
49            olaBudget~lbActual~
50            tfSales Expenses by Manager~
51            q{windowson}vrgq{panelon}{indicate}
52            {menubranch main_menu}
53
54
55  OVER      {indicate "OVER"}{paneloff}{windowsoff}{goto}crit~+remaining<0
56            /dqeq{goto}out~{panelon}{windowson}{indicate}
57            {menubranch main_menu}
58
59  UNDER     {paneloff}{windowsoff}{goto}crit~+remaining>=0~
60            /dqeq{goto}out~{panelon}{windowson}
61            {menubranch main_menu}
62
63  MEMOS     {goto}start~{paneloff}{windowsoff}
64            {r 6}tempman{r}
65            tempbud{r}tempact{r}temprem{r}temperr~
66            /rnld{end}{l}{end}{l}~
67            {goto}start~/rfd1~@now~
                                  UNDO
```

Figure 14.39 The final OVER routine

Now add the {INDICATE} commands to the UNDER routine.

Move to: cell AB59
Press: EDIT (F2)
HOME
→
Type: {indicate "UNDER"}
Press: ↓
EDIT (F2)
Type: {indicate}
Press: ↵

Figure 14.40 The final UNDER routine

Try these routines again. Hold down Alt and type m. Then select the Over and Under options. The mode indicator changes to OVER or UNDER and then the correct list appears. Select Exit Yes to leave the menu and edit the MEMOS routine.

Save the worksheet before you continue.

Now add {INDICATE} commands to the MEMOS routine. The MEMOS routine illustrates one situation in which you don't use the on and off version of {PANELOFF}, {WINDOWSOFF}, and {INDICATE} in tandem. The first line of the MEMOS routine contains {PANELOFF} and {WINDOWSOFF} commands. So does the first line of the TEXT routine.

The second-to-last line of the TEXT routine contains {PANELON} and {WINDOWSON} commands. Each time the TEXT routine runs, these {PANELON} and {WINDOWSON} commands restore the screen. To freeze the screen for subsequent memos, the first line of the TEXT routine must repeat the {PANELOFF} and {WINDOWSOFF} commands that appear in the first line of the MEMOS routine. (The MEMOS routine issues the {PANELOFF} and {WINDOWSOFF} commands twice the first time it runs, but the second command has no effect.)

You must enter {INDICATE "MEMOS"} before the {PANELOFF} command in the MEMOS routine *and* the {PANELOFF} command in the TEXT routine. You need to enter {INDICATE} only once, in the last line of the MEMOS routine.

Move to: cell AB63
Press: EDIT (F2)
HOME
BIG RIGHT (Ctrl-Right) twice
→ three times to move the cursor after ~
Type: {indicate "MEMOS"}
Press: ↵
Move to: cell AB69
Press: EDIT (F2)
HOME
BIG RIGHT (Ctrl-Right) twice
→ to move the cursor after r
Type: {indicate}
Press: ↵
Move to: cell AB71
Press: EDIT (F2)
HOME
BIG RIGHT (Ctrl-Right) twice
→ three times to move the cursor after ~
Type: {indicate "MEMOS"}
Press: ↵

Figure 14.41 The final MEMOS routine

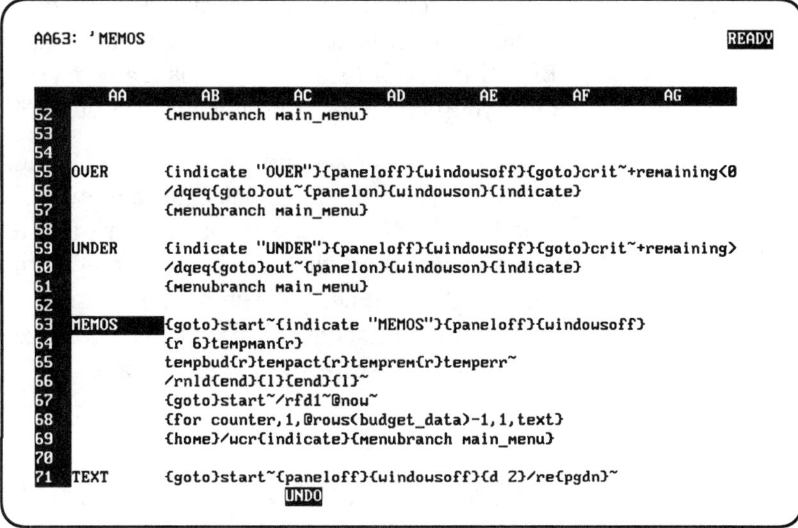

```
AA63: 'MEMOS                                                          READY

      AA        AB        AC        AD        AE        AF        AG
52               {menubranch main_menu}
53
54
55  OVER         {indicate "OVER"}{paneloff}{windowsoff}{goto}crit~+remaining<0
56               /dqeq{goto}out~{panelon}{windowson}{indicate}
57               {menubranch main_menu}
58
59  UNDER        {indicate "UNDER"}{paneloff}{windowsoff}{goto}crit~+remaining>
60               /dqeq{goto}out~{panelon}{windowson}{indicate}
61               {menubranch main_menu}
62
63  MEMOS        {goto}start~{indicate "MEMOS"}{paneloff}{windowsoff}
64               {r 6}tempman{r}
65               tempbud{r}tempact{r}temprem{r}temperr~
66               /rnld{end}{l}{end}{l}~
67               {goto}start~/rfd1~@now~
68               {for counter,1,@rows(budget_data)-1,1,text}
69               {home}/ucr{indicate}{menubranch main_menu}
70
71  TEXT         {goto}start~{paneloff}{windowsoff}{d 2}/re{pgdn}~
                           UNDO
```

Figure 14.42 The final TEXT routine

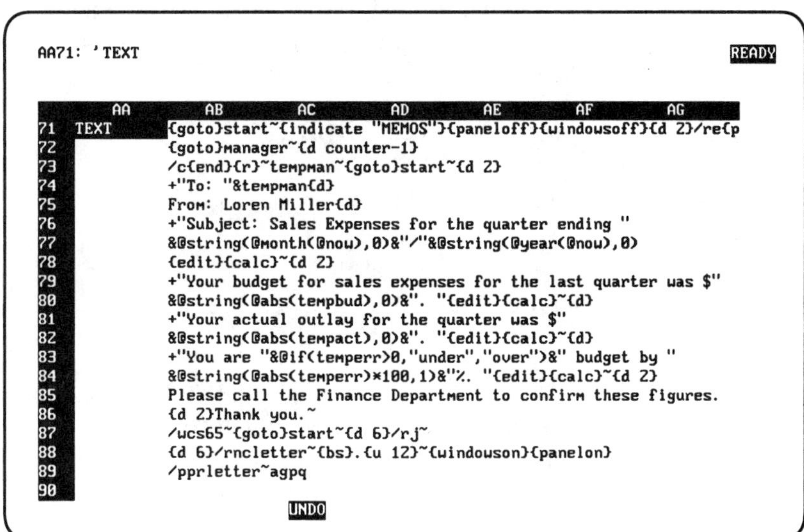

```
AA71: 'TEXT                                                           READY

      AA        AB        AC        AD        AE        AF        AG
71  TEXT         {goto}start~{indicate "MEMOS"}{paneloff}{windowsoff}{d 2}/re{p
72               {goto}manager~{d counter-1}
73               /c{end}{r}~tempman~{goto}start~{d 2}
74               +"To: "&tempman{d}
75               From: Loren Miller{d}
76               +"Subject: Sales Expenses for the quarter ending "
77               &@string(@month(@now),0)&"/"&@string(@year(@now),0)
78               {edit}{calc}~{d 2}
79               +"Your budget for sales expenses for the last quarter was $"
80               &@string(@abs(tempbud),0)&". "{edit}{calc}~{d}
81               +"Your actual outlay for the quarter was $"
82               &@string(@abs(tempact),0)&". "{edit}{calc}~{d}
83               +"You are "&@if(temperr>0,"under","over")&" budget by "
84               &@string(@abs(temperr)*100,1)&"%. "{edit}{calc}~{d 2}
85               Please call the Finance Department to confirm these figures.
86               {d 2}Thank you.~
87               /ucs65~{goto}start~{d 6}/rj~
88               {d 6}/rncletter~{bs}.{u 12}~{windowson}{panelon}
89               /pprletter~agpq
90
                           UNDO
```

Before you continue, save the worksheet.

You can try the memos routine again to see the mode indicator. Hold down Alt, type m, and select Memos. The mode indicator changes to MEMOS and the routine prints five memos.

The NEW routine doesn't contain {PANELOFF} and {WINDOWSOFF} commands because you need to see information as you enter it. The READY indicator tells you 1-2-3 is ready to accept your entries; therefore, you don't need to enter any {INDICATE} commands.

If you stop a macro before it reaches the {INDICATE} command, 1-2-3 doesn't restore the mode indicator automatically. For example, if you stop the MEMOS routine before it prints all five memos, the MEMOS mode indicator remains on the screen even though you're no longer running the routine. To restore the normal 1-2-3 indicator, create a macro that consists of the {INDICATE} command alone. Running such a macro will restore the mode indicator.

INVOKING THE MENU MACRO AUTOMATICALLY

A menu that you create may be intended for use by many people. If so, you may want to have the macro start automatically whenever someone retrieves the file. To do this, you must name the macro \0 (backslash zero).

Move to: cell AB40
Press: /
Select: Range
Name
Create
Type: \0
Press: ↵

The starting macro now has two names: \0 and \M. Document the name \0 in cell Z40. Although you can't run a \0 macro manually with the Alt key, you can do so with Run (Alt-F3). In this case, you can run the macro with Alt-m also.

Use the file saving macro to save the worksheet. After you've saved it, retrieve it to start the macro automatically:

Press: /
Select: File
Retrieve
SALESEXP

The macro starts as soon as you retrieve the file, and the macro menu appears in the control panel. If you don't want to use the macro right now, select Exit Yes.

(2.2) You can use \0 only once in each worksheet. 1-2-3 Release 2.2 is set up to start a \0 macro (called an **autoexecute macro**) automatically when you retrieve the worksheet that contains the macro. If you don't want the macro started automatically when you retrieve the worksheet, you have the option of selecting **/Worksheet Global Default Autoexec No** to change the default setting.

Appendix A: Working with 1–2–3 Add-In Programs

Add-in programs are programs that run with 1–2–3 to extend its power and functionality. You can start an add-in with a single keystroke and return to 1–2–3 just as quickly.

The 1–2–3 package includes two add-ins:

- Allways (described in Chapter 6) lets you format and print presentation-quality worksheets.
- The Macro Library Manager (described in Chapter 12) lets you store macros and data in a library so they can be used with any worksheet.

Numerous add-ins are available from other manufacturers. Always read the documentation that accompanies the add-in to be sure you set up and use the add-in correctly.

To use an add-in, you must first attach and invoke it. **Attaching** means loading the add-in into memory. **Invoking** means activating the add-in so you can use its commands.

Once you finish working with an add-in, you can **detach** it, or unload it from memory.

You attach, invoke, and detach add-ins by using the Add-In commands.

This appendix explains how to attach, invoke, and detach add-ins manually, as well as how to attach and invoke add-ins automatically at the start of each 1–2–3 session.

> NOTE: The instructions that follow assume you work with add-ins by using the Add-In commands from the 1–2–3 main menu. You can also, however, display the Add-In commands by pressing App4 (Alt-F10) if you haven't assigned this key to an add-in. Key assignments are discussed in the next section.

ATTACHING AN ADD-IN

Attaching an add-in loads it into memory. The add-in will remain in memory until you detach it or end the 1–2–3 session.

During the process of attaching an add-in, 1–2–3 will ask you to select a key for invoking the add-in. You have a choice of App1 (Alt-F7), App2 (Alt-F8), App3 (Alt-F9), App4 (Alt-F10), or no key. If you don't assign the add-in to a key, you will have to invoke it using **/Add-In Invoke**.

1–2–3 must be running before you can work with add-ins.

If you have a two-diskette computer, place the disk that contains the add-in you're attaching in one of the disk drives. On a hard-disk computer, the add-in will generally be in the directory that contains the 1–2–3 program files.

Press: [/]
Select: Add-In
Attach

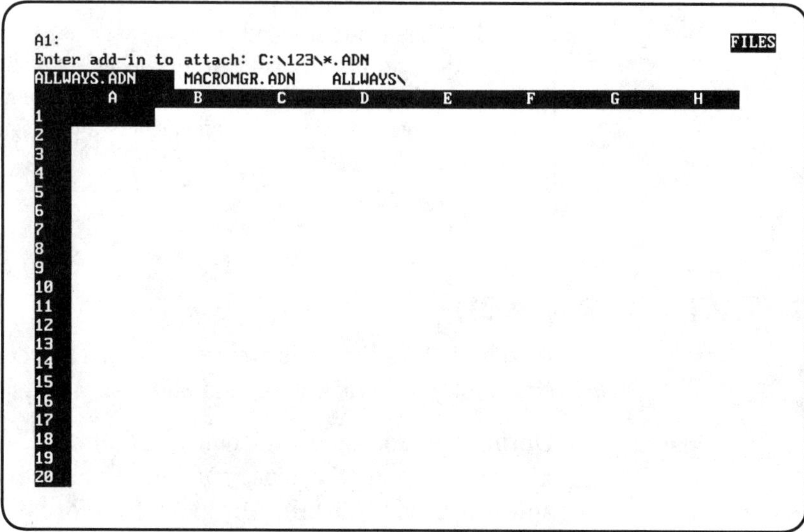

Figure A.1 Add-ins listed

1-2-3 displays all the files with a .ADN extension in the directory from which you started 1-2-3. An .ADN extension indicates an add-in program. To see files in another drive or directory, press Esc to clear the file names and enter the new drive and/or directory.

Select: the add-in you want to attach

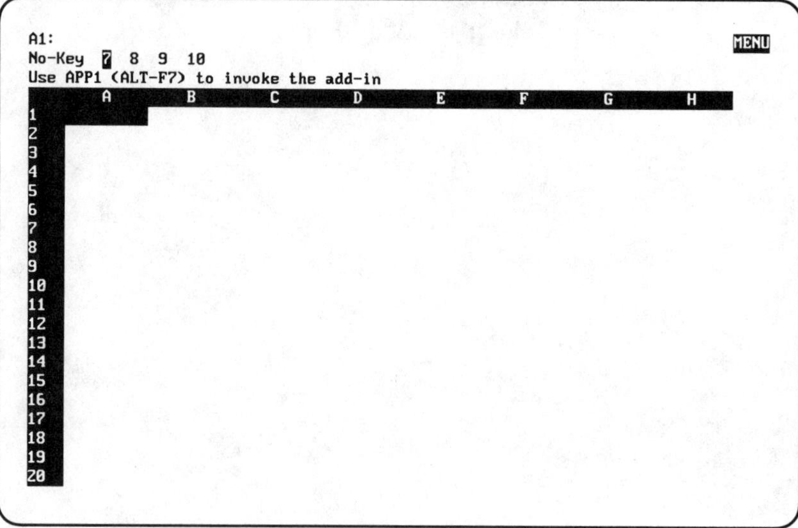

Figure A.2 Key choices for invoking the add-in

1-2-3 now displays a menu listing the key choices for invoking the add-in. If you've already assigned a key to another add-in, it won't appear in the menu 1-2-3 displays.

Select: the key you want to use or No-Key

The add-in is now in memory, ready to be invoked (activated).

If you use an add-in frequently, you may want to consider attaching it automatically each time you start 1-2-3. See "Attaching and Invoking Add-Ins Automatically" later in this appendix.

INVOKING AN ADD-IN

Once you're ready to use an add-in you've attached, you must invoke it.

You can invoke an add-in in one of two ways: with the key you selected when attaching the add-in or with the **Add-In Invoke** command.

To use a key:

Press: the key you selected when you attached the add-in (App1 (Alt-F7), App2 (Alt-F8), App3 (Alt-F9), or App4 (Alt-F10))

To use the **Add-In Invoke** command:

Press: /
Select: Add-In
Invoke

1-2-3 will display the names of all the add-ins currently attached.

Select: the add-in you want to activate

What happens after you invoke the add-in depends on the particular add-in. Each add-in works differently. For example, when you invoke the Macro Library Manager, its menu appears.

DETACHING ADD-INS

Add-ins take up memory, so it's usually a good idea to remove them from memory once you finish working with them. This will give you more room for large worksheets, other add-ins, or the undo feature. (Unless you have expanded memory—memory for which you've purchased special software and hardware—you may run out of memory if the undo feature is on and a particular add-in is invoked. You can turn off undo with **/Worksheet Global Default Other Undo Disable**.) You can remove, or detach, either a specific add-in or all add-ins currently in memory.

To detach a single add-in:

Press: /
Select: Add-In
Detach
the add-in you want to detach

The add-in is no longer in memory. To use it again, you must attach and invoke it once more.

To detach all add-ins:

Press: /
Select: Add-In
Clear

1–2–3 removes all add-ins from memory.

ATTACHING AND INVOKING ADD-INS AUTOMATICALLY

If you use one or more add-ins frequently, consider having them attached automatically whenever you start 1–2–3. This will save you from attaching the add-in(s) manually each time. You can attach up to eight add-ins automatically and invoke one of them automatically at the start of a 1–2–3 session.

The setting for automatically attached add-ins is one of 1–2–3's default settings that is stored in the 1–2–3 configuration file. 1–2–3 reads this file at the start of every session to set up all the defaults correctly.

Just as when you attach an add-in manually with **/Add-In Attach**, 1–2–3 will ask you to choose a key for invoking the add-in when you specify the add-in to attach automatically. You have the choice of Appl (Alt-F7), App2 (Alt-F8), App3 (Alt-F9), App4 (Alt-F10), or no key.

To attach an add-in automatically:

Press: /

Select: Worksheet
Global
Default
Other
Add-In
Set

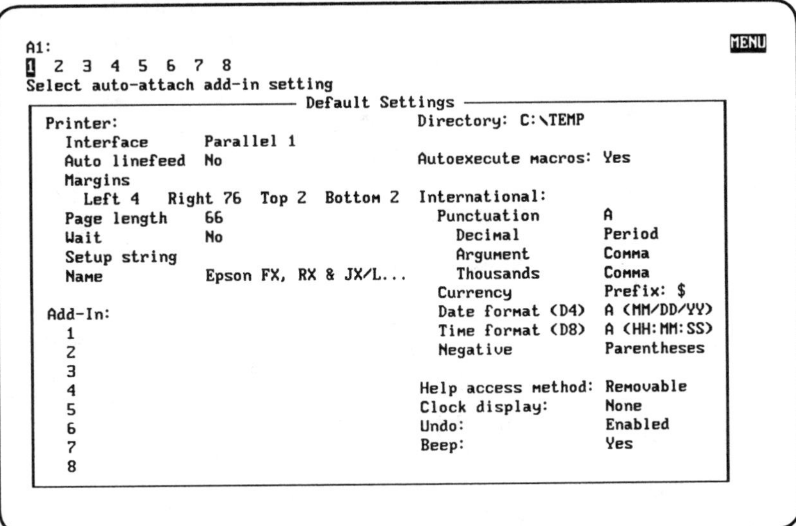

Figure A.3 Prompt for add-in to attach automatically

1-2-3 displays the default settings sheet and asks you to indicate which add-in you want to attach automatically. 1-2-3 displays the add-ins it finds in the directory from which you started it. To indicate a different directory, press Esc and type the new directory name.

Select: a number for the add-in
the add-in you want attached automatically

1-2-3 prompts for the key assignment.

Select: the key you want to use to invoke the add-in (or No-Key)

1-2-3 now asks if you want the add-in to be invoked automatically at the start of each session. This would mean that the add-in would be running as soon as you started 1–2–3. Generally, you would select No unless the add-in was designed to start running at the start of a 1–2–3 session.

Select: Yes or No
Quit

To make this default setting apply to all 1–2–3 sessions (not just the current one), you must update the 1–2–3 configuration file by selecting **/Worksheet Global Default Update**. If you don't do this, the add-in you specified won't be attached at the start of the next 1–2–3 session.

If you no longer want an add-in attached automatically at the start of every 1–2–3 session, proceed as follows:

Press: [/]
Select: Worksheet
Global
Default
Other
Add-In
Cancel
the number (1 to 8) of the add-in you wish to cancel

Then update the 1–2–3 configuration file with **/Worksheet Global Default Update** to make the change apply to future 1–2–3 sessions.

Appendix B: Using 1–2–3 Over a Network

1–2–3 Release 2.2 lets you share data files on a network that Lotus supports, thus making it easy to share data with other 1–2–3 users. You can also print your worksheets on a network printer if your computer is connected to the printer. Both activities are possible with the standard 1–2–3 Release 2.2 package.

If your company or department wants to share 1–2–3 program files as well as data files on a network, it must purchase the 1–2–3 Release 2.2 Server Edition. This package allows a certain number of licensed users to share 1–2–3 program files.

This appendix describes:

- How to share files with other 1–2–3 users
- How to print on a network (shared) printer

SHARING DATA FILES

To share data files on a network, your computer must be connected to the network and you must know how to specify the path to the shared files. (Your network administrator can help you with this.) You must also have DOS version 3.10 or higher.

When files are being shared, it's often important to limit access to them. For example, in some cases you may not want all users to see privileged information (such as salary information) that a file contains. In other cases, it may be fine for users to see the contents of the file, but you may want to limit the number of users who can change its contents.

In addition, when several users can change the contents of a file, it's important to make sure (through **concurrency controls**) that they don't inadvertently write over one another's changes.

The privilege of seeing the contents of a file is also known as **read access**. The privilege of changing a file is known as **write access**.

Limiting Read Access

You can limit who reads shared files in two ways:

- You can use 1–2–3 to save a file with a password. That way, only users who know the password can retrieve the file. For information about saving files with a password, see the description of **/File Save** in the *1–2–3 Reference* manual.
- Your network administrator can use the network software to limit access to files through the use of passwords.

Limiting Write Access

You can prevent users from changing shared files in the following ways:

- Your network administrator can use the network software to give a directory that contains shared files read-only status. This would prevent anyone from changing the files.
- You can give a file read-only status through the DOS ATTRIB command. For details, see your operating system manual.

Concurrency Controls and File Reservations

Concurrency controls don't prevent users from changing a file, but make sure that users who share files don't accidentally write over one another's changes. 1–2–3 provides concurrency controls through file reservations.

A **file reservation** is a kind of lock; it prevents different people from saving different versions of the same file with the same name at the same time.

Each file has one reservation. The reservation lets you save any changes you make in the file. When you retrieve a file on a network, you will automatically get its reservation unless someone else has retrieved the file with its reservation. If you try to retrieve a file and someone else has the reservation, 1-2-3 will inform you and give you the option of retrieving the file without a reservation. In this case, you will be able to look at (read) the file, but not save changes in it (unless you save the file under a different name). An RO (meaning *read only*) indicator at the bottom of the screen reminds you that you don't have the reservation.

NOTE: If a shared file has read-only status due to the DOS ATTRIB command or a network password, the RO indicator will appear even if a reservation is available.

Getting a Reservation

To retrieve a shared file, use **/File Retrieve** as usual, but be sure to specify the path to the file correctly. If the file reservation is available, it will automatically become yours. If someone else is using the file and has the reservation, select No to cancel the command without retrieving the file or Yes to retrieve the file without the reservation (you will be unable to save changes in the file, however).

If you're working on a file without the reservation and want to get the reservation, select **/File Admin Reservation Get**. If the reservation has become available, you will get it. (You may have to try the command more than once.) If you get the reservation, 1-2-3 removes the RO indicator from the screen. If you don't get the reservation because someone else has it, the file has changed since you retrieved it, or you don't have write access to the file, 1-2-3 will display a message.

Releasing a Reservation

If you're working on a file, but don't need the reservation (because you're not planning to save changes in the file), you can release the reservation so it's available to others. Select **/File Admin Reservation Release**. 1-2-3 will release the reservation and display the RO indicator at the bottom of the screen.

PRINTING ON A NETWORK

If your computer is connected to a network printer, you can print your worksheets on it by taking the following steps:

- Include a driver for the network printer in your driver set (see the *Setting Up 1-2-3* manual for details of installing printer drivers).
- Set up 1-2-3 so it can print on the network printer. First use **/Worksheet Global Default Printer Name** to select the network printer. Then select **/Worksheet Global Default Printer Interface** to select the printer port through which your computer connects to the network. (If necessary, ask your network administrator for help with these settings; you won't be able to print anything if they're not defined correctly.) Lastly, use **/Worksheet Global Default Update** to save the settings in the 1-2-3 configuration file so 1-2-3 uses these settings every time you start 1-2-3.
- Use the Print commands as usual to print the worksheet, but be sure to select Quit after you finish so 1-2-3 closes the connection to the printer.

Appendix C: Quick Reference

This appendix summarizes Lotus 1-2-3 Release 2.2 keys, file extensions, label prefixes, arithmetic and logical operators, @functions, and macro commands. It also contains menu trees for main menu commands in Allways, PrintGraph, and Macro Library Manager. (The 1-2-3 menu trees for the Add-In, Data, File, Graph, Print, Range, and Worksheet commands appear on the foldout card at the back of this book.)

1-2-3 KEYS

The following tables briefly describe some of the groups of keys you can use in 1-2-3: keys for moving around the worksheet, editing keys, and function keys.

Keys for Moving Around the Worksheet

Name	Description
←	Moves cell pointer left one column.
→	Moves cell pointer right one column.
↓	Moves cell pointer down one row.
↑	Moves cell pointer up one row.
BACKTAB (Shift-Tab)	Moves cell pointer left one screen.

Excerpted from Lotus 1-2-3 Release 2.2 *Quick Reference*. Used with permission of Lotus Development Corporation.

Name	Description
BIG LEFT (Ctrl-Left)	Moves cell pointer left one screen.
BIG RIGHT (Ctrl-Right)	Moves cell pointer right one screen.
END ←	Moves cell pointer left to intersection of a blank and a nonblank cell.
END →	Moves cell pointer right to intersection of a blank and a nonblank cell.
END ↑	Moves cell pointer up to intersection of a blank and a nonblank cell.
END ↓	Moves cell pointer down to intersection of a blank and a nonblank cell.
END HOME	Moves cell pointer to lower right corner of active area.
HOME	Moves cell pointer to cell A1.
PGDN	Moves cell pointer down one screen.
PGUP	Moves cell pointer up one screen.
TAB	Moves cell pointer right one screen.

Editing Keys

Name	Description
→	Moves cursor right one character.
←	Moves cursor left one character.
↑	Completes editing and moves cell pointer up one row.
↓	Completes editing and moves cell pointer down one row.
BACKSPACE	Erases character to left of cursor.
CTRL – → or TAB	Moves cursor right five characters.
CTRL – ← or SHIFT – TAB	Moves cursor left five characters.
DEL	Erases current character.
END	Moves to last character in entry.
↵	Completes editing.

Name	Description
ESC	Erases all characters in entry.
HOME	Moves to first character in entry.
INS	Switches between inserting text by moving existing text to right (INS mode), and writing over existing text (OVR mode).
PGUP	Completes editing and moves cell pointer up one screen.
PGDN	Completes editing and moves cell pointer down one screen.

Function Keys

Name	Description
ABS (F4)	**POINT and EDIT modes:** Cycles a cell or range address between relative, absolute, and mixed.
APP1 (Alt-F7)	**READY mode:** Activates add-in program assigned to key, if any.
APP2 (Alt-F8)	**READY mode:** Activates add-in program assigned to key, if any.
APP3 (Alt-F9)	**READY mode:** Activates add-in program assigned to key, if any.
APP4 (Alt-F10)	**READY mode:** If no add-in program is assigned to key, displays the Add-in menu. Otherwise, activates add-in assigned to key.
CALC (F9)	**READY mode:** Recalculates all formulas in worksheet. **VALUE and EDIT modes:** Converts a formula to its current value.
COMPOSE (Alt-F1)	**READY, EDIT, and LABEL modes:** When used in combination with alphanumeric keys, creates international characters and other characters you cannot enter directly from keyboard. For a list of compose sequences, see Appendix A.

Name	Description
EDIT (F2)	**READY mode:** Puts 1–2–3 in EDIT mode and displays contents of the current cell in control panel, so you can edit entry.
	EDIT mode: Switches between EDIT mode and LABEL mode, if entry displayed in control panel is a label, or VALUE mode, if entry displayed in control panel is a value.
GOTO (F5)	**READY mode:** Moves cell pointer directly to cell or named range you specify.
GRAPH (F10)	**READY mode:** Displays current graph.
HELP (F1)	Displays a 1–2–3 Help screen related to task you are performing.
	HELP mode: Displays first Help screen you viewed.
	ERROR mode: Displays a Help screen that explains error message 1–2–3 is displaying.
LEARN (Alt-F5)	Turns on learn feature and records subsequent keystrokes in learn range. Press LEARN (Alt-F5) again to turn off learn feature.
NAME (F3)	**POINT mode:** Displays a menu of named ranges.
	FILES and NAMES modes: Switches between displaying a menu of names in third line of control panel and displaying a full-screen menu of names.
	VALUE mode: When pressed after typing + – / ^ (or * in a formula, displays a menu of named ranges.
QUERY (F7)	**READY mode:** Repeats last /Data Query you specified.
	FIND mode: Switches 1–2–3 between FIND mode and READY mode.
RUN (Alt-F3)	**READY mode:** Displays a list of range names so you can select the name of the macro you want to run. If you press ESC after pressing RUN (Alt-F3), 1–2–3 switches to POINT mode so you can highlight the first cell of the macro you want to run.

Name	Description
STEP (Alt-F2)	Turns of STEP mode, which executes macros one step at a time for debugging. Press STEP (Alt-F2) again to turn off STEP mode.

ALLWAYS KEYS

In Allways, you can use many of the same pointer-movement keys and special keys that you are accustomed to using in 1–2–3. The following tables contain descriptions of additional keys you can use in Allways.

Allways Function Keys

Name	Description
DISPLAY (F6)	**ALLWAYS mode:** Switches screen display between graphics mode and text mode.
ENLARGE (Alt-F4)	**ALLWAYS mode:** Enlarges display. Keep pressing ENLARGE (Alt-F4) to enlarge cells up to 140% of their normal size.
GOTO (F5)	**ALLWAYS mode:** Moves cell pointer directly to cell or named range you specify.
GRAPH (F10)	**ALLWAYS mode:** Turns on graph display so you can see actual graphs on the screen. Press again to turn off graph display and display only hatched boxes that indicate range in which a graph is positioned. NOTE: Your screen display must be in graphics mode in order for you to see the actual graphs when you use GRAPH (F10).
HELP (F1)	Displays an Allways Help screen.
NAME (F3)	**POINT mode:** Displays a menu of named ranges in the worksheet. **FILES mode:** Displays a menu of file names.
REDUCE (F4)	**ALLWAYS mode:** Reduces the display. Keep pressing REDUCE (F4) to reduce cells down to 60% of their normal size.

Allways Accelerator Keys

You must specify the range you want to format before pressing an accelerator key:

- To format a single cell, move the cell pointer to that cell and press the accelerator key.
- To format a range, press . (period) to anchor the cell pointer, highlight the range you want, and then press the accelerator key.

Many of the keys listed in the following table cycle among two or more formats—keep pressing the accelerator key until the choice you want appears.

Name	Description
ALT – B	Boldface: Set/Clear
ALT – G	Print grid: On/Off
ALT – L	Lines: Outline/All/None
ALT – S	Shading: Light/Dark/Solid/None
ALT – U	Underline: Single/Double/None
ALT – 1	Sets Font 1
ALT – 2	Sets Font 2
ALT – 3	Sets Font 3
ALT – 4	Sets Font 4
ALT – 5	Sets Font 5
ALT – 6	Sets Font 6
ALT – 7	Sets Font 7
ALT – 8	Sets Font 8

FILE NAMES

Each operating system has its own guidelines for naming files, which are described in detail in your operating system documentation. In general, however, file names can be any combination of uppercase and lowercase letters, numbers, _ (underscores), and - (hyphens). They should not include spaces or contain more than eight characters. File names can also have extensions that consist of a . (period) followed by three characters.

1-2-3 automatically adds an extension appropriate to the type of file you are naming as shown in the following table:

File Type	Extension
Backup worksheet file	.BAK
Graph file	.PIC
Print or text file	.PRN
Worksheet file	.WK1

Allways automatically adds an extension appropriate to the type of file you are naming as shown in the following table:

File Type	Extension
Allways format file	.ALL
Encoded print file	.ENC
Font set library file	.AFS
Layout library file	.ALS

Macro Library Manager automatically adds the extension .MLB to macro library files when you name them.

LABEL PREFIXES

The following table lists 1-2-3 label prefixes:

Prefix	Result
'	Aligns label with left edge of cell.
"	Aligns label with right edge of cell.
^	Centers label in cell.
\	Repeats characters in label to fill cell.

> NOTE: The ¦ (split vertical bar) is also a label prefix. It is used primarily for embedded setup strings (see Appendix B of *1-2-3 Reference*) and **/Data Parse** format lines (see Chapter 4 of *1-2-3 Reference*). If used as a label prefix for a label that is located at the beginning of a row of data, the ¦ tells 1-2-3 not to print the row. If, however, the label is located elsewhere in a row (such as between other labels), the label will be left-aligned and will not print.

OPERATORS AND PRECEDENCE NUMBERS

The following table shows the arithmetic, string, and logical operators you can use in formulas and their order of precedence. The lower the precedence number, the earlier 1-2-3 performs the operation. Operations with the same precedence number are performed sequentially from left to right.

Operator	Operation	Precedence number
^	Exponentiation	1
– or +	Identification of value as negative or positive	2
* or /	Multiplication or division	3
+ or –	Addition or subtraction	4
= or <>	Equal-to or not-equal-to tests	5
< or >	Less-than or greater-than tests	5
<=	Less-than-or-equal-to test	5
>=	Greater-than-or-equal-to test	5
#NOT#	Logical-NOT test	6
#AND# or #OR#	Logical-AND or logical-OR tests	7
&	String concatenation	7

1–2–3 @FUNCTIONS

This section lists the 1–2–3 @functions in alphabetical order. Arguments for each @function are in italics. You must provide the required arguments.

@@(*location*) returns contents of the cell *location* refers to.

@ABS(*x*) calculates absolute (positive) value of *x*.

@ACOS(*x*) calculates arc cosine of *x*.

@ASIN(*x*) calculates arc sine of *x*.

@ATAN(*x*) calculates arc tangent of *x*.

@ATAN2(*x*,*y*) calculates four-quadrant arc tangent of *y*/*x*.

@AVG(*list*) averages values in *list*.

@CELL(*attribute*,*range*) returns information about an *attribute* for the first cell in *range*.

@CELLPOINTER(*attribute*) returns information about an *attribute* for current cell.

@CHAR(*x*) returns the character that corresponds to LICS code *x*.

@CHOOSE(*offset*,*list*) returns value or string in *list* specified by *offset*.

@CLEAN(*string*) removes control characters from *string*.

@CODE(*string*) returns LICS code for first character in *string*.

@COLS(*range*) counts columns in *range*.

@COS(*x*) calculates cosine of angle *x*.

@COUNT(*list*) counts nonblank cells in a *list* of ranges.

@CTERM(*interest*,*future-value*,*present-value*) calculates number of compounding periods for an investment (*present-value*) to grow to a *future-value*, given a fixed periodic *interest* rate.

@DATE(*year*,*month*,*day*) calculates date number for *year*, *month*, and *day*.

@DATEVALUE(*string*) calculates date number for a *string* that looks like a date.

@DAVG(*input,field,criteria*) averages values in a *field* of a database (*input* range) that meet criteria in the *criteria* range.

@DAY(*date-number*) calculates the day of the month, an integer from 1 to 31, in *date-number.*

@DCOUNT(*input,field,criteria*) counts nonblank cells in a *field* of a database (*input* range) that meet criteria in the *criteria* range.

@DDB(*cost,salvage,life,period*) calculates depreciation allowance of an asset using the double-declining balance method.

@DMAX(*input,field,criteria*) finds the largest value in a *field* of a database (*input* range) that meets criteria in the *criteria* range.

@DMIN(*input,field,criteria*) finds the smallest value in a *field* of a database (*input* range) that meets criteria in the *criteria* range.

@DSTD(*input,field,criteria*) calculates population standard deviation of values in a *field* of a database (*input* range) that meet criteria in the *criteria* range.

@DSUM(*input,field,criteria*) adds values in a *field* of a database (*input* range) that meet criteria in the *criteria* range.

@DVAR(*input,field,criteria*) calculates population variance of values in a *field* of a database (*input* range) that meet criteria in the *criteria* range.

@ERR returns the value ERR (error).

@EXACT(*string1,string2*) returns 1 (true) if *string1* and *string2* are the same; 0 (false) if not.

@EXP(*x*) calculates value of *e* (approximately 2.718282) raised to the power *x*.

@FALSE returns the logical value 0 (false).

@FIND(*search-string,string,start-number*) calculates first occurrence of *search-string* in *string*, beginning with *start-number.*

@FV(*payments,interest,term*) calculates future value of a series of equal *payments*, given a periodic *interest* rate and number of payment periods (*term*).

@HLOOKUP(*x,range,row-offset*) returns contents of cell in specified row (*row-offset*) of horizontal lookup table (*range*).

@HOUR(*time-number*) calculates the hour, an integer from 0 to 23, in *time-number.*

@IF(*condition,x,y*) evaluates *condition* and returns *x* if *condition* is true; *y* if false.

@INDEX(*range,column-offset,row-offset*) returns value in cell located at specified *column-offset* and *row-offset* in *range*.

@INT(*x*) returns integer portion of *x*, without rounding the value.

@IRR(*guess,range*) calculates internal rate of return for a series of cash flows in *range*, based on the percentage *guess*.

@ISAAF(*name*) returns 1 (true) if *name* is a defined add-in @function; 0 (false) if not.

@ISAPP(*name*) returns 1 (true) if *name* is an attached add-in @function; 0 (false) if not.

@ISERR(*x*) returns 1 (true) if *x* is the value ERR; 0 (false) if not.

@ISNA(*x*) returns 1 (true) if *x* is the value NA; 0 (false) if not.

@ISNUMBER(*x*) returns 1 (true) if *x* is a value or a blank cell; 0 (false) if *x* is a string.

@ISSTRING(*x*) returns 1 (true) if *x* is a string; 0 (false) if *x* is a value or a blank cell.

@LEFT(*string,n*) returns first *n* characters in *string*.

@LENGTH(*string*) counts characters in *string*.

@LN(*x*) calculates natural logarithm (base *e*) of *x*.

@LOG(*x*) calculates common logarithm (base 10) of *x*.

@LOWER(*string*) converts all letters in *string* to lowercase.

@MAX(*list*) finds largest value in *list*.

@MID(*string,start-number,n*) returns *n* characters from *string*, beginning with character at *string-number.*

@MIN(*list*) finds smallest value in *list*.

@MINUTE(*time-number*) calculates the minutes, an integer from 0 to 59, in *time-number.*

@MOD(*x,y*) calculates remainder (modulus) of *x/y.*

@MONTH(*date-number*) calculates the month, an integer from 1 to 12, in *date-number.*

@N(*range*) returns the entry in first cell of *range* as a value.

@NA returns the value NA (not available).

@NOW calculates date and time numbers that correspond to the current data and time based on your computer's clock.

@NPV(*interest,range*) calculates net present value of a series of future cash flows (*range*), discounted at a fixed, periodic *interest* rate.

@PI returns the value π (calculated at 3.1415926536).

@PMT(*principal,interest,term*) calculates amount of periodic payment needed to pay off a loan (*principal*), given a specified *interest* rate and number of payment periods (*term*).

@PROPER(*string*) converts letters in *string* to proper capitalization; the first letter of each word uppercase with remaining letters lowercase.

@PV(*payments,interest,term*) calculates present value of a series of equal *payments*, discounted at a periodic *interest* rate and given a number of payment periods (*term*).

@RAND generates random number between 0 and 1.

@RATE(*future-value,present-value,term*) calculates periodic interest rate necessary for investment (*present-value*) to grow to a *future-value*, given a number of compounding periods (*term*).

@REPEAT(*string,n*) duplicates *string n* times.

@REPLACE(*original-string,start-number,n,new-string*) replaces *n* characters in *original-string* beginning at *start-number,* with *new-string.*

@RIGHT(*string,n*) returns last *n* characters in *string.*

@ROUND(*x,n*) rounds value *x* to *n* places.

@ROWS(*range*) counts rows in *range*.

@S(*range*) returns the entry in first cell of *range* as a label.

@SECOND(*time-number*) calculates the seconds, an integer from 0 to 59, in *time-number.*

@SIN(*x*) calculates sine of angle *x*.

@SLN(*cost,salvage,life*) calculates straight-line depreciation allowance of an asset for one period.

@SQRT(*x*) calculates positive square root of *x*.

@STD(*list*) calculates population standard deviation of values in *list*.

@STRING(*x,n*) converts value *x* into label with *n* decimal places.

@SUM(*list*) adds values in *list*.

@SYD(*cost,salvage,life,period*) calculates sum-of-the-years'-digits depreciation allowance of an asset for a specified *period*.

@TAN(*x*) calculates tangent of angle *x*.

@TERM(*payments,interest,future-value*) calculates the number of payment periods in the term of an investment necessary to accumulate a *future-value*, assuming *payments* of equal value, when the investment earns a periodic *interest* rate.

@TIME(*hour,minutes,seconds*) calculates time number for *hour, minutes*, and *seconds*.

@TIMEVALUE(*string*) calculates time number for a *string* that look like a time.

@TRIM(*string*) returns *string* with no leading, trailing, or consecutive spaces.

@TRUE returns the logical value 1 (true).

@UPPER(*string*) converts all letters in *string* to uppercase.

@VALUE(*string*) converts number entered as *string* to its actual numeric value.

@VAR(*list*) calculates population variance of values in *list*.

@VLOOKUP(*x,range,column-offset*) returns contents of cell in specified column (*column-offset*) of vertical lookup table (*range*).

@YEAR(*date-number*) calculates the year, an integer from 0 (1900) to 199 (2099), in *date-number.*

MACRO KEY NAMES

1–2–3 Key	Macro Keystroke Instruction
↓	{DOWN} or {D}
↑	{UP} or {U}
←	{LEFT} or {L}
→	{RIGHT} or {R}
ABS (F4)	{ABS}
APP1 (Alt-F7)	{APP1}
APP2 (Alt-F8)	{APP2}
APP3 (Alt-F9)	{APP3}
APP4 (Alt-F10)	{APP4}
BACKSPACE	{BACKSPACE} or {BS}
BIG LEFT (Ctrl-Left) or BACKTAB (Shift-Tab)	{BIGLEFT}
BIG RIGHT (Ctrl-Right) or TAB	{BIGRIGHT}
CALC (F9)	{CALC}
DEL	{DELETE} or {DEL}
EDIT (F2)	{EDIT}
END	{END}
↵	{
ESC	{ESCAPE} or {ESC}
GOTO (F5)	{GOTO}
GRAPH (F10)	{GRAPH}
HELP (F1)	{HELP}
HOME	{HOME}

1-2-3 Key	Macro Keystroke Instruction
INS	{INSERT} or {INS}
NAME (F3)	{NAME}
PGUP	{PGUP}
PGDN	{PGDN}
QUERY (F7)	{QUERY}
TABLE (F8)	{TABLE}
WINDOW (F6)	{WINDOW}
/ (slash or < (less-than symbol)	/, < or {MENU}
~ (tilde)	{~}
{ (open brace)	{ { }
} (close brace)	{ } }

ADVANCED MACRO COMMAND SUMMARY

This section lists the 1-2-3 advanced macro commands in alphabetical order. Arguments in [ ] (brackets) are optional. When an argument is italicized, you must substitute something else when you enter the command. When an argument is not italicized, you must include the exact word.

{*subroutine* [*arg1*],[*arg2*],. . .,[*argn*] performs a subroutine call.

{?} suspends macro execution, letting you type any number of keystrokes.

{BEEP [*tone-number*]} sounds computer's bell or tone.

{BLANK *location*} erases contents of *location*.

{BORDERSOFF} turns off display of the worksheet borders.

{BORDERSON} redisplays worksheet borders.

{BRANCH *location*} transfers macro control from current macro cell to *location* for further macro instructions.

{BREAK} returns 1-2-3 to READY mode.

{BREAKOFF} disables Ctrl-Break.

{BREAKON} restores use of Ctrl-Break.

{CLOSE} closes the open text file.

{CONTENTS *target-location,source-location,*[*width*],[*cell-format*]} copies as a label the contents of *source-location* to *target-location*.

{DEFINE *location1,location2,. . . ,locationn*} stores arguments passed in a subroutine in a {*subroutine*} command so those arguments can be used later in the subroutine.

{DISPATCH *location*} performs an indirect branch by transferring macro control to the cell whose name or address is in *location*.

{FILESIZE *location*} determines number of bytes in the open text file and enters number in *location*.

{FOR *counter,start-number,stop-number,step-number,subroutine*} creates a for loop—it repeatedly performs a subroutine call to *subroutine*.

{FORBREAK} ends a for loop.

{FRAMEOFF} turns off display of the worksheet borders. Same as {BORDERSOFF}.

{FRAMEON} redisplays the worksheet borders. Same as {BORDERSON}.

{GET *location*} suspends macro execution until you press a key, then records keystroke as left-aligned label in *location*.

{GETLABEL *prompt,location*} displays *prompt* in control panel, waits for your response, and stores whatever you typed as a left-aligned label in *location*.

{GETNUMBER *prompt,location*} displays *prompt* in control panel, waits for your response, and stores whatever you typed as a number in *location*.

{GETPOS *location*} enters as a number in *location* the current byte pointer position in the open text file.

{GRAPHOFF} removes a graph displayed by {GRAPHON}.

{GRAPHON [*named-graph*],[nodisplay]} displays the current graph or a named graph.

{IF *condition*} evaluates *condition*. If *condition* is true, macro moves to instruction immediately following {IF} command in the same cell; if false, moves to next cell.

{INDICATE [*string*]} changes mode indicator to *string*.

{LET *location,entry*} enters number or left-aligned label (*entry*) in *location*.

{LOOK *location*} checks the keyboard buffer for keystrokes and enters as left-aligned label in *location* the first keystroke (if any).

{MENUBRANCH *location*} displays in control panel the macro menu found at *location*, waits for you to select an item, then branches to the associated macro instructions.

{MENUCALL *location*} displays in control panel the macro menu found at *location*, waits for you to select an item, then performs a subroutine call to the associated macro instructions.

{ONERROR *branch-location,*[*message-location*]} continues macro execution at *branch-location* if an error occurs.

{OPEN *file-name,access-type*} opens a specified text file for read-only or read-and-write processing.

{PANELOFF [clear]} freezes control panel and status line, optionally clearing contents.

{PANELON} unfreezes control panel and status line.

{PUT *location,column-offset,row-offset,entry*} enters number or left-aligned label (*entry*) in specified column and row in a range (*location*).

{QUIT} immediately ends the macro and returns 1-2-3 to READY mode.

{READ *byte-count,location*} starts at byte pointer position in the open text file, copies *byte-count* number of bytes to *location*, and advances byte pointer *byte-count* bytes.

{READLN *location*} starts at byte pointer position in the open text file, copies remainder of current line to *location*, and moves byte pointer to beginning of next line.

{RECALC *location*,[*condition*],[*iterations*]} recalculates values in *location*, proceeding row by row.

{RECALCCOL *location*,[*condition*],[*iterations*]} recalculates values in *location*, proceeding column by column.

{RESTART} clears subroutine stack during subroutine execution.

{RETURN} affects flow of control in subroutines by returning macro control to the next instruction after {*subroutine*} or {MENUCALL}, or by ending the current iteration in a for loop and starting the next iteration.

{SETPOS *offset-number*} positions byte pointer in the open text file *offset-number* bytes from the first byte.

{SYSTEM *command*} temporarily suspends the 1-2-3 session and executes the specified operating system command.

{WAIT *time-number*} suspends macro execution and displays WAIT as the mode indicator until the time specified by *time-number.*

{WINDOWSOFF} freezes worksheet area of screen during macro execution and suppresses setting sheet display.

{WINDOWSON} restores normal updating of worksheet area and turns on setting sheet display during macro execution. To turn on setting sheet display if a {WINDOWSOFF} command is in effect, use {WINDOWSON} twice: once to redisplay the worksheet area and the second time to redisplay setting sheets.

{WRITE *string*} copies *string* to the open text file, starting at current byte pointer position.

{WRITELN *string*} copies *string*, carriage return, and line feed to the open text file, starting at current byte pointer position.

MENU TREES

The following pages provide graphic representations of the commands available in Allways, Macro Library Manager, and PrintGraph. The 1-2-3 menu trees for the Add-In, Data, File, Print, Range, Graph, and Worksheet commands appear on the foldout card at the back of this book.

ALLWAYS MENU TREES

The Display Commands

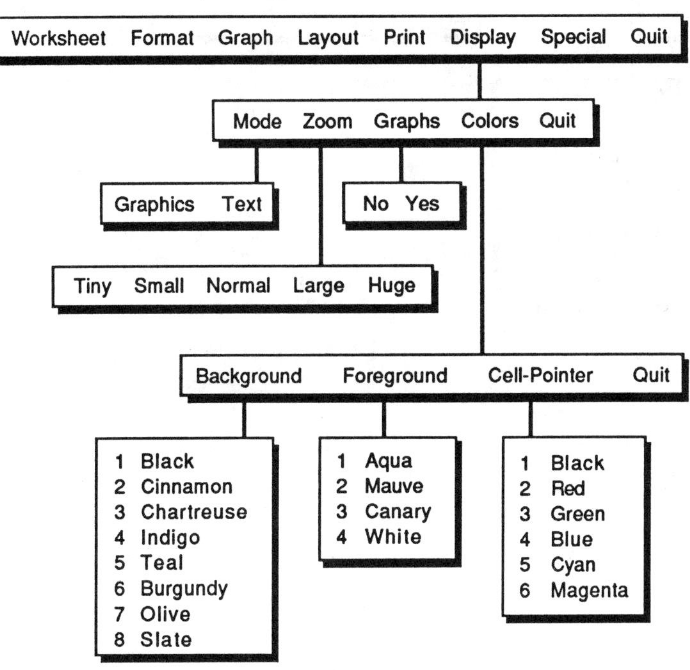

The Format Commands

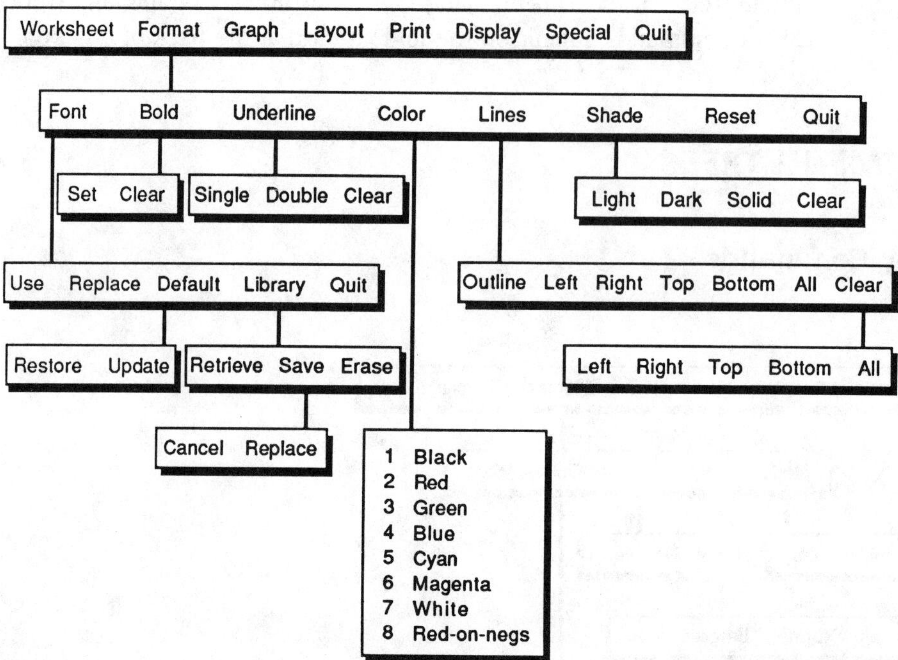

The Graph Commands

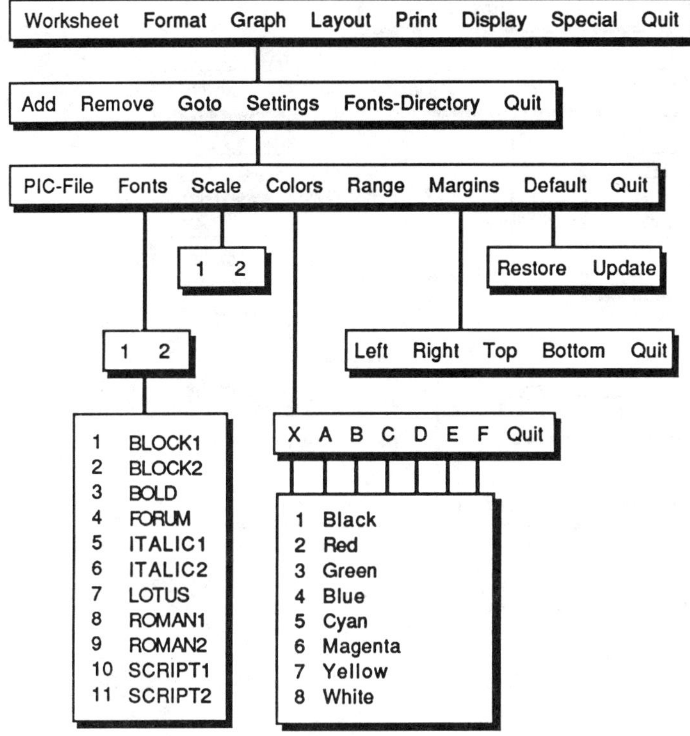

The Layout Commands

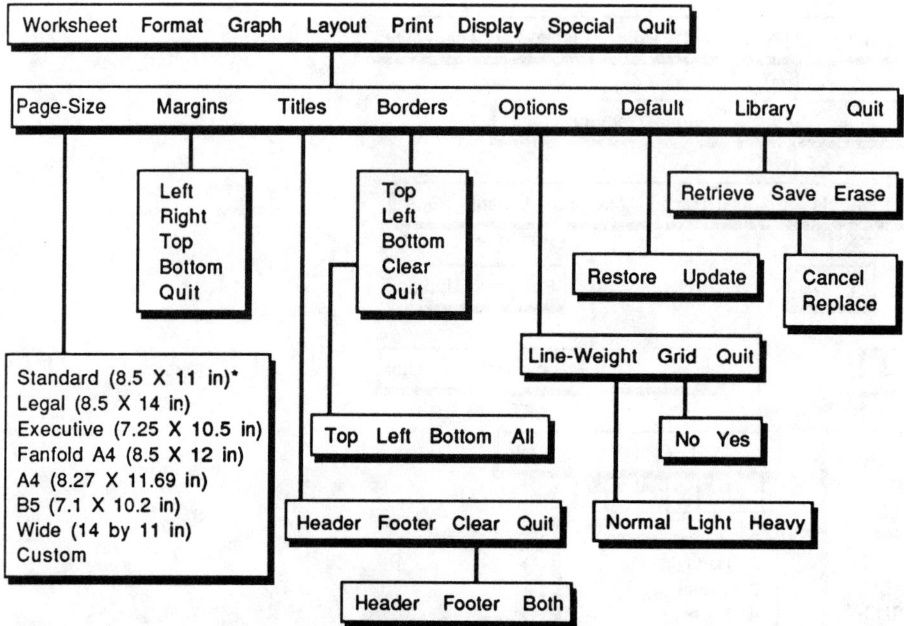

* Your available selections may be different depending on the type of printer you selected.

The Print Commands

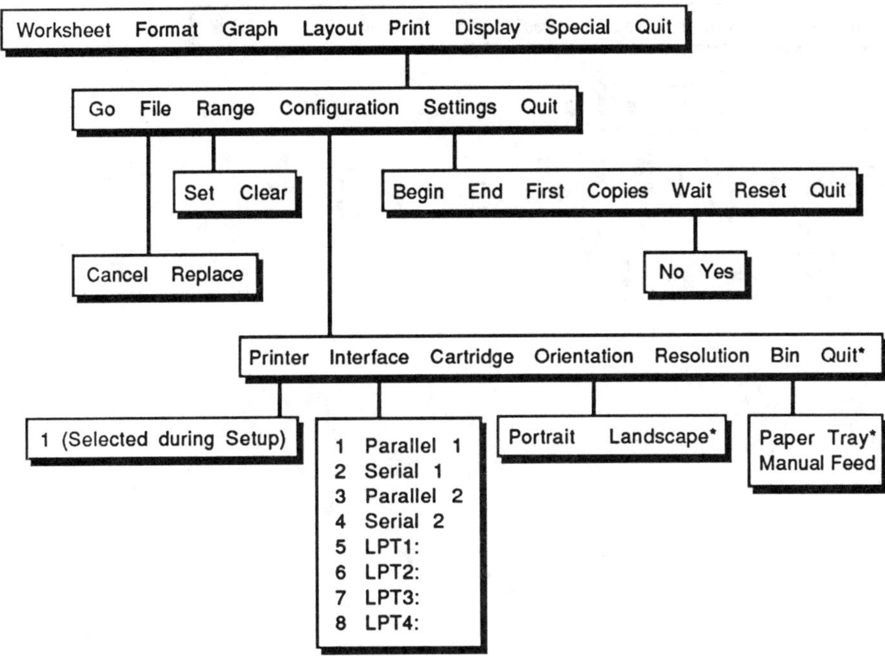

* Your available selections may be different depending on the type of printer you selected.

The Special Commands

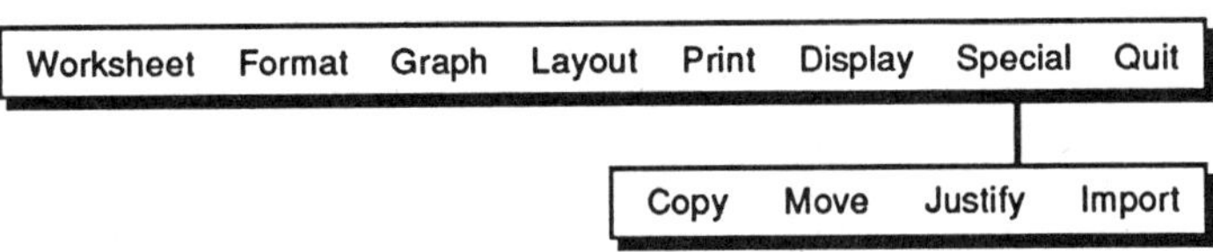

The Worksheet Commands

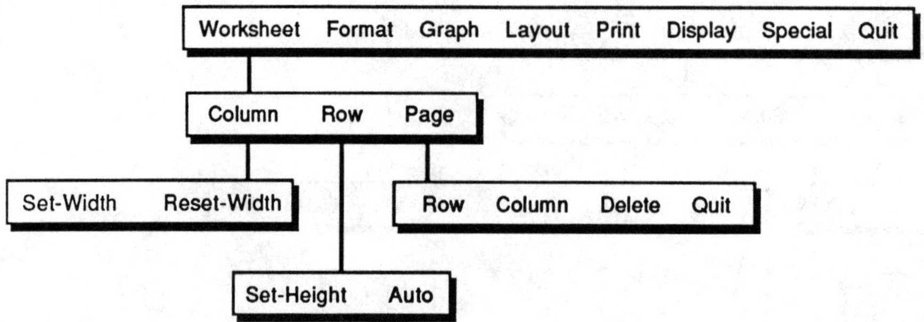

MACRO LIBRARY MANAGER MENU TREE

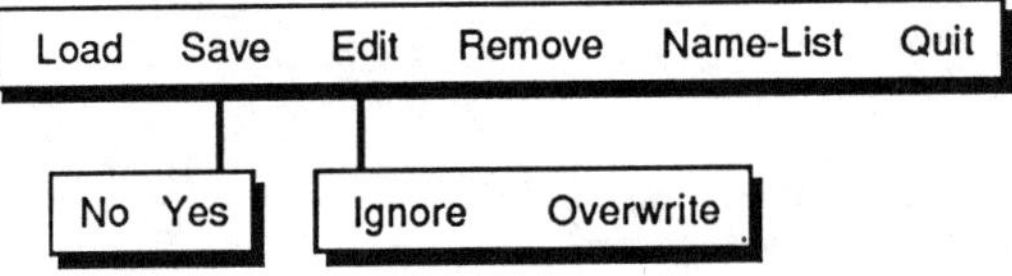

PRINTGRAPH MENU TREE

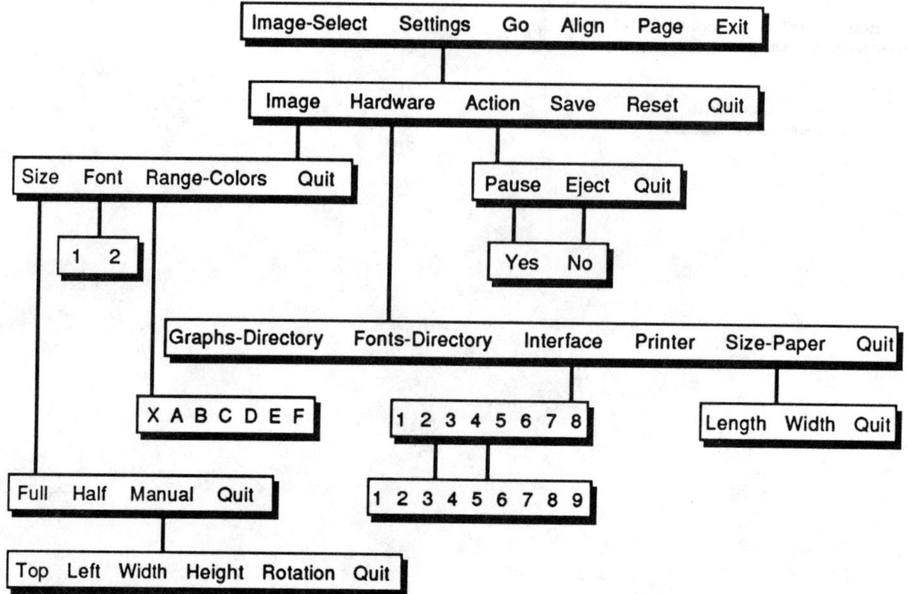

Index

~ (tilde), 331, 332, 340, 341
{ { }, 341
{ } }, 341
{ }, 341
{?}, 388, 420–423, 515
/ (slash) key
  macro key name for, 341
  and menus, 10, 14, 22, 236

1-2-3
  configuration file, 280, 290
  customizing, 278–280
  global settings, 65
  Help facility, 45, 91
  initializing, 4, 5
  installing, 5–6
  leaving, 16, 168
  menus, 22–24
  and networks, 603–606
  screen, 20–22
  starting on hard-disk computer, 11–15
  starting on two-diskette computer, 8–11
123.SET file, 5

{ABS}, 340, 569–571
Abs (F4) key, 84–85, 284, 340
Absolute cell address, 76, 82–86, 294
Accelerator keys, Allways, 318–319
Access system. *See* Lotus Access system
Add-In commands, 231, 443
  Attach, 232–234, 445–446, 597–599
  Clear, 128, 600
  Detach, 238, 464, 600
  Invoke, 232, 234, 444, 447, 599
Add-in programs, 230, 596–602
  assigning to function key, 597
  attaching, 597–599
  attaching automatically, 600–602
  detaching, 599–600
  invoking, 599
  invoking automatically, 601–602
  and undo feature, 600
  See also Allways add-in; Macro Library Manager add-in
Adding
  blank columns, 241
  blank rows, 62–63, 239–240
  boxes with Allways, 263–264
  data labels to graphs, 312–314
  to learn range, 365
  lines with Allways, 254–255
  page breaks, 308
  shading with Allways, 255–256
Advanced macro commands, 368–402
  argument separators, 370
  arguments, 368–369, 370–371, 385–386
  defined, 325, 326–327
  keywords, 368, 386
  and learn feature, 348
  listed, 621–624
  and macro libraries, 466
  rules for, 385–386
  syntax, 369
  troubleshooting, 381–387
  See also individual advanced macro commands
Aligning labels, 63–64
  See also Label prefixes; Range Label commands
Allways add-in, 230–273
  and 1-2-3 formats, 242–243
  accelerator keys, 318–319, 612
  adding boldface with, 252–253
  adding boxes with, 263–264
  adding graphs to worksheet with, 257–266
  adding lines with, 254–255
  .ALL files, 251
  assigning to function key, 232–234
  attaching, 231, 232–234

attaching automatically, 234, 320
changing fonts with, 244-251
changing graph size with, 260-262
changing graph text size with, 262-263
changing row heights with, 315-316
default font, 245-248
display settings, 259-260
displaying graphs with, 259-260
exiting, 238, 256
font set, 244-245
formats and 1-2-3, 319-320
formatting with, 242-256
function keys, 237, 611
graph settings, 261
Help facility, 237-238
indicating ranges in, 252
invoking, 231, 234
installing, 6
keeping attached, 242, 251, 319-320
leaving, 238, 256
main menu, 236
menu command structure, 270-273
and printer drivers, 267
printing with, 266-269
requirements for running, 231
returning to 1-2-3 from, 238, 256
saving your work, 251
screen, 235, 235-236
selecting from lists in, 247-248
Setup program, 6
shading with, 255-256
suppressing display of graphs with, 259-260
tips, 315-320
underlining with, 253
and undo feature, 238-239

ALLWAYS indicator, 235, 236
Alt key
and running a macro, 326, 336, 337, 376
{ADD1}, 340
App1 (Alt-F7) key, 232, 340, 444
{ADD2}, 340
App2 (Alt-F8) key, 232, 340, 444
{ADD3}, 340
App3 (Alt-F9) key, 232, 340, 444
{ADD4}, 340
App4 (Alt-F10) key, 232, 340, 444
Application macros, 468-535
database, 493-517
form letter, 517-536
graph presentation, 470-492
Arguments
in advanced macro commands, 368-369, 370-371, 385-386
in @functions, 72
in subroutine calls, 391
Arrow keys, 25
At functions. *See* @Functions
Attaching add-ins, 596, 597-599
Allways, 231, 232-234, 320
automatically, 600-602
Macro Library Manager, 443, 444-446
@AVG, 73

{BACKSPACE}, 340
Backspace key, 61, 282, 340
Backup files, 42
Bar graph, 129-130
creating, 142-154, 481-484
data labels, 312
data ranges for, 145-146, 148
legends for, 151-152
naming, 155
negative values in, 167
saving for printing, 156
titling, 153-154
viewing, 147
X-axis labels for, 145
{BEEP}, 370, 388-389
Big Left key, 27, 28, 340
Big Right key, 27, 28, 340
{BIGLEFT}, 340
{BIGRIGHT}, 340
{BLANK}, 369, 389, 502
Boldface
adding to worksheet, 252-253
Borders
displaying worksheet, 393
printing, 304-307
suppressing worksheet, 392

{BORDERSOFF}, 389
{BORDERSON}, 389
Boxes
    adding with Allways, 263-264
Braces
    and advanced macro commands, 325, 328, 369
    and key names in macros, 325, 328, 339
    macro key names for, 341
{BRANCH}, 372, 389, 420-423, 495, 521-522, 558-559
{BREAK}, 390
{BREAKOFF}, 390
{BREAKON}, 390
{BS}, 340, 501
Byte pointer position, 394, 400

{CALC}, 276, 331, 340, 373, 414
Calc (F9) key, 276, 277, 340
CALC indicator, 276
    and learn feature, 353
Calculations. *See* Formulas; @Functions
CAPS indicator, 21, 29
Caps Lock key, 29
Cell
    current, 20
    defined, 20, 49
    printing contents of, 303-304
    protection, 283-284
    source, 100
    target, 100
Cell address, 20
    absolute, 76, 82-86, 294
    mixed, 294
    relative, 75-78, 83, 294
Cell format. *See* Formats
Cell pointer, 6, 20
    macros for moving, 341-343, 420-423
@CELLPOINTER, 302-303, 533-534
{CLOSE}, 390
CMD indicator, 326, 376
Color graphs, 154-155, 309
Columns
    adding blank, 241
    changing width of, 55-56, 192-193, 432
    changing width of globally, 65-66, 542
    changing width of group of, 193, 359
    changing widths with Allways, 316-317
    deleting, 416
    displaying hidden, 289
    hiding, 287-289
    printing as borders, 304-305
Comma, in macros, 370
Condition argument, 371
Conditional statements, 395, 494-495
    See also {FOR}; {IF}
Configuration file (123.CNF)
    updating, 234, 280, 290, 602, 606
{CONTENTS}, 390-391
Control panel
    1-2-3, 21
    Allways, 235-236
    freezing in macros, 398, 583-587
Converting
    formulas to labels, 295
    formulas to values, 297-298
    values to labels, 391, 423-428
Copy command, 30-34, 94
    and cell formats, 281
    and formulas, 74-75, 85-86
    and Name (F3) key, 94
    and range specification, 281-282
    tips, 281-282
@COS, 73
Counter
    in {FOR} command, 426, 437
Criteria, 207
    entering, 213, 216
    formulas in, 221-222
    range, 210-213, 550
    wildcards in, 298-299
Ctrl-Break key
    and {BRANCH}, 422
    controlling with {BREAKOFF}/{BREAKON}, 390

and stopping printing, 269
and {WAIT}, 401
Customizing 1-2-3, 278-280

{D}, 340, 421, 429, 430
Data
copying, 30-34, 94, 281-282
editing, 59-62
entering, 26-27
erasing, 34-35, 94, 114-115, 241
making bold with Allways, 252-253
moving, 281-282
shading with Allways, 255-256
storing in macro library, 443, 453-459
storing with macros, 398
underlining, 253
updating links to, 105-107
See also Labels; Values
Data commands
Fill, 305
menu structure, 228
Data entry form, 493, 498-500, 506-507
Data labels
adding to graphs, 312-314
Data Query commands, 208, 549-550
Criteria, 212-213, 551
Extract, 217, 219-220, 552, 565
Find, 213-217
Input, 209-210, 551
Output, 219, 551
Data range
in databases, 198-200, 205-206
in graphs, 135, 137-138, 144-146, 157
Data record. *See* Record
Data Sort commands
Data-Range, 199, 205
Go, 203, 207
Primary-Key, 200-201, 203, 515
Secondary-Key, 200, 516
Database, 180-228
adding a record to, 205
criteria range, 210-213
data range, 198-200
defined, 180, 493
entering field names in, 185-187
entering records in, 187-189
extracting records from, 217-223
field name, 183
field, 180, 183, 493
finding records in, 213-217
input range, 209-210
querying, 182, 207, 207-223
record, 180, 183, 493
replacing information in, 223-227
sort keys, 200-203, 514-515
sorting, 181, 197-207, 514-517
tips, 298-300
Database application macro, 493-517
creating the data entry form, 506-507
entering records with, 501-506, 508-514
setting up ranges for, 496-498
setting up the data entry form, 498-500
setting up the database, 500-501
sorting routine, 514-517
@DATE, 189, 196, 296-297, 378-379, 381
Date
entering, 189-190, 296-297, 377-381, 410-412
formatting, 190, 292, 360
including in header/footer, 301
recording with macro, 414-416
Debugging. *See* Troubleshooting
Default font, 245-248
Default settings sheet, 9-11, 14-15, 279-280
{DEFINE}, 391
{DEL}, 340
Del key, 61, 340
{DELETE}, 340
Detaching add-ins, 596, 599-600
Directory
changing default, 10-11, 14-15
creating, 12
root, 11
{DISPATCH}, 391
Display commands, Allways
Graphs, 259-260

menu structure, 273
Display (F6) key, Allways, 237
Display settings sheet, Allways, 259-260
Displaying
graphs in Allways, 259-260
hidden columns, 289
negative values, 289-290
Dividing the screen, 111-114
{DOWN}, 340
See also {D}
Down key, 27, 62, 340
Driver set, 5
Drivers, 5
and Allways, 267
ASCII collating, 505, 522, 535
network printer, 606

{EDIT}, 340
Edit command, Macro Library Manager, 447, 452-453, 457-458, 460
Edit (F2) key, 59-60, 295, 340
and learn range, 363-364
and macros, 339
and range names, 286
EDIT indicator, 59, 61, 67, 289
Editing
data, 59-62
and FIND mode, 299-300
and Ins key, 289
and insert mode, 289
keys for, 61-62, 608-609
learn range, 363-364
macro library, 459-464
macro, 338-339
and overstrike mode, 289
range names, 286
{END}, 331, 340
End key, 28, 61, 331, 340
Enlarge (Alt-F4) key, Allways, 237
Enter key, 7, 340
and editing, 61
and macros, 331
Entering
data, 26-27
date, 189-190
field name in database, 186-187
formula, 70-73
label, 54-55
line with macro, 416-420
macro, 327-330, 334
record in database, 187-189
value, 57-59
Erasing
with {BLANK}, 389
data, 34-35, 94, 114-115, 241
worksheet, 39, 50
Error handling in macros, 397
ERROR indicator, 371
{ESC}, 340
Esc key
and {BREAK}, 390
macro key name for, 340
and menus, 24
and ranges, 282
and returning to 1-2-3 from Allways, 238
Executing a macro. *See* Running a macro
Exiting
1-2-3, 16
Allways, 238, 256
Macro Library Manager, 448
@EXP, 73
Extracting records from database, 217-223
indicating the output range, 217-219

Field, 180, 183, 493
Field name, 183, 185-187
in criteria range, 210-212
in input range, 209
in output range, 217-219
File, 37-44
1-2-3 (.WK1), 39
123.CNF, 280, 290
add-in (.ADN), 598
Allways (.ALL), 251
ASCII, 121
backup (.BAK), 42
byte pointer position in, 394, 400
closing text, 390
configuration, 280, 290, 446
graph, 134, 156, 164, 257

linking, 99–108
listing information about, 107–108, 290–292
listing with Name (F3), 44, 287
macro for saving, 408–410
macro library, 442–443, 448
.MLB, 442–443, 448
naming rules, 612–613
opening text, 397–398
.PIC, 134, 156, 164, 257
print, 121
reading text, 399
reserving on network, 604–605
retrieving, 40–41, 43–44, 105–107, 605
saving, 39–40, 41–42, 68–69, 82
sharing on network, 603–605
size of, 107–108, 291–292, 392
source, 100
table, 291–292, 356–363
target, 100
types, 613
.WK1, 39
writing to text, 402

File Admin commands
Reservation, 605
Table, 290, 291, 356–359

File commands, 46

File List command, 107–108, 287, 290–291

File Retrieve command, 40–41
and Allways, 251
and linked data, 105–107
and Name (F3) key, 44
and networks, 605

File Save command, 39–40, 68–69, 82
and Allways, 251
and modified worksheet, 41–42

FILES indicator, 287

{FILESIZE}, 391–392

FIND indicator, 214, 299, 300

Finding records in database, 213–217
editing while, 299–300

Flow control in macros, 388, 389, 391, 400

Fonts in Allways, 243–251
default font, 245–248, 317
defined, 243–244
font set, 244–245, 318
for graphs, 262
printer, 245, 317–318
scaling in graphs, 262–263
soft, 245, 318

Fonts in PrintGraph, 172–173

Footer
aligning, 301
including cell data in, 302
including date in, 301
including filename in, 302–303
printing on last page, 301

{FOR}, 392, 425–426, 436–438, 502–503, 568–569

{FORBREAK}, 392

Form. *See* Data entry form

Form letter macros, 428–434, 519–536

Format commands, Allways
Bold, 253, 265
Font, 246–250, 265, 317–318
Lines, 254–255, 263
menu structure, 271
Shade, 255–256, 316
Underline, 253

Formats
+/–, 87
, (comma), 86, 88–89
Allways, 243, 319–320
Currency, 86, 90, 188
Date, 87, 190, 195, 292, 360, 411
Fixed, 86, 293, 481
General, 87
Hidden, 87
Percent, 87, 544–545
Reset, 87
Sci, 86
Text, 87
Time, 292, 412

Formatting
with Allways, 230–273, 242–256
globally, 544
macro, 351–356
values, 86–91
See also Range Format commands

Formula
changing to value, 297–298

- copying, 74-78, 85-86
- in criteria, 221-222
- defined, 69
- editing, 295-296
- entering, 70-73
- linking, 100, 103-105
- mathematical operators in, 70, 614
- range names in, 95-96
- string, 567, 571
- tips for, 293-298
- using Name (F3) when creating, 287

{FRAMEOFF}, 370, 392
{FRAMEON}, 393
Function keys
- 1-2-3, 7, 28, 609-611
- Allways, 237, 611
- to invoke add-ins, 232-234, 444-446

@Functions
- arguments in, 72
- defined, 71-72
- listed, 615-620
- tips for, 293-298

@FV, 73

{GET}, 325, 393, 518, 521
{GETLABEL}, 373, 373, 374, 393, 499, 504, 505, 521-522
- and zip codes, 510

{GETNUMBER}, 373, 374, 377-379, 393-394, 574
{GETPOS}, 394
Global settings sheet, 65, 279
{GOTO}, 325, 333, 340, 342, 362, 499
Goto (F5) key, 25, 340
- Allways, 237
- and checking macro names, 346
- and ranges, 96-97, 439, 508

{GRAPH}, 340
Graph, 127-178
- adding data labels to, 312-314
- bar, 129-130, 142-154, 481-484
- changing size of with Allways, 260-262
- changing text size in with Allways, 262-263
- color, 154-155, 309
- creating with /Graph Group, 135-140
- data ranges, 135, 144-146, 157
- displaying with Allways, 259-260
- displaying with macro, 394
- file (.PIC), 134, 156, 257
- fonts for printing, 172-173, 262
- including with worksheet data, 257-266
- legends for, 140-141, 151-152
- line, 128-129, 137-138, 487-489
- macro for presenting, 489-492
- moving with Allways, 260
- naming, 134, 155
- pie chart, 131-132, 156-164, 484-487
- printing, 134, 168-176, 266-269
- printing density for, 171-172
- removing with macro, 394
- saving for printing, 156
- selecting for printing, 174
- selecting type of, 144
- stacked bar, 130-131
- suppressing display of with Allways, 259-260
- table of names, 314-315
- tips, 309-315
- titling, 153-154, 157, 482, 487-488
- types, 128-133, 470
- viewing, 139-140, 166, 259-260
- what-if, 164-167
- X-axis labels, 137, 144, 309-310, 482
- XY, 132-133
- Y-axis scale indicator, 310-311

Graph application macro, 470-492
- creating the graphs, 481-489
- creating the macro, 489-492
- entering data for, 472-481
- running, 492

Graph commands
- Group, 135, 137-138
- menu structure, 177
- Reset, 157, 484
- Save, 156, 257
- Type, 144, 157
- View, 139-140

Graph commands, Allways
Add, 257-258
menu structure, 271
Settings, 260-263
Graph (F10) key
1-2-3, 166, 340
Allways, 237, 260
PrintGraph, 174
Graph Name commands
Create, 155
Delete, 155
Table, 314
Use, 155, 166
Graph Options commands
B&W, 155, 309
Color, 154, 309
Data-Labels, 312, 313
Format, 487
Legend, 140-141, 151-152
Scale, 309-310, 311
Titles, 153-154, 157, 482, 487-488
Graph Settings commands, Allways
Range, 260-261
Scale, 262-263
Graph settings sheet
1-2-3, 133-134
Allways, 261
{GRAPHOFF}, 394
examples of use, 490-492
{GRAPHON}, 394
examples of use, 490-492

Header
aligning, 301
including cell data in, 302
including date in, 301
including file name in, 302-303
{HELP}, 340
Help (F1) key
1-2-3, 45, 340
Allways, 237
Help facility
1-2-3, 45, 91
Allways, 237-238
Hiding columns, 287-289
Highlighting ranges, 31-32, 252, 282-283
{HOME}, 329, 331, 340
Home key, 28, 61, 340

@IF, 73, 567
{IF} 395, 494-495, 504, 505-506, 521-522, 533
Image-Select command, PrintGraph, 174
Income statement, 51-52
{INDICATE}, 395, 518, 521-522, 587-594
Indicator
date-and-time, 22
mode, 21, 395, 521-522, 587-594
status, 21
See also individual indicator names
Initializing 1-2-3, 4, 5
Input range, 209-210
{INS}, 340
INS indicator, 62
Ins key, 62, 289, 340
{INSERT}, 340
Inserting
blank columns, 241
blank rows, 62-63, 239-240
page breaks, 308
Installing
1-2-3, 5-6
Allways, 6
Instructions
macro, 329
@INT, 293
Interactive macros, 330, 372, 373-381
Invoking a macro. *See* Running a macro
Invoking add-ins, 596, 599
Allways, 231, 234
automatically, 601-602
Macro Library Manager, 443, 444

Keyboard, 6-7
buffer, 396
Keys
abbreviations for in macros, 339-341
accelerator in Allways, 318-319, 612
editing, 61-62, 608-609
function, 7, 28, 237, 609-611

names of, in macros, 325, 328, 339–342, 620–621
not available in macros, 330
pointer-movement, 6–7, 26–28, 607–608
See also individual key names

Keystroke macros
defined, 325, 326
entering, 330–338
troubleshooting, 346

Keystrokes
capturing with macros, 325, 388, 393–394
checking for with {LOOK}, 396

{L}, 340, 421

LABEL indicator, 54, 68

Label prefixes, 63, 613–614
and Allways, 242
centered, 192
left-aligned, 54, 68
and macros, 325, 328, 344
and numeric labels, 67–68
right-aligned, 64

Labels
adding to graphs, 312–314
aligning, 63–64
beginning with numbers, 67–68
centering, 191–192, 196–197
defined, 53
entering, 54–55
and entering macros, 325, 328
frozen as titles, 277–278
long, 57
right-aligning, 63–64, 102
storing with macros, 393
transposing, 110–111

Layout commands, Allways, 266
menu structure, 272

Learn (Alt-F5) key, 352–353, 357, 361

Learn feature, 344, 348, 348–366
and advanced macro commands, 348
advantages of, 348
guidelines for using, 349–350
recording keystrokes with, 352–353, 357–362
restarting recording with, 365–366
turning off, 353, 361
turning on, 352–353, 357

LEARN indicator, 352–353

Learn range, 348
adding to, 365–366
and CALC indicator, 353
cancelling, 357
correcting mistakes in, 363–364
defining, 349, 351, 357
expanding, 365
running out of room in, 366

Leaving
1-2-3, 16, 168
Allways, 238
Macro Library Manager, 448

{LEFT}, 340
See also {L}

Left key, 27, 62, 340

Legends
adding, 151–152
adding as group, 140–141
using cell address in, 152

{LET}, 370, 371, 396

Line graph, 128–129
creating, 137–138, 487–489
data labels, 312
legends for, 140–141

Lines
adding with Allways, 254–255, 316
adding with macros, 416–420

Linking files, 99–108
and Macro Library Manager, 466

Linking formulas, 100
entering, 103–105

Listing
files, 44, 290–291
range names in macro library, 448

Load command, Macro Library Manager, 447, 459

Location arguments, 371, 386, 387, 495

Logical functions, 73

Logical operators, 614

{LOOK}, 396

Looping. *See* {FOR}

Lotus Access system, 8, 9, 12, 13

Macro
- advanced macro commands, 325, 326-327, 368-402
- autoexecute, 594
- changing in a library, 460-464
- debugging, 346, 381-387
- defined, 324
- documenting, 335-336
- editing, 338-339
- end of, 327
- Enter key in, 331
- entering, 327-330, 334
- error handling, 397
- instructions, 329
- interactive, 330, 372, 373-381
- invoking automatically, 594-595
- key names in, 325, 328, 339-342
- keystroke, 325, 326
- learn feature, 348-366
- and manual recalculation of worksheet, 276
- menu, 396-397, 538-595
- names, 325, 335, 345
- naming with /Range Name Labels, 354, 375
- protecting, 329, 344-345, 349
- range, 325
- range names in, 332
- recording with learn feature, 344
- repeating keystrokes in, 341
- returning to DOS from, 401
- rules, 343-345
- running, 325-326, 336-337
- running automatically, 594-595
- saving, 339, 345
- STEP mode, 381-385
- stopping, 390, 399
- storing in library, 442-443
- suspending execution of, 388, 393, 401
- transfer of control, 372, 388, 389, 391, 396, 397, 400, 495, 517-518
- troubleshooting, 346, 381-387
- using, 330
- *See also* Application macros; Interactive macros; Utility macros

Macro library, 339, 345, 436, 442-443
- and advanced macro commands, 466
- editing, 447, 459-464
- file, 442-443, 448
- listing range names in, 448
- loading into memory, 447, 459, 469
- names, 465
- range names in, 466
- removing from memory, 448, 453
- saving macros in, 448-451
- saving range in, 447
- and storing data, 453-458
- updating, 462-464
- using, 451-453

Macro Library Manager add-in, 442-466
- assigning to function key, 444
- attaching, 443, 444-446, 469, 542
- attaching automatically, 446
- commands, 447-448
- detaching, 464
- invoking, 443, 446-447, 469, 542
- leaving, 448
- menu, 447-448
- rules, 464-466

Macro menu
- and 1-2-3 menus, 554
- creating, 554-560
- entering data for, 543-547
- entering descriptions, 557
- entering items for, 556
- routines, 560-577

Main menu
- 1-2-3, 22-23, 124
- Allways, 236
- Macro Library Manager, 447-448
- PrintGraph, 169

Mathematical operators, 70, 614

Memory
- loading add-ins into, 596
- loading Allways into, 231, 232-234
- loading macro libraries into, 447, 459
- loading Macro Library Manager into, 443, 444-446
- removing add-ins from, 596

removing macro libraries from, 448, 453, 464
and undo feature, 238–239, 600
usage and @REPEAT, 476
and worksheet, 38
{MENU}, 341
Menu
creating own, 396–397, 538–595
getting out of, 24
selecting from, in 1-2-3, 23
selecting from, in Allways, 236–237
MENU indicator, 22, 236
{MENUBRANCH}, 396, 554, 558
{MENUCALL}, 396, 397, 400
Minimal recalculation, 119, 275
Mixed cell address, 294
Mode indicator
1-2-3, 21
Allways, 235, 236
changing, 395, 518, 521–522, 587–594
See also individual indicator names
Move command
and Name (F3) key, 287
Moving
around worksheet, 25–28
cell pointer macro, 341–343
data, 281–282
graphs with Allways, 260

{NAME}, 341, 342
Name (F3) key, 44, 93
Allways, 237
and erasing data, 94
and formula creation, 95–96, 287
and full-screen menus, 287
and listing range names, 287, 463
and locating ranges, 96–97
macro key name for, 341
and specifying data ranges, 146
tips, 287
when running macros, 345
Name-List command, Macro Library Manager, 448
NAMES indicator, 287
Naming
files, 612–613
graphs, 155, 164
macros, 325, 335, 345, 354, 375
ranges, 91–99, 101
ranges with macros, 406–408
Negative value display, 289–290
Networks, 603–606
printing on, 606
sharing files on, 603–605
@NOW, 410, 411, 414, 490–491
NUM indicator, 29
Num Lock key, 29
Numbers. *See* Values
Numeric argument, 371

{ONERROR}, 397
{OPEN}, 390, 397–398
Operators, 614
Outlines
adding with Allways, 263–264
Output range, 217–219, 549–550
OVR indicator, 62, 289

Page breaks, 308
{PANELOFF}, 398, 401, 490–491, 568, 569–570, 583–587
{PANELON}, 398, 583–587
Password
file, 604
macro library, 450, 465
{PGDN}, 341
PgDn key, 27, 341
{PGUP}, 341
PgUp key, 27, 341
Pie chart, 131–132
creating, 156–164, 484–487
data range for, 157
exploding, 162–163
naming, 164
saving for printing, 164
shading, 159–162, 484
titling, 157
viewing, 158
Pitch, 244
@PMT, 73
POINT indicator, 31, 236, 282
Pointer. *See* Cell pointer

Pointer-movement keys, 6-7, 26-28, 607-608
Points in fonts, 244
Precedence of operators, 614
Print commands, 121-123, 125, 435
Print commands, Allways, 266
  Go, 269
  menu structure, 272
  Range, 267-268
Print Configuration commands, Allways
  Interface, 267
  Printer, 267
Print Printer Options commands
  Borders, 278, 304, 307
  Footer, 302, 303
  Header, 301
  Other As-Displayed, 304
  Other Cell-Formulas, 303-304
Print settings sheet, 120-122
PrintGraph program, 168-176
  fonts and Allways, 262
  menu structure, 178
  previewing graphs with, 174
  printing density, 171-172
  saving settings for, 172
  screen, 169-170
  selecting fonts, 172-173
  selecting graphs to print, 174
  settings, 170
  specifying directory for graph files, 170-171
  specifying fonts directory, 172
  specifying printer, 171-172
  starting, 169
Printing
  adding page breaks, 308
  with Allways, 266-269
  borders, 304-307
  cell contents, 303-304
  column and row borders, 304-305
  date in header/footer, 301
  file name in header/footer, 302-303
  footer on last page, 301
  graphs, 168-176, 266-269
  macros for, 435-438
  non-adjacent columns, 287-288
  on networks, 606
  options, 122
  stopping, 269
  tips, 301-308
  worksheet, 120-123
Protecting
  data from macros, 329, 344-345, 349
  library with password, 450, 465
  worksheet, 283-285
{PUT}, 398

{QUERY}, 341
Query (F7) key, 341
Query settings sheet, 208
Querying a database, 182, 207-223
  criteria for, 207, 213, 216
  identifying the criteria range, 210-213, 551
  identifying the input range, 209-210, 551
  identifying the output range, 219, 551
{QUIT}, 327, 399, 525, 577
Quit command
  1-2-3, 16, 168
  Allways, 256
  Macro Library Manager, 448

{R}, 341, 421, 501
Random access memory (RAM), 38
  See also Memory
Range
  anchored, 31, 282
  and Backspace key, 282
  copying, 30-34
  criteria, 210-213, 550
  data, 198-200, 205-206
  defined, 29-30
  erasing, 34-35, 114-115
  and Esc key, 282
  highlighting, 31-32, 252, 282-283
  indicating, 31
  indicating in Allways, 252
  input, 209-210, 551
  justifying text in, 115-117
  learn, 348, 349, 351, 357, 365-366
  macro, 325

names, 91-99
output, 217-219, 549-550
print (1-2-3), 122-123, 305
print (Allways), 267-268
saving in library, 449
saving in macro library, 447
transposing, 109-111
unanchored, 31, 282
Range commands
Erase, 34-35, 94, 114-115
Justify, 115-117, 432-434, 532-534
menu structure, 125
Protect, 285
Search, 223-227
Trans, 109-111, 501
Unprot, 284
Value, 74, 297-298, 428, 476
Range Format commands, 86-90, 242
, (comma), 88-89
Currency, 90, 188
Date, 190, 195, 292, 360, 411
Fixed, 293, 481
Percent, 87, 544-545
Range Label commands, 242
Center, 191-192, 196-197
Right, 64, 102
Range Name commands
Create, 91-94, 285, 286, 335, 346, 407-408
Delete, 286
Labels, 354, 375, 406-407, 547
Reset, 286
Table, 98-99, 438-439
Range names, 91-99
changing, 286
and copying, 94
creating, 92-94, 101, 354, 407-408
deleting, 286
and erasing data, 94
and formulas, 95-96
and macro libraries, 466
and macros, 325, 332
table of, 96-99, 438-439
tips for, 285-286
{READ}, 399
{READLN}, 399
READY indicator, 21, 50, 61
{RECALC}, 276, 399
{RECALCCOL}, 276, 400
Recalculation of worksheet 275-276, 399-400
Record, 180, 183, 493
adding to database, 187-189, 204
extraction, 217-223
finding in database, 213-217
Reduce (F4) key, Allways, 237
Relative cell address, 75-78, 85, 294
Remove command, Macro Library Manager, 448, 453
@REPEAT, 417-418, 473, 476
Repeating
keystrokes in macros, 341
Replacement string, 225-226
Reservation
file, 604-605
{RESTART}, 400
Retrieving files, 40-41, 43-44, 105-107
{RETURN}, 400, 533-534
{RIGHT}, 319, 332, 341
See also {R}
Right key, 27, 62, 341
RO indicator, 605
@ROUND, 293
Rounding off numbers, 293
Rows
adding, 62-63, 239-240
adjusting heights with Allways, 315-316
deleting, 416
examples of use, 502-503, 568-569
inserting blank, 462
printing as borders, 304-305
Run (Alt-F3) key, 325, 336-337, 342-343, 362
and Name (F3) key, 345
Running a macro, 325-326, 336-337

Save command, Macro Library Manager, 447, 448-451, 456, 463-464
Saving
files, 39-40, 41-42, 68-69, 82, 408-410
macros, 339, 345, 447, 448-451

Screen
- 1-2-3, 20–23
- Allways, 235–236
- freezing, 583–587
- moving around, 25–28
- PrintGraph, 169–170
- splitting, 111–114
- windows, 111–114

SCROLL indicator, 29
Scroll Lock key, 29
Search string, 224
Searching and replacing, 223–227
Semicolon in macros, 370
{SETPOS}, 400
Settings Hardware commands, PrintGraph
- Fonts-Directory, 172
- Graphs-Directory, 170–171
- Printer, 171–172

Settings Image commands
- Font, 172–173

Setting sheet
- default, 9–11, 14–15, 279–280
- display, Allways, 259–260
- displaying with {WINDOWSON}, 402
- global, 65, 279
- graph, 133–134
- graph, Allways, 261
- print, 120–122
- query, 208
- sort, 199, 206
- suppressing with {WINDOWSOFF}, 401

Shading
- pie chart, 159–162, 484
- worksheet with Allways, 255–256

Sort settings sheet, 199, 206
Sorting a database, 181, 197–207
- identifying the data range, 199–200
- indicating sort keys, 200–203
- macro, 514–517
- new records and, 204–207
- sort order, 198, 201, 514–515

Source cell, 100
Source file, 100, 105
Spreadsheet
- defined, 48–49
- *See also* Worksheet

@SQRT, 72, 73 SST indicator, 382
Stacked bar graph, 130–131
- data labels, 312

Starting
- 1-2-3 on hard-disk computer, 11–15
- 1-2-3 on two-diskette computer, 8–11
- Allways, 234
- learn feature, 352–352
- Macro Library Manager, 446–447
- PrintGraph, 169
- STEP mode, 382

Status indicators, 21
- *See also* individual indicator names

Status line
- in Allways, 236
- freezing in macros, 398

@STD, 73
Step (Alt-F2) key, 382, 384, 385, 508
STEP indicator, 382
STEP mode, 381–385, 508
- SST indicator, 382
- turning off, 384
- turning on, 382

@STRING, 567, 569–571
String
- argument, 371
- formulas, 567, 571
- operators, 614
- replacement, 225–226
- search, 224

{subroutine}, 388, 389, 400
Subroutine, 517–518
- clearing stack, 400
- returning from, 400

Subroutine calls, 388, 397
- arguments for, 391
- and for loops, 426

@SUM, 72, 73, 76
{SYSTEM}, 401

Tab key, 62, 340
{TABLE}, 341
Table
  file, 290-292, 356-363
  graph name, 314-315
  range name, 96-99, 438-439
Target cell, 100
Target file, 100, 105
Templates
  and Macro Library Manager, 453-459
Text
  editing, 115-117
  files, 390, 382, 394, 397-398, 400, 402
  justifying, 115-117, 432-434, 532-534
  See also Labels
@TIME, 490-491
Time
  entering, 412-414
  formatting, 360
  recording, 414-416
Titles
  graph, 153-154, 157, 482
  worksheet, 277-278
Transposing ranges, 109-111
Troubleshooting
  advanced macro commands, 386-387
  keystroke macros, 346
  macros in STEP mode, 381-385
Typeface, 244

{U}, 341, 420
Underlining data
  with Allways, 253
  with macros, 416-420
Undo feature, 35-37, 78
  and Allways, 238-239
  turning off, 239, 600
  and writing over data, 282, 291
UNDO indicator, 21, 36
{UP}, 341
  See also {U}
Utility macros, 404-440
  to convert values to labels, 423-428
  to enter current date, 410-412
  to enter current time, 412-413
  to enter lines, 416-420, 473
  to move cell pointer, 420-423, 473
  to name ranges, 406-408
  to print, 435-438
  to produce form letter, 428-434
  to record date or time, 414-416
  to save files, 408-410, 472
  using, 469, 471, 496, 519, 541-542

VALUE indicator, 57
Values
  converting to labels, 295, 391, 423
  defined, 53
  entering, 57-59
  formatting, 86-91
  negative, 289-290
  rounding off, 293-294
  storing with macros, 394
@VAR, 73

{WAIT}, 401, 490-492
WAIT indicator, 41, 236, 401
What-if calculations, 117-119
What-if graphics, 164-167
Widening columns, 55-56, 192-193
  with Allways, 316-317
  as group, 193, 359
  globally, 65-66, 542
  macro for, 332-333
Wildcard characters in criteria, 298-299
Window (F6) key, 112-113, 341
Windows, 111-114
{WINDOWSOFF}, 401, 535, 568, 569-570, 583-587
{WINDOWSON}, 401, 402, 535, 583-587
Worksheet, 49, 50
  adding boldface to, 252-253
  adding columns to, 241
  adding graphs to, 257-266
  adding lines to with Allways, 254-255
  adding rows to, 62-63, 239-240
  changing fonts in, 243-251
  displaying frame of, 393

erasing, 39, 50
formatting with Allways, 230–273
freezing in macro, 401
moving around, 25–28
planning, 283
printing, 120–123
printing with Allways, 266–269
protecting, 283–285
recalculating, 119, 275–277, 399–400
replacing data in, 223–227
retrieving, 39–40, 43–44, 105–107
saving, 39–40, 41–42, 68–69, 82
shading with Allways, 255–256
suppressing frame of, 392
tips, 275–292
titles, 277–278
underlining with Allways, 253
unfreezing display of, 402
windows, 111–114
Worksheet Column commands
Column-Range, 193, 359
Display, 289
Hide, 288
Reset-Width, 434
Set-Width, 56, 66, 192–193, 432
Worksheet commands
Delete, 308
Erase, 39, 50
menu structure, 124
Page, 308
Status, 238
Titles, 277–278
Window, 111–114
Worksheet commands, Allways
menu structure, 270
Row, 316
Worksheet Global commands, 279
Column-Width, 65–66, 542
Format, 544
Protection, 284
Recalculation, 276
Worksheet Global Default commands, 10, 14, 279
Autoexec, 595
Directory, 10, 14
Other Add-In, 234, 320, 446, 601-602
Other Beep, 280
Other International Negative, 290
Other International Punctuation, 370
Other Undo, 239, 600
Printer, 606
Update, 234, 280, 290, 602, 606
Worksheet Insert commands
Column, 241
Row, 62, 239–240, 462
Worksheet Learn commands
Cancel, 357
Erase, 364
Range, 349, 351, 357, 365, 366
{WRITE}, 402
{WRITELN}, 402

X-axis labels, 137, 144, 482
skipping, 309–310
XY graph, 132–133
data labels, 312

Y-axis
scale indicator, 310–311

Zip codes
and {GETLABEL}, 510